Carlos Lacerda, Brazilian Crusader
Volume I: The Years 1914–1960

JOHN W. F. DULLES

Carlos Lacerda, Brazilian Crusader

Volume I: The Years 1914–1960

UNIVERSITY OF TEXAS PRESS, AUSTIN

Printed in the United States of America

First Edition, 1991

♾ The paper used in this publication meets the minimum requirements of American National Standard for Information Sciences—Permanence of Paper for Printed Library Materials, ANSI Z39.48-1984.

Library of Congress Cataloging-in-Publication Data

Dulles, John W. F.

Carlos Lacerda, Brazilian crusader / by John W. F. Dulles. — 1st ed.

p. cm.

Includes bibliographical references and index.

Contents: v. 1. The years 1914–1960

ISBN 0-292-71125-5 (cloth)

1. Lacerda, Carlos. 2. Brazil—Politics and Government—1930–1954. 3. Brazil—Politics and Government—1954–1964. 4. Brazil—Politics and Government—1964–1985. 5. Journalists—Brazil—Biography. 6. Politicians—Brazil—Biography. I. Title.

F2538.22.L3D85 1991
981.06'092—dc20
[B] 90-38782
CIP

For CC
whose encouragement has been a blessing

Contents

Prologue

When Major Rubens Vaz, who would be killed in 1954 by bullets meant for Lacerda, suggested that Lacerda soften his scathing attacks, the journalist and orator defended his bruising political style by insisting that "Brazil needs to be shaken up." It was a course of action for which Lacerda was admirably fitted. Placing himself at the center of one political crisis after another, many created by his own pen and oratory, he aroused passions as few others have done in Brazil's republican history.

Historian José Honório Rodrigues has written that "no single person exerted as much influence on the Brazilian historical process as Carlos Lacerda from 1945 to 1968." Political attacks, a key to that vast influence, forced lawyer Thomas Leonardos to conclude that Lacerda was a tempest. Another prominent lawyer, Dario de Almeida Magalhães, points out that Lacerda was "the most fearful and implacable adversary known in this country, at least in the last fifty years."[1]

The newspaper columns of Lacerda, unsparing in their denouncements and frequently sensational, reveal the broad interests, diligence, and intelligence of a man full of ardor. But every person has a number of facets, and the newspaper columns tend to hide the man who was compassionate. The sight of suffering often brought tears to his eyes. Besides, his friends are constantly speaking of how he went out of his way to be considerate. Former Finance Secretary Mario Lorenzo Fernandez says that generosity was the outstanding personal characteristic of Lacerda.

Banker and politician Herbert Levy mentions two Lacerdas, the "monster" behind the journalist's typewriter and the pleasing, understanding conversationalist. It was the latter I came to know, gracious and interesting. His descriptions of situations in which he had found himself were spiced with a sense of humor, touched with satire, that I found delightful. If he was quick in his columns to hammer away at the shortcomings of political figures, in these conversations I heard more about lovable idiosyncrasies. He reached an all-time high in overlooking shortcomings when he surprised me by asking me to become his biographer.

With financial assistance from the Andrew W. Mellon Foundation and the

Institute of Latin American Studies at the University of Texas at Austin, information about Lacerda's life has been collected. The work was greatly assisted by Daphne F. Rodger, Fernando Goldgaber, Vera Lacerda Paiva, and Cacilda M. Rêgo, by letters in the hands of the Lacerda family and others, and by the documents at the University of Brasília and in the Walter Cunto collection in Rio de Janeiro.

The work indicates that Lacerda's life can be divided into four stages: (1) the years until 1955 when journalism predominated; (2) the 1955–1960 period, when, according to Congressman Paulo Pinheiro Chagas, he was "the greatest tribune to have taken a seat in the Chamber of Deputies"[2]; (3) his years as a constructive governor (1960–1965), presidential candidate, and participant in the events that saw two presidents fall from office; and (4) the years in which he became a political outcast while battling the military regime that ended only after his death in 1977.

A narrative like the present one, which seeks to cover the first two periods of Lacerda's life, would be incomplete without references to the literary circle that included Carlos, an aspiring playwright and literary critic. And it would be incomplete without a few scenes from the life of his father Maurício, both because the difficult relationship between father and son is part of the biography and because the two were so similar. Neither was underhanded and each owed his political support to voter appeal rather than to deals with power groups. They were exceedingly independent, regardless of the cost. Maurício, one of the most passionate orators of his generation, stirred the masses in the streets against "the oligarchy" and never hesitated to antagonize the top political figures.

Carlos, zealously pro-Communist in his youth, became, like his father, the object of attacks originating in the Communist Party. In 1954, when the curtain was falling on the first period of his life, his strident anti-Communism and role in the events that led to the suicide of President Getúlio Vargas were so provocative that mobs in the streets shouted "Death to Lacerda." But the ballot boxes made it almost immediately apparent that the appeal of the courageous campaigner against corruption was extraordinary. He received more votes than had ever been cast in Brazil for a congressional candidate.

Former Foreign Minister Afonso Arinos de Melo Franco, who was prominent in the federal legislature when Lacerda was there, states that Lacerda's activities affected adversaries and supporters to such an extent that "no one will be able to be compared with him."[3] Some of Lacerda's congressional speeches have been published in an 800-page volume with introductory comments by José Honório Rodrigues, who asks us to bear in mind that writings by Lacerda, and especially his speeches, were remarkable in that they had effects that were "instantaneous."[4] In the hope of producing a companion to that fat volume and report on some of those effects, I have tried to reconstruct the settings in which the pronouncements were made and, thus, have given attention to politicking.

Thanks in large measure to Lacerda, politics were turbulent in 1955, his first year as a congressman. It was a presidential election year, and he hoped to deliver a blow to the leading candidates by his disclosure of the "Brandi letter." The letter, which he considered authentic, was a forgery, and he was described by his adversaries as a forger himself.

Already Lacerda had advocated a postponement of elections in favor of an "emergency regime" to reform political ways and thus had gained the reputation of desiring a coup and dictatorship. When he demanded in November 1955 that the election victors, Juscelino Kubitschek and his running mate, João Goulart, be prevented from taking office, he did nothing to diminish that reputation. The pro-Kubitschek "counter-coup" of War Minister Henrique Lott led him to exile himself abroad, thus ending what he later considered the worst year of his life.

Following his return to Brazil in 1956, and for most of his career in Congress, Lacerda was barred from using radio or television because Kubitschek feared that broadcasts of his oratory might bring about the fall of the government. So combative was the freshman congressman that he was awarded the post of leader of the opposition party. The government, hoping to have him jailed, argued that his attempt to uncover corruption had impaired the national security. Thus he became the central figure of a parliamentary drama that stirred the nation. "A traitor is loose in the streets," the pro-government *Última Hora* screamed after Lacerda's stunning victory in the Chamber of Deputies.[5]

The congressman was constantly on the campaign trail. He stirred up crowds as his father had done, but with more literary polish. The campaign of 1958 in an old truck, the Caminhão do Povo, attracted enormous attention and led Afonso Arinos to observe, "Never have I experienced anything as stimulating, as fantastic."[6] The campaign in 1960 for the governorship of the new state of Guanabara was the roughest of all, with Lacerda's opponents on the Left distorting his controversial past to call the "author of the shameful Brandi letter" a fascist agent of foreign imperialism. Journalist David Nasser rudely and inaccurately wrote that Lacerda as a friend was "horrible"; but he had to admit that the candidate was honest, intelligent, and patriotic and had faced the kind of struggle "in a corrupt country" that perhaps justified "his excesses."[7]

The narrow victory of Lacerda in Guanabara coincided with the sweeping victory of Jânio Quadros for the presidency. No one individual, not even Quadros himself, showed as much determination as Lacerda to place the temperamental former governor of São Paulo in the presidential palace. Lacerda, who had once called Quadros a "virtuoso of felony," similar to Hitler, was therefore accused of revealing, and not for the first time, inconsistency. The accusation was accurate. But in the bizarre business of political alliances, forged and broken by men belonging to thirteen parties, inconsistency was commonplace. If it appeared startling in the case of Lacerda, it was because the journalist-politician used such strong language to express, almost daily, his views about everybody and everything.

Lacerda, in making his alliance with Quadros, remained consistent with his long cherished goal of crushing an "oligarchy" he had reason to consider corrupt. With the achievement of that goal in the elections of 1960, he attained, at the age of 46, a new peak in his tumultuous political career. The governor-elect and foremost orator of the republic appeared to be destined to reach the presidency before long.

J. W. F. D.

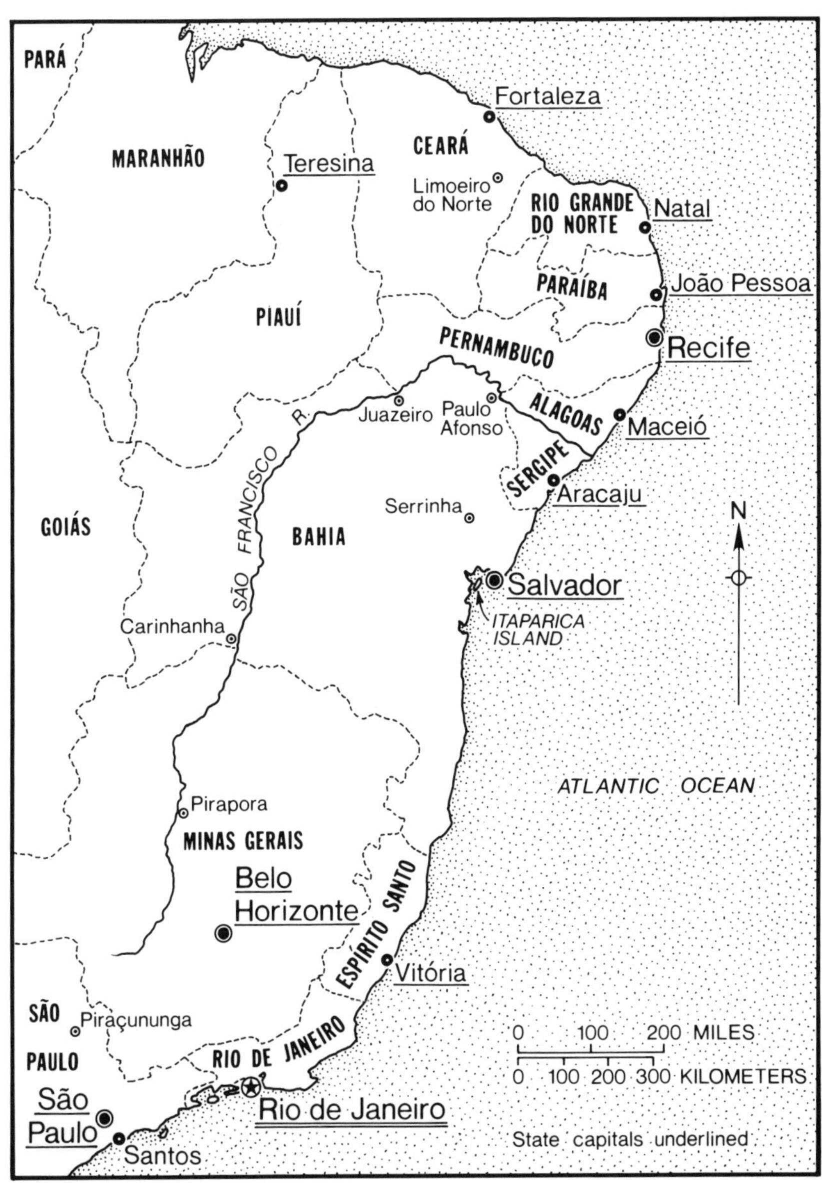

Eastern Brazil and the São Francisco River

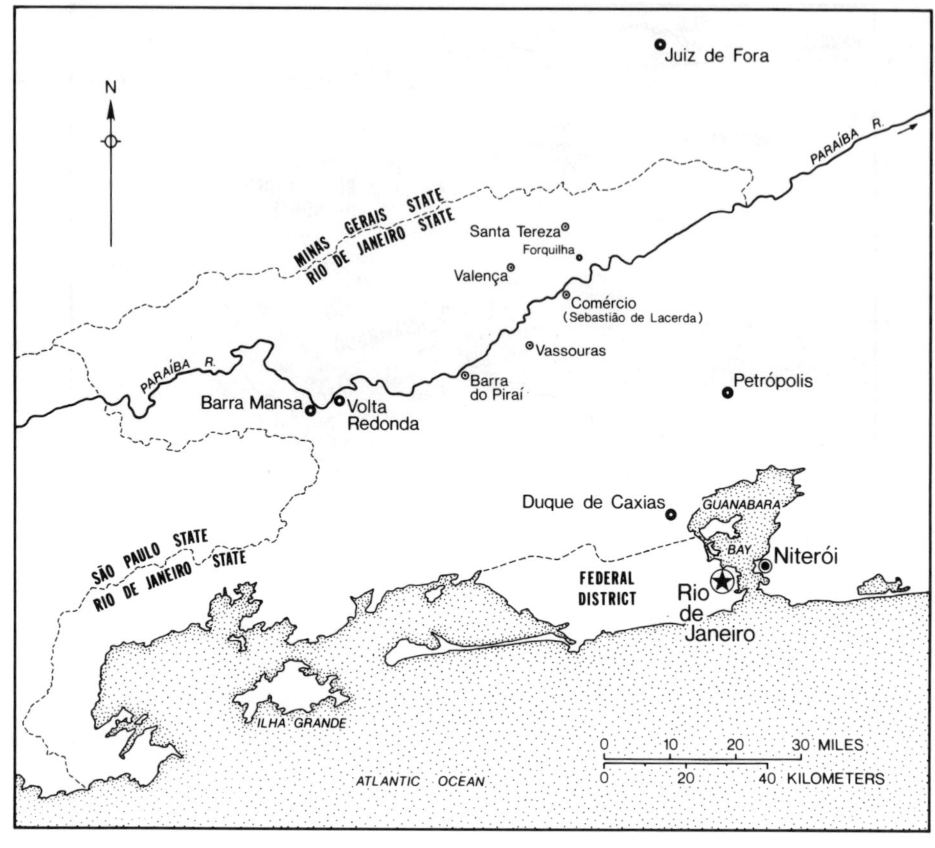

A part of Rio de Janeiro state and the Paraíba River

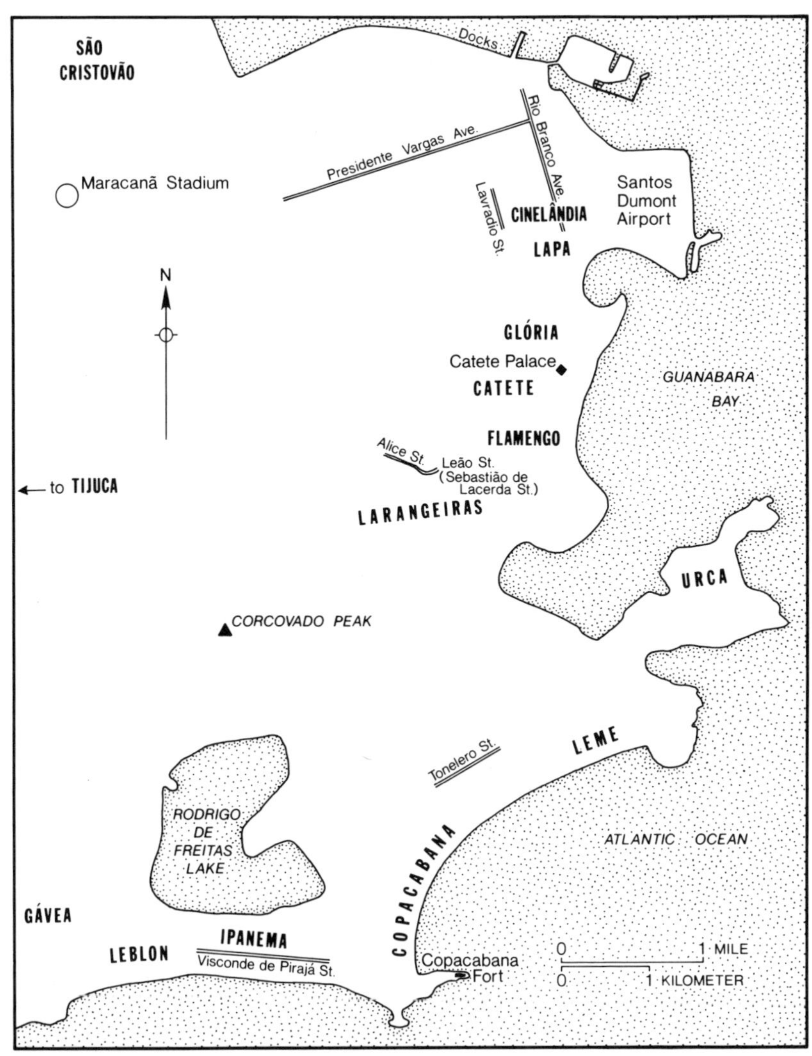

A part of the city of Rio de Janeiro

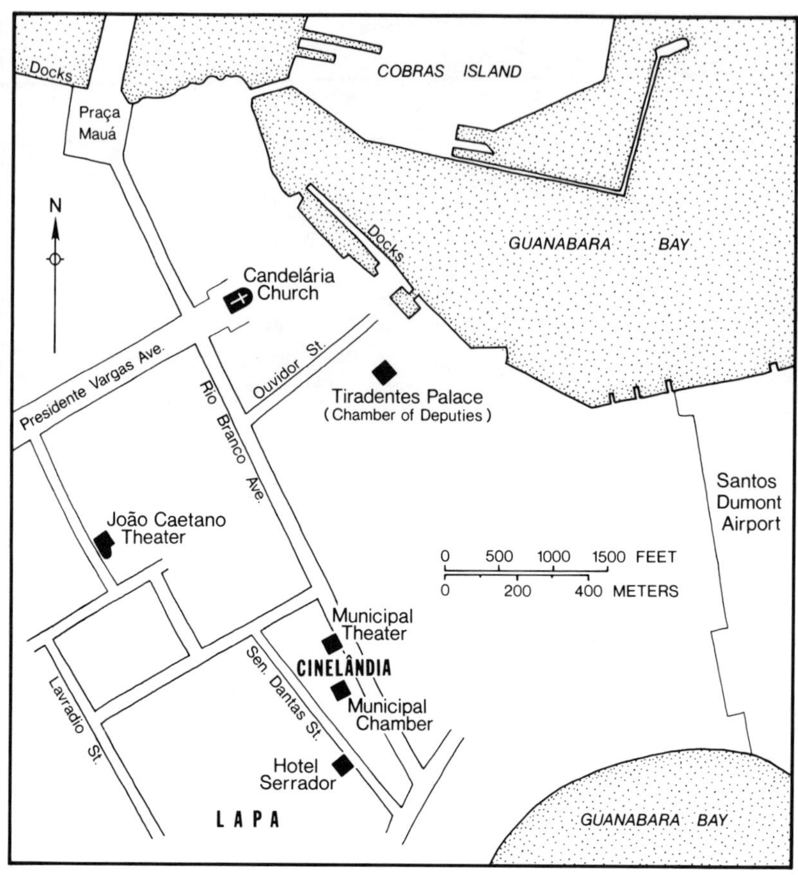

Downtown Rio de Janeiro

Carlos Lacerda, Brazilian Crusader
Volume I: The Years 1914–1960

I.

Son of Maurício (1914–1931)

1. Family Background (1860–1900)

Soon after Carlos Lacerda was born in the city of Rio de Janeiro in 1914, his father, Maurício, registered the birth as having occurred in Vassouras, a municipality that includes a stretch of the Paraíba River, about forty miles north of the infant's real birthplace.

The Lacerda family's loyalty to the hilly municipality was equaled by the loyalty that the people of Vassouras showed to the Lacerdas, particularly to Maurício during difficult moments of his colorful political career. As for Carlos, Vassouras came to be associated with unforgettable scenes in the days when he grew up. Recalling those days, he observed that the Paraíba River was as important to his boyhood as the Mississippi was to Mark Twain's.[1]

Vassouras became the home of the Lacerdas because Maurício's grandfather, João Augusto Forjaz Pereira de Lacerda, settled there after crossing the Atlantic from the Azores. João is described by Carlos as a modest, good-natured baker and bookkeeper who found a wife in the city of Vassouras, the seat of the municipality, in the early 1860s. His bride, Maria Emília Gonçalves de Andrade, had come from Madeira Island.

In 1877 João found work in the riverside village of Comércio, which boasted a station on the recently extended Central do Brasil Railroad, not far from the city of Vassouras. The work allowed João to acquire an old coffee property, or *chácara,* across the river from the railroad station, and there he built a bakery. He would have been content simply to make and sell bread, but his wife, whose uncles and brothers were prominent in São Paulo educational and religious affairs, was ambitious and energetic. With the help of a mentally disabled slave, she drained swamps on the *chácara* and turned the swampland into a profitable orchard, featuring mangos that were sold to train passengers.[2]

Thus it was possible to provide the couple's two boys, Sebastião and Edmundo, with university educations. Edmundo received a medical degree in Rio and established a practice in Petrópolis. His older brother, Sebastião Eurico Gonçalves de Lacerda, grandfather of Carlos, was attracted to the São Paulo Law School by a maternal uncle, a professor. In São Paulo, where

Sebastião studied in the early 1880s, the professor took such a liking to the youth that he gave him his 7,000-volume library. But the warm relationship ended when the austere professor, a rabid supporter of the Brazilian monarchy, learned that his nephew favored republicanism.[3]

Returning to Vassouras in 1884 with a law degree and a dislike of slavery and the empire, Sebastião opened a law office and, four years later, founded the Partido Republicano of Vassouras municipality. Following the success of the emancipation and republican movements in Brazil in 1888 and 1889, Sebastião had a distinguished career, assisted by friendships made at the São Paulo Law School, trainer of political leaders. He was a member of the constitutional assembly of the state of Rio de Janeiro (1892), federal congressman (1894–1896), justice secretary of his state (1897), and transport minister (1897–1898) in the cabinet of President Prudente de Moraes. Then, after a ten-year absence from public life, his reaction to the death of his 29-year-old wife in 1898, Sebastião became president of the Vassouras Municipal Chamber, state assemblyman, and secretary-general of the state government. In 1912 he was named to the lifetime post of minister (justice) of the federal Supreme Court by Marshal Hermes da Fonseca, president of Brazil.[4]

The Sebastião de Lacerda known to young Carlos Lacerda was apt to be irritable. Lacking the outward calm of his father, João, and brother, Edmundo, he was given to fits of fury. Inclined to be unsociable, he never hid the deep hurt brought about by the early death of his violin-playing wife, "Pequetita." He wore a small beard, dressed invariably in black suits, and, in the words of Carlos, looked like a studious Jew. Attached to his watch chain was a medallion with a picture of his late wife. The great vocation of Sebastião, Carlos has written, was to be a widower.[5]

Pequetita (Maria da Glória Paiva) was a daughter of Sílvio dos Santos Paiva, a hard-boiled, successful rancher. In 1854, at the age of sixteen, he had come from cattle-raising Rio Grande do Sul to the coffee-growing state of Rio de Janeiro, and there he married into a wealthy family. Sharing Sebastião's ideas, Sílvio became a prominent abolitionist. He ran his estates (*fazendas*) with Italian immigrants and slaves whom he freed long before the emancipation decree of 1888, thus avoiding troubles with newly freed slaves that emancipation brought to other *fazendeiros*.[6]

After the death of Pequetita in 1898, Sebastião tried his hand, without much pleasure, at managing one of his father-in-law's ranches. Meanwhile, his three sons were brought up in the national capital, Rio de Janeiro, by their aunt, Maria das Dores, another daughter of Sílvio. The boys, born between 1888 and 1893, were Maurício, Fernando, and Paulo. The large house, of old Portuguese-style architecture, was in Rio's Laranjeiras district on Leão Street, named after the marble lion on the building's front wall.[7] It had an enormous yard where flowers (once tenderly cultivated by Pequetita)[8] and fruits were grown.

Maria das Dores ruled the establishment with an iron hand that was much needed because the residence was generally filled with the boys' cousins who came to Rio to attend schools. At the plays the children put on, the willful Maurício Paiva de Lacerda, Sebastião's oldest son, was always the leading "prince," and he was undisguised favorite of his grandfather, Sílvio dos Santos Paiva.[9]

2. A Multitude of Relatives (1900–1914)

Maurício, an ardent reader, was fiery in speech and action. He was not a tall man and has been compared with Napoleon by his son Carlos, who wrote that Maurício was out to conquer the world, had the necessary charms, and was proud of them. He became an emotional orator, one of the foremost in Brazil in his generation, and was, according to another observation of Carlos, the center of events wherever he was.[1]

Maurício has written that in 1907, when he was nineteen, he first raised his voice against Brazil's political bosses and that in 1909, while still studying law in Rio, he turned twice to military men to banish what he considered oppression by professional politicians. In the first episode he used weapons and soldiers, furnished by his friend Colonel Manuel Carneiro da Fontoura, to rid Vassouras of the "thugs" of federal Congressman Henrique Borges Monteiro, who opposed his father's electoral hopes. Later that year he participated in his first conspiracy. Learning from Fontoura about a soldiers' plot to rid the nation of professional politicians, he joined it.[2] But President Afonso Pena, who was to be overthrown, died before the plot materialized.

During these years Maurício welcomed opportunities to be with Olga Caminhoá Werneck,[3] who lived in a house on Alice Street, practically an extension of Leão Street. Olga's father, Ignácio Avellar Werneck, was a relative of rancher Sílvio dos Santos Paiva's wife (making Olga a cousin of Maurício) and had died in his early thirties, in 1900, after a business failure.[4]

Visiting the Alice Street house, Maurício found women, poverty, and pride in the achievements of two men who had died. Olga's grandmother "Yayá" (Delmira Monteiro Caminhoá) ran the house, trying to make ends meet by economies, such as restricting the use of lights, and by selling land around the house. It had been built by her husband, Joaquim Monteiro Caminhoá (the first of the illustrious pair). A medical doctor from Bahia, Caminhoá had taught the daughters of Emperor Pedro II and become a distinguished botanist. The manuscript pages of his botanical dictionary, never completed because of his death in 1896, were preserved with reverence in the study.

The three generations of Caminhoá women in the house included sisters of Olga's mother. One of them had died a few years back, and so had her husband, surgeon Eduardo Chapot-Prévost (the second of the illustrious pair). At the turn of the century, the surgeon had achieved fame by performing, for the first time in Brazil, an operation separating Siamese twins. Maria, one of the twins, did not live long, but Rosalina, the other, survived and was brought up as a member of the family.

When Maurício, having graduated in law late in 1909, married Olga at the

Alice Street house in June 1910, Colonel Carneiro da Fontoura served as *padrinho* (sponsor) for the groom.[5] For *madrinha,* Olga chose a niece of Yayá who had been raised by Yayá before marrying a rich sugar mill owner in Bahia.

Paivas, Wernecks, Lacerdas, Caminhoás, and assorted relatives and acquaintances gathered together from time to time in the countryside after Sílvio dos Santos Paiva ("the old plowman," as he called himself in letters to newspapers) sold his small farms and used the proceeds to purchase Forquilha, a huge *fazenda* in Vassouras municipality about fifty miles north of the Brazilian capital. The five-hour trip from Rio was made partway by the wide-gauge Central do Brasil, followed by a narrow-gauge train to Santa Teresa de Valença, and then by horse or carriage. Besides its housing for 150 workers' families, Forquilha offered an elaborate main house, with large windows and an elegant entrance staircase, and was constructed in the form of a chalet. It had a chapel in one wing. The fourteen bedrooms were particularly useful because Sílvio's son, Júlio dos Santos Paiva, was a hospitable man and the father of fifteen children.[6] Júlio's wife, Silvina, known as Vinoca, was a sister of Sebastião de Lacerda.

Forquilha was very imposing, but Sebastião's Comércio property did not remain insignificant. In 1914 Sebastião greatly enlarged the building there, giving it three high-ceilinged floors surmounted by a pinnacle, with a circular staircase inside, so that the Supreme Court minister could look out over the trees.[7] This house, too, had fourteen bedrooms. But the bedrooms were small, and the Comércio fruit *chácara* could not compare with vast Forquilha, with its cattle, corn, and abundant coffee. When Sílvio, "the old plowman," died at the age of 77 in 1915, Forquilha passed on to his son, Júlio dos Santos Paiva. With Júlio's death in 1920, his wife, Vinoca, the myopic sister of Sebastião de Lacerda, became the owner of Forquilha.[8] She presided over the vacation-time gatherings at which cousins played with each other, fell in love with each other, and not infrequently married each other.

3. Maurício Enters Politics (1910–1918)

In 1909, while completing his law studies, Maurício worked for the presidential election of Marshal Hermes da Fonseca, who was promising to rid Brazil of oligarchical political bosses. The youth was rewarded in 1910 (the year of his marriage) with a post in the new president's office, and from there he followed the regional conflicts that accompanied the marshal's efforts to make good on his promises.[1] Maurício participated in the political conflicts in Rio state, where he ran a publication, *O Vassourense,* and gained election to the state assembly. In 1912, when the marshal named Sebastião to the Supreme Court, Maurício was elected federal congressman from Rio state and left the president's office.

Continuing to attack the political establishment, Maurício turned against President Hermes da Fonseca because he came to distrust the influence that Senator Pinheiro Machado exerted on the president. Joining such well-known oppositionists as Rui Barbosa, Irineu Machado, and Pedro Moacyr, Maurício unleashed blistering attacks on the administration.[2]

During the four years of the marshal's term (1910–1914), Olga gave birth to her three children: Maurício ("Mauricinho"), born in 1911; daughter Vera, born in 1912; and Carlos Frederico Werneck de Lacerda, born on April 30, 1914. Maurício was reading a book in the study once used by botanist Caminhoá when Carlos was born, shortly after midnight, in Yayá's upstairs room at the Alice Street house. In choosing the names Carlos and Frederico for his son, Maurício paid tribute to Marx and Engels.[3]

Maurício's brother Fernando, who became godfather of Carlos, was embarking on a medical career. With the outbreak of the war in Europe in August 1914, he planned to join the French fighting forces as a doctor. But he was an obedient son and abandoned the idea when his father objected.[4] Fernando was always trying to make up, in the eyes of Sebastião, for the disappointments provided by the judge's other sons, Maurício and Paulo. Paulo was merely wild as a law student, and Fernando, a prude, kept assuring Sebastião that he was straightening his younger brother out.[5] After Paulo graduated in law and married into the Bhering chocolate manufacturing family, he was, in the words of Carlos, sent to do legal work for the São Paulo police in the state's interior, as a "cure" for the fondness for "wild follies" he had revealed as a student. He became a devout Catholic, a serious scholar of Jesuit literature, and was soon writing his father to complain about the spiritualist doctrines embraced by Fernando.[6]

Neither Sebastião nor Fernando could do anything to curb the independence and irreverence of Maurício. Fernando, writing his father in 1912, could only express the hope that time would cure him of his "rotten" behavior toward his father. After Maurício upset Sebastião with an unfilial letter in 1915, Sebastião concluded that Maurício was drinking too much. Fernando expressed his loathing for the letter but added that his older brother was simply suffering a "mental imbalance" and was not an alcoholic.[7]

This was the year when Maurício was elected mayor of Vassouras and was first reelected to Congress. Also in 1915 he was chosen to lead a "sergeant's revolt," planned after the government majority rejected his proposed legislation to benefit sergeants. The "revolt," which Maurício later maintained had the objective of giving Brazil a parliamentary form of government, never broke out. But it was thoroughly investigated. Maurício proudly spurned an offer of Rio state Governor Nilo Peçanha that would have taken him on a sugar study mission to Chile and spared him possible reprisals. Replying to allegations that Sebastião had harbored conspirators, Maurício pointed out that he and his father were not on speaking terms and added that Sebastião received so many guests at Comércio that he did not know who some of them were.[8]

Maurício's friends were anarchist and socialist writers for *Na Barricada* (1915) and *O Debate* (1917), populist politicians, and labor leaders who defied President Venceslau Brás and the police during the great strikes of mid–1917.[9] These friends and Maurício's negligence of his home had become a severe trial to Olga. Desperate, she wrote her father-in-law as early as 1914, just before Carlos was born, to complain that Maurício spent all his time with vulgar "riff-raff," such as politicians Irineu Machado and Pedro Moacyr, and came home infrequently and then only to change his clothes. Olga pleaded with Sebastião to persuade Maurício to forsake, and stop imitating, his companions. She could not, she added, continue putting up with the role of abandoned wife.[10]

Maurício, who resented Olga's opinions of his companions in battle, had plenty of admirers away from home. He could be charming. Orating in a manner that Carlos has said was captivating, audacious, and more appealing to emotion than to reason,[11] he built up the reputation of being "adored by women." His enemies—and he did not seem to care how many his unyielding positions brought him—called him a demagogue. But Maurício's campaign against the power of the oligarchy was a sincere one, and he was as strictly honest in his mission to help the underprivileged as he was in money matters. As early as June 1917 he was calling for the government to create a labor department and by the year's end was expressing admiration for the Bolshevik revolution.

Having been reelected congressman in 1918, Maurício traveled to Europe to inform himself about the social question there and the problems of post–World War I peace.[12] Cables from Olga and Sebastião, reaching him in Paris in December, advised that his family was suffering from the epidemic of "Spanish flu" that, as early as mid-November, had already afflicted half of Rio's population of 900,000 and killed 14,500 Cariocas.[13] He wrote a tender letter to Olga and promised to take a steamer to Brazil in January.[14]

Olga and two of her three children (7-year-old Mauricinho and 6-year-old Vera) were among those stricken at the Alice Street house. Sebastião resolved that 4-year-old Carlos, the cute imp who was becoming his favorite grandchild, should be taken by the children's nanny, Clara Freitas, to the home of Sebastião's brother Edmundo in Petrópolis. But Carlos fell ill in Petrópolis. Clara, devoted to the boy, nursed him during eight worrisome days.[15] Like the rest of the family, Carlos recovered before Maurício was back in Brazil.

4. Tribune of the Proletariat (1919–1924)

Maurício returned from Europe to find Brazil preparing for a special presidential election to be held because the "Spanish flu" had killed the winner of the contest of 1918. Contemplating the race between Epitácio Pessoa, a northeasterner friendly to his father, and oppositionist Rui Barbosa, Maurício declared that he would henceforth put the social question ahead of political matters.[1]

During Epitácio Pessoa's three years in the presidency, Maurício's "speeches, articles, polemics, and battles,"[2] gained him the reputation of being a Bolshevik as well as a demagogue. He descended, in his words, from the tribune of the parliament "to the popular tribune of the proletariat." In the anarchist-slanted workers' newspaper *Voz do Povo* (which he supported

Incendiary Maurício de Lacerda. (*A Maçã*, August 5, 1922)

with part of his congressman's paycheck),[3] Maurício suggested that the police clashes against labor and the whipping of arrested workers, combined with the refusal of the government majority to enact legislation he introduced, increased the likelihood of changes being wrought by violent revolution.[4] He did all he could to get workers to organize and strike. Although he was the choice of unions to represent Brazilian labor in Washington at the postwar International Labor Congress, he declined the mission (officially offered by the government) because labor's representatives would be in a minority there. Using his well-known irony, he ridiculed remarks made at the Congress by representative Afrânio de Melo Franco.

Writing in *Voz do Povo* about the violent Leopoldina Railway strike of 1920, he deplored what he called the Brazilian president's failure to observe labor practices recommended in the Versailles Peace Treaty, signed by Epitácio Pessoa himself.[5] The president and his men retaliated by arranging to have Maurício excluded from the Partido Republicano Fluminense and replaced in Congress in 1921 by Henrique Borges Monteiro, whose "thugs" Maurício had dispersed from Vassouras in 1909.[6] Amidst a throng of admirers, Maurício was conducted from the Chamber of Deputies to the street, where he made another of his impassioned speeches—this one declaring that it was in the streets, and not Congress, that the truly representative voices were to be heard.[7] It was hard to disagree with this position after the administration-controlled majority of congressmen refused to seat oppositionist Nicanor do Nascimento (elected in the Federal District in 1921) because he attacked President Epitácio Pessoa's ethics.

Maurício and former President Hermes da Fonseca, both furious with Epitácio Pessoa, made their peace and gave their support to Nilo Peçanha's campaign to win the presidency in 1922 from the official candidate, dour Artur Bernardes. Maurício, indignantly rejecting a bribe offered by Bernardes' supporters, had the temerity to go to Bernardes' own state of Minas Gerais on behalf of the opposition. Speaking in Juiz de Fora, he was struck on the head by one of the stones hurled by ruffians brought there by the political party of Bernardes. Later he was photographed, his head well bandaged, as he entered the Supreme Court building to plead (successfully) for a writ of habeas corpus that would give him protection when speaking in Minas.[8]

Early in June 1922, not long after the official election count made Bernardes president-elect, a few unhappy military officers spoke to Maurício about a planned revolt. But Maurício declined to support it upon learning that its objectives did not include prolabor measures. The revolt took place on July 5, 1922, principally at Rio's Copacabana Fort, and was subdued in a few days, during which Maurício tried to help arrested civilians by drawing up a habeas corpus appeal that suggested that both Epitácio Pessoa and Rui Barbosa (who voted for a state of siege following the uprising) were traitors to their earlier pronouncements.

Then Maurício himself, accused of conspiring, was arrested at the Leão Street house, much to the indignation of Sebastião, who phoned the police to object to the invasion of the home of a Supreme Court minister and the arrest there of a legislator of Rio state (his son). Maurício was released within a couple of days, during which he was elected municipal councilman of Vassouras. But, with his foes in control of his native state, he did not long remain in any legislative post. His alleged conspiring in 1922 was given as the reason for depriving him of his councilman's seat.[9]

Now a former congressman, Maurício directed the Rio daily, *A Nação*.[10] He conspired with retired General Isidoro Dias Lopes, whose plans for rebellion appeared to include a supportive uprising by labor. "Only cannons," Maurício told the depressed and dying Nilo Peçanha, "can resolve the Brazilian case."[11]

When the rebellion was set to break out in Rio in September 1923, Maurício arranged for his brothers, Fernando and Paulo, to take their ill father to Comércio. Fernando had long ago turned from spiritualism and was a puritanical Catholic who did much more than Maurício or Paulo to care for Sebastião. Paulo had become active in the Communist Party of Brazil, much to the exasperation of his wife.[12]

The Army conspirators postponed the rebellion and made plans for it to break out in São Paulo, to which Maurício objected. He also objected to a purely military movement and made it clear, in an article in *A Rua*, that he would back only a social revolution.[13]

Before the uprising of July 5, 1924, occurred in São Paulo, with Isidoro as its chief, Maurício was advised by a fellow member of the Masonic Order to flee from Rio. He chose not to flee and was arrested on July 5 by the police of Marshal Carneiro da Fontoura, once the *padrinho* at his wedding and now an implacable foe of the Lacerdas. The effect of Isidoro's revolution was a state of siege and considerable turmoil, lasting until late in 1926, when Bernardes' term ended and Maurício was at last released.

5. Carlos and His Relatives (1919–1924)

If Maurício's interest in journalism, labor unions, and politics kept him often from home, so did his devotion to his mistress, Aglaiss Caminha, the schoolteaching daughter of novelist Adolfo Caminha. In 1920, when she bore Maurício a son in Rio, the proud father named the boy Maurício and registered his birth as occurring in Vassouras. (Later Aglaiss had the registration of the boy's name changed to Maurício Caminha de Lacerda and therefore confusions with Mauricinho were usually avoided.)[1] Olga, her life shattered by Maurício's behavior, tried to defend "her lost world" by keeping up appearances and thus, Carlos has written, postponed the moment "when the truth burst into our lives" and made it easier to "resist the impact."[2]

Recalling his boyhood, Carlos has admitted that "in the rare but fascinating interventions of my father in our life . . . , he brought us news of the world, a new book, an idea, the description of a scene, the culminating moment of a debate, an intelligent word, an interesting, unusual vision of things and personalities, a jubilant good faith, the love of human beings, not of abstract entities." Carlos' sister, Vera, remembering her father's visits during her girlhood, mentions sea captains, who, "when they appear now and then, are the most enchanting of fathers."[3] For Vera these appearances became less frequent after February 1922, when she began her six-year stay at the Assunção Boarding School, run by nuns in Rio's Santa Teresa district. Her stay there was financed by her wealthy godfather in Bahia, whose wife, Yaya's niece known as Nhanhã, had been *madrinha* at Olga's wedding. Vera, separated from family life at an early age, was happy to see Carlos each Sunday, even if her younger brother, during the Santa Teresa streetcar rides, ate all the chocolate he was supposed to bring her.[4]

Carlos received his first lessons at home (the Alice Street house) from his nanny, Clara Freitas, who shared a bedroom with him, and from his godmother, a sister of Olga.[5] Then, in 1922, at the age of eight, he went to the José de Alencar public school, which Vera had attended earlier.

He was an active, imaginative boy, who would use the old blackboard of botanist Caminhoá when he pretended to be a teacher or turn furniture into "space ships" with his brother, Mauricinho. He inherited, more than Mauricinho, the willfulness of his father. Vera, speaking of young Carlos' determination to get others to do what he wanted, says he was so persistent that in the end the others would give in simply to end the argument.[6]

He could be a terror—in which case the family would call the nanny, saying "Clara, come and do something about Carlos." Frequently she was fierce with him and sometimes spanked him until he cried. But she looked after him with affection for she was crazy about him.[7]

Cutting classes, Carlos would make his way to a tourist agency where he gathered brochures to add to the collection of pictures and magazine clippings that represented his secret, better world. All was destroyed when a periodic housecleaning reached his secret hiding place in a cupboard. Recovering from his tears, he set about making albums by using the backs of discarded medical records of surgeon Chapot-Prévost. Exasperated when the albums were burned by his aunt in the backyard, he turned to vengeance. Running into the living room, he "messed up all the furniture, turned chairs upside down, pulled the tablecloth, overturned the sofa (supreme humiliation for the pride of the furniture), and enjoyed the suffering of the pieces, which are not as inert as they say."[8]

It was not difficult for Carlos to see himself as a martyr. He has written that the tears produced by a spanking gave an iridescence to the halo he pictured above his head. But a very different experience was in store when his mother learned that he had discovered her hiding place for cash and had been stealing from it. Summoned by the disconsolate Clara Freitas to go to the formal, seldom used room for receiving visitors, Carlos found his mother and soon saw that she was deeply hurt. Tenderly she explained how little she had to cover expenses. During the tearful session she treated him as an equal, as one she depended on for help, and he found himself determined to be her protector. She promised to tell no one of his transgression, and when Maurício "returned from one of his many trips," the boy became convinced, by his father's attitude, that Olga had kept her word.[9]

By dropping in at the editorial office of *A Tribuna,* of which Maurício was a director in 1922, Carlos became acquainted with his father at work. Sometimes the boy joined his father and other *A Tribuna* officers, such as Austregésilo de Athayde and Gustavo Garnett, at the latter's home. Carlos, the directors found, was inquiring and alert and sometimes expressed more aggressive opinions than one would expect from a boy of eight. He did not hesitate to disagree with his elders and even seemed eager to do so.[10]

Carlos' uncle and godfather, Fernando, went out of his way to be attentive to Maurício's children. But he had his own family to consider after 1923, when he married Ericina Borges, of a family of wealthy Pará rubber merchants.[11] He stopped providing Carlos and his other godchildren, cousins of

Carlos, weekly issues of *Tico-Tico,* and this led Carlos to compose his "first letter of protest"—a complaint about a step that would, he wrote, deprive "three innocent children" of salutary reading. He turned for additional signatures to the other two godchildren, Léa Villares Paiva, a granddaughter of Júlio dos Santos Paiva, and Stellinha, a daughter of Edmundo de Lacerda. When Léa asked whether *afilhada* (goddaughter) should be spelled with one or two *f*s, Carlos gave a novel reply: "with three, you fool!"[12]

It was a pleasure to be with playful Uncle Paulo, who did not behave as an adult and became one of the heroes of Carlos' youth.[13] But Carlos' best friend in these years was his grandfather, and he saw much more of him than of Paulo because Sebastião, imitating the undisguised favoritism once shown by Sílvio dos Santos Paiva for Maurício, insisted that the boy be with him frequently in Comércio. At the *chácara* Carlos came to feel close to the Paraíba River and characters he fancied as having inhabited the old, crumbling slave quarters. The characters were not all imaginary: "Aunt Colodina," the cook with enormous hips, was a former slave and a great storyteller.[14]

In Comércio in 1921, Carlos had one of his most memorable early impressions of his father. Maurício, his head bandaged after his speaking engagement in Juiz de Fora, arrived in a special railroad car filled with his political cronies. At the crowded *chácara,* Maurício explained how he had put his hand to his head in Juiz de Fora and, upon becoming aware of blood, had told a nearby politician that the speechmaking was over. Carlos, proud of his father, was filled with wounded pride when he overheard the whispers of members of the family who criticized the theatrics and suggested that the injury had been slight.[15]

So many political friends of Maurício arrived in the special car and in other trains that Carlos and Clara Freitas had to sleep on the floor of Sebastião's study. The room was filled with framed family photographs. It also contained the notebooks into which newspaper articles were transcribed by hand. Carlos, who could never understand why his grandfather did not simply paste newspaper clippings into the albums, was exempted from copying because his handwriting was considered atrocious. But Sebastião, marking articles about Clemenceau, Lloyd George, or Bolshevik "horrors," found plenty of relatives satisfactory for the chore. Chief among them was the fashionably dressed César de Oliveira, son of a sister of Sebastião's mother and a permanent guest at the *chácara.* Sebastião himself did some copying in a minute, almost illegible hand.[16]

Surrounded by people, the melancholic and sometimes explosive judge was close to none of them. Carlos, the exception, received Pequetita's violin when the judge learned of his grandson's violin lessons. The two of them would listen to the Caruso records that Sebastião liked, or they would take walks, accompanied by Sebastião's dog. Sebastião, in his battered black hat, might be silent much of the time but Carlos felt a closeness in the silence. Then suddenly the judge would start reciting poetry, as he would also do sometimes during the annual train rides with his grandsons and dog to "take the waters" of Caxambu.[17]

Sebastião, a conscientious Supreme Court minister, loathed politics and what he considered the despicable bargaining by politicians. His second son, Fernando, shared Sebastião's ideas. Writing to his father in 1923, Fernando said that Maurício was continuing with his "extremely dubious work" of trying to straighten out the "petty politicians" of Brazil. Considering the "tricks and intrigues" in which these men "wallowed," Fernando told his father that "abstention" was the recommendable course. Before long Fernando and Maurício got into such a bitter dispute that Maurício moved from the Leão Street house to the Hotel Majestic on Laranjeiras Street. He took Olga, Carlos, and the nanny with him.[18]

Carlos must have received a poor opinion of political ways from Sebastião and Fernando, but it was Olga's experience that persuaded the boy to have nothing to do with politics. At the age of nine he brought comfort to his mother by writing her: "I have chosen my profession. It is to be an agronomist. I shall not get involved in politics, I have made this vow. I shall neither defend nor attack. I know that such things upset you because it was with this accursed politics that my father became lost." Following many "kisses" for his "adored mother" was a signature that may have pleased her, for she would have liked to have seen him bear her grandfather's name. He signed: Carlos Frederico Caminhoá Werneck.[19]

6. The Death of Sebastião (July 5, 1925)

Carlos' imagination was stirred by the deeds of the *tenentes*—the military rebels who agitated Brazil in the 1920s. Following the short-lived uprising of July 5, 1922, at Copacabana Fort, he started a notebook of clippings about its participants. On July 5, 1924, he arrived at the José de Alencar School with a copy of Isidoro Dias Lopes' revolutionary manifesto hidden in his boot. Interrupting the schoolwork, he read it aloud. The tolerant teacher simply smiled and Carlos was delighted with the scene he had caused.[1]

With the long imprisonment of Maurício that began on July 5, 1924, Carlos and his nanny went from the Hotel Majestic to live with Sebastião. The judge, already saddened by the recent death of his brother, Edmundo, was about to be shaken by events that would hasten his own death. They included the jailing of his Communist son Paulo and the illness of Maurício, which became serious with the prison's inept and unsanitary medical treatment following the break of a needle in his arm during an injection. Sebastião arranged that his two arrested sons, both ill, be held at his expense as prisoner-patients at a private clinic, the Casa de Saúde São Sebastião.[2]

Maurício, feverish and suffering from kidney trouble, septicemia, and a tumor in the infected arm, was allowed to receive a few family visitors at the Casa de Saúde. It was there that his mistress and their boy, Maurício Caminha de Lacerda, first met Carlos. "Are you Carlos?" Aglaiss Caminha asked him. "Who was that?" the 4-year-old later asked his mother, and she replied that Carlos was his brother.[3]

Police Chief Carneiro da Fontoura let Maurício know that an early release might be possible if Sebastião, no friend of President Bernardes, would keep away from the Supreme Court when it considered the habeas corpus petition submitted on behalf of Edmundo Bittencourt, the *Correio da Manhã* director who, like Maurício, had been held without charge for over six months. Maurício's response was to write to his father to suggest he vote for the release of the courageous journalist. Fernando, fearing for the health of Sebastião, did not deliver the letter, but, anyway, the court was so loaded with administration men that Sebastião's vote would not have helped Bittencourt. According to Maurício, the court was even worse than President Bernardes or the state of siege.[4]

Another letter from Maurício warned Sebastião that Fontoura planned to have the Comércio *chácara* searched for conspirators. Conspirators were there, brought by a friend without the sick judge's knowledge, and, as Maurício's warning was not delivered by the messenger, they were still there when Rosalina, the former Siamese twin, noticed the arrival of a military police brigade on March 28, 1925. Its leader, taken to the bedside of the judge, claimed to be acting in accordance with a verbal authorization of Justice Minister Afonso Pena Júnior. But Sebastião exclaimed: "Search the residence of the Supreme Court minister? Never!"[5]

During the two days that the soldiers remained in the area, the conspirators considered turning themselves in. The judge would not hear of it and said if he were stronger he would join the revolutionaries. Nevertheless, the conspirators decided to leave. Some eluded the police and others were captured.[6]

Dictating sometimes to Fernando, who was taking care of him, Sebastião wrote warm letters of praise to Maurício and Paulo. He let them know that "the two sons separated from me are and will be my reason for pride."[7] When the government threatened to use his absence from the court as a reason for retiring him, he disregarded the advice of his doctor, Miguel Couto, and took the train to Rio, as of old, to participate in the court's deliberations. Carlos was with him at the Leão Street house when he received a visit from cadets who had been expelled from the military academy for having participated with their instructors in the 1922 uprising. The boy heard his grandfather, thin and pale, agree to vote for their reinstatement when the court met on June 25, 1925. But, despite Sebastião's vote, the court ruled against the cadets. So disgusted was Sebastião that he instructed Maurício not to let him be buried in his robe of Supreme Court minister.[8]

Sebastião died on July 5, 1925. According to *Correio da Manhã*, which had renewed publication after a ten-month occupation by the police, Sebastião expressed his farewell thoughts to Maurício, who was permitted to be at his side. "We have," he was reported to have said, "suffered much because we are upright. My son, continue my work! Always remain on the side of the persecuted, the humble, and those who need protection."[9]

The Leão Street house was filled with people, including journalists, when Carlos was taken to Sebastião's side. Lifting lightly a hand of his dying grandfather, the boy found it swollen, repugnant. But he kissed it, as he felt he ought, and then ran tearfully to the Alice Street house.[10]

7. Hard Times for the Family (1925–1927)

After the death of Sebastião, Carlos and the nanny moved to Alice Street. There on August 24 Yayá died. Writing about 1925, Carlos said: "Suddenly I felt myself an adult and expelled from paradise."[1] Family gatherings at Comércio were discontinued and a heavy mourning was observed at the Alice Street house.

Gloom was accompanied by the family's economic distress, occasioned by Maurício's imprisonment and Sebastião's death. It was out of the question to continue paying the bills of the Casa de Saúde São Sebastião. Even with Olga pawning her jewelry, piece by piece, the unpaid bills accumulated, bringing "panic" to the women. Violin lessons for Carlos became a thing of the past.[2]

Nhanhã, following her husband's death, continued to pay for Vera's education but otherwise limited her help to sending the suits of her late husband to be cut down to make clothing for the boys.[3] The Masonic Order's Grande Oriente do Brasil, to which Maurício belonged, paid for educating Mauricinho and Carlos at the Liceu Francês, a middle-upper-class school on Laranjeiras Street.

Classmates noticed that Carlos never took lunch to school, and he was fortunate that one of the pupils brought enough to provide him with snacks.[4] He was considered intelligent but not outstanding in his studies, one of his troubles being that the headmaster expected too much of the precocious boy and put him in the second grade, which he had to repeat. He found arithmetic difficult but excelled in history and languages. He shied away from sports and was one of the few boys who did not kick a soccer ball around during the breaks from lessons. Instead of following publicized soccer competition, he followed the Long March of the anti-Bernardes rebels throughout the Brazilian interior. He found a hero in its leader, the bearded Luís Carlos Prestes.[5]

Another hero of Carlos, his Uncle Paulo, was allowed to return from the Casa de Saúde to his home, where his distraught wife demanded that he choose between her and that "scum of the earth, Communism."[6] Paulo chose Communism and, in 1926, made a gift of Bukharin's *The ABC of Communism* to his 12-year-old nephew Carlos. Uncle Fernando's wife, Ericina, unlike Paulo's, was devoted to the Communist movement[7] and had more influence over her husband. Fernando joined Paulo in the party and served it with a zeal reminiscent of his earlier dedication to Catholicism.

In September 1925 Maurício appeared before the Supreme Court and a capacity crowd of visitors to argue that he had been jailed illegally, had "absolutely no responsibility for the armed movements," and wanted freedom to campaign for the March 1, 1926, election to the Municipal Council of Rio de Janeiro. After he lost his case, by an 8-to-3 vote, he advised Justice Minister Pena that he could no longer pay the Casa de Saúde for the treatment of wounds inflicted by "doctors of the state of siege." He was jailed again and transferred from prison to prison. He read books, writing notes in the margins, and saw practically nothing of his family. Justice Minister Pena, prohibiting visits, answered an appeal from Olga by asserting that "when men conspire they do not think of their families or children."[8]

After a rare visit to his father, made before the minister became inflexible, Carlos returned to Alice Street. There in the backyard he was treated to pro-Bernardes taunts by João Daudt d'Oliveira, the Bromil cough medicine manufacturer from Rio Grande do Sul who had built on a property sold by Yayá. Olga, scolding Carlos later, called the language used in his retorts inappropriate for addressing an older person.[9]

Vera had been able to exchange a glance with her jailed father after a prison doctor had told him when her school bus would pass the prison hospital. Seeing him behind bars brought tears to the 12-year-old girl. At her boarding school, not much later, Vera was told by the daughter of one of the prison doctors that Bernardes had been forced to jail Maurício to cure him from addiction to intoxicants.[10]

Maurício's imprisonment did not prevent his running for the Rio Municipal Council. His manifesto, published in the clandestine, revolutionary *5 de Julho,* declared that "the city, by electing the prisoner, will condemn the permanent state of siege used to scourge it ever since the establishment of the republican regime."[11] On March 1, 1926, he won his council seat easily. In long letters written first from the São Clemente Street police barracks and, after May 1, 1926, from the barracks of the Fire Department, he revealed immense satisfaction with his electoral victory. It would have been impossible, he wrote socialist Agripino Nazaré, if he had allowed himself to be crushed by suffering or fear—or if he had accepted promises of liberty in return for desisting. Continuing to resist, he called President Bernardes "a coward." He was barred, by a Supreme Court decision, from taking the seat given him by the voters.[12]

Maurício's letters to Communist leaders, such as Otávio Brandão and Everardo Dias, made it clear that he wished to remain independent of political parties, including the Partido Comunista do Brasil (PCB) and its electoral front, the Bloco Operário, but would cooperate in "parallel action" as a friend of the PCB. After Washington Luís Pereira de Sousa became president of Brazil on November 15, 1926, and promised a prompt end of the state of siege, Brandão visited Maurício. He urged the haughty prisoner to declare his support for the program of the Bloco Operário.[13]

Maurício, released on November 27, learned of the Bloco Operário program from the pages of his own newspaper, *A Nação,* on January 3, because *A Nação*'s co-owner, Leônidas de Rezende, had turned it over to the PCB. Maurício's annoyance with Leônidas and refusal to support the Bloco Operário's Communist program brought upon him the wrath of *A Nação* and the PCB when he ran unsuccessfully for Congress from the Federal District's second district early in 1927. Before the campaign ended on February 24, Maurício suddenly launched the candidacy of far-away Luís Carlos Prestes for congressman in the first district, infuriating Communists, who saw the move as designed to draw votes away from their own first-district candidate. Paulo Lacerda, now a PCB Central Executive Commission member, spoke savagely against his brother, as required by the party, and was therefore frequently jeered by Maurício's supporters.[14]

8. Pio Americano and Forquilha (late 1920s)

Vinoca, the widow of Júlio dos Santos Paiva and owner of Forquilha, received her brother Sebastião's *montepio* (life insurance income).[1] It helped her pay for the schooling of Mauricinho and Carlos at the Ginásio Pio Americano in the late 1920s. The *ginásio,* a large institution for boarders and day students in Rio's São Cristóvão district, was attended also by some of the Forquilha cousins, such as Odilon Lacerda Paiva (a son of Vinoca) and Moacir Werneck de Castro (more distantly related).

For the most part Carlos was a day student at the *ginásio,* going there from the family's new residence, the home of Olga's deaf mother on São Clemente Street. After the deaths of Yayá and Sebastião, the Alice Street house had been rented and the Leão Street house sold, with Maria das Dores moving from Leão Street to Visconde de Pirajá Street in the Ipanema district (and taking the marble lion with her). According to Carlos, proceeds from the sale of the Leão Street house made it possible for Fernando and Paulo to help finance the Communist Party.[2]

Carlos had an unhappy interval as a boarder at the *ginásio* following a suggestion made to Olga by the school's mathematics teacher Luís Werneck de Castro, older brother of Moacir.[3] Hating what he called the conformity forced on him as a boarder, Carlos ran away. With money borrowed from a schoolmate, he bought a second-class railroad ticket to Comércio and surprised the *chácara*'s administrator, Antônio Bello. Within two days his irate father ordered Bello to bring the boy back to Rio.[4]

Carlos had learned from Sebastião of Maurício's running away from school, and he was quick to remind his father of the episode. Maurício, beside himself with fury, threatened to have Carlos placed in the custody of the Juiz de Menores (judge for wayward or homeless children), whereupon Carlos declared he welcomed the idea. With the help of Olga, a compromise was reached whereby Carlos completed his year as a boarder and then resumed being a day student.[5]

Carlos, whose grades at Pio Americano were generally excellent[6] notwithstanding his difficulty with mathematics, showed great interest in history and literature. Writing an aunt, he praised *Flor del Fango* and *La Demencia de Job* by Vargas Vila and said he had also been reading Machado de Assis and Graça Aranha; he explained that he was getting through the Spanish books with the help of Spanish-French and French-Portuguese dictionaries.[7] He continued to show no interest in sports. At the beach at Urca when he was fourteen he tried to swim, but failed.[8]

It was a surprise to Emil Farhat, a fellow student, to find Carlos reading Euclides da Cunha's *Os Sertões* in the Pio Americano library because he supposed the Lacerdas were well off and must have had a collection that included *Os Sertões.* Farhat and others at Pio Americano considered Carlos talented and restless. They knew him best as the son of Maurício,[9] the oppositionist orator who was easily elected to the Rio municipal council in October 1928.

Carlos skipped classes to attend the sessions of the Municipal Council, in which his father took his seat after adding "with reservations" to the customary pledge to uphold the laws. The sessions were frequently animated and, in Carlos' opinion, more educational than the schoolwork.[10] The two Communist councilmen, Otávio Brandão and Minervino de Oliveira, adhered to the party line and were therefore less friendly to Maurício than he was to them. Maurício, supporter of underdogs, had served as lawyer of Minervino, a marble worker, during the difficult contest to determine whether he should be seated. Carlos often enjoyed telling of how Minervino showed less interest in the legal aspects of the case than in the splendid marble of the building in which it was debated.[11]

Municipal councilmen (*vereadores*) had the use of reserved boxes at the Teatro Municipal, and Carlos took full advantage of the privilege. In an independent frame of mind, he upset his family by attending a theater performance instead of the departure of his mother and Nhanhã to Europe around the middle of 1928 on a trip paid for by Nhanhã. Olga, writing her children from Europe in September, suggested that Carlos study arithmetic and algebra and postpone recreations until vacation time, and she added that "your father has not sent me a single line during the entire trip."[12]

Vacations were spent at Forquilha, where, Carlos has written, "I found liberty and love. With their animated companionship, the many children and grandchildren of Uncle Júlio and Aunt Vinoca ended the solitude of my boyhood."[13] During the vacations at Forquilha, Carlos, with the help of his brother and his cousin Moacir Werneck de Castro, produced a newspaper, *O Forquilhense,* written by hand in notebooks. A sort of holiday diary, it was filled with family news, gossip, and humor. It also called attention to new books, mentioning, among others, *O Circo* by Álvaro Moreyra. The drawings were supplemented by photographs taken with Carlos' small Kodak. Writing to his mother in Europe early in August 1928, he informed her that her picture had accompanied the *Forquilhense* article about her departure for Europe with Nhanhã.[14]

The foremost outlet for his imagination and leadership lay in creating and directing theatrical performances at Forquilha for an audience of relatives and some of the *fazenda* workers. Turning his girl cousins into dancers and giving them Russian names, Carlos would present a serious ballet. It would be followed by a satire, such as "Box Flower," featuring a tall boy who would emerge from a box dressed as a flower while another boy, his sox suspenders showing, would dance as Carmen with a flower between his teeth. Short sketches would contain political and family commentaries. For a "Dance of Death" around a coffin and candlesticks, Carlos wanted everything in red and therefore gathered all the red blankets at Forquilha. For the production of "In a Persian Market," he composed words for the music and dressed his cousins as sheiks, using white sheets and headbands. From swamps on the property, Carlos gathered lilies for a scene appropriate for a "Swan Lake" dance by Júlio dos Santos Paiva's granddaughter Léa Villares Paiva, the talented dancing star of the Forquilha theater.[15]

Carlos participated, without skill, in the Forquilha soccer games. He was chosen goalkeeper, but his poor vision, caused by myopia, was a handicap, and his soccer career ended after the opposing team scored its seventh goal. He did not join the others in taking after-lunch naps. Explaining that sleeping was a waste of time, he would go to his bedroom and write stories ("lightning tales")—a different story for a different person each day.[16]

Elza Werneck de Castro, sister of Moacir and Luís, became very fond of Carlos. But her moralistic views led to squabbles. Finding him reading Émile Zola's *Germinal* at Forquilha, she stole the book before he could finish it.[17]

9. Maurício, Carlos, and the 1930 Revolution (1928–1930)

With the approach of the presidential and congressional elections of March 1930, Maurício, a congressional candidate in the Federal District, devoted his energies to the national situation as a representative of the restless *tenentes.* Their military operations had ended early in 1927 with the retirement of the so-called Prestes Column to Bolivia.

Luís Carlos Prestes himself was in Argentina in March and April 1928 when Maurício was in Rio Grande do Sul helping opposition politicians form "a national united front" against President Washington Luís. After Maurício, still in the south, explained that he was "sowing the seeds of a renovating movement and preaching a loathing of professional politicians," Prestes declared that he and Maurício thought alike and were convinced of the need for a united front to face the pressure organized by the dominant classes.[1]

Maurício, following the advice of Prestes, worked his way northward, spreading his propaganda.[2] Upon reaching Rio, he defended Prestes, "the Cavalier of Hope," against the attacks of Communists Otávio Brandão and Minervino de Oliveira. Presenting himself as Prestes' representative, in October 1929 he called on the Communist Party (PCB) to urge people to vote for Getúlio Vargas, presidential candidate of the opposition.[3] Thus he irritated Prestes, who had a poor opinion of Vargas and his party, the Aliança Liberal.

Maurício's step also irritated the PCB, whose Bloco Operário e Camponês (BOC) named its own presidential candidate, marble worker Minervino de Oliveira. The BOC slate included congressional candidate Paulo de Lacerda. Paulo had represented Brazilian Communism in Moscow at the Sixth World Congress of the Comintern (Communist International) in 1928 and served briefly as PCB secretary-general in 1929 (before being succeeded, also for a short time, by a troika that included Fernando de Lacerda).[4]

The elections of 1930 brought few surprises. Washington Luís' favorite presidential candidate was declared the victor over Vargas. Like all the Communist candidates, Paulo de Lacerda did poorly. On the other hand, his popular brother Maurício won by a large vote.

Back now in the federal Chamber of Deputies, Maurício criticized the May 30 manifesto in which Prestes, turning gradually to Communism, condemned as "insignificant" the purposes of the revolution being planned by *tenentes* and Aliança Liberal supporters of Vargas. A few days later, after learning that Prestes had attacked him in a letter late in 1929, Maurício defended himself against the charge of opportunism made by "the man I most admired and best served." The galleries of Congress were filled when Maurício explained that, in seeking votes for Vargas, he had acted as agent for the revolutionary current and at the request of such outstanding *tenentes* as Antônio de Siqueira Campos and Juarez Távora.[5]

Maurício was at the Rio docks with an enormous crowd on August 7 to receive the coffin of João Pessoa, Vargas' running mate, who had been shot in Recife. His eyes wet, Maurício delivered his most famous speech, calling the dead man's body "the corpse of the nation." "João Pessoa," he cried out, "God willed you the immortal name of martyr of liberty. You are the red banner of our revolt. Citizens, . . . die for this man who gave his life for you. . . . You, Gaúchos and Mineiros, fulfill your promise. The people are ready to die for liberty."[6] Masses of people, some carrying the coffin, advanced defiantly toward a contingent of mounted police that had orders to prevent their using the main avenues. The police drew swords and a bloody clash seemed imminent. But, at the last minute, Maurício climbed on the hood of a car and, in a stirring speech, asked the crowd to interpret the police as a guard of honor and the drawn swords as a gesture of homage to the assassinated hero. He was able to divert the masses and lead the procession along the itinerary established by the authorities.[7]

Gaúchos, Mineiros, and northeasterners started the Aliança Liberal revolution on October 3, and presently its successes led the government of Washington Luís to crack down in Rio on prominent supporters of the movement. After Maurício was arrested in front of the Chamber of Deputies building on October 9, Olga submitted a habeas corpus petition that cited the immunities congressmen were supposed to enjoy. The government denied that it had arrested him, but Vera, thanks to a friendly guard, sent a note to her father and received a reply revealing where he was being held. He was released on the thirteenth, before the Supreme Court ruled on Olga's petition.[8]

While successful revolutionaries—*tenentes* and Aliança Liberal partisans—approached Rio, Washington Luís called up the reserve forces (which included Mauricinho). Then Maurício, at Olga's suggestion and with a little help from Carlos, drafted a proclamation addressed to reservists by their "mothers, wives, and daughters," who said (according to the proclamation) that they would be the first to understand a call to defend Brazil from a foreign attack but not a call to preserve the sinister rule of a group of politicians. "Do not present yourselves," the proclamation admonished. To make hundreds of copies (some handwritten, some typed), a group of young people joined Carlos at the Lacerda home. Later the group went through the streets, delivering copies at residences.[9]

On October 24, before the revolutionaries from the north and south reached Rio, Washington Luís was overthrown by a so-called Pacification Junta of local military leaders. Rio was in delirious turmoil. Mobs sacked stores and burned the buildings of newspapers that had supported the fallen regime. *A Esquerda,* a leftist newspaper, appeared with a headline screaming *vivas!* for Maurício de Lacerda, Getúlio Vargas, and the Revolution.

Carlos donned an old Pio Americano school uniform that had a somewhat military appearance, added a shoulder strap, and went into the streets with his older brother. They grabbed places on a passing truck and, when it took them to Rio Branco Avenue, saw their father in the car of a friend, surrounded by an admiring throng. Maurício told the mob that instead of destroying newspaper buildings it should set fire to prisons and liberate political prisoners. The mob turned to the prisons, freeing more than political prisoners, and Maurício made his way to the presidential palace, where he was joined by his family. Delivering a speech there, he told the presidential guardsmen that, instead of pointing their rifles at the crowd, they should cooperate with his idea of moving the president to a fort where he would be out of danger of being killed by the irate populace. Still at the palace, Maurício had the opportunity to express this thought to members of the ruling Pacification Junta.

After the cardinal, at the Junta's request, persuaded Washington Luís to go to Copacabana Fort, Maurício went there. Carlos was at his side when a car brought Washington Luís. The boy was gleeful at the prospect of seeing the fallen president interned in the fort, but Maurício spoke to his son with words that Carlos would always remember: "Never humiliate someone who has fallen."[10]

With less admiration Carlos would remember his own role that turbulent night of wild celebrations and acts of personal vengeance. He joined a *Diário de Notícias* archivist who wore a red neckerchief of the revolution and who was determined to give expression to his hatred of politicians from his home state of Pará. One of the politicians had disappeared, but Carlos and his acquaintance found a senator from Pará asleep in a hotel room in the downtown Cinelândia district. The archivist pronounced him prisoner and they took him, philosophical and unresisting, to the police headquarters, where he was locked up with other newly made prisoners by João Cabanas, colorful leader of the revolutionary "Column of Death" of the 1920s.[11]

10. The Uruguay Trip and Its Aftermath (1930–1931)

On October 27, during the worst of the disorders in Rio, the exuberant Osvaldo Aranha arrived from Rio Grande do Sul as Vargas' representative. In paving the way for Vargas to take over the government without dispute, he agreed that the military ministers and foreign minister, already named by the Pacification Junta, would continue in office. From the north, *tenente* hero Juarez Távora reached Rio at the same time; and Carlos, whose sister, Vera, had been a schoolmate of Távora's fiancée,[1] was able to meet the revolutionary about whom he had collected newspaper clippings in the 1920s.

Juarez Távora. (Drawing by Appe in *O Cruzeiro,* reproduced in Vol. 4 of Herman Lima, *História da Caricatura no Brasil*)

Carlos was struck by Távora's height and his "handsome face of a pre-Columbian idol, cut in hard rock."[2] Khaki uniforms and red neckerchiefs, such as Távora wore, were becoming commonplace in Rio, and so was the talk of a new era, free from the dominance of Brazilian oligarchies and foreign interests. Olga and other women, responding to a campaign of the recently founded *Diário de Notícias,* solicited money in the Rio streets to pay off Brazil's foreign debt.[3]

Wildly enthusiastic multitudes welcomed the short, stocky, affable Vargas. As he turned to the task of appointing his cabinet, it was rumored that Maurício, like his father, Sebastião, would be named transport minister, and therefore the house on São Clemente Street became packed with job seekers and friends.[4] But a more appropriate possibility came his way after Vargas decided to create a new ministry, the ministry of labor, commerce, and industry, usually simply called the labor ministry. Aranha, who became the new justice minister, and Lindolfo Collor, a former congressman from Rio Grande do Sul, spoke to Maurício, in the name of Vargas, about his becoming Brazil's first labor minister. Maurício, recalling the conversation, has written that his socialist views were incompatible with the corporativist ideas of Brazil's new rulers, influenced by Italian facism.[5] The position was given to Collor.

Maurício did not seek appointive posts and was averse to any that would take him from the center of the Brazilian scene. Therefore Foreign Minister Afrânio de Melo Franco had to exert pressure before Maurício agreed to accept a brief mission in December 1930 to represent Brazil, with the rank of ambassador, at the ceremonies marking Uruguay's centenary. He was to inaugurate a bridge, consider treaties, and explain the Brazilian revolution of 1930, whose objectives, he felt, were entirely misunderstood in Uruguay. In choosing official assistants to accompany him, he included navy officer Hercolino Cascardo, a revolutionary of the 1920s, and the 19-year-old Mauricinho (Maurício Lacerda Filho), a member of the student directorship at Rio's medical school. Olga, Vera, and Carlos also went along, but at the expense of Maurício.[6]

The mission opened on a disturbing note. Even before Maurício stepped off the boat in Montevideo, someone came aboard with one of the leaflets that were being distributed and that repeated, in Spanish, charges made against Maurício in the late 1920s by *A Nação,* the PCB's *A Classe Operária,* and Otávio Brandão, who had become a Communist martyr, languishing in jail for his attacks on the new Vargas government. From a group of Communist youths, which had joined official greeters on the dock, two girls came forward with flowers when Maurício stepped ashore. One of them hit him forcefully in the face while the Communists shouted "fascist" and "We want the liberty of comrade Brandão." Embarrassed Uruguayan officials arrested the mischief-makers.[7]

Maurício, during his short mission, gave speeches and interviews that defended the new Brazilian regime. He pointed out that it was headed by a civilian and had shown clemency to overthrown members of the old regime. He insisted that the Vargas government, which had closed Congress and set the constitution aside, would rapidly return Brazil to democratic ways.[8]

At a reception at the Park Hotel in Montevideo, a diplomat's wife said to Olga, "I didn't know you had four children." Following this remark Olga learned that Maurício had gone to the docks to greet Aglaiss Caminha and their 10-year-old son Maurício Caminha de Lacerda. The incident contributed to the decision of Maurício and Olga, reached in Uruguay, to separate definitely—a decision that left Carlos furious at his father. Ambassador Maurício de Lacerda, upon returning to Rio, established his permanent residence with Aglaiss Caminha and their boy in a small house on Buarque de Macedo Street.[9]

Maurício's return to Rio coincided with the Communists' plans for a "hunger march" to call wide attention to the desperate economic situation of the masses. The Rio police prevented the march and rounded up its instigators. Because Fernando de Lacerda had signed an aggressive bulletin calling on the people to participate in the march, the Rio police invaded his home on January 19, 1931, seized his correspondence, and put him in prison. In São Paulo, Paulo de Lacerda was arrested after a copy of Fernando's bulletin was found in his possession. Maurício, although Fernando and Paulo had broken with him, acted on a dying wish of Sebastião that the brothers defend one another. Visiting Justice Minister Aranha to explain that his brothers were ill, he learned that Vargas wished to have their cases handled to Maurício's satisfaction. Within a week both brothers were at liberty, as were all those accused of involvement in the plans for the "hunger march."[10]

Maurício began to doubt his assurances, given in Uruguay, that Brazil was on the verge of becoming a democracy. Speaking again with Aranha, he argued that the 1930 revolution was making itself unpopular by giving the people no clear idea of when constitutional ways would be resumed. And he used his columns in *Diário de Notícias* to attack the expulsion of foreign leftist agitators from Brazil and the ideas of Aranha that he considered fascist. The primary purpose of the columns, he maintained, was to correct mistaken paths of the Vargas regime, particularly in economic matters, and thus prevent the revolutionary government from becoming discredited. The government, displeased with the articles, offered Maurício the ambassadorship to Bolivia. Citing his dislike of high altitudes, he rejected the offer.[11]

In May 1931 the government forced *Diário de Notícias* to announce that "circumstances" required the discontinuance of Maurício's articles. At the same time, the newspaper reported that police agents had invaded a printing shop to prevent the publication of Maurício's new book. The report, denied by the police, helped the book, *Segunda República,* become a best-seller. But Maurício's passages assured him the enmity of the Vargas regime, which he described as a "fascist dictatorship" that was collapsing because of inattention to social problems. He called on his fellow revolutionaries to form an organization to struggle for radical social programs.[12]

Maurício became a lawyer in the municipal government of Rio. There, after a careful historical and legal investigation, he won an important case when he demonstrated that the Santo Antônio Hill in the federal capital belonged to the government, which could therefore go ahead with plans to open up the area without making payments to an industrial company that claimed ownership.[13]

Popular as ever, Maurício drove on June 1, 1931, from Comércio (renamed Sebastião de Lacerda after the 1930 revolution) to Vassouras city to attend the unveiling of a bust of himself in the main square. In reply to the speeches honoring the municipality's "greatest son," he said that Vassouras had been the foremost inspiration of his ideas.[14] He became mayor of Vassouras in 1932.

II.

Crusader for Communism (1931–1939)

1. The First Publications of Carlos (1931–1934)

The 16-year-old son of Maurício who reported for work at the *Diário de Notícias* in the latter part of 1930 was tall and lean, with a rich head of hair that contrasted with his father's baldness. Carlos had not started to wear glasses, and his new acquaintances were struck by his eyes, which appeared to protrude and contributed to the ardent expression on his angular face.

In return for 150 milreis a month, which came not from the newspaper but from the pocket of Carlos Alberto Nóbrega da Cunha, one of its founders, the adolescent was expected to assist Cecília Meireles by furnishing material for her daily page about education. Cecília Meireles, a 29-year-old former schoolteacher with talent for poetry and drawing, took kindly to Carlos and he came to have a deep affection for her.[1]

Starting in 1931 Carlos could easily contribute items about the Rio Law School (Faculdade Nacional de Direito). His graduation from Pio Americano was assured when the Vargas government, considering the turmoil of late 1930, decreed that all students should be recorded as having passed their courses that year. During 1931 Carlos attended the prejuridical course of the law school, and in February 1932 he started the regular five-year study of law.[2] With his help, *Diário de Notícias* kept its readers informed about the law students' activities, such as their protest following police action against Professor Luís Frederico Carpenter, accused of introducing Communist ideas in his classes.[3]

The first article to show a Carlos Lacerda by-line was a long one, appearing on August 29, 1931. The young reporter discussed in an ornate style the aspirations of youth and the "sins" of "encyclopedists" and egotists who ignored those aspirations. In subsequent signed articles Carlos called for "the abolition of the privileges of tenured professors," the free expression in classes of "the ideologies of the present," and a law school building better than the old one on Catete Street, constructed "for 300 students and handling over 1,000." In a series revealing investigative work, irony, and contempt for authorities, Carlos campaigned against the way children were treated by the Juiz de Menores. To further this campaign, he spoke on Rádio Diário de Notícias.[4]

Cecília Meireles' husband, artist Fernando Correia Dias, became interested in the profile of an Indian apparent in a view of jutting rocks on a slope of Rio's Corcovado Peak. He took Carlos with him on a climb of the pinnacle, and, during the outing, Carlos gathered notes for a story, the artist made sketches, and they both took photographs. The idea of an article appealed to wealthy Álvaro Moreyra and therefore on January 2, 1932, his weekly *Para Todos* published the "sensational report" of Carlos Lacerda and Correia Dias. Carlos' story, "The Other Statue on Corcovado," described the Indian—Carlos called him Tupan—as three times the size of the statue of Christ recently set atop the peak.[5]

The author of the Forquilha "lightning tales" wrote so much about Tupan, the climb, and a chauffeur said to have "discovered" the Indian that *Para Todos* ran a second installment on January 16. After *Diário de Notícias* hailed the "revelation" and reprinted some of Carlos' account, Álvaro Moreyra suggested making a musical record about the Indian. His friend novelist and poet Luís Martins easily persuaded composer Joubert de Carvalho to carry out the task. Joubert's "Maringá," composed hastily to put something on the back of the Victor record, became a hit, whereas "O Índio do Corcovado," sung by Gastão Formenti, did not.[6]

Carlos found broader possibilities for his literary interests after his mother took him to the Casa do Estudante do Brasil (House of the Brazilian Student). "See if you can do anything with this rascal," she said to Ana Amélia Queiroz Carneiro de Mendonça, the Casa's zealous director and benefactor.[7] The rebellious Carlos was prepared to dislike the 36-year-old, socially prominent Ana Amélia, known as the "Queen of the Students," but he agreed to join her group and visited the Casa frequently. If at first the Casa's chief attractions for him were the inexpensive meals and the typewriter that Ana Amélia placed at the disposal of students, gradually he found himself admiring her spirit, revealed in her reactions to his arguments, and he came to recognize her sincere desire to help students, even when admonishing them. Besides, Ana Amélia, like many women, perceived the timidity that lay behind Carlos' aggressiveness and became fond of him.

After Ana Amélia obtained a government subsidy for a monthly publication of the Casa, Carlos worked on it with her and other students. Placed in charge of the project,[8] Carlos named the magazine *rumo,* gave it a modernistic appearance by doing away with capital letters, and turned it into a vehicle in which students and well-known writers expressed their views. The first number, published in May 1933, featured an article by Anísio Teixeira, director of public education in the Federal District, and contained an article by Carlos that denounced the "cowardly indolence" of Alceu Amoroso Lima, secretary of the Catholic Electoral League. Carlos was unkind to Catholicism also in other articles, such as *mosquitos inconvenientes* and his amusing "posthumous interviews" with Eça de Queiroz (written eça de queiroz). In one of his early articles for *rumo,* Carlos turned to his "almost native land," Vassouras. Describing the old slave quarters, mill wheel, and corrals, he argued that Brazil's "intermediate zone" had been neglected by

Drawing by "carlos frederico" (Lacerda). (*rumo*, September 1933)

foreigners who wrote about the country as though only the backlands (*sertões*) and coastal areas existed.[9]

Carlos' illustrations, drawn in a primitive manner and signed "carlos frederico," took their places in *rumo* alongside those of Di Cavalcanti, Cândido Portinari, and Paulo Werneck, cousin of Carlos' mother. Cousin Elza Werneck de Castro, who had taken Émile Zola's *Germinal* from Carlos at Forquilha, was not pleased with *rumo*. "At least you could put in capital letters," she scolded.[10]

Carlos designed the cover of *sensacionalismo*, the Casa do Estudante's first book. Published in 1933, it was a collection of articles and speeches prepared for the campaign of the law students' association, the Centro Acadêmico Cândido de Oliveira, to combat undesirable sensationalism in the media. Cecília Meireles' article praised the campaign. Carlos contributed remarks, given by him on Rádio Sociedade, about scandalous police reports

Plínio Salgado. (Drawing from João Mellão Neto, *Jânio Quadros: 3 Estórias para 1 História*)

used by newspapers to increase sales. It was up to the readers, Carlos concluded, to show better taste and pave the way for a clean and serious press.[11]

While writing for *rumo,* Carlos participated in the world of artists by taking an interest in Pro-Arte, an association launched lavishly by the German embassy in January 1932 to foster artistic interchange. Cecília Meireles' drawings were exhibited at Pro-Arte. *Rumo* promoted a talk that author Mário de Andrade, a *rumo* contributor, gave at Pro-Arte, and Carlos Lacerda delivered the opening remarks at Pro-Arte's exhibit of Lasar Segall's paintings. But in 1933 Carlos played a role in the demise of Pro-Arte because he discovered that the organization had fallen into the hands of Nazis. Attending a meeting called to elect a slate of officers proposed by the German embassy, he denounced the plan of Nazis to expel Jewish members from the association. Dramatically he walked out and was followed by a large group.[12]

Rumo, which ridiculed Hitler and Mussolini almost from the start of its existence, left the Casa do Estudante in the first part of 1934, following differences of opinion between its editors and Ana Amélia.[13] Carlos, hoping to keep the monthly alive without the government subsidy, moved it to the office of Evandro Lins e Silva, who, before graduating in law in December 1932, had played a role in the successful defense of Professor Luís Frederico Carpenter.[14] *Rumo*'s number 8 (June 1934), showing Carlos, Evandro, and Moacir Werneck de Castro as editors, contained Carlos' stinging article about Plínio Salgado and his growing fascistlike Ação Integralista Brasileira, whose members paraded in green shirts. In a reference to Salgado's assertion that cowardly, "subterranean" resisters to the green-shirt movement would be listed and dealt with implacably, Carlos called on Plínio to include those, like himself, who attacked the movement openly. For addition to Plínio's list, he gave his name and description: law student, 20 years old, thin, tall, dark-complexioned, with a shirt of many colors except green. He invited friends and relatives to attend the third-class burial that, he said, Salgado would be preparing for him. In *rumo*'s last number (9 and 10, of July–August sensacionalismo

conferencias de:
roberto lyra
carlos sussekind de mendonça

artigos de:
cecilia meirelles
benjamin lima
abiud cardoso

palestras de:
roquette pinto
nelson hungria
carlos lima
carlos lacerda
césar luchetti
h. o. sant'anna
fernando castro rebello
joão bosco de rezende
celio loureiro

prefacio de:
anna amelia queiroz carneiro de mendonça

Title page of *sensacionalismo,* first book published by the Casa do Estudante do Brasil, 1933.

1934), Carlos described Salgado's new book, *Voz do Oeste,* as a "marvel of historical dishonesty and ignorance."[15]

With the financial failure of *rumo,* Carlos became a contributor to *Revista Acadêmica,* founded in September 1933 by his classmate Murilo Miranda with the help of Lúcio Rangel and Moacir Werneck de Castro, also classmates.[16] Carlos' first article in *Revista Acadêmica,* published late in 1934, reviewed *São Bernardo* by Graciliano Ramos. Criticizing the novel for its lack of attention to the lives of the oppressed, he praised it for its descriptions of the "wormy world" of the inhuman oppressors. "When the Revolution comes," Carlos wrote, "it will find a system to destroy—but not men, because these, the members of the dominant class, will already have dissolved in their own mud."[17]

2. Carlos, Law Student (1932–1934)

Student associations at the Rio Law School were weak before the 1930 revolution and even the Centro Acadêmico Cândido de Oliveira, open to all the students, was not functioning.[1] A spectacular revival of interest occurred in

1932, when Carlos was a first-year law student. In large part it was due to a tiny minority to which Carlos belonged that was active in awakening an interest in programs and ideas. Officerships in student organizations were often determined by this small group.[2] It was invincible in the annual elections of the members of the official law student directorship, made up of two representatives from each of the five classes.

A majority of the students decided to participate in the directorship election of 1932 in order to support a program that called for evening courses, scholarships, and more-convenient library hours. The program, organized by the tireless Ivan Pedro de Martins, was launched, together with a slate of candidates, by Ivan, Carlos, Donatelo Griecco, Eliezer Schneider, and Edmundo Moniz.[3] Among the candidates, put up by the little group, were Carlos, whose earnestness and intelligent wit won admiration, and Adalberto João Pinheiro, a friend of Carlos from Minas, who belonged, like Carlos, to a politically prominent family.[4] Their landslide victories were mostly a reflection of the effectiveness of a clique that had set to work where a vacuum had existed.

The student association to which Carlos devoted the most attention during his first year was the Clube da Reforma, which tried to practice a parliamentary form of government. The Clube's founder, monarchist-minded Alceu Marinho Rego, served as president and ruled autocratically with the help of a Chamber of Peers, or ministry, of which Miguel Lins was prime minister. At the meetings, held in 1932 in a theater, Carlos discovered himself as an orator. Discussing the problems of young people finding their way in the world, and urging them to choose a path at the side of the weak, Carlos was eloquent and moving. Later his growing following of admirers hung on his every word as he presented his unexpected appeal for a vote of no confidence in the Clube's officers. The 18-year-old speaker ridiculed his adversaries and provided such a biting and lengthy account of their "abuse" of power that his surprising motion was overwhelmingly adopted. Alceu Marinho Rego resigned in fury and Miguel Lins called the assembly "a bunch of imbeciles." Elegant leftist Evandro Lins e Silva became the next Clube da Reforma president.[5]

To participate in a student excursion to Minas, the Clube da Reforma chose Evandro, Carlos, Adalberto João Pinheiro, and Antônio Gomes da Cruz. While they were in Belo Horizonte on July 9, 1932, the unsuccessful three-month São Paulo anti-Vargas revolution broke out, but it failed to attract Carlos because he was still partial to the regime established by the 1930 movement.[6]

Turning his attention to affairs of the heart, Carlos went to Forquilha to be near the cousin he loved, Nedda Villares Paiva, granddaughter of Júlio dos Santos Paiva and younger sister of Forquilha dancer Léa. Carlos, always intense, was passionate about the girl, and his mother, Olga, was fond of her. Nedda's mother, on the other hand, and three pious aunts concerned with the girl's upbringing had the worst opinion of the leftist, anti-Catholic Carlos. Noting his lack of interest in his studies and fearing he was unstable, they predicted that he would be a poor husband.

Carlos persisted and late in 1932 he and Nedda became engaged. The lovesick Carlos happily showered attentions on the girl. But the flirtatious Nedda filled him with so much jealousy that he finally retaliated by avoiding her. Carlos suffered acute agony in 1933 after a conversation with Nedda brought the short engagement to an end. She returned the ring and bracelet Carlos had given her. The bracelet had belonged to Olga, and Olga asked her to keep it.[7]

At the law school in 1933 Carlos became the chief organizer of the opposition to Catholic leader Alceu Amoroso Lima, who aspired to become professor of the introduction to the science of law. Thus Carlos followed the example of Marxist Professor Edgardo Castro Rebello, who had used all the power at his command in 1931 to make sure that Leônidas de Rezende, another Marxist, defeated Amoroso Lima in the contest to gain the appointment of professor of political economy.[8] By 1933 Castro Rebello and Leônidas de Rezende were the professors with the greatest influence on the students.

In 1933 ten candidates for the science of law professorship faced an examining board of five professors, but in the end the contest was between Catholic Alceu Amoroso Lima and Hermes Lima, the favorite of the Left. The audience, made up mostly of Hermes Lima supporters brought in by Carlos, filled the examining room. During the questioning of the candidates, students booed, shouted, and chanted derisive songs when Alceu Amoroso Lima tried to respond. They applauded examiners and even hurled rolls of toilet paper when Alceu was trapped by questions, as not infrequently happened. For the most part the examiners were sympathetic to the Left, and a few of them were rude to Alceu. Hermes Lima, whose responses were greeted by noisy approval, was declared the winner.[9]

Young criminal lawyer Evandro Lins e Silva, who was present at the contest won by Hermes Lima, received an appeal for legal help in 1934 when Maria Werneck de Castro, wife of Luís, became concerned about the fate of Castorina Ramos Teixeira, a prostitute accused of killing her newborn baby by asphyxiation. Maria also appealed to Carlos. After the president of the court appointed Evandro and Carlos as defense lawyers, without pay, Carlos threw himself into the case. Far into the nights he consulted treatises on medical law from the libraries of Sebastião de Lacerda and Afrânio Peixoto, a professor who gave him advice. Appearing before the jury, he presented a scholarly discussion of medical tests to show that it was impossible to determine whether the infant had died before or after birth. And he appealed so effectively to the emotions that two women of the jury were in tears. Evandro addressed the jury forcefully. Even the prosecuting attorney decided to ask for the woman's acquittal. After the jury agreed, a note from a visitor in the courtroom was delivered to Carlos by his cousin Odilon Lacerda Paiva. It said: "In the forty years that I have frequented this forum, I have never witnessed a debut as auspicious as yours. You are a worthy grandson of Sebastião de Lacerda!"[10]

By this time Odilon Lacerda Paiva had married Carlos' sister, Vera, and they had a baby daughter, Lygia. The home on São Clemente Street, also occupied by Olga's mother and sister and the sister's family, had become so crowded that Olga, Mauricinho, Carlos, Odilon, Vera, and Lygia moved back to Alice Street, where they rented a small house.[11] Nearby Leão Street had been renamed Sebastião de Lacerda Street.

At the new Alice Street residence in 1934, Carlos wrote his first book. The fifty pages took him only two nights and were based on research done in 1933 when he spent a little time with his father, the mayor of Vassouras. In the Vassouras municipal library he gathered information about slavery in the area in the 1800s: the *fazendeiros'* patrol for capturing runaway slaves, the whipping posts, stocks, and gallows.[12] With this material he described the flight in 1839 of three hundred slaves to a *quilombo* (hiding place), from which they made their way to one of Manuel Francisco Xavier's *fazendas* and burned the buildings down, leading to their capture by federal troops. After tracing subsequent events, including another unsuccessful slave uprising, Carlos concluded that "slavery still exists"—in the form of the miserable treatment of the poor, hungering, and abandoned masses. Arguing that "the history of Brazil has been the history of the dominant classes," he called on the Paraíba River to remain unnavigable so as not to serve the oppressors.[13]

The little book, dedicated to the Paraíba River and illustrated by Paulo Werneck, was called *O Quilombo de Manoel Congo* and was published in 1935 by Editôra Revista Acadêmica. By then Carlos' Communist activities were giving him trouble with the police and, therefore, his articles began appearing under pseudonyms.[14] His book showed the name Marcos as the author.

After his visit to his father and the Vassouras library in 1933, Carlos was shocked to learn that Maurício had ordered João, an employee at the *chácara,* to send Sebastião's books to Vassouras for the establishment of a Sebastião de Lacerda room in the library. Carlos sent a countermand to João and a severe letter to Maurício. Besides pointing out that he needed the books, Carlos expressed regret that he and his father should have to resort to letter-writing to handle such matters. He added that from time to time he had to straighten his father out by telling him truths that "others either dare not, or wish not, to say." "I lack neither courage nor frankness," Carlos wrote.[15]

Carlos' interest in the books was for his self-education, for he was not pleased with what he was receiving at the law school. Despite his brilliant defense of Castorina in 1933, he was given a failing grade in penal law, an indication of his indifference toward his studies. Reflecting on the Castorina case, he declared that "the cases that interest me do not bring in any money." Making a further excuse for abandoning his law school work, he said, "I am opposed to the existing juridical system."[16] Olga, determined that Carlos receive his law degree,[17] kept urging him to return to university study, following the example of the less rebellious Mauricinho, whose medical education brought an appointment in the Federal District hospital organization in September 1934.[18] Carlos, however, stopped attending law school in 1935.

Cover of *O Quilombo de Manoel Congo*, the first published book of Carlos Lacerda. The author, whose name is given as Marcos, wrote the fifty-page book in a few days in 1934. Editôra Revista Acadêmica published it in 1935.

Carlos felt he could not conform to the "suffocating rules" of the world—rules that seemed to "swallow the soul, like a crusher grinding cane." He tried to commit suicide in his basement room at the small Alice Street residence. Writing later about the attempt, he pictured himself as a youth with a Messianic mission, suffering torment and panic because "all appeared to be lost."

Vera, intending to wake him in the morning, found that he had cut a wrist and was fainting. She summoned their father and he brought one of his cousins, who sewed up the cut. The suicide attempt immediately became a subject never to be mentioned in the family.[19]

3. Communism Beckons (1932–1934)

The economic situation was appalling in 1932. Communist Everardo Dias, living in a Rio slum, raising chickens, and searching for work, wrote to his daughter about the "sordid, nauseating" living conditions of the poor and the suffering caused by the "bourgeois organization."[1] Most of the law students, although hardly members of the downtrodden proletariat, had a difficult time making ends meet and frequently told the sympathetic cashier of the inexpensive Café Lamas that he would have to wait before they could pay him for meals. Carlos Lacerda always seemed in bad straits. Olga, hoping that the Lacerda *chácara* might provide income, wrote administrator Antônio Bello, but the results were insignificant. Like other students, Carlos became dependent on small payments occasionally received for his articles.[2]

Marxism was popular at the law school, due in part to the instruction. Carlos has written that, in Professor Leônidas de Rezende's course on political economy, "I learned Marxism and nothing else."[3] Of even greater influence were the nights that students spent in discussions at the homes of Professors Leônidas de Rezende and Castro Rebello. In 1932 and 1933 at the home of Leônidas de Rezende, who had given *A Nação* to the Communists in 1926, such students as Carlos, Ivan Pedro de Martins, Evandro Lins e Silva, and Antônio Chagas Freitas gathered to discuss, often until dawn, Marx, Engels, and positivism. The professor was convincing. According to Carlos, only Chagas Freitas was not "contaminated" and this was because Chagas Freitas had a "weak head" for beer.[4]

Carlos was among those who were persuaded to join the Communist movement. His first mission, painting "Down with imperialism, war, and fascism" on a statue of Pedro Alvaro Cabral, was a success, and in 1933 he was assigned a second mission: to go with Moacir Werneck de Castro, Tobias Warschawski, and others to the gate of the Lloyd Brasileiro steamship company and start a rally of workers. Policemen, led by Cecil Borer, prevented the rally and arrested several students, including Carlos. Taken in a patrol wagon to the local police station, he was held only long enough for the police to register him as a Stalinist.[5]

Carlos might have had more trouble with the police in 1933 on account of his articles in the pro-Communist *Jornal do Povo* of Aparício Torelli, which flourished for a couple of weeks when Brazil was on the road to returning to democratic constitutional ways. The authorities considered the newspaper a Communist threat and closed it down. For a while they went after people associated with it, and Carlos therefore spent a little time hiding at the home of a cousin in Uberlândia, Minas Gerais.[6]

In Rio, Carlos associated with about twenty students who formed the Federação Vermelha dos Estudantes (Red Federation of Students). But he did not formally become a member. Nor did his friend Ivan Pedro de Martins, who remarked to a veteran Communist, "If you want to alienate the students, then call something red." The Federação Vermelha disappeared and Ivan formally joined the Communists, concentrating now on the preparations to hold a congress of proletarian and student youth (Congresso da Juventude Proletária, Estudantil, e Popular).[7]

Carlos came close to joining the Federação da Juventude Comunista, the young people's section of the PCB. To become eligible, he was required to follow an example of his Uncle Paulo, who, in the late 1920s, had issued a public attack on Maurício. Carlos, agreeing to act as a "heroic Communist," prepared to type an appropriate letter for publication in *rumo.* But his typewriter, the victim of his severe pounding with two fingers, was broken down. When he asked Vera for the use of hers, she declared, "You won't type such a letter on my machine." Brother and sister argued and in the end Carlos acknowledged that a public attack on his father would hardly be a worthy act.[8]

The opinions of Communist Uncles Fernando and Paulo were unavailable to Carlos for they were far from Rio. Fernando, like Luís Carlos Prestes, was in the Soviet Union. Paulo, his whereabouts unknown to his family, had gone out of his mind after arrests in São Paulo and Rio Grande do Sul and was an indigent in an insane asylum in Uruguay.

Continuing to be attracted to the Federação da Juventude Comunista, Carlos worked for the youth congress, a pet project of the Federação and a vehicle for uniting all the antifascist currents of young people. The directive committee for organizing the congress consisted of Ivan Pedro de Martins (president), Carlos Lacerda (vice-president), Edmundo Moniz (secretary), Cláudio Medeiros Lima, and Jorge Amado, already a published novelist who had transferred from Bahia to the Rio Law School.

These students signed a manifesto of the committee, and then most of them, including Carlos, called on Mayor Pedro Ernesto Batista in search of financial assistance for their cause. After the good-hearted mayor contributed five contos (5,000 milreis), Carlos suggested that this generous sum be used to published a magazine for young people. Ivan Pedro de Martins obtained approval of the idea from Communist colleagues and thus *Juventude* (Youth) was born. Carlos, a "veteran journalist" in the eyes of the others, became editor-in-chief. He wrote with so much enthusiasm that Ivan had to caution him to be briefer to allow space for other writers.[9]

In preparation for the youth congress, Rio law students stirred up interest at other colleges, in Rio and elsewhere. Although the congress was never held, the propaganda and preparatory meetings were effective. One especially fervent convert, a poet fond of dramatic gestures, ripped off his green shirt at a public meeting and proclaimed that he was replacing "God, Country, and Family," the refrain of Plínio Salgado's Integralistas, with "Bread, Land, and Liberty," the slogan of the far leftists.[10]

One of the contributions of Carlos to the cause was his translation into Portuguese of the small book by Ilya Ehrenburg about the bloody suppression in Austria of the strikes of February 1934. In a long preface to the published translation, *Fevereiro Sangrento,* Carlos pointed out that fascism was strong in Austrian rural areas just as it had been strong in Italy's nonindustrial south. Likewise in Brazil, he wrote, the strength of fascism was to be found in the predominantly agricultural north, where it was promoted by pro-Vargas rulers in union with the Church and the large landowners. And he added that the movement was assisted by war-minded foreign imperialists and members of the Brazilian industrial bourgeoisie who favored a directed economy. "May the report of Ehrenburg serve, dear reader, as a lesson. At this time, indifference is more than treason: it is suicide."[11]

4. The Aliança Nacional Libertadora (1935)

Late in 1934, Carlos and some of his friends went to a labor union meeting hall in Niterói to participate in a convention of the recently formed Committee against War and Fascism. The purpose of the convention was to organize a Youth Committee against War and Fascism. The official slate of young people, favored by the parent organization to become the Youth Committee, was surprised to find itself challenged by a united group led by Carlos and Moacir Werneck de Castro. Carlos, charming the convention delegates with his oratory and making it clear that his ideas coincided with those of the official slate, was so effective that the official candidate for the top post, law student Eliezer Schneider, felt that Carlos deserved to win. After the official slate was declared victorious, Schneider arranged for the collaboration of Carlos and his group. An opportunity to discuss the collaboration arose when Carlos and Schneider, upon returning to Rio by ferry, found themselves in the same prison cell. Like all the delegates who had come from the convention, they were arrested by Rio's Delegacia de Ordem Política e Social (DOPS), held overnight, and then released after questioning.[1]

The Committee against War and Fascism was absorbed early in 1935 by the more formidable Aliança Nacional Libertadora (ANL), an organization that stemmed from the decision of the Comintern to encourage and support antifascist popular fronts. Presented in January 1935 by Brazilian oppositionists and discontented *tenentes* as a movement to oppose a proposed national security law and free Brazil from foreign economic domination, the ANL issued a program in February that included repudiation of the foreign debt, nationalization of imperialist companies, and the parceling of large landownings to make plots available to peasants.

Carlos became so involved in the work of the ANL that he later maintained that his participation in it was his first important political activity.[2] As the official student orator of the local ANL directorship, he appeared frequently at rallies with *Juventude* Director Ivan Pedro de Martins, official student orator of the national directorship. Carlos, a flaming young Apollo given more to gesticulating than Ivan, often alternated roles with Ivan and therefore spoke at meetings sponsored by the national organization.[3]

Brazil had returned to democracy with the promulgation of the 1934 Constitution and was operating with a Congress that generally supported President Getúlio Vargas. But the Comintern, even before Congress passed the national security law, classified the government of Getúlio as reactionary and oppressive and hoped to use the ANL to generate an uprising. The connection between the Comintern and ANL, however, was unknown to the masses in Brazil who flocked to join the new movement. It was unknown to the throng of anti-Integralistas and anti-Getulistas that filled Rio's João

Caetano Theater on Saturday night, March 30, to hear ANL President Hercolino Cascardo, Maurício de Lacerda, Carlos Lacerda, and other speakers, including discontented workers.

Maurício declared to the audience that the "monster law" (national security law) had brought him into the arms of the ANL, where he would serve as a soldier.[4] Carlos, about to speak as representative of the students, was approached by Major Carlos da Costa Leite, an ANL director. The veteran revolutionary suggested to the young man that he nominate Luís Carlos Prestes for honorary president of the ANL. Carlos was delighted.[5] When he closed his speech by making the nomination, the crowd roared its approval and banners were unfolded proclaiming "Luís Carlos Prestes, Honorary President."

The name of the "Cavalier of Hope" helped bring tens of thousands to the ANL. The new front established chapters throughout Brazil. Participating in the work, orators Maurício, Carlos, and Ivan Pedro de Martins took a train to the Paraíba Valley. In a small movie theater in Barra do Piraí, not far from Vassouras, the principal speech was given by Carlos. Maurício, stunned by the eloquence and beautiful presentation, gazed admiringly at his son and remarked to Ivan, "Can this be possible? Can I have fathered this miracle?"[6]

On to Vassouras went the ANL propagandists, but there the train was met by Green Shirts. After a bitter fight, the followers of Plínio Salgado fled and Maurício, Carlos, and Ivan spent the night at the local newspaper office, composing the copy and setting the type for an edition devoted largely to the ANL and the recent fracas.[7] Green Shirts, retaliating a little later, removed the bust of Maurício from the square where it had been placed in 1931. But the bust was recovered and set up in its former position during a ceremony in which Congressman Otávio da Silveira, an ANL leader, addressed a crowd of Maurício's admirers.[8]

ANL-affiliated organizations sprang into existence. One of them, for intellectuals, was the Clube da Cultura Moderna that attracted Maurício, Professor Hermes Lima, lawyer Maria Werneck de Castro, young writer Rubem Braga, Rio journalist Aparício Torelli, and Brasil Gerson, editor of *A Platéia* of São Paulo. For women, the União Feminina do Brasil was established with the help of Maria Werneck de Castro, Mary Mercio (who married Ivan Pedro de Martins), and Eugênia Moreyra, the flamboyant, cigar-smoking wife of Álvaro Moreyra. The ANL's major daily, *A Manhã,* which began publication in Rio in April, was directed by Pedro Mota Lima with assistance from Otávio Malta, admirer of Maurício and *tenentismo.*[9]

Carlos, using his pen for the cause, wrote occasionally for *A Manhã* and more extensively for *Revista Acadêmica,* where he specialized in literary criticism. Listing the works he considered most important for the formation of a socialist culture, he placed books by Marx, Engels, and Stalin in his top priority category, followed by books by Lenin, Manuilski, Rosa Luxemburg, Plekhanoff, and Bela Kun, and the Program and Statutes of the Communist International. His article condemning the Catholic conversion of poet Murilo Mendes was pitiless in its sarcastic references to Catholics like

Juarez Távora, lawyer Heráclito Fontoura Sobral Pinto, and "the godmother of the troop and police agent" Alceu Amoroso Lima.[10]

Meanwhile, in April, Carlos' hero, Luís Carlos Prestes, together with his German, Jewish wife, Olga, entered Brazil clandestinely, as did Comintern agents from several countries who would work for a leftist revolution headed by Prestes. In his place of hiding, the Cavalier of Hope signed a thunderous manifesto to recapture the spirit of the *tenente* uprisings of July 5, 1922 and 1924, and to call on the people to arise. The situation, he wrote, was one "of war," and he closed by exclaiming, "Down with the odious government of Vargas! For a popular national revolutionary government! All power to the Aliança Nacional Libertadora!"

Although the intellectuals in the Clube da Cultura Moderna favored the release of the manifesto, the ANL national directorship, fearing that it would bring government reprisals, ordered that it not be released.[11] However, army Captain Henrique Oest, of the ANL municipal directorship, approached Carlos on July 4 to inform him that, as ANL student orator, he had been chosen to read Prestes' manifesto the next day at the ANL headquarters. When Carlos, unaware that Prestes was in Brazil, expressed surprise at the existence of the manifesto, the tall, athletic army captain told him that Prestes had sent it from Barcelona, Spain.[12]

Despite some arrests at labor unions, a crowd gathered at the ANL headquarters and heard Carlos read the manifesto. The arrests, condemned by the ANL, led to a lively session in the Chamber of Deputies, where a motion was adopted to honor "the heroes of the two July 5s" and where Congressman Otávio da Silveira also read the Prestes manifesto.[13] The manifesto was published on July 6 in *A Manhã* together with a front-page photograph of Carlos reading it. As a result of the publicity given to the manifesto, the government closed the ANL on July 11. ANL cells fell under the control of the PCB, which claimed that the recent leftist publicity had raised party membership to eight or ten thousand.[14]

A Manhã, which continued to circulate, published the protests of Álvaro Moreyra, lawyer Luís Werneck de Castro, and others who condemned the government for closing the ANL and its affiliated organizations. Carlos used *A Manhã* to denounce the bourgeoisie and the arrest, in São Paulo, of Communist Brasil Gerson.[15] And he attended meetings at which plans were made to organize public demonstrations in favor of the ANL. He even went around Rio's downtown area at dawn with law students Hélio Walcacer and João Condé sticking ANL posters on walls. But near the João Caetano Theater the police arrived on horseback. Although Walcacer scattered corks on the street to make it difficult for the horses, Carlos and Walcacer were caught and held briefly at a police station.[16]

Carlos participated in the plans for launching new popular fronts, such as the Popular Front for Bread, Land, and Liberty. Although public support was weak,[17] an encouraging—but unrealistic—view of the situation was given Carlos by PCB Secretary-General Antônio Maciel Bonfim, whom he met in August along with other Communists at the home of Henrique Oest. Bonfim, a former army sergeant, described the Brazilian northeast as ripe for revolution. Moscow published similar reports. There, Fernando de Lacerda wrote inaccurately that the Brazilian people, infuriated by the government, had "rallied by the millions" around the closed ANL and would "proceed to decisive battles for bread, land, and liberty, and for the power of the ANL."[18]

When ANL organizer Francisco Mangabeira, rich young member of an oppositionist family in Bahia, launched the weekly *Marcha* in Rio in October 1935, Carlos joined the editorial staff together with Rubem Braga, Di Cavalcanti, Newton Freitas, and São Paulo ANL leader Caio Prado Júnior. *Marcha* advocated a broad front to achieve "a popular revolutionary government with Prestes at its head." Carlos, signing as Marcos in *Marcha,* acclaimed the effort of the União Popular Autonomista Fluminense to persuade various oppositionist currents to stop squabbling at a time when "the enemy sets up its murderous machine guns in the streets and prepares to sack, pillage, and massacre a heroic people." He warned that the united front was threatened by the rift between the wing associated with Gaúcho Governor José Antônio Flores da Cunha and the Aliancista wing, supporter of the Bread, Land, and Liberty movement and a Prestes-headed "popular national revolutionary government."[19]

On November 11, ANL leaders used the João Caetano Theater again, this time to launch what they called the Popular Front for Liberties. Maurício wrote the hidden Luís Carlos Prestes to advise that "companions have chosen me president" of the new front. It would, Maurício promised, do everything possible to strengthen the forces congregated around Prestes' name. "Our past separation thus finds a point of national conciliation for our struggle for the good of Brazil. I extend my hand to you."[20]

5. In Hiding (1935–1936)

Carlos was a rebel with an insatiable appetite for intellectual stimulation and a craving for an affectionate relationship with a father figure. He found his answer at the house of Álvaro and Eugênia Moreyra, in Copacabana. Although in November 1935 he shared a tiny apartment with friends, he resided much of the time with the Moreyras, whose home was the leading meeting place of intellectuals. The 47-year-old poet treated Carlos as a son.[1] Eugênia, Carlos has written, was the link between literature and a libertarian, romantic communism.[2] A colorful nonconformist, she wore her hair in bangs and used vivid colors on her lips and long fingernails. Everything about her was large, including her handbags and the cigars she smoked.

Pleasant days for Carlos were rudely jolted by a summons for induction into the army. Taking a ferry to Niterói on November 22, he reported, as ordered, at the Second Infantry Battalion. There he was told by the officer of the day to return on the twenty-third but he decided not to go back. He loved the books, music, and conversation at the Moreyra home. He reflected on his unhappy boarding school experience and the reputation of Battalion Commander Euclides Zenóbio da Costa for assigning cleaning chores to students. Above all, Carlos was "horrified at the prospect of passing empty hours." If he needed further reasons for not returning to the barracks in the

Eugênia and Álvaro Moreyra. (Drawing by Álvarus in *Vamos Ler*, 1940, reproduced in Adelar Finatto, *Álvaro Moreyra*)

pouring rain on the twenty-third, he found them by considering that he might be called to fight against a movement he favored, and that Álvaro and Eugênia, both suffering temporary ailments, needed his help. He became a deserter.[3]

During that night and the next day, Communist uprisings broke out in the northeast of Brazil. Although they were crushed within two days, the information about them was not clear in Rio when Prestes and Antônio Maciel Bonfim ordered revolts to break out there on the twenty-seventh. Carlos on the twenty-sixth was advised by an individual, unknown to him, that he would be told later where he should take up arms for the revolution.[4] By this time Congress had declared a state of siege and the Communist plans were no secret to the Vargas regime, thanks to police work carried out with the cooperation of British Intelligence agents.

Carlos spent the night at the Moreyras'. With them he kept close to the radio on the morning of the twenty-seventh, listening to reports about the success of government troops in smashing the uprisings in Rio. During subsequent announcements, which revealed the names of captured rebels, Carlos and his hosts were startled to hear of the arrest of "student Carlos de Lacerda." Álvaro Moreyra, knowing that Carlos would have to go into hiding, observed simply that it was time for him to "get out."[5]

Mauricinho agreed to notify Adalberto João Pinheiro, the generous and occasionally violent law school friend with whom Carlos had participated in student politics and interminable late-night conversations at the Café Lamas and Sereia Bar.[6] Although Adalberto's father, son of former Minas Governor João Pinheiro, was conservative, and Adalberto's mother was very Catholic, they agreed to hide the "dangerous Communist."[7] Assuming the name of Pedro, Carlos spent a few weeks at their Rio home, mostly in an upstairs room because the Pinheiros received many visitors. There he ate his meals, brought by the Pinheiros' daughters, and started a series of notebooks in which he recorded his impressions of books, his fantasies, and his effort to devise a mathematical formula based on the capital formation theory of Marx and Engels. As his window looked out on the yard of the Copacabana police station, nights were sometimes interrupted by the screams of the victims of barbaric police "interrogations," carried out to gain information that would lead to the arrest of more Communists.

In the opening pages of his first notebook, Carlos wrote that "in the midst of the greatest anguish, the most delightful thing is to find paper and a soft pencil," and he mentioned his "overwhelming will to write, write, write." He also noted that while he had found it a pleasant sensation to be at liberty while hearing a radio broadcast of his own arrest, it had been even more pleasing "to feel like a sort of double personality."[8]

Not wishing to give the Pinheiros trouble with the police, Carlos became the guest of Heitor Monteiro Espínola, a cousin of Olga. Heitor was cooperative, despite his leaning toward Integralismo, and Carlos spent several weeks in his home in the Santa Teresa district. Besides teaching French to Heitor's children, Carlos made a poor translation of La Bruyère's *Caractères* that was published by Editôra Athena in 1936 with the translator's name shown as Luís Fontoura.[9]

Unfortunately for Carlos' sojourn in the Santa Teresa house, a niece of Heitor's wife came to visit from Paraná and fell in love with Pedro, as Carlos continued to be called. Carlos was uninterested, being in love with Léa Figueiredo, daughter of Olga's cousin Lúcia Werneck de Castro Figueiredo.[10] Determined not to tell the lovesick girl from Paraná that he was wanted by the police, he found it difficult to give her reasons why he would not attend parties and picnics she organized or go to movies with her.[11]

Seeking a new hiding place, Carlos dismissed the idea of going to the Copacabana apartment on Duvivier Street occupied by Olga, Mauricinho, and Vera and her family. The apartment had recently been searched by the authorities, whose zeal for repressing "the red peril" had created an anti-Communist terror. After the capture of Luís Carlos Prestes, his wife, and his papers in March 1936, Brazil was declared to be in a "state of war," thus eliminating the few remaining individual guarantees, such as the immunities of legislators. Even before the "state of war," the 47-year-old Maurício had been dismissed from his Federal District legal post and locked up. The subsequent inspection of Prestes' papers disclosed Maurício's letter to him of mid-November 1935, adding to Maurício's problems.

Carlos moved from Heitor's house to the Rio home of his great-aunt Vinoca (owner of Forquilha). For six months he was alone in a room, leaving it only occasionally at night to chat with Vinoca and her family when they had no visitors. Troubled by insomnia and a poor appetite, he spent his time reading and writing in his notebooks. "I have forgotten how to live," he wrote. "I need to say something to my fellow creatures. . . . Already I have spoken to books, chairs, tables, walls, to the piece of sky that I see, to the wall of ivy. No one answered." When he did have an opportunity to converse with a human being, he "talked and talked and talked" and found his listener, unable to interrupt, wanting to leave him.[12]

The messages Carlos received from his family did little to raise his spirits. He learned that the mother of Léa Figueiredo had told Olga that Léa would not be a suitable companion for him. And Olga's mother, in a letter to Carlos, urged him to continue with his legal career and thus give her the happiness that Mauricinho had done with his medical work. "Abandon everything unconnected with your career," she asked him to promise.[13]

Calling himself Carneosso (Flesh and Bones) in his notebooks, Carlos left no doubt about his contempt for bourgeois life. For the most part, however, he filled the notebooks with episodes and facts taken from his reading. He developed stories out of brief items, such as a newspaper reference to two girls who sought death by lying on railroad tracks only to have the oncoming train turn off on a siding.[14]

Books that held particular interest for Carneosso were biographies and histories of Brazil and Europe. He enjoyed Stefan Zweig's *Marie Antoinette* but concluded that the author had the soul of a lackey and did not understand the reasons for the French Revolution. Ridiculing the "established types" used by some writers, Carneosso brought some of them out of "the museum": Marie Antoinette "with those fatal airs she assumed after they put the republican knife through her neck," constantly unfastening her head and placing it between her knees, and Joan of Arc playing cards with Charles I, Vasco da Gama, and Messalina (a wife of Emperor Claudius). Napoleon, Lord Byron, Josephine Baker, and Julius Caesar (looking for a biographer and signing autographs) became members of the eccentric group in Carneosso's account.[15]

Seeking a pseudonym for his articles in *Revista Acadêmica,* Carlos chose the first three names of a journalist he knew, Caio Júlio César Vieira, because he thought them ridiculously pompous.[16] Signing Caio Júlio César Tavares, Carlos attacked Oswald Spengler and praised José Lins do Rego's *Usina* and Jorge Amado's *Jubiabá* ("one of the five best Brazilian novels"). Soon he was abbreviating the ridiculous pseudonym to C. J. C. Tavares and Júlio Tavares and using other names as well: Nicolau Montezuma, Marcos Pimenta, and Marco Aurélio Júnior. He kept *Revista Acadêmica* well supplied; in one issue, three of his articles appeared under different names.[17]

Writing for *Unidad* of Buenos Aires under his own name, Carlos argued that the epoch of bourgeois development, once favorable for literature, was about to collapse and had reached a stage where it offered only "a false standardized literature." "The true intellectual production of our time," Carlos maintained, "is on the side of the revolution." He quoted Lenin as saying that art "must unite the feeling, thought, and will of the masses."[18]

Desperate for moments in the open, Carlos took advantage of Carnaval to put on a costume, change the color of his hair, and join crowds in the streets with a cousin, thus "getting the rust out of my system." Later he decided on another change: to go ahead with an earlier plan to join his immediate family. The move, made at night, took him to the apartment to which the family had moved on Leme Beach. Carlos was introduced to Vera's 3-year-old daughter Lygia as her Uncle Pedro.[19]

Carlos' urge to get away from hiding in Rio became intense and he turned for help to his cousin Nestor Barbosa. Nestor made an arrangement with a smuggler who brought coffee illegally from Rio state to the Federal District. The hiding place in the smuggler's small vehicle was used to conceal Carlos when the vehicle, on a return trip from the national capital, approached the police inspection point. Thus Carlos reached the family *chácara* on the Paraíba River.[20]

6. *O Rio* (1937)

At the *chácara* Carlos had the company of Moacir Werneck de Castro, who was writing a historical study, and an Argentine Communist, whose lectures on Marxism delighted Carlos. Paulo de Lacerda, in a deplorable condition, was also there. Uncle Paulo, who had spent the early 1930s in a Rio Grande do Sul prison, was said to have gone crazy there when he faced a firing squad (which never fired). The root of his insanity was the failure to treat his syphilis, and when he reached Uruguay he was placed in an asylum for the destitute and insane.[1] Maurício, learning in the mid-1930s of Paulo's situation, arranged to have him brought to Rio. There, and later at the *chácara,* Paulo drank heavily when he felt a bad mental spell was approaching.[2]

Paulo, Carlos noted, was wearing soiled bandages on his infirm legs and fondling a guitar he was unable to play but had asked Maurício to buy for him. With a twisted mouth he explained to Carlos that he had come from a trip to the stratosphere. As usually happened when he spoke, he fell into an unintelligible mumble before completing what he had to say.[3]

The condition of Paulo gave Carlos ideas for a character, Lucas, in a play he commenced writing at the *chácara* at the suggestion of Álvaro Moreyra, whose Companhia de Arte Dramática received a subsidy from the education ministry for a series of amateur performances.[4]

In the play, which Carlos called *O Rio* (The River), the demented and caustic Lucas participates in the desultory life of some rural people, living by a river in the tumbledown shacks of old slave quarters. The arrival of the tubercular Manuel, released after fourteen years in the penitentiary, elicits little comment in the drab community. But no one ignores the return of Idalina, niece of a ragged, alcoholic former slave. The obstinate Idalina, attractive to men, is unsuccessful in her attempt to drown her baby in the river, leading Lucas to remark that the child had found its beginning where the rest of the people ended up. Explaining to Idalina that "the river is a friend, the only one," Lucas tells her that the day is coming for him to be taken away by it.[5] By the time Lucas tries to bring Idalina together with the ailing, timid Manuel, she has become devoted to her baby and turns away from Manuel or anyone whose presence might not be good for the child. At the end of the theatrical piece, she displays uncharacteristic humility when she appeals to a talkative traveling peddler of herbs to tell her how she and her baby can live.[6]

O Rio lacks a plot with a dramatic or satisfying conclusion. But Carlos, a great mimic, was able to reproduce the vernacular of the shabby, rural individuals and depict their concerns. Their subtle malice, he wrote later, was "the result of disillusionment and, to a certain extent, discernment."[7]

With Álvaro and Eugênia Moreyra planning to produce his play and act in the roles of Lucas and Idalina, Carlos wrote to Vera to say he was in a good mood and determined to put up no longer with isolation. The affectionate letter, written in April 1937, ended a month of silence following a disagreement in which he had expressed annoyance at his family. "It is no small matter," he wrote, "to spend so much time as I have spent it." He mentioned psychological problems "that conversation alone can clear up" and begged his family not to remain irritated at him. Revealing that he was determined to make a change in his life, he observed that "to continue counting the stars here is impossible."[8]

The change was facilitated by the government's decision in June not to extend the "state of war." With the start of the presidential election campaign of 1937, congressional supporters of the candidates favored an end to repression. José Carlos de Macedo Soares, the new justice minister, canceled "preventive imprisonment" orders, including the one against Maurício, much to the disgust of Police Chief Filinto Müller, who declared that the release of Maurício would "cause alarm in the public spirit."[9]

Carlos, while in hiding in Rio, had exchanged letters with Maurício and had read his book about the legal case of the Santo Antônio Hill. Now he looked forward to seeing him for the first time in two years and hoped that the National Security Council would absolve him in the still-pending matter of his letter of November 1935 to Prestes.[10]

Although the author of *O Rio* was shown as Júlio Tavares in the program prepared for São Paulo's Boa Vista Theater, Carlos had no hesitation in attending rehearsals or granting preperformance interviews. Above all, the identity of Júlio Tavares became public when, amidst the applause following the first performance on July 28, Carlos went on stage ("*em carne e osso*"—in flesh and bones—as Moacir Werneck de Castro wrote in *Revista Acadêmica*). Olga, in Bahia, received a telegram from Vera saying, "Father absolved, play successful."[11]

Moacir's review called *O Rio*'s theme a departure from the conventional presentations of rural life with their emphasis on buffoonery and rustic hicks. He praised the stage settings by Santa Rosa and Oswald de Andrade

Filho and the acting of the Moreyras. He attributed poor reviews to the "ill will" of the Paulista press toward Moreyra's Companhia de Arte Dramática.[12] But neither the reviews nor the attacks of professionals, displeased with subsidized amateur competition,[13] dissuaded Moreyra from bringing his plays to Rio. There, in mid-September, *O Rio* was offered at the Regina Theater with the original cast.

Correio da Noite wrote that the audience, its attention glued to the characters, was waiting for the plot to move forward when the final curtain fell; and *Jornal do Brasil* said the author of the "vanguard piece" should write with more effort to "harmonize the literary work with what is intrinsically theater." Graciliano Ramos, questioning whether *O Rio* was a theatrical work, called it a "strange thing" whose miserable characters were almost always in the shadows. In other reviews the young playwright was described as talented, brilliant, and "one of those restless spirits of the modern Brazilian generation." *O Globo*'s reviewer expressed enchantment with the author's "absolute disrespect for all the age-old rules established in the theater."[14]

7. The Merry Smile of Ziloca (1937)

Before Carlos came out of hiding, he fell in love again. The romance began after Moacir Werneck de Castro spoke to him about two girls from the town of Marquês de Valença who had been hired to give lessons to the children at the Forquilha *fazenda*. On horseback the two young men covered the hills and valleys between the *chácara* and Forquilha. At the *fazenda* Carlos made his choice as soon as he saw the 20-year-old Letícia Abruzzini, known as Ziloca. He was captivated by her merry smile and "eyes that sang." At the same time, while chatting in the sunshine of that first afternoon, he reached the conclusion that her smile hid a feeling he had come to know too well, loneliness.[1]

Moacir and Carlos returned to Forquilha frequently to the delight of the schoolchildren, who welcomed long recesses. In the garden Carlos and Letícia embraced and kissed and learned about each other. Letícia, Carlos found out, was the daughter of an Italian surveyor who had come to Brazil and worked for a railroad company. He had died when Letícia was two, leaving his widow, Henriqueta, with four children to raise. The family was poor.[2]

Carlos, after leaving the *chácara*, devoted himself happily in Rio and São Paulo to political meetings, conversations with literary figures, and the *O Rio* rehearsals. And he dashed off a stream of letters to Gatinha (Kitten), his pet name for Letícia. "I love you, I love you, I love you," he wrote and asked for photographs and letters. He also wrote enthusiastically about what he was doing. In her replies Letícia expressed her fear that their relationship was a mere passing dream, and she contrasted the sadness she felt at their separation with his obvious enjoyment of life. "Carlos," she said in one of her letters, "I don't wish to write to you any more. It seems to me that the Carlos who is in Rio is not the same one I knew in Forquilha. You are all wrapped up in your life." He tried to assure her that it was "our life" that concerned him. What satisfaction, he asked, could be found in struggling in a vacuum, without his loved one at his side. "You say you are alone. What about me?"[3]

Early in August 1937, Carlos was writing to Letícia of plans that would bring them together. But he was also becoming involved in political work that would keep them apart. Still calling himself Júlio Tavares, he joined the União Democrática Estudantil (UDE—Democratic Student Union), which supported the presidential candidacy of José Américo de Almeida, an intellectual from the northeast and former Vargas cabinet minister.[4] José Américo's electoral opponents were Integralista leader Plínio Salgado, who had little political backing, and former São Paulo Governor Armando de Sales Oliveira, a strong anti-Vargas candidate. The José Américo candidacy, although launched by most of the governors and considered at first to be favored by the Vargas administration, was unwelcome to Vargas, particularly after José Américo delivered speeches pleasing the Left and criticizing the government. José Américo was backed by the Communists.

The UDE sent a group of six or seven students, among them Carlos, Hélio Walcacer, and Luís Pinheiro Paes Leme, to Belo Horizonte, Minas Gerais. "The pretext," Carlos explained later, "was to spread José Américo propaganda and combat Armando Sales as a reactionary, etc. But, in reality, what we carried out was a campaign that was anti-Integralista and, as goes without saying, just a little bit Communist."[5] In Belo Horizonte, Carlos suggested that the group spread its propaganda in the interior, to the north, with the result that Minas Governor Benedito Valadares, then a José Américo supporter, arranged passages by rail to Pirapora and from there by ship down the São Francisco River to Juazeiro, Bahia. Carlos, writing Letícia from Belo Horizonte on August 15, said the trip to Bahia would take five or six days and he would soon be back, holding her in his arms in Rio, which she was planning to visit. Even after the students reached Pirapora and saw the tiny, ancient boat, built during the Brazilian empire, Carlos had no idea that it would take twenty-two days to reach Juazeiro.[6]

8. Bahia (1937)

The old boat stopped at towns on the São Francisco River, and there the students participated in pro–José Américo rallies. At these stops and at the unscheduled ones, when the boat went aground, Carlos questioned the local inhabitants and, when he could overcome their reserve, obtained information for his new series of notebooks. Writing quickly with the softest pencils he could find, he became a reporter preparing for future articles. He recorded his findings about diseases, death rates, land fertility, and mental attitudes, and he recorded the prices of foodstuffs, medicine, freightage, and real estate.[1]

Carlos found the Integralista movement surprisingly strong, perhaps because it often constituted the only opposition to the backland chieftains on whom, Carlos discovered, Bahia Governor Juracy Magalhães relied for support.[2] In Carinhanha, Carlos spent hours with one of the chieftains, "Colonel" João Duque, a 67-year-old ruffian about to marry a 15-year-old girl. Grinning malevolently, Duque explained that "in politics one does not speak of assassinations, but the removal of obstacles." Communists, he revealed, had been "removed" after the 1935 uprisings. "As for Armando Sales supporters, or Integralistas, or Protestants, we have none here; we have only relatives and friends," the Al Capone of the Minas-Bahia frontier remarked. Carlos, disgusted, devoted pages of a notebook to outlining the plot for a new play that he planned to call "the King of the Backlands."[3]

As the boat at last approached Juazeiro, where the river trip was to end, Carlos wrote to Letícia to say that the "horrible voyage" had left the student campaigners "half dead." At the Juazeiro post office he found a letter from her. It was a sad one, and he hastened to assure her that he would soon be at her side.[4] Also, in Juazeiro, he filled pages of his notebook with his thoughts about the political behavior of young people and the role of the true revolutionary. Reflecting on aimless discussions, he wrote that "a revolutionary has no right to waste his time in this way." It was, he added, easier for a revolutionary to become a reactionary than for a reactionary to become a revolutionary, because all a revolutionary had to do to become a reactionary was to stop acting as a revolutionary. "This is the secret of desertions," he concluded.[5]

The weary students were greeted at Juazeiro by Communist Diógenes de Arruda Câmara and other UDE delegates. All were provided with railroad passages to Salvador, supplied by Governor Juracy Magalhães. At Serrinha, one of the stops on the rail trip of several days, Carlos witnessed the suffering of people deprived of water. And he learned that the Integralistas, finding no instruction there for children, had opened a school.[6]

Carlos was in Salvador late in September when the Vargas government announced untruthfully that it had discovered a ghastly Communist plot, the so-called Cohen Plan. Congress was quick to enact a "state of war" again, and the repression of Communism went into high gear.

Thanks to Professor Álvaro Dória and a brother of the governor, arrangements were made for Carlos to hide on Itaparica Island in the beach house of another professor, who was in Europe. Carlos, pretending to be a student of medicine, found himself prescribing aspirin and mint tea to ailing fishermen and their families. At night, while winds stirred the palm trees outside the beach house and built up large waves in the ocean, he sat by a kerosene lamp and banged away on a borrowed typewriter, hoping to produce a play based on *Os Sertões* by Euclides da Cunha. He was fed by a cook who worked for Professor Dória and was kept supplied with cigarettes by an unknown friend.[7]

One evening when Carlos returned from the beach, the cook announced the presence of two police agents. They seized his papers, the typewriter, and *Os Sertões,* and took him to the Salvador jail. Transferred soon to the barracks of the Guarda Civil, he met other leftists and faced interrogators who sought to prove that his map of Canudos, used for his *Os Sertões* work, was a subversive map. He penned an unfair note to Governor Juracy Magalhães, whom he had never met, accusing him of capitulating to the oncoming Vargas dictatorship.[8]

The Bahia police, following the recommendation of Rio Police Chief Filinto Müller, shipped Carlos and two arrested former military men to Rio aboard the *Itanagé.* Olga, seeing a photograph of the three disembarking "extremists," published in Rio's *Diário da Noite* on November 2, rushed to the police headquarters and asked Müller what the charges were. "Your son," she was told, "is very intelligent and can be a serious nuisance to the government."[9]

Carlos was in the Casa de Detenção (detention prison) on November 10, when the Vargas government and its military leaders canceled the presidential election, closed Congress, and promulgated a new constitution, thus ushering in the dictatorial Estado Novo, with Vargas at its head. Transferred a few days later to the Casa de Correção (penitentiary), Carlos mingled with an assortment of Vargas haters. One of them, anarchist Professor José Oiticica, gave Portuguese lessons in prison. Both he and Carlos created language problems for the prison censors because Carlos asked his family for books in French, and Oiticica was correcting notes in Greek.[10]

Carlos, who had not heard from Letícia since September, sent her a note telling her where she could address him. But he received nothing and had to be content with rereading old letters.[11]

9. Marriage (March 1938)

A friend of Maurício persuaded Filinto Müller to allow Carlos to spend Christmas Eve with his family at the Rio home of Vinoca on condition that he go immediately afterward to the Lacerda *chácara* and not leave it. During the brief holiday reunion, the family found Carlos a revolutionary in a quarrelsome mood.[1]

Carlos was preoccupied with his need to converse with Letícia, in whose old letters he saw hesitations in accepting the idea of a life together. As soon as he reached the *chácara,* at 1:00 A.M. on Christmas day, he wrote her ten pages. He had, he told her, been chasing all over the place, putting his life together to share it one day with her. "You know everything that has happened to me. About you I know nothing except that your affection appears to have diminished and many seek to take over my empty place beside you." He asked her not to believe those who might be telling her that if he traveled so much it was because he did not really care for her.[2]

Carlos hesitated to risk imprisonment by visiting the town of Valença (Marquês de Valença), where Letícia lived. A trip to Forquilha, he felt, was less dangerous, and there on January 11 the lovers were reunited in a setting full of memories. "You are mine," he wrote exultantly after the meeting. He was thrilled about her plan to make a one-day visit to the *chácara* beginning the next Saturday night.[3]

Carlos confided in his father, who had come to the *chácara* with the unrealistic hope of turning it into a profitable producer of fruits, vegetables, chickens, and firewood. Maurício, working in boots as a farmer, with a straw hat to protect his bald pate from the summer sun, struck Carlos as a sort of Napoleon in exile.[4]

Letícia, during her visit, enchanted Maurício and made a good impression on Antônio Bello, the *chácara*'s administrator. Carlos, in heaven because she agreed to marry him, took her to see Uncle Paulo, ill in bed in Sebastião's old room. "This is my Italiana," Carlos announced. Paulo peered at her for a minute with his one good eye and then smiled and said, "You look like a gypsy, my girl." Moved by the news that the young people were engaged, Paulo recited verses of Ada Negri, socialist poet.[5]

After Letícia left, promising to return the next weekend, Carlos wrote to her to say that "everything here is still filled with your presence." Writing to his mother of his decision to marry "that girl from Valença," Carlos said that after the wedding, which "tiresome formalities" were delaying until March, the couple would live at the *chácara* "until things get better." Explaining that he wanted his mother's opinion, he promised that the girl would be a lovely addition "to our small family," and expressed his conviction that his marriage would "resolve a large part of my problems and put my life on a better foundation."[6]

Olga, taken by surprise, expressed pleasure in her son's happiness and suggested that Carlos not let romanticism close Letícia's eyes to the problems of living in the "solitude" of the *chácara.*[7] Carlos agreed with his mother. He felt the isolation despite occasional visits by friends he had known at law school, such as Evandro Lins e Silva, Adalberto João Pinheiro, Antônio Chagas Freitas, Antônio Gomes da Cruz, and Alceu Marinho Rego. Sometimes Moacir Werneck de Castro brought Samuel Wainer, who idolized Carlos and was organizing a new monthly, *Diretrizes.* Seventeen-year-old Maurício Caminha de Lacerda came to see his father and developed a good relationship with his half brother, whom he sought to emulate in romance by turning to a friend of Letícia.[8]

When Letícia said she was delighted with the *chácara,* Carlos thanked her for her "kind hypocrisy" and mentioned his mother's concern. He told her also that she would be fond of Olga, whom he described as "a child who has been obliged by life to live as an adult." "She is," he added, "a sister to whom I give advice that is never followed."[9]

"For the first time," Carlos wrote to Letícia, "I have found happiness in love."[10] His letters, which Letícia hid under her mattress, were found by her mother, Henriqueta. "A man who can write letters like these can't be bad," Henriqueta said to her brother when he asked whether Henriqueta was going to "let Ziloca be courted by that crazy, unemployed, young Communist." "She is going to marry him," Henriqueta declared.[11]

Maurício gave his son 200 milreis for a wedding present, and with the money Carlos bought a razor and a piece of soap. After Maurício went to Valença to help with the formalities, Carlos made the trip there for the ceremony, a civil one, at the home of Letícia's brother-in-law, Osvaldo Fonseca. Olga, who attended in the company of Carlos' sister, Vera, was not on speaking terms with the father of the groom. Carlos, writing later to Olga, said that Letícia was fully informed about the poor relations between Maurício and Olga and would become a warm friend of Olga.[12]

At the *chácara,* Carlos was charmed by the beauty and "new life" that Letícia, "with her confident smile," brought to what had formerly been "a cold cave." His joy was evident to the couple's first visitors, Jorge Amado and music composer Dorival Caymmi, who found Letícia in a fluffy white bathrobe, one of the few garments in her wedding trousseau.[13]

Letícia took French lessons from Carlos and helped him plant vegetables and convert a little-used room into a dining room. But she was not well, the result, Carlos felt, of undernourishment. He regretted not having the money to send her to a specialist in Rio[14] and was determined to remain no longer unemployed.

In mid-May, while Communists congratulated Vargas on the failure of a rebellion by Green Shirts and Armando Sales supporters, Carlos advised Rio's *delegado* (commissioner) of political order that he was leaving the *chácara.* His need of a job, the message said, forced him to move to Rio.[15] There he and Letícia resided with Vinoca, Olga, and Vera's family while he looked for permanent work.

10. Writers and Beer Drinkers (1938–1939)

Carlos, an ascetic-looking young hero of the Left, had established himself as an outstanding orator during his work for the ANL. His other great talent, writing for the press, was a more reliable source of income and emerged in mid-1938, when he became associated with *O Observador Econômico e Financeiro.*

O Observador, a successful imitation of *Fortune* magazine, had been founded in 1936 by Valentim Bouças, member of the finance ministry technical board, IBM director in Brazil, and friend and golfing companion of Vargas. Bouças, owner of the monthly, put its management in the hands of handsome Olímpio Guilherme, who had written books critical of the United States after seeking a movie career in Hollywood.[1] Guilherme asked Carlos to do a piece on the government's proposed National Confectionery Institute, which was to issue regulations to prevent an alleged overproduction of sweets. Carlos' article, published in August 1938, showed that no overproduction existed and led to the abandonment of the plans for the institute.[2] It landed him a steady job on *O Observador* and allowed him and Letícia to move into their own apartment, the first of four that they occupied in a two-year period.

The *Observador* work did not prevent Carlos from contributing to newspapers and other magazines. Samuel Wainer's *Diretrizes,* which was fast becoming a popular outlet for articles by talented leftist writers, published articles by Carlos about the region of the São Francisco River.[3] Carlos' articles were lengthy because he was apt to get carried away by his interest in his subjects; but his interest was infectious and readers found themselves sharing his feeling that the mass of evidence he presented, the result of painstaking research, was important.

For *O Observador,* Carlos spent twelve days in Santos, gathering material for an article about the docks. For another *O Observador* article, he interviewed Education Minister Gustavo Capanema, whose "pseudomethodical" exposition and looseness with statistics he did not admire.[4] In October, he went to the state of Santa Catarina[5] to obtain information for articles in *O Observador* and *Diretrizes* about German colonization and influence in Brazil. In adding historical background, which he found at the National Library in Rio, he mentioned legislation introduced by his father in 1911 and 1912 to revise concessions of German colonizing companies and to make the use of the Portuguese language obligatory in schools. The articles stirred up the public, with their accounts of organized pro-Hitler infiltration under "the principal chief of Nazism in Brazil, Hans von Cossel," as revealed by arrested German infiltration agent Otto Schinke. Although Carlos' articles in *O Observador* were unsigned, they greatly enhanced his reputation. He became editor of *O Observador.*[6]

Returning to the National Library, Carlos embellished his São Francisco River material and early in 1939 gave *O Observador* a piece that analyzed the studies and work done on behalf of the region in the past. As he liked to do, he condemned past practices and advocated new ones. He wrote that feudalism should be eradicated and Brazil should reject simplistic solutions advanced by those who had "a false perception of the problems of the country's interior." "It is not," he wrote, "a problem of irrigation, property ownership, health, or production, but a question of all these things at the same time."[7]

Carlos' relations with Olímpio Guilherme were good, but he enjoyed a much warmer relationship with the group of pro-Communists that worked under Samuel Wainer at *Diretrizes.* Wainer, after making a success of a Jewish almanac, had secured financing for *Diretrizes* from the foreign-owned Light and Power Company thanks to the intervention of his friend, blind journalist Azevedo Amaral. The arrangement soon ended because the leftist orientation of the magazine became evident. The editorial office was moved from Azevedo Amaral's residence to the small apartment of Wainer and his pretty wife, Bluma, on Senador Dantas Street in the downtown Cinelândia district, a sort of Greenwich Village of Rio.[8] The street, Orígenes Lessa writes, had a provincial atmosphere, and the apartment shook when streetcars went by.[9] There the hospitable Wainers gathered with *Diretrizes* collaborators Otávio Malta, Jorge Amado, Rubem Braga, Moacir Werneck de Castro, Carlos Lacerda, Dorival Caymmi, and Eneida Costa de Morais.[10] Malta, who had helped run *A Manhã* and secretly represented the PCB in his *Diretrizes* editorial work, has recalled that "Carlos was one of us; he was poor like the rest of us, and had holes in his shoes."[11]

Carlos and Moacir were also close to the intellectuals associated with Murilo Miranda and his *Revista Acadêmica.* Outstanding among them was Mário de Andrade, Murilo Miranda's best friend, who came to Rio in April 1938 after changes brought about by the Estado Novo cost him his position of director of culture of São Paulo city. He became director of the Institute of Arts of the University of The Federal District and took an apartment close to it on Catete Street. After Yedda, sister of Rubem Braga, married Murilo Miranda in 1939, the couple lived for a month in Mário de Andrade's apartment.[12] The apartment was not far form the Taberna da Glória. There Mário de Andrade spent several nights a week drinking beer with his young intellectual friends, who called him *mestre* (master) because of his reputation and age (he was in his forties). The "undisputed leader of modernism"[13] enjoyed prodding Carlos and his other drinking companions with questions, or provocative remarks, about Beethoven, Goethe, and Dante.[14] Sometimes the group gathered at the Brahma Restaurant downtown, and occasionally it visited the noisy bars and cabarets in the Lapa district, known as the Carioca Montmartre. Writing to Paulo Duarte in São Paulo, Mário de Andrade said "the drinking sprees, held two or three times a week," were "colossal."[15] They often lasted until dawn.

Although Guilherme Figueiredo had been a law school classmate of Carlos, it was through Mário de Andrade that he came to know Carlos. Figueiredo's work with the *Diário de Notícias,* where Mário de Andrade became head of the literary supplement, usually kept him busy until 11:00 P.M., when he was able to join Mário de Andrade, Murilo Miranda, Carlos, Moacir, and music critic Lúcio Rangel.[16] Poet and novelist Luís Martins, who had known Carlos since the days of "O Índio do Corcovado," joined these beer-drinking friends on his visits from São Paulo state, where he had recently moved. With them he would roam from bar to bar in the Lapa district, while all sang discordantly.[17]

11. Expulsion from the Communist Party (February 1939)

The government observed the first anniversary of the Estado Novo with a public exposition showing accomplishments of its ministries. An exhibit about the justice ministry's work against the Communist threat was housed in a pavilion filled with captured documents and photographs—including one of Carlos reading Prestes' manifesto of July 5, 1935.[1]

Assisted by funds from the government's Press and Propaganda Department (DIP), *O Observador Econômico e Financeiro* cooperated by publishing articles about the ministries. When Olímpio Guilherme told Carlos that the DIP wanted the inclusion of a historical study of the Communist Party of Brazil (PCB), he said Carlos would probably be uninterested in view of his Communist connections. Carlos agreed that Guilherme should find another writer.[2]

By the time Carlos spoke of the matter to his friends in Wainer's apartment, he was able to inform them that Guilherme was planning to turn to a fiercely anti-Communist writer, such as Heitor Muniz or Odete de Carvalho e Souza.[3] During a discussion about whether the PCB might be better off with Carlos doing the writing, Otávio Malta said he would consult the PCB leadership. A few days later Carlos was advised to accept the *Observador* assignment and handle it in a manner that would indicate that Communism was no danger to Brazil and, therefore, steps to repress it were needless.[4]

Carlos' article, "The Anti-Communist Exposition," pointed out that knowledge of PCB history was indispensable for those who wanted to crush the movement, and he mentioned the sources he used for his account: Communist documents seized by the police after the 1935 uprisings and revelations made to the National Security Tribunal by defendants. Some of the documents cited by Carlos contained the PCB's criticism of Prestes in 1930.[5] In dealing with the ANL, Carlos quoted Communist International (Comintern) executive Van Min to show that it had been created "in accordance with confidential instructions of the Soviet legation in Montevideo." Carlos wrote that the ANL had resulted from "the interference of the Comintern" in Brazil's internal affairs. It was, his article said, "a maneuver" of the International, "in national terms," for the hegemony of the PCB.

Carlos was careful not to include names of Communists other than Prestes and Comintern agents from abroad, most of whom, like the Cavalier of Hope, were in Brazilian prisons. He also stressed the PCB's inability to act subversively. He attributed this in part to the government's "enlightened labor legislation, which has removed the worker from the Muscovite mirage," and in part to the PCB's recently adopted mild program of supporting "national union" and abandoning insurrectional activities. The Brazilian Trotskyites, Carlos pointed out, had reacted to this policy by writing that "the Communist Party has ceased to be the party of the working class, and become a small-bourgeois party." In conclusion, Carlos stated that "in the present regime, with the centralization of power, the prestige of its leader, and the national union of all forces favoring progress and peace, it is improbable that Communism can develop again."[6] Carlos gave a copy of the article to Malta. Malta discussed it with Astrojildo Pereira, a former party leader, and then told Carlos that it seemed "reasonable."[7]

Carlos had made it clear to Olímpio Guilherme that he could accept no special compensation for the article. He was, however, in need of additional income, especially as Letícia, late in 1938, was expecting their first child. The income came just in time, not from journalism, but from Carlos' courtroom ability. Following the trial of Castorina in 1934, Carlos had participated successfully in other legal cases, first when he defended, at the request of cousin Nestor Barbosa, a truck driver accused of murder and then when he collaborated with Letícia's brother-in-law Osvaldo Fonseca in defending four tenant farmers who had killed an overseer.[8]

These defendants could only reward Carlos with some chickens and cheese. But he was better remunerated in the case he handled, also with Osvaldo Fonseca, in December 1938—defending a young man who, while protecting his sister from ill-treatment by her *fazendeiro* husband, killed the *fazendeiro.* Carlos received 500 milreis, enough to obtain a room for Letícia at the Santa Casa Hospital in Valença.[9] On Christmas day she gave birth to Sérgio Carlos Abruzzini Lacerda.

The January 1939 issue of *O Observador* carried Carlos' unsigned article, illustrated with photographs that the police had furnished the exposition. The editing had been light but not insignificant. The "genius" of Lenin appeared as the "degenerate genius," and a reference to the party appeared as "the terrible party." The government, well pleased, printed thousands of extra copies for distribution at the exposition.[10]

In February, during Carnaval, Carlos learned from Moacir at Cinelândia's Café Amarelinho that an emissary of the PCB's Central Committee wished to speak with him at a dairy in the suburbs. Carlos made the trip and met "Baby Face," who asked him whether he belonged to the Party. Carlos replied that in the past he might have joined the Federação da Juventude Comunista had it not been disbanded. Baby Face, showing some relief on learning that Carlos was not a PCB member, said the party directorship was furious with his *Observador* article. When Carlos pointed out that he had done the work at the party's suggestion, Baby Face explained that Carlos, in his article, had gone too far, "showing that the party has no importance whatsoever any more, and therefore causing the bourgeois opposition to lose interest in PCB support." Baby Face demanded a written statement giving the reasons why the article had been written. Carlos refused, saying that such a document, falling into the hands of the police, would be troublesome to both of them and to anyone mentioned in the explanation.[11]

The party, finding any number of reasons to be furious, worked on an analysis of the article. In the meantime Eneida Costa de Morais, who did not like Carlos,[12] spoke to intellectuals at José Olympio's bookstore, saying that it was inconceivable that the author of such an article should be connected with the PCB. Many agreed.

Wainer and Moacir Werneck de Castro were surprised by the appearance, in downtown Rio one afternoon, of mimeographed leaflets announcing the expulsion of Carlos from the PCB for being an agent of fascism, Trotskyism, and imperialism and a provocative informer responsible for the deaths of militants. Moacir and Wainer, shocked, went to the modest apartment above the Roxy Movie Theater in Copacabana, where Carlos lived with Letícia and their baby. Carlos, stunned by the news, turned pale. He emphatically denied any intention of hurting the party. Wainer, as a gesture of friendship, asked him to direct the literary section of *Diretrizes*, which had blossomed into a weekly, and write reviews.[13]

Carlos accepted Wainer's offer, but the party's reaction to his *Observador* article left him shattered. He drank too much at a bar and then, after midnight, arrived at the Wainers' apartment where he collapsed on the floor. Put to bed by Samuel and Bluma, he cried during a fitful sleep and kept repeating that he had been left an orphan, deprived of a "mother," a reference to the PCB.[14]

Although Carlos had not been a member of the PCB, it would have been difficult to find anyone who had been more romantically dedicated to it. In the lines of free verse that he enjoyed jotting down, he had written passionately that only the PCB could provide mankind with all that it needed for life. Poetically, he had idolized the Soviet Union along with the "heroism of the illegal struggle" against oppression and fascism.[15]

No less agonizing than the reputation of traitor to the party was the prospect of being ostracized and condemned by those whose company had been dearest to him. In the expulsion order, which was reprinted in the PCB's *Re-*

vista Proletária, the Party ordered "all friends and sympathizers of the PCB—especially the intellectuals—to keep away from that dangerous provocative agent at the service of the worst enemy of the people and of Brazil: fascism!"

Revista Proletária's expulsion order and warning were accompanied by a list of charges. Carlos, that "despicable adventurer of fascism who managed for a while to dupe the good faith of revolutionary and democratic circles," was accused of writing "an undisguised appeal to the police to infiltrate the PCB" and of "even having the impudence to assert that the PCB directorship supervised his provocative work." According to *Revista Proletária*, Carlos' reference to cells of maritime workers had been followed by the jailing and brutal beating of hundreds of such workers and the killing of one.

"Carlos de Lacerda," *Revista Proletária* wrote, "insults the memory of Marx, calling him a 'deformer,' storms against Luís Carlos Prestes . . . the most beloved Brazilian," and calls Lenin a "degenerate genius." Carlos' "slander" against the ANL, his "falsified version" of Van Min's speech, and his description of the "terrorist plans" of the Comintern were denounced as copied from reports of Brazilian police authorities, "all instructed by the Gestapo." Furthermore, the PCB accused Carlos of defending "the Trotskyite agents of the Gestapo" by presenting them as forming a "political current in the labor movement" and not recognizing that their "supposed disagreement about tactics" was nothing but a desire to "stab the PCB in the back."[16]

The warning of the PCB to its sympathizers was not to be taken lightly by those who wanted a good standing in pro-Communist circles. Friends whom Carlos had seen daily and joined at cafés and bars turned their backs on him, and they made remarks that discredited him and Letícia.[17] Moacir's brother, Luís Werneck de Castro, the lawyer representing Olga in her case against Maurício, phoned Olga on the night before a scheduled court appearance to say that he would not be present and could no longer represent her. "I cannot talk to Carlos," he explained.[18]

Wainer's appointment of Carlos to head the literary section of *Diretrizes* was a mistake. After members of the magazine's staff complained, Carlos made things worse with his sharply critical reviews of the works of well-known leftists. "See what you have done, bringing that low scoundrel here," Jorge Amado said to Wainer. With Moacir and other *Diretrizes* officers upset and some of them threatening to resign, Wainer dismissed Carlos several months after the appearance of the PCB leaflets that had called Carlos a fascist.[19]

The PCB made sure that Carlos' "Trotskyite activities" were reported to the authorities, and therefore two police agents arrived one night at his new residence in Laranjeiras. They searched everywhere for documents, not omitting Sérgio's cradle, and came away with some well-annotated Communist books that had belonged to Carlos' uncles.[20]

As ordered, Carlos reported the next day to Serafim Braga, *delegado* of social order. The *delegado* had already called in Carlos a few months earlier when someone had denounced a nonexistent Stalinist plan in which Carlos was allegedly associated. Now the *delegado* seemed amused to learn that Carlos had apparently become a Trotskyite, or anti-Stalinist. He explained that he had been advised that a search of Carlos' home would uncover Trotskyite manifestos, such as those Carlos was said to have been distributing in Cinelândia. Carlos retorted that the denouncement was ridiculous for he had passed the age of distributing manifestos and reached the age of writing them. He denied being a Trotskyite. Serafim Braga said he had received the accusation against Carlos from a "good source," but he released him.[21]

Drawing by "carlos frederico" (Lacerda). (*rumo,* September 1933)

III.

Crusader for Democracy (1939–1945)

1. With Inter-Americana (1940–1941)

Carlos hoped to have his *O Observador* articles about German colonization and the São Francisco region published in book form. He therefore sent them to his father, who was busy at the *chácara* suing its former administrator, Antônio Bello, for laziness, disobedience, and theft. Replying to his son, Maurício pointed out that publishers of books like Carlos had in mind expected to be paid by the authors.[1]

This was an impossibility for Carlos, who found it difficult to make ends meet despite all he did to supplement his *O Observador* paychecks by writing articles for other publications and making translations. Desperate for money, he finally wrote Olímpio Guilherme in November 1939, arguing that an increase in pay would allow him to eat better, think more calmly, and thus serve *O Observador* more efficiently. However, neither Guilherme nor Carlos continued much longer with *O Observador*. After *O Estado de S. Paulo* was closed by the government in March 1940, Guilherme, president of the National Press Council and officer of the DIP, urged Vargas and DIP Director Lourival Fontes to allow the newspaper's owners to reopen it. Unsuccessful in his appeal, Guilherme left his government and *O Observador* posts. Carlos, expressing support for Guilherme, also resigned from the monthly.[2]

It was a difficult time for journalists, especially those with leftist reputations. Fortunately for a handful of them, the United States Bureau of the Coordinator of Inter-American Affairs, headed by Nelson Rockefeller, made arrangements in Brazil to counteract Nazi propaganda. As a result, Armando d'Almeida, head of a public relations firm, set up Agência Inter-Americana to translate material from the United States and publish it throughout Brazil.[3] The *agência,* which paid salaries above those received by journalists, hired Carlos in June 1940. Letícia, away from Rio, received the good news in a letter in which Carlos devoted most of his pages to reporting ecstatically on the activities and beautiful features of 18-month-old Sérgio.[4]

Agência Inter-Americana broadened its program to include the publication of appropriate articles written in Brazil by Carlos and others and the financing of lectures to strengthen cultural ties between Brazil and the

United States. The apparent sponsor of the lectures was the recently formed Instituto Brasil–Estados Unidos (IBEU). Carlos, organizer of the lectures, discussed the IBEU arrangement in his letter of October 11, 1941, to Mário de Andrade, after the eminent poet had given a lecture at the institute on the music of the United States.

"You made an insinuation," Carlos wrote to Mário de Andrade, "about my position in the campaign of developing close relations with the United States when you stated, in a friendly way, that I do this because I 'have to live.'" Carlos admitted that, during the debate about the enactment of the National Security Law, he had combatted American imperialism. But, he wrote, he had become convinced that "only with American stimulus can there be organized a force of democratic resistance to Nazism in Brazil." Resenting the implication that he had "sold himself to the Americans," Carlos explained that "supporting the Americans, and the British, too, is a duty, considering the common enemy, the only enemy, which is Nazism."

Carlos' letter distressed Mário de Andrade because it called him "the worst sort of slanderer" for having remarked that Armando d'Almeida, considering Professor Paul Vanorden Shaw a competitor of Agência Inter-Americana, had turned to the DIP and police to have the American professor persecuted. Carlos wrote that Shaw, unknown to Almeida, was no competitor but only a "vulgar hustler" who had misinformed Americans that all was well in São Paulo during the "savage brutalities" of the Armando de Sales Oliveira state government. "In whose name," asked Carlos, "can you condemn Jorge Amado, your declared enemy, if you stab, for amusement or a lack of intelligence, your friends and friends of your friends?"

Mário de Andrade had made his unjust remark about Almeida while drinking too much beer in São Paulo with writers Sérgio Milliet, Rubem Braga, Mário Neme, and Edgar Cavalheiro. After receiving Carlos' letter, he wrote Moacir Werneck de Castro of his "unimaginable suffering" and resolve to drink less. Carlos, he told Moacir, continued to be "one of the few thoroughly correct individuals whom I admire and am deeply devoted to. . . . I think Carlos was right when he said that all of us, unable to accomplish more and dissatisfied with ourselves, are in an explosive state that any little thing can ignite."[5]

On behalf of Agência Inter-Americana, Carlos made a study in June 1941 of Japanese farmers in the state of São Paulo. Then, in newspaper articles entitled "The Japanese Penetration of Brazil," he sought to demolish what he called Nipponese propaganda, presented with "obsequious smiles," about the virtues of Japanese immigration. The series, published in eleven installments just after the attack on Pearl Harbor, described Japanese settlers as failing to integrate and bringing diseases, such as glaucoma. Their wives, trained in Japan to be obedient, were pictured as putting up with the institution of concubinage, along with beatings when the men drank sake. Worst of all, according to Carlos, the Japanese settler was an automaton controlled by the expansionist aims of the Mikado. Brazil, Carlos wrote, should "unite against the Nazi, fascist, and Nipponese assassins."[6]

Armando d'Almeida, whose public relations firm was foreign-oriented, spoke of making Carlos its representative in New York. The idea of a foreign assignment appealed to Carlos, who had observed, in his letter of November 1939 to Olímpio Guilherme, that "abroad, everything has the flavor of adventure, difficulties are fleeting, and social commitments, the bonds that tie us to daily misery, are more brilliant." With bitterness Carlos had added that "in our own habitat those bonds are made with poor quality bakery twine."[7]

The idea of an assignment in New York appealed also to Rubem Braga and he hoped that Almeida would consider him if Carlos were uninterested. Rubem Braga was doing boring work for *O Estado de S. Paulo,* now in government hands. "I would give half my life," he told Carlos, "to get out of newspaper work and other public functions."[8]

After the Japanese attack on Pearl Harbor, which brought the United States into the war, no more was said about the New York assignment. Carlos, who had been spending much of his time in São Paulo, developing friendships and a new life,[9] obtained a challenging position organizing and supervising the publication of a weekly bulletin of the São Paulo Commercial Association.

2. Friendships in São Paulo (1939–1942)

Early in 1939, just after his "expulsion" from the PCB, Carlos began making frequent trips to São Paulo, where he wrote for magazines and newspapers.[1] He stayed at the home of 35-year-old poet Paulo Mendes de Almeida and his wife, Aparecida. The poet, whom Carlos had come to know in Rio at Álvaro Moreyra's house, was soon collaborating with Carlos on plans to produce a radio series of adaptations of the works of the world's "best authors." Carlos' proposal for a "Theater of a Thousand and One Tales" listed foreign and Brazilian writers and suggested that the programs, to be broadcast once or twice a week, be sponsored by commercial firms. The proposal was accepted by Rádio Gazeta of São Paulo and in 1941 the station presented adaptations, by Carlos and Paulo, of stories by Honoré de Balzac, W. Somerset Maugham, Guy de Maupassant, and other creators of "universal literature."[2]

For Paulo and Aparecida, Carlos' visits were intellectually exciting. Carlos, when he was not banging out articles on his typewriter, loved conversation. Sitting on Paulo's bed until around 3:00 A.M., he told such fascinating stories that Paulo came to feel that his young friend was "almost a genius." Carlos, Paulo noted, needed little sleep. Even after coming in at 4:00 A.M., so drunk he could hardly walk, he was ready for a day's work three hours later. He had, Paulo and Aparecida decided, an "iron constitution."[3]

Writing to Carlos in April 1939, Paulo confided that Rubem Braga "has been saying you are succumbing to the vice of drunkenness"—and "there are," Paulo added, "worse vices," such as being an Integralista.[4] Luís Martins, one of Carlos' São Paulo drinking companions, was finishing his novel *Fazenda* and living with painter Tarsila do Amaral at her country home, Santa Teresa do Alto. When Luís Martins and Tarsila and some of their friends, such as the artist Di Cavalcanti, sent a "collective letter" urging Carlos to visit the place, Luís Martins excited Carlos' interest by mentioning that he and art critic Sérgio Milliet were arranging for a series of small books to be published by Editôra Guiara. But, as it turned out, the series was not to include theatrical works, thus eliminating *O Rio,* and the payment to authors of only 200 milreis per volume seemed to Carlos ridiculously small for his German colonization and São Francisco studies.[5]

Sometimes Carlos brought Letícia and Sérgio with him to São Paulo, and on other occasions Sérgio was left in Rio in the care of Olga and Carlos' old nursemaid, Clara Freitas, who was considered a part of the family.[6] In São Paulo, when Carlos and Letícia made calls on painter Lasar Segall, they were often accompanied by Paulo Mendes de Almeida, art critic as well as poet, and Aparecida. Paulo was delighted with the company of Carlos' Italiana and when she was away from São Paulo he wrote her letters, often tender and sometimes witty or silly. Writing to Carlos, who asked his opinion of his prose, Paulo recommended simplicity. The "whirlwind" treatment, he said, should be "the exception and always related to the matter at hand."[7]

Carlos' interest in adapting literature for the radio gave him an association in São Paulo with Edgar Cavalheiro, a friend of famed author Monteiro Lobato. Cavalheiro and Carlos, at Monteiro Lobato's home one evening, requested the author's permission to use characters from his children's stories in a radio series. Monteiro Lobato, after talking all night, finally wrote an authorization allowing Carlos and Cavalheiro to compose the dialogue for "No Sítio do Pica-Pau Amarelo" (At the Farm of the Yellow Woodpecker). The series, sponsored by a clothing store and presented on Rádio Gazeta in 1943, featured Lúcia ("the girl with the snub nose"), Prince Fish, a beetle, and a spider, along with Master Shrimp, Dona Oyster, and Dona Wood Louse.[8]

Carlos obtained his full-time position in São Paulo in 1941 after he and Brasílio Machado Neto, of the São Paulo Commercial Association, discussed the launching of a weekly bulletin of the association. To overcome Machado's doubts, Carlos worked feverishly several days and nights drafting five numbers, and the result was a contract with the Unidas public relations firm for Carlos to run the bulletin, called the *Digesto Econômico.*[9]

With the help of Paulo and Aparecida, Carlos found a small house on the same little street as theirs. He and Letícia settled in it soon after the birth of their second son, Sebastião, in June 1942. Sérgio, active and bright at $3\frac{1}{2}$ years, was full of confidence when he set off for kindergarten with his teacher, a neighbor.[10]

All four Lacerdas joined Paulo Mendes de Almeida and Aparecida in accepting the invitation of Tarsila do Amaral and Luís Martins to spend several days at Santa Teresa do Alto. There Carlos showed off his good horsemanship. He was, however, the butt of good-natured jokes at the swimming pool, where Paulo, a former São Paulo swimming champion, won the honors.[11]

Intellectuals were friendly to Carlos in São Paulo. This was evident at the Livraria Jaraguá, a bookstore founded at that time by Alfredo Mesquita, whose anti-Vargas brothers had been prevented from publishing the family's *O Estado de S. Paulo.* The bookstore became a gathering place for writers and artists, mostly impoverished, such as Cândido Portinari. Among the writers there, the closest to Alfredo were Carlos and Vinícius de Morais. Alfredo had organized the Grupo de Teatro Experimental and was pleased to discover that Carlos shared his passion for the theater.[12]

Carlos at last found a publisher for *O Rio,* after Alfredo formed Editôra Gaveta (Drawer), named after a drawer in the bookstore where painter Clóvis Graciano kept rare old books. For the publication, Carlos wrote a 21-page preface containing thoughts that he said had come to him on the fishermen's beach in Bahia. It was a reply to critics who said the play lacked a plot. Movies, he argued, were better suited for action, whereas the legitimate stage, with its stronger humanizing power, was appropriate for enacting the realities of life. Editôra Gaveta's *O Rio,* illustrated by Lívio Abramo, appeared in 1943.[13]

Soon after settling with his family in São Paulo, Carlos had an argument with the São Paulo Commercial Association and left the *Digesto Econômico.* Vera was surprised when her brother, appearing unexpectedly in Rio, asked to stay with her and Odilon until a new position would allow him to rent a Rio apartment. He was a confident young man and expressed the certainty that he would find something quickly.[14]

Thanks to Olímpio Guilherme, director of the A.D.A. public relations firm, Carlos found work handling the firm's advertising layouts. The advertising, ostensibly done on behalf of Rio casino shows featuring Marlene Dietrich and other stars, was, as Carlos discovered, a method of making payments to newspapers to keep them from undertaking campaigns against gambling. Mário Rolla, owner of A.D.A., was brother of wealthy Joaquim Rolla, who held the gambling concessions at the Urca and Icaraí casinos.[15]

3. Union with Vargas for the War Effort (1942–1943)

After Brazil broke diplomatic relations with Germany, Italy, and Japan in January 1942, Brazilian ships were torpedoed by the Germans and Italians. Amid the resulting fury in Brazil, Carlos turned to *Revista Acadêmica* to accuse prominent writers of taking advantage of the crisis for self-serving ends. He dismissed the visiting Waldo Frank as "arrogant" and called Orson Welles a "street vendor of sub-panamericanism." He railed at French author Georges Bernanos for blaming the fall of France on a lack of world understanding of that country, when in fact, Carlos wrote, France had been the victim of its own reactionaries, such as Bernanos, André Maurois, and Jules Romains. "The French intelligentsia," he concluded, was "a slovenly, ragged gang using the calamity as a means of livelihood."[1]

In June 1942 Carlos joined about one hundred Brazilian intellectuals in signing a "declaration of Principles" that was published in *Diretrizes* and the daily press. It described the war as nothing more than "the historic clash" between regimes of oppression and the progressive forces favoring democratic liberties. War Minister Eurico Gaspar Dutra, who considered the declaration an expression of discontent with the Estado Novo, told President Vargas emotionally that its signers, some of them Communists released from jail, were using "the excellent pretext of the war" to spread Communist propaganda.[2]

Carlos was not satisfied to earn his living designing displays to promote casino shows. Bringing him news of a welcome change, Leão Gondim de Oliveira, factotum of newspaper magnate Francisco de Assis Chateaubriand, told him that Chateaubriand wanted Carlos to reorganize and direct Agência Meridional, the telegraphic agency of the huge Diários Associados newspaper chain. To accept this new position, paying 4,000 milreis a month plus 1,000 for expenses, Carlos left A.D.A. on August 5, 1942. He rented an apartment on Avenida Copacabana and brought Letícia and the children from São Paulo.[3]

Carlos was in his stimulating new post in mid-August when a German submarine sank five Brazilian ships off the northeast coast, causing about six hundred deaths. As soon as the first ship was lost, Agência Meridional telephoned the news to Chateaubriand's Rádio Tupi, where Raul Brunini made the shattering broadcast.[4] The anti-German demonstrations turned into popular cries for war and on August 22 Vargas and his cabinet declared that Brazil was at war with Germany and Italy.

Carlos decided to enlist in the army. His situation with the military had been irregular following his desertion in 1935 but could be cleared up by the amnesty promised to all who presented themselves promptly. He sent Letícia and the children to live in Valença and made arrangements for them to receive an income from Companhia Editôra Nacional in return for his writing reviews of some of its books and translating a biography of Thomas Jefferson. During the dismantlement of the Copacabana apartment Carlos wrote to his wife to say that he "did not have the courage to watch the departure of the last things. . . . That is too much. . . . Everything there is so much connected with you, with our life there!"[5]

Upon presenting himself to the war ministry, Carlos was instructed to submit to a medical examination and return within a month. When he reported again, he was told to await a call for induction between December 1 and 15.[6] In the meantime he got together with his godfather, Uncle Fernando, who was back in Brazil.

Fernando de Lacerda, after a long stay in the Soviet Union, was in Argentina with Brazilian Communist exiles when Brazil entered the war. The exiles, mostly former military officers, returned to Brazil hoping to fight for their country. But they were arrested and ordered to complete prison sentences resulting from their participation in the 1935 uprising. Even Jorge Amado, a returning civilian, was sent to a prison camp. Fernando de Lacerda, who was not arrested, brought what he said was the view of the Comintern: Brazilian Communists should abandon Communist activities and close ranks in support of the Vargas government for the sake of the war effort.[7]

When Carlos discussed his "expulsion" from the PCB with Fernando, he was told not to worry about it and that his standing with the PCB would be good if he would publish an article supporting the line Fernando advocated. Carlos' article, "The Intellectuals and the National Union," affirmed that all complaints should be forgotten and the Vargas regime viewed as "our friend." It called for defending the government "against anyone who might seek to intrigue against it." The call for union, Carlos wrote, had been made by Vargas, political prisoners, Hermes Lima, and many writers.[8]

Carlos took the article to Samuel Wainer and emphasized that it was important for him to have it published in *Diretrizes*. "It is a matter of my survival," he is reported to have told Wainer. Wainer appeared agreeable and kept the article. But, like most Brazilian writers, Wainer was against giving Vargas "unconditional support." Guessing that Carlos had turned to his godfather about his problem with the PCB, Wainer sought the opinions of the Communists at *Diretrizes*. They all opposed the article, and Wainer, after two weeks of giving excuses to Carlos about the delay in publication, finally told him that *Diretrizes* could not possibly publish it.[9] Carlos, furious with Wainer, turned to *Revista Acadêmica*, which had only a small circulation and which published the article in November 1942.

Carlos had to contend also with anti-Communists, and in doing so he emphasized his advocacy of cooperation with the government. Hearing in November 1942 that the police wanted to jail him "for the sake of general order," he wrote a long letter about his beliefs to the police chief, Colonel Alcides Etchegoyen. He admitted that he had been held by the police three times, during 1937 and 1938, on "vague" accusations, never proved, of professing "leftist ideas"; but, he pointed out, he had written about German and Japanese penetration in Brazil and had, one month before the war declaration, urged that differences be set aside so that Brazil might become an "indestructible bloc" for defeating the enemy. Even before September 1939, Carlos told the colonel, he had come out in favor of "the most solid, loyal, and patriotric union at the side of President Vargas."[10] Carlos was not jailed. But his request for induction into the army was never acted upon despite his constant appeals, made in person, at the war ministry.[11]

Fernando de Lacerda carried his national union concepts to a point where few Communists could accept them. In an interview with Wainer, after Stalin ended the Comintern, he argued that the Communists should not try to reorganize their party lest this create difficulties for the government. The interview, published by *Diretrizes* in July 1943, earned Fernando the epithet "liquidationist" in Communist circles and was condemned by Communist leaders, including the jailed Luís Carlos Prestes. It also led to the imprisonment of Fernando and Wainer for four weeks for violating the government's prohibition of the publication of the views of Communists.[12]

In 1943 Carlos abandoned the thesis that Fernando had urged on him a year earlier and became a widely known opponent of the Estado Novo. Called on to speak in August 1943 at a lunch given in Belo Horizonte by Mayor Juscelino Kubitschek, he told the gathering that the large number of bureaucrats in Minas was no reason for the state not to conspire against the Vargas dictatorship. The discomfiture caused by his remarks was broken when Kubitschek laughingly told Carlos, "You are terrible!"[13]

Later in 1943 Carlos accused *Diretrizes* of being pro-Vargas. His remarks, given to Mauricinho to pass on to Samuel Wainer, followed a *Diretrizes* article condemning his attack on poet Manuel Bandeira. "Tell Samuel," Carlos wrote his brother, "that I am not willing to receive scoldings from *Diretrizes.*" If, he added, *Diretrizes'* idea of wartime unity meant unity around Vargas, he would have none of it and *Diretrizes* could, if it wanted, denounce him as a Gestapo agent. In a parting shot, Carlos suggested that *Diretrizes* was afflicted by "an ideological (or psychological?) automatism" that allowed it to express its love of Vargas in the same way that, "during the German-Soviet Pact, it discovered 'revolutionary potential' in Hitler."[14]

4. Working for Chateaubriand (1943–1944)

Love of Vargas was not a characteristic of *Diretrizes,* but the weekly had to be careful. Its secretary, Joel Silveira, after publishing an anti-Vargas interview with Monteiro Lobato, went to his home state of Sergipe to avoid arrest. Returning to Rio, he found a job with Chateaubriand's Diários Associados and thus was again in touch with Carlos, whom he had known earlier at gatherings at the Amarelinho Bar.[1]

When Chateaubriand unexpectedly chose Joel Silveira to be war correspondent in Europe for his newspaper chain, he ended the dispute among his three leading writers, Carlos Lacerda, David Nasser, and Edmar Morel, as to who would get the coveted opportunity of accompanying the Brazilian Expeditionary Force (FEB).[2] In Italy, Joel joined Rubem Braga of *Diário Carioca,* Egídio Squeff of *O Globo,* Raul Brandão of *Correio da Manhã,* and João Batista Barreto Leite Filho, who had been reporting on the war in Africa for the Chateaubriand chain.

"I need you here, Dr. Lacerda," Chateaubriand told Carlos.[3] Carlos, crushed, turned in January 1944 to the next best opportunity, coverage of military activities in the Brazilian northeast, where American forces had set up air and naval bases. As space on aircraft was scarce, he used his Agência Meridional credentials to board the *Rio Branco,* an old hydrographic vessel converted into a warship that formed part of a convoy of merchant ships making their way northward along the coast through seas infested with German submarines. The laconic commander, Paulo Bosísio, allowed no smoking at night because he feared that the glow of a cigarette in the darkened ship might alert the enemy. The inquisitive Carlos, collecting facts and statistics about the *Rio Branco* and the navy, was limited in what he could record lest his notebooks fall into enemy hands. Finding the ship's library deplorable, he resolved to ask the National Book Institute to supply reading matter for navy vessels.[4]

In the bedlam at Recife's crowded Grande Hotel, Carlos was accosted by Aderbal Jurema, a *Revista Acadêmica* correspondent, and he proposed to Aderbal that they travel overland to Fortaleza, Ceará. Carlos arranged for a government agency to place a car and driver at their disposal; thus he was no longer in Recife when the police there searched for him in connection with the "crime" of having called on sociologist Gilberto Freyre after stepping ashore. The motorists stopped in João Pessoa, Paraíba, where Carlos persuaded Aderbal's brother, Abelardo Jurema, a local Diários Associados reporter, to open a Meridional office.[5]

After the drive to Fortaleza, Carlos made use of introductions from United States Press Attaché William Wieland to become acquainted with air and naval bases. It was an exhilarating experience. At one of the bases, in the territory of Amapá, he was taken aloft in an assortment of planes used to protect the sea for navigation. A flight in a dirigible gave him the impression of being in a "plaything," so "light and graceful" was the craft. On the ground he joined Amapá Governor Janari Gentil Nunes in a volleyball game and visited with gypsy washerwomen as well as American soldiers. When he left for Belém, his low priority for plane travel saved his life; from the Douglas Lockheed on which he finally secured space, he saw below, wrecked in a marsh, the Grumman of the Canadian air force he had originally expected to take.[6]

As "the first South American reporter" at the bases, Carlos sent the Chateaubriand chain articles that focused on the customs and conditions of the people and that were nevertheless censored by Americans (who cut out references to places) and the DIP. Back in Rio in March 1944 he wrote to São Paulo to tell Décio de Almeida Prado that in Amapá he had found a "magnificent story" for a play involving American enlisted men, whose club in the marshes was close to the laundry of a gypsy. Décio had been hoping that Carlos would contribute a short piece to be produced by a university student theatrical group.[7]

Chateaubriand, keeping Carlos in charge of Meridional, gave him the additional position of editor of *O Jornal*, the chain's leading daily. Wainer was also doing well, and when Carlos spied him in Cinelândia, he congratulated him on the success *Diretrizes* was having. "You'll be the future Chateaubriand!" he exclaimed to his one-time friend, but the remark brought a nasty retort from Wainer, who felt that any comparison with Chateaubriand was an insult. Wainer, on top of the world as the result of a sensational *Diretrizes* article about unscrupulous promoters of shares of nonexistent steel companies, was about to go too far in publishing articles distasteful to the authorities. In mid-1944 the government cut off the paper supply of *Diretrizes* and Wainer left Brazil, going to the United States via Argentina.[8]

Carlos, the twenty-first editor of *O Jornal* in as many years, reorganized the editorial staff. He increased the number of reporters, appointed Vinícius de Morais to head the literary supplement, and named *O Jornal*'s former editor, Geraldo Ferraz, art critic.[9] He worked long hours on stories related to the war. To give *O Jornal* a full page in May 1944 about the exercises carried out by the FEB artillery, which was about to go overseas, Carlos went to the Gericinó training grounds; there he considered asking Vargas, who was nearby, to let him serve in the FEB, but the president left before he could speak with him.[10] In June, when the Allies invaded France, Carlos typed for thirty-six hours without rest. *O Jornal* director Austregésilo de Athayde, impressed with the hard work, admired above all the enormous flow of ideas that led Carlos to write at great length without being baroque. The editor of

O Jornal, he concluded, used just the right words, kept to the point, and wrote what was necessary and interesting.[11]

Carlos himself, in *Publicidade* magazine, made suggestions for improving newspaper writing. Commenting on the belabored use of "illustrious" and other adjectives, he said Brazilian newspaper writing was fifty years behind the times. The "difficult art" of presenting good interviews, he wrote, required that the person being interviewed have the necessary credentials, have something to say, and say it well; and he suggested that photographs accompanying interviews not always show the newspaper reporter. Carlos was particularly critical of the way in which material, paid for by interested parties, was presented. It resulted, he pointed out, in the appearance of articles that sometimes conflicted with the newspaper's editorial policy, thus damaging the newspaper's role of "friend, adviser, and confidant of the reader." Furthermore, Carlos decried the low pay of Brazilian journalists, "probably the poorest paid in the world."[12]

In his *Publicidade* articles Carlos used his experience at *O Jornal* to discuss the problems of a newspaper editor, and he even mentioned messy articles delivered by government ministries. But it was in a letter resigning as *O Jornal* editor, written to Leão Gondim de Oliveira in July 1944, that Carlos most fully unburdened himself. He said that the "bureaucratic, sedentary, listless, and thankless" work left him no time for reading or music or "for simply living" and paid only 2,000 cruzeiros a month, less than some reporters received and far less than he could earn writing articles for other publications were he not so busy being editor. He complained that the authority he enjoyed at Meridional was lacking in his *O Jornal* position and added that further improvement of the daily would require a "unified command."[13]

Carlos, who continued directing Meridional, was asked by Chateaubriand for an article giving the views of Fernando Costa, federal *interventor* in charge of São Paulo. David Nasser and Jean Manzon, chosen for the job by Carlos, found the *interventor* on the veranda of his ranch in Piraçununga, São Paulo. Their article, appearing in *O Jornal* on November 30, 1944, described the *interventor* as "a happy peasant in pajamas and house slippers" and bore a sensational headline quoting him as predicting "the disappearance of coffee from the world." His point was that the production of coffee sapped vitality from land that could better be used for cereals, and that São Paulo's great export opportunity lay in cultivating real silk. Nasser, recalling the repercussions of his story, says that Vargas got in touch with Chateaubriand and insisted on a rectification.[14]

Chateaubriand phoned Carlos to object to the article's "disrespectful" reportage about Fernando Costa and to a news item about the consumer goods tax. The Commercial Association had called to say that the tax story was not exactly accurate and had upset Vargas and the finance minster. The DIP ordered *O Jornal* to deny the tax item and rebuke the reporter.

Carlos wrote at once to Chateaubriand, resigning from the Diários Associados. He resented not having been given the opportunity to explain the two matters, but did so in his letter. The tax information, he said, was based on the "guarantee of its source, the Commercial Association." The treatment of Interventor Fernando Costa, he added, "seemed to me picturesque but friendly" and was "signed by a reporter who must be responsible for what he writes."[15]

5. At the First Writers' Congress (January 1945)

Carlos, a free-lance writer for *Correio da Manhã* and *Diário Carioca* at the end of 1944, was under police surveillance because his name was on the list of approximately one hundred "enemies of the regime," drawn up by the Rio police of Coriolano de Góis. Sharing this distinction were some of the signers of the "Manifesto of the Mineiros," a call for democracy issued in Belo Horizonte a year earlier. Three of the Mineiros—Virgílio de Melo Franco and lawyers Dario de Almeida Magalhães and Adauto Lúcio Cardoso—were arrested in December 1944, together with journalists Austregésilo de Athayde and Rafael Corrêa de Oliveira, after Virgílio de Melo Franco prepared to launch the presidential candidacy of Brigadeiro Eduardo Gomes, the only surviving officer of the 1922 uprising at Copacabana Beach.[1] During the ten days the five democrats were held at the barracks of the First Cavalry Regiment of the Police, Carlos sent them a Christmas basket of delicacies from the elegant Lidador store.[2]

The wave of repression of December did not dampen the conviction that the forces of democracy, ringing up victories in Europe, would soon prevail in Brazil. This conviction dominated more than two hundred writers who met in São Paulo from January 22 to 27 for the First Writers' Congress, held at the suggestion of Communists belonging to the Brazilian Writers' Association (ABDE).[3]

The Communists, in a minority at the congress, were influential. They did nothing to disrupt the congenial atmosphere inspired by the common desire to proclaim the need for democracy.[4] If any friction was evident it came from Guilherme Figueiredo, critical of José Lins do Rego and Álvaro Lins for having failed to attack the Estado Novo and critical also of Communist writers Jorge Amado and Oswald de Andrade for their "strange excursion," during the German-Soviet alliance, "to the pages of *Meio-Dia*, a newspaper favoring Hitler." *Meio-Dia*, owned in 1940 by businessman Joaquim Inojosa, had been subsidized by the German agency Transocean and had published a literary supplement run by Jorge Amado.[5]

The spirit that prevailed at the 1945 Writers' Congress was not represented by Guilherme Figueiredo's critical remarks, but, rather, by the burial of old quarrels. Carlos Lacerda and Manuel Bandeira became reconciled in a São Paulo bar. Luís Martins embraced Álvaro Moreyra, from whom he had been separated, and made his peace with Osório Borba,[6] the emotionally violent anti-Vargas journalist and former congressman from Pernambuco.

"Carlos Lacerda," Luís Martins writes, "was, without a shadow of a doubt, the dominating figure of the Congress."[7] Carlos became known as a leader and not just a writer. Sleeping but little at night at the home of Paulo Mendes de Almeida,[8] he participated with extraordinary energy in the discussions held during and outside the sessions of the congress. At the official meetings he was constantly on his feet, from the first plenary business session until the closing ceremonies, when he served as spokesman for the Carioca delegation. At the opening business session he proposed that the conclusions of the five commissions be discussed and acted upon at plenary sessions. The clarity of the proposal led to the withdrawal of other suggestions,[9] and, after that, whenever Carlos argued for a position he was supported by a majority.

During the discussions of theses about education, Carlos secured the adoption of clauses calling for free secondary education "in the shortest time possible."[10] On the other hand, he argued at length, and successfully, against a thesis supporting the National Institute of Education's plan for a coordinated nationwide campaign against illiteracy. Speakers congratulated him for pointing out that "such a campaign could be carried out in a fascist country to benefit fascism" and that an earlier national literacy crusade had been "an instrument of demagoguery."[11]

As the commentator on a thesis about immigration, Carlos made a significant modification to put the congress on record as favoring a liberal policy. He refused also to support the restriction of the use of foreign comic strips, a proposal he felt was too nationalistic and inspired by commercial interests. But he warned against "Superman" and other comics that "contribute to the systematic deformation of child mentality." During the debate about whether the agrarian reform thesis of Aguinaldo Costa lay within the scope of the congress, a majority agreed with Carlos when he said he saw no reason not to include it as a matter to be studied.[12]

Carlos was a member of the powerful fifteen-man commission for political matters, whose Osório Borba achieved acclamation by insisting that Brazilian intellectuals should "participate more fully and effectively in political affairs," particularly when the country, as Borba put it, was about to recover its tradition of a free people, "suffocated and butchered for so long."[13] A Declaration of Principles, the crowning achievement of the congress, was drafted by the political affairs commission, principally José Eduardo Prado Kelly and Caio Prado Júnior.[14] The Declaration, which the DIP would not allow the press to publish, stressed the urgency for Brazil to adjust its political organization to allow complete liberty of expression along with a government elected by the people through direct and secret universal suffrage.[15]

6. The Interview with José Américo (February 1945)

Returning to Rio from the writers' congress, Carlos continued his practice of dropping in at the home of Luís Camilo de Oliveira Neto, whose work on behalf of the Manifesto of the Mineiros had cost him his position of director of the Foreign Ministry library. More recently Luís Camilo had turned his home into an oppositionist center where he and his friends typed propaganda for mimeographing and mailing to victims and adversaries of the regime.

Carlos, interested mainly in picking up information, was considered an outsider by the members of the group. They were older than Carlos and suspicious of his leftist reputation. When they spoke to Luís Camilo about "that insane Communist," Luís Camilo admitted that Carlos might be "a little crazy"; but, he pointed out, Carlos was intelligent. Luís Camilo was fond of Carlos and became one of those men whom Carlos would later describe as having been like a father to him.[1]

Luís Camilo, wanting a newspaper article that would stagger the Estado Novo, proposed that Carlos interview José Américo de Almeida, whose presidential ambition had been crushed by the establishment of the Estado Novo. Luís Camilo assured his friends that "Carlos won't give us trouble" and overcame their objections to the choice of José Américo, favorite candidate of the Communists in 1937. A more serious problem was José Américo's reluctance to give an antigovernment interview.[2] However, the former candidate showed less resistance in the second week of February, following the government's failure to punish anyone for the publication of a prodemocracy, proamnesty interview given to the *Correio da Manhã* by Vargas foe José Antônio Flores da Cunha.[3]

Finally, in mid-February, Carlos joined the bespectacled José Américo on the porch of his Rio home and took notes. The politician from Paraíba, invoking the decision of the writers' congress that thoughtful people should assume positions about the country's problems, spoke of the government's failures. Painting a distressing picture of general disorganization accompanied by inflation, speculation, antiquated transport, food shortages, and production decreases, he blamed the Estado Novo, which, he told Carlos, lacked the confidence of the people and had become impotent. Turning to labor legislation, "atrophied by bureaucracy and deformed by propaganda," he argued that the compulsory contributions of employers and employees had been misused. The failure of the legislation, he added, could be verified by observing "the condition of squalor into which the middle and working classes have fallen."

Answering Carlos' questions about politics, José Américo affirmed that the elaboration of a valid constitution required a setting in which free discussion prevailed. He went on to say that he and his chief opponent in 1937, Armando de Sales Oliveira, ought not to repeat their contest in 1945 because that would divide opinion just when political unification was necessary. In remarking that "the national political forces already have a candidate, a man who has served the country well," José Américo left the uninitiated guessing because he did not give the name of Eduardo Gomes. He also complicated the picture when he suggested that, in case of a contest between the unnamed candidate and Vargas, the best solution would be the avoidance of a heated campaign by finding a "third," or compromise, candidate. He noted that he himself would be "suspect" in speaking of this "third" possibility and explained that he was considering "solutions, not men."[4]

Carlos typed the interview, cleared it with José Américo, and read it aloud to a group of Vargas opponents in the office of Virgílio de Melo Franco.[5] But, in the days that followed, Luís Camilo found newspapers reluctant to publish it. Orlando Dantas, whose *Diário de Notícias* had the worst relations with the DIP, agreed to use it if other newspapers would do the same. *Diário Carioca*'s Horácio de Carvalho Júnior showed interest but was overruled by José Eduardo de Macedo Soares.[6] More promising, however, was the outlook at *Correio da Manhã,* whose Pedro da Costa Rego had a letter from the absent owner, Paulo Bittencourt, telling him not to let consideration of "my interests" prevent him from assuming "courageous positions." Costa Rego said the *Correio da Manhã* already had an unpublished interview with Maurício de Lacerda that could be used for testing the water.[7]

Maurício's interview had been given to his youngest son, *Correio da Manhã* writer Maurício Caminha de Lacerda, and was published on February 21. According to the 57-year-old veteran of political strife, "the unrestrained aspiration for liberty . . . reveals itself once more by words that no censorship can enchain." Maurício called for restoring the vote, but not before the attainment of freedom of opinion and unrestricted political party organization. Like Flores da Cunha, Maurício advocated amnesty. He also argued for diplomatic relations with the Soviet Union, "this ally whom we have joined in the war," and reminded readers that in 1926, when he was in prison, he had recommended such a step in an article in *A Rua.*[8]

Carlos, beginning to feel that his interview with José Américo would never appear, took a vacation with his family in Petrópolis. There on February 22 he bought a copy of *Correio da Manhã* and found the interview, with no mention of himself, spread all over the important last page.[9]

In Rio, excited intellectuals filled the home of Luís Camilo, while opposition politicians, among them Virgílio de Melo Franco, flocked to the house of José Américo. "I simply feel," José Américo told them, "the relief of one who gives an unrestrained cry in the desert." Expressing the belief that he had spoken for millions who had been forced to be silent, he said he was proud to have been "of service to future generations."[10]

O Globo had recently shown an interest in publishing the sensational interview but had wished to make changes unacceptable to José Américo. Disappointed at having been beaten by *Correio da Manhã,* it sent a reporter to ask José Américo to identify the unnamed opposition candidate. "The candidate," José Américo replied, "will be Brigadeiro Eduardo Gomes, who will accept if there is a milieu of liberty and one that guarantees the functioning of a democratic regime."[11]

The publication of Carlos Lacerda's strongly antigovernment interview with José Américo marked the onset of that milieu because it brought no reprisals from the DIP. Opponents of Vargas quickly filled the newspapers with their views and rallied with unusual unity behind the candidacy of Eduardo Gomes. Vargas, after opening the way for the election of congressmen and a new president, announced on March 2 the end of the DIP's censorship role, the forthcoming initiation of diplomatic relations with the Soviet Union, and a study of the amnesty question.

Maurício, orator from the past, and Carlos, rising star in journalism, found themselves together on a speakers' platform, along with Flores da Cunha and student leaders, when oppositionists gathered for their first rally in Rio after the end of the repression there. The rally, held in the rain on March 7 in front of the Municipal Theater, was to protest the killing of student Demócrito de Souza Filho by the Pernambuco police four days earlier in Recife.

Maurício, after receiving a particularly warm ovation, declared that freedom of opinion had been achieved by the newspapers, without government decrees. He praised Eduardo Gomes and told the people that the greater the fervor in their souls, the sooner the burial of the fetters of fascism in Brazil. Admirers embraced "the tribune of the people," and one youth, expressing the gratitude of the people of Pernambuco, threw himself into Maurício's arms. Carlos also stirred the crowd with his speech hailing the achievement of national union "in the streets" at the side of Eduardo Gomes.[12]

During the pro–Eduardo Gomes campaign of the União Democrática Nacional (UDN), organized by Virgílio de Melo Franco, the 31-year-old Carlos was frequently called on to speak "in the name of the young people."[13] Virgílio took Carlos with him in April when a *caravana* of campaigners visited Recife to decry the recent shooting of the student there. Carlos, speaking at the law school in front of a portrait of the fallen student, told the audience that former Pernambuco Interventor Agamenon Magalhães, after being defeated in the forthcoming congressional elections, should be "dragged to this room with pincers" and placed in front of the portrait so that all could see that it was the student who lived while the former *interventor* died.[14]

7. The Break with Prestes (April–July 1945)

João Alberto Lins de Barros, the new police chief, announced in March that Communist prisoner Luís Carlos Prestes would be allowed to receive visitors. For his steady stream of callers, the Cavalier of Hope had a message: the Communist Party (PCB) should support Vargas.

As Carlos found out, when he tried to tell Prestes that everyone should join the anti-Vargas front, Prestes was more of a talker than a listener. Prestes, with plans for a strong PCB, continued to be annoyed at Fernando de Lacerda's "liquidationist" position, and he paid little attention to Carlos, who had come with a group of visitors.[1]

Wainer, who has remarked that Prestes never forgave him for the Fernando de Lacerda interview, also found Prestes difficult when he visited him in jail. Wainer, back in Brazil after giving *O Globo* a story about Prestes' daughter in Mexico, was shocked to be condemned by Prestes for "exploiting small bourgeois sentimentalism" with his *O Globo* story.[2]

Set free on April 18 along with other political prisoners, PCB Secretary-General Prestes denounced the two presidential candidates, Eduardo Gomes of the UDN and War Minister Dutra of the PSD (Partido Social Democrático). At well-attended rallies "the great martyr" advocated national union with Vargas and a postponement of the presidential election. In heading a remarkable revival of the PCB, he was assisted by his own fame, admiration of Russia's wartime struggle, the legality attained by the PCB, and its moderate program. Nor was his alliance with Vargas insignificant. Vargas was more popular with the masses than was realized and his government was able to assist PCB work in the labor unions.

Carlos, shocked to learn that Prestes considered Vargas a patriot, contributed to the press campaign against the president in articles that often demonstrated brilliant investigative work. After *Diário Carioca* founder José Eduardo de Macedo Soares, another anti-Vargas columnist, was assaulted in May by a giant of a man, Carlos solved the mystery of his identity when he recognized the label on a suit he found in the assailant's apartment. With help from the tailor and lawyers Adauto Lúcio Cardoso and Heráclito Fontoura Sobral Pinto, Carlos discovered that the assailant worked for the personal guard of the president. Then, after searching the *Correio da Manhã* files, he arranged to have the *Correio da Manhã* publish a photograph of Macedo Soares' attacker in the company of Vargas.[3]

Carlos publicized his break with Prestes and the PCB political line, known as the *linha justa,* in a prominent *Correio da Manhã* article on May 27. The article, "The extended hand and the moral liquidation," was a bombshell, read and discussed in political and intellectual circles and praised by leftists and others who were shocked by Prestes' pro-Vargas position. Alfredo Mesquita, writing to Carlos of the excited interest the article aroused in São Paulo, called it a "stupendous" display of intelligence and courage.[4]

Carlos opened his article by saying he would continue to fulfill his duty with inflexible determination "even when all my old friends, intimidated, turn away from me." Taking issue with Prestes' claim that Vargas had "sided with the people," Carlos wrote that the people had forced the "usurper" to break with the Axis but that Vargas had maintained, within Brazil, "fascist terror and immorality." Prestes, Carlos said, should not forget that Vargas, as shown by lawyers Sobral Pinto and Luís Werneck de Castro, had acquiesced to the crime of shipping Prestes' wife to Germany, where she had died in a concentration camp. In reply to Prestes' condemnation of the "agitation of the last few months," Carlos accused Prestes of supporting "the disorder installed in the government" and of ignoring the fact that the recent agitation had secured the freedom of the press and of Prestes himself.[5]

Unkind remarks about Prestes began appearing in Carlos' columns in *7 Dias em Revista,*[6] a weekly launched in June to support Eduardo Gomes and imitate *Time.* The unsigned columns, collections of short notes, were hardly appropriate for Carlos' style, and Carlos used the *Correio da Manhã* to publish a full-fledged criticism of the united front ideas of Prestes and Earl Browder. The correct ideas, he wrote, could be found in the program of the Brazilian socialists as expressed by their political party, the Esquerda Democrática (ED—Democratic Left). The ED, a movement supported by João Mangabeira, Professors Hermes Lima and Castro Rebello, and former ANL President Cascardo, worked for the election of Eduardo Gomes. It charged that fascism sought to destroy popular liberties and defeat socialism in order to save the capitalist regime. The ED program, Carlos wrote, reflected the views of Henry Wallace, supported the basic needs of the Brazilian people, and had an advocate in UDN President Otávio Mangabeira, brother of João. "It is there," Carlos said, "that we have the platform of National Union."[7]

But Carlos became disenchanted with the ED when, in his words, it failed to organize the equivalent of the British Labour Party and, instead, assumed a stupid and spiritless position lest it offend Prestes. "It plays the role of vehicle of the *linha justa* in the UDN," Carlos wrote Osório Borba in July.

After ED President João Mangabeira said that Carlos was not welcome in the ED, Carlos told Borba he had no interest in participating in it both because of the views he held and because "I am not a politician; I am merely a journalist who plays a political role . . . when actors are lacking." He would, he told Borba, return to the peanut gallery "where I reserve the right to applaud and boo—unfortunately more to boo than applaud. The journalist role is all I want."[8]

8. Unsuccessful Playwright (October–November 1945)

In August Carlos telephoned Alfredo Mesquita to say he had written a farce for Alfredo's Grupo de Teatro Experimental. Alfredo therefore went to Rio and there, in his Copacabana Palace Hotel room, listened while Carlos, lying on the floor, read the two-act play to him. It presented, in caricature form, individuals with whom Alfredo was familiar, such as a theatrical agent.[1] In Carlos' story, *A Bailarina Solta no Mundo* (The Ballerina Loose in the World), a fearsome master of a traveling ballet company, Major Michael Stanislas Katinski, faces a crisis when his favorite ballerina runs into passport difficulties, brought about by a young industrialist who finds her infatuating and wants to prevent her departure. The major tries to browbeat an ambassador and, before the farce ends, loses the ballerina, not to the young industrialist but to the theatrical agent, who offers her a role in a local casino show.[2]

The amusing dialogue, well read by Carlos, kept Alfredo in stitches. After Alfredo's group of amateurs in São Paulo agreed that the play was hilarious, arrangements were made to produce it, under Alfredo's direction, at São Paulo's Municipal Theater.[3]

During *A Bailarina* rehearsals early in October, Alfredo wrote to Carlos that Décio de Almeida Prado hoped Carlos would be in São Paulo on October 10, when the Grupo Universitário de Teatro would present Carlos' one-act *Amapá*. Alfredo felt that the shutdown of the *Diário Carioca*, occasioned by the government's refusal to free its paper supply at customs, should allow Carlos to leave Rio. With lawyer Adauto Lúcio Cardoso's "victory over the dictatorship," the *Diário Carioca* resumed publication on the tenth, but Carlos went to São Paulo anyway.[4]

Amapá, presented at the Municipal Theater on the tenth and fourteenth, received compliments for the loose and authentic dialogue of American soldiers. Some of the soldiers' dreams were interpreted by a ballet, such as Carlos might have created in his Forquilha days, with dancers representing a blonde stenographer, a gangster, and a dish of ham and eggs. At the junk-filled shed of a drunken gypsy, where laundering is done, a half-witted civilian photographer, posing as an air force pilot who served in Italy, impresses the soldiers with his philosophic views[5] and makes as much sense as Lucas in *O Rio.*

Décio de Almeida Prado considered the play first-rate journalism, clever and amusing, with a plot that was weak for the stage. Athos Abramo's review called it "the fruit of the imagination of an authentic poet" but no masterpiece.[6]

To attend rehearsals of *A Bailarina,* Carlos was in São Paulo on October 29, the day Getúlio Vargas was overthrown by military leaders who feared a move to call off the presidential election—a move demanded by mobs of Queremistas shouting "We Want Getúlio" (Queremos Getúlio). Carlos described his reaction to the historic overthrow in a letter written from the Mesquita family *fazenda* to his mother (whose separation from Maurício had recently become legal). His first inclination, he wrote, had been to return at once to Rio, but the prospect of attending boring matters there had persuaded him to refrain from newspaper work "until I feel willing and able to go forward on all fronts." Contributing principally to his delay in returning home was an amorous affair with the young woman he had loved about ten years earlier, as reflected in passages scribbled in notebooks while hiding from the police early in 1936.

He would, he wrote his mother, remain for a while at the Mesquitas' *fazenda,* located in Louveira, a 1½-hour drive from São Paulo city. He called it "an ideal place to rest and put body and soul in order: eucalyptus trees, orchids, swimming pool, good food, good horses, good phonograph, good books, and solitude or good company." The company included Júlio de Mesquita Filho, pleased with the prospect of getting *O Estado de S. Paulo* back, and his sons, one of whom, Ruy, was to play the young industrialist in *A Bailarina.* Carlos told Olga that *A Bailarina* would be presented on November 13 and would probably be a success. He spoke of returning to Letícia and the boys in mid-November.[7]

The high hopes of Carlos and Alfredo for *A Bailarina* came to naught. Alfredo, admitting the play was "a flop," attributed the public's apathy to unfamiliarity with the people and incidents in Rio on which it was based. One of the reviewers, looking for something meaningful, guessed that Carlos had departed from the theme of his heroine's liberation and allowed casual circumstances to dominate situations. Chateaubriand's *Diário da Noite* criticized Carlos for long and hollow declamations and added that "the figure of the ambassador has no basis in reality."[8]

9. "Fiuza, the Rat" (November–December 1945)

In Alfredo Mesquita's Jaraguá bookstore on November 15, Carlos learned that Luís Carlos Prestes had named, as PCB presidential candidate, Yeddo Daudt Fiuza, mayor of Petrópolis in the 1930s and, since 1937, director of the National Highway Department.[1] Fiuza, no Communist, was a friend of Vargas and a cousin of another friend of Vargas, Rio de Janeiro Commercial

Association President João Daudt d'Oliveira (Yayá's Alice Street neighbor, whose praise of Bernardes had upset young Carlos). Communist leaders hoped that Vargas, irritated at the two military candidates for their roles in deposing him, would throw his support to Fiuza.[2]

Carlos returned to Rio where campaigning was vigorous with the approach of the December 2 elections. Leftist admirers of Brigadeiro Eduardo Gomes, such as ED-UDN congressional candidate Hermes Lima, tried to convince voters that their presidential candidate was a friend of labor[3] and had never said, as reported by Queremista leader Hugo Borghi, that he was uninterested in the vote of *marmiteiros* (low-wage workers). Maurício de Lacerda, a founder and congressional candidate of the Federal District UDN,[4] spoke at rallies for the *brigadeiro,* whose party backing came not only from the UDN but also from the smaller ED, Partido Libertador (PL), and Partido Republicano (PR). Dutra, presidential candidate of the PSD, founded by Vargas politicians, received support from Plínio Salgado's small Partido de Representação Popular (PRP). The pro-Vargas Partido Trabalhista Brasileiro (PTB—Labor Party) finally entered the presidential contest on November 28, when Hugo Borghi, disappointing the Communists, read an appeal of Vargas asking his followers to vote for Dutra.[5]

Carlos worried lest votes for the PCB's Yeddo Fiuza hurt Gomes.[6] He acted decisively when his cousin Nestor Barbosa brought information, damaging to Fiuza, from Nestor's brother Ary, a former mayor of Petrópolis.[7] Carlos' research about Fiuza, carried out with help from Nestor, Mauricinho, Sobral Pinto, and Adauto Lúcio Cardoso,[8] allowed him to publish dramatic investigative articles in the *Diário Carioca* each day between November 22 and election day. They appeared on page 1, under large headlines, and were accompanied by photographs showing documents and the real estate holdings of Fiuza and his business partners. Written savagely, they dismayed Prestes, brought consternation to Fiuza, and introduced the public to a journalistic style that became a part of Lacerdismo.[9] They made Carlos famous as Brazil's most sensational political journalist and as an anti-Communist crusader.

Fiuza, thanks to Carlos, became known as "the rat," the Communist candidate who had supported Integralista (Green Shirt) activities against Communists and made a fortune by dishonest dealings while in office. On November 23, the *Diário Carioca*'s headline proclaimed that "Prestes exhibits Fiuza the Rat," and on November 30, an enormous picture of a rat filled much of a front page that was entirely devoted to Fiuza. Carlos explained in his opening article that around 1926 *A Pacotilha* of Maranhão had described Fiuza as a "hotel rat." Later, in the introduction to his book *O Rato Fiuza,* Carlos wrote that he had learned of the Fiuza candidacy after coming from the Mesquita *fazenda* where children would sometimes kill "immense, repugnant rats" in an abandoned coffee storehouse. The association of "Fiuza, the rat," with Integralistas, known by their enemies as "green chickens," led Carlos to write that he was reminded of a dilapidated zoo.[10]

Carlos maintained that if Dutra, supported by Plínio Salgado and his PRP, achieved the presidency, Prestes would be responsible for a government in which the Integralistas participated. In his explanation, Carlos said that Prestes, the "Guiding Genius" of the "Integral-Communist Party," had acted treasonably and played the Integralistas' game by presenting a third presidential candidate—and a "Nippo-Nazi-fascist" candidate at that. Carlos went on to say that this candidate—this "rat disguised as a person"—this "geisha girl of Petrópolis"—had flown the Integralista flag in his Petrópolis residence at the side of the Brazilian flag. Fiuza, Carlos also revealed, had made the municipal palace of Petrópolis available for a Green Shirt exhibition while Green Shirts in the city attacked ANL adherents, wounding many and killing one. Carlos added that ANL Secretary-General Roberto Sisson, "intimate friend of Prestes," had been denounced to the police as a Communist by Fiuza and had reacted by calling Fiuza a police agent and Integralista demagogue.[11]

Carlos' well-founded[12] charges against Fiuza's honesty stemmed in part from an official investigation begun in 1944 after the "absurdly" high cost of road construction and Fiuza's nickname of "Ten Percent" had aroused comment. Although the investigation's findings had become tied up in government offices and classified as secret ("stifled by Vargas"), Carlos picked up passages from bureaucrats who had seen them. With this help and other information, some supplied by unknown admirers who telephoned, Carlos showed that Fiuza's 10 percent was only a part of the citizenry's loss, because Fiuza had converted the firm of G. Fiuza & Co. and another firm, belonging to his secretary, Augusto Filpo, into suppliers of trucks, cement, and streetcar tracks to the National Highway Department (DNER). The tracks, sold by Petrópolis to Filpo when Fiuza was mayor, had been resold to the DNER. Filpo, Carlos declared, had operated a modest mechanical repair shop until his association with Fiuza had made him "one of the richest men in the state of Rio." Carlos maintained that the "poor and honest" Fiuza, despite a modest salary, had become a leading owner of real estate and buildings in Rio's southern zone, and he stated that at least one of the houses had been constructed by the DNER's grateful suppliers.[13]

Carlos called "the rat" a liar for professing to be a simple citizen living exclusively on what he earned, and he ridiculed Prestes for praising the "experienced administrator" and "candidate of the workers" in speeches that were monotonous and poorly worded. Prestes, Carlos wrote, had "forgotten Portuguese and not learned Russian" and was issuing pro-Fiuza propaganda that was suitable for launching an insecticide.[14]

The Communist daily, *Tribuna Popular,* explained that Fiuza's sale of Petrópolis streetcar tracks had been authorized by the local legislature, whereupon Carlos retorted that the legislature had acted on a report by an engineer chosen by "the rat."[15] *Tribuna Popular,* which Carlos called "Mentira Popular" (Popular Falsehood), was run by Pedro Mota Lima. It wrote that the "desperate" *Diário Carioca* favored a general strike on December 2 to prevent the elections.[16]

In its pro-Fiuza campaign, aided by Hélio Walcacer, Paulo Werneck, and other old friends of Carlos, *Tribuna Popular* reported excitedly about the throngs attracted by Prestes and Fiuza. The PCB rally of November 30, it reported, had been South America's largest, attended by "half a million *marmiteiros.*" Prestes, speaking about Carlos to the crowd, said that "yesterday we heard the old mischief-maker Lacerda, who is no longer a young politician, say that if his candidates are not elected, they will use the weapons of the nation against the people!"[17]

Prestes ignored Carlos' invitation to appoint five members of a ten-man commission to study Fiuza's wrongdoings. Instead, he described Carlos as a "hired writer at the service of hidden interests." Fiuza, who felt like killing Carlos, decided to sue him for slander. But the lawsuit was never undertaken, to the disappointment of Carlos. According to the press, Prestes opposed legal action because the charges against Fiuza were too well founded. Carlos, citing a "perfectly informed source," reported that Prestes, after seeing Fiuza's reaction to the first article, concluded that Fiuza was guilty but could not be abandoned as PCB standard-bearer without harming the party.[18]

10. The Defeat of the UDN (December 1945)

Carlos, campaigning on the radio for Brigadeiro Eduardo Gomes, said that members of the Brazilian Expeditionary Force who had given their lives for democracy could not rest in their graves because Dutra "wants to rule Brazil with the support of Nazism." "To vote for Dutra," he declared, "is to vote with the ghost of Adolf Hitler."[1]

Most of the press and intellectuals believed the *brigadeiro* would win. For the "thoughtful people," described by writer Carolina Nabuco as solidly behind the *brigadeiro,*[2] the results of the elections were a shock and showed that the labor legislation of the Estado Novo had been more effective than José Américo had supposed when he gave his interview to Carlos.

Dutra, assisted by Vargas' last-minute appeal, was easily elected president. Vargas proved to be enormously popular among workers as was evident in the votes cast for him in the congressional and senatorial races in São Paulo; he accepted a senatorship from Rio Grande do Sul. As for the PCB, Prestes was the most successful senatorial candidate in the Federal District, and Fiuza, after his short presidential campaign, received about 570,000 votes, 10 percent of the national total. Of the 286 seats in the lower chamber the PSD won 151, the UDN 77, the PTB 22, and the PCB 14. Hermes Lima was the most popular UDN congressional candidate in the Federal District. Maurício de Lacerda, president of the local UDN, went down to defeat when party representation rules permitted PTB candidates, with fewer votes than Maurício, to gain seats because of the large number of votes for Vargas. Maurício said he was disillusioned with politics.[3]

Unhappy UDN leaders agreed with the *Diário Carioca* when it wrote that "most of the population is still a long way from the level of political education necessary for a truly democratic regime." "The people," one of the *udenistas* wrote, "revealed themselves unprepared to use the right to vote" and could not "distinguish authentic statesmen from vulgar demagogues."[4] Losers also mentioned regimentation of workers' votes by labor unions.

Carlos, discussing the election years later, criticized the "immensely juridical speeches" written for the solemn-looking *brigadeiro* by Prado Kelly and acknowledged also that "a barbarous dictatorship, like that of Getúlio, was able to gain the support of the masses by giving them things they needed."[5]

The 1945 election results meant that Carlos would continue as an oppositionist, a role to which he was well suited. His daily columns in the *Diário Carioca* in December did not spare interim President José Linhares, accused of "Vargas-like" nepotism, but lashed out chiefly at Getulismo and Communism. With cutting sarcasm he described an imaginary session of parliament in which the wealthy Hugo Borghi, "recipient of over 300 million cruzeiros" from the Vargas government for cotton operations, called himself a *marmiteiro* and was deliriously applauded. Prestes was described in the same scene as coming to the support of Borghi in a five-hour speech in Spanish that praised "Eurico Gaspar Dutra, wearer of the Red Star awarded by the Guiding Genius of the World Proletariat, His Serene Highness Joseph Gabriel Rafael Micael Stalin de Orleans e Bragança."[6]

To honor "journalist Carlos Lacerda" for his "fearless and brilliant performance during recent political events," a luncheon was given on January 2, 1946. Among the more than one hundred admirers who gathered at the restaurant of the Casa do Estudante do Brasil were UDN President Otávio Mangabeira and UDN Secretary-General Virgílio de Melo Franco, who had invested his life savings in the unsuccessful campaign of Eduardo Gomes.[7] One of the speakers, Guilherme Figueiredo, represented "the leftist intellectuals who understood the combative position of Carlos Lacerda in opposition to the political line of the Communist Party." His speech, recalling Carlos' role at the First Writers' Congress, was followed by that of Senator-elect Hamilton Nogueira, a Catholic leader who considered it significant that Catholic thinkers were attending a gathering to pay tribute to "a sincere and outstanding representative of the Left." Catholicism and the Left, he said, could work together to provide a sense of dignity to human beings.[8]

When Carlos rose, his applauding admirers saw a courageous-looking, strikingly handsome man, with shell-rimmed glasses, whose wide smile displayed a fine set of teeth.[9] Always having a lot to say, he turned his words of thanks into an hour-long political essay.[10]

Congressman Maurício de Lacerda in the town of Comércio in 1914, the year his son Carlos was born. (*Manchete*)

Maurício's father, Supreme Court Justice Sebastião de Lacerda, among the mango trees at his *chácara* (country place) near Comércio. (*Manchete*)

Alice Street, Rio de Janeiro, in 1919. The boy in dark clothing is Mauricinho, the older brother of Carlos. (Kindness of Vera Lacerda Paiva)

Sebastião de Lacerda with his grandchildren Vera, Carlos, and Mauricinho. (Kindness of Vera Lacerda Paiva)

Maurício de Lacerda, father of Carlos. (*Manchete*)

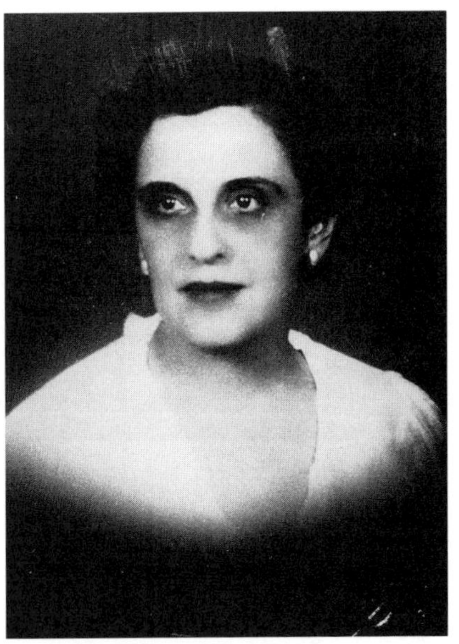

Olga Werneck Lacerda, mother of Carlos. (*Manchete*)

Carlos, Vera, and Mauricinho. (Kindness of Vera Lacerda Paiva)

Carlos Lacerda. (Kindness of Vera Lacerda Paiva)

The main house at the Forquilha ranch, where many of Carlos' relatives gathered in the 1920s. (Kindness of Vera Lacerda Paiva)

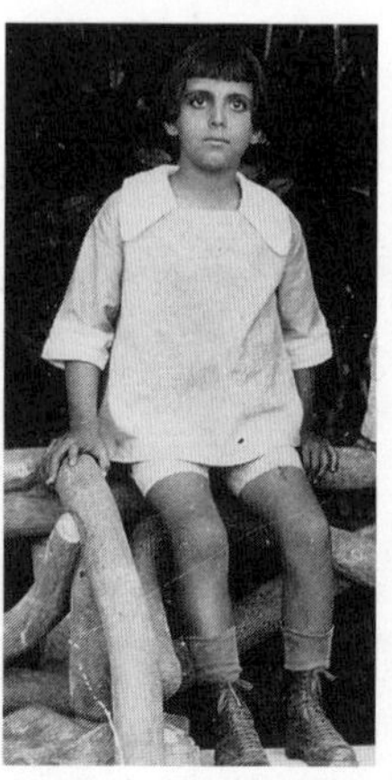

Carlos. (Kindness of Vera Lacerda Paiva)

Children at Forquilha. (Kindness of Vera Lacerda Paiva)

Delmira Caminhoá Werneck, mother of Olga, with Olga's boys, Carlos and Mauricinho. (Editora Nova Fronteira)

Carlos, eight years old, in Caxambu, which grandfather Sebastião liked to visit. (*Manchete*)

Carlos and Mauricinho in Caxambu. (*Manchete*)

Olga and her children in 1930. The names (and dots on the noses) were supplied years later by the daughter of Carlos. (*Manchete*)

Carlos. (*Manchete*)

Dressed for a costume party in Valença. (*Manchete*)

In 1930 Maurício de Lacerda was named ambassador to head the delegation to observe the 100th anniversary of Uruguay's independence. Top row (*left to right*): Carlos, H. Saddock de Sá, Mauricinho, Hercolino Cascardo, Sílvio V. Freire, and Vicente Perrota. *Bottom row, excluding the men at each end:* Vera Moscoso Fragoso, Maurício de Lacerda, Olga Lacerda, Riva Saddock de Sá, Murillo Tasso Fragoso, and Vera Lacerda. (*Manchete*)

Leaving for Uruguay in 1930. *From left to right:* Mauricinho, Olga, Carlos, Maurício, and Vera. (Kindness of Vera Lacerda Paiva)

At the Aliança Nacional Libertadora on July 5, 1935, Carlos reads the manifesto of Communist Luís Carlos Prestes. (Agência O Globo)

Carlos, in hiding from the police in Rio in 1936, at 258 Visconde de Pirajá Street. (*Manchete*)

At the *chácara* near Comércio in 1937, Carlos is visited by his cousin Moacir Werneck de Castro (*right*) and Alceu Marinho Rego, both of whom had attended law school with him. (Agência JB)

Carlos is visited at the *chácara* by Evandro Lins e Silva, another companion of law school days. (Editora Nova Fronteira)

On horseback in 1937 Carlos rode from the *chácara* to Forquilha to meet with Letícia Abruzzini, whom he married in March 1938. (*Manchete*)

In July 1937, Álvaro Moreyra (*left*) and his wife, Eugênia (*center*), played the lead roles in Carlos' play *O Rio*. (Arquivo Yedda Braga Miranda)

Carlos and Letícia with Sérgio, born on Christmas day, 1938. (*Manchete*)

President Getúlio Vargas (*right*), shown with his son Lutero and father. Carlos, journalist, assailed Getúlio and Lutero. (*O Estado de S. Paulo*)

João Batista Luzardo (*left*) was a Vargas man whom Carlos attacked. In 1937 Carlos campaigned for presidential candidate José Américo de Almeida (*center*) and in 1945 he published a sensational anti-Vargas interview with him. (*Correio da Manhã*)

Anti-Vargas newspaper publisher Júlio de Mesquita Filho, São Paulo friend of Carlos. (*O Estado de S. Paulo*)

Carlos was also close to Virgílio de Melo Franco, organizer in 1945 of the anti-Vargas UDN political party. (*Correio da Manhã*)

Communist Party Secretary-General Luís Carlos Prestes (*right*) with two of the Communist candidates in 1945: presidential candidate Yeddo Fiuza (*center*) and senatorial candidate Abel Chermont. (*Scliar*)

Eurico Gaspar Dutra (*left*) and Gustavo Capanema, embracing. Dutra, with Vargas' support, won the presidency in 1945. (*Manchete*)

Before leaving for Europe in 1946, Carlos dines with Letícia at the Copacabana Palace Hotel. (*Manchete*)

From the Arab world, which he visited in 1948, Carlos brought costumes for his sons, Sérgio (*left*) and Sebastião. (Kindness of Vera Lacerda Paiva)

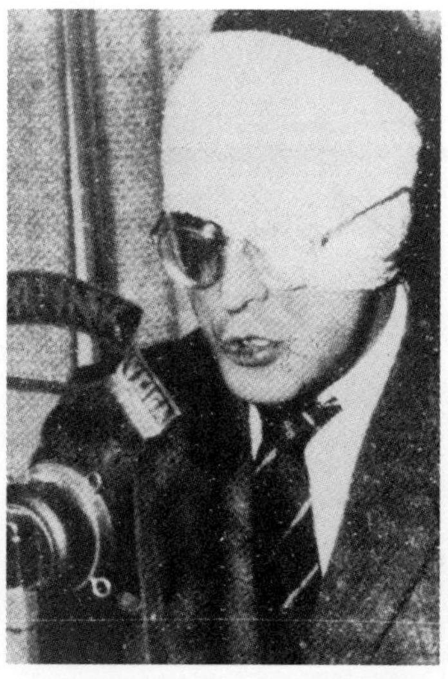

Carlos speaks in 1948 on Rádio Mayrink Veiga about the thrashing given him by five municipal thugs after he had accused the mayor of Rio of corruption. (Editora Nova Fronteira)

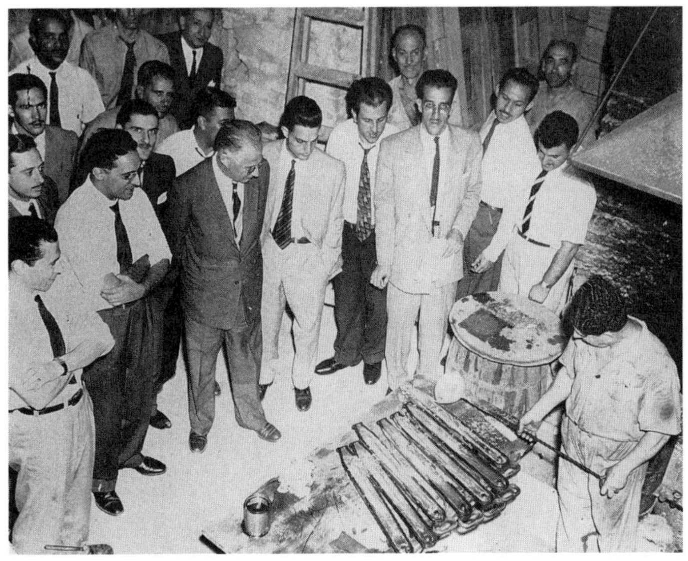

At the *Tribuna da Imprensa,* a daily founded by Carlos in 1949, preparations are made for printing the first number. UDN leader Eduardo Gomes (*in front, in dark suit*) stands between Carlos and *Tribuna* reporter Walter Cunto. (Kindness of Lamy Cunto)

The revelation by Carlos in 1950 of the corruption of an air force colonel led to a physical assault on Carlos by the colonel and a crony. Here Carlos testifies about the assailants. (Agência O Globo)

Carlos and lawyer-politician Adauto Lúcio Cardoso during the inquiry about the assault of 1950. Both had resigned in 1947 from the Rio Municipal Council after the federal legislature had curtailed its power. (Agência O Globo)

The *Tribuna da Imprensa* observes its first anniversary late in 1950. At the far left is Dario de Almeida Magalhães. Next to him (*and in front of pillar*) is Heráclito Fontoura Sobral Pinto. At Sobral's other side is Catholic intellectual Gustavo Corção (*wearing glasses, both hands visible*). Carlos sips. (Kindness of Lamy Cunto)

Getúlio Vargas announces in 1950 that he will seek to return to the presidency. Next to him is João Goulart (*center, in dark suit*). Journalist Samuel Wainer is directly in front of the tree at the left. Vargas won the election. (*O Cruzeiro*)

General Juarez Távora (*left*) with Brigadeiro Eduardo Gomes, the unsuccessful UDN presidential candidate in 1945 and 1950. (Agência O Globo)

Otávio Mangabeira, first head of the anti-Vargas UDN and governor of Bahia, 1947–1951. (*O Estado de S. Paulo*)

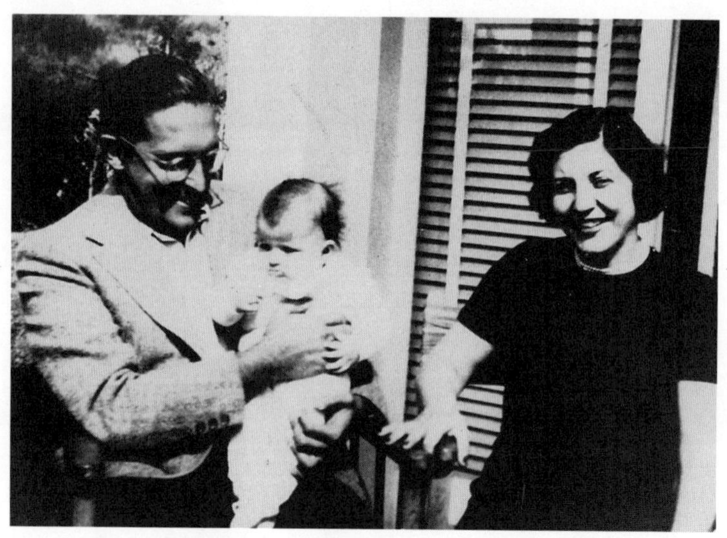

Carlos and Letícia with their daughter, Maria Cristina, born in May 1951. (*Manchete*)

Carlos, imprisoned in 1952 after revealing police corruption, is visited by Colonel Napoleão de Alencastro Guimarães. (*Manchete*)

The *Tribuna da Imprensa* building is decorated to receive Carlos upon his release from prison. (*Manchete*)

At a dinner organized by the *Tribuna da Imprensa* in 1953: former President Dutra (*in black suit*), Vice President João Café Filho (*center*), and Carlos Lacerda. (*Manchete*)

From left to right: Afonso Arinos de Melo Franco, Carlos Lacerda, and Artur Bernardes Filho. (*Manchete*)

In May 1953, Samuel Wainer, director of the pro-Vargas *Última Hora*, prepares to sue Lacerda's *Tribuna da Imprensa* for publishing an untrue story about his newspaper. (*Manchete*)

Lacerda's disclosures about "the *Última Hora* scandal" resulted in a Parliamentary Commission of Inquiry that condemned Samuel Wainer, Lutero Vargas, and officials of the Vargas government. Here Lacerda testifies. (*Manchete*)

Journalist Carlos Lacerda with Congressman Armando Falcão, who helped investigate *Última Hora.* (Agência O Globo)

Orator Carlos Lacerda. (*Manchete*)

Samuel Wainer in prison in 1953. (Agência O Globo)

Founding the Lantern Club at the home of Amaral Netto in August 1953. *From left to right:* Letícia Lacerda, Stella Amaral Netto, and *Tribuna* employees José Carlos Pires, Ruth Alverga, and Amaral Netto. (Kindness of Ruth Alverga)

Lutero Vargas, having sued Lacerda for slander, leaves a court hearing while Lacerda, on top of a vehicle, tells the crowd outside the court that Lutero is a thief. June 1954. (Agência O Globo)

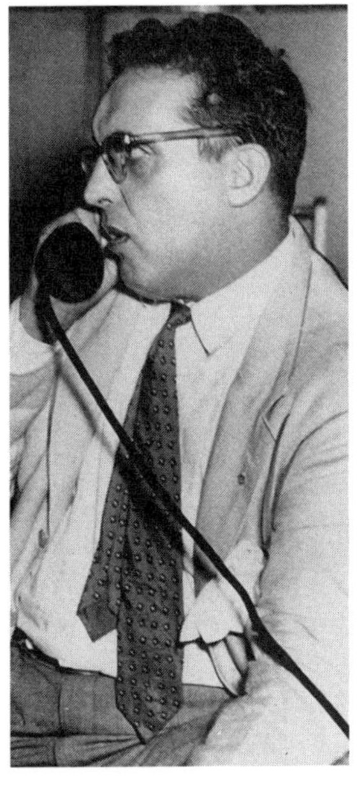

Carlos Lacerda, UDN congressional candidate in 1954. (Agência O Globo)

Gregório Fortunato, head of the personal guard of President Vargas, being decorated by War Minister Zenóbio da Costa. (*Manchete*)

The Tonelero Street apartment building where the Lacerdas lived. Near its entrance, bullets wounded Carlos and killed air force Major Rubens Vaz after midnight on August 5, 1954. The shots were fired after Gregório Fortunato ordered the assassination of Carlos. (*Manchete*)

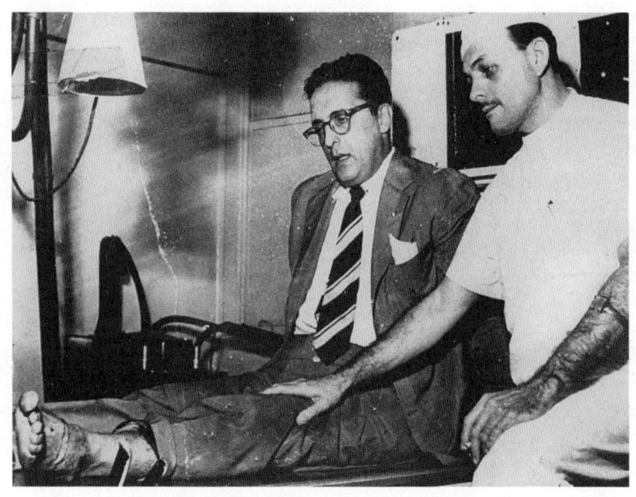

Carlos has been driven to a hospital and is attended by Dr. George Sumner Filho. (Kindness of George Sumner Filho)

Carlos, after receiving a cast on his foot. (*Manchete*)

Carlos, his sister, Vera, at his side, is visited by General Juarez Távora. (*Manchete*)

Rally in front of the Municipal Theater to protest the shootings at Tonelero Street. (Agência O Globo)

Carlos Lacerda with reporters. (Agência O Globo)

Cover of *Manchete* magazine after the suicide of Getúlio Vargas on August 24, 1954: "From Catete Palace to History." (*Manchete*)

Lacerda calls on João Café Filho, who took over the presidency following the suicide of Vargas. (*Manchete*)

São Paulo Governor Jânio Quadros (*left*) persuaded Juarez Távora (*right*) to run for president in 1955 against Ademar de Barros, Juscelino Kubitschek, and Plínio Salgado. Távora became candidate of the UDN, PDC, and PL. (*Correio da Manhã*)

Election of 1955: Ademar de Barros–Danton Coelho rally. (*O Globo*)

The forged "Brandi letter," which Lacerda considered authentic and disclosed during the election campaign, stated that Kubitschek's running mate, Goulart, had received instructions about "worker shock brigades" from Argentine President Perón. Here Lacerda, accompanied by reporters and Rádio Globo broadcaster Raul Brunini (*far left*), discusses the letter with Ignacio Pinedo in Argentina. (Agência O Globo)

Carlos Luz (*right*), interim president during Café Filho's illness, presides at a cabinet meeting. *From left:* War Minister Lott and Justice Minister Prado Kelly. November 1955. (*O Globo*)

Lacerda (*far left*) aboard the *Tamandaré* with Carlos Luz and members of his administration who were driven from office by the November 11, 1955, coup of Lott. The coup, unwelcome to Lacerda, assured the inauguration of election victors Kubitschek and Goulart. (*Manchete*)

Lacerda with Admiral Pena Boto (*left*) and Marcondes Ferraz, companions on the *Tamandaré*, which returned to Rio after two days at sea. (*O Globo*)

Lacerda on November 17, 1955, leaves for an exile that took him to the United States and Portugal. (Editora Nova Fronteira)

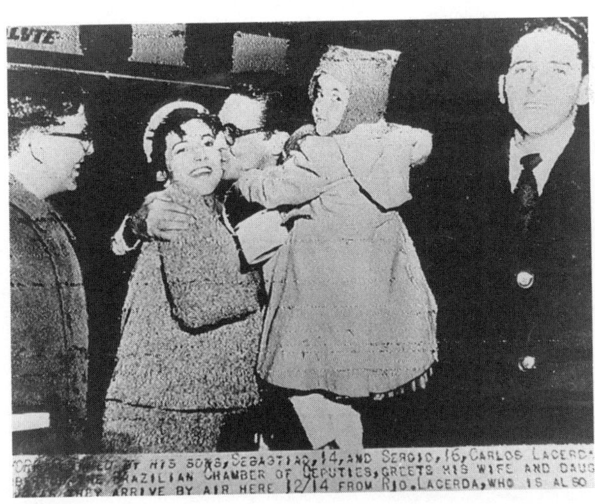

Carlos Lacerda is joined in New York in December 1955 by son Sebastião (*left*), wife, Letícia, daughter, Maria Cristina, and son Sérgio. (United Press)

The police close down the *Tribuna da Imprensa* on August 24, 1956, for publishing a manifesto sent by Lacerda from Portugal. (*Manchete*)

Returning from Portugal to Rio in October 1956. Raul Brunini, at the top of the steps with Letícia, greets the Lacerdas. (Kindness of Lamy Cunto)

Agência Estado

Manchete

Manchete

Agência O Globo

Congressman Carlos Lacerda became UDN congressional leader in March 1957.

Letícia and the children at their Tonelero Street apartment. (*Manchete*)

Carlos and daughter, Maria Cristina. (*Manchete*)

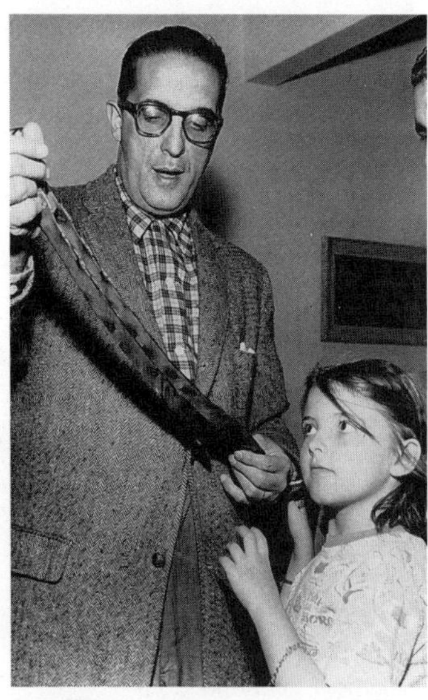

Carlos and daughter. (*Manchete*)

Letícia and daughter at Lacerda's place in Samambaia, near Petrópolis. (*Manchete*)

Carlos, devoted to animals and plants, is shown here at Samambaia with his daughter and his friend João Condé. (*Manchete*)

Lacerda, seated between Adauto Lúcio Cardoso (*at left, wearing glasses*) and Milton Campos, in the congressional justice commission, which was considering whether he should be deprived of his congressional immunities and tried for disclosing a secret foreign ministry cable. May 2, 1957. (Agência O Globo)

Lacerda presents his defense to the justice commission in a ten-hour speech. The commission, dominated by Kubitschek supporters, decided against Lacerda and forwarded the matter to the full Chamber of Deputies. (Agência O Globo)

In Congress on May 15, 1957, Afonso Arinos de Melo Franco defends Lacerda. Much of the nation, aroused by rallies and the publicity given to the case, heard the oratory on radios. (Agência O Globo)

Vieira de Melo closes the oratory by presenting the government's case against Lacerda. (Agência O Globo)

The outcome was in doubt; and the Chamber of Deputies, in Tiradentes Palace, was a quiet place during the voting. (Agência O Globo)

With the outcome favorable to Lacerda, handkerchiefs are waved in a jubilant gallery. Early morning, May 16, 1957. (Editora Nova Fronteira)

Lacerda and UDN President Juracy Magalhães, wearing white neckerchiefs, return to Rio after an antigovernment Caravana da Liberdade trip of speechmaking in the south. September 1957. (Agência O Globo)

President Juscelino Kubitschek with São Paulo Governor Jânio Quadros. (*Jornal do Brasil*)

The publication of this photograph of a pleading Kubitschek, taken during the visit of Secretary of State Dulles to Rio in August 1958, infuriated leaders of the Brazilian administration. After it first appeared in *Jornal do Brasil*, the *Tribuna da Imprensa* ran it twice, with Lacerda writing that the Brazilian president appeared as "a subordinate, a beggar." (Agência JB)

Carlos Lacerda and Jânio Quadros, 1959. (Editora Nova Fronteira)

Lacerda, Juracy Magalhães, and José de Magalhães Pinto, March 1959. (Editora Nova Fronteira)

Returning from conversations with Quadros in Europe in August 1959, Lacerda displayed his pet black crow, obtained in Portugal. He had often been called "the crow" by the hostile *Última Hora.* (Editora Nova Fronteira)

UDN presidential nominating convention, Rio, November 7, 1959. Quadros supporter Lacerda (*at right*) has been replying to arguments of the backers of Juracy Magalhães and is interrupted by a plea for harmony by Cid Sampaio (*left*). Quadros won the nomination. (Editora Nova Fronteira)

Lacerda, having been nominated in June 1960 for the Guanabara governorship by the UDN and PTN, accepts the nomination of the PL. Rio, June 21, 1960. (Agência O Globo)

Confident of his election victory, Lacerda bids farewell to the *Tribuna da Imprensa* on September 30, 1960, three days before the election. He is given a special copy of the *Tribuna*, already dated October 4, announcing his triumph. Mário Franqueira (*tall, with mustache and dark jacket, facing Lacerda*) has spoken on behalf of the *Tribuna* employees. (Kindness of Lamy Cunto)

After turning the *Tribuna* presidency over to his son Sérgio, Carlos sits for the last time at his *Tribuna* desk. *Left to right*: Ruth Alverga, Celso Castro, Nilton Ribeiro, Walter Cunto (*leaning forward in front of unidentified man*), Mário Franqueira, Sérgio Lacerda, José Machado, Luiz Ernesto Kawall, Stefan Baciu (with glasses and dark jacket), Ledo Ivo, Luiz Garcia, Lincoln Machado, and Emiliano Castor. (Kindness of Lamy Cunto)

After a narrow victory, Lacerda is received with flowers when he goes to the Maracanã Stadium to thank supporters who audited the counting of votes there. In the same election, Quadros won the presidency and Goulart was reelected vice-president. (Agência O Globo)

IV.

Indefatigable Columnist (1946–1949)

1. Launching "Na Tribuna da Imprensa" (1946)

General Eurico Gaspar Dutra took over the presidency on January 31, 1946, and on February 2 the congressmen and senators held their first meeting as members of the constitution-writing assembly.

To cover the proceedings of the assembly, Carlos started a column, "Na Tribuna da Imprensa," which appeared daily in the *Correio da Manhã*.[1] The column's coverage of the assembly, however, was meager. It was devoted to analyzing national and international events and issues from the point of view of the anti-Getulistas and to hurling journalistic bombs at those considered responsible for the defeat of the UDN in December. Thus, in its open letter to that "livid man," Senator Luís Carlos Prestes, the column discussed the "sinister consequences" of the Communist line and announced that PCB Congressman Jorge Amado had accepted money from the German embassy during the war.[2]

An early target of the column was Hugo Borghi, who had run for Congress with spectacular success in São Paulo, stirring up vast throngs of workers who banged loudly on their lunch pails (*marmitas*). Borghi prided himself on having financed the Queremista ("We Want Getúlio") movement,[3] but the anti-Vargas press and politicians lost no time in proclaiming that the money had come from the 267 million cruzeiros loaned to Borghi's cotton business by the Vargas government. A commission, appointed by Interim President Linhares, concluded in June that the loans had been improper, but no action was taken.[4]

Carlos called Borghi "the bollworm" (*curuquerê*), the pest that feeds on cotton, and wrote that for every Brazilian soldier killed in the war Borghi had received 500,000 cruzeiros.[5] In his daily column he gave publicity to the remarks of anti-Borghi Congressmen Otávio Mangabeira, Flores da Cunha, Aliomar Baleeiro, Prado Kelly, and Amando Fontes. He also supplied them with ammunition, sometimes with the help of admirers, who wrote him letters volunteering information about Borghi's alleged transgressions. So upset was Carlos with the electioneering methods Borghi had used that he called for legal measures to prevent the broadcasting of "slanders" of the type he attributed to Borghi.[6]

Carlos viewed the *marmiteiro* movement as akin to that of Argentina's *descamisados* (shirtless ones). Still worse, he wrote, the two movements had become allied through a deal struck by Vargas and the "uncouth" Juan Domingo Perón to create a neofascist South American bloc. Brazilian Ambassador João Batista Luzardo, described by Carlos as acting for Vargas in the deal, was consistently referred to as Juan Bautista Luzardo in the column.[7]

After Luzardo was reappointed to Buenos Aires, Carlos published an open letter to Dutra calling the president a prisoner of the Getulistas.[8] The "contrabandist ambassador," like "the monstrous, smiling Hugo Borghi" and the "inveterate criminal" Agamenon Magalhães (former *interventor* of Pernambuco), became one of the Rebequistas of "Na Tribuna da Imprensa." With the success of the movie, *Rebecca, the Unforgettable Woman,* Carlos had begun to use the name "Rebeco" in referring to Vargas, "the unforgettable dictator," and Rebequistas in referring to men close to Vargas.[9]

Carlos' ferocious writing style so enraged individuals who were pilloried that he was in physical danger. Members of the Rio Special Police, regarded by him as "hoodlums of the ex-dictator,"[10] decided to kidnap and at least pummel the pugnacious journalist, no small matter as some of them were not above killing. The first effort, that of June 1, failed because the thugs had their eyes on the apartment of Odilon Lacerda Paiva. Odilon, prevented by a strike from using a bus to reach his workplace in the municipal government, accepted an automobile ride from men who pulled a revolver on him after he stepped into the car. On their way to a deserted area they learned of their mistake and brought Odilon back to the city and released him. Later in the day Odilon, Mauricinho, and Virgílio de Melo Franco told Police Chief José Pereira Lyra of the threat to Carlos, but Lyra did no more than listen.

On his way downtown on the morning of June 18, Odilon passed the Copacabana apartment where Carlos lived and recognized, in front of it, two of his captors and the car they had used on June 1. He telephoned Carlos, who got in touch with Horácio de Carvalho Júnior, of the *Diário Carioca,* and lawyer Clóvis Ramalhete, persuading them to come to the Copacabana Avenue apartment building. Odilon, at Carlos' suggestion, went to the office of Virgílio de Melo Franco, where, with the help of Adauto Lúcio Cardoso and Sobral Pinto, arrangements were made for newspaper photographers to go also to the apartment building.

At a shop in the apartment building, an accomplice of the two thugs, Telmo Augusto Batista, said he was looking for Carlos. Telmo, seen there by Carlos, Ramalhete, Horácio, and others, was identified by the shopkeeper as a Special Police soldier. Because of the crowd, the man could do nothing and left with his cronies in the car, but not before Carlos and his friends noted the licence plate number. Horácio and his chauffeur found the car later in a fleet of official vehicles at the service of the Special Police commander.

Adauto Lúcio Cardoso and Sobral Pinto, unable to prod Police Chief Lyra into action, put the facts in a letter, copies of which they delivered to leaders of the constitutional assembly. On July 6 the *Correio da Manhã* published the letter, and Carlos, in his column, lashed out at the inability of Dutra to deal with the Special Police. He wrote that Police Chief Lyra, a confidant of Dutra, protected bandits. And he called the Special Police a breeding ground of rascals who lived off the milk that children lacked and whose exclusive function was to beat and kill people.[11]

2. Studying European Cooperatives (July–August 1946)

Valentim Bouças, *O Observador* founder and IBM vice-president, spoke one evening to his son Jorge, his son-in-law Fernando Cícero da Franca Velloso, and Carlos about his wish to form a large cooperative to help the employees in some of his businesses. After he suggested that Carlos study cooperatives in England and Scandinavia, Carlos discussed the idea with UDN leaders and *Correio da Manhã* officers and found them agreeable. Arrangements were made for the *Correio da Manhã* paychecks to go to Letícia and for Carlos to send reports to *O Observador*, the *Correio da Manhã*, and *O Estado de S. Paulo*.[1]

Carlos, who relished the idea of traveling abroad, left Brazil with a stack of letters of introduction. Minas politician Mário Brant, in his letter to Sir Otto Niemeyer, called Carlos "Brazil's foremost journalist." Letters from Alceu Amoroso Lima, whom Carlos had loathed in his youth, were addressed to British Catholic leaders.[2]

At the Hyde Park Hotel in London, Carlos felt flattered when an elevator operator, struck by his good looks, asked if he were a movie actor. He could barely reply "not yet" because his English was poor. But he understood enough to be fascinated by the debates in Hyde Park, where it was a pleasure to him to find the police protecting extremes of freedom of speech. "I saw," he wrote lawyer Fernando Velloso, "tattooed Negroes insulting the English, calling them bloodsuckers." He added: "Bombed houses are up for sale. So are the Lords. The difference is that the latter no longer find buyers."[3]

Carlos, predicting radical social changes, was attracted to the program of the Labour Party, which was in power. "In England," he reported to the *Correio da Manhã*, "a revolution is under way. It is not visible at first sight because everything occurs as though the English had never known anything different." Significantly, he also wrote that "the act of placing the permanent rights of justice out of the reach of what might be convenient to the government is the cardinal virtue of England."[4]

The stimulation of being in his first European city, evident in the abundance and length of his observations to family, friends, and the Brazilian press, was tempered by disappointments. In his opinion the only redeeming feature of life in London was the theater. Otherwise, he wrote to his mother and Virgílio de Melo Franco, the city was depressing. "In England," he told Velloso, "Brazil does not exist. Most of the people don't even know we were in the war."[5]

The IBM man in London had little familiarity with cooperatives and considered them a danger to England.[6] However, thanks to friends made at the

Co-operative Union, the Labour Ministry, and the Trades Union Council, Carlos collected opinions and documents and was given introductions he used in visiting cooperatives in Manchester and Leicester.[7]

If London seemed expensive, Sweden seemed more so, and if IBM was disappointing in London, it was the same in Sweden. But Carlos persevered, visiting workers' houses "almost in the polar zone" and studying the program of the Social Democratic Party of Sweden. A find that excited him was a copy of the United States government's 1937 *Report of the Inquiry on Co-operative Enterprises in Europe.*[8]

Carlos planned to continue his mission by flying to Denmark and Holland and revisiting England. But he canceled his August 20 reservation to Copenhagen upon receiving a cable from Jorge Bouças instructing him to cover the Paris Peace Conference for the publications that had been financing his study of cooperatives.[9]

3. Trieste and the Paris Peace Conference (August–October 1946)

From Paris on August 21 and 22 Carlos wrote to Velloso that "it is not easy, arriving in the middle of a disorderly conference, to do something serious and coordinated." He described the Brazilian delegation as in complete confusion and put the blame on delegation head João Neves da Fontoura, Dutra's foreign minister and friend of Vargas. João Neves, he wrote, coordinated nothing and lost several "excellent opportunities" for Brazil. "The delegation head does not know what he is doing; he goes to the Folies Bergère while his wife distributes small images of saints to the delegates." Carlos added that the Brazilians had some good men at the conference, the best being the UDN's Raul Fernandes (a distant cousin of Carlos), but that they had little influence.[1]

At the Grand Hotel, where the foreign correspondents were lodged, arguments raged about the Soviet Union and the positions it took. Carlos had a supporter in anti-Stalinist Barreto Leite Filho, the Diários Associados correspondent with stories about the misbehavior of Russian troops in Europe.[2]

Once again the path of Carlos crossed with that of Samuel Wainer, who was in Paris as correspondent for *Diretrizes,* which had become a daily but was no longer under his control. This time the quarrel between the two journalists, about the role of the Soviet Union at the peace conference, would make reconciliation difficult. Carlos, in an article in the *Correio da Manhã,* wrote that Wainer "became a sort of press agent of the legations of the satellites of Stalin, taking unwary correspondents to cocktail parties and press conferences of the Bulgarians, Yugoslavs, etc." He also accused Wainer of ridiculing Raul Fernandes.[3]

The dispute between Carlos and Wainer was reflected in their contrasting positions regarding Yugoslavia's claim to Trieste. Wainer, some of whose articles appeared in the French Communist press, was asked by a Yugoslav correspondent to support Yugoslavia's claim, and he agreed in return for having an interview set up with Josip Broz Tito, who had not given interviews.[4] Carlos regarded Yugoslavia as the "instrument of Russian expansion" and wrote that the United States, owing to the incompetence of its State Department, was abandoning Italy on the Trieste question. As he saw it, the Italians could count only on the support of the Brazilian delegation, which was outvoted on all the proposals it submitted about the matter.[5]

Difficulties mentioned to Velloso could not prevent Carlos from sending Brazil a reportage that was both "serious and coordinated." He told his readers that Trieste was "the frontier of the two enormous and hostile worlds that are going to emerge from the Peace Conference."[6]

To describe the situation in Trieste, he set forth on September 26 in the Orient Express, accompanied by Arlindo Pasqualini, of the *Correio do Povo* of Porto Alegre. In articles in the *Correio da Manhã,* he explained that Brazilians should be interested in Italy's sorrowful experience because it had been similar to their own, except that, in the end, Mussolini's body had hung from a gasoline station girder whereas Rebeco (Vargas) had become a "senator making suggestions about the republic he disgraced." Above all, Carlos argued that the Italian problem was of fundamental importance to the world: Italy should not be hurt but should be given the opportunity to reorganize as a democratic republic, thus showing weak nations, such as the feudal Balkans, that they need not submit to Russia in order to have "their pocket-size French revolutions."[7] Passing through Pistoia, Italy, where the FEB dead were buried, he said that the "stupid smile" of a Getúlio or the peace treaty to be signed in Paris "are not the sort of answers that should be given to men who gave their lives to end cynicism in the world."[8]

In Udine, a military stronghold forty miles northwest of Trieste, Carlos and Pasqualini failed to obtain the passes to Trieste they had been expecting from the Allied military government. Carlos, angry at a "Victorian" British major who gave them no help, told his Brazilian readers that the British army in Italy was "stupidly, absurdly" behaving as it might have done in India in the past. With all of Udine's hotels requisitioned, Carlos and his companion passed the night in the railroad station, crowded with civilians who slept on benches or the cement floor.[9]

Carlos reported on the anti-Tito apprehension of the people he interviewed in the railroad station. Quoting statistics to show that the area's population was overwhelmingly Italian, he wrote that Tito's argument about Yugoslavia's need of a port made as much sense as if Paraguay were to demand the port of Santos. Even the Communist Party of Trieste, Carlos disclosed, had defied Moscow by opposing Yugoslavia's claim and therefore had been closed down, together with its newspaper, by Italian Communist leader Palmiro Togliatti.[10]

Despite his opinion of the British major, Carlos credited the Anglo-American troops with preventing Tito from being able to announce at the peace conference that the Yugoslav invasion of Trieste was an accomplished fact. While saying that such an invasion would signal a new war, Carlos argued that an undeclared war existed already in the area, with unknown heroes dying daily. He told his readers that "the hordes of Tito, manipulated by Russian expansionism . . . , behave as true barbarians," committing crimes "equal to Nazi crimes that have been verified." He called Wainer "the agent of Tito."[11]

Carlos was back in Paris on October 7, just after the commissions of the conference had completed their work. The problem of Trieste, he cabled to the *Correio da Manhã* on the tenth, had not been solved, because Trieste and the neighboring area were to be taken from Italy and made into free territories. He reported that, while the "brutish" Yugoslav delegate spoke in Paris, "his countrymen continued to expel, kill, corrupt, and coerce" the terrified people of the area.[12]

João Neves objected to the free territory decision in a speech that Carlos said should have been given at the opening of the conference. Although Carlos faulted the speech for its verbosity and poor French, he considered it praiseworthy and concluded that João Neves and some of the Brazilian delegates had done as well as could be expected considering the handicap of having at home a government without authority, headed by a man "who could have been a great mediocre president but is content to be a great mediocrity."

But then, Carlos asked, who could have played a brilliant role "at this listless and sulky conference . . . , destined to be simply an insipid farce?" He pointed out that, while the commissions were at work in the Luxembourg Palace in Paris, the important developments, such as Secretary James F. Byrnes' speech in Stuttgart about Germany, occurred elsewhere.[13]

In August, Carlos had been so engrossed in his study of cooperatives that he had been reluctant to lay it aside;[14] but his switch to reporting from abroad on international politics gave his columns, formerly devoted so much to the Rebequistas, a new dimension. Writing further about the Paris conference on October 15, he said: "The plenary comedy will end, and, on the twenty-third the comedy season will continue in New York, in the UN general assembly, with the completion of this fine work of preparation for the third world war, begun efficiently here by Messrs. Molotov, Byrnes, and others, with the precious help of . . . the experienced executioner Vyshinsky." Carlos agreed with the *New Statesman and Nation,* which had written that the Russians and Americans were constructing regional security organizations. And he criticized Henry Wallace, who felt that peace would be more likely if thc "imperialistic" British would stop trying to draw the United States into a war with Russia. Carlos wrote that Wallace's "puerile" speech, given in the United States, advanced the cause of peace no further than Chamberlain had done in dealing with Germany.[15]

Upon returning to Brazil, Carlos agreed to the suggestion of a new São Paulo publisher, the Instituto Progresso Editorial, that his articles about the Paris Peace Conference be published as a book, and he named it *Como Foi Perdida a Paz* (How the Peace Was Lost). The new authority on world problems, happy when he could show friends the neckties and musical records he had brought from Europe,[16] was ready to participate in the Brazilian elections of January 1947 for governors, state legislators, and some additional federal legislators. Political work took precedence over completing the study about cooperatives.[17]

4. Election to the Municipal Council (January 1947)

By the time Carlos returned to Brazil, the constitution of September 18, 1946, had been promulgated and the constitutional assembly had turned itself into the Chamber of Deputies and Senate. Politicians were heatedly debating President Dutra's offer of a formal UDN-PSD alliance, an extension of the UDN's recent association with anti-Vargas supporters of Dutra in the constitutional assembly. Dutra's offer, which would give the UDN two cabinet posts, was favored by UDN President Otávio Mangabeira and condemned by UDN Secretary-General Virgílio de Melo Franco.

Carlos, known as a "colt" of the UDN,[1] agreed with Virgílio that the party should remain oppositionist and "uncontaminated." To promote that view, he worked with the Resistência Democrática, in which Catholic intellectuals, such as lawyer Sobral Pinto, were influential. Explaining his position in the *Correio da Manhã*, Carlos wrote that "a nation in which Hugo Borghi can be a candidate for anything except prison cannot be saved by 'coalitions' or 'accords.' . . . What does it matter if the government party formally attacked Rebeco yesterday, if it feeds on the same errors and lives for the same ambitions?"[2]

A majority of the UDN directors favored the alliance with Dutra and in December Raul Fernandes was named foreign minister and Congressman Clemente Mariani, of Bahia, minister of education. Virgílio de Melo Franco resigned as UDN secretary-general.

The response of Carlos was to get together with Adauto Lúcio Cardoso and others to organize the anti-Dutra Movimento Renovador of the UDN so that Carioca voters would be able to vote against the government without having to turn to the Communist Party (PCB) or the pro-Vargas Labor Party (PTB). In the Movimento Renovador, the Resistência Democrática joined a small, vocal group of socialists, such as longtime Trotskyites Mário Pedrosa and Edmundo Moniz, who used *Vanguarda Socialista* and the *Correio da Manhã* to attack Stalin and Prestes and criticize the "capitulating liberals" of the Esquerda Democrática (ED).[3] At the same time, the Movimento Renovador attracted Catholic thinkers independent of the Resistência Democrática, among them Alceu Amoroso Lima and Gustavo Corção.[4]

As a candidate of the Movimento Renovador for one of the fifty Municipal Council seats, Carlos led the campaign against the UDN's chief rival in Rio, the PCB. Even more popular than he had been when he defended the PCB eleven years earlier, he drew large crowds. He told them that the "fanatics" of Luís Carlos Prestes belonged to a totalitarian party, which, he charged, was guilty of assaulting the Movimento Renovador headquarters during the night. Prestes, Carlos warned, was determined to turn a PCB victory in Rio into a springboard for Communist control of Brazil. Warning also that the PCB, fundamentally subversive, used demagoguery in its fight for a victory in Rio, he ridiculed what he called the claim of the PCB that it would construct a subway "in twenty-four hours."[5]

But Carlos insisted that "we are not calling on the people simply to be anti-Communist. . . . It is necessary to be in favor of something, and that can only be democracy." He also gave the Movimento Renovador a positive program to take to the Municipal Council (Câmara dos Vereadores) so that the Cariocas might obtain a law about cooperatives, a law to prevent the adulteration of foods or pharmaceutical products, a law to give the municipality control of transport to the islands of Guanabara Bay, and a ruling to transfer workers, employed at "sumptuous municipal construction," to more urgent projects, such as those for supplying the city with water.[6]

At a UDN rally at the Largo do Machado on January 8, the throng acclaimed Eduardo Gomes, Senator Hamilton Nogueira, and Carlos Lacerda. Carlos, who had not been scheduled to speak, gave an impromptu address in which he mocked leaders of the PTB, suddenly friends of the people "after exploiting them for fifteen years." The Communists, Carlos said, wanted to turn Brazil into a Russian base of influence in the Americas. During the parade of January 13, which closed the UDN campaign, Carlos rode in an open car, grinning broadly. Mobbed by admirers, he signed autographs and handed out ballots to be used in the election, as was the practice. Upon reaching Ouvidor Street, which was filled with "Vote for Carlos Lacerda" signs, he spoke to a multitude.[7]

The Communists, with their marching song glorifying Prestes and their "slate of the common people," also waged a lively campaign. In the *Tribuna Popular,* illustrated by Paulo Werneck, Moacir Werneck de Castro extolled the PCB ticket. The PCB's enormous closing rally was a testimony of the party's appeal.[8]

The election returns made it clear that the PCB was the leading party in the Federal District and Carlos Lacerda the leading political figure. His 34,762 votes amounted to 42.5 percent of the total cast for the forty-nine UDN candidates for the Municipal Council. His extraordinary popularity gave him three times the number of votes received by his closest competitor in all twelve parties and gave the UDN a grand total that allowed it to seat four or five more councilmen than would otherwise have been possible.[9] Nevertheless, the PCB, with 24 percent of the Federal District vote, gained the most seats in the Municipal Council, eighteen. The UDN and PTB, about even with 19 percent of the vote, were awarded nine seats each.

Borghi's campaign for the São Paulo governorship was set back when PTB leaders, including Vargas, turned against him and when his chief rival, former Interventor Ademar de Barros, of the Partido Social Progressista (PSP), obtained the backing of the Communists. After Ademar de Barros won a narrow victory, Borghi called Vargas a traitor and said the PCB was fascist.[10] The PCB also had successful alliances elsewhere, some with the UDN, its archenemy in the Federal District. It boasted that it was responsible for the UDN victories that made jurist Milton Campos governor of Minas Gerais and Otávio Mangabeira governor of Bahia.[11]

Before Mangabeira turned the UDN presidency over to José Américo, Carlos assured him that the Movimento Renovador had no intention of causing a split in the UDN.[12] But the success of the Movimento Renovador, due in large part to Carlos, presented a problem to the Dutra-allied UDN. Senator

Hamilton Nogueira declared that the success of the Movimento Renovador gave it the right to represent the "entire" UDN in the Federal District.[13]

Early in February, a phone call from the Dutra government's war ministry informed Carlos that he could not take his seat in the Municipal Council because he had been a military deserter and therefore did not have the required certificate showing him to be a member of the armed forces reserve. Carlos pointed out that he was covered by the amnesty granted to all who reported for service after Brazil declared war. The problem was resolved at an army recruitment station on February 8, when he swore allegiance to the flag and signed a form that made him a "third class reservist" in the army.[14]

Even before this formality was out of the way, Carlos began preparing for serious legislative sessions by taking groups of incoming UDN municipal councilmen on trips to study hospital services and rural conditions in the Federal District.[15] He also worked to have Adauto Lúcio Cardoso elected president of the Municipal Council *mesa* (board of officers). The Communists, however, arranged to have the post go to former Police Chief João Alberto, of the PTB, a man Carlos accused of having created the Special Police, torturer of Communists during the Estado Novo.[16]

5. The PCB's Loss of Legality and Representation (1947–1948)

While the Municipal Council held its first meetings, the Superior Electoral Tribunal considered the government's case against the PCB. Already in 1946, Luís Carlos Prestes had infuriated the Dutra administration by stating that the Brazilian Communists, "opposing an imperialist war against the Soviet Union," would take up arms to resist the Brazilian government if it joined another nation in waging such a war. Dutra's lawyers argued that the PCB, a party with international ties, had gained legality in 1945 by presenting false statutes to the electoral tribunal and insincerely denying allegiance to Marxism-Leninism.[1]

In the Municipal Chamber and in his columns, Carlos opposed depriving the PCB of its legal status, despite his view that it was the "only large reactionary party in Brazil." He argued that its closure would open the way for the government to make political arrests and legislate about the press so that it could shut down "Popular Falsehood" (*Tribuna Popular*). A better course for Dutra, he said, would be to ban the participation of civilian and military government personnel in the PCB, close the Communist Youth organization, prevent Communist infiltration in labor unions, and mobilize popular support by presenting a bold plan for improving Brazil. When Dutra moved against Communist Youth in April, Carlos commended his step and asserted that the young should be educated at school and at home, neither of which should be invaded by the PCB's "deforming" and "totalitarian" propaganda.[2]

Like Carlos, the UDN national directorship did not favor ending the legality of the Communist Party. But on May 7 the electoral tribunal closed the PCB.

Carlos, forecasting a furious government repression that would help Communism in the long run, pledged impetuously in his column on May 8 that "while the Communist Party is closed I shall not write one word against it or any of its members." On the next day he repeated the sensational pledge during a long Municipal Chamber speech, which was so vigorously acclaimed that João Alberto had to call on the gallery to be quiet.[3]

Lawyer Sobral Pinto, described by Carlos as "a sort of Catholic Voltaire," wrote to Carlos on May 10 to blame him for being the most responsible for the PCB's closure. Citing Carlos' campaign to portray the PCB as Russian and Prestes "as a Soviet citizen," he expressed the hope that the episode would teach Carlos something about his responsibilities as a writer. Sobral went on to say that Carlos should not interpret the letter as implying support for Communism or Prestes and added that in letters to Prestes and other Communists he had written "truths even harsher" than those published by Carlos.[4]

Carlos was hurt by the scolding from his friend. As usual, his reaction was to assume an offensive position in which he attacked the scolder for more than unfairness. "I do not," Carlos wrote to Sobral, "give you the right to judge problems of conscience from the comfortable position of being truthful only in letters and leaving the people to be delivered to the Communist lie." "If," he added, "the price of the existence of the Communist Party is the cessation of all democratic combat against it, then you, my dear Dr. Sobral, are giving support to General Dutra."[5]

The pledge of Carlos not to write one word against the PCB in his column was broken in June when he criticized the PCB for calling Perón's regime democratic and ridiculed Prestes' "ludicrously puerile" campaign for a popular front that would force "the resignation of Dutra." Carlos and the PCB also quarreled about the petroleum question, with Carlos maintaining that it would be good for Brazil to accept minority holdings from foreign investors, as suggested by General Juarez Távora.[6]

By August and September the war of words was as venomous as ever, with Carlos writing that "the PCB directorship has no interest in having Communists know the truth about their party or the wretched fanaticism that led to crimes, such as the ruthless murder of Elza Fernandes, ordered by Luís Carlos Prestes." Carlos reiterated that Jorge Amado and Samuel Wainer had received German money and issued German propaganda after the Stalin-Hitler pact. Returning to the petroleum question, he wrote that it would be "better to have American help under the control of the Brazilian government than Russian help supervised by the Russian subject Prestes."[7]

Communist members of the Brazilian Writers' Association (ABDE) were so angry at Carlos that they threatened to abandon the Second Writers' Congress, held in Belo Horizonte in mid-October, in case he were seated. A compromise was reached, at the suggestion of Júlio de Mesquita Filho, whereby Carlos was seated with the understanding that he would not speak at the sessions.[8]

The congress, which lacked the importance of the 1945 Writers' Congress, was torn by political dissension. After the writers acclaimed a resolution protesting the closing of the PCB, a resolution was proposed to condemn the treatment of intellectuals in the Soviet Union. At length all political resolutions were withdrawn and a rule was adopted barring the presentation of political matters.[9]

Carlos participated in the all-night meetings at the Pingüim Bar with Carlos Drummond de Andrade, Décio de Almeida Prado, Luís Martins, Arnaldo Pedroso d'Horta, and Antônio Cândido de Melo e Souza. After the congress ended, he drove Murilo Miranda, Luís Martins, and Alceu Marinho Rego in his recently acquired Ford, his first car, on the dirt road to Rio. His lack of practice at driving was evident to his frightened companions, especially when he rounded curves at excessive speed.[10]

Soon after the writers' congress, the Dutra administration broke diplomatic relations with the Soviet Union under circumstances that led crowds to assault the *Tribuna Popular* plant and office. Carlos, explaining the situation to his readers, wrote that "the entire nation" was insulted harshly by a Soviet article slandering the Brazilian government and military, including the FEB. Carlos maintained that, after the Soviet Union returned Brazil's letter of protest, calling it unworthy of a reply, Brazil was forced to become the first democratic nation to sever relations with the Soviet dictatorship. He also wrote that the step, "sad but necessary," led him to suppose that Prestes, in the Senate, was uttering his usual "drivel." "But no," he added, "Stalin has assured us that Prestes has been murdered. Therefore Prestes should consider himself very much murdered and shut up, repeating no more of the nonsense that has led to the ruin of the PCB."[11]

When Communist Municipal Councilman Amarílio Vasconcelos called the break in relations welcome news to "North American warmongers and monopolies," Carlos, in a speech of rebuttal, said that neither the UDN nor the people would allow the break to be used to the advantage of fascists and reactionaries. Outside the chamber, five men wearing green neckties held up signs reading "Down with the Lackeys of Moscow," and one of them shouted that UDN Councilman Luís Paes Leme (husband of Carlos' former fiancée Nedda Paiva) was a "Communist in disguise." Carlos was quick to declare that the break in relations with the Soviet Union would not be used for the resurrection of dead "green chickens."[12]

The year 1947 ended with the government majorities in the Senate and the Chamber of Deputies preparing to enact legislation, of questionable constitutionality, depriving all PCB legislators, federal and local, of their mandates. Carlos, who had already defined the mandates as derived from the same secret vote that put Dutra in the presidency, offered advice to Dutra after the Senate passed the government's bill. With the proposed legislation still needing the approval of the lower house, Carlos told Dutra, in an open letter, that he should not waste the time of Congress with the question of the Communist mandates, "which will resolve nothing," but should turn, instead, to a petroleum law, an immigration law, and banking reform.[13]

The Dutra administration, however, was eager to deal a new setback to the PCB and it found the necessary congressional votes (including those of Juscelino Kubitschek, Artur Bernardes, and Juracy Magalhães). All who had reached legislative chambers on the PCB ticket lost their mandates on January 7, 1948.[14]

6. Combative Municipal Councilman (1947)

Soon after taking his Municipal Council seat, Carlos joined three other councilmen in proposing that Presidente Vargas Avenue be renamed Castro Alves Avenue to honor the romantic poet, born in 1847. He called for a commission to investigate "persecutions" by Vargas police agents in the municipality. And he worked to bring about drainage, canal, and river improvements in Jacarepaguá, Guaratiba, Campo Grande, and Santa Cruz, frequently flooded suburbs in the Federal District.[1]

Early in June 1947, President Dutra appointed General Ângelo Mendes de Morais mayor of the Federal District. Writing in *Correio da Manhã* about this "incredible nomination," Carlos began his long feud with the general. He called him the government's *gauleiter,* or area ruler, and one of Dutra's poker-playing "kitchen animals," a reference to the "pantry and kitchen" (*copa-e-cozinha*) group, intimate with the president. When Mendes de Morais, in conflict with the Municipal Chamber, defended his positions on the radio, the municipal councilmen passed the Carlos Lacerda Law, requiring Rádio Roquete Pinto, the municipal government station, to broadcast the Municipal Chamber debates.[2]

A pet project of Mendes de Morais was to construct the huge Maracanã soccer stadium within two years, in time for use during the 1950 world soccer championship matches. Carlos argued against this popular idea, citing the high cost of such speedy construction in the urbanized area not far from the São Cristóvão railroad station. "I ask you sports people," he wrote, "if you have 400 million cruzeiros, and if you do, why you do not spend them on petroleum extraction that will provide you with profits and enrich the nation to such an extent that it will be able to afford several monumental stadiums."[3]

UDN Municipal Councilman Ari Barroso called Carlos an "enemy of sports." But Carlos proposed an alternative to Maracanã: a suburban sports complex that could be built at less cost next to Jacarepaguá Lake. The area, off the Barra da Tijuca beach, was expected to become developed, especially with a railroad extension and highways already under consideration. Carlos pointed out that his alternative, the result of a study made in 1938 by engineer Antônio Laviola, had the support of former Transport Minister Maurício Joppert, who had declared that the construction of Maracanã and its complementary facilities within two years would be practically impossible and would "disorganize the market for materials and labor."

In arguing for his alternative, Carlos was farsighted. He spoke of the need to decongest traffic-burdened Rio and called it idiotic to use costly land in the city for the stadium parking facilities he said would become necessary. For Jacarepaguá he visualized the world's most complete Olympic City, suitable for water sports, and he added that the urbanization of the area and completion of contemplated transport links would stimulate the production of foods in the valley.[4]

The Communist majority presented a resolution calling for six (!) soccer stadiums: five in the suburbs and one (Maracanã) in the city. This solution found widespread support. Enacted by the Municipal Council, it was approved by Mendes de Morais in November. Carlos said the Communists were demagogues, seeking popularity "among those who place soccer ahead of everything."[5]

During the debate about stadiums, the federal Senate worked on an Organic Law for the Federal District that would diminish the authority of the municipal councilmen by enabling the federal Senate, not the Municipal Chamber, to decide whether to uphold the mayor's vetoes of the chamber's legislative bills. Carlos, in a letter to João Alberto, said he would resign if the proposal about vetoes, known as the Melo Viana Amendment, were put into effect. He wrote that the voters would not forgive him if he remained in a chamber that was "totally subordinate to the dictatorship of the executive." Adauto Lúcio Cardoso assumed the same attitude.[6]

Fernando de Melo Viana, the recipient of one of the telegrams that Carlos sent to senators, denied that his position was dictated by his PSD affiliation and told Carlos that he would not yield to acrimonious personal attacks. After Melo Viana cited former presidents of Brazil who had taken positions similar to that expressed in his amendment, Carlos reprinted articles by Rui Barbosa that railed against forcing the great city to be administered by the central government.

During the final turbulent debate in the Senate, the municipal councilmen were permitted to seat themselves among the senators. The Vivaqua Amendment, similar to that of Melo Viana, was approved, 22–17, and the Organic Law was forwarded to the Chamber of Deputies for final approval.[7]

While the *deputados* considered the Organic Law, Carlos got into trouble with the UDN of the Federal District. The dispute began after the municipal councilmen approved a project of the PCB's Amarílio Vasconcelos, first secretary of the chamber, to create one hundred new jobs: a special corps of guards and new assistants for the chamber's secretariat. Carlos, given the opportunity by a UDN councilman to name a cousin or friend, was furious that the UDN had "yielded to temptation" in the "scandal," which gave the Municipal Chamber more bureaucrats than the much larger federal Chamber of Deputies. He wrote that "the UDN reveals that it is not yet politically or morally prepared to assume the responsibility of the government of the city." "The flesh is weak," he also said.[8]

Senator Hamilton Nogueira, of the executive commission of the Carioca UDN, wrote to Carlos to reprimand him for the display of party "indiscipline" shown in his article. Then Adauto Lúcio Cardoso made public a letter to Carlos agreeing that the UDN was not yet mature (and adding that the PSD and Mendes de Morais were even less mature, and the PTB and PCB were "thoroughly putrid"). Adauto, in receipt of a warning from the executive commission of the Federal District UDN, replied that five members of the commission, along with some of the UDN councilmen, had used the Amarílio Vasconcelos resolution to give jobs to relatives and "electoral clients," thus violating public promises about political ethics. Luís Paes Leme, who joined three other UDN municipal councilmen in resigning from the executive commission, wrote Senator Hamilton Nogueira to ask how men who had received approximately three hundred votes in the election could interpret the will of the UDN electorate.[9]

Carlos, in response to a letter suspending him from the UDN for thirty days, addressed a letter, which he published, to the "Senhora Comissão." "My dear woman," he wrote, "you forgot to tell me until what date I am deprived of your delicious company." He reminded the *senhora* of the pledge, once signed by all the UDN municipal councilmen, to "create only strictly indispensable jobs," and asked her what moral grounds she had for "censuring, then suspending, and even planning to eliminate from the UDN, your representatives who disapprove of filth."[10]

Carlos, like his father before him, was apt to be the center of attention, and his fight with the UDN was the talk of Rio. The popular councilman, however, dismissed politics from his mind and became the family man on Sundays when he happily loaded his new Ford with his and Vera's families and set forth to picnic. A traffic policeman, wondering where the well-known political figure would turn after separation from the UDN, stopped the crammed car to ask, "Now where are you going?" Carlos, oblivious to everything except the picnic, replied, "Tijuca Forest."[11]

In mid-December the Chamber of Deputies approved the Organic Law of the Federal District as written by the Senate. Adauto resigned at once from the Municipal Council.[12] Carlos, who was in Bahia, telegraphed his resignation as soon as he heard the news and wrote a letter saying that the Senate had destroyed the Municipal Chamber with the help of the immorality of a majority of the councilmen themselves. But, he added, most of the state legislatures were just as bad. In Pernambuco, which he had recently visited, the representatives of the people had voted to increase their own pay. Carlos' letter was addressed to the acting president of the Municipal Chamber because João Alberto, wishing to support Dutra, had left the PTB and the chamber.[13]

In a final address to the chamber, Carlos said he was casting his last vote in favor of a bill demanding the expulsion of Mayor Mendes de Morais, whose failings in the army had been demonstrated in an inquiry "filed away by Dutra when he was war minister." Rejecting appeals that he delay his resignation, Carlos told the councilmen that a novice in public life could make no greater sacrifice than bid farewell to that life to demonstrate the existence of men able to fulfill their word at a time when parties and public men were abdicating honor and dignity, when the chamber was hurrying to comply with a congressional law that would expel eighteen Communist councilmen, when chamber leaders were bowing to an unpopular arrangement "made in the dark," when the UDN, in a series of retreats and maneuvers, was turning itself over to a false democracy, and when days of bloodshed and fear were being prepared for Brazil.[14]

When the picnicking Carlos was asked, "Now where are you going?" he might have mentioned the Movimento Renovador, which he and Adauto Lúcio Cardoso helped revive during their squabble with the Carioca UDN. The Movimento Renovador, established in the Federal District in December 1946 to play a role in the January 1947 Municipal Council election, sought in November 1947 to become a national movement. Its manifesto of November 20, written with the help of Resistência Democrática Catholics and longtime Trotskyites Mário Pedrosa and Marino Besouchet, described the movement as above political parties. It called for the adherence of reformers in all parties, every opponent of totalitarianism, to join its struggle against what it considered a deadly new form of capitalism: excessive government control (*estatização*) in the form of "technicians, bureaucrats, and professional politicians," who "take possession of the state as though it were their private property, transforming themselves into a new dominant social caste." More dangerous than fascism or Communism, the manifesto said, was the abdication by citizens of their responsibilities, demonstrated by their constant appeals to the "all-providing state, the state that is the father of all things." Carlos, promoting the Movimento Renovador at meetings and in newspaper columns, became its president.

Engineer Eduardo Borgerth, a member of the commission that wrote the manifesto, hoped that the result would be "a great democratic movement—something never seen in South America." Carlos, he wrote in his diary, was the most talented and impetuous journalist and probably the most widely read in the Federal District and at meetings had revealed himself a brilliant, combative, well-educated, young orator who disclosed facts and conditions "that few people have the courage to mention." "If he succeeds in maintaining his moral conduct and physical strength, he will play a dominant role in the elevation and reconstruction of this country. Last night he had a great success. The audience, during every moment he spoke, was captivated by his thoughts."[15]

7. Visit to the Arab World (February–March 1948)

For Carlos, the urge to be a storyteller was never altogether subdued by politics. On the contrary, literary creativity became a pastime to which he turned sometimes for relaxation during political crises. While serving as a municipal councilman, he put together seven short stories that were published as a book early in 1948 by Murilo Miranda's Editôra Revista Acadêmica.

The book, dedicated to Yedda and Murilo and illustrated by Axl Leskoschek's woodcuts, bore the title of its opening story, *Uma Luz Pequenina* (A Tiny Light). The story, in keeping with earlier writings of Carlos, made use of the drawl of the most uneducated and destitute to portray their superstitions and tribulations. Poet Carlos Drummond de Andrade, in a prepublication commentary, called attention to the "unforgettable death of the boy Xanam" in the first story and the "delicate exposure of psychological truth" in the second story, which described scenes in the Alice Street house when

Carlos (José in the story) stole money set aside for household expenses. Discussing the collection further, Drummond wrote of the "versatility of a literary talent, perhaps excessive in the richness of its sounds, which sometimes transgress the principles of economy, as is valid in all art."[1]

The author of *Uma Luz Pequenina* continued battling the authorities in his "Na Tribuna da Imprensa" column. In January he rebuked Osvaldo Aranha, UN General Assembly president and Brazilian delegation chief, for agreeing with the United States that Palestine be partitioned to establish the state of Israel. Arguing that Brazil should have abstained instead of participating in the vote to create Israel, Carlos wrote that Judaism "is not a nation or race, or even a complete culture; it is a religion common to the sons of different peoples, different races." He condemned Zionist propaganda and said that the UN vote, contrary to the true interests of the Jews, would benefit the Zionist oppression of the Arabs of Palestine.[2]

In February, while the question was hotly debated, Carlos went to the region as correspondent for the *Correio da Manhã, O Estado de S. Paulo,* the *Jornal do Comércio* of Pernambuco, and Rádio Mayrink Veiga. He spent much of his time in Egypt and wrote from there of the urgent need for Brazil "to recognize the existence of the Arab world." That world, he affirmed, was experiencing a rebirth, "to the benefit of Egypt, converted by the political skill of young King Farouk into the principal political center of the Arab movement."[3]

At the Cairo headquarters of the year-old Arab League, Carlos interviewed the League's secretary-general, Abdur Rahman Azzam Pasha, an Egyptian who shared Carlos' views. The interview, providing material for many columns and ideas that Carlos often repeated, was the most important of his trip. As Carlos reported, Azzam believed that Russia had voted for the partition of Palestine because it felt that the gratitude of Jews in the United States would prevent a premature war against the Soviet Union, and also because it recognized that the partition would lead soon to disturbances and local wars in the Middle East that Russia wanted. Azzam recommended the cessation of Jewish immigration to Palestine and an election for a Palestinian constitutional assembly to be made up of Jews and Arabs.[4]

Carlos, marshalling his own arguments to support these recommendations, wrote that the immigrants going to Palestine were mostly young Jews equipped and trained for war. He called the Judaic nationalism in Palestine "an aggressive, fierce nationalism, supported by fascists and terrorists who destroy peaceful life." He defined Zionists as "those Jews who want to send the other Jews to Palestine."[5]

Calling Harry S. Truman one of those "inferior people" who "unfortunately govern," Carlos said the American president's quest for the Jewish vote had resulted in an error "for which American citizens will pay with their blood after shedding the blood of others."[6] The Arabs, Carlos reported, knew they could count on the support of Russia "in case the United States tries to hew the line of the UN decision—because that was the reason Russia gave the victory to the Zionists." Abdel Krim, the septuagenarian fighter for Moroccan independence, agreed with Carlos that the United States "has made a grave error" and "opened the Arab world to Russia."[7]

Carlos, wondering how his articles were being received in Brazil, wrote to his mother from Beirut on February 24: "I suppose many people will say I am sold to the Arabs—but this is of little importance."[8] He informed his readers that the Saint Joseph Jesuit University and the American University, both in Beirut, made it possible for Lebanon to furnish the Arab world with outstanding intellectual leaders, equipped with Arab and Western culture. In Jerusalem he was so pleased to receive a copy of the declaration of the Christian churches of Palestine that he sent a translation by cable, enabling the Brazilian media to be the first in the world to make it known. The signers of the document opposed the UN plan to partition Palestine and said it had caused "grievous and bloody events."[9]

After returning to Brazil on March 23, Carlos arranged to have his articles from abroad published as a book, *O Brasil e o Mundo Árabe.* In the preface he wrote that his conclusions resulted from investigation and reasoning and that impartiality was not possible "in the face of the conquest of Palestine by Zionism, supported by American money and Russian politics."[10]

In the *Correio da Manhã* Carlos warned Brazilians that the dominant press agencies in the United States "systematically poisoned" the news to make it suitable for the Zionist groups.[11] But these were not the only agencies to differ with Carlos about the question. Assis Chateaubriand, deciding to publish reports favorable to the creation of Israel, sent several reporters to the area.[12] One of them was Samuel Wainer, who added to the reportorial laurels he had already won in Mexico, Nuremberg, Spain, Portugal, and Yugoslavia. Upon returning from the Middle East, he gave speeches that contradicted the views of Carlos.

Carlos, commenting later on the reaction to his own pro-Arab position, said that, although he had always been antiracist and anti-Nazi, "the Jewish colony in Rio was almost solidly against me." Citing an example, Carlos recalled that "Lasar Segall, the painter who had been my close friend, acted coldly toward me for many years." Samuel Wainer, Carlos said, was one of the members of the Jewish community who "exploited" the so-called anti-Jewish stand revealed in the writings of Carlos about the creation of Israel.[13]

8. Municipal Thugs Pummel Carlos (April 1948)

Carlos, returning from the Middle East, found petroleum extraction an emotional issue in Brazil. Dutra had proposed a statute that would, as suggested by Távora, allow minority investments of private capital, national and foreign, while placing a majority interest and control in government hands. Supporters of a monopoly, 100 percent in government hands, organized a Study Center to Defend Petroleum and the National Economy, and named, as its honorary president, General Júlio Caetano Horta Barbosa, former director of the National Petroleum Council. The monopoly idea gave rise to the slogan "The Petroleum Is Ours" and had many vocal adherents, especially in the PCB. Hermes Lima, speaking for the Brazilian Socialist Party (PSB—formerly the ED), supported the idea.[1]

Carlos, attacking the idea, wrote in April that a sluggish, costly, inept government apparatus would require thirty, forty, or fifty years to solve the problem, and, even with "ruinous" new taxes and funds from the pension institutes, would lack money and equipment. After a PCB supporter declared that the government project "was elaborated in the United States in the offices of Standard Oil," Carlos ridiculed propaganda of that nature published in the PCB's new *Folha do Povo* (Newspaper of the People), which Carlos called the "*Rolha do Povo*" (Gag of the People). When PSB Municipal Councilman Osório Borba brandished a promonopoly manifesto signed by "two hundred journalists," Carlos said many of them were not journalists and fifty-two were "militant Communists" who "defend the thesis that petroleum should not exist in Brazil as long as it might be used against Russia in war." He quoted Monteiro Lobato as saying that Brazil was the only nation that had petroleum and did nothing with it. And he wrote that General Horta Barbosa, as director of the National Petroleum Council, had jailed Monteiro Lobato and closed down petroleum exploration companies.[2]

The general who suffered most at the hands of Carlos was Mendes de Morais, the mayor. In nightly broadcasts on Rádio Mayrink Veiga, Carlos blamed him for "maladministration" and "corruption" connected with the Maracanã Stadium project. According to Vera's son Cláudio, Carlos pried into the mayorship's "every nook and cranny," not even sparing the "scandalous purchase of a pair of giraffes for the Carioca zoo."[3] When the mayor said he wanted to discuss the *favelas* (slums) with Carlos, Carlos agreed to meet him at the home of *Correio da Manhã* owner Paulo Bittencourt. But, Carlos wrote later, when "I discovered" that the real purpose of the meeting was "to tame the campaign against his administration . . . , I redoubled the intensity of my denouncements." Critical of the Rio police, Carlos on April 16 published an appeal to Dutra to investigate policemen allegedly torturing political prisoners.[4]

On Saturday evening, April 17, Carlos arrived as usual at the Mayrink Veiga radio station, just off Rio Branco Avenue, but this time, when he got out of his Ford, he was assailed by five individuals. Held from behind, he was hit in the face by fists and pistol butts. His eyes, especially the left one, were damaged, and a wound was opened on his chin. The assailants used coarse words of insult, and one of them said, "This is to teach you not to attack the army." Carlos fought off an effort to get him into the assailants' car. His cries brought people to windows and doors. Although the spectators were kept at a distance by revolver shots, one of them phoned the Radio Patrol Service for help. Finally, after seven minutes of bludgeoning, Carlos broke loose and the culprits left in their car.[5]

Carlos delivered the radio talk he had prepared, a warning against "the two conflicting totalitarianisms," the power-hungry Communists and the anti-Communist government forces that unleashed brutal police terror. Then he made his customary visit to the *Correio da Manhã* to leave the typescript of a new column.[6] At the newspaper office a warm handshake was given him by columnist Maurício Caminha de Lacerda. Carlos recalled later, "We gazed at each other, he who looked so much like my father, and I with a bloody eye and pains that were growing worse. Years of suffering and misunderstanding were set aside in that handshake."[7] From the newspaper office, Carlos went home.

Letícia was at the Italian embassy with Murilo and Yedda Miranda attending a reception that Carlos had left early. Learning from the ambassador of the assault, she hastened to the Lacerdas' Tonelero Street apartment, where she found 9-year-old Sérgio and 5-year-old Sebastião trying to help their father. Blood flowed into the glass of water they had given him.[8]

Visitors were shocked by the sight of Carlos' badly injured face. "It was terrible, swollen and all out of shape," according to UDN congressman and writer Afonso Arinos de Melo Franco, younger brother of Virgílio.[9] By the time Eduardo Gomes arrived, the apartment was full of people. Eagerly awaiting a comment from the *brigadeiro* about the thrashing of Carlos, at length they heard him say that it would be good "to put raw meat on the wounds."[10]

Under large headlines, the Sunday newspapers described the assault and criticized the ineffectiveness of the Radio Patrol. Throughout the day Rádio Mayrink Veiga received anonymous phone calls with threats to destroy the station if Carlos continued to broadcast. But he appeared that evening on schedule, a large bandage on his head and left eye. He read his broadcast, attacking terror in Brazil, in a studio filled with admirers, among them society women and representatives of the Movimento Renovador.[11]

Carlos was able to furnish columns to the *Correio da Manhã* for April 21 and 22, one of them calling attention to efforts to kidnap him in 1946, and the other, an open letter to Dutra, complaining about the slow pace of the investigation of the recent assault. But on April 23, pain from the wounds made it impossible for him to write or dictate, and, on medical orders, he suspended his activities for five days. "Mule Kick," an unsavory guard assigned by the authorities to protect him, hung around the apartment.[12]

Expressions of support for Carlos, such as those from the Egyptian chargé d'affaires and Elza Werneck de Castro, filled the press. Among the municipal councilmen who publicly deplored the incident were Osório Borba and Ari Barroso, Adauto Lúcio Cardoso's successor as head of the UDN bloc. In the Chamber of Deputies the beating was denounced by *udenistas* Prado Kelly, Euclides Figueiredo, and 26-year-old Aluísio Alves, of Rio Grande do Norte. Government leader Acúrcio Torres told the lawmakers that the Rio police chief had been called to Catete Palace and ordered, by President Dutra himself, to carry out an investigation.[13]

The Senate was silent about the matter. Therefore Sobral Pinto, president of Resistência Democrática, published critical telegrams he was sending to UDN national President José Américo and UDN local President Hamilton Nogueira, senators who had been on poor terms with Carlos. José Américo, in reply to Sobral, explained his decision to make no statement about Carlos, "my gratuitous and truculent offender." Carlos, he wrote, had interpreted his statements about the forthcoming 1950 presidential election as motivated by a desire to extinguish the Eduardo Gomes candidacy in favor of a José Américo movement. Referring to the injuries received by Carlos, José Américo compared them with the hurt Carlos had caused him: "Those who suffer physical pains cannot appreciate how very excruciating, also, are pains of the spirit."[14]

Carlos, defying a summons of the Rio police to answer questions, said he would not participate in a farce; the true nature of police investigations, he said, was revealed when the inquiry into the 1946 kidnapping attempt had been dropped because a leading transgressor had been found to be a member of the Special Police. In the case of the 1948 assault, the licence plate on the car used by the thugs had been noted, allowing Sobral, Adauto Lúcio Cardoso, and *Correio da Manhã* reporters to trace the car to the Rio police. A justice ministry attorney, assigned to head an inquiry, agreed that the car had been loaned by the municipality for use in the aggression; but he found himself short of funds and investigators, and his preliminary report was pigeonholed by the chief prosecutor for the Federal District.[15]

Not much more was learned until 1950, when Carlos, after being assaulted again, confronted suspects and recognized two who had clobbered him in 1948: a municipal guard and an illiterate thug, known as Kangaroo, who had joined the municipal police in 1935. After Kangaroo broke down in tears in 1950, Carlos was able to name all of his assailants of 1948 and publish a chart showing whom they served. A key boss was Renato Meira Lima, "the prosperous head of city control and inspection . . . , gasoline black marketeer during the war," and accomplice of "Mussolini de Morais."[16]

While Sobral Pinto and Adauto Lúcio Cardoso took legal steps in 1950 against Carlos' assailants, Carlos wrote that "nobody in this country can any longer doubt that General Mendes de Morais ordered the assault at the door of Mayrink Veiga." Late in his life, Carlos declared that while he could not guarantee that the order for the 1948 assault had been given by Mendes de Morais, "everything leads one to believe this was the case."[17] Many, like Afonso Arinos de Melo Franco and journalist Walter Cunto, have asserted that, without a shadow of a doubt, the order was given by the mayor.[18]

9. Conversion to Catholicism (1948)

Carlos in bandages evoked memories of his father, wounded in the 1920s. Like Maurício, he came across as rashly courageous in attack, honest, and unwilling to compromise or scheme underhandedly. Also like his father in the past, he had an enormous capacity to instill excitement in the public and become excited himself. If there was a difference between the railings of father and son against "the oligarchy," it could be found in the literary quality that Carlos gave his speeches and articles. They were often praised for sonorous phrasing and sparkling humor or irony.[1]

Carioca voters liked the image of the intense crusader, merciless in denouncing the perpetrators of crimes against the public. If physical danger could not deter Carlos, neither could lawsuits, such as those brought against him in June 1948 by the director of the naval academy, whom he called corrupt, and the minister of the navy. Carlos, who had been denouncing naval leaders for expelling four hundred cadets, was accused by Senator Vitorino Freire of inciting indiscipline, but the accusation only prodded Carlos into retorting that he was in no need of lessons in discipline from members of Dutra's "pantry and kitchen" group.[2]

Newspaper readers were not wrong if they supposed that Carlos was the sort of crusader who might explode in exasperation at associates he considered uncooperative. When he was absorbed in his work he was both detail-conscious and impatient and had little time for stupidity, mediocrity, or a lack of interest. But this was only one facet of a man who could be charming socially, delighted friends with favors, and provided unexpected help to people in need. He was gentle to all who were fragile. Deeply sensitive, he was frequently moved to tears, particularly in the presence of suffering.[3]

The Carlos Lacerda who relaxed with music and whiskey, who assumed the role of an epicure, and who participated in all-night discussions was the same Carlos Lacerda who was a productive dynamo at work. He was determined to live life to the fullest. "My profession is to live," he told friends.

He was, in many respects, the small boy, scornful of routine, who had cut classes in order to collect brochures at a travel bureau. With an enthusiasm for adventure, a happy wonder at discovering the world, he was forever, in reading and conversation, searching for ideas. His mind was not closed to what telepathy, fortune telling, or astrology might offer. He pored over volumes of philosophy, with the hunger of one in need of ideas that would give meaning, and therefore richness, to life.

In speaking of his growing interest in Catholicism in 1947, Carlos sometimes mentioned his disillusionment with Communism[4] in a way to suggest that the disillusionment had left him, to his regret, without the sustaining help of a commitment to a superior institution devoted to justice and the alleviation of ills.

By 1947, when Movimento Reformador work put him in constant touch with dedicated Catholics Hamilton Nogueira,[5] Sobral Pinto, Alceu Amoroso Lima, and Gustavo Corção, Carlos was familiar with the Bible, having been attracted to the Psalms as literature.[6] Of his Catholic political friends, more than willing to discuss religion with him, the ascetic Gustavo Corção and the less conservative Alceu Amoroso Lima were the most influential in his decision to join the Catholic Church. Corção, described by Carlos in 1947 as "one of the most intelligent men in this and other countries," had been converted to Catholicism in 1939, thanks in part to Alceu Amoroso Lima, president of the Centro Dom Vital, a Catholic study and discussion group.[7]

"It is difficult," Carlos wrote Corção, "to return alone, with bleeding feet, to the house of God. Without support. Without the company of those in the lead." Corção offered no illusions about conversion being an easy step, but he made himself, in Carlos' words, "a fraternal guide."[8] Corção, an admirer of Carlos' journalism, had studied theology at Rio's São Bento Monastery and he agreed to give, as suggested by Carlos, a course on religion. At the classes, held at Corção's house, Carlos came to be regarded as "the chosen son" of the group.[9]

Corção took Carlos to call on Dom Lourenço de Almeida Prado, the Benedictine monk who ran the school at the São Bento Monastery. Dom Lourenço, once a student of medicine in Rio, recalled the days when Carlos had directed the leftist *rumo* while Lourenço had directed a rival publication, *Vida,* organ of Catholic students.[10] After their meeting in 1948, Carlos was frequently seen at the monastery, an athletic-looking figure making the sign of the cross with zeal and carrying a book of daily Catholic devotions. He conversed much with Dom Lourenço and became fanatical about Catholicism.

In mid-1948, during a talk with Dom Lourenço that lasted until 2:00 A.M., Carlos asked to partake of communion as a sign of his conversion. But the monk pointed out that he and Letícia should first be married in the Church. Letícia, who was agreeable, received the necessary instruction; and on August 17, 1948, after Sérgio and Sebastião had been baptized, Carlos and Letícia were married religiously by Dom Lourenço at a small ceremony in the monastery. Virgílio de Melo Franco, who had become godfather of Sérgio, and Alceu Amoroso Lima served as *padrinhos* (sponsors). Carlos, thinking of Clara Freitas, his Catholic nanny who had died in 1945, wrote that the religious marriage was a victory for her "because she never believed in our lack of faith."[11]

Carlos' fanaticism for Catholicism in 1948 did not translate itself into a lifetime of what Dom Lourenço would call being a "very disciplined church member" or a "very practicing Catholic." Dom Lourenço, who came to consider Carlos "disorganized" but "faithful in his search for justice," offered him some advice as early as September 1948. He wrote that "Your own confidence in your opinion, reached rather impetuously, leads you to lose generosity, which is the best feature of your character." At the time that Dom Lourenço wrote these words, the philosophical discussions at Corção's home were becoming unpleasant for Corção because the argumentative Carlos continually interrupted him. Before long they were held without Carlos.[12]

Among those to whom Carlos made confession were Dom José Távora and Dom Hélder Câmara, about whose work in Rio he was enthusiastic for a while. He enrolled Sérgio and Sebastião in the school of the São Bento Monastery. Whenever, later in life, he was asked if he had doubts about the existence of God, he was always quick to declare he had none.[13] His faith was evident in his letters and in the interest he showed, from time to time while traveling, in attending Mass.[14]

In his reflective study about the moments in the life of Christ between the judgment of Pontius Pilate and the crucifixion, Carlos wrote that "without faith, our life is nothing more than an obscure and monotonous obligation; with faith it is transformed into a fascinating pilgrimage." "The son of God," he also declared, "became man so that men might know who they are, recognize their origin, and understand where they are going." "One day," he concluded, "all people, like Jesus, will be resurrected."[15]

Carlos revealed his faith in 1951 when he published a long letter to Congressman Oswaldo Costa, commenting on *Oração da Humildade,* a brochure by Corrêa Pinto. In the brochure, the author wrote of God as a universal God to be found in nature and attacked "the detestable Creed of the Church, that Creed which demands the adoration of God embodied restrictively, in the human figure, God of one single species, . . . a dead God, God of suffering and sadness, a God who promises good things to some and Purgatory and the Inferno to others, and who uses ambition and fear to have Himself worshipped." Carlos replied that Corrêa Pinto did not understand that "the death of Christ on a cross did not give us a dead God but a God more living than anything because he is a resurrected God and not a God of suffering and sadness, and by no means one of ambition and fear because He is a God of love."[16]

Writing in 1967, Carlos said, "Today, I must admit I am somewhat perplexed. My faith has not diminished. Only—how shall I put it?—it seems to have hibernated." One of his problems stemmed from what he felt was a new tendency of priests and other churchmen, "in this tumult of a sociological-economic bazaar," to forget the need of people to pray and lead personal Christian lives. While recognizing the importance of a militant church, opposed to injustice, he rejected the idea that all churchmen should "necessarily transform themselves into economists, sociologists, and amateur reformers." "I observe," Carlos wrote, "that most of those who applaud the social and political position of the recent encyclical letters do not believe in God and only believe in the Pope to the extent that they feel he confirms the tendency that everyone has to believe in Utopia, instead of believing in . . . eternal life."[17]

10. Predicting the Election of Dewey (October–November 1948)

Following their religious marriage, Carlos and Letícia took the SS *Uruguay* to New York. During four months of discovering what life was like in the United States, Carlos found a new Catholic hero, Monsignor Fulton J. Sheen. After lunching for three hours in Washington with the influential Catholic author and broadcaster, the Brazilian journalist devoted nine *Correio da Manhã* articles to Sheen's ideas and his own.[1]

Quoting Sheen as saying that Communism sought to turn individuals into slaves of the state, Carlos ridiculed the ideas of "that goofy 'dean of Canterbury,' who keeps repeating, like a perfect simpleton, the statistics of Stalinist propaganda."[2] But what Carlos chiefly emphasized was Sheen's belief that "the true Christian must free himself from the illusion that the Church, in opposing Communism, opposes all who seek to modify the present economic system." Carlos pointed out that Sheen supported Catholic doctrine favoring workers' participation in the profits, administration, and ownership of industries in which they worked. Admitting that many Catholics disagreed with Sheen on this point, Carlos argued that, in doing so, they broke with the Pope and the Church.[3]

A primary purpose of the trip was to cover the American presidential election campaign, but it allowed Carlos to report on a good deal more. And, like all Brazilians visiting the United States, Carlos and Letícia seized the opportunity to purchase things that would have cost much more in Brazil. The chief acquisition, as Carlos proudly wrote Sérgio, was a 1949 Ford. But much that they wanted to get for themselves and Olga was beyond their means. Carlos, a compulsive buyer when traveling, wrote to lawyer Fernando Velloso, Sebastião's godfather, that "to be unable to purchase a little of what is being sold here is a cruelty for one with my fondness for buying things."[4]

The 34-year-old boy who enjoyed discovering the world was delighted with the United States. "Washington," he wrote to his mother, "is probably the prettiest city I have seen in my life." "The best things here are the trains," with their bar cars, good food, comfortable air conditioning, and telephone service.[5] He was immensely impressed, as he told his *Correio da Manhã* readers, by the size of Ford's River Rouge steel plant. To understand the United States, he also told his readers, they should appreciate that "a large part of the proletariat thinks and acts like the middle class. In fact, a plumber, neighbor of a Brazilian consul in the United States, lives in a house identical to the consul's, has an automobile like his, and earns more than he does."[6]

Critical remarks were reserved for the presidential candidates. Norman Thomas was "pig-headed," Henry Wallace had accepted the "kiss of death" of Bolshevism, and Republican candidate Thomas E. Dewey "should be considered a big ass unless some facts emerge to reveal, to himself included, unknown facets of his personality."[7] Truman, "the Dutra of the United States," headed an administration that was so interested in the Marshall Plan for Europe that it had forgotten continental economic development.[8]

"The election," Carlos wrote to Fernando Velloso, "is losing interest because everybody already knows it will be won by Dewey." Analyzing "Dewey's victory" for his newspaper readers, he said that Wallace was going off with the Democratic Party's left wing and Strom Thurmond with the right wing and that the Americans were "tired of domination by the Democratic Party since the time of Roosevelt."[9] A few of Carlos' articles were sent by cable, such as one from Truman's campaign train, but he was reluctant to run up large cable bills for the *Correio da Manhã.* Noting that articles he mailed were not printed promptly, he concluded that Brazil had little interest in news beyond that provided by São Paulo Governor Ademar de Barros and Dutra's "pantry and kitchen."[10]

After Truman's victory Carlos telephoned a report, which appeared on the *Correio da Manhã*'s first page, describing the outcome as "the most astounding in American history" since Woodrow Wilson's defeat of Charles Evans Hughes. He called the result a victory for Roosevelt's New Deal and the labor forces and saw, as possible results, a reappearance of Roosevelt's Good Neighbor policy and an impetus for social reform in the world, strengthening "the struggle against capitalist and Communist slaveries." He could not have given the Democratic victory a greater tribute than when he wrote in the *Correio da Manhã* that it was a pity that Virgílio de Melo

Franco "could not witness the triumph in the United States of the ideas to which he dedicated his noble life in Brazil: the formation of a great democratic party, alive and acting independently of the powerful, and bringing together all the sincere reformers to fight Communism 'by action rather than by reaction.'"[11]

The murder of Virgílio on October 29, shot by one of his former employees, left Carlos so shocked that, as he wrote to his mother, he "spent nights without sleep." In lines written for Sérgio, Carlos suggested that the boy spend some time with Virgílio's widow "and take pride in the godfather you had, as I do in the friend I lost. When I return I'll speak with Adauto about your religious confirmation, and so he will be your second godfather." "Don't be sad," Carlos wrote to the boy a little later, "your godfather is in heaven, thanks to God, because he was always so good and useful."[12]

11. Communists Disrupt the ABDE (March–April 1949)

Returning to Brazil in December 1948, Carlos found the Communists in an aggressive mood. He agreed with the Rio police chief that Communists had "infiltrated" the National Union of Students (UNE) and pointed out that he had warned of this when he had opposed declaring the PCB illegal. But he maintained that the police and Education Minister Clemente Mariani went too far in shutting down the UNE after students tried to wreck a streetcar while protesting an increase in streetcar fares.[1]

Mariani, Carlos wrote, was a crafty Francisco Franco–like conservative who lacked any understanding of youth and was capable of "the most sordid acts," such as using his ministry's budget to further his ambition to become governor of Bahia. Affiliation with the UDN, such as Mariani enjoyed, was no protection from Carlos' invective. Carlos wrote that "feudal baron" Juracy Magalhães, also of the Bahia UDN, relied on the *Reader's Digest* and Stefan Zweig's *Marie Antoinette* for his political education and that Minas Interior Secretary Pedro Aleixo, another "feudal baron" of the UDN, lacked national "political vision."[2]

When the UNE was reopened, Carlos received an invitation to attend its cocktail party. He declined in a letter condemning the UNE for remaining silent in the face of the sentencing of Cardinal Joseph Mindszenty by a Communist court in Hungary to serve a long prison term. Carlos, who filled columns about the Mindszenty case, told the UNE that "nowhere in the world . . . is there a greater enemy of liberty than Stalin, or in Brazil a more hateful and repugnant adversary of free institutions . . . than Sr. Luís Carlos Prestes," who, Carlos added, was as worthy of admiration as Nazi "ruffian" Horst Wessel. He told the UNE that "no one today so much resembles a Nazi as does a Communist."[3] Commenting in his column on a Communist-inspired "Manifesto for the Preservation of Peace," he praised Suzanne Labin's *The Russia of Stalin* and scolded the manifesto's signers, from Artur Bernardes to "the candidates for the post of local Henry Wallace."[4]

The Communists were ready for battle not only to show their strength in cultural and professional associations but to use the clashes for agitation and propaganda. Wishing to create the impression that Marxism dominated the intellectual sector,[5] the PCB ordered a major effort at the election of officers of the Brazilian Writers' Association (ABDE) on March 26, 1949. They stimulated the enrollment, in the association, of individuals hardly known for their writing, such as a former driver of Luís Carlos Prestes, a milkman, and a Jockey Club stableboy. Their electoral slate, made up mostly of militant Communists, was headed by Professor Homero Pires, a non-Communist.[6]

Poet Carlos Drummond de Andrade, bitter about his experience as a *Tribuna Popular* editor four years earlier, was alarmed at the Communists' desire to use the ABDE for purposes unrelated to the reasons for its formation. Therefore, in opposition to the ABDE Communist electoral slate, he organized a "democratic" slate and became its candidate for first secretary. Minas Congressman Afonso Arinos de Melo Franco was persuaded by Álvaro Lins, managing director of the *Correio da Manhã,* to head the democratic slate. Others on the slate of seven were Alceu Amoroso Lima, Hermes Lima, and Manuel Bandeira.[7]

Afonso Arinos was surprised by the hostility shown him by those favoring the Communist slate, including some of the outgoing officers. The Communists, he writes, used every possible means to achieve their ends, such as "extreme lack of loyalty," the breaking of agreements, and "the most scurrilous intimidation." Carlos, writing in the *Correio da Manhã* before the election, praised Carlos Drummond de Andrade and said, "We have seen what happened to the UNE . . . and shall see what happens to the ABDE."[8]

The election meeting, held at the Brazilian Press Association (ABI), found the democrats outnumbered because most of them had given proxies to friends who were present. Unable to get one of their members accepted as presiding officer, the democrats agreed to Communist Astrojildo Pereira's suggestion of Marxist Professor Castro Rebello. He was a good choice, showing impartiality during six hours of debate about proposed Communist motions, unrelated to the election and introduced for propaganda purposes. Carlos, in his shirtsleeves, spiced his oratory with witty remarks. José Lins do Rego used less finesse and was called a Special Police agent by the Communists.[9]

During the balloting, Afonso Arinos observed with chagrin that some of his friends voted for his opponent although they did not know him. He left for home before the outcome was known and was in bed when Carlos phoned to say, "Afonso, we won."[10]

The meeting of April 7 to install the new officers was not attended by Carlos because the outgoing officers, hoping for a quiet affair, limited invitations to the incoming and outgoing officers. But the recently victorious slate of seven, reaching the small ABDE headquarters for the ceremony, was dismayed to find that its election opponents had arrived with a group of sixty. The group, in Afonso Arinos' words, contained only half a dozen "true writers," such as sectarian Communist Graciliano Ramos, the rest being "young men and women of newspapers and mere thugs."[11]

Following Álvaro Lins' announcement of the officership transfer, Afonso

Arinos could not express the customary words of thanks because, he says, pro-Communist writer Dalcídio Jurandir, "as though he had gone crazy," gesticulated wildly and shouted insults at him. Insult hurling became general while motions were presented to invalidate proxies voted on March 26 and to have outgoing officers remain in office until a new assembly could review the election results. A metalworker struggled without success to seize the official record book from Rubem Braga and then began to attack Carlos Drummond de Andrade physically. The bedlam, according to Afonso Arinos, lasted several hours.[12]

The aftermath, suggested by Carlos Drummond de Andrade, was the collective resignation of the recently elected slate and the exodus from the Carioca ABDE of practically all writers who were not Communist. About five hundred of them signed a declaration, written by Carlos Drummond de Andrade and dated April 28, that described the recent turmoil and blamed the PCB. It concluded that the Carioca ABDE could no longer carry out its legitimate mission of defending writers.[13]

A year later, when Communist publications announced that the ABDE would hold the Third Writers' Congress in Salvador, Bahia, Carlos pointed out that the ABDE of São Paulo refused to participate in the "farce" and that the ABDE of Rio was simply a Communist cell whose literary work was limited to issuing statements worshiping Russia. Carlos berated Bahia Governor Otávio Mangabeira for giving the state's official recognition and blessing to the Salvador meeting.[14]

12. Carlos Leaves the *Correio da Manhã* (April 1949)

Using his column to advocate one of his favorite themes, a liberal immigration policy, Carlos criticized lawmakers who clamored for restrictions that would develop in Brazil "the most desirable characteristics of European stock." When at last the Senate passed a law placing immigration decisions in the hands of the central government, Carlos called the law "simply idiotic" because it left no initiative to the states and because, he said, it would mean a continuation of the Vargas policy of keeping immigration to a minimum.[1]

Carlos also favored an influx of foreign capital. Arguing that Brazil's capital formation was insufficient for its needs, he outlined a formula whereby the Brazilian government, in return for concessions to foreigners, would be given fifty percent of the original capital of the enterprises; if the enterprises prospered, the foreign investors were to receive cash dividends on their shares whereas the Brazilian government's shares, which might be sold to Brazilian individuals, were to be increased in number, making for gradual nationalization. The idea, Carlos wrote, had been given him by Belgium's former Minister Paul Van Zeeland and had been used successfully in the development of the Belgian Congo.[2]

To Carlos' regret, the government's proposed petroleum statute, which would have allowed a minority participation in petroleum extraction by international companies, died in Congress. The death, celebrated at a *Car-*

naval do Petróleo in Bahia in February 1949, was attributed by Carlos to Communists and what he called banana republic nationalists (*nacionalistas do bananismo*), such as "morbid" Artur Bernardes and General Horta Barbosa, president of the Study Center to Defend Petroleum and the National Economy. Carlos maintained that Brazil, lacking petroleum production, would remain at the mercy of the international oil companies, who ought to erect a plaque to glorify "the honorable Communist Party" and the "meritorious" men responsible for the Petroleum Carnival merrymaking.[3]

Petroleum refining, Carlos insisted, should be in the hands of the government, and he described as "scandalous" the refining concessions granted by the Dutra government to two private national groups, the Soares Sampaio and Drault Ernâni groups. Carlos demanded that the government "annul the concessions and construct the refineries on its own account and by public subscription, in the form adopted for the Volta Redonda steel plant." He joined Congressman Hermes Lima in denouncing "favors" granted to the two groups and said "the episode reveals how the government is overrun by influence peddlers and crooks."[4]

Under the heading "A group milking Brazil," Carlos published articles on April 26 and 27 about the Soares Sampaio group, which, he wrote, was "the leader of the circle of businessmen who took over the Dutra government, compromise it, . . . advise it, and blacken its reputation." Naming members of the group, he mentioned the Soares Sampaio family, Senator Artur Bernardes Filho ("general representative of Westinghouse"), and a son and son-in-law of the finance minister.[5] Bernardes Filho, after reading Carlos' article of April 26, spoke in the Senate to deny being a shareholder of any refinery.[6]

Correio da Manhã owner Paulo Bittencourt was in Araxá, Minas Gerais, on April 27 when he read Carlos' article of the twenty-sixth. Having long been a close friend of the Soares Sampaios, he telephoned Pedro da Costa Rego, editor-in-chief of the *Correio da Manhã,* and gave orders that further articles on the subject by Carlos not be published. With the failure of the newspaper to print the next in his series, Carlos took the matter up with Costa Rego and then with Paulo Bittencourt, who came to Rio.[7]

At the request of Carlos, Bittencourt published, on May 1, an explanation of Carlos' separation from the *Correio da Manhã.* It opened by saying: "Bad news: Carlos Lacerda has stopped collaborating with this newspaper. That we shall miss his collaboration—ardent, personal, a bit romantic and subjective, but always courageous and honest—there is no doubt." Bittencourt wrote of his decision to suspend what he felt was a series of articles that harmed friends "who were described in the columns of my newspaper in a way that conflicts completely with my personal opinion of them. Is this fair? Unfair? I do not know and it does not matter. Carlos Lacerda felt hurt by me, and from his point of view, I do not deny that he has reason. In my place, however, he would do what I did. I believe that we have both lost out."[8]

V.

Director of a New Newspaper (1949–1953)

1. Prescription for Better Journalism (1949)

The columns of Carlos in the *Correio da Manhã* had been so combative that other newspapers were unwilling to take him on as a columnist. Speaking early in May 1949 to Aluísio Alves, young UDN congressman from Rio Grande do Norte, Carlos said, "No newspaper wants me; I think I'll write fiction for Rádio Mayrink Veiga." During a conversation at the home of Luís Camilo de Oliveira Neto, he talked about going into real estate brokerage. This was not a new idea for the journalist who had spent several months desperately seeking a business connection to augment his income.[1] Now Aluísio Alves and Luís Camilo urged him to establish his own newspaper. Others did the same.[2]

Carlos had well-founded doubts about starting a daily in a city oversupplied with newspapers, but friends connected with the UDN and the Catholic Church offered encouragement and help. After discussions at the law office of Adauto Lúcio Cardoso and the home of UDN Congressman Carlos de Lima Cavalcanti, Carlos set to work in a small office to organize an afternoon newspaper.[3] It was to be called *Tribuna da Imprensa* because Paulo Bittencourt agreed to let him have the name he had made famous with his columns.[4]

Luís Camilo, who had been appointed a director of the Banco de Crédito Real de Minas Gerais by UDN Governor Milton Campos, arranged a loan from the bank to the Sociedade Anônima Editôra Tribuna da Imprensa.[5] To provide capital, a campaign was begun on May 12 to raise eight million cruzeiros by selling the public eight thousand shares at one conto (a thousand cruzeiros) apiece, payable in installments.[6] The campaign, "to support Carlos Lacerda," was so successful that a second office was opened to handle it. Luís Camilo, Alceu Amoroso Lima, and lawyer Dario de Almeida Magalhães were effective in getting people to buy shares. Significant help was also rendered by businessman Lauro de Carvalho and his son, José Vasconcelos Carvalho, both friends of Gustavo Corção.[7]

Nine thousand shares were sold to 3,404 individuals, most of whom bought one share. The two largest stockholders, with five hundred shares each, were Adauto Lúcio Cardoso and Luís Severiano Ribeiro, owner of a

Rio theater chain.[8] This method of launching a Rio daily by popular subscription and without any principal owner was practically unheard of and resembled the founding, in 1920, of the anarchist-slanted workers' daily, *Voz do Povo,* which Maurício de Lacerda had assisted.

Carlos promoted interest in the *Tribuna da Imprensa* when he delivered a speech about journalism, first at the ABI in Rio at the invitation of the Resistência Democrática, then in Belo Horizonte at the invitation of the State Student Union (UEE) of Minas, and then at the São Paulo Law School at the invitation of Juventude Universitária Católica (JUC). Criticizing prevailing practices, he told his audiences: "You may be sure that untruthful advertisements will not be published in the *Tribuna da Imprensa.* . . . You will appreciate that a newspaper with this standard is the most suitable for advertisements of all genuine products that abide by commercial ethics, and thus you will discover one of our trump cards."[9]

In his speech, Carlos said he had happily managed to escape the tendency of journalists to become skeptics. To those who accused him of being pessimistic and insufficiently constructive, he replied that conditions in Brazil justified pessimism and that construction by journalists did not consist of laying cornerstones for projects costing twice their value but in revealing such facts and creating "a well-informed public opinion, thoughtful, alert, and enlightened."[10]

Speaking of the Communist daily *Imprensa Popular,* which had succeeded the *Tribuna Popular* in 1948, Carlos condemned the "Popular Falsehood" for making the truth subservient "to the interests of a class, or, more precisely, the group that dominates in the name of that class." And he denounced the "more subtle" form of Communist work: infiltration, such as that in Geraldo Rocha's *O Mundo,* "where the editor is a member of the Communist Party," or in the *Diário de Notícias,* where the education section "is in the hands of a Communist."[11]

He attacked also the anti-Communist campaign of PSD Congressman Euvaldo Lodi, president of the National Confederation of Industry and director of SESI (Serviço Social da Indústria). The Diários Associados of Chateaubriand, he said, had received millions of cruzeiros of SESI money, wrung by government decree from Brazilian consumers. "When an editorial, in bold type . . . in a prominent afternoon newspaper, observes the birthday of Euvaldo Lodi as though it were a national holiday, you can be sure—because it is a fact—that it was paid material (*matéria paga*), financed by SESI."[12] Describing *matéria paga* as "a running sore of Brazilian journalism," Carlos pointed out that newspapers, for a higher than ordinary price, would publish propaganda in a way to make it appear indistinguishable from their regular news and editorials.[13]

According to Carlos, another Brazilian weakness was large, sensational headlines, which, he said, had generally been done away with abroad. Calling sensational pictures and headlines the result of irresponsibility, he said that "in Brazil, where we pay for paper in dollars, sometimes half the first page, in millions of pages, is wasted in expressing nonsense or lies." He likened enormous headlines to cries in the street, which, if made daily, cease to alarm and become less effective than a quiet voice.[14]

The Brazilian press, Carlos said, was afflicted by extreme nationalism, scant effort to verify information, attention to what was superficial, and a tendency to exaggerate in attacks and praise. These faults, he explained, revealed "instability of judgment, a characteristic not of journalism alone but of the whole country." "If our press is rotten, the blame can be attributed to the elite, who read, write, pay for propaganda, are afraid to deal with issues, indulge in excesses, and cheat."[15]

Carlos warned that complacency, which had led an uncensored press in 1937 to accept the Cohen Plan as genuine, was returning to Brazil.[16] But he was not hopeful of improvement by the press. "Most of the presidents of leading newspapers are not, or do not wish to be, journalists." Some, he said, had inherited their newspapers, others had become rich and still others, "due to strange combinations of fate, possess instruments they do not want to manage."[17]

2. Launching the *Tribuna da Imprensa* (December 27, 1949)

Fernando Velloso, regarded as Carlos' best friend,[1] joined lawyers Dario de Almeida Magalhães and Ignácio Piquet Carneiro in setting up the Tribuna da Imprensa Company statutes and organization. Lest too many of the widely distributed shares fall into the hands of political opponents, they made it mandatory for sellers of shares to give preference to bids submitted by remaining stockholders. It was also decided that "political and spiritual control" of the newspaper would be guaranteed if ownership of its name would remain with Carlos. Therefore Carlos did not sell the chief asset, the name *Tribuna da Imprensa,* to the company; instead, the stockholders assigned him a royalty of one percent of the company's gross income in order to use the name.[2]

At the stockholders' meeting of September 2, Carlos was chosen *diretor-presidente* of the company with a monthly salary of five thousand cruzeiros and was voted additional payments for directing the newspaper: ten thousand cruzeiros as salary and ten thousand for expenses. Lawyer Ignácio Piquet Carneiro became the company's *diretor-gerente* (managing director). The fiscal council was made up of former Pernambuco Governor Carlos de Lima Cavalcanti, businessman José Vasconcelos Carvalho, and Dario de Almeida Magalhães.[3]

"To ensure the continuity of the orientation of the newspaper and the faithful observance of its program," a consultive council was established: Adauto Lúcio Cardoso, Alceu Amoroso Lima, Gustavo Corção, Heráclito Fontoura Sobral Pinto, and Luís Camilo de Oliveira Neto.[4] It drew up thirty-five points for giving the newspaper a campaign for "the moralization of politics." One of the first to resign was Sobral Pinto, who concluded, within a year, that Carlos was violating restraints contained in the thirty-five points.[5]

Rents were so high that the company purchased an old two-story building at 98 Lavradio Street in a downtown district full of carpentry and upholstery shops. The upper floor was transformed from cheap dwellings into the newspaper offices, mostly a large reporters' room. The ground floor, formerly a paper deposit, became the *Tribuna da Imprensa* printing and distribution area. It received a small rotary press, which Listas Telefônicas had found unsatisfactory for printing the telephone directory and had been pleased to sell. Carlos called the troublesome old press a "sugar cane crusher."[6]

O Estado de S. Paulo's José Maria Homem de Montes (who has remarked that "everyone on our side in São Paulo bought Tribuna da Imprensa shares") visited Rio, at Carlos' suggestion, to give advice.[7] He found Carlos full of ideas about a newspaper that would avoid sensationalism and check the reliability of advertisers. Carlos even drew up, for publication in the first number, a "commercial code of ethics" banning indecent advertisements or commercial propaganda that attacked competitors, offered quack cure-alls, or gave opinions that might be misinterpreted as those of the *Tribuna*. "The views of this newspaper," he wrote, "are not for sale."[8]

Trotskyite Hilcar Leite, an experienced journalist, left the *Diário Carioca* to accept, at Carlos' invitation, the post of head of reporting (*chefe de reportagem*). In the newspaper's editorial hierarchy, he was listed, at the start, under Editor-in-chief (*Redator-chefe*) Aluísio Alves and Editor Wilson de Oliveira, former editor of the *Diário Carioca*. Young men whom the *Tribuna* took on as early reporters, such as Fidélis Amaral Netto and Hermano Alves, found in the newspaper a school of journalism that paved the way to political careers. But they began their work with an organization that had no automobile for reporters and whose printing equipment could give no clear reproductions of pictures taken by Diogenes, the sole photographer.[9]

The first number, supposed to appear before Christmas, was delayed by obstacles attributed to Mayor Mendes de Morais, such as the difficulty in arranging for the receipt of gas to heat the boiler. The *Tribuna* resolved the problem by burning wood, and therefore, when the old rotary press began printing the newspaper on December 27, the employees were in tears more from smoke than emotion. The smoke, filling the ground floor, spread to the reporters' room.[10]

In a first-page commentary, "At Last We Get Started," the daily's directorship wrote that exciting pictures, large headlines, and "false respectability" did nothing useful for the reader. The *Tribuna*, the reader was told, would give him honest information, keep him company, share his grievances, and perhaps guide him, preparing him for victory "so that when it comes, it will be just and well used." In accordance with the directorship's pledge that the *Tribuna* would dedicate itself to "the Christianization of society," the first number devoted a page to Cardinal Mindszenty and offered the opinions of Fulton Sheen, Gustavo Corção, and Alceu Amoroso Lima. The newspaper opposed divorce. A note from the editors promised that the weekly children's page, supervised by Darcy Evangelista, would avoid the use of comic strips featuring gangsters or frightening stories.[11]

Turnover of personnel was heavy in the executive area. Ignácio Piquet

Flier announcing that the *Tribuna da Imprensa* will finally be available.

Carneiro's successor, Walter Ramos Poyares, was a journalist and advertising agency executive brought in to promote sales and better administration at the suggestion of José Vasconcelos Carvalho. Poyares found Carlos a disorganized genius, defiant of routine and sometimes explosive, and he therefore withdrew in the belief that Carlos' brother Mauricinho might be a more suitable choice; but Mauricinho had the same difficulties and left after a few years.[12] On the other hand, the reserved Odilon Lacerda Paiva remained with the *Tribuna* despite the unenviable task of being treasurer of a daily whose advertising revenues were restricted due to the lack of a wide circulation and the disinclination of government-associated companies to assist it. Cláudio Medeiros Lima, who had participated with Carlos in law school politics, was brought in by Carlos to improve the *Tribuna* as a newspaper. Under his management the reporters' room was filled to overflowing with new faces, but the infusion was more than the *Tribuna* could finance and Medeiros Lima departed.[13]

More than once Carlos' principles contributed to the financial problems of the newspaper. When the state of Amazonas sent the *Tribuna* money to pay for publicity, Carlos rejected the proposal and returned the money because he was engaged in a campaign against the Amazonas state government.[14]

Like all newspapers, the *Tribuna* had its share of reporter turnover. Lindolfo Collor Filho, its first writer on labor affairs, left dissatisfied.[15] But most of the reporters, although not very well paid, were devoted to "Ugly Duckling," Carlos' nickname for the *Tribuna*. They, along with the other employees, became a highly motivated team, deeply involved in the campaigns of the daily. They shared the enthusiasm of Carlos, who seemed more concerned with writing and investigation than administration and who did not hesitate to spend days and nights at work in order to have the *Tribuna* demonstrate, for example, that the city's milk was contaminated. Carlos frequently rewrote articles by others when he felt they could be improved. His dedication was such that when the news of a Brazilian World Cup soccer victory turned the *Tribuna* offices into a scene of wild jubilation, he simply went on with his dictation as if nothing had happened.[16]

Ayrton Baffa, a prize-winning reporter who began his career at the *Tribuna* in 1958, points out that Carlos was oblivious to commotion while bent over a keyboard, his glasses pushed back to the top of his forehead. Murilo Melo Filho, who has become executive director of the Bloch publishing enterprise and was on the *Tribuna* team from 1952 to 1959, writes of Carlos: "Never have I seen such an extraordinary person or one so filled with passion. Everything about him was on a grand scale, his good qualities and his defects." The Bloch executive says that Carlos was "idealistic, with an enthusiasm appropriate for a youngster" and was so absorbed in his *Tribuna* work that sometimes, instead of going home at night, he slept on reporters' room tables covered with newspapers.[17]

The *Tribuna* campaigns, vividly recalled today by Murilo Melo Filho, became dramatic battles against the authorities and followed one upon another, making life at the *Tribuna* a continuous tumult. All hoped the campaigns would increase the circulation beyond the 19,000 figure reached early in the *Tribuna*'s life. When this circulation, lower than that of the major Rio dailies, gained the newspaper the label of *lanterninha,* the lantern at the end of trains, Carlos, in a characteristic response to detractors, placed a drawing of a lantern, symbol of truth-seeking, on the *Tribuna* masthead.[18]

By then the *Tribuna,* usually twelve pages, had abandoned its resolve to eschew sensational headlines. The first page, frequently dominated by one headline, contained many smaller ones above articles that were often rather brief. Pictures, spread all over the first page, might occupy half the space (and more than that when a train wreck was illustrated by views of dead bodies). But the chief attraction was the long, hard-hitting editorial by Carlos, usually on page four and sometimes on page one.

Among the mainstays was Hilde Weber, the well-dressed woman from Germany who drew the political cartoons.[19] Another was chief photographer Ernesto Santos, who did photographic work concurrently for the war ministry[20] and whose team at the *Tribuna* included Fernando Bueno. Among the hundreds who worked at the *Tribuna* over the years were Walter Cunto, Carlos Castello Branco, Hélio Fernandes, João Duarte, filho, Odilo Costa, filho, Villas-Bôas Corrêa, Mário Pinto Franqueira, Waldemar Lopes, Nilson Viana, Waldyr Figueiredo, Nertan Macedo, José Carlos de Macedo Miranda, Borba Tourinho, Caio Pinheiro, Ledo Ivo, Luiz Garcia, Carlos Lemos, Quintino Carvalho, José J. Veiga, José Calheiros Bonfim, Walter Fontoura, Faustino Porto Sobrinho, Luís Jorge Lobo, Araújo Neto, economist Luís Brunini (brother of broadcaster Raul), Stefan Baciu (foreign news), Elpídio Reis (management), Geraldo Sinval Montalvão (publicity), Lincoln de Sousa Machado (advertising), and Emanuel Fonseca (printing-plant superintendent).

Eventually Carlos' son Sérgio and nephew Cláudio joined the *Tribuna.* So did sons of Carlos' friends Luís Camilo de Oliveira Neto and Marcelo Garcia. Carlos had so much esteem for medical doctor Marcelo Garcia, whose

Tonelero Street apartment adjoined his own, that he customarily left typed editorials under Marcelo's door so that the doctor could comment on them before the typescripts went to the *Tribuna.* Some were toned down at Marcelo's suggestion.[21]

A key role was played by Ruth Alverga, who joined the *Tribuna* in July 1950 at the age of 21. She began her work as secretary of Ignácio Piquet Carneiro and then helped Darcy Evangelista, who started "Tribuninha" for children, at first a single page and later a separate section, or insert. Ruth became the secretary of Carlos, using a desk in his simple office, which adjoined the reporters' room and had a noisy air conditioner and a large, well-filled bookcase. A loyal admirer of "Dr. Carlos," she was known for her efficiency, glamour, and, when she felt it necessary, bossiness and directness of speech. "Ruth," Stefan Baciu writes, "appeared at the office punctually at 8:30 A.M., impeccably dressed in a style very much her own, with high-heeled shoes, and the hairdo and make-up of a star." He adds that she was "mysteriously well organized, being the only person, outside of Lacerda, who could locate easily any paper lost in a veritable sea of documents, letters, and telegrams, and decipher any manuscript of 'Dr. Carlos.'" Thousands of letters poured in, many from women expressing their undying love for Carlos and others from readers irritated by the *Tribuna.*[22]

Carlos, Baciu recalls, would arrive and leave the *Tribuna* loaded with papers. "He would enter the reporters' room like a gale. Throwing his jacket over a chair, he would roll up his sleeves, unfasten his necktie, and start to use the first typewriter he saw, without opening the door of his own office, which was always kept shut" because of the air conditioner.[23]

3. Assaulted by an Air Force Colonel (May 14, 1950)

On May 11 the *Tribuna da Imprensa* unleashed a barrage against Artur Pires, the president of the Carioca Serviço Social do Comércio (SESC) who was preparing to run for the Senate on the Labor Party (PTB) ticket. Pires, the *Tribuna* said, had a SESC subordinate, air force Colonel Guilherme Aloísio Teles Ribeiro, who headed the air force purchasing department and bought so much for the air force from the Pires family firm that "Pires . . . is the air force's chief supplier of canvas, boots, socks, khaki cloth for uniforms, etc."[1]

The reply to the article was physical attack on Carlos on Sunday morning, May 14, after he attended church services with his family. Having left Letícia at a pharmacy, Carlos went to his Tonelero Street apartment with his sons, aged 11 and 7, and the 11-year-old son of Senator Vitorino Freire, who lived on the eighth floor of the same building. The two would-be assailants, strangers to Carlos, joined him and the boys in the elevator and remained in it after the Freire boy left on the eighth floor. When the elevator reached the top floor, the tenth, where the Lacerdas lived, Carlos opened the elevator door, letting his sons out, and replied in the affirmative when one of the strangers asked if he were Carlos Lacerda. Then one of the men held him while the other tried to close the elevator door. But Carlos pushed one of them out and therefore the struggle took place in the vestibule, where Carlos fell to the floor and was kicked and hit in the face. Sérgio joined Carlos in the fight while Sebastião used the stairway to reach the eighth floor. Senator Freire, after phoning the Radio Patrol from his apartment, went with his son and Sebastião to the tenth floor. The assailants fled in the service elevator and got away in a waiting car. Carlos' wounds were not serious.[2]

As had happened after the more damaging assault near the Mayrink Veiga building in 1948, the Lacerdas received visits from friends and politicians who wished to show support. Among the first were Prado Kelly, Gabriel Passos, and Eduardo Gomes, all of the UDN, and they were followed by Paulo Bittencourt and José Americo. Five *Tribuna da Imprensa* consultive council members met at the apartment to plan legal action. Sobral Pinto drew up a writ, or *mandado de segurança,* which Carlos sent to the Supreme Court, accusing President Dutra of being responsible for the successive assaults, starting with the brief kidnapping of Odilon Lacerda Paiva, and demanding that he set an effective investigation in motion and have the Federal Department of Public Security take steps to protect Carlos' life and liberty.[3] The accusation was reported in the press under headlines about the "new criminal assault against journalist Carlos Lacerda."

In the Senate on the fifteenth the "cowardly vandalism" was denounced by José Américo and Hamilton Nogueira, both of whom had remained silent after the 1948 assault. Hamilton Nogueira said that he was one of those who did not always agree with Lacerda's "bruising" style but that the attack, the third against "one of the most important figures of the Brazilian democratic rebirth," was a disgrace. Likewise Senate UDN leader José Ferreira de Souza declared that while people might disagree with the "vivaciousness" with which the journalist handled facts and men, "no one can deny the purity of his ideas and his good faith."[4] Writing in the *Tribuna da Imprensa,* Carlos asked, "How can one rely on a government that produced the perpetrators of the assaults?" No words from the government, he wrote, "can return to my children the vision of peace I have sought for them." And he suggested that the police were simply waiting for him to be killed, as had happened in the case of the unsolved murder of Virgílio de Melo Franco when he had tried to defend his home.[5]

The investigation of the 1950 crime—an investigation carried out under the direction of police Delegado Fernando Schwab with Adauto Lúcio Cardoso acting as Carlos' lawyer—allowed Carlos to identify men who had beaten him up in 1948.[6] Renato Meira Lima, whom Carlos called the prosperous accomplice of Mayor "Mussolini de Morais" and accused of involvement in the 1948 assault, gave the police information that did much to clear up the attack of 1950.[7] Carlos, summoned to the *delegado*'s office to look at suspects, went there with Sérgio. A large crowd, which included journalists, saw Carlos, and then Sérgio, point to Colonel Guilherme Aloísio Teles Ribeiro as being one of the two assailants who went up with them in the elevator. Adauto Lúcio Cardoso pounced on inconsistencies when the colonel tried to show that Carlos was mistaken. It was learned that the colonel and his SESC boss, Artur Pires, had been together just before and after the colonel had made his foolhardy trip to Tonelero Street.[8] "The colonel," *Tribuna da Imprensa* wrote on June 9, "confesses that he made a mistake."

The revelation of the names of those involved in the 1948 crime—a revelation assisted by the tearful confession of assailant "Kangaroo"—provided material for enormous headlines in the *Tribuna da Imprensa.* The Ugly Duckling denounced "to the Brazilian nation" the "hoodlums of Mendes de Morais, led by Meira Lima," and lashed out at "mellifluous" Senator Bernardes Filho and *O Globo*'s "mercenary" Roberto Marinho for supporting the mayor. At the same time, the *Tribuna* accused both Artur Pires and air force Colonel Teles Ribeiro of having enriched themselves from the sales to the air force. Carlos, writing about the incident in 1967, said: The "air force colonel . . . wanted to prove he was not a thief by attacking me in the elevator at my apartment. He did not prove anything."[9]

4. Presidential Election (October 1950)

Late in 1949 Carlos told Brigadeiro Eduardo Gomes that he did not favor his renomination for president by the UDN because he hoped the PSD and UDN would agree on a joint candidate and thus make it possible to stop Vargas from returning to the presidency on the PTB ticket.[1]

The joint candidate suggested in March 1950 by Milton Campos, UDN governor of Minas, was Afonso Pena Júnior, who, as Bernardes' justice minister in the mid-1920s, had made life difficult for the Lacerdas. Carlos wrote in the *Tribuna* that Pena seemed to lack the energy and disposition to carry out a reform program and break with the "conservatism that asphyxiates this country." But he supported Pena as a means of creating a PSD-UDN bloc against Vargas. And when some PSD politicians appeared cool about Pena, Carlos put the blame on Senator Vitorino Freire and then on Dutra himself, who, Carlos wrote unfairly, wanted to create confusion in order "to remain, criminally, in the government."[2]

UDN leaders threatened to abandon Pena unless he obtained the support of São Paulo Governor Ademar de Barros, strongman of the PSP (Partido Social Progressista). Carlos and Afonso Arinos de Melo Franco therefore called on Pena at his Rio home to discuss the situation. During the three hours it took to obtain a telephone connection to Milton Campos in Belo Horizonte, Carlos was more impressed with the jurist's library than with his candidatorial attributes. About all Pena would say was "the problem is yours, not mine." After they learned from Milton Campos that Ademar de Barros would not support Pena, Pena rejected Carlos' suggestion that he would do better to withdraw his candidacy than have the UDN drop it. Pena said he would not withdraw a candidacy he had not put forward.[3]

In April, while the Dutra people considered other possible coalition candidates, the UDN directorship, headed by Prado Kelly, resolved to launch the candidacy of Eduardo Gomes. Carlos was vexed at the precipitous step but he nevertheless attended the UDN nominating convention, held in Rio in May. His speech there was a warning that the party could reach the people only if it courageously adopted a program to reform "the moral order, administrative planning, production and distribution methods, the behavior of public figures, and governing methods." Writing in the *Tribuna,* he challenged staid *udenistas* "who seem to think they own the *brigadeiro*" to turn him into a "revolutionary candidate," offering "the basic reforms," including agrarian reform.[4]

After the PSD settled on the relatively unknown Cristiano Machado, described by Carlos as the world's most timorous man, it was no surprise to Carlos to learn that Vargas decided to oppose Machado and Gomes as candidate of both the PTB and Ademar de Barros' PSP. Carlos said the Machado candidacy was nourished by the Bank of Brazil and he called the Vargas candidacy a demagogic, totalitarian movement similar to that employed by Perón in Argentina. He did not deny that years of Estado Novo propaganda had given Vargas popularity, but most of his reasons for predicting a narrow victory for Vargas were based on what he called UDN errors.[5]

So angry was Carlos at the UDN that he addressed a long letter to its President Odilon Braga, withdrawing from the party. He accused the UDN of making itself "impermeable to the working classes" by limiting its campaign to an abstract discussion of liberty and ignoring the Movimento Renovador program of social reform "that I have been preaching for five years."[6]

Carlos was also furious because the Carioca UDN had not accepted the conditions he had laid down as necessary if he were to run for Congress. He refused to be a candidate, he said, as long as the Carioca UDN slates included individuals unworthy of "the confidence of the *udenista* electorate." He especially condemned Luís Paes Leme and Ari Barroso, renominated to run for municipal council seats.[7]

The most scathing of Carlos' remarks about the UDN were reserved for what he called its "sinister" deal with Plínio Salgado's Partido de Representação Popular (PRP). After Eduardo Gomes joined Salgado in speechmaking at the PRP convention, Carlos wrote that the *brigadeiro* was reviving the Green Shirt movement and had become the perfect candidate of Integralismo and the favorite of the far Right. His severe open letter to Gomes, calling his deal with Salgado immoral, was followed by the refusal of Gomes to speak with *Tribuna* reporters. Writing of "the hostility of the *brigadeiro,* because we told him the truth," Carlos said "we are prepared to suffer such blows." "The *brigadeiro*'s men understood nothing," Carlos said later when speaking of the distraught Alceu Amoroso Lima, who complained that he had worked hard to sell Tribuna shares only to discover that the newspaper was critical of his favorite candidate.[8]

In the *Tribuna* Carlos wrote that the UDN had renounced its ideals and that "any difference between the *brigadeiro* and Cristiano Machado has disappeared completely." Therefore, he argued, either Machado or Gomes should withdraw. But the UDN ignored his plea that it "fuse at once with the PSD" to end the split of the anti-Vargas front. Then late in July, Carlos spoke to Machado, asking him to step aside in favor of Gomes. The PSD standard-bearer refused.[9]

Carlos had recently declared that if Vargas should be elected he ought to be denied the presidency and if he assumed the presidency "we must turn to revolution to prevent him from governing." Determined to do what he could to defeat the 68-year-old Gaúcho, on August 3 he published an editorial: "With the *brigadeiro* in spite of everything." He wrote that João Mangabeira, presidential candidate of the Partido Socialista Brasileiro (PSB), was doing well to criticize the other candidates "but we are not socialist and . . . above all his candidacy is not viable."[10]

While Samuel Wainer became close to Vargas, covering his election campaign for the Diários Associados, Carlos attacked the old "dictator." Nor did he spare Vargas' wife Darcy, whom he accused of wasting "26 million cruzeiros, taken from the funds of the people," to build what he called a wretchedly planned Girls' Town, "in the days when the DIP called her the 'mother of the Brazilians.'" Carlos told the *Tribuna* readers that Girls' Town, inspired by Father Edward Flanagan's Boys Town in the United States, "is not a town and has no girls."[11]

With the approach of election day, October 3, Carlos wrote that the voting would be "the most corrupt in the political history of Brazil." He listed "the indiscriminate use of the radio for insidious propaganda," the "delirious expenditure" of public money and gambling money, and the "shameless rush of state and municipal candidates to join the adversaries of their own candidates on the national level."[12]

Noting daily adherences that strengthened Vargas' candidacy, Carlos began to adopt the position that drastic measures were necessary to prevent an electoral victory by a dictatorial machine established, over many years, by censorship, propaganda, radio monopoly, and, "above all, the opposition's inability to communicate." According to this thesis, elections should be held only after electoral legislation had been reformed and the dictatorship's machine dismantled. "But," Carlos has observed, "to explain this to the jurists of the UDN was an impossibility." "The thesis," he found, gained him "the reputation of being a '*golpista*' [supporter of coups] and even a 'fascist,' etc."[13]

Vargas achieved the presidency, as he wished, "on the arms of the people." His vote was 3,849,040, compared with 2,342,384 for Gomes, 1,697,193 for Machado, and fewer than 10,000 for João Mangabeira. Vargas' running mate, João Café Filho of the PSP, narrowly defeated Odilon Braga of the UDN. In the Federal District, Vargas' son Lutero (PTB) won a congressional seat by an overwhelming margin.

Carlos supported the effort of the UDN's Aliomar Baleeiro to convince the Superior Electoral Tribunal that Vargas ought not to be inaugurated because he had not received an absolute majority. After this effort failed, Afonso Arinos de Melo Franco (UDN) said that Vargas would "undoubtedly carry out a coup," and Carlos wrote that it was unlikely that Vargas or his companions would be guided by the constitution.[14]

Carlos reported, however, that Vargas would find it difficult to reestablish the DIP. Writing in mid-October from New York, where he played a leading role at the Sixth Conference of the Inter American Press Association,[15] Carlos pointed out that the conference had voted to establish an Inter American

Ademar de Barros: I'm going to America to study election propaganda methods to use in the 1955 elections.
Vargas (*with cigar*): Where will there be elections in 1955?
(Drawing from *Careta,* Rio de Janeiro, June 16, 1951, reproduced in Adelina Alves Novaes e Cruz et al., *Impasse na Democracia Brasileira, 1951–1955*)

Freedom of the Press Tribunal to deal with moves that might restrict the press. "Getúlio Vargas," Carlos told the *Tribuna,* "will no longer enjoy his previous delicious situation."[16]

5. Vargas Returns to the Presidency (1951)

With Vargas preparing to return to Catete Palace at the end of January 1951, the *Tribuna* came out against UDN collaboration with the incoming administration. Such collaboration, the *Tribuna* said, would make it necessary for the newspaper to "create a democratic movement" favoring social reform and "displacing" the UDN. But the threat was not carried out because the UDN directorship rejected the offer of two cabinet posts, made by PTB President Danton Coelho on behalf of Vargas.[1]

As inauguration day drew near, the *Tribuna* had second thoughts about Paes Leme after he tried to prevent a further "assault on the public coffers" by Rio municipal councilmen. And Carlos had second thoughts about the outgoing president. In an open letter to "citizen Dutra," he admitted that, in the heat of pointing out errors, he had sometimes been unjust to the general and his government. Carlos spoke well of the Dutra government's work at the Paulo Afonso hydroelectric project, beneficial to the northeast, and praised Dutra especially for adhering to the constitution, leaving office at the end of his mandate, and allowing the publication of criticism in a free press.[2]

The fire of the *Tribuna* was now directed at the new regime, including Finance Minister Horácio Lafer, Justice Minister Francisco Negrão de Lima, and Foreign Minister João Neves da Fontoura. When a *udenista,* João Cleofas, agreed to become minister of agriculture, he was described by Carlos as a "Judas of the UDN." Above all, the *Tribuna* went after the new Bank of Brazil president, Ricardo Jafet, a heavy contributor to Vargas' election campaign. Carlos disclosed financial operations in which the Jafet companies had benefited from favors provided by top São Paulo officeholders and wrote that Vargas, having promised to get rid of "the exploiters of the people," was putting them "in key posts."[3]

In the *Tribuna* office early in 1951, few were unaware that Carlos was expecting to become a father again. With the infectious enthusiasm that characterized his work, Carlos raved about the daughter he and Letícia would have. Dismissing any suggestion that they would have another son, he wrote poems about the unborn girl and showed them around the office. He was not disappointed. On May 21 Letícia gave birth to Maria Cristina Lacerda. She was baptized by Dom Lourenço de Almeida Prado in August.[4]

Hoping to give his newspaper the reputation of being constructive, Carlos directed campaigns in 1951 in favor of a Rio slum (*favela*) improvement program that would not "stupidly" move slum dwellers from their areas of employment and an agrarian reform that would attack Brazil's "large landholdings, a national calamity."[5] Declaring that it wished to be more than "simply an opposition newspaper," the *Tribuna* sponsored a round table on agrarian reform. It gave particularly good coverage to the views of Bahia Congressman Nestor Duarte, a round-table participant who defined agrarian reform as a revision of the juridical and economic relations between landowners and rural workers and who interpreted the constitution as allowing gradual, rather than prompt, indemnification payments for expropriated land.[6]

Most of the newspaper's campaigns, however, were in opposition to one thing or another. It objected to Vargas' appointment of Yeddo Fiuza to a post in the Federal District water department, calling it submission to Communism, and it opposed Bahia Congressman Nelson Carneiro's effort to legalize divorce.[7] It reacted unfavorably to the United Nation's request that Brazil send troops to Korea. Arguing that Brazil had a real interest in Europe and Africa but not in Korea, Carlos described Vargas' reply to the UN as "covering Brazil with shame" because it implied that Brazil, lacking the capacity to send even a symbolic force overseas, might do so if it were to receive financial assistance.[8]

Although Carlos opposed sending Brazilian troops to Korea, he defended the role played by United States soldiers in the conflict and thus ran into trouble when he participated in a debate early in August during the UNE's Fourteenth National Student Congress. His debate was with Giovanni Berlinguer, secretary of the International Union of Students, with headquarters in Prague. Berlinguer, Carlos wrote in July, was a Cominform professional and so-called Italian student who had been "lugged" to Brazil by José Colagrossi Filho, head of the "pro-Communist" Paulista delegation to the student congress and a recent participant at Peace Congresses held in Prague, Peking, and Paris. Berlinguer, using an interpreter, insisted that the Korean War had been started by the aggression of South Korea. He declared that the International Union of Students favored peace, and he persuaded Brazilian students to attend its forthcoming Youth Festival in Berlin's Russian zone.[9]

It was late at night when Carlos told the students that they, and all Brazilians, should speak out in favor of the Western democracies, "to whose destiny Brazil is linked," and he added that it was cowardice "not to speak here of the American students who are dying in Korea." By that time the pro-Communists, thanks to new arrivals, were in the majority. They stirred up so much disorder that the meeting broke up.[10]

Carlos wrote that Communist views among the students were understandable because they had "the right to be inexperienced," but he added that it was a serious matter to find military officers "following the example of the students." In an open letter to Vargas, Carlos called War Minister Newton Estillac Leal "a Communist Party accomplice," useful to the party and "not innocent."[11] In part this was because the directorship of the Military Club, of which Estillac Leal was president, favored the "nationalist line," which, Carlos said, was part of the "game of the Communist Party" to create rifts in the preparation of the defense of the Western bloc. Carlos maintained that the "nationalism" of the PCB and the Military Club was harmful to Brazil, which, he wrote, needed foreign capital and technical assistance in petroleum and other areas. Arguing in favor of "loyal and legitimate understandings between Brazil and the United States," Carlos described as "a crime against the national interest . . . all the intrigue presently carried out by people associated with the Vargas government in opposition to an understanding and alliance with the United States." Carlos suggested that the Military Club was offering a deplorable picture "to the world—that is, if the world still takes Brazil seriously" following the nomination of Luzardo (the "Centaur of the Pampas," half man and half horse) to return as ambassador to Buenos Aires.[12]

Early in December 1951 the Vargas administration presented Congress a proposed petroleum law for creating Petrobrás, a government-controlled petroleum extraction company. It would levy a tax on petroleum products to be used for road building and petroleum production, with 80 percent of the shares of Petrobrás going to the central and local governments. The central government's shares, never less than 51 percent, would increase as it took its dividends and interest in the form of new shares. Shares not owned by the central or local governments would be available for sale to nongovernment persons and companies, Brazilian and foreign, and would be represented by one member of the board of directors. The other four board members, appointed by the president of Brazil, would include the Petrobrás president, who would have the right to veto decisions of the board or the executive directorship. Appeals against vetos could be forwarded to the president of Brazil by the board or the executive directorship, in which case he would give his decision after consulting the National Petroleum Council.[13]

Although these arrangements gave more than ample protection against foreign control and left only a small stock interest available to investors other than the Brazilian central and local governments, a veritable furor of condemnation greeted the proposed Petrobrás Law. The PCB, bent on attacking everything Vargas did, was joined by "nationalists" and Vargas opponents, such as UDN leaders. Aliomar Baleeiro (UDN) declared that "Vargas is a prisoner of the oil trusts."[14]

Rômulo de Almeida, author of the proposed law, presented arguments reminiscent of some of Carlos' articles. Pointing to the strict provisions to prevent domination by private capital, Brazilian or foreign, he could see no reason to deprive the enterprise of the participation of that capital. But the *Tribuna*, publishing cartoons of a plump, cigar-smoking Vargas in the arms of foreign trusts, declared sensationally that the projected legislation would give "control of the industry to the trusts without risk or expense." It screamed about "foreign directors" and imagined "capital increases that could deprive the state of control of the company."[15] Vargas, Carlos warned, was proposing an arrangement whereby the money of the Brazilian people would be used so that the "foreign trusts" could participate in Petrobrás and set up their businesses using Brazilian petroleum, not only without financial risk but also without responsibility and without much investment. Seeking to criticize the project in as many ways as possible, Carlos said that Vargas had tried to conciliate two opposing points of view (government monopoly and free competition), "forgetting that synthesis is not a mixture of opposites."[16]

6. The Specter of *Última Hora* (1951–1952)

Among those attacked by the *Tribuna* in 1951 were journalist Samuel Wainer and Gregório Fortunato, chief of the president's 102 palace guards. The *Tribuna* wrote that the "sinister" Gregório, a poorly educated black from Vargas' home town of São Borja, profited from the sale of contraband trucks in an operation assisted by Rio Grande do Sul Interior Secretary João Goulart, friend and São Borja neighbor of Vargas.[1]

More distressing to Carlos, hoping to make a success of the money-losing *Tribuna*, was the activity of Samuel Wainer. Wainer, as a Chateaubriand reporter in 1950, had been practically alone in giving the Vargas candidacy helpful notices in the press, and immediately after the election he explained to the president that the new administration would need some favorable coverage because "in Brazil it is the press that decides." Vargas suggested to the "prophet," as he fondly called Wainer, that he start a newspaper. "Exchange ideas with Alzira, and do so quickly," Vargas said, in a reference to his daughter, the wife of Rio state Governor Ernâni do Amaral Peixoto.[2]

Thus emerged a powerful competitor to the *Tribuna* and all the existing newspapers—powerful because of financial backing supplied by men associated with the new administration, and especially serious to Carlos because Wainer decided on an afternoon newspaper.

Wainer's first task, to find a newspaper printing plant, was facilitated by the bad financial situation of the *Diário Carioca*, which had supported Cristiano Machado for president. The *Diário Carioca*'s directors, José Eduardo de Macedo Soares and Horácio de Carvalho Júnior, were interested in selling Editora de Revistas e Publicações (Érica), which had built a four-story building on Presidente Vargas Avenue for publishing the *Diário Carioca* and which was deeply in debt to the Bank of Brazil and the Caixa Econômica Federal.[3]

The sale of the elaborately furnished building and its less elaborate press for approximately 58 million cruzeiros to a group associated with Wainer was made possible by the members of this new group, mainly Bank of Brazil Superintendent of Money and Credit Walter Moreira Salles, Congressman Euvaldo Lodi, and Bank of Brazil President Ricardo Jafet, all of them past targets of the *Tribuna.* Moreira Salles, whose Banco Moreira Salles had already invested heavily in Érica, took 10 million cruzeiros of the new stock; Jafet used his family bank to put up a similar amount; and Euvaldo Lodi loaned 7 million cruzeiros and furnished a contract whereby SESI would spend 9 million cruzeiros for advertising. The new owners of Érica agreed to assume its old debts and print the *Diário Carioca* for two years.

Following the transfer of Érica, money was needed to launch the newspaper. Some of it came from the Bank of Brazil's initial loan of 63 million cruzeiros, of which 17 million helped complete the Érica purchase and about 10 million was retained by the bank in payment of a loan made to Érica when Dutra was president of Brazil. Industrialist Francisco Matarazzo Júnior, enemy of Assis Chateaubriand, put up 3 million cruzeiros. The financing arrangements were not known at the time and some of the stock purchasers, like Moreira Salles, transferred their shares to the names of third parties. Wainer was especially careful not to allow disclosure of loans from three banks totaling 3 million cruzeiros (to be paid off in advertising in the newspaper) arranged by Minas Governor Kubitschek after Cláudio Medeiros Lima took Wainer to see Kubitschek.[4]

The officerships and shareholder lists of Érica and the new newspaper company revealed the names of Ambassador Carlos Martins Pereira de Souza (president of Érica), Luís Fernando Bocaiuva Cunha (son-in-law of Education Minister Ernesto Simões Filho), Armando Daudt d'Oliveira (son of João), Dinarte Rey Dornelles (nephew of Vargas), a nephew of Matarazzo, and brothers of Senator Napoleão de Alencastro Guimarães and Governor Amaral Peixoto. Bocaiuva Cunha, who left the Bank of Brazil to become vice-president of the newspaper, arranged to purchase, for an insignificant sum, an abandoned title, *Última Hora.*[5]

In April and May 1951, Bank of Brazil President Jafet and Congressman Lutero Vargas assisted the Wainer group in its takeover of an ailing broadcasting company, the Rádio Clube do Brasil, whose debts included about 54 million cruzeiros owed the Bank of Brazil. The arrangement was beneficial to the Rádio Clube's previous owner, Hugo Borghi. Late in 1951 and in 1952, when money was raised to start the São Paulo edition of *Última Hora,* Wainer received much additional financial assistance from Matarazzo and the Bank of Brazil. Congressman Olavo Bilac Pinto (UDN), speaking in Congress in August 1952, announced that altogether the Bank of Brazil had loaned 160 million cruzeiros to Érica and *Última Hora.*[6]

Última Hora's paper supply was assured after João Alberto, on a government trip to the United States and Canada in 1951, entered into agreements at Wainer's request. As a result, the Atlanta Corporation of Canada offered five-year newsprint contracts in Brazil on condition that payments be made or guaranteed by the Bank of Brazil. The only company to make such an arrangement was Érica, on whose behalf the Bank of Brazil guaranteed a payment equivalent to more than 100 million cruzeiros over five years.[7]

Wainer, paying journalists more than they could get elsewhere, put together a talented team, some of whom, like Chief Editor Otávio Malta, Editor Paulo Silveira, and Francisco de Assis Barbosa, had been with *Diretrizes.* Editorial writer Otávio Malta became a right-hand man of Wainer, as did the imaginative superintendent João Etcheverry. Edmar Morel and Nelson Rodrigues joined the reporting staff, along with Medeiros Lima, who broke with Carlos. Wainer found an exceptional page diagramer in André Guevara, a Paraguayan who had worked in Argentina, and talented political cartoonists in Augusto Rodrigues and Lanfranco Vaselli, from Italy, who signed: LAN.[8]

The first number of *Última Hora,* appearing in Rio on June 12, 1951, featured the facsimile of a letter of praise from Vargas. The newspaper had far more pages than the *Tribuna da Imprensa* and its circulation climbed to over 100,000 (and over 150,000 on Mondays when morning papers were not published). Wainer, seeking money for his São Paulo edition even before the Rio *Última Hora* reached its peak, was able to tell Matarazzo that it had "achieved first place or at least second place" in Rio.[9]

Carlos was quick to tell *Tribuna* readers that the "notorious" Wainer had "served the German embassy during the war" and was for sale to the highest bidder. The *Tribuna* stepped up its attacks on Lutero Vargas ("a nonentity"), called Wainer "a Brazilian of the last minute" (*de última hora*), and described *Última Hora* as a newspaper "established by Getúlio for the Communists." At the Seventh Conference of the Inter American Press Association, held in Montevideo in October 1951, Carlos participated in an appeal to parliaments to curb government-subsidized newspapers that competed "in sale and advertising with the independent press." Early in November, when the *Tribuna* disclosed the names of Érica directors and *Última Hora* stockholders, Carlos accused the newspaper of "dumping," by which he meant paying "unreasonably high" salaries, offering advertising space at low rates, and selling the equivalent of 2 1/2 newspapers at a price below the cost of one.[10]

Última Hora accused Carlos of having dismissed *Tribuna* economics reporter Juvenile Pereira in May 1951 for writing an anti-SESI article just when "the last place" *Tribuna,* "influential in foreign capitalist circles" and "a small ultra-reactionary part of the UDN," was about to sign a big "publicity contract" with SESI. The *Tribuna* blamed this "completely untruthful" allegation on Vargas' administrative chief, Lourival Fontes, who, it wrote, had tried to destroy the *Tribuna* by planting two infiltrators among its reporters, Juvenile Pereira and Adão Carrazoni. The dismissal of Pereira, who had been trying to stir up *Tribuna* employees against Carlos, was explained dramatically by Carlos when he called a special meeting of *Tribuna* reporters and read them a letter from Adão Carrazoni to his cousin, Vargas admirer André Carrazoni, describing the work for "resisting" Carlos done by himself and Pereira within the *Tribuna.* After the meeting, Adão Carrazoni left the *Tribuna* to become assistant editor of *Última Hora.*[11]

Replying to questions drawn up by *Última Hora,* the *Tribuna* revealed that its expenses of about a million cruzeiros a month left it with a deficit "common to all newspapers in their first three years." It denied being connected with any foreign group but expressed admiration for the Christian Democratic movements of Italy, France, and Uruguay, respect for the Labour Party of England and the Social Democratic Party of Sweden, and support for many ideas of Franklin D. Roosevelt. It added that it received no political party money and that its director, Carlos Lacerda, had withdrawn from the UDN.[12]

Reporting to the Editôra Tribuna da Imprensa shareholders in March 1952, Carlos said the company's loss in 1951, due to "unfair competition" and soaring paper costs, was 888,282 cruzeiros, compared with a deficit of 1,700,000 cruzeiros in 1950. He went on to tell the stockholders that their company had no debts beyond 2,000,000 cruzeiros loaned by the Bank of Brazil and a 1,150,000 cruzeiro Caixa Econômica loan secured by the Lavradio Street property, whose 4,000,000 cruzeiro value, Carlos said, would increase with the urbanization that was to follow the demolition of the Santo Antônio Hill.[13]

7. *Bamba* and Other Headaches (1951–1952)

The idea of replacing the weekly children's supplement of the *Tribuna* with a separate children's weekly magazine, similar to Catholic magazines successful in France, was encouraged by Bishop Hélder Câmara.[1] Arrangements were made for the magazine, *Bamba,* to be sold at churches and for Geneviève Flusin, who ran the publications in France, to send appropriate material to Graça Carvalho Pierotti, chosen by Carlos to direct the magazine. The publication of the first number, that of June 10, 1951, was celebrated at a balloon-filled party at the Municipal Theater, with entertainment for children, who received their invitations through the schools.[2]

Four of *Bamba*'s eight tabloid pages were devoted to colored comic-strip-form stories and adventures ("to be continued"), with the other pages supplying articles on science, past heroes, and letters from readers. Poet Manuel Bandeira headed a committee of intellectuals, formed for judging the best letters written by schoolchildren in observance of Mother's Day and Father's Day.[3]

In São Paulo, Cardinal Carlos Carmelo de Vasconcelos Mota hailed the appearance of *Bamba.*[4] But it did not catch on. Some found it too sugary, while others argued that Catholicism in families in Brazil was not as strong as in France. Carlos, addressing the Editôra Tribuna da Imprensa stockholders in March 1952, revealed that *Bamba* lost 263,000 cruzeiros in its first six months, but he expressed the hope that it would be possible to continue with the "wholesome" weekly that featured "heroes and not gangsters, adventure and not crime." While vacationing with Letícia in Paris in April 1952, he sent word to Mauricinho, who was running the *Tribuna* with Aluísio Alves, that Geneviève Flusin would be crossing the Atlantic to give new impetus to *Bamba.*[5] But, despite all the French educator could do, *Bamba* by the end of 1952 was such a financial drain that Carlos resolved to

Page one of the first number of *Bamba*, June 10, 1951.

drop it. If he had expected financial assistance from Ação Católica, he was disappointed.[6] He wrote to Dom Hélder Câmara that he had been faithful to the agreement he had made with the bishop to provide "good reading for children" and closed his letter by speaking of the lesson he had learned, "bitter" but "useful."[7]

Already Carlos had broken with the Catholic group associated with the establishment of the *Tribuna.* Dom Lourenço de Almeida Prado, writing to Carlos in April 1952, criticized him for the break and expressed regret at the few opportunities he had to converse with Carlos. Replying on July 30, Carlos said he had not established a newspaper to serve a group, and he reprimanded the group, "morbidly conceited," for its lack of humility and generosity. He complained of the "prima donna Corção" who "disregards the souls that generously approached the Church, and, instead, goes around attracting followers for the informal discussion groups at which he pontificates." Corção, Carlos wrote, "is best seen and read from a distance, and better seen than read, to judge from his last articles." Asking Dom Lourenço where one could find "the group," he said it was not in the Resistência Democrática, which had fallen apart due to "conflicting vanities." Nor, Carlos added harshly, was it at the São Bento Monastery where people "in truth know very little. They know of themselves, and very poorly, or else excessively well, and have . . . , like the Marxists, replies for all questions, prefabricated solutions for all problems, by means of the simple application of a code."[8]

Carlos' break with "the group" coincided with the disintegration of the *Tribuna*'s consultive council, which, Walter Cunto has remarked, "tried to patrol even minor matters."[9] Sobral Pinto had already left, stating that the council's rules had been ignored. Gustavo Corção and Dario de Almeida Magalhães resigned in February 1952 after Carlos, without consulting them, assailed Assis Chateaubriand's candidacy to be senator from Paraíba.[10] More departures followed. The last to leave was Alceu Amoroso Lima, who did not participate in deliberations because he spent two years in the United states directing the cultural department of the Organization of American States. He returned to Brazil in April 1953 to find that the *Tribuna*'s experiment with a consultive council had been abandoned. Carlos, unwilling to put up with interference, also scuttled plans to start a São Paulo weekly magazine when it developed that business leaders there, who were to finance it, demanded an effective voice in the editorial policy.[11]

Sales of the *Tribuna* depended so much on Carlos' editorials that his travels abroad in 1952 had an adverse effect, as Mauricinho, writing to Paris, told him in April. The decline was no fault of the alert, 13-year-old Sérgio, who wrote to his vacationing parents that, on Copacabana Avenue, he found a youthful newspaper vendor shouting "*Cruzeiro, Globo, Última Hora.*" "I gave him five cruzeiros," Sérgio wrote, "to yell '*Tribuna da Imprensa!*' It was a marvel. The *Tribuna* went ahead of *O Cruzeiro, O Globo,* etc."[12]

The European vacation, following an Inter American Press Association trip to Panama, lasted almost three months. Writer João Condé, who joined

Carlos and Letícia in Paris, found that Carlos, more than Letícia, enjoyed staying up all night, fraternizing in restaurants with natives and tourists.[13]

Late in July, after returning to Rio, Carlos wrote to Andrew Heiskell, of Time-Life, that his long absence in Europe and battle with *Última Hora* made it unlikely that he could get to Chicago for the Eighth Conference of the Inter American Press Association. But Carlos had been elected secretary-general of the association at the Montevideo conference in 1951, and in the end he yielded to pleas that he go to Chicago.[14] There he worked to have the 1953 conference take place in São Paulo. And he gathered information for the *Tribuna* about the Dwight Eisenhower–Adlai Stevenson presidential election. "What Brazil needs," he concluded, "is a Brazilian who is like Stevenson."[15]

Stopping in Washington after the Chicago meeting, Carlos was visiting *Time*'s William W. White and his wife Connie when he met John Dos Passos. "From the livingroom," Dos Passos wrote, "I could hear a voice with a foreign accent pronouncing the words 'Oopaylong Ca-seedy.' Immediately I was introduced to a tall strikingly handsome man. In one hand he was brandishing a pearlhandled cap pistol. A glittering holster was draped over one shoulder. Perched on his head above his shellrimmed glasses was a small boy's cowboy hat. . . . His high spirits were catching. He shared our taste for the absurd." After Carlos left, the Whites told Dos Passos, "He's the nicest man in Brazil."[16]

8. Widely Heralded Prisoner (December 1952)

For several days in September 1952 the *Tribuna*'s first page was filled with facsimiles of documents showing lists of policemen and the monthly payoff received by each for overlooking prostitution.[1] Therefore the police, in a position to jail the two women who had written the payoff lists, persuaded them to deny the authenticity of the lists. The police also invaded the office of lawyer Hilário Ruy Rolim, who had furnished the lists to the *Tribuna*, and, by threatening him with a revolver, obtained his signature on a statement describing the lists as false. "This newspaper," the *Tribuna* then wrote, "has the complete collection of autographed lists of the two brothel associates of the Thirteenth Police District." "19 creatures exploited by official ruffians!" the *Tribuna* screamed.[2]

At courtroom hearings in October and November, the two women said the lists were false and Rolim told of the threat to his life by the police. Carlos, summoned early in November by Delegado José Picorelli to testify in court, wrote Picorelli that such testimony was unnecessary to prove police corruption, revealed in detail in the *Tribuna*, and that he would not "participate in any farce." Asserting that Rolim was not alone in receiving threats, Carlos said the Lacerda family had been receiving them constantly on the telephone ever since the *Tribuna* had published the lists of policemen.[3]

Late in November Carlos telegraphed Justice Minister Negrão de Lima to advise that, after being summoned again by Picorelli, he had replied that he would appear only under arrest. The guilty parties, he told Negrão, were turning the inquiry into a show in which the accusers were becoming the accused and the victims, due to fear, were becoming accomplices of criminals.[4]

The judge who presided at the inquiry, now chiefly a police case against Rolim, gave Picorelli an order for Carlos' arrest based on the Estado Novo's national security law of 1938. The arrest, made at the *Tribuna* on the afternoon of December 1 by police investigators and a court officer, was not unexpected in journalistic and political circles. It was announced by a long blast of the *Tribuna*'s siren and then, more explicitly, by radio stations. Many people accompanied Carlos and most of the *Tribuna* personnel when they went in the rain to the police headquarters on Relação Street.[5]

In getting himself arrested during his campaign against police corruption, Carlos gained admirers and, Wainer would add, increased the sales of the *Tribuna*.[6] The crowd at Relação Street was enormous. It was filled with congressmen, three of whom asked Picorelli the reason for the arrest. Picorelli complained that Carlos had scrawled a note on the back of a judicial summons, refusing to comply unless arrested. "The judge," Picorelli added, "decreed his arrest for slandering and insulting public authority." "But," PSD Congressman Armando Falcão persisted, "what is the legal basis?" Picorelli spoke of the 1938 National Security Law, whereupon Carlos declared that he felt honored to be held under a "fascist law of the Estado Novo."[7]

Using microphones of radio station broadcasters, Carlos delivered a speech. In a scene reminiscent of those in which his father had participated, he expressed pride at being jailed for "the crime of defending the interests of the people of the Federal District." He told the crowd and radio listeners that Brazilian soldiers had fought in Italy so that the Mussolini-like fascist laws of the Estado Novo would be exterminated.[8]

The crowd, still growing, went with Carlos from prison to prison while orders about the place of his confinement were altered. Finally a small room at the barracks of the Military Police on Evaristo da Veiga Street was made available.

The room could not possibly hold all the representatives of political groups that wished to show support for the prisoner. One group after another, such as the Rio state assembly, the PSB, the PL, and the Resistência Democrática, resolved to send representatives. Former President Dutra sent PSD Congressman Lopo Coelho. UDN leaders Prado Kelly and Odilon Braga went to the barracks, where visitors included members of Rio society who had never met Carlos. Among the writers were Carlos Drummond de Andrade and Manuel Bandeira. Lawyers phoned the *Tribuna*, offering their services to help defend Carlos.[9]

The press condemned the arrest, with Aluísio Alves writing in the *Tribuna* that the denouncement of crimes had resulted in the imprisonment only of the journalist who had revealed the "cancer that corrodes the Federal District police." Congressmen affixed their signatures to a habeas corpus petition, drawn up by Adauto Lúcio Cardoso and Sobral Pinto, that pointed out that Carlos was not a defendant in the accusation filed against

Rolim by thirty-two policemen. In the Municipal Council, where UDN leader Mário Martins described all Brazilian newspapers as threatened, even PTB and PCB councilmen went along with the motion to send a commission to the barracks to express support for Carlos.[10]

Supporters of Carlos filled the meeting room of the Supreme Court on December 2, when the justices, considering the habeas corpus petition, heard Sobral Pinto argue that the imprisonment order amounted to an unjust sentence. In a unanimous decision the court ruled that Carlos should be released.[11]

In front of the barracks, Carlos delivered a speech to a rejoicing throng, thanking the people for their support. The throng, joining Carlos in a triumphant march to Lavradio Street, was greeted by a celebrating blast from the *Tribuna*'s siren. Carlos' handwritten statement, thanking God for the opportunity to serve the cause of liberty, was reproduced on the first page of the next day's *Tribuna.* On the editorial page, the political cartoon showed a ball and chain attached to a typewriter. The editorial column was a large blank space above the signature of Carlos Lacerda.[12]

A week later, Rio Police Chief Ciro de Rezende was replaced by General Armando de Morais Âncora.

9. "Help Your Brother" (February–March 1953)

Corruption and mismanagement, Carlos maintained, were characteristics of government programs to deal with the drought that started, in 1951, to ravage the already backward and impoverished northeast. The reports that he wrote about his trips to Ceará and Rio Grande do Norte in 1951 and 1953 described thousands of scrawny people living in the equivalent of sheep corrals and dying so fast that he asked a doctor, the only doctor in a community of thirty thousand, whether he had time to sign all the death certificates.[1] A relief station in Ceará, he reported, was run by a crook, appointed by the labor ministry, who enriched himself by selling in Fortaleza both the food sent to the relief station and the truck-farm produce raised by unpaid drought victims.[2]

According to Carlos, funds announced by the government for building dams and roads had not been provided and therefore the contractors and equipment suppliers made charges that ate deeply into the fifteen cruzeiros (fifty cents U.S. currency) per day that workers were supposed to receive.[3] In the south of Rio Grande do Norte, where people tried to survive on *macambira,* a kind of cactus, a local legislator suggested that Vargas, "the father of the poor," had better come quickly if he wanted to see his "children" before they died.[4]

In Limoeiro do Norte, Ceará, in February 1953, Carlos and Victor Coelho Bouças, son of Valentim Bouças, found children using tin cans, trying to deepen a hole in the ground in the hope of reaching water. In nearby Ibicuitinga, a village of about five hundred, tears rolled down the cheeks of Carlos as he looked at the children, their faces marked by extreme suffering and untimely maturity.[5] The *Tribuna* carried gruesome accounts.

In his talk at the ABI in 1951, which was published as a book, Carlos proposed that engineering projects be accompanied by programs that would lead to "the social and human recuperation of the northeasterner."[6] His audience at the ABI in 1953, which included congressmen, heard him criticize Vargas' plan to redistribute land by expropriating large holdings adjoining dams built with government help. The danger, Carlos said, lay in dividing the land excessively, with the creation of "legions of semifamished owners" of small, unviable parcels.[7]

Carlos' talk in 1953 was accompanied by photographs and tape recordings that vividly revealed the plight of drought victims. A purpose was to raise money for the "Help Your Brother" (Ajuda Teu Irmão) campaign, begun on February 12, 1953, by the *Tribuna*. The campaign started out well, with the governors of Minas and São Paulo expressing support and Aviation Minister Nero Moura offering planes to carry food to the stricken area.[8]

Soon after the campaign began, *Última Hora* published an article harmful to "Help Your Brother" and signed by Vargas' wife Darcy, who headed the assistance campaign of the Legião Brasileira de Assistência (LBA). Concerned about the bickering between the two campaigns, Carlos arranged to call on Darcy at Catete Palace.[9] He was accompanied by the 14-year-old Sérgio, whom he planned to take, later that night, to the house he had been building in Samambaia, near Petrópolis.

Darcy had an injured ankle, and Carlos and Sérgio found her in bed, with copies of the pro-government *Última Hora* and *O Radical* on the bed covers. After Sérgio gallantly kissed Darcy's hand, she said, "So you are the son of that demon who makes his living by attacking us." Carlos said she would see that he was not as devilish as he had been described to her, and he proposed that the efforts of the government in the northeast be augmented by those of oppositionists.[10]

"I have come," Carlos said, "from the northeast, where I saw airforce planes taking avocados sent by the LBA. Those people have never seen avocados and won't eat them. As a result . . . , they are being offered for sale at any price in the Mossoró market without finding buyers." Carlos added that

"Help Your Brother" campaign twenty-cruzeiro note.

some people, not playing their role properly, sold provisions sent to the northeast by the LBA.

Darcy agreed that not everything worked out perfectly and agreed also to Carlos' suggestion that he and she continue to do the best they could. Asking Carlos not to create obstacles for the LBA, she reminded him that he had written articles against her and her pet charity, Girls' Town. Carlos warned her against reading the newspapers he saw on her bed and said his chief criticism of Girls' Town was its excessively expensive entrance gate. He claimed his opposition to the Vargas government, made without hatred for Vargas, was a useful service. Before her visitors left, Darcy told Sérgio, "I hope you won't grow up to be like your father. Use your intelligence, which you must have inherited from him, for more constructive things."[11]

On February 24, the *Tribuna* applauded the LBA and announced that Darcy supported "Help Your Brother." In the month that followed, the *Tribuna*'s front page carried news of contributions to its campaign, such as trucks loaned by Drault Ernâni and fifty tons of condensed milk donated by the Nestlé Company. Money sent to the *Tribuna* helped move flour, beans, corn, beef jerky, and manioc meal to the northeast by steamer, trucks, and planes.[12]

Before long, Carlos said later, the LBA "absorbed everything." But he concluded that the *Tribuna*'s campaign "forced the official government organs" to take steps that were necessary. The campaign also marked the initiation of the politically important association of Carlos with Rádio Globo broadcaster Raul Brunini, who interviewed him about "Help Your Brother" and assisted the campaign.[13]

10. Precarious Relations with Jânio Quadros (1953)

When the Vargas administration abandoned its original Petrobrás project in July 1952 and joined the UDN and others to ensure the enactment of a government petroleum extraction monopoly, Carlos accused the president of trying to use "an obsolete and suicidal nationalism to save what remains of his popularity." The UDN, Carlos said, was "inventing a new type of conspiracy against the regime: the conspiracy of adhering to the government."[1]

But when the UDN, rejecting the "nationalism" of the Left, joined the government in calling for legislative approval of the Brazil–United States Military Agreement, the *Tribuna* was pleased. It was also pleased that UDN leaders, early in 1953, defeated the bid of "nationalist" Gabriel Passos to head the party. Welcoming the selection of Congressman Artur Santos, the *Tribuna* described Gabriel Passos as having been backed by Vargas and *Última Hora* in a move to weaken the UDN.[2]

In São Paulo early in 1953, the UDN joined the major parties in nominating Professor Francisco Antônio Cardoso for mayor. Although the *Tribuna* wrote that Cardoso was certain to win,[3] Carlos kept his eye on Jânio Quadros, the thin, indignant state legislator who, as the candidate of the Socialist and Christian Democratic Parties (PSB and PDC), was making a spirited race for mayor—the campaign of "the nickel (*tostão*) against the million" of

Jânio Quadros. (Hilde Weber drawing in Hilde Weber, *O Brasil em Charges, 1950–1985*)

the powerful. Thousands of humble voters, stirred by Jânio's call for a change, brandished the brooms that he cried out were necessary to sweep away the thieves, the shady dealers, and the inept who took personal advantage of power instead of serving the people.[4]

As far back as 1951, Carlos had sent a note to young journalist Luiz Ernesto Kawall, head of the *Tribuna*'s small São Paulo office, saying "Who is that Jânio Quadros, who is becoming so noticeable in São Paulo? Interview him."[5] Kawall, calling on Quadros again in March 1953, reported in the *Tribuna* that the candidate for mayor had "the mustache of Nietzsche and the eyes of Bette Davis." Quadros promised to wipe out Ademarismo, Kawall wrote, and kept a picture of Vargas at his campaign headquarters "for stimulating the work of the labor group."[6]

Quadros' surprising victory over Cardoso, by 284,922 votes to 115,055, gave the "Jânio Quadros phenomenon" an assured political future. What worried Carlos was Quadros' evident connection with the PTB, which, although a member of the Cardoso coalition, had picked Quadros' successful running mate. Equally worrisome were the reports that Jânio, immediately after his victory, had secretly visited Vargas. Carlos, in an editorial on March 26, wrote: "Jânio Quadros with Getúlio Vargas? Only an insane suicidal person would unite his ascending career with the declining one of the demagogue." Carlos suggested that Quadros not capitulate to temptation and insisted that the election outcome had been a defeat for Getúlio, Ademar, and the PCB as well as a good lesson for the UDN and PSD. A Hilde cartoon on March 28 showed a perplexed Quadros between the bulky figures of Ademar de Barros and Getúlio Vargas, who seemed to be trying to control him.[7]

Deciding to take the matter up directly with Quadros, Carlos called on him at his home in São Paulo early in April. He found the mayor-elect in the company of local Socialist Party leaders and was impressed by his "incredibly rapid mind" and interest in problems affecting the public. But Carlos failed to obtain the clear anti-Vargas statement he wanted from Quadros.[8]

Carlos stuck close to the new mayor when he came to Rio on April 20 to address the Municipal Council and touch base with PSB and PDC leaders. At the *Tribuna* office, Quadros made a reference to "the illustrious Carlos Lacerda" in a handwritten message expressing hope for the "abandoned multitudes." Carlos, after seeing Quadros off at the airport, wrote a column in which he said he well appreciated how Municipal Councilman Mário Martins felt when he remarked that Quadros "appears to be a man prepared to die for his beliefs."[9]

After Quadros visited the São Paulo office of *Última Hora* and lavished praise on the pro-Vargas daily, an irritated Carlos phoned him. During the phone conversation, Carlos reported, Quadros dictated a statement of support for Carlos' campaign against Wainer and said that the visit to *Última Hora* had been a mere matter of routine. But then *Última Hora* published another declaration—also authorized by Quadros—in which the mayor contradicted the statement recently dictated to Carlos.[10]

Late in 1953 Carlos was aware that Quadros, considering PTB support for his gubernatorial bid, had been calling on Vargas. Nevertheless he and Otávio Mangabeira met with Quadros at the São Paulo home of anti-Vargas writer Paulo Duarte to ask him to speak at, and help promote, a "non-party" Moral Recuperation rally to be sponsored by São Paulo university students. Quadros, in accepting, suggested the Ipiranga independence monument as the location. When Carlos asked why the rally should be held so far from the center of the city, Quadros replied that he would make sure plenty of people got there.[11]

Carlos, returning to São Paulo for the December 12 rally, was surprised to find the city devoid of posters announcing it. Later, at the hotel where Mangabeira was staying, he was shocked to learn from Janistas that Jânio would not attend. Jânio's gubernatorial candidacy, he was told, "will be liquidated if he goes to a rally with you people, sworn adversaries of the government."

Carlos, indignant, replied that Quadros could not deal so falsely with old Mangabeira, often jailed and long exiled for his ideals. "Go tell that miserable wretch that either he goes to the rally . . . , or I'll turn it into the greatest attack he has ever received in his life. I'll dedicate my life to unmasking that bum. I'll say everything I know and even things I don't know. Never will I allow a quiet moment for him, deceiver of the people!"[12]

At the Ipiranga monument only about five hundred people showed up. Antigovernment speeches were under way when Jânio, bundled in a dark coat and scarf, made his entrance. After embracing Mangabeira he spoke to Carlos to criticize São Paulo Governor Lucas Nogueira Garcez for having decided to stay away. He said he had come despite being sick.

The UNE president attacked the corruption of Ademar, Paulo Duarte attacked Vargas, and Mangabeira attacked immorality. When Carlos attacked

Última Hora, the audience, in a chorus, shouted "thieves, thieves." Quadros told the gathering that, no matter what the cost, he would never refuse invitations "such as this one" made to him by students.

Back in Rio, Carlos published an editorial, "The fear of being honorable," which attributed the "unpopularity" of Governor Garcez to his timidity. The *Tribuna* described the rally as a great success notwithstanding the efforts of *Última Hora.* São Paulo, it said, had been filled with the appropriate posters and a multitude of six thousand had attended.[13]

VI.

Dethroner of Vargas (1953–1954)

1. Congress Investigates the Wainer Group (June–November 1953)

The turn in events that would give a new dimension to the career of Carlos and play a role in the collapse of the Vargas administration began with the *Tribuna's* publication on May 20, 1953, of an interview that never took place. It appeared under a headline announcing that the Bank of Brazil had recently named an *interventor* to take a hand in the affairs of Érica and try to recover "squandered" money loaned when Jafet headed the bank. Natalício Norberto, a young *Tribuna* reporter, quoted Herófilo Azambuja, the "*interventor*" whom he had not interviewed, as saying that the bank had for some time been planning this step.[1]

During the ensuing denials, Carlos tried unsuccessfully, by telegrams and phone calls, to reach Azambuja, who was in Rio Grande do Sul. *Última Hora* and Érica sued the *Tribuna de Imprensa* for twenty million cruzeiros, saying they would use the money to build a hospital for journalists. The credit manager and president of the Bank of Brazil declared that no intervention existed.

Reporter Norberto left the *Tribuna* and joined *Última Hora,* where he issued a statement saying that Lacerda had pressured him into writing the false interview and accusing the *Tribuna* of failing to support him. In the *Tribuna,* Carlos Castello Branco wrote that Norberto's complaints were unfounded and that when he had expressed fear of being seized and beaten by enemies of the *Tribuna,* members of the *Tribuna* staff had offered him protection in their homes.[2]

Carlos, whose reaction to a reverse was to take the offensive, met with the *Tribuna* reporters. He enlisted their support for a full-scale campaign against *Última Hora,* a move that prompted his brother Mauricinho to tell him, "You are in a canoe trying to sink a cruiser."

Carlos turned to Armando Falcão, gave him information about the "*Última Hora* scandal," and suggested he speak in Congress. Falcão, delivering the speech two days after the Azambuja "interview," said that the finance ministry was reducing credits for public works in his home state of Ceará at the same time that government money was flowing to the Wainer group. He suggested that the time had come for an investigation.[3]

Within the next few days Falcão collected 110 signatures of congressmen on his petition for a CPI (Parliamentary Commission of Inquiry) about the Wainer group. To counter this move, Education Minister Simões Filho, father-in-law of *Última Hora*'s "Baby" Bocaiuva Cunha, persuaded another congressman to collect signatures on a petition for a CPI to investigate the financing of all the Brazilian media. Pleased that this new proposal attracted the signatures of 122 congressmen, Wainer wrote Vargas that "the rat has been caught in his own trap" and that, "as we have liquidated Lacerda in the area of journalism, our plan now is to give him a knockout in the congressional area." In a letter to Alzira Vargas do Amaral Peixoto, Wainer wrote that he would appreciate some help. It would be well, he said, to have the Bank of Brazil president refuse to allow that confidentiality, or secrecy, in banking operations be violated and to have the PSD bear in mind, in appointing members of the commission, that a "decent commission" was necessary. "The PTB," he added, "has already chosen Frota Aguiar, our friend."[4]

As it developed, Anésio Frota Aguiar was less than helpful to Wainer and played a key role as *relator* (official reporter) of CPI 313 that investigated Érica. The commission's seven-man membership (the same as that of the inactive commission to study all the media) consisted of three PSD congressmen and two from the UDN, in addition to Frota Aguiar (PTB) and commission president Carlos Castilho Cabral (PSP, São Paulo). While CPI 313 was getting organized, the *Tribuna* published a letter from Wainer to Lutero Vargas about a block of Rádio Clube shares that Lutero had received in April 1951 as a gift from Wainer and had decided in August 1952 to return to Wainer. The *Tribuna* used the expression "sea of mud" to describe the Bank of Brazil's business with the "chief of the Mangue Gang"—a reference to Wainer and the Mangue prostitution district near the Érica building.[5]

For five months the CPI kept the media supplied with revelations as it questioned Carlos, Wainer, Lutero Vargas, Walter Moreira Salles (ambassador to the United States), Jafet, Lodi, Count Matarazzo, João Alberto, Bank of Brazil President Anápio Gomes, and eighteen other witnesses. It became evident that the Wainer group owed the Bank of Brazil almost 200 million cruzeiros including the 64 million Rádio Clube debt and excluding money the bank put up for newsprint contracted by Érica. The country gradually learned about the SESI publicity contracts and the financial involvements of Moreira Salles, Jafet, and Lodi, and it learned that 12 million cruzeiros were supplied by Matarazzo for *Última Hora* of São Paulo.[6] This Matarazzo money, transferred with the help of Lutero Vargas, had made it possible to start the São Paulo newspaper in March 1952 in a plant purchased from Jafet.[7] Transactions for establishing *Última Hora* of Porto Alegre, the country learned, were still being negotiated.

During the CPI hearings, Carlos spoke to the nation several nights a week on the radio, usually Rádio Globo. He commented on the testimonies of the CPI witnesses and introduced newly discovered documents about Wainer, dug up in large part by the inspired *Tribuna* team. People gathered on the streets at places where his voice on the radio could be heard. The places in Rio were many, according to Stefan Baciu, who writes that "the voice of the crusader, preaching the salvation of Brazil and denouncing the 'sea of mud,'" could be heard from "all the windows." Listeners wrote or telephoned the *Tribuna* (its phones rang constantly) to submit information they felt would be harmful to Wainer, and some even sent money. Reporter Hermano Alves was put in charge of making a daily résumé of developments.[8]

In April 1953 the ambitious Wainer had started publishing a popular weekly Rio magazine, *Flan.* Therefore Assis Chateaubriand, whose empire included the weekly *O Cruzeiro,* intensified attacks on Wainer in the Diários Associados and made TV Tupi available to Carlos.[9]

Although Carlos had not broadcast on television before, it was soon apparent that his personality and delivery, described by Professor Marvin Alisky as "slightly conversational but authoritative" in tone, would make him Brazil's leading political television figure. Techniques that Carlos had learned from watching Fulton J. Sheen in the United States were put to good use. Marcelo Garcia concluded that "Carlos Lacerda's handling of blackboard charts on television was the most effective part of the campaign against Wainer." Viewers, who might have been puzzled by the complicated financial dealings and relationships between companies, publications, and individuals, watched Carlos explain organization charts whose lines connected the presidential palace and Bank of Brazil with the "*golpista* clique," the "group of shady dealers," and the Érica companies.[10]

Radio and television were also used by PTB politicians who sided with Wainer. They told their listeners that the defense of *Última Hora* was as patriotic as the "Petroleum Is Ours" campaign, and they described opponents of Lodi and Matarazzo as men who worked for foreigners. São Paulo State Assemblyman José Antônio Rogê Ferreira declared on television that Lacerda, "at the service of Chateaubriand," was an "antinational monster."[11]

Labor union members, meeting at Rio's João Caetano Theater, called for the invasion of the *Tribuna.* Such calls, coupled with rumors about plans to beat up or kill some of its reporters, led *Tribuna* printers to turn to iron bars as arms and reporters to consider carrying revolvers. Carlos obtained a licence to carry a revolver and brought one to the office, although he remarked casually that he did not know how to use it. Perhaps the revolver was a good idea. A retired police investigator was offered 100,000 cruzeiros to murder Carlos, but he declined the offer and the man who made it killed himself playing Russian roulette before he could proceed further with his scheme.[12]

Wainer, recalling that not a single newspaper defended *Última Hora,* has told of the bitterness he felt when *Correio de Manhã*'s Antônio Callado concluded that Carlos Lacerda was sacrificing himself for Brazil whereas Wainer would give the country nothing. José Eduardo de Macedo Soares, writing in the *Diário Carioca,* praised Lacerda for having discovered and denounced the "scandal" brought about by Vargas, who, Macedo Soares said, "never understood the intangibility of the moral power of the free press." In *O Jornal,* Assis Chateaubriand scolded Vargas for "not believing what I told

Vargas sitting on the investigation of the Bank of Brazil. (Hilde Weber drawing in Hilde Weber, *O Brasil em Charges, 1950–1985*)

him and insisting on traveling" with only one journalist, Wainer, who, Chateaubriand said, was now using that relationship for the worst sort of blackmail, threatening the free press. In the *Diário de Notícias,* Rafael Corrêa de Oliveira condemned "the crooks of the presidential palace." This was a favorite theme of the PCB's *Imprensa Popular,* which delighted in picturing Vargas in the company of "embezzling sharks," such as Matarazzo. It called Wainer a lackey of the Vargas regime, a swindler, and the beneficiary of an assault on the Bank of Brazil.[13]

Carlos, the first witness of the CPI, spoke in a calm, pleasant manner hardly in keeping with his editorials. Discussing his own financial situation, he mentioned his income from his work and his debt of 200,000 cruzeiros, most of which had been spent on his Samambaia home near Petrópolis. He owned six shares of *Tribuna* stock and a one-eighth interest in the *chácara* that had belonged to his grandfather. He explained also that he, Mauricinho, and Vera had owned a small plot in Vassouras but had given it and a house, financed by the sale of a part of the plot, to their mother. Speaking of the Wainer group, he had so many details to offer that his appearance in June occupied the commission for three days.

The lanky Wainer, second CPI witness, said the Bank of Brazil carried on financial operations with many newspapers and radio stations. "The great crime of which we are accused," he said, "is that of being loyal friends of Getúlio Vargas. The most deceitful insinuations have been made about our supposed prestige in the government, but no one has shown that we have obtained any personal advantages or privileges."[14]

After Wainer sent Frota Aguiar a memorandum explaining that "professional secrecy" prevented him from revealing the names of his financial backers, the CPI went to the courts to force him to talk. Wainer's lawyer, Hariberto de Miranda Jordão, argued that the CPI was not "a juridical personality," but he lost the case in the Seventh District Court, whose judge punished Wainer with a fifteen-day prison sentence.

Starting to serve his term on July 20 at the barracks of the Military Police, Wainer gave a lively interview to an *Última Hora* reporter, in which he called Assis Chateaubriand "that old gangster of the yellow press," UDN Congressman Aliomar Baleeiro "a sordid criminal," and Armando Falcão "a rat" and a thief. Carlos Lacerda, he said, was a moral degenerate, director of an insignificant, failing little bulletin, who had contributed nothing to journalism and was known throughout Brazil for mudslinging. Taking his cue from reports that Carlos had testified against Maurício in the case of the latter's separation from Olga, Wainer added that Carlos did not hesitate to smear his own family.[15]

One day later, the judge of the twenty-fourth District Court, who had put Carlos in jail in December, issued a habeas corpus decree freeing Wainer from prison and from the obligation of answering questions about his financial backers. The CPI, calling the author of the decree a "manifestly incompetent" judge, stopped questioning witnesses and awaited a superior court decision about the conflict between the judges of the seventh and twenty-fourth districts. This decision, delivered by the local superior court on July 27, unanimously supported the habeas corpus decree. At the Military Police barracks, rejoicing *Última Hora* employees greeted the released Wainer with fireworks. However, on August 5, the Supreme Court, in a unanimous decision, upheld the original fifteen-day prison sentence. Wainer, still refusing to disclose names sought by the CPI, returned to prison. The CPI called witnesses again.[16]

On July 30, while the Supreme Court decision was awaited, Vargas signed a decree, recommended by Transport Minister José Américo, closing the financially troubled Rádio Clube because Wainer had transferred most of the shares to writer Marques Rebello without obtaining permission from the transport ministry. The decree, based on this technicality, left Wainer with the Rádio Clube debt. Even worse, it informed the public, including *Última Hora* advertisers, that Vargas could not be counted on to help Wainer.[17]

With newsprint prices declining, Érica bought paper from sources less costly than the Atlanta Corporation, leaving the Bank of Brazil with an abundance of invoices and newsprint, whose dimensions were inappropriate for newspapers other than *Última Hora.* Marcós de Sousa Dantas, who replaced General Anápio Gomes as the bank's president in August 1953, was unable to get Érica to pay for the paper, storage, and interest charges, and therefore the bank renegotiated the contract with Atlanta, which agreed to reduce the price and supply a more conventional size of newsprint.[18]

Érica, like the Rádio Clube do Brasil and the company publishing *Última Hora* of São Paulo, was in arrears on payments due the bank. *Última Hora* of Rio, however, was up-to-date, thanks to financial assistance received from two former Vargas cabinet ministers who became officers of the organization, Danton Coelho and Simões Filho (father-in-law of "Baby" Bocaiuva Cunha).[19]

With Danton Coelho, Carlos exchanged nasty letters, which were made public. He also went after Bank of Brazil President Sousa Dantas, accused by the *Tribuna* of not taking action against Wainer for numerous crimes, such as issuing checks without funds, not complying with the Atlanta contract, and buying Érica shares with a Bank of Brazil loan intended for buying equipment. When Carlos learned that Sousa Dantas was to be offered a dinner by friends who disapproved of the *Tribuna* attack, he sent him a telegram calling him "the protector of public thieves" and adherent "to the corrupt oligarchy that devours this country."[20]

The CPI's final report, issued on November 3, said that the loans to Wainer could only be explained as the result of influence in high places and it quoted witnesses who attributed the loans to the interest of Vargas. Wainer's lawyer, in a rebuttal written on November 4, called the report a political document, full of personal opinions and lies, that described acts by private companies as "criminal" although no laws had been broken. He accused the CPI of seeking to have the federal legislature exceed its constitutional powers. He could find no legal reason why Wainer should reveal the names of his financial backers, and he said that Érica, months before, would have secured a price reduction for Atlanta paper except that former Bank of Brazil President Anápio Gomes had ruled against the modification.

Congressman Orlando Dantas, defending *Última Hora* and Lodi, alluded to "hidden interests." The attacks, he said, began after *Última Hora* and Lodi supported the "Petroleum Is Ours" campaign and after Lodi urged that Brazilian resources be protected from American industries. Lutero Vargas, presenting Carlos Lacerda as an agent of anti-Vargas United States diplomats, cites Wainer and others who have argued that the campaign against *Última Hora* was guided by the "Momsen law firm of Rio de Janeiro, an American firm that was closely associated with Standard Oil" and "whose Brazilian partner was José Nabuco."[21]

In March 1954 the CPI findings were forwarded to the Eighth District Court, together with the accusations of a prosecuting attorney against Wainer, Lutero Vargas, Lodi, Bocaiuva Cunha, Jafet, and a Bank of Brazil loan officer. Jafet and two of his relatives were charged with improper handling of public money, Lutero with lying, and Wainer with "dumping," fraud, and false testimony. Lutero Vargas and Lodi, the judge pointed out, were protected by congressional immunities.[22]

2. "Samuel Wainer, Born in Bessarabia" (1953–1954)

According to Carlos, the *Tribuna*'s interest in investigating Wainers' nationality was sparked at the height of the *Última Hora* controversy, when suggestions "from all directions" were reaching the *Tribuna*. A woman, who felt it safer to remain anonymous, phoned to say that a study of the records of prewar immigration from Russia or Romania would reveal that Wainer was not a Brazilian.[1]

Proof of Wainer's foreign nationality would make it impossible, under Brazilian legislation, for him to run a Brazilian newspaper. Therefore, after the anonymous call, the *Tribuna* team set to work, in Rio and São Paulo, to find documents about the Wainer family. Some of the work was done in the government registries of foreigners and marriages.[2]

The result was a bombshell, described by the *Diário de S. Paulo* as "the most sensational statement made since the *Última Hora* scandal burst upon us." Speaking on TV Tupi in Rio on July 14, 1953, in front of a blackboard showing family names and dates, Carlos declared that Samuel Wainer was neither a native nor a naturalized Brazilian but had been born in Bessarabia at a time when the former Russian province had been a part of Romania. Carlos accused Wainer and two of his brothers of having made false declarations about their Brazilian nationality.

Carlos held up documents to show his audience that Wainer's father Chaim (Jaime in Portuguese), on obtaining his foreigner's identity certificate in 1943, had declared that he had arrived in Brazil in 1920 and that Wainer's mother Dora, when applying for a similar certificate in 1942, had stated that she had arrived for the first time in 1915 on the *Valdivia*. The couple, obtaining a Brazilian marriage certificate in São Paulo in 1943, had confirmed those arrival dates. And since Samuel Wainer was born in 1912, Carlos explained, he could not have been born in Brazil. Therefore, Carlos charged, Samuel had committed a falsehood in declaring, for his 1935 marriage certificate and other papers, that he was a native of São Paulo. Carlos added that Samuel's brothers Artur, José, and Marcos, born in 1903, 1905, and 1914, were also foreigners. Dora Wainer, after viewing Carlos' television presentation, asked her son Samuel, "Why does he hate you so much? He was always at our home and was such a nice young man."[3]

According to Carlos' later testimony, a second phone call from the unknown woman suggested a search of records at the German School or Pedro II School in Rio. Carlos was thrilled when reporter Hermano Alves told him about the records at the Pedro II School, where Artur Wainer had enrolled his 14-year-old brother Samuel in 1927. Artur had informed the school, in statements signed in February and April 1927, that Samuel was a native of Edenitz, Romania. Speaking on television in São Paulo on July 17, Carlos showed the public the photographs of the relevant pages from the Pedro II records.[4] Artur Wainer, in reply, said he had been untruthful when he had enrolled Samuel at the school. "My father," Samuel explained, "considered his children as having his own nationality; he was planning to return to Europe, which he never did."[5]

The director of the Department of Immigration, a section of the labor ministry, furnished a certified copy of the list of passengers who had disembarked in Rio on January 5, 1905, after crossing the Atlantic on the *Canárias*, and it included the names of Jaime and Dora Wainer. *Última Hora* published this certified list and announced that it settled the matter, conclusively and definitively.[6] But on July 20, Carlos expressed the conviction that the list was false for two reasons: (1) Chaim Wainer could not have disembarked with the Brazilian name of Jaime, which he only adopted after deciding to stay in Brazil, and (2) the director of the Department of Immigration had obstinately refused *Tribuna* reporters access to the documents.

Carlos also pointed out that the labor ministry, supervisor of the Department of Immigration, was being run by Vargas' young friend, João Goulart.[7]

In the company of Congressman Armando Falcão and *O Cruzeiro*'s David Nasser (who had helped investigate Wainer's nationality), Carlos went to look at the original *Canárias* passenger disembarkation list. Without hesitation Carlos asserted that the names of Samuel's parents had been added. David Nasser, more cautious, felt it would be well to have the old list examined by a manuscript expert and this was done although the tampering was obvious. The *Tribuna* announced that the list was false, and, on July 20 and 21, Carlos used radio and television to reveal that, with the inclusion of the Wainer names, the list had more people on it than the Rio press reported disembarking from the *Canárias* on January 5, 1905. Carlos went on to say, "I publicly accuse João Goulart, the minister of labor, as the principal person responsible for the scurrilous falsification of the document of the Department of Immigration."[8] The head of the Department of Immigration hastened to explain that he had given *Última Hora* the certified copy of the *Canárias* list before learning of its "adulteration," but he was dismissed from his post.[9]

Congressman Falcão, who had already brought legal action against the Wainer brothers for making false statements, joined Carlos in a search for the forger of the *Canárias* list. The two of them led thirty reporters in an invasion of the Municipal Council on July 28. Not finding the man they wanted, they marched with the reporters into the education ministry, where *Tribuna* reporter Araújo Neto had previously located papers about Samuel Wainer's days as a pharmacy student. The journalists ended up with photographs of papers, dated 1929 and 1930, showing Samuel as a native of Romania. The documents, one signed by Samuel, included letters of recommendation and a registration statement. On the radio that night, Carlos demanded the dismissal of Goulart if the falsifier of the passenger list were not punished.[10] A few days later Carlos asked for police protection at the door of his apartment, because, he said, "three unidentified individuals tried unsuccessfully to enter in order to steal a collection of documents."[11]

Early in August, *Última Hora* announced that Bocaiuva Cunha would be legally responsible for running the newspaper in the place of Wainer.[12] *Tribuna* reporter Amaral Netto, pleased with developments, used his house in Niterói to hold the "first celebration of the results obtained by the *Tribuna da Imprensa* in its struggle for freedom of the press in Brazil." It was called the "Celebration of the Lantern," a reference to the masthead emblem used in reply to *Última Hora*'s "*lanterninha*" remark. Over a hundred people applauded when Carlos was given a gold tie clip and Letícia a gold brooch, each with a lanternlike decoration. Later in August, Amaral Netto founded, and became president of, the Lantern Club. *Tribuna* readers were asked to join by sending dues to the Lavradio Street address. Soon it was so successful that it set up an office on Senator Dantas Street.[13]

Carlos, honorary president of the Lantern Club, attracted members by speaking at meetings. In 1954, intellectual Padre (Father) Benedito Calasans, a UDN assemblyman, became president of the Lantern Club of São Paulo, and Carlos announced the list of candidates for federal and state elective offices who had the blessing of the club because, he said, "they fight against the oligarchy of Getúlio." Participants in the club's activities included Odilon Braga, Prado Kelly, Hamilton Nogueira, and Frota Aguiar, *relator* of the *Última Hora* CPI.[14]

While the Lantern Club was being organized in August 1953, the investigation of the Department of Immigration forgery revealed that an archivist of the department had allowed "an *Última Hora* reporter" to have access for several days to the department's old records. The so-called reporter was identified by three Department of Immigration employees as José Wainer, older brother of Samuel.[15] He became a new client of able criminal lawyer Evandro Lins e Silva, who had defended Castorina with Carlos in 1934 and was now at work with Hariberto de Miranda Jordão defending Samuel Wainer.

While the role of José Wainer made headlines late in September, Carlos was in New York. There on October 2, at Columbia University's Graduate School of Journalism, he received one of the four Maria Moors Cabot gold medals awarded in 1953 for outstanding journalistic contributions "to the progress of international friendship in the Americas." He went on to Mexico City for the Ninth Inter American Press Association Conference, where he completed his stint as the association's secretary-general and obtained approval for holding the Tenth Conference in Brazil.

In his correspondence with Letícia about the meetings in Mexico City, Carlos complained of Júlio de Mesquita Filho's "inability to get along with anybody." But the Mexicans, he told her, were delightful. Letícia, whose suggestions about her husband's work were infrequent but good, wrote him that she found the *Tribuna* devoting too much space to the case of protection for UDN Congressman Tenório Cavalcanti, accused of having ordered the machine-gunning of two police officers. And she asked Carlos not to drink to excess during his trip.[16]

The esteem in which Carlos was held by his American journalist friends is reflected in letters he had received earlier in Rio, with Bill White asking him to "stomp for me on Sammy Wainer when you get him down" and Heiskell's reminder that "all of us are praying for your success." "The *lanterninha* shines in the Americas," Carlos cabled the *Tribuna* from Miami after the conference in Mexico.[17] Furthermore, the campaign against *Última Hora* was beneficial to the *Tribuna* circulation, which had dropped from 19,050 in June 1951 to 14,900 in June 1952 (because of *Última Hora*'s competition) but which rose to 24,700 in July 1953, leading Carlos to observe to stockholders that "Wainer is right in saying that crime helps to sell newspapers."[18]

Government investigator Antenor Lírio Coelho, studying findings about the Wainer brothers' birthplace and the forgery of the *Canárias* passenger list, declared on September 15 that he agreed with Falcão's accusation. But the government investigation lasted until March 1954. Carlos, apparently convinced that it was not a "farce," testified on March 15, after recovering from a duodenal ulcer that kept him "practically out of life . . . and in a tiresome mood" during much of February.[19]

On March 18 the findings were forwarded to the criminal court of the Eleventh District, whose judge, Valporé Caiado de Castro, was a nephew of the head of the presidential Casa Militar (Military Staff). During the trial, the *Tribuna* reported the discovery at the Department of Immigration of records showing that Dora Wainer had brought her children to Brazil on the *Sofia*, which had docked on November 1, 1920; the seven children included Brucha, whose age corresponded to that of Samuel. Wainer, in a short testimony before the judge, reaffirmed that he had been born in São Paulo and charged that the campaign against him was a personal one waged by Armando Falcão and Carlos.[20]

Última Hora, whose masthead showed that it was directed by Danton Coelho as president and Bocaiuva Cunha as superintendent, lacked the affluence of the past.[21] The newsprint problem that it shared with the Bank of Brazil was solved, at least in part, by a decision to have Atlanta Corporation paper go to government agencies, such as the Imprensa Nacional and the *Diário Oficial*. The *Tribuna* denounced Finance Minister Osvaldo Aranha for thus assisting Danton Coelho and not taking *Última Hora* to the courts.[22]

3. Trying to Impeach Vargas (April–June 1954)

In November 1953 Carlos Castello Branco left the *Tribuna* and was replaced as general editor by Hélio Fernandes, who had been directing the recently established magazine, *Manchete*.[1] During Hélio Fernandes' five months with the *Tribuna*, it continued to collaborate with the ultra-oppositionist group of UDN congressmen, known as the "Musical Band" (*Banda de Música*), that included Afonso Arinos de Melo Franco, Aliomar Baleeiro, and Olavo Bilac Pinto. The *Tribuna* and the *banda* called attention, late in 1953, to corruption in the Bank of Brazil's Carteira de Exportação e Importação (CEXIM), whose bureau for granting import licences had become a bureau of bribery. Congressman Raimundo Padilha's charges led to the establishment of a CPI, whose *relator*, Aliomar Baleeiro, was soon demanding the dismissal of CEXIM Director Coriolano de Góis.[2] Not only was Coriolano forced to resign, but also CEXIM itself was closed down in December 1953.

To add to the troubles of the president, called "Farouk Vargas" by the *Tribuna*, a manifesto was signed in February 1954 by eighty-two Army colonels and lieutenant colonels, complaining of labor agitation, conditions in the army, and corruption in political life. Vargas, as a result, appointed his third war minister, Zenóbio da Costa, and accepted the resignation of Labor Minister Goulart. But Congressman Goulart, president of the PTB, continued to run the ministry, through its interim head, and to advocate a 100 percent increase in the minimum wage. The *Tribuna*, opposed to the minimum wage increase, wrote that Vargas, "like all totalitarians and demagogues, thinks the poor and humble are attracted only by money." After Vargas signed his decree of May 1, doubling the minimum wage, Carlos wrote that the president, "an incurable *caudilho*," had handled the matter unconstitutionally because he did not wish to share popularity with Congress.[3]

In the *Tribuna,* Carlos called Getúlio Vargas a monster, Lutero Vargas the degenerate, rich son of "the father of the poor," and Finance Minister Aranha a liar and a thief. The intensity of feelings provoked by such attacks was reflected in an incident at the Copacabana Palace Hotel's Bife de Ouro Restaurant when Carlos dined there in March 1954 with a UDN congressman and Agriculture Minister João Cleofas, a Pernambuco UDN leader accused by Carlos of serving "the Vargas oligarchy." During the meal, Aranha's son Euclides came to the table and insulted Carlos. Carlos, rising from his chair, was struck in the face by Euclides and on the forehead by a member of the presidential Casa Militar. Although his spectacles fell to the floor, Carlos was able to grab a revolver that Euclides aimed at him before being pulled away from Carlos by friends.

Carlos noted that Cleofas had disappeared during the melee, and he therefore published an open letter to the Pernambucano to say that his retreat revealed a good deal about his temperament and "vacillation." In Congress, Bilac Pinto declared, in a reference to Osvaldo Aranha, that "anyone called a thief by the press should limit his response to proving the contrary." But Flores da Cunha, an old friend of Aranha, said that Carlos' violent articles about the finance minister made the attack understandable, and Maurício Joppert, another UDN congressman, expressed doubt that Osvaldo Aranha approved his son's action.[4]

During the offensive against CEXIM, Sobral Pinto warned UDN leader Afonso Arinos de Melo Franco against the "danger of systematic disparagement of all men in public office."[5] But it was Afonso Arinos, the disparager, who was next on the list to be disparaged by Carlos. After the UDN leader accepted the invitation of the foreign ministry to be a delegate to the Tenth Inter-American Conference of diplomats, which met in Caracas in February 1954, Carlos accused him of having succumbed to "blandishments," pleasing to his "vanity," offered by Vargas.[6] Afonso Arinos has written that he received the approval of the UDN's directorship and congressional bloc before he agreed to join the large Brazilian delegation, which included Alceu Amoroso Lima and Hermes Lima. However, the *Tribuna* wrote that "all the UDN directorship, except for Secretary-General Virgílio Távora, advised Afonso Arinos not to go to Caracas." Echoing an observation of Carlos, Otávio Mangabeira remarked that Afonso Arinos, "after saying he was going to the barricades, embarked for Caracas."

At the conference, Afonso Arinos received a cable from Carlos telling him to resign his UDN leadership position. "Your disastrous absence," Carlos said, "would become real treason should you continue in the leadership." Afonso Arinos cabled back to say that he had never served better as opposition leader than in his Caracas delegate post. He expressed his distaste for unjustified attacks and told Carlos he would never be intimidated by them. Alceu Amoroso Lima, also attacked by Carlos for attending the Caracas conference, left off collaborating with the *Tribuna.*[7]

In foreign affairs, Carlos supported the overthrow of Jacobo Arbenz of Guatemala, calling his regime an agent of Russia. This led *Última Hora* to write that Lacerda had lied in declaring himself "a Hindu, a Bessarabian, or an American." His first cradle, it said, had been a banana tree of the United Fruit Company in Guatemala. Lacerda, *Última Hora* added, was an ex-Communist, ex-Trotskyite, ex-ANL member, and ex-son (he "rejected even his own father") and had learned his irony on the United Fruit plantations.[8]

It was from Argentina that Carlos received information that gave him his greatest opportunity to strike at Vargas in foreign affairs. In February 1954, Argentine exiles in Uruguay published a copy of the secret speech of Perón, delivered in November 1953 at the Argentine War College, and they sent a copy to the *Tribuna*. As revealed by the *Tribuna* and by Carlos on Rádio Globo, Perón had told the war college that Vargas, before his election in 1950, had promised to join him in an ABC (Argentina-Brazil-Chile) bloc in opposition to the continental hegemony of the United States. According to the speech, Vargas had authorized Perón to go to Chile and sign the appropriate treaty with President Carlos Ibáñez, which Perón did. "When Vargas became president," Perón said, "he promised me that we would meet in Buenos Aires or Rio and carry out this treaty." Perón added that Vargas, in accounting for his failure to fulfill his promise, had explained that he could not act rapidly because he had "a somewhat complicated situation with Congress."[9]

In mid-March the Argentine embassy announced that Perón had not given the speech, but the denial was difficult to believe, especially after João Neves, Vargas' foreign minister until 1953, proclaimed that the speech was authentic. João Neves wrote about secret letters between Vargas and Perón and Vargas' promise to Perón to dismiss João Neves. Carlos then wrote in the *Tribuna* that "sometimes we criticized the performance of João Neves, but today we must be fair about the virtuousness of his position."[10]

Bilac Pinto called for a CPI to look into the relations between Vargas and Perón. Herbert Levy, another UDN congressman, suggested that Vargas had illegally accepted campaign money from Perón. After Aliomar Baleeiro accused Vargas of "high treason" and asked for impeachment proceedings, an interparty commission was established to study grounds for impeachment.[11]

Afonso Arinos, following his trip to Caracas and a visit to the United States, returned on May 19. He found Eduardo Gomes adamant that the UDN congressional leader present a bill to impeach the president. Afonso Arinos told thc *brigadeiro* that impeachment was the wrong course to follow and that the bill would probably be defeated, leaving the president the beneficiary. But the *brigadeiro* insisted and so Afonso Arinos introduced the bill. The *Tribuna,* hailing the "battle of impeachment" begun late in May, wrote that the chief "crimes" of Vargas were his "pact with Perón," inflationary government spending, and "responsibility for the Bank of Brazil–*Última Hora* affair." *Última Hora* described the impeachment battle as election year demagoguery and wrote disparagingly of the leading anti-Vargas participants in the "comic opera." Banker and Congressman Herbert Levy was pictured as a black market dollar operator and Afonso Arinos as a member of "one of the families most costly for the republic to support." Frota Aguiar was called a traitor.[12]

Former President Dutra came out against impeachment. In doing so, he

Vargas in trouble. (Hilde Weber drawing in Hilde Weber, *O Brasil em Charges, 1950–1985*)

gave his approval to a statement, written by Armando Falcão, that defined the position of the Dutristas: "For the good of democracy . . . , Getúlio Vargas must be endured and sustained in the government until the last minute of his constitutional mandate."[13] This view gained support beyond the Dutristas and left Afonso Arinos directing a losing battle.

In the final tally, 35 congressmen voted for impeachment, 136 opposed it and 132 did not vote. The *Tribuna*'s Murilo Melo Filho wrote of "treason" among the *udenistas,* with 6 of them opposing impeachment and 40 abstaining. Outside the UDN, Afonso Arinos' bill attracted only 5 votes, including those of Frota Aguiar, who was about to leave the PTB, and Roberto Morena, a Communist elected on the ticket of a minor party. Afonso Arinos, criticized by Artur Santos and other *udenistas* for having introduced his bill, offered to resign his party leadership in Congress. But the offer was rejected.[14]

4. "The Crow" (May–June 1954)

Young reporters who wrote about the Rio police considered *A Noite*'s 44-year-old Nestor Moreira an amiable associate and a veteran. Policemen, however, resented his articles stressing their incompetence. When he dropped in at the Second District police station to seek information after midnight on May 11, 1954, he was attacked by members of the *guarda civil* and savagely beaten by Mule Kick, the guard who had been assigned to protect Carlos and his family in 1948. While Nestor Moreira lay in the Miguel Couto Hospital, a taxi driver who had accompanied the journalist denounced Mule Kick, and *Última Hora* reporter Edmar Morel, after interviewing Nestor Moreira and prisoners held at the Second District police station, gave an account of the beating. While the press howled about police brutality, journalists met at the ABI and planned a protest march.[1]

Nestor Moreira died on the morning of Saturday, May 22. That afternoon, sports activities were suspended and movie theaters observed a minute of silence. On Sunday thousands accompanied the casket when it was taken, with ABI President Herbert Moses and outgoing Military Club President Alcides Etchegoyen as foremost pallbearers, first to the *A Noite* building, then to the ABI building, and finally to the São João Batista cemetery. Funeral speeches were broadcast by Rádio Globo. Carlos, one of the graveside speakers, condemned police barbarism and suggested that Police Chief Morais Âncora be replaced by anti-Communist General Alcides Etchegoyen. In a front page *Tribuna* editorial, Carlos mentioned Vargas' declaration that the crime had been monstrous and added that everything was monstrous in the Vargas government of corruption and violence.[2]

Wainer, accompanied by a reporter, called on Antonieta, the widow of Nestor Moreira, and argued that it was undesirable to have Nestor's death used for "political exploitation." She signed a letter that he composed saying that Nestor had always kept apart from political passions and that she and her children hoped that political exploitation, "begun after his death," would cease. Wainer sent copies of the letter to the newspapers and arranged to have some of them use the words "begun at the side of his grave" instead of "begun after his death."[3]

Following the publication of the letter, Nestor's friends at *A Noite* persuaded Antonieta that she had made a mistake. She explained that Wainer "told me the government was disposed to grant me a lifetime pension and suggested I write a letter to the newspapers." But she added that she had not accused the newspapers of exploiting her husband's death for political purposes. During an interview broadcast by Rádio Tupi, she was asked about the press campaign that had followed Nestor's death and replied that "it should continue in order to end this barbarism." The *Tribuna* wrote that Wainer, who "continues, in fact, to direct *Última Hora*," had pretended to be a friend of Nestor but had never known him. The Communist *Imprensa Popular* called the publication of the letter, "attributed to the widow," an "infamous maneuver of the government." It quoted a son of Nestor as saying that Wainer, acting "falsely," had sought to discredit the family in the eyes of Nestor's colleagues.[4]

Wainer, when attending Nestor's funeral in the company of Otávio Malta and Moacir Werneck de Castro, had been struck by Lacerda's black clothing and solemn air. Speaking to Malta, he had called Lacerda a crow, and he had told *Última Hora* reporter Edmar Morel that Carlos was no journalist and had never seen Nestor Moreira in his life. Returning to *Última Hora*, Wainer asked political cartoonist LAN to draw Lacerda as a crow and suggested to Paulo Silveira the publication of an editorial about *o corvo* (the crow).[5]

LAN's drawing of a black crow, with Lacerda's face, shedding tears at the side of a coffin, appeared in *Última Hora* on May 25 and 27 alongside editorials. The first of these said that when Nestor Moreira, surrounded by his

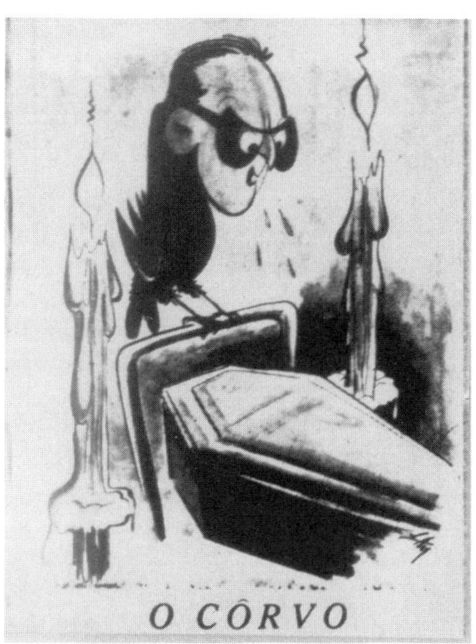

The crow shedding tears by the coffin of Nestor Moreira. (Drawing by LAN in *Última Hora,* May 25 and 27, 1954)

family and companions, "exhaled his last breath, the form of the crow appeared at the hospital door. Until then he was simply lurking, awaiting the opportune moment to satiate his black, exhibitionist, and hypocritical buzzard's soul." It added that the modest, humble, and honest Nestor Moreira could never be understood by a man who was his exact opposite, "a miserable informer on his companions, a wretch frustrated in his own profession, with a stool-pigeon's soul at the service of all antipopular, antihuman, antinational movements." According to *Última Hora,* the "noble letter" of Antonieta Moreira, published in the press, was a "tremendous protest against the *corvos* who prowled about the body of Nestor Moreira, transforming it into a repast to nourish their mean, personal interests and electoral ambitions."[6]

The *corvo* of Lavradio, *Última Hora* wrote on May 29, was about to feel the weight of the law because Lutero Vargas, president of the Federal District PTB, was suing the *Tribuna* director for defamation and slander. "Lacerda will be submitted to a sanity examination," *Última Hora* gloated on May 31, after Lutero's lawyer, Alfredo Tranjan, asked the court to determine whether Carlos could be considered mentally responsible for his acts. *Última Hora* said that "the lunatic of Lavradio," after a "recent crisis," had

OS ARTISTAS são profetas: LAN advertiu que o h
trião estava louco e a justiça agora vai confirmar.

"Artists are prophets: LAN warned that the buffoon is insane and the court of law will confirm it." (Drawing by LAN in *Última Hora,* May 31, 1954)

The insane crow. (Drawing by LAN in *Última Hora,* June 10, 1954)

confided to "two illustrious coup club members," Armando Falcão and Frota Aguiar, that he was being "persecuted by visions, in the form of immense flying saucers, falling en masse on his head, . . . and entering his heart." Falcão and Frota, *Última Hora* added, consulted a psychiatrist and learned that the saucers were phonograph discs, with the recordings of the insults and slanders that would send the mad *corvo* to jail. LAN illustrated the article with a drawing of the Lacerda-faced black crow, wearing a Napoleon hat, in a birdcage with flying saucers above it.[7]

Among those who would testify in court about Carlos' sanity, *Última Hora* announced, was Sobral Pinto, "a *Tribuna da Imprensa* founder who left it." Sobral hastened to write Lutero to say that, as Carlos' lawyer, he could not appear as a witness for Lutero, which was to be regretted because he would tell the court that "if any trace of decency remained in our land, your testimony about your participation in the *Última Hora* financial scandal would have brought about the fall of Getúlio Vargas." In a letter to Lutero's lawyer, Sobral criticized those who sought to make use of divergences between himself and Carlos. He told of his admiration for "men of honor, who struggle disinterestedly, and not without risk, for the improvement of public life."[8]

After the *Tribuna* published Sobral's letters, *Última Hora* published Lutero's sensational reply, a reminder of the extramarital love affair that had led to Sobral's resignations, in 1928, as prosecuting attorney of the republic and Federal District. Among his witnesses in court, Lutero wrote, he wanted no one who, "calling himself a Catholic religious leader, had desecrated a home, . . . going off with the wife of his friend and protector, and who, when

The crow broadcasting. (Drawing by LAN in *Última Hora*, June 3, 1954)

caught red-handed, had been whipped in the very center of Rio by his betrayed friend." Carlos condemned Lutero's "brutal and nasty aggression," and Adauto Lúcio Cardoso praised Sobral for having resigned in 1928, thus punishing himself after his "hour of temptation." Sobral's response to Lutero, published on July 14, discussed his "indescribable agony" in 1928 and decision not to remain in an accuser's post. Lutero, he said, had found it impossible to deny his own crimes and was storming furiously because Sobral would not cooperate in trying to jail a brave journalist.[9]

Sobral Pinto and Adauto Lúcio Cardoso accompanied Carlos to court in June and July. Asked whether he had called Lutero a thief, Carlos replied in the affirmative, and, with the judge's permission, expressed his view about the "group of gangsters" that had a "monopoly on Brazilian public life." Lutero, he told the judge, was merely a "bit player" in the drama.

Carlos spoke also to the crowd outside the courthouse and to the audience of Rádio Globo, whose announcer, Raul Brunini, was on the spot. Using the microphone after one of Carlos' court appearances, Brunini exclaimed, "This is a great day for us because Carlos Lacerda faced Lutero and confirmed what he said previously, 'he is a thief,' and the people, at the door of the court, repeated 'he is a thief.'" Carlos took the microphone from Brunini to express his appreciation to the people, who, he said, had always supported him "in the struggle against robbery and corruption by the oligarchy that has taken possession of this country."[10]

5. Candidate Lacerda and the Air Force Majors (January–August 1954)

Carlos liked to say that *Última Hora,* in financial trouble, looked forward to May 1954, when campaigning would begin for the October 3 elections to choose congressmen and some of the senators and governors. Danton Coelho and "Baby" Bocaiuva Cunha, Carlos wrote, could then meet payrolls with the help of candidates and political parties interested in purchasing the newspaper's support.[1]

As early as December 1953, Carioca UDN President Maurício Joppert wrote Carlos asking him to be a congressional candidate of the party. Carlos set the letter aside and worked to form a local popular front, which he considered "the key for success in the struggle to defeat the oligarchy in the national capital."[2]

Carlos' manifesto for the front, called the Popular Alliance against Thefts and Coups (Aliança Popular contra o Roubo e o Golpe), stressed the need to work against a government that lived by means of corruption and planned a coup to keep itself in power. The candidates of the Popular Alliance, according to the program written by Carlos, would favor the stimulation of individual initiative and would seek to make the municipalities the recipients of most of the taxes. They would work to abolish the *imposto sindical,* the tax that supported the labor union setup, and would espouse a union system "free of the labor ministry." They would advocate separation of the Bank of Brazil from the government and would support an agrarian reform whose primary attention would be directed to agricultural loans and technical assistance. Carlos visualized a lot of productive properties, owned by "middle class farmers," on the outskirts of consuming centers.[3]

Late in February, the Carioca UDN agreed to join the smaller Partido Republicano (PR) and Partido Libertador (PL) in the new alliance. This step and the UDN's "expulsion of undesirable individuals" were praised by Carlos in March when he agreed to be a UDN congressional candidate.[4]

Among his opponents in the congressional race was Lutero Vargas, whose lawsuit against Carlos added to the interest of the press and public in the campaign. The *Tribuna,* offering more pages than formerly, cited reports of fiscal authorities who claimed that Lutero had cheated on tax payments, a charge made earlier by Lantern Club founder Amaral Netto. Displaying pictures of Lutero at dances and surrounded by actresses, the *Tribuna* pointed out that in 3 1/2 years Lutero had been in Congress only on fifty-three days. *Última Hora* retaliated by giving publicity to statements by labor leaders who described Carlos as the principal enemy of the workers. And it warned against people connected with what it called the "Club for Coups and Thefts"; they planned, it wrote, to carry out an anti-Vargas coup before the elections.[5]

In July the Popular Alliance against Thefts and Coups listed eighteen Federal District candidates who had its support. The list included several PR candidates and every one of the twelve congressional candidates announced by the UDN early in June, men such as Adauto Lúcio Cardoso, Carlos Lacerda, Euclides Figueiredo, Mário Martins, Maurício Joppert, Odilon Braga, and Frota Aguiar.[6]

Carlos, campaigning for the UDN in Rio state, told an audience at Barra Mansa that workers should participate in company profits. In São Paulo, where he helped build up the local Lantern Club, he was asked his opinion of gubernatorial candidate Jânio Quadros. "Never," Carlos said, "have I seen a Brazilian politician lie so much to so many people in so short a time."[7] Quadros, candidate of the PTN and PSB, had broken with the PDC, whose São Paulo leader, André Franco Montoro, joined the Lantern Club. Jânio's strongest opponents were Ademar de Barros (PSP) and Governor Garcez's candidate, Francisco Prestes Maia (UDN-PSD-PR-PDC-PRP). Some support from members of the fragmented Paulista PTB could be expected by Quadros.[8]

Carlos followed with interest the gubernatorial race in Pernambuco, where João Cleofas, nominated by the local UDN, was backed by the PTB, Goulart, *Última Hora,* and the Communists. The anti-Vargas candidate, General Osvaldo Cordeiro de Farias (PSD), was backed by the incumbent, Etelvino Lins, whom Carlos had assailed in 1945 and now praised. After the *Tribuna,* along with Adauto Lúcio Cardoso and Joppert, called for the expulsion of Cleofas from the UDN, *Última Hora* quoted Cleofas as saying that "Pernambuco politics are handled in Pernambuco and not by the sleek gentlemen of the Federal District."[9]

Carlos, campaigning in the Federal District against corruption and Communism, attracted throngs of admirers. None shared his concerns more than a group of about ten air force officers, mostly majors in the Air Transport Command. Through a third party in 1950 some of them had given him information leading to his denouncement of air force Colonel Teles Ribeiro for improperly purchasing khaki canvas from the Pires family. Recollecting, with shame, the air force colonel's assault on Carlos in the elevator and learning about threats to Carlos' life as he campaigned in 1954, they delegated one of their group, Major Luciano Souza Leão, to speak to Carlos at one of his rallies and explain that armed members of their group wanted to take turns accompanying him.[10] Soon afterward, four of the majors presented themselves to Carlos when he was at Rádio Tupi: Gustavo Borges, Américo Fontenelle, Moacir del Tedesco, and Rubens Florentino Vaz. Within the next few days Carlos met, also for the first time, more members of the group: Colonel Alfredo Correia, Majors Haroldo Veloso, Paulo Victor da Silva, Jorge Diehl, and Francisco Lameirão, and Lieutenant Antônio Carrera. The officers hoped to deter assassination attempts by the presence of one of them during each speaking engagement, not overlooking "the most vulnerable moments," when the intended victim left his home for a meeting and returned home after it.[11]

The program worked fairly well, but, as Carlos and the officers recognized, was far from foolproof. Good luck was a factor on Sunday, July 14, when Carlos, Raul Brunini, and others went by boat to a political rally on Paquetá Island. A dynamite explosion at the Paquetá dock made the boat inoperable but failed to harm any people.[12]

At the rallies, the air force officers began to be noticed by enemies of Carlos who had assassination in mind. Each officer, when his turn came to guard Lacerda, examined the meeting place and its exits and assessed "the danger spots." On the night of August 4, when Carlos was scheduled to speak to over a thousand at the auditorium of the São José School in the Tijuca district, the examination was carried out by Major Gustavo Borges together with Major Rubens Vaz because Borges had unexpectedly been called by the Air Transport Command to fly a mail plane to Goiás before dawn and was therefore turning his guard duty over to Vaz. At 9:30 P.M. Borges left for home to sleep before making his flight.[13]

Major Vaz, who would drive Carlos home in his small car, was not as concerned as some of the others about assassination threats,[14] and he lacked the pugnaciousness of Major Fontenelle. Vaz had sometimes suggested that Carlos might use more moderation in his speeches, only to be told by Carlos that the campaign would be ineffective if it were not violent. The country, Carlos felt, needed to be "shaken up."[15]

6. "My Friend Vaz Is Dead" (August 5, 1954)

Gregório Fortunato, the large-framed, 54-year-old head of the presidential personal guard, was devoted to Getúlio and Benjamim Vargas. "Colonel" Benjamim, Vargas' younger brother, had promoted the uneducated peon to the rank of lieutenant in the provisional battalion of São Borja, Rio Grande do Sul, in 1932 and had brought him into the presidential guard when he had organized it in 1938. Following Vargas' election in 1950, Gregório had rebuilt the guard with the assistance of money from SESI and a secret fund of the Federal Department of Public Security.[1]

Known as "the Black Angel of Catete Palace," Gregório Fortunato exerted extraordinary influence. Lutero Vargas stated that the selection of Colonel Dulcídio Cardoso as mayor of the Federal District in December 1952 was made by Gregório and that Dulcídio, distributing more municipal posts to Gregório's followers than to Lutero's PTB followers, was quick to attend to Gregório's wishes. Influence brought wealth to Gregório, who received commissions for favors such as CEXIM licences and Bank of Brazil loans. In 1953 he used a three million cruzeiro loan himself to purchase a São Borja *fazenda* from Vargas' son Manuel ("Maneco"), the secretary of agriculture of Rio Grande do Sul.[2]

Gregório was constantly flattered. In 1954 he was decorated by the war minister. Even more stirring were the words of General Mendes de Morais to Gregório, giving him the title of "minister of defense" of Brazil and the responsibility for preventing calamities.[3] Deeply moved, Gregório took to heart the scathing denunciations of Carlos Lacerda by Mendes de Morais, Euvaldo Lodi, and Danton Coelho. He came to feel he had an assignment and duty to arrange for the elimination of the journalist whose brutal attacks on the president and his circle would, according to Mendes de Morais, lead to civil war.[4]

Plans made in April 1954, for a good "thrashing" of Carlos, gave way to more sinister ones in June. Gregório spoke about Carlos to presidential guard Climério Euribes de Almeida, a former peon on the Vargas property and, like Gregório, a soldier under "Colonel" Benjamim Vargas in 1932. Climério's driver, José Antônio Soares, knew just the man to shoot Carlos: Alcino João do Nascimento, who had already been used by Soares on March 1 to commit a murder, the investigation of which had been called off, thanks to the intervention of Gregório. In the "case of Carlos Lacerda," Gregório approved the choice of Alcino because he was not a member of the guard.[5]

After driver Soares offered Alcino 200,000 cruzeiros to kill Lacerda, presidential guard Climério discussed the amount with Gregório and then told Alcino he would receive 100,000 cruzeiros, a house in the suburbs, and a job as police investigator. Climério, often seen in public at Lutero Vargas' side, also guaranteed that Gregório would protect Alcino from trouble and even said, untruthfully, that Congressman Lutero was interested in the crime and would help cover it up. From driver Soares, Alcino received on loan a Smith & Wesson 45-caliber revolver, the type carried by members of the presidential guard. On Gregório's instructions, the secretary of the guard, João Valente de Sousa, made 80,000 cruzeiros available to Climério for some of the expenses of the project.[6]

To point out the "man to be killed," presidential guard Climério and his driver Soares took murderer Alcino to Nova Iguaçu, Rio state, on July 11, when Carlos spoke there. After that, several plans to kill the journalist came to naught. One was in front of the Tonelero Street building where Lacerda lived; but Carlos, instead of coming out alone, was accompanied by

Letícia, and the would-be assassins, not wishing to kill "an innocent person," decided to try again. On August 1, Climério and Alcino, driven by Soares, set out for Barra Mansa, where Carlos gave his speech advocating worker participation in company profits. The car broke down before reaching Barra Mansa.[7]

Another attempt was to be made at the São José School in Tijuca on the night of August 4. But Municipal Council candidate José Cândido Moreira de Souza, who had brought Carlos to the school and was on the speaker's platform, was obviously carrying a revolver; besides, Carlos has written, Alcino and Climério were thwarted at the school because of the crowd that surrounded Carlos, seeking autographs and asking questions.

From the school, Climério phoned Nelson Raimundo de Sousa, Catete taxi driver and barber, asking him to come and drive Alcino and Climério to the vicinity of Carlos' apartment on Tonelero Street and then wait at a corner until he was needed again. Climério told Nelson Raimundo to keep his mouth shut about the affair in which an individual was going to be "thrashed." As compensation, the taxi driver was offered 20,000 cruzeiros and a police investigator's job. In the meantime, air force Major Rubens Vaz insisted on driving Carlos from the school to Tonelero Street. Jokingly he told Municipal Council candidate José Cândido Moreira de Souza, "If you don't let Carlos come with me, I won't vote for you."[8]

It was a bit past midnight when Major Vaz brought Carlos and 15-year-old Sérgio to their apartment building. Vaz, before saying goodnight, repeated his admonition that Carlos "be calm and understand ideas held by other people." Carlos, who spotted some men across the street, went to the front door. Finding he had forgotten his keys, he sent Sérgio to the service entrance to ask the building's garage man to let them in through the garage door.[9]

Carlos was to have been shot from across the street when his silhouette became still against the building's illuminated front hall, but, like Sérgio, he moved toward the garage door. Alcino, troubled by the poor lighting at the garage door and the plants in the flower bed in front of it, crossed the street to shoot from closer range. One of his two shots pierced the navicular bone of Carlos, near the ankle of the left foot. After Sérgio tried to shield Carlos, both found protection in the garage. Carlos sent his son upstairs to phone for help and prepared to use his 38-caliber revolver to shoot the attackers. He believed there were several.[10]

In the meantime Vaz jumped from his small car. With his revolver resting in the glove compartment, he struggled unarmed against Alcino. Trying to grab Alcino's 45-caliber revolver, he was shot twice by Alcino and died at once.

Carlos, despite the pain in his foot, made his way from the garage to the building's main hall and opened the front door from the inside. Seeing Alcino, he started shooting at him. But he missed and Alcino rushed to the waiting taxi. Before the assassin made his getaway he was spotted and ordered to stop by a municipal watchman who was running toward the scene from a police station. The watchman, felled by a shot in the leg by

Alcino, fired five shots from the ground at the departing taxi, making it recognizable later, and he noted its licence number.[11]

Alcino, after being driven downtown by taxi driver Nelson Raimundo, made his way to the home of Climério. But Climério, who had left the scene of the crime earlier than Alcino in a taxi he had picked up, was at Catete Palace, where he was soon joined by the nervous Nelson Raimundo. Climério told his friend Gregório Fortunato what had happened and then went home. There he gave 10,000 cruzeiros to Alcino.

On Tonelero Street three *Diário Carioca* reporters, in the neighborhood after returning from work, came to the scene of the crime. They found Carlos kneeling by the body of Vaz and exclaiming, "My God, my friend Vaz is dead." To Sérgio, who was coming from the building, Carlos said, "For God's sake, phone First Aid to get a doctor." Ten minutes later, one of the *Diário Carioca* reporters wrote, there were five hundred people on Tonelero Street. An automobile, offered by a neighbor, was used to take Carlos and the body of Vaz to the Miguel Couto Hospital.[12]

Gustavo Borges, who had received a phone call from Sérgio, rushed to Tonelero Street and then went to the hospital, where Carlos was on a table receiving a provisional bandage on the lower part of his left leg.[13] Also at the hospital were Armando Falcão, advised by journalist Murilo Melo Filho of the shooting, and Eduardo Gomes, director of the Air Transport Command in which Vaz had been serving.

Falcão, driving with Carlos in a taxi from the hospital to Tonelero Street, writes that the wounded journalist exclaimed, "I think I'm going crazy! What a horrible thing. I may have killed Vaz. I shot at random without my glasses. I think Vaz was in front of me. How terrible!"[14]

In his crowded apartment, Carlos was interrogated by the *delegado* of the nearby police station. As the questions made it clear that the *delegado* wanted to show that Carlos and Vaz had had an altercation, Carlos ordered him out of the apartment and refused to turn over his revolver to him. Falcão, who had been consulting police technicians in front of the building, came to Carlos with the news that Vaz had apparently been killed by bullets from one of the powerful 45-caliber revolvers that were restricted to the military and fifty of which had been made available to the president's guard. Carlos showed immense relief.[15]

In the meantime, taxi driver Nelson Raimundo decided to make a partial confession before the clues provided by the wounded municipal watchman led to his arrest. Going to the police at 3:30 A.M., he told the story as though he had no idea who his passengers had been. But it was a simple matter for the police to discover that Nelson Raimundo's work consisted in serving the presidential guard.[16]

With the news of the Tonelero Street affair, Maurício de Lacerda resolved to act dramatically on behalf of his son. Readers of *Última Hora* might have been misled into thinking that Maurício, a leading lawyer of the municipal government, was not on the side of Carlos. To give that impression, Wainer's daily had used a photograph of Maurício warmly embracing Mendes de Morais to illustrate a news item about a dispute between Carlos and the general. Now Maurício, learning of the attempt to shoot his son, grabbed a revolver and set out to see the top police authorities. But his youngest son, Maurício Caminha de Lacerda, would not let the immensely agitated Maurício take the revolver with him.[17]

7. Investigation of the Crime (August–October 1954)

Aureliano Leite, speaking for the UDN in Congress on August 5, said this would not be the first time the president had covered his hands with blood. "Before God," Carlos wrote in the *Tribuna,* "I accuse one man as responsible for the crime. He is the protector of thieves whose freedom from punishment gives them the audacity to commit such acts. That man is named Getúlio Vargas. . . . Rubens Vaz, our dear friend, died in the most insidious of wars: that of a defenseless people against the bandits who make up the government of Getúlio Vargas."[1]

While five hundred people demonstrated outside Catete Palace, demanding punishment of the assassins, Vargas questioned Gregório Fortunato.[2] After Gregório denied the involvement of the presidential guard, Vargas issued a statement for Majority Leader Gustavo Capanema to read in Congress: "Until now I considered journalist Carlos Lacerda my principal enemy, but now I consider him my Number Two enemy. Because the Number One, the person who has most harmed my government, is the man who tried to kill him and assassinated that young air force officer."[3]

Afonso Arinos de Melo Franco, interrupting his election campaign in Minas, drove to Rio to assume the leadership of the congressional denouncers of the Vargas regime. After Mauricinho Lacerda brought him up to date, he spoke in Congress on August 9. Recalling Carlos' attacks during his trip to Caracas, he said he had quarreled and would probably quarrel again with the journalist whose unbridled passion often led to imprudence and tumult. But, he said, he could not understand the government's use of hired assassins. Congressman Augusto Amaral Peixoto, brother of the Rio state governor, warned against making grave charges before all the facts were known. As for the facts, Afonso Arinos replied, the civilian police investigation was accomplishing so little that its failure seemed deliberate.[4]

Infuriated air force officers, after meeting on August 5, persuaded the government to authorize air force Colonel João Adil de Oliveira to "accompany" the civilian police investigation. But, despite the replacement of Police Chief Morais Âncora by army Colonel Paulo Torres, the air force majors were not disposed merely to accompany the police. They set up their own investigative headquarters at the air force communications section of Rio's Santos Dumont Airport. In assigning missions to hundreds of officers and volunteers in the search for the assassins, they made use of helicopters, planes, and 120 vehicles and received cooperation from other branches of the military. Gustavo Borges, who worked day and night alongside Major Paulo Victor da Silva, recalls that "everything we requested was provided, without consultation of *brigadeiros.* We ran the country for twenty days. We kept our headquarters secret."[5]

Colonel Adil was still "accompanying" the civilian police investigation on August 7 when the police made their chief contribution, the disclosure by taxi driver Nelson Raimundo de Sousa that he had driven Climério to Tonelero Street. With this development, Casa Militar head Aguinaldo Caiado de Castro ordered Gregório to send for Climério. But Gregório, instead, sent word to Climério that he was being sought by the authorities. Climério and assassin Alcino fled from Rio and separated.[6]

Gregório then arranged to meet Benjamim Vargas on Sunday, the eighth, on the road between Petrópolis and Rio while Benjamim was on his way to Catete Palace. The Black Angel admitted having ordered Climério to arrange for the elimination of Lacerda and said he was confessing to Benjamim as he would to a father, blood related or religious.

At the palace, Benjamim did not reveal the confession to Getúlio, perhaps because he heard his brother say that, with Nelson Raimundo's disclosure about Climério, "it is impossible that Gregório did not participate." Benjamim simply said, "That is also my opinion."[7] Getúlio disbanded the personal guard and confined Gregório to his suite of rooms at Catete Palace. As he put Gregório and Gregório's files at the disposition of the investigators, the oppositionists soon had a field day disclosing papers about shady deals.

At the Air Force Club on the tenth, hundreds of officers were stirred by the irate Eduardo Gomes and heard another officer repeat remarks of Nelson Raimundo's brother that pointed to Lutero Vargas as responsible for the death of Vaz. Colonel Adil promised that rapid progess would result from Justice Minister Tancredo Neves' agreement to authorize the air force to make arrests. This was done on the twelfth, with the creation of a Military Police Inquiry (IPM), headed by Colonel Adil.[8]

The IPM was set up at the Galeão Air Base, thirteen kilometers to the northwest of the centrally located Santos Dumont Airport. Holding prisoners there and calling in witnesses, the IPM became known as the "Republic of Galeão." On the thirteenth, Alcino was brought in by air force searchers, who were reported to have carried out "140 missions in 8 days." On the fourteenth, presidential guard secretary João Valente de Sousa confessed to the IPM that he had, on Gregório's orders, facilitated the getaway of Alcino and Climério.[9]

With Alcino and much of the press implicating Lutero Vargas, the president's son set aside his congressional immunity and went on August 13 to Galeão, where he offered to give any information that might be helpful. On that same evening he addressed the nation by radio and spoke of the "lunacy of bad Brazilians, working for personal hatreds, trying to involve my name in their plot." In conclusion he said, "I swear before God and the nation that I had no part . . . in the deplorable event." But the *Tribuna* kept on calling Lutero the instigator of the Tonelero shootings. Lutero's declaration, Carlos wrote on the fourteenth, was "a maneuver to break the impetus of today's Military Club meeting," at which fifteen hundred army officers rose to their feet to applaud deliriously a major's proposal that the club insist on the president's resignation.[10]

In the search for Climério, areas in the states of Rio de Janeiro, São Paulo,

Paraná, and Rio Grande do Sul (including São Borja) were combed. A lead from a Catete taxi driver sent investigators to a banana grove in Rio de Janeiro state. Roads were blocked and a helicopter hovered overhead while military vehicles and two hundred well-armed men, under the orders of air force Colonel Délio Jardim de Matos, closed in. On the chilly morning of August 18, at the end of what was described as "the greatest manhunt in Brazilian annals," a hungry and exhausted Climério was captured. "Those in whom I most trusted betrayed me," he said.[11]

Climério was found in possession of 53,000 cruzeiros bearing the same serial number as the 225,000 cruzeiros found on Gregório and the 7,000 found on Alcino. Like Alcino, Climério made a full confession to the IPM. Gregório, transferred to Galeão and accused by Climério of ordering the crime, put the blame on Congressman Euvaldo Lodi and General Mendes de Morais.

Gregório charged, on August 21, that former presidential secretary Roberto Alves had brought him Lodi's request for the elimination of Carlos. Alves confirmed Gregório's charge and described a scene, at which he said he was present, in which Lodi pleaded with Gregório that Lacerda be killed. When the investigators put Alves and Gregório together with Lodi, the two energetically insisted that Lodi had incited Gregório to homicide. Lodi called them liars.[12]

Gregório also received support in his charge against Mendes de Morais. He maintained that the general, after asking him one day about the steps he had taken against Lacerda, had told him that he had engaged someone else to shoot Lacerda, whereupon Gregório had exclaimed, "Let's see who does it first!" Following this disclosure, publicity was given to information received by DOPS Inspector Cecil Borer from Mendes de Morais' former driver, songwriter José Alcides, who told Borer that he had been asked by Mendes de Morais to murder Lacerda. Alcides, questioned by the investigators, said the general had given him a Colt 45 revolver for this purpose and had emphasized that excellent opportunities occurred when Carlos went to and from the War College (Escola Superior de Guerra), where the journalist was enrolled in a course. Alcides told the investigators that he had refused to kill Lacerda. Confirming his story later in court, he delivered the Colt 45 to the judge.[13]

Mendes de Morais called the accusations "the greatest infamy ever articulated against a public man in Brazil" and declared that he had "not the slightest connection with Gregório and his people." Unable to sustain his denial of connection with Gregório, he argued that he had done nothing more than tell him that Lacerda was pernicious and very dangerous. In drawing up his legal defense, Mendes de Morais wrote that "Carlos Lacerda and his accomplice Adauto Cardoso transformed the crime and the investigation into a hideous attack on my reputation," and he maintained that the government prosecutor, a relative of some of his political foes, had not been impartial. Mendes de Morais suggested that the instigator of the crime was Benjamim Vargas and wrote that "it is strange that Benjamim Vargas did not ask Gregório the name of the instigator."[14]

Cláudio Lacerda Paiva writes that "Carlos Lacerda died with the conviction that the instigator of the crime was Bejo [Benjamim Vargas]; the conviction was based on the loyalty of Gregório, testified by everyone, and on the violent, arbitrary, and even cruel personality of Getúlio's brother, a fact known to all from the days of the Estado Novo." However, Hugo Baldessarini, lawyer of the widow of Vaz, takes a "completely opposite" position, and argues that Benjamim acted always with discretion during the Vargas administration that began in 1951. Baldessarini also points out that, during that administration, Gregório became so important that he "proclaimed his independence of the influences of the past."[15]

During the investigation, Major Fontenelle or Major Borges, hoping to get a fuller account from Gregório, persuaded Carlos to print a few copies of the *Tribuna* containing an untruthful story with a headline reading "Bejo Vargas Flees to Montevideo, Abandoning His Friends in the Hour of Peril." A copy was left where Gregório would see it. "When he read it," Carlos recalled later, "he caved in. With that he began saying things. . . . But he never would agree to incriminate Bejo Vargas. He always maintained that Getúlio knew nothing and that Bejo only learned later. That is to say, the man was loyal to them until the end."[16]

When the IPM was closed down early in October 1954, Gregório Fortunato and the other prisoners were transferred from Galeão to the police jail. Information collected at the IPM was used by the police for its report, forwarded in October to the civilian judiciary and the war ministry. Four individuals, who were not prisoners, were cited in the report as the instigators of the crime: Benjamim Vargas, Danton Coelho, Euvaldo Lodi, and Ângelo Mendes de Morais. Evandro Lins e Silva, lawyer of Lodi and Mendes de Morais, the two most seriously implicated, argued successfully that Lodi should make no deal that would strip his congressional immunities, and he was eventually successful in preventing a civilian court trial of Mendes de Morais by maintaining that a four-star general could be judged only by the military justice system. The Superior Military Tribunal decided to drop the case against Mendes de Morais.[17]

The civilian judiciary sentenced Alcino and Climério, who had gone to Tonelero Street, to thirty-three years of imprisonment. Taxi driver Nelson Raimundo, who had driven them there, was sentenced to eleven years, and José Antônio Soares, the driver who had asked Alcino to kill Lacerda, received a twenty-six-year sentence. Gregório Fortunato was condemned to serve twenty-five years.[18]

8. Demanding the Resignation of Vargas (August 1954)

After the assassination of Major Vaz, Carlos asked Hermano Alves to cover the war ministry for the *Tribuna* and he told Hilcar Leite to assign a special group of reporters to help Luís Jorge Lobo cover Catete Palace. Carlos himself, in articles and broadcasts, led the campaign to drive Vargas from office. He spoke frequently on Rádio Globo but no longer used Rádio Mayrink Veiga, whose owner, Victor Costa, ran the government's Rádio Nacional and was accused by the *Tribuna* of having given Gregório Fortunato 500,000 cruzeiros.[1]

In the *Tribuna* on August 9, Carlos wrote that Vargas was hiding the criminals and had lost his authority to be president when the assassins were found to be his own men. In Congress that afternoon Aliomar Baleeiro demanded that Vargas resign so that the crime could be investigated with impartiality and safety. Transport Minister José Américo, also on the ninth, went to Catete Palace and advised Vargas to step aside in view of the disorders in the country. But the president, speaking a few hours later to Casa Civil head Lourival Fontes, vowed to serve out his mandate and said that, if necessary, he would "fight in the streets and only leave here dead."[2]

At the Brazilian Press Association (ABI) on the night of August 9, members of the Lantern Club heard Odilon Braga add "a new hero to the glory of the Eighteen" of the Copacabana Fort uprising of 1922: Major Vaz. To the crowd at the meeting, which included opposition senators and congressmen, a transmitter brought the voice of Carlos Lacerda, speaking to a radio audience from his home.[3] Carlos, in a reference to his wound, explained that he could not be with the club members "for reasons that you know" but could address them "thanks to Rádio Globo and Raul Brunini."

The speech was one of the most stirring ever delivered by Lacerda. After reading a message from Cardinal Jaime de Barros Câmara about the seventh-day Mass for the soul of Vaz to be celebrated on the eleventh, Carlos read the psalm beginning "The Lord is my refuge and strength" and then expressed the hope that the psalm would be with the soul of Vaz, "who fell for me, who fell for us." Carlos called Vaz, father of four small children, the father of the year, sacrificed on behalf of the liberty and safety of all Brazilian children.

Picturing himself as a man without hatred, Carlos in his speech forgave Getúlio Vargas for his "lack of conscience." Expressing forgiveness also for Lutero Vargas, he explained that the president's son could not help being associated with crime for he had been brought up in a setting in which crime was practiced daily.

Carlos quoted much that Vaz had said in response to dangers, such as the Paquetá Island explosion. If he should die at the side of Carlos, Vaz had said, "the people will have to decide between their desire to live in peace and their condition of a people enslaved by terror and corruption." Was it necessary, Carlos asked, for this simple, warmhearted father to be killed in order to have Vargas dissolve his illegal band of so-called personal guards and, after almost twenty years of promiscuity with bandits, realize that he was surrounded by thugs and criminals? "If," Carlos said, "there remains a trace of patriotism in the soul of Getúlio Vargas, he will understand . . . that his presence in the government at this moment constitutes a threat to the tranquility of the Brazilian family, and that his presence at the head of the government is a defiance and an intolerable insult to the conscience of Brazilians."

Problems with the ABI loudspeaker sent the Lantern Club members into the street where they joined the crowd that listened to Carlos' speech as delivered by automobile radios. Following the speech, the crowd, shouting "Viva Lacerda," went to the square in front of the Municipal Chamber for an improvised rally with oratory provided by candidates of the Popular Alliance against Thefts and Coups.[4]

When Cardinal Jaime Câmara spoke to Vargas on the tenth about a possible presidential resignation, Vargas continued to resist. But his problem was accentuated by the rage of military officers, particularly in the air force. On August 11, leaders in all three branches asked War Minister Zenóbio da Costa to persuade Vargas to resign. But the war minister refused.[5]

Carlos on the eleventh also tried to exert pressure on the war minister. One step was to look up Vice President Café Filho and ask him to tell Zenóbio that Vargas should resign. With his foot in a plaster cast and with the physical support of two navy officers, Carlos went to the Hotel Serrador, where Café Filho agreed to receive him. There Carlos suggested that Café Filho assure Zenóbio that if he, Café Filho, took over the presidency, he would not alter the military setup except in cases where guilt was found. But the vice-president refused to take any step that might bring himself to the presidency.

With the help of the navy officers, Carlos then went to the war ministry, and, in the minister's waiting room, startled Mendes de Morais by his arrival. Zenóbio, described by Carlos as neither brilliant nor cultured, received the journalist and pointed out that they were cousins, having a common Madeira Island ancestor. Carlos asked him to persuade Vargas to resign or else depose him, and, when the minister said he could not betray the president, Carlos argued that Zenóbio had the choice of betraying the country or the president.[6]

Zenóbio, answering a phone call, learned of disorders downtown where thousands, having assembled around Candelária Church during the Mass for the soul of Vaz, marched to Cinelândia, tearing down Lutero Vargas campaign posters. When Zenóbio heard that the mob was in conflict with the police, he said to Carlos: "See what you are doing to the country." Carlos replied that the conflict had arisen because the minister was not assuming his responsibilities, and he offered to end the disturbance in five minutes "if you will authorize me to go there and say that you will ask Vargas to resign." Without that authorization, Carlos made his way to Cinelândia, where the police were using tear gas. He helped disperse the crowd by proclaiming, from the steps of the Municipal Chamber building, that the people could rely on the armed forces to handle the crisis.[7]

Vargas, scheduled to speak at the new Mannesmann steel plant in Minas in the company of Governor Kubitschek, flew on August 12 to Belo Horizonte, where law students were demonstrating against him. In his speech, the president condemned those who, he said, used lies to bring discord, chaos, and anarchy to Brazil.[8]

Afonso Arinos de Melo Franco was furious. In Minas, he recalls, "Getúlio called me a liar." His reply, one of his most famous speeches in Congress, was given in "a sort of hysteria" on August 13. He asked if the term "lies" should be applied to the Tonelero Street bloodshed, the *Última Hora* investigation, import licence corruption, or the "disgraceful spectacle of the submission of our international relations to the orders and whims" of Perón.

The Mineiro politician claimed to be fulfilling his duty, expressing the views of the people and not the words of an oppositionist, when he asked the president to recognize that his government was a sea of mud, a sea of blood. In words for Vargas, Afonso Arinos said he had no choice but to resign. Following the well-applauded speech, Congressman Antônio Pereira Lima (UDN, São Paulo) embraced Afonso Arinos and told him, "You have overthrown the government."[9]

As orators, the administration had none who could compare with oppositionists Carlos Lacerda and Afonso Arinos. Novelist Josué Montello wrote in August 1954 that "two orators are leading the events or are led by them: Carlos Lacerda and Afonso Arinos. Whenever one of the two speaks, the floodgates open and the dammed-up waters, in a violent torrent of words, seem to inundate the country, sending it into convulsions." "Lacerda," Montello wrote a little later, "is truly a great journalist. However, as an orator he is even greater. . . . The fluency of the journalist, occasionally excessive, gained a new vigor in the fluency of the tribune." Marcelo Garcia has observed that Afonso Arinos, known for his profundity, was the second-best orator after Carlos, known for his charm and artistry. Carlos spoke in a very pure Portuguese, without faltering, and in a voice that essayist Fernando Pedreira calls fantastic. His physical presence, clarity of elocution, agility of expression, and perfect phrasing, noted by Montello, helped give him what José Américo has called a matchless and seductive ability. He was, Catholic writer Antônio Carlos Villaça points out, a genius at combining vehemence and irony and "liked to improvise in the heat of momentary emotion. He was a mixture of coldness and passion. . . . Passion predominated. . . . It is impossible to imagine Carlos without the passion that characterized him."[10]

Oppositionist oratory, inflaming the people, strengthened the resolve of much of the military to demand the resignation of Vargas. Sentiment among air force and navy officers was overwhelmingly in favor of formally presenting this demand. The fifteen hundred army officers who had demonstrated a similar attitude at the Military Club on August 14 had been advised by the club's president and vice-president, Canrobert Pereira da Costa and Juarez Távora, to await further disclosures.[11] After that, confessions of participants in the crime were made public along with documents from the files of Gregório Fortunato.

Anti-Vargas demonstrations, such as those in Cinelândia and around Catete Palace, were inspired in part by the Communists, eager for an uprising to remove the "agents of North American imperialism," a term that referred to "the Vargas government of national treason, the UDN *golpistas,* and the fascist generals." According to the PCB, United States imperialism could be found behind the recent shootings because the corrupt Brazilian government imported "the methods of gangsterism from the North Americans." The party's *Imprensa Popular* called Goulart "one of the largest landholders of Brazil." PCB Secretary-General Luís Carlos Prestes reminded newspaper readers of the "sanguinary instincts" of Vargas, whose Estado Novo terror, he wrote, had been unforgettable and whose recent government, he added, had used the police to "barbarously torture and even assassinate not a few workers." While demanding the overthrow of Vargas, the Communist press also condemned Carlos Lacerda, whom it called an FBI "spy" and the "mouthpiece" of a group that wished to displace the Vargas "gang."[12]

Communist Fernando de Lacerda, uncle and godfather of Carlos, had the temerity to suggest that the PCB should not insist on overthrowing Vargas. Prestes therefore wrote that Fernando's "presence in our party is inadmissible." He called him "an instrument of the enemy, infiltrated in our ranks." Fernando's position, Prestes also said, "is exactly that of a person who fears the revolution."[13]

By August 20, when Carlos went to São Paulo, Café Filho was trying to get the military ministers and congressional leaders to accept his suggestion that both he and Vargas step aside simultaneously. Dutra had declared that Vargas' resignation would "tranquilize the nation." The Brazilian Order of Lawyers and the board of directors of the University of the Federal District had added their voices to the calls for resignation.[14]

Carlos, during his full speaking schedule in São Paulo, exhibited copies of papers from Gregório's files and stated that he had come to São Paulo to preach a "revolution of peace" to be made by the people within the constitution and for the resignation of the "puppet president, already morally deposed." Speaking at the São Paulo UDN convention, he supported Prestes Maia, running for governor against Ademar de Barros and Jânio Quadros.[15]

In Rio, officers of the air force gathered to hear Major Gustavo Borges read a report of Colonel João Adil de Oliveira about the IPM findings. Shocked by the revelations, the air force officers met again on the next day, the twenty-second, and agreed unanimously with Eduardo Gomes' assertion that Vargas had to resign. After thirty *brigadeiros* signed a brief message demanding resignation, for armed forces Chief of Staff João Batista Mascarenhas de Morais to present to Vargas, admirals met and agreed unanimously to follow the example of the air force. At the home of General Álvaro Fiuza de Castro, a manifesto was drawn up and began circulating for the signatures of army generals. Dated August 22, it cited criminal corruption among those close to the president and stated that the "political-military crisis" was "irreparably worsening the economic situation."[16]

Vargas, who had rejected Café Filho's joint resignation proposal, received the message of the air force on the evening of the twenty-second. In reply he told General Mascarenhas de Morais that "even if I should be abandoned by the navy, army, and air force, and by my own friends, I'll resist alone . . . I have had a full life. Now I can die. Never, however, will I give a demonstration of pusillanimity."[17]

For five hours on August 23, Paulistas participated in a "resignation march" organized by students. São Paulo women and lawyers issued appropriate manifestos. Meanwhile in Rio, Vice President Café Filho delivered a Senate speech describing the nation's situation as calamitous, with "order and the regime itself" apparently "hanging by a thread, on the edge of a cliff." Catete Palace was surrounded by a shouting anti-Vargas mob. Late that night radios brought the news that, "after successive meetings of top officers of the air force, navy, and army," the resignation of Vargas had been "imposed by the armed forces."[18]

At 4:00 A.M. on the twenty-fourth, following this news, Carlos was carried by admirers to the crowded apartment of Café Filho. The victorious Lacerda, warmly applauded, said on a radio microphone that Vargas "ought to rot" at the Galeão Air Base. Later, Carlos and Letícia joined festive friends at the home of José Nabuco and his wife Maria do Carmo. Bottles of champagne were opened.[19]

9. "Death to Lacerda" (Late August 1954)

Around 8:30 A.M. on August 24, radios broadcast the news of the suicide of Vargas, who had shot himself in the heart at Catete Palace. Almost as soon as the suicide was announced, Rádio Nacional broadcast two sentences based on excerpts from a penciled note of Vargas that had been found in the palace a week earlier: "To the fury of my enemies I leave the legacy of my death. I have the sorrow of not having done all I wanted for the humble."[1]

Carlos was thunderstruck. On his way home from José Nabuco's house, he stopped at a church to pray for the soul of Vargas.[2] At home a radio brought the spirited farewell message of the late president. It opened by mentioning insults and slanders unleashed by "the forces and interests which work against the people." According to the message, an "underground campaign of international groups" had joined with national groups in opposing freedom for the workers and independence for the people:

> I have fought month after month, day after day, hour after hour, resisting constant pressure, suffering everything in silence, forgetting everything, giving myself in order to defend the people who are now left deserted. There is nothing more I can give you except my blood. If the birds of prey want someone's blood, if they want to go on draining the Brazilian people, I offer my life as a holocaust. I choose this means of being always with you. When they humiliate you, you will feel my soul suffering at your side. . . . My sacrifice will keep you united and my name will be your battle standard.
>
> Each drop of my blood will be an immortal flame in your conscience and will uphold the sacred will to resist. To hatred, I answer with pardon. And to those who think they have defeated me, I reply with my victory. I was a slave of the people, and today I am freeing myself for eternal life. But this people whose slave I was will no longer be slave of anyone. My sacrifice will remain forever in their souls and my name will be the price of their ransom.

Vargas, in his final act, had done more than avoid "a demonstration of pusillanimity." He had assured a popular following for Getulismo. In the words of Carlos, the climate changed completely, with Vargas becoming "the Julius Caesar of Shakespeare. . . . The same multitude that had acclaimed Brutus and the killers of Caesar," Carlos explained, "began to demand the death of Caesar's assassins."

Vargas' farewell message, Carlos noted at the time, was read and reread sensationally on the radio to the accompaniment of appropriate funeral music. Therefore Carlos, upon joining air force friends at their Santos Dumont Airport quarters, phoned members of the new Café Filho administration. "What you are doing is crazy," he said. "You are throwing the people against the Café Filho government and soon we shall have riots in the streets."[3]

For the most part, the people were sorrowful. The crowd around Catete Palace, once anti-Vargas, grew in size and shifted in sentiment, becoming tearfully pro-Vargas.[4] But throughout Brazil the tears were accompanied by disorderly demonstrations, some stimulated by Communists who received PCB orders to lead the masses in revolution with the help of Vargas' farewell message.[5] In Porto Alegre four people were killed during the destruction of an opposition radio broadcasting studio and two opposition newspaper installations and during attacks on the American consulate and the local headquarters of the Partido Libertador and the Coca-Cola Company. The police in São Paulo prevented a mob, estimated at twenty thousand, from wrecking the building housing the Diários Associados. Riots in Belo Horizonte damaged the quarters of the United States Information Agency.[6]

In Rio, Afonso Arinos secured Army Police protection of his home after receiving messages that it would be invaded. Downtown, the police wounded three people while firing on a throng that tried to attack the buildings of the United States embassy and Standard Oil. In Cinelândia, locale of the PTB headquarters, a vast crowd listened to a reading of the farewell message. Then, after shouting "Vivas" for Vargas and foul epithets for his enemies, they screamed, "Down with the Air Force," "Down with the Amcricans," and "death" to Lacerda, Eduardo Gomes, and *O Globo*'s Roberto Marinho. They set two *O Globo* trucks on fire and resolved to assault Rádio Globo and the *Tribuna da Imprensa.*[7]

From the Santos Dumont Airport, Carlos made phone calls to secure police protection for the *Tribuna* and was fortunate that the appeal reached Cecil Borer, chief of the labor sector of the DOPS (who had arrested him for Communist activity in 1933). Borer, alone among the police officers, decided that policemen had to be sent to defend the *Tribuna.* While Borer set to work, air force officers flew Carlos in a helicopter to the Galeão Air Base.

The mob that went from Cinelândia to Lavradio Street, shouting "Death to Lacerda," was led by Communist Municipal Councilman Aristides Saldanha. *Tribuna* Secretary Nilson Viana, taking charge of the newspaper's defense, locked the front door and phoned the nearby *Correio da Manhã* to arrange an emergency exit via an adjoining roof. While Trotskyite journalist Hilcar Leite prepared Molotov cocktails to help the defenders, immense rolls of newprint were placed behind the door to serve as barricades.[8]

Members of the Special Police were of no help. They joined the mob and demanded that the *Tribuna* open its front door and hoist the Brazilian flag.

As the door continued shut, they entered an adjoining building and, from its windows, pointed machine guns into the windows of the *Tribuna*'s reporters' room. A few of them used a balcony to enter the *Tribuna* and hoist the flag. But the front door remained closed and the mob, unable to invade the building, was turned away by the police sent by Borer.[9]

Mauricinho Lacerda, Hermano Alves, Amaral Netto, Nilson Viana, Walter Cunto, and others at the *Tribuna* signed copies of the historic number announcing Vargas' suicide, but the circulation, like that of other Rio oppositionist dailies, was restricted by demonstrators, leaving *Última Hora* with practically a monopoly. The *Tribuna* was not printed on the twenty-fifth, the day on which an enormous crowd, said to have been the largest in Rio's history, accompanied Vargas' coffin to Santos Dumont Airport for shipment to São Borja. The procession to the airport was accompanied and followed by disorders resulting in several deaths, and many injuries and arrests. Air force soldiers made use of rifles to defend their installations.[10]

The *Tribuna* on the twenty-sixth blamed the disorders on Communists and hoodlums and condemned what it called the demagogic reaction of gubernatorial candidate Jânio Quadros to the Vargas suicide.[11] It listed the men whom Café Filho, without cooperation of the Getulistas, named to the new administration—conservatives such as Aviation Minister Eduardo Gomes and Foreign Minister Raul Fernandes. Generals who had signed the demand that Vargas resign did well. Thus Juarez Távora became head of the Casa Militar and Henrique Duffles Teixeira Lott became war minister.

Café Filho, sounding out currents in his search for a new mayor of the Federal District, sent Aluísio Alves (like himself a native of Rio Grande do Norte) to the Galeão Air Base to discuss with Carlos the possible appointment of engineer Alim Pedro. Carlos expressed support for Alim Pedro and also his concern lest Café Filho try to govern without considering that Brazil had experienced a cataclysm. Writing in the *Tribuna* on the twenty-seventh, Carlos said that the new administration should deprive the "oligarchy" of the control it had "abusively obtained" over financial organs and propaganda vehicles. To act otherwise, he said, would mean a repetition of the failure that had followed the overthrow of Vargas in October 1945.[12]

Carlos, in the article, wrote that the *marmiteiro* (low-wage worker) calumny against Eduardo Gomes in 1945 was "nothing compared with the typewritten document, attributed to the man who committed suicide, that contains the outrageous slander that the armed forces and an enormous part of the Brazilian people are traitors to their country." "The falseness" of the farewell message, Carlos wrote, "is evident." He declared it to be "attributed to Vargas by those who, in his lifetime, exploited his authority and popularity for the most sordid acts." Calling a little later for an investigation of the authenticity of "this new Cohen document of the oligarchy's falsifiers," Carlos said it was a document of hatred and vengeance, a testament worthy of Roman Emperor Nero, who had also committed suicide.[13]

The farewell message was, in fact, authentic. Vargas had worked on the text over a period of several days with the help of his industrialist friend and speechwriter, José Soares Maciel Filho. Maciel had typed the copies in the belief that Vargas was preparing a message to be read in case he were killed in a struggle.[14]

From the Galeão Air Base Carlos cabled an account of the situation to the *Observer* of London; it said that the "plot" of the Vargas administration against him had been inspired by the wish "to create street brawls," a state of siege, and the suppression of the October elections. Then on August 28, after the plaster cast had been removed from his foot, he returned to the city, using a cane.[15]

He was ready to defend himself against the charges of bringing on Vargas' death and of behaving more recently as a coward. The first charge gained him the title of *corvo-assassino* in *Última Hora.* Nor did the Communists spare him despite Luís Carlos Prestes' assertion that the overthrow of Vargas had been carried out on "direct orders of the North American embassy," for Carlos continued to be described by them as a Yankee police agent and embassy spy. He was pictured by the Communists as in such fear of the people that he had fallen convulsively, in recent days, at the feet of the American ambassador, while Yankee marines used machine guns in compliance with the embassy's order for a "massacre of the people." Getulistas, too, made much of Carlos' disappearance. *O Radical* wrote of the cowardice of the "skunk and cheater," the "false moralizer."[16]

In the *Tribuna* on August 28, Carlos wrote: "It was not we who killed Getúlio Vargas, as is insinuated by Osvaldo Aranha, in chorus with the Communists and *golpistas.* It was in part Aranha himself. It was he, friend, confidant, and collaborator, who did not open in time the eyes of his boss to the crimes of the clique."

Using the airwaves that night for the first time since the suicide, Carlos made the same point to his Rádio Globo audience when he said that the real enemies of Vargas were not the thousands whom the late president had cruelly tortured but were the false friends who kept him misinformed. "In order to have the people forget the terrible situation of Brazil," he also said, "these same people who reduced Getúlio to despair now seek to call us responsible for his death and demand our head in the streets." And he predicted that Vargas' "false friends" would now "take their oaths and shed their tears" on the body of the late president, "which means more conflicts, tortures, infamy, slander, and devastation." The well-typed farewell message, Carlos argued, "cannot be authentic" and was a harbinger of evil and intrigue that sought to throw Brazilian against Brazilian.

Carlos told his radio audience that he had not gone to the American embassy but had "left the streets" to avoid being killed and to get a rest. Deep reflection during the rest, he said, had led him to conclude that the suicide would be explicable if one could learn what Benjamim Vargas had confessed to his brother to leave him so "crushed" at 8:00 A.M. on the twenty-fourth, when Benjamim had received a summons to testify at Galeão.[17]

Carlos' radio address did nothing to silence the blare of PTB loudspeakers in the streets that echoed the charge that Lacerda, the UDN, and military officers had executed Vargas on the orders of Wall Street. To Olga, worried about her son's safety, Carlos wrote a note on September 1 to say that he was with friends and perfectly safe. At a Lojas Brasileiras store, he reported, the people had been friendly to him. "Everything will soon be normal," he assured her.[18]

10. Most Voted-for Congressman (October 1954)

Carlos gave the Café Filho government good marks for selecting administrators. He looked forward to firm and "inflexible action" from the new Federal District police chief, anti-Communist Lieutenant Colonel Geraldo de Meneses Cortes, whom he had come to know at the War College before the events of August had forced him to stop attending his course there. Writing in the *Tribuna* about banker Clemente Mariani, the new Bank of Brazil president, Carlos noted that he had developed into a highly respected statesman since the days when "we criticized him for his participation as a *udenista* in the Dutra government." The new finance minister, Professor Eugênio Gudin, had called the Vargas 100 percent minimum wage increase a disaster and was praised in a speech by Aliomar Baleeiro that was reported in the *Tribuna*.[1]

Carlos feared that the new government, respectable as it was, would succumb to "the temptation of not acting" and would behave like a disinterested judiciary when conditions demanded strong action against "the gregórios and gregoriovitchs" who planned to use the electoral system to reestablish the domination of the "oligarchy." The temptation of "abstentionism," of passivity, Carlos wrote, was "no less dangerous" than the ignoble temptations to which the previous government had succumbed.[2]

Campaigning for the defeat of the "gregórios" in October 3, 1954, elections, Carlos denounced PTB municipal candidate José Gomes Talarico, described by the *Tribuna* as a Vargas labor ministry "falsifier of documents" who had "demanded the head" of Carlos on August 24. In São Paulo, where the PTB distributed badges showing a drop of blood next to the party's initials, Carlos found supporters of the Jânio Quadros–Porfírio da Paz ticket promoting the refrain:

With Jânio and with Porfírio
And with the dead body of Getúlio.

In Rio, 174 candidates contended for 17 congressional seats.[3] There the Lantern Club organized a campaign finale in the form of a "Liberty Procession" of 482 vehicles. Carlos, speaking that night despite a painful callus in his throat, delivered what he was discovering to be his most effective message: Vargas' many sincere followers among the poor forgave the errors of the late president because they understood his inability to govern, surrounded as he had been by false friends who only wished to enrich themselves and who should not be returned to power.[4]

At the Maracanã Stadium the counting of the results from the 2,761 Federal District ballot boxes was done by hand. They showed Carlos Lacerda and Lutero Vargas far ahead of their 172 competitors, with Carlos outdistancing Lutero, 159,707 votes to 120,913.[5] Among the UDN winners were Adauto Lúcio Cardoso in the congressional race and popular Rádio Globo broadcaster Raul Brunini in the Municipal Council race.

In São Paulo the Lantern Club's Calasans lost his bid for a Senate seat and Quadros edged Ademar de Barros in the contest for the governorship; the feeble showing of Prestes Maia was attributed to the alleged role of the UDN in the suicide of Vargas. If the anti-Getulistas were disappointed also at the strong showing of the PSD-PTB combination in Rio state, they found consolation in the outcomes in Rio Grande do Sul, where Goulart failed to win a Senate seat, and in Pernambuco, where Cleofas lost the governorship race to General Cordeiro de Farias.[6] The 326-member Chamber of Deputies in which Carlos was to serve would have 114 from the PSD, 74 from the UDN, and 56 from the PTB.

The election results were not yet in when delegates from abroad arrived for the Tenth Conference of the Inter American Press Association that began in São Paulo on October 4 and was transferred to Rio on the ninth. The delegates and their wives, almost two hundred in all, attended a lunch at the Mesquita *fazenda* in Louveira before going to Rio. Carlos, fond of sending flowers, delighted the wives of the delegates with his thoughtfulness. Flowers held a fascination for him and he seemed happiest when cultivating roses at his country place in Samambaia. But months had passed since he had had time to relax in that way.

Despite his bad throat, Carlos addressed the delegates at a banquet and argued, at business meetings, that the regular systems of justice, and not the government powers, should decide on freedom of the press matters. He was chosen by the Inter American Press Association's Mergenthaler Prize committee to receive the first Mergenthaler award for "meritorious achievement in Latin American press activities."[7]

Carlos' plan to depart with his family by ship for Portugal on October 15 led Lutero Vargas to go to court with petitions saying that Carlos, as the defendant in a slander suit, should not be permitted to leave the country. But the judge ruled against Lutero, and the Lacerdas left on the SS *Vera Cruz*.[8] Before sailing, Carlos spoke on Rádio Globo and promised that, on his return, he would meet with the Carioca people in their districts to debate the problems to be studied by Congress when it opened its session in the first part of 1955. He called the October 3 elections a repudiation of the Gregórios despite the "intense emotional impact, exploited tremendously and with money robbed from the people." After he left Brazil, Rádio Globo broadcast a recording in which he expressed his confidence in those who governed Brazil and explained that he had chosen Portugal as a place to rest because of the warm reception given him there two years earlier. "I owe it to my children to show them the land of their forefathers," he said.[9]

INTERMISSION

Journalist and Orator

The Lacerdas were in need of a vacation. While the exhausted Carlos handled countless details for the Inter American Press Association Conference, he and Letícia moved from their rented apartment at Tonelero Street to another, purchased with borrowed money, in the same building.

"I went abroad," Carlos said later, "because I was really in deplorable physical condition and I even suspected that I had cancer of the throat." The pain, it turned out, was caused by callused vocal cords, strained by campaign speeches, often made without the aid of microphones.[1] His energy was immense, but so also had been the intensity of his involvement in the dramatic events of 1954 both as an emerging political figure and as the publisher and editorial writer of the *Tribuna da Imprensa*. Like his physical condition, his nervous condition was poor on the eve of his departure for Portugal.[2]

The departure came at a time when Carlos, 40 years old, was about to begin a new career that would make him Brazil's most exciting congressman. He had, until then, been known primarily as a journalist.

A review of Lacerda's career as a journalist brings to mind the youth who filled notebooks while traveling down the São Francisco River and who had the ability to report at length on his findings in a manner that aroused the interest of readers. Journalist Emil Farhat, citing the São Francisco articles, has observed that Lacerda was a pioneer of objective reporting in Brazil.

Articles by Lacerda in *O Observador Econômico e Financeiro,* along with other descriptive pieces such as some of the reports sent from abroad in the 1940s, reveal the painstaking observer. Like the more combative columns characteristic of a later phase, they have not escaped the charge of being prolix. The articles about Japanese penetration go on and on and would have filled a book. One commentator remarked maliciously that Lacerda's articles were for people who were ill at home and had little to do but read, while another criticized Lacerda's inability to synthesize. "Prolix but not baroque," Brazilian Academy of Letters President Austregésilo de Athayde explained when he pointed out that the nonstop typist had an enormous flow of ideas, used just the right words, and was interesting. Lacerda's own intense interest, which kept him pounding away, had an infectious quality.

When the author of articles in *O Observador* became a well-known columnist associated with a political position, his writing was inclined to be sensational. Shocking disclosures were often the result of first-class research, as in the case of articles about Yeddo Fiuza and *Última Hora*. On other occasions the author was moved more by bias than facts, as when he accused President Dutra of plotting to remain in office beyond his mandate.

Journalist David Nasser has written that Lacerda's adjectives were charged with nitroglycerin.[3] Savagery was commonplace, not only in the Communist reporting that Lacerda came to know well in his youth and later, but also in the leading Rio newspapers. Unbridled invective, of the type used by *Última Hora* in assailing him, was a journalistic way of life. According to political commentator Fernando Pedreira, "Carlos Lacerda was the last and perhaps the most brilliant example of a type of journalism that has died. It was a time when journalism was more personal, factious, and aggressive than today."[4] Lacerda was careful, however, not to include remarks about the private side of the lives of the men he attacked.

Lacerda's secretary Ruth Alverga was sorry to see him run for Congress in 1954 because she believed he was the world's most accomplished journalist and should remain in that field. Her view of his ability was shared by David Nasser, who called Lacerda "the greatest journalist of our time."[5] He was, however, a much greater orator. As an oppositionist congressman, the leading vote-getter in the Chamber of Deputies, and potential candidate for higher office, he had opportunities for oratory that were unsurpassed and he made full use of them. In the words of novelist Josué Montello, "the fluency of the journalist, sometimes excessive, gained a new force in the fluency of the tribune."[6] Lacerda, actor and artist, spoke clearly and fearlessly with the ardent voice that Fernando Pedreira described as fantastic. Using phrases that some found marked by "a sense of poetry," he seemed to speak directly to "the heart of the people" about matters that he convinced them were serious. He was a genius at improvising,[7] much better at this than Rui Barbosa or Otávio Mangabeira, and became, without doubt, the greatest orator of his day and probably the greatest in the history of the Brazilian republic.

Lacerda's quick mind brought him fame for incisive and cutting remarks during debates, delighting crowds that filled the congressional galleries to hear him. He loved also the direct contact with the masses that campaigning brought, and welcomed opportunities to address hostile audiences. Such were the spellbinder's powers of persuasion that these audiences sometimes carried him in triumph on their shoulders after he finished speaking.

It is easy to agree with Emil Farhat that Lacerda's experience in journalism contributed to his success as an orator. The reporter, concerned about pleasing structures for sentences, became the tribune finding a way to express himself with literary polish. The young journalist was also like the more mature orator in Congress in that he described with urgency what was wrong and presented himself as the person who knew the remedy and how to apply it.

Lacerda's journalism was notable for its independence, especially evident when he left his secure position as the *Correio da Manhã*'s leading columnist in 1949 in protest against a restriction. The same independence would mark the freshman congressman, leading him to take positions that embarrassed the leaders of his party.[8]

The characteristic of Lacerda's journalism that served him best as a politician was courage. He became, in the eyes of much of the electorate, an individual who did not hesitate to jeopardize his safety or life in defense of the public interest. The people also saw an individual who, instead of fearing to take positions on issues, was eager to do so. This is not to say that consistency marked his views. He could praise the Democratic Left (ED) and its supporters in an article and denounce them a few months later. He left the impression, however, of remaining steadfast in his devotion to his principal themes, the eradication of corruption and the dismantlement of what he called the ruling oligarchy.

Samuel Wainer liked to say that Carlos Lacerda was not a great reporter and was a poor journalist, and he would point out that Lacerda's idea of making the *Tribuna da Imprensa* a new type of newspaper was a failure.[9] Lacerda, running the *Tribuna* with little financial backing, did have to abandon his dream of a daily that shunned prominent headlines. But he kept the *Tribuna* true to his promise that its views were "not for sale," a statement that could not be made about all of Rio's dailies. The Ugly Duckling was a success as a training ground for future journalism stars and had, among its reporters, an esprit de corps that reflected the hard worker in Lacerda. It kept his name and views before the public and helped him shake up Brazil.

The *Tribuna* losses were much reduced in 1954, partly because of increased receipts stemming from the role of Lacerda and the newspaper in the events of that year. The reduction in losses could be attributed also to the program of curbing expenditures instituted by Mauricinho. Lacerda's older brother, before turning over his *Tribuna* post to Elpídio Reis in May 1955, was able to report that the daily had actually made a little money in

January and March that year, only failing to do so in February because the short month and Carnaval limited the number of issues.

In watching expenses, Mauricinho early in 1955 irritated Carlos by suggesting that invoices for photographic equipment might be for Carlos' personal account rather than the *Tribuna* account. Carlos scribbled a reply to say he was not out to rob the *Tribuna,* for which he had purchased the equipment, and that Mauricinho's "disagreeable" and "rude" note, "inopportune, unfair, and untrue," had offended him. Mauricinho, generally calm as well as witty, was taken aback. He answered, "I would never have written you a note such as the one I received." He added that he would prefer to return to the less turbulent life he had known before coming to the *Tribuna* than continue risking a friendship with clashes that revealed Carlos' lack of confidence in him and his effort to do his duty.[10]

Turbulence, encountered by Mauricinho at the *Tribuna,* was frequently a characteristic of the Chamber of Deputies, and, with Carlos taking his seat there early in 1955, turbulence was assured.

VII.

Advocate of an Emergency Regime (1955–1956)

1. The Etelvino Lins Candidacy (April–June 1955)

On October 15, 1954, Carlos and Letícia sailed from Rio on the SS *Vera Cruz* with their sons, 15-year-old Sérgio and 12-year-old Sebastião. Their 3-year-old daughter, Maria Cristina, would be well cared for in Rio by Carlos' sister, Vera, and mother, Olga.

While in Portugal, Carlos was urged to undergo a throat operation, but he refused. Still troubled by hoarseness when he returned to Brazil after his ten-week vacation, he consulted his friend, physician Marcelo Garcia. Marcelo introduced him to a former actress, Ester Leão, who supplied the remedy in the form of a course that taught him to use his voice without tiring his vocal cords.[1]

The vacationing Lacerdas did not confine their European visit to Portugal. In Rome, Carlos made use of Bishop Hélder Câmara's introductions to meet Cardinal Montini (who was to become Pope Paul VI) and Monsignor Tardini. Tardini reacted unfavorably to Carlos' expressed desire to help build a strong Christian Democratic Party in Brazil. "Don't do that," Tardini said, "Don't mix the Church with the inevitable corruption of political parties."[2]

In Europe, Carlos kept in touch with the political maneuvering that preceded Brazil's 1955 presidential election. Even before he left Brazil, observers were concluding from the 1954 election results that the Getulistas, associated with the memory of the late Getúlio Vargas, were likely to win the presidency in October 1955, a prospect that dismayed Carlos. Getulismo was especially strong in the Brazilian Labor Party (PTB) and flourished also in the Social Democratic Party (PSD), Brazil's largest. Juscelino Kubitschek, the exuberant governor of Minas Gerais and one of the favorites of the Getulistas, was making a strong bid to become the standard-bearer of the PSD.

Kubitschek's friend Hugo Gouthier, consul general in New York, phoned Lisbon to inform Lacerda that, if he would not oppose the Kubitschek candidacy, he would be named mayor of the Federal District. Lacerda declined the offer.[3] He felt that if a presidential election were to be held, the UDN should join the anti-Vargas sector of the PSD to defeat the "oligarchy" established in 1930 by Vargas. That oligarchy, he felt, had given Brazil's demo-

Juscelino Kubitschek. (Drawing by LAN in Sebastião Nery, *Folclore Político,* 2)

cratic system such serious defects that the wisest course would be to suspend the election and concentrate on reforming the system.

Writing from Lisbon to outgoing Pernambuco Governor Etelvino Lins, of the PSD anti-Vargas wing, Carlos argued that the Juscelino Kubitschek candidacy embodied "a personalist and opportunist formula, destitute of authentic popular content" and would be dependent on populism. "You have the qualities," he told Etelvino Lins, "to bring about a solution of true democratic unity and national salvation." Lacerda, in his letter, also criticized the administration of João Café Filho, who had reached the presidency with the suicide of Vargas. It was an anti-Getulista administration, but Lacerda wrote that it failed to "perceive the need to promote a unity solution" and was making itself unpopular unnecessarily with an austerity program that "asks sacrifices of the people but does not impose them on the members of the oligarchy."[4]

When Carlos stepped off the *Vera Cruz* in Rio on December 27, he told reporters that Juscelino Kubitschek had violated the constitution by initiating electoral propaganda while still in the Minas governorship. In Congress, Carlos said, he would work for a revision of the election laws and advocate that Portuguese citizens, with over five years' residence in Brazil, have the right to vote in Brazil.[5]

President João Café Filho. (Hilde Weber drawing in Hilde Weber, *O Brasil em Charges, 1950–1985*)

Carlos has written that he returned to a country governed by a timid administration that failed to understand its mission to complete the August 1954 "revolution" by postponing the elections and setting up an "emergency regime," during which the electoral ways and constitution would be modified to provide "true democracy" and "destroy" the long-dominant "oligarchy." "I have come from Portugal," he told President Café Filho in Catete Palace, "and find an unrecognizable country because the real country is not what is here." He added that the administration's resolve to hold the 1955 elections on schedule meant that the nation would be "committing suicide" by allowing the return of the same group from which "we thought we freed it." When Café Filho said he was not in the presidential chair to carry out a coup, Carlos pointed out that Brazil was in no condition for normalcy because it was "intoxicated" and "traumatized" by the events of 1954.[6]

Carlos had an opportunity to touch on his ideas in public on February 5 at a ceremony naming a street after Major Rubens Vaz. At the ceremony Carlos declared, "Our nation has been reduced to a swampland that must be drained . . . ; its institutions must be reorganized and its men rehabilitated." In the *Tribuna da Imprensa* he wrote that the elections would be a farce and result in misery unless changes were first made in the constitution and election laws. If elections should be held, he said, the people should not choose the "personally dishonest" Kubitschek, "the candidate of inflation who cannot explain his own fortune"—the "sly dandy" who had secretly backed the Labor Party's Vargas in 1950, thus "betraying" the presidential candidate of the PSD that year. Nor, Carlos added, should support go to President Café Filho's favorite "unity candidate," Paraná Governor Bento Munhoz da Rocha Neto, the relatively unknown "counterfeit candidate of a counterfeit president."[7]

Carlos, participating for the first time in congressional activities early in February, saw some hope for an anti-Getulista "national union" because Carlos Luz (PSD, Minas) defeated Kubitschek's candidate for presiding officer of the Chamber of Deputies. Despite this outcome and a call by the military ministers for interparty collaboration to avoid a violent campaign, the PSD nominated Kubitschek on February 10. But the PSD organizations in three states, Pernambuco, Santa Catarina, and Rio Grande do Sul, refused to support Kubitschek and became likely adherents to a "unity slate" in which PSD dissidents would join the UDN.[8]

Months earlier Carlos would have supported a move to nominate legendary General Juarez Távora, a rebellious *tenente* (lieutenant) in the 1920s, who, in August 1954, had signed the generals' manifesto demanding the resignation of Vargas. But Távora, now head of the Casa Militar of President Café Filho, had declared himself uninterested in running for president, and Carlos, respecting the general's declarations, had been promoting the candidacy of the less glamorous Etelvino Lins.

Early in April 1955, Carlos was shocked to learn that President Café Filho had decided on a Távora–Munhoz da Rocha ticket and was working to get the cooperation of São Paulo Governor Jânio Quadros; as part of the arrangement, Jânio promised to eliminate himself as a candidate in return for Café Filho administration favors for São Paulo. Távora, like Carlos, was dismayed at this development. He upset Café Filho by refusing to allow his name "to be advanced . . . as part of such commitments."[9]

Following Távora's declaration, the PSD dissidents joined the UDN, Carlos, and the Lantern Club in supporting Etelvino Lins. Lins, PSD leader from Pernambuco, was nominated on April 28 at the UDN convention that selected jurist Milton Campos to head the anti-Getulista party. Carlos and UDN Congressman Adauto Lúcio Cardoso, meeting with Etelvino Lins in his Rio apartment during the convention, discussed naming Munhoz da Rocha as Etelvino's running mate. Etelvino favored this choice, which Adauto Lúcio Cardoso said would please President Café Filho, but Carlos expressed his resolve to combat it lest the ticket became known as "the slate of the presidential palace." Etelvino then observed that his position would be difficult if Munhoz da Rocha, nominated for vice-president by the UDN, were subsequently attacked by the *Tribuna da Imprensa.* Some of the UDN delegates, noting that Munhoz da Rocha's ties were with the small Partido Republicano (PR), wanted a genuine *udenista* on the party ticket and were therefore cool to President Café Filho's favorite. The UDN convention failed to name Munhoz da Rocha, leaving Café Filho offended by its hostility to his wish to play a role in the deliberations.[10]

Carlos praised Etelvino Lins as a courageous, undemagogic candidate who had resisted Vargas in the 1950s and was devoted to the "basic reforms." If the presidential palace would "simply fulfill its duty of dismantling the oligarchy's machine," he wrote, the people would defeat the PSD-PTB alliance that had been forged with the selection of Labor Party (PTB) President João Goulart to be the running mate of Kubitschek.[11]

The presidential contest between Kubitschek (PSD-PTB) and Etelvino Lins (UDN) became a four-way race with the entry of two more aspirants. Anti-Communist Plínio Salgado, who had led the fascist-like Integralista "Green Shirts" in the 1930s, became candidate of the PRP (Party of Popular Representation), and big, gruff São Paulo populist Ademar de Barros was nominated by the PSP (Progressive Social Party). São Paulo Governor Jânio Quadros, worried lest his local adversary Ademar de Barros become president, told General Juarez Távora that it was his duty to prevent such a "disaster" by entering the race and splitting the São Paulo vote. Távora, the towering, conscientious "*tenente* with the white hair," searched his soul and then agreed that Ademar was "even worse than Kubitschek." Therefore he became the candidate of the Christian Democratic Party (PDC) on May 18 and quickly was endorsed also by the Brazilian Socialist Party (PSB).[12] Thus Brazil found itself with five presidential candidates, a far cry from the original desire of the military leaders for a single "national unity" candidate with enough support to avoid a violent campaign.

Carlos used strong language to express his disgust for São Paulo Governor Jânio Quadros and disappointment in Távora for involving himself with Quadros and weakening the Etelvino Lins candidacy. He called Quadros a "childish egocentric," a "delirious paranoid," a "virtuoso of felony" with the "smile of a grotesque Mona Lisa," and a charlatan, whose political morals were those of a Communist. Távora was described as a simple-minded idiot whose lack of political ability prevented him from resisting "the demoniac demagoguery and morbid cynicism of that dangerous, reckless adventurer who presently governs São Paulo."[13]

Aviation Minister Eduardo Gomes, the revolutionary *tenente* of the

Juarez Távora (*left*) and Jânio Quadros. (Drawing from *Careta*, October 15, 1955, reproduced in Adelina Alves Novaes e Cruz et al., *Impasse na Democracia Brasileira, 1951–1955*)

1920s who had been UDN presidential candidate in 1945 and 1950, asserted that "my candidate is Etelvino." Carlos, helping to inaugurate a weekly Etelvino Lins television program, spoke in June on TV Tupi to an audience estimated optimistically at 600,000 by the candidate's backers.[14] But late in June the Santa Catarina PSD, led by former Vice-President Nereu Ramos, deserted Etelvino in favor of Kubitschek. Etelvino thereupon withdrew as a candidate. He cited the "surprising" decisions of Távora and Nereu Ramos, both of whom, he said, had promised to support him.[15] The withdrawal allowed the UDN to turn, as many of its members had wanted, to the renowned Távora.

Carlos praised Etelvino's sincerity and denounced those who had contributed to his withdrawal. He said that the "sinister" Jânio Quadros was "a much greater danger to Brazil than a dozen Ademars," and that Távora, "an instrument of irresponsible forces," would have to "whitewash" an election in which he participated and defend the inauguration of the victor, either Juscelino Kubitschek or Ademar de Barros. Calling Etelvino's withdrawal "the grimmest warning received by this country since August 24," he pictured Brazil as moving to a civil war being prepared by the ambition and stupidity of its politicians, "unconscious puppets of the Communists, who depend on disunity to get the disorder they need for achieving their final objectives."[16]

Carlos' statement that the election would be won by Kubitschek or Ademar hardly supported the value of the poll conducted among readers of his *Tribuna da Imprensa.* The poll, which put Plínio Salgado, the anti-Communist former Green Shirt, in first place, served only to disclose how drastically the sentiments of the *Tribuna* readers differed from those of the general public. Conducted before Etelvino's withdrawal and published on June 6 and June 25, it showed:

	June 6	*June 25*
Plínio Salgado	2,567	5,066
Etelvino Lins	2,194	5,028
Juarez Távora	1,971	4,130
Ademar de Barros	153	159
Juscelino Kubitschek	119	148

Carlos, returning in June from a visit to the Amapá manganese mine, owned jointly by Bethlehem Steel and private Brazilian interests, praised the development of the area by private initiative and scolded Távora for supporting the government petroleum extraction monopoly. Távora, in defense of his new position, explained "the law is the law," but Carlos retorted that the candidate should offer to modify bad laws. If, Carlos asked, mediocrity, cowardice, and opportunism "are reasons for not voting for Kubitscheck or Ademar, how then can we vote for General Juarez Távora, who has renounced all he learned and taught . . . , and adheres to the sophism of 'the Petroleum Is Ours.'"[17]

"Juarez Távora and legality." (Drawing by Otávio in *Folha de S. Paulo*, October 1955, reproduced in Prefeitura do Município de São Paulo, *História das Eleições: Memória da Democracia*)

2. The Panair Strike (January–March 1955)

Carlos, branded as the enemy of the workers, began his congressional career at the side of employees who went on strike against Panair do Brasil in mid-January 1955. The airline management had imposed a fifteen-day suspension on one of its troublemakers—a pilot who told the management (thus bypassing his immediate superior) that if he did not hear from it promptly he would pick up meals for his flights in Fortaleza instead of Belém, which provided "rotten" food. The pilot's subsequent discourteous behavior in the presence of the company's superintendent of pilots cost him his job. Of the 152 pilots who went on strike to support him, 18 were dismissed.[1]

After two of the pilots persuaded Carlos to support their cause, the freshman congressman proposed legislation for suspending government subsidies to Panair during the strike. He also began to collect signatures for the formation of a CPI (Parliamentary Commission of Inquiry) to investigate the airline.[2]

When Carlos spoke in Congress on February 18, the strike was still in effect despite the unanimous decision of the regional labor court in favor of the company. Carlos, describing the "rotten" food and insisting on the right of employees to defend "the dignity of their labor," lamented the failure of Panair's other 4,000 workers to support the strike. He argued that the government ought not to subsidize the struggle of the company against its employees. And he accused Panair of taking on incompetent new pilots and of wanting to be rid of the 152 because they were familiar with a plane, the DC-3, that was going to be replaced.[3]

Panair President Paulo Sampaio, in a published reply, expressed regret that Carlos, interested in only one side of the case, had made so many untrue and unjust remarks. The pilots, he said, resented disciplinary steps, such as those taken to prevent them from flying planes at half the normal speed in order to build up their hours of flying time.[4]

Wealthy Antônio Carlos de Almeida Braga, whose insurance company did business with Panair, arranged for Carlos to meet with Paulo Sampaio, a commercial aviation enthusiast accused by the *Tribuna da Imprensa* of having lost touch with his employees. During the meeting, at the home of lawyer José Nabuco, the Panair president emphasized the need for discipline. Carlos explained that he had been authorized by the strikers to call off the congressional inquiry if Sampaio would agree to accept the return of all but twelve pilots. Because Sampaio was unbending, Carlos said: "You don't know what a CPI is like. . . . You are playing with fire." "I'm not afraid of you," Sampaio replied.[5]

It was the aviation minister, Brigadeiro Eduardo Gomes, who worked out the settlement, early in March, whereby 140 of the 152 pilots returned to work. The returning pilots expressed their confidence in the word of the eminent *brigadeiro* and said that the CPI and its repercussions could be expected to improve the lot of the employees.[6]

The CPI, of which Carlos was *relator,* turned its attention to the investigation of tax exemptions and subsidies enjoyed by Panair. During the study, the *relator* received long, technical letters from Canada in which his friend, Brazilian air force Major Gustavo Borges, discussed foreign legislation affecting Panair and the relations between Panair and Pan American World Airways. Pan American, which was owed more than two million dollars by Panair, owned 48 percent of the Brazilian company's stock, a fact that led the CPI to study the possibility of recommending that legislation deprive airlines of subsidies unless they were at least 80 percent in Brazilian hands. When Paulo Sampaio testified, Carlos asked him about his large stockholdings in other airlines, domestic and foreign. In a reference to the daughter of Getúlio Vargas, he also asked, "How do you explain the use of Panair planes to bring contraband to Alzira Vargas?"[7]

The situation, Carlos has observed, created difficulties for leftist writers, because they loved neither Carlos nor the company. When journalists failed to support the strike, Carlos attributed their silence in part to arrangements made by Panair to give them free passages to Europe and back. But Paulo Sampaio, in a letter to the CPI, denied the charge. Trips by journalists to Europe, he admitted, were made in March 1955, when Café Filho visited Portugal, but most of the journalists traveled with the president on the cruiser *Tamandaré* and if any went by Panair it was at their own cost.[8]

Carlos, continuing to maintain that Panair paid for the European trips, blamed such a trip for what he called the pro–Paulo Sampaio attitude of journalist Antônio Maria. Antônio Maria, writing against Carlos at the time of the congressman's conflict with the Panair management, coined the term *mal-amadas* (poorly loved women) to describe the multitude of women who adoringly followed the career of Carlos. The term, implying that these admirers were insufficiently satisfied by their husbands or boyfriends, came to be applied with affection for the women and was even used by many of them with pride.[9]

When Carlos turned on his charm, a charm marked by a fetching simplicity, women became crazy about him. Serious affairs, however, were infrequent. An exception was his relationship with actress Maria Fernanda, who played the leading role at Rio's Copacabana Theater in 1955 in the revival of Carlos' play *O Rio*, originally presented in 1937.[10] Carlos, intense in his enthusiasms, was strongly attracted to the talented young actress who shared his zest for life and ideas and whose mother, poet Cecília Meireles, had given him affection when he started to work at the age of sixteen at the *Diário de Notícias*. The close relationship between Carlos and Maria Fernanda became a long-lasting one, regarded by some as a romance. In Carlos, Maria Fernanda saw a man with charming personal qualities and a rich imagination, whose talents and interest in everything, particularly in matters of culture, gave him the dimensions of a Victor Hugo. She saw a genius, a mortal blessed with the divine qualities of Zeus.[11]

For those who shared his broad cultural interests, Carlos was much more than a fiery newspaper columnist and gifted orator—more even than a handsome knight with delightful manners and a sparkling intelligence. He was the advocate of the opening of windows for the enrichment of life, and he helped open the windows.[12]

3. Contentious Congressman (July–September 1955)

Paulo Pinheiro Chagas, longtime PSD congressman from Minas, has written that "Carlos Lacerda was the greatest tribune to have taken a seat in the Chamber of Deputies. In my opinion, no one has surpassed him since the days of the empire. . . . He was an orator who gripped and dominated his audience with his cultured eloquence, characterized by beautiful expression and the sparkle of courage. He spoke with the spontaneity of running water, and like it, not infrequently overflowed in violent whirlpools."

The quickness of Carlos' mind allowed him to prepare well in a short time for subjects new to him. It also made him famous for incisive, cutting replies during debates. When a congressman called him a thief, who took away the honor of others, Carlos shot back that his accuser could relax because he had nothing for Carlos to steal. Better known was the reply of Carlos when a PTB congressman, in an interruption, called a speech of Carlos a purgative. "And your interruption," Carlos retorted, "is the effect of it."[1]

Carlos' participation in congressional debates was carried out with more stress than he or his observers realized. The stress frequently produced a physical reaction, evident after his return home. His blood pressure low, he would sweat and feel cold.[2]

The galleries were packed when Carlos spoke on July 4, 1955, about the coming election. Addressing the supporters of vice-presidential candidate João Goulart (known as "Jango"), he said their man was likely to win but the victory would take the country to civil war. He called on Congress to find a formula to allow the executive branch, made up of honorable men, "to carry out the political reforms essential for a viable democratic regime in Brazil." An emergency regime, he said, would prevent a coup d'état, certain to result from electoral practices that featured false promises and the corraling of voters and that amounted simply to a whitewash to cover up "arbitrariness, corruption, and coercion."

Visitors in the galleries were treated, as they had expected, to deft repartee and unconventional ideas from Carlos. In response to the groans that greeted his proposal that Congress surrender its legislative powers, Carlos remarked that the protests came from the very people who had submitted to such a situation during the Estado Novo dictatorship of Vargas. When a PSD congressman asked if Carlos wanted Congress to annul itself, he replied that Congress was already "completely annulled." Communist-backed Antônio Bruzzi de Mendonça, critical of Carlos for presenting no clear ideas about the measures of salvation to be enacted by his "emergency regime," said, "As far as I can see, your only program is to establish a regime that will turn Brazil's wealth over to foreign trusts." "Your Excellency," Carlos answered, "is mistaken; I am not proposing a Communist regime."[3]

Afonso Arinos de Melo Franco writes that Carlos, with support among young military officers, defended the establishment of a two-year regime of "exception" that would "really be a dictatorship." This attitude, he adds, made "my position of UDN congressional leader terribly difficult" despite the objection of most of the UDN congressmen to Carlos' "ideas for a coup." According to Afonso Arinos, Carlos' "tirades and proposals, almost always senseless but almost always brilliant, had a greater repercussion than my explanations."[4]

It seemed possible that Carlos had considerable military support when Military Club President Canrobert Pereira da Costa, chief of staff of the armed forces, delivered a thunderous speech at the Air Force Club's August 5 meeting in memory of Major Vaz. For two months Canrobert had been confined to his home by the illness that was about to kill him. He was in a pessimistic mood when he spoke to his military audience about the "maleficent, embittered forces of passions, of parties, and of all the uncontrolled ambitions of individuals and groups." He denounced the "multiple scandals" and the failure of Brazilian justice to punish the guilty. The general created a furor when he condemned "the democratic falsehood in which we insist on living" and when he spoke of "pseudo-legality," which he said was used to promote corruption and satisfy the appetites of the power-hungry. Canrobert forecast that, after the election, the denouncements of "frauds and lawlessness, imaginary or real," would ignite the furnace of "intranquility and disorder in our unhappy Brazilian land."[5]

Carlos proposed that Canrobert's speech be inscribed in the congressional record. But UDN Congressman Aliomar Baleeiro expressed his displeasure at the speech and joined Adauto Lúcio Cardoso in appealing to UDN leader Afonso Arinos to work with the leaders of other parties to uphold the institutions and oppose any "extralegal solution." On August 11, the UDN congressional bloc, in a slap at Lacerda, issued an official note "reaffirming its determination to defend the democratic regime and applauding the performance of Afonso Arinos."[6]

Afonso Arinos was trying to bring about electoral reform by following conventional procedure. It was a slow procedure, with law projects usually languishing unattended in congressional commissions. Such was the fate of most of the fifteen projects introduced by Carlos between February and July. The dynamic Carioca congressman had not been inactive but he could see no likelihood of anything beyond quiet death for the legislation he proposed to require the use of nominative and not bearer stock certificates, to make information in income tax returns available to Congress, to require administrators of government-dominated companies to declare their wealth, and to give Brazil a new labor code. The proposed labor code would end government control of unions, abolish the *imposto sindical* (the tax that financed Brazil's paternalistic union system), and provide workers with their long-promised participation in company profits; workers would be guaranteed rights at least as extensive as those enjoyed theretofore, and these rights would be extended to rural workers.[7]

Carlos was quick to introduce proposals to revise voter lists and institute an officially printed ballot, the *cédula oficial,* bearing the names of all the candidates for an office, to be given each voter by the electoral justice system at the time each entered the booth. The *cédula oficial* was to replace the prevailing method condemned by the UDN and *udenista* Justice Minister José Eduardo Prado Kelly, whereby ballots, separate ones for each candidate, were distributed ahead of time by the parties. They were hardly secret, being of different sizes, and had apparently been used with excessive zeal in the PSD-dominated interior, where, according to Prado Kelly, the number of ballots cast exceeded the number statistically eligible to vote.

Lacerda's *cédula oficial* proposal, presented in February, was rejected in May by the commission for elaborating a new election law. But the idea was kept alive by *udenistas* during heated debates with supporters of the Kubitschek-Goulart ticket. PSD leaders maintained that the time remaining before the election was too short to allow adoption of the change. They also contended that the electoral justice system was not extensive enough to carry out the required distribution and that, for political reasons, local election officials might refuse to pass out ballots.[8]

While congressmen wrangled about the proposed *cédula oficial,* Adauto Lúcio Cardoso and UDN vice-leader Oscar Dias Correia exhibited documents that they felt supported their claim that Kubitschek had enriched himself improperly in real estate while serving as mayor of Belo Horizonte. Adauto arranged to require that presidential candidates submit declarations of assets. After Ademar and Kubitschek disclosed that they were well off financially, in contrast to Távora and Salgado, Adauto took the lead in setting up a congressional commission to investigate the origin of the assets of the candidates. He obtained, as required, the signatures of one-third of the 326 congressmen. But the UDN, with only 74 members in the Chamber, was outflanked by the combination of the PSD (114 members) and the PTB (56 members). It was assigned only two places on the commission. Tarcilo Vieira de Melo (PSD, Bahia), named *relator* by commission president José Maria Alkmin (PSD, Minas), persuaded a majority of the members that the commission's constitutionality depended on an affirmative ruling of the congressional justice commission, a ruling that was never received.[9]

Alkmin, the adroit Kubitschek floor leader, worked with Afonso Arinos on a presidential election ballot compromise that had the blessing of Superior Electoral Tribunal President Edgard Costa. A so-called *cédula única,* listing all the candidates for president and vice-president, would be printed but was to be distributed by the parties as well as the electoral justice system and could be marked well ahead of election day. "A partial victory," thought Afonso Arinos. But, he writes, Carlos described the outcome as a "total defeat" and called "me a boob, deceived by the tricks of the PSD. He was diabolical."[10]

Carlos, emphasizing the role of the Communists in the Kubitschek-Goulart movement, was sensationally aided by labor leader Ari Campista. Campista, who resigned in August from the Communist-dominated Movimento Nacional Popular Trabalhista (MNPT), declared that Kubitschek supporters had bought Communist support for eight million cruzeiros, of which two million went to the MNPT and six million to the illegal but active Communist Party of Brazil (PCB). Speaking in Congress, Carlos said that "with the nation debating the problem of the alliance between the PCB and certain candidates for president and vice-president, I believe it important to incorporate in the annals of the Chamber" the interview given by Eudocio Ravines to the *Tribuna da Imprensa* about that alliance. Carlos explained that Ravines, former head of the Latin American Bureau of International Communisim and more recently author of the anti-Communist *The Yenan Way,* had given the *Tribuna* the international Communist reasoning for supporting Kubitschek and Goulart. When a PTB congressman from the far south belittled the speech Carlos was giving, Carlos suggested that his colleague could surely appreciate that the PCB was motivated by more than money in supporting the two candidates. The Ravines interview, Carlos insisted, revealed the tactic of the Soviet Union to use people like Perón and "the type we are cultivating in vivariums in Brazil." Congressman Bruzzi de Mendonça called Carlos a "shameless agent of American imperialism," and Carlos called Bruzzi a "jackass."[11]

Speaking in Congress again on September 5, Carlos asserted, on his "word of honor," that in São Paulo three days earlier he had listened to a recording of conversations in a hotel room there, during which leaders of the Communist MNPT had received money and instructions from Goulart, PTB Congressman José Artur da Frota Moreira, and Tancredo Neves, the last justice minister of Vargas.[12] A few days later Carlos created a stir by carrying into the Chamber of Deputies four machine guns, property of the army; the guns, Lacerda said, had been discovered in a Rio building by *Tribuna* reporters and had been intended for use by groups associated with Goulart. The denouncement of the theft from the army gained Carlos the title of "Best Congressman of the Week," a selection made by twenty-one political reporters. General Emílio Maurell Filho, secretary-general of the war ministry, was placed in charge of an inquiry about the theft.[13]

To combat possible coups, lawyers Heráclito Fontoura Sobral Pinto and Evandro Lins e Silva helped form a League to Defend Legality (Liga da Defesa da Legalidade).[14] The conflict between the league's objectives and those of Carlos, advocate of a "regime of emergency," led to a television debate between Carlos and Evandro that attracted wide attention during several broadcasts starting on August 25. Evandro, on the defensive throughout the debate, was described by Carlos as a crypto-Communist and a "useful innocent" of the PCB. When Evandro, in reply to a question of Carlos, said he could not recall whether he had belonged to the Partido Popular Progressista (PPP), a Communist front that was denied registration in 1946, Carlos exhibited records to prove that Evandro, one of the PPP's provisional directors, had submitted the registration application of the front. Evandro, complaining about those who called him a Communist, said Carlos was acting like "any Pena Boto"—a reference to Admiral Carlos Pena Boto, president of the Brazilian Anti-Communist Crusade. Evandro criticized Pena Boto for attacking lawyer Sobral Pinto, and Carlos criticized Evandro for attacking Pena Boto.

Carlos maintained that Evandro, member of the League to Defend Legality, defended "gangsters" and "an illegality that assures that impunity of criminals." Listing the "criminals," all clients of Evandro, he named former São Paulo Governor Ademar de Barros, former Federal District Mayor Ângelo Mendes de Morais, former Bank of Brazil President Ricardo Jafet, and Congressman Euvaldo Lodi. The discussion, in which Carlos had the upper hand, led Evandro to remark, "It is not easy to have a discussion with you, Carlos."

When Evandro said his own ideas coincided with those expressed in an article by Hélio Jaguaribe, Carlos asked Evandro if he knew who Jaguaribe was. Evandro replied in the negative, whereupon Carlos described Jaguaribe as a former official in the Vargas dictatorship who belonged now to the Itatiaia group (named because the group, a sort of "nationalist brain trust," had met in the early 1950s at the agriculture ministry's Itatiaia property between São Paulo and Rio). Carlos called the group "neo-totalitarian" and told Evandro (and the television audience) that it was "in charge of preparing the climate for a coup by Jango Goulart." Evandro said he did not know about those things. Carlos replied: "Well, I know. I am a journalist and it is my duty to know. If you don't know, it is not my fault. You ought to know about them to discuss them. . . . If you don't know about those things, read the *Tribuna da Imprensa* and become informed."[15]

4. The Brandi Letter (September–October 1955)

In June 1955 a *Tribuna da Imprensa* reporter put Carlos in touch with Alberto Mestre Cordero, who introduced himself as an anti-Peronist Argentine exile with a fortune that the Perón government kept blocked in Argentina. Cordero told Carlos that the Perón government had learned of the plans of anti-Peronists to stage an uprising in June and he therefore asked Carlos to arrange to have the Brazilian Catholic Church advise the Argentine Catholic Action movement to cancel the uprising. As it turned out, the uprising took place and was crushed.[1]

In July an Argentine friend of Cordero, Fernando Malfussi, called on Carlos at the Tonelero Street apartment to show him a document that purportedly confirmed Goulart's treasonable ties with the Perón government.[2] The document was a letter of August 5, 1953, to Labor Minister Goulart, typed on the stationery of the legislature of the Argentine province of Corrientes, and apparently signed by Antonio Brandi, a member of that legislature. It opened by saying that the writer had received Goulart's message, transmitted by Iris Valls, mayor of Uruguaiana, Rio Grande do Sul, and had divulged its contents, together with ideas that Brandi and Goulart had exchanged in Buenos Aires, to an Argentine cabinet minister. The minister, according to the document, had shown great interest and, after a discussion with Perón, had decided that further communications were to be handled through the Argentine embassy in Rio with Rio "lawyer F. A." acting as intermediary. It had been decided, Carlos also read, that Corrientes Vice Governor Clementino Forte, former General Labor Confederation leader of northern Argentina, would "coordinate all the labor union activities between Brazil and Argentina." The document went on to say that "the bearer of this letter, Sr. Ignacio Pinedo, who will go to Rio on an apparent business trip," had been authorized by Corrientes Vice Governor Forte to convey verbally to Goulart the Argentine minister's recommendations about "worker shock brigades" together with instructions too delicate to be put in writing. The closing sentences concerned "the merchandise which Your Excellency acquired at the Military Manufacturing Plant of Córdoba" and that was to be disguised as foodstuff and consigned to Uruguaiana Mayor Valls for delivery to Goulart.[3]

Carlos showed the document to Afonso Arinos, Congressman Armando Falcão, Police Chief Geraldo de Meneses Cortes, and war ministry Secretary-General Emílio Maurell Filho, but he did not reveal his source, having agreed with Cordero not to do so. They advised Carlos to check the letter's authenticity, as did several people at the *Tribuna.*[4] Inquiries made at the Rio hotels revealed that Ignacio Pinedo, the alleged bearer of the Brandi letter, had indeed been at Rio's Novo Mundo and Ambassador hotels from August 9 to 13, 1953. Cordero, who had spoken to Carlos in June about the unsuccessful uprising, told Carlos that "lawyer F. A." was Fortunato Azulay and that the lawyer's office ought to be raided by the police for the seizure of other documents bearing on Brazilian security. But Rio Police Chief Geraldo de Meneses Cortes refused to authorize the raid.[5]

With the approach of the October 3 elections, Carlos made the Brandi letter public. During a dramatic TV-radio broadcast on the night of September 16, just before the Perón government was overthrown, he said that the letter, proof of Goulart's treason, had been apprehended at the Ambassador Hotel during Pinedo's stay there.[6] On the next day a facsimile of the letter appeared on the first page of the *Tribuna.*

In Congress, Lopo Coelho (PSD, Federal District) said "the document proves once again, as though that were necessary, the preposterousness of the Goulart candidacy." But caution characterized the comments of *udenistas,* such as Afonso Arinos and Mário Martins, who called for an investigation of the letter's authenticity. Carlos, in Congress, presented demands that the Brazilian ministries of labor, war, foreign relations, and finance supply all sorts of information about Peronist agents and contraband arms from Argentina, together with the full text of what Carlos called the expression of concern of former Labor Minister José de Segadas Viana, made to Vargas in 1953, about the interference of Peronists and Communists in Brazilian labor matters with the help of Goulart.[7]

Goulart declared that if the Brandi letter, said to have been seized at the Ambassador Hotel in 1953, was not a recent forgery, it would have been made public by Vargas' enemies during their furious campaign of 1954, and he added that he would not debate the matter because of his reluctance to deal with blackmailers. The Communist *Imprensa Popular* called the "new falsification, by the American embassy's agent" Lacerda, one more "chapter in the vast Yankee conspiracy against Latin America."[8] PTB congressmen argued that "worker shock brigades" could hardly be organized in secret and they denied that Goulart or their party had anything to do with contraband arms alleged to have come from Argentina. Following a request by a group of congressmen, War Minister Henrique Lott formed a Brandi letter IPM (Military Police Inquiry) on September 22 and named General Emílio Maurell Filho to head it.[9]

Carlos, about to carry out his own investigation, sent a *Tribuna* reporter to speak with Uruguaiana Mayor Valls. After Valls criticized Carlos and called the Brandi letter a forgery by the Rio daily *O Globo,* Carlos went to Buenos Aires with police officer Cecil Borer and Rádio Globo broadcaster Raul Brunini.[10] Using the opportunity to do more than look into the controversial letter, he obtained confirmation of Perón's secret speech of November 1953 to the Argentine War College, reported by the *Tribuna* in March 1954, mentioning the plans of Vargas to join Perón in a move against the continental hegemony of the United States. And Carlos informed the *Tribuna* about Argentina's "return to democracy," being celebrated in demonstrations in Buenos Aires. A leader of the anti-Perón revolution, Carlos reported happily, asked that Getulista Ambassador João Batista Luzardo "be sent to us again so we can throw him into the river." Carlos also criticized Milton Eisenhower for what he called recent United States friendship with Perón, resulting in a deal allowing "Standard Oil to exploit the petroleum."[11]

With Brunini and seven Brazilian reporters, Carlos spent two hours interviewing Ignacio Pinedo, said to have given "delicate" information verbally to Goulart. Although Pinedo admitted being a good friend of "Joãozinho" Goulart, he denied his alleged role, including delivery of the letter to Goulart. Carlos attributed his denial to Pinedo's fear of being known as a Peronist or a smuggler, "just about synonymous." Pinedo, learning that Brandi disclaimed knowing him, showed Lacerda his marriage certificate, signed by Brandi as a witness. After Carlos found the signature similar to that on the Brandi letter, the *Tribuna* proclaimed the letter authentic. Carlos, back in Rio on September 27, told reporters "I have proofs of the treason of Goulart."[12]

On October 1, when General Maurell Filho reached Buenos Aires, the Argentine police were looking for Brandi and Clementino Forte, the Peronist vice-governor of Corrientes. The police chief of Buenos Aires gave Maurell a handwriting study that concluded that the signature of the Brandi letter was "almost certainly" Brandi's. Maurell cabled the information to War Minister Lott and it reached the Brazilian public on October 3, the day of the election.[13]

The Argentine police located Brandi and Clementino Forte in Corrientes, and Maurell was able to interrogate them there but not in time to communicate again with Brazil before the election. The general, as a result of his findings in Argentina and later in Uruguaiana, returned to Rio on October 12 with reasons to be suspicious of Cordero and Fernando Malfussi. They were both arrested and held in Rio.[14]

On October 17 Maurell disappointed Carlos. He announced that contraband arms were not reaching Brazil from Argentina and that the Brandi letter was a forgery. He analyzed the differences between Brandi's real signature and the false one and added that he could not say who had committed the crime.[15]

A more complete story was made public early in November when Maurell released his report. It became clear that the Brandi letter, typed by Cordero in July 1955 in the office of a Rio bank, had been given the Brandi-like signature by Malfussi. Cordero, a Peronist forced to leave Uruguay by anti-Peronists, had come to Brazil in 1953. There, according to Maurell, his swindling had become known to Fortunato Azulay—a reason advanced by Maurell for Cordero's insistence on a raid to seize papers in that lawyer's office. Cordero and Malfussi were found also to have forged a postcard from Brandi, giving Azulay's full name, and a letter from Goulart. To copy the signature of Goulart, Malfussi had borrowed a Goulart letter in Uruguaiana and knowledge of this incident had made Maurell suspicious of him.[16]

Maurell's findings were greeted joyfully by *Última Hora.* It proclaimed that "Malfussi and Cordero were inspired to act by Carlos Lacerda." The Communist *Imprensa Popular* wrote that, in "the scandalous Brandi letter hoax," the "forger Lacerda" had been associated with Aviation Minister Eduardo Gomes, Rio Police Chief Meneses Cortes, Foreign Minister Raul Fernandes, and Navy Minister Edmundo Jordão Amorim do Vale.[17] More frequently, Goulart supporters pointed to air force Colonel Adil de Oliveira, investigator of the Major Vaz murder, as Lacerda's accomplice in the Brandi letter affair. Carlos, speaking on Rádio Globo on October 18, said that "Maurell, so protective of the reputations of Jango Goulart, Brandi, Forte, and Valls," had done nothing to dispel the claims of the "Jango-Peronist newspapers" that Carlos and Colonel Adil were the falsifiers.[18]

The *Tribuna* called Maurell "infantile" for disregarding serious charges of subversion made by Lacerda and for attributing a matter of international intrigue to a personal feud between Cordero and lawyer Azulay.[19] Carlos, trying to turn the Brandi letter setback into an occasion for a vast offensive, maintained that Maurell took too limited a view in his investigation and was wrong in denying that contraband arms reached Brazil from Argentina.

In a letter written a little later to War Minister Lott, Carlos said that Maurell, "in his effort to incriminate us, decided to wash his hands of the crime of political groups against Brazil and the peace of the American continent—whereas, to be precise, he dirtied his hands in a report that would be pharisaical were it not pathetic, for it is the work of an emotionally repressed person." "Your Excellency," Carlos also told Lott, "tried to dishonor my name . . . by placing in charge of the inquiry . . . a general who . . . has personal hatred of the air force and the Lantern Club."[20]

Carlos, working on a deposition in October, received a letter from Segadas Viana to confirm that "really some of my reasons for resigning" as Vargas' labor minister "were related to the gravity of Peronist infiltration in our country." Segadas Viana revealed that Vargas himself had been "preoccupied and even irritated to learn of the interference of Peronist agents in Brazilian labor unions."[21]

Carlos' 168-page deposition was made public at the same time as Maurell's report. It quoted the Brazilian attaché in Buenos Aires as confirming the shipment of contraband arms to Brazil. Carlos also called attention to what he described as the "preparation of the laboring masses by Goulart in order to hurl them against the military." Further, Carlos suggested that the falsification of the Brandi letter might have been done by the Goulart group, "interested in discrediting me and promoting the idea of the innocence of João Goulart."[22]

O Globo analyzed Maurell's report and Carlos' deposition and found nothing in either that would please Janguistas (Goulart followers) who were accusing Lacerda and Colonel Adil of conniving with forgers. Roberto Marinho's anti-Goulart daily said emotions were "turbulent" and the time had come to "do away with any presumption of evil intentions on the part of our colleague." Commenting on Lacerda's methods, *O Globo* wrote that even when it had most highly praised his "patriotic action," it had always deplored his "temperamental excesses." So much ardor in campaigns of public interest, it wrote, had led Lacerda sometimes to commit "serious errors of judgment about people and facts." But, *O Globo* pointed out, even the bitterest enemies of the young congressman and journalist would be unjust if they denied his spirit of sacrifice. He was pictured as spurning corruption, living modestly, and risking his only material asset, his newspaper, in extraordinary combats. *O Globo* closed by saying, "These are the thoughts we want to present about Carlos Lacerda at a time when an aggressive and unjust campaign in sectors of the press and Congress is unleashed against him."[23]

5. The October 1955 Elections

On September 10, Communist Party Secretary-General Luís Carlos Prestes issued an appeal to the voters to save Brazilian petroleum from Standard Oil and defeat "the coup-minded generals by giving an overwhelming victory to Kubitschek and Goulart." Carlos, in a *Tribuna da Imprensa* editorial two days later, called attention to the order of the Central Committee of the Communist Party (PCB) for party activists to "mobilize the people" to vote. But he maintained that the people, having witnessed one election after another that resolved nothing, showed little interest in the October 3, 1955, "farce," which was to choose half the governors as well as the nation's president and vice-president. He wrote that the nation, "intoxicated by demagoguery and defiled by corruption," had reached a condition that could not be cured by votes or the "hullabaloo of electoral rallies."[1]

Kubitschek had recently told Communist leader Pedro Pomar that as president he would regard Petrobrás as sacred and untouchable but would oppose legalization of the PCB, just as he had done while in Congress. The *Tribuna,* probably unaware of that conversation, reported that votes for Juscelino and Jango would be votes for a ticket that demanded legality for the Communist Party.[2] But, Lacerda argued, votes for anti-Communist Juarez Távora would contribute to "the future success of Jânio Quadros—and this is a calamity for the future at least as serious as the one that threatens Brazil today." Besides, he wrote, such votes would not guarantee Távora's victory or change the makeup of Congress (determined in 1954) and would not separate Távora from his "malign tutors and sinister campaign 'allies.'" The only solution, according to Carlos, was an "intervention" by the forces eager to preserve Brazil from decomposition, and, if this step were not taken quickly, more drastic measures, such as a "pure and simple military dictatorship," would have to be adopted.[3]

With no "intervention" materializing, Carlos at length yielded to a pro-Távora appeal of Milton Campos, UDN president and running mate of Távora. The appeal of Campos, broadcast on Rádio Globo on September 19, was addressed to Lacerda, the Federal District UDN, and the Lantern Club, of which Lacerda was honorary president. It was followed by the broadcast of a speech in which Carlos gave his "unconditional" support to Távora and Campos and promised to lead the local UDN and Lantern Club in an electoral battle to defeat Juscelino Kubitschek and Ademar de Barros in the Federal District. Addressing his old foe, anti-Communist Plínio Salgado, Carlos pleaded with the former Green Shirt leader to withdraw in favor of Távora, not because Salgado was unworthy of votes but because Salgado could not win. Following Lacerda's closing call for a "revolution by the vote," the radio audience heard Lantern Club President Fidélis Amaral Netto, a long-time *Tribuna* reporter, announce the club's pro-Távora position. And it heard Municipal Councilman Raul Brunini, a founder of Rádio Globo, announce that Etelvino Lins had just phoned Rádio Globo to congratulate Lacerda on his decision.[4]

Távora discussed Lacerda's declaration with Quadros, who had taken a leave of absence from the São Paulo governorship to campaign for the pro-Távora National Renovation Front, a coalition of the UDN, PDC, PL (Partido Libertador) and dissidents of the PSD. After Quadros advised Távora to accept Lacerda's help, the austere "*tenente* with the white hair" told the press, "I receive with open arms the adherence of my old friend Carlos Lacerda." Carlos, preparing at that time to make his trip to Argentina, telegraphed Távora that he would prove the treason of the "Peronist candidates for president and vice-president, associated with corruption and Communism." During the trip, he said, he would send recordings so that his daily pro-Távora broadcasts, begun on Rádio Globo on the twentieth, would continue uninterrupted.[5]

Lacerda was back in Rio for the closing pro-Távora rallies there, mobilized by the UDN and the Lantern Club. Audiences, the presidential candidate found, were more interested in hearing what Lacerda had to say than in what he had to say.[6] The upright Távora, having declared that "I have nothing to offer and ask only for sacrifices," had campaigned with less optimism than Kubitschek, advocate of a vast program of development goals. Ademar de Barros, posing also as a builder, was contending in his own state and elsewhere with Quadros, who cried out emotionally that "no thief will wear the sash of the presidency of the republic." Quadros, stating that his eyes were "brimming with tears," made a last-minute appeal in São Paulo for the voters to reject "vice in all its repellent forms" and turn the regime over to Távora.[7]

On election day, October 3, Rádio Globo disclosed the opinion, received from Argentina, that the Brandi letter was almostly certainly authentic, and this led the PTB and PSD to accuse the radio station of violating electoral legislation prohibiting electoral propaganda on election day. Voters, often waiting in long lines at polling places, were so orderly that PSD Con-

Ademar de Barros. (Drawing in João Mellão Neto, *Jânio Quadros: 3 Estórias para 1 História*)

gressman Armando Falcão, citing the need of harmony in Brazil, expressed hope that the inaugurations of the victors would be carried out in the same tranquil climate.[8]

But on October 6 *O Estado de S. Paulo* predicted that a Juscelino-Jango victory would give Brazil a "permanent climate" similar to that which had prevailed in Congress on October 5, when PTB congressional leader Fernando Ferrari had kicked Lacerda during an exchange of insults. While congressmen and journalists had separated the antagonists, Military Police Captain Alfredo Tomé, called a "thug of Lacerda" by Congressman Bruzzi de Mendonça, had rushed onto the floor of Congress apparently intending to protect Lacerda.[9]

Even before preliminary results gave a good idea of the outcome of the voting, Carlos insisted that the election, under the existing structure, was "a process of national decomposition." He called for a bloodless revolution that would set up a "government by a cabinet," which was to free Brazil from political bandits and disintoxicate the people by speaking to them frankly, loyally, and even harshly. "The hour has come," he wrote, "to decide" and not sit by radios recording votes that would simply tell whether "Ademar de Barros sauce or Kubitschek sauce" would be served at the meals of pleasure seekers.[10]

It was clear, a week after the election, that the results would favor the PSD-PTB ticket, and this was confirmed later:

For president	
Juscelino Kubitschek	3,077,411
Juarez Távora	2,610,462
Ademar de Barros	2,222,725
Plínio Salgado	714,379
For vice-president	
João Goulart	3,591,409
Milton Campos	3,384,739
Danton Coelho	1,140,261

6. "Kubitschek Will Not Be President" (October 1955)

Carlos wrote on October 10 that when the members of the Café Filho government, especially the military members, had taken office following the fall of Vargas, they had entered into a contract with the nation to prevent the return of the Gregórios.

The election victors, Lacerda said, would not be in first place except for the work of the illegal Communist Party (PCB), which, he added, had been barred from electing congressional representatives and therefore should not elect the president and the person who, as vice-president, would preside over Congress. Labor Party (PTB) Secretary-General José Artur da Frota Moreira, he remarked, had recently left with novelist Jorge Amado to visit Moscow.[1]

A memorandum by Foreign Minister Raul Fernandes maintained that the PCB had acted illegally as a body and therefore the election victory should be "given to Juarez Távora and Milton Campos." The same position was taken by the *Diário de Notícias* and *O Estado de S. Paulo* and their columnist, UDN Congressman Rafael Corrêa de Oliveira. Rio's popular afternoon daily, *O Globo,* published Admiral Pena Boto's message to "Brazilian Patriots" saying "it is indispensable to prevent the inauguration of Juscelino and Jango to posts to which they have been improperly elected." But Rio's *Correio da Manhã* defended the inauguration and published, along with the PCB's *Imprensa Popular,* a declaration of Luís Gallotti, Electoral Tribunal president, critical of "unjust" references by anti-Getulistas to "corrals and vivariums of voters."[2]

The *Correio da Manhá,* replying to Lacerda's denouncement of its position, wrote that "everything about Carlos Lacerda is small, mean, and despicable." Calling him Gregório II, it argued that he, like Gregório I, was moved by a feeling of unbridled power and believed he should be allowed to get away with anything, including the incitement of people to carry out a slaughter and a putsch. In truth, the *Correio da Manhã* wrote, he had behaved in a cowardly way on August 5, 1954, fleeing to the garage on Tonelero Street while Major Vaz had died defending him and fleeing again after Vargas' suicide on August 24, "abandoning his fellow-workers" at the *Tribuna.* Lacerda, according to the *Correio da Manhã,* had lied to Congress about the discovery of army weapons by *Tribuna* reporters, had duped the *Tribuna* shareholders when he secured a large Caixa Econômica loan for the newspaper, and had obtained the loan for purchasing his Tonelero Street apartment through the influence of Gilberto Marinho, whom he had supported for election to the Senate in opposition to his own party's candidate.

Calling Lacerda "a false journalist, false congressman, false man of virtue, false Catholic, false Communist, . . . totally false," the *Correio* portrayed him as a cold "simulator of tumultuous passions." "The only real thing real about him is a conceit that is paranoid and a cruelty that reaches a murderous fury. His ideal would be to provoke suicides semi-annually."

These remarks led Carlos to publish "The ills of alcoholism" about Paulo Bittencourt, owner of the *Correio da Manhã.* "In recent times," Lacerda wrote, "his personality has rotted due to alcohol, wanton living, and a horror of old age." According to Carlos, "the rattlebrained dissipated sexagenarian"—born "the owner of the newspaper"—had allowed the *Correio da Manhã* to become defiled by the squalor of those who flattered and deceived him—those who filled his cup. One of the men who gave orders to Bittencourt, Carlos wrote, was pro-Kubitschek writer and businessman Augusto Frederico Schmidt, described by Carlos as a thief. But Carlos blamed Bittencourt himself for developing what he called a tactic of using personal insults to divert Carlos from the matter that, Carlos felt, required all his attention: the prevention of Kubitschek and Goulart from taking office. "His editorials these days will be useful to show my grandchildren when they come home from their first parties. Take care, children; do not drink so much lest you end up like Paulo Bittencourt!"[3]

PTB Congressman Ari Pitombo set to work to get Congress to cancel Lacerda's mandate on the ground that he was seeking to "abolish the regime." At the same time, an army colonel in the northeast denounced Lacerda for violating laws by inciting the armed forces to undertake a rebellious movement. Carlos, undaunted, wrote that the armed forces had no choice but to preserve peace by acting against "the democratic falsehood." Using his strongest language, he wrote that Kubitschek "cannot be president and will not be president." In Congress, Carlos raised the issue of electoral fraud, a favorite thesis of the National Renovation Front. He spoke of "the dead people who vote, the electors who vote more than once, and those who vote with false identification papers."[4]

To help ensure that Kubitschek would become president, PSD congressional leader Alkmin negotiated alliances with Ademar de Barros (PSP) and Plínio Salgado (PRP) and let General Lott know that he could continue as war minister in Kubitschek's cabinet. Lott, esteemed for his devotion to the constitution, also received appeals on behalf of Kubitschek's inauguration from Augusto Frederico Schmidt, Congressman Armando Falcão, and Senator Vitorino Freire.[5] But Lott's fellow military ministers had other ideas, with Aviation Minister Eduardo Gomes insisting that electoral victory required an absolute majority and Navy Minister Edmundo Jordão Amorim do Vale referring to fradulent voting and financial transactions that he said had been carried out by Goulart and Communists at the home of Osvaldo Aranha, longtime associate of Vargas. The views of the aviation and navy ministers prompted PTB Congressman Leonel Brizola to accuse them untruthfully of using secret government funds to finance the deficits of the *Tribuna da Imprensa*.[6]

War Minister Lott, who had the full backing of Café Filho, dismissed furiously anti-Kubitschek Coastal Artillery Inspector Alcides Etchegoyen and hotheaded pro-Kubitschek Army Inspector-General Zenóbio da Costa for making political pronouncements.[7] Aviation Minister Eduardo Gomes then imposed ten days of imprisonment on an air force officer who had declared that the military should back those who had been elected.

In the Municipal Chamber, supporters of Lacerda spent a week trying to give a reading to a manifesto of the Lantern Club, issued on October 12; supporters of the Left, among them Lacerda's old friend Hélio Walcacer, created such turmoil that the reading was not possible.[8] The Lantern Club had written the manifesto in order to persuade the people to resist the return of "the thieves and traitors," whose candidates, it said, were supported by "10 percent of the adult population, 20 percent of the electorate, and a little more than 30 percent of those who voted." Mentioning Juscelino, Jango, Mendes de Morais, Lodi, Gregório Fortunato, Getúlio's brother Benjamim, daughter Alzira, and son Lutero, the manifesto declared: "Here they are, back again, . . . triumphant, audacious, vile, and shameless; threatening and vindictive; ravenous and insatiable . . . , ready to fling themselves like rats, along with the Reds, on a Brazil that is divided and defenseless."[9]

Thousands of Lantern Club members filled the auditorium of the Brazilian Press Association (ABI) on October 20 to hear the club's president,

Amaral Netto, express these views. Its honorary president, Carlos Lacerda, called the club the true defender of legality and said the violators of the law were Kubitschek and Goulart and Congressmen Alkmin, Vieira de Melo, and Frota Moreira. Stating that "we do not fear Communism," Lacerda explained "what we do fear is that Brazil will be turned over to Communists. We fear that General Lott will turn the country over to João Goulart so that João Goulart can govern with the Communists."

"They say," Lacerda informed the club, "that I am beaten down, ever more isolated, and that I betray the democracy to which I have devoted the best of my life. They affirm that I am dishonest and a coward, and they use, as a veiled threat, the charge that I carried out a forgery." But, Lacerda maintained, he had never asserted "categorically" that the Brandi letter was authentic. What was to be regretted, he said, was the effort to make a martyr out of that "cruel, inhuman" Goulart and use Maurell's inquiry to destroy the investigation of 1954, headed by Colonel Adil de Oliveira, which had disclosed criminal activities by members of the recent Vargas administration.[10]

From the ABI auditorium, Lacerda went with a crowd to the steps of the Municipal Chamber building for a reading of the Lantern Club manifesto. The physical clashes in the streets that followed the reading foretold the verbal clashes in the Municipal Chamber the next day, when insults and threats caused such a tumult that a new attempt by a UDN councilman to read the Lantern Club manifesto was only partially successful. Meanwhile, in the Chamber of Deputies, UDN leader Afonso Arinos repeated that his party opposed solutions that contravened the laws and the constitution. UDN Congressman Adauto Lúcio Cardoso came out in favor of inaugurating the election winners, no matter how bad they might be.[11]

With *Última Hora* founder Samuel Wainer in the headlines in October 1955, Lacerda repeated his charge, made in 1953, that Goulart had allowed the falsification of the 1905 *Canárias* passenger list—a falsification inspired by the wish to show that Wainer's parents had reached Brazil before Wainer was born, thus exempting Wainer from the ban against foreigners running Brazilian newspapers. The new headlines stemmed from the decision of Judge Valporé Caiado de Castro that sentenced Wainer, a strong supporter of Kubitschek, to a year in prison for having told authorities untruthfully in 1935 that he was a Brazilian and sentenced his brother José to three years for a similar crime and for falsifying the *Canárias* list. Lawyer Evandro Lins e Silva, maintaining that the statute of limitations applied to the old declarations to authorities, described the judge as "intellectually dishonest" and turned to the Federal Court of Appeals. The *Tribuna* predicted the expulsion of Wainer. But expulsion appeared doubtful because Wainer, after marrying model Danusa Leão in 1954, had become the father of a Brazilian.

Wainer, as a result of Judge Caiado de Castro's sentence, was a prisoner at the barracks of the Military Police on November 7, 1955, when the Court of Appeals, in a 4-to-3 decision, upheld the sentence. Evandro Lins e Silva expressed faith in "more favorable jurisprudence" from the Supreme Court. He could perhaps also take comfort from a *Time* article that predicted that if Wainer's lawyers did not secure his release prior to Kubitschek's inauguration, the new administration would surely arrange to do so.[12]

"Many things," Lacerda wrote Marshall Field, Jr., had happened in October and therefore he would be unable to attend the forthcoming Inter American Press Association meeting in New Orleans. "For the first time in my life I feel tired. Just a little. And I will recover soon—so help me God." *O Estado de S. Paulo,* denying rumors that Lacerda had suffered a heart attack, blamed his health problem on low blood pressure and added that it was a condition not difficult for doctors to cure.[13]

7. Lott's Coup (November 11, 1955)

The death of Military Club President Canrobert Pereira da Costa on October 31 was a bitter blow to those who had hoped he would lead a movement against the inauguration of Kubitschek and Goulart. Carlos sought to prevent the new development from becoming a setback by showing that the memory of the general's leadership and views gave the remaining leaders the duty to act. In his broadcasts and columns, Carlos made repeated references to the general's August 5 speech and more than once quoted Canrobert as saying, "You can be certain, comrades, that we, your chiefs, will not let you down." Carlos chided "leaders unable to lead." Calling the August 5 speech the general's "political testament," Carlos wrote, "How can anyone forget the emotion with which he ended it, when we saw tears on the face of the man pronouncing those words in the tone of one who leaves no doubt, in the tone of a commander?"[1]

Carlos praised the bold funeral oration of Colonel Jurandir de Bizzaria Mamede, delivered in the pouring rain on behalf of the Military Club. The colonel, emphasizing the wisdom of Canrobert, asked if it would not surely be a "democratic falsehood" to sanction "a victory by the minority" and "pseudo-legality" to rely on "a mechanism intentionally prepared to assure voting by illiterates, prohibited by law." Mamede, Lacerda said, had expressed "the thought and feeling of the conscientious nation" and had interpreted the views of the military officers.[2]

War Minister Lott, among the orators at the rain-drenched burial, was furious when he heard Mamede's speech and none too pleased to observe Chamber of Deputies President Carlos Luz warmly congratulating the colonel.[3] After Lott let it be known that he would punish Mamede, Carlos Lacerda wrote that Lott's decision, like his dismissal of General Alcides Etchegoyen and "the campaign" against Police Chief Meneses Cortes, was "a step on the road of the moral disarmament of the military."[4]

The War College (Escola Superior de Guerra), where Mamede taught, reported directly to the president, and therefore Lott turned to Catete Palace to have the colonel removed from his post. But he learned that Café Filho had been afflicted by a cardiovascular disturbance on November 2 and was under an oxygen tent at the Hospital for Public Servants.

On November 5, while the Mamede case continued unresolved, Távora and Milton Campos released a statement to point out that fraud and pressure on voters had been so widespread that it would appear that rejection of the *cédula oficial* had been a deliberate plan to "falsify the popular will." The National Renovation Front candidates complained that many districts in the interior had lacked electoral judges. They expressed the hope that drastic, courageous action by the electoral justice system would correct the published results and punish the guilty.[5]

Távora, meeting a little later with leaders of the parties that had supported him, heard Afonso Arinos say that the UDN, in its "judiciary battle," stood for the absolute majority thesis and the annulment of the results because of the Communists' role. But neither Távora nor the representatives of the PDC, PL, and PSB (Brazilian Socialist Party) agreed with these two points. Therefore the UDN, initiating the "judiciary battle" at the Superior Electoral Tribunal, emphasized fraud. It presented evidence for rejecting the results reported from the states of Espírito Santo and Rio de Janeiro and prepared to submit more serious evidence from Minas Gerais.[6]

Carlos scoffed at the "judiciary battle," calling it a "joke in poor taste in a country whose major crisis is, precisely, the failure of the judiciary." Writing that "no legal formula exists for making a revolution," he maintained that "the hour has come for the military chiefs to decide whether to turn Brazil over to the enemy in the name of a false 'legality.'"[7] Heráclito Fontoura Sobral Pinto, a founder of the League to Defend Legality, objected to declarations of this sort, and therefore Carlos sent him a terse note on November 8, revoking all authorizations he had given the lawyer to defend him in legal cases. The step ended a close professional relationship dating from 1946.[8]

It seemed on November 8 that "the hour" of which Lacerda had spoken had at last arrived. Café Filho, finding he would have to remain in the hospital, transferred the presidency, on a temporary basis, to the next-in-line, Carlos Luz, well known for his aversion to the apparently victorious candidates.[9] In a page 1 editorial on the ninth, Lacerda wrote: "It is important that it be clearly—very clearly—understood that the president of the Chamber did not take over the government in order to prepare the inauguration of Juscelino Kubitschek and João Goulart. These men cannot take over, should not take over, and will not take over. It is important to tell everything truthfully. The government inaugurated yesterday, under the aspect of a routine succession, is a government that was born and will be maintained solely by the consensus of the military chiefs who were responsible for" the August 1954 overthrow of Vargas and who, having afterwards made a mistake, "are now in a position to rectify that mistake." Excessive legalistic zeal, Lacerda said, had brought the Gregórios to the doors of power, opening the way to a return to the "river of mud and blood." Prevention of that return, Lacerda said, was the purpose of the Luz government. But, Lacerda warned, the Gregórios, "the greatest conspirators of this country," were still at work, with Generals Zenóbio da Costa and Mendes de Morais "meeting openly under the complacency of Minister Lott, a man gone astray in his profession and perplexed by political situations."[10]

While Lott prepared to see Luz about the Mamede case, the Military Club made its position clear by choosing, as successor of Canrobert, a member of the anti-Getulista Democratic Crusade. The Mamede case, discussed by everyone in the club, had assumed such political importance that radios carried the news of Lott's visit to Catete Palace on November 10 and even described his annoyance at being kept waiting forty-five minutes while Luz received more recent callers ahead of him. When Lott was finally admitted he learned of Luz's decision not to punish Mamede and to replace Lott with General Álvaro Fiuza de Castro, the first to sign the generals' demand of August 1954 that Vargas resign.

That evening Lott agreed to join General Odílio Denys, the laconic commander of the Rio-based Eastern Military Zone, in a coup against the Luz government. The generals under Denys, loyal to him and Lott, shuddered at the prospect of Fiuza de Castro in the war ministry, and so did the impetuous Zenóbio da Costa, whose pro-Kubitschek Movimento Militar Constitucionalista appealed to Communists. Denys and his men ordered troops to come from the nearby Vila Militar barracks and take over Catete Palace, the police headquarters, telephone and telegraph operations, the *Tribuna da Imprensa,* and the Lantern Club. Lott wired commanders of the military zones and regions: "As the presidential solution of the case of Colonel Mamede is considered by the army chiefs here . . . to be an act of positive provocation, I decided to try to reestablish the application of disciplinary precepts in order to prevent the breakdown of unity in the army."[11]

Carlos was at home, before dawn on November 11, when he learned of the coup. He phoned the *Tribuna,* but already its building on Lavradio Street was in the hands of soldiers who brandished weapons, seized papers, and forced the employees to leave. After an unfriendly army captain answered his call to the newspaper, Carlos phoned military friends because he wanted to find a place "in some barrack" where he might "defend the legitimate government."[12]

Carlos asked the Marcelo Garcias, whose apartment was in the same building as his, to take care of his family, and then he set forth with a few clothes that Letícia and the boys had helped him gather. But before he could get his car out of the garage, Senator Vitorino Freire, coming from Catete Palace, cheerfully advised that Luz was already as good as deposed and suggested that Carlos, his life in danger, seek refuge in an embassy. Carlos, using the phone again, asked two of his military friends, Major Heitor Caracas Linhares and navy Commander Carlos Balthasar da Silveira, to meet him at Afonso Arinos' home.[13]

At Afonso Arinos' home, Carlos found oppositionist congressmen planning an early morning session of the UDN bloc at Tiradentes Palace. Carlos decided not to attend the session because he felt he might be killed on trying to enter the Chamber of Deputies and because he wanted to be at the side of Luz. With Heitor Linhares and Balthasar he set out for Catete Palace in the navy officer's car. As Carlos' car remained in front of Afonso Arinos' home, the UDN leader received threatening phone calls from people who thought he was harboring the agitator.[14]

In the meantime Lott's soldiers, headed by Generals Emílio Maurell Filho and Floriano de Lima Brayner, reached Catete Palace only to find that Luz had left. But they were not too late to arrest General Fiuza de Castro, who was supposed to become war minister, and General Alcides Etchegoyen, who was so enraged that he collapsed while expostulating and had to be sent to a military hospital. Besides occupying Catete Palace and the *Tribuna,* the soldiers of Lott and Denys arrested police officer Cecil Borer and Police Chief Meneses Cortes. An army major was ordered to arrest Lacerda.[15]

Lacerda and his companions, on their way to Catete Palace, learned that Luz had gone to the navy ministry building. Revolvers in hand and aided by Balthasar's connections, they entered the crowded navy building, where Ministers Eduardo Gomes and Amorim do Vale were issuing a manifesto placing the air force and navy at the side of Luz. While Eduardo Gomes left, to get an air squadron moving to São Paulo, Luz received advice from navy Squadron Commander Pena Boto, who attributed the coup to just four generals: Denys, Lott, Zenóbio, and Mendes de Morais. Pena Boto, the erudite head of the Brazilian Anti-Communist Crusade, persuaded the president and his supporters that their position in Rio was untenable and that they would do well to travel on the cruiser *Tamandaré* to Santos, São Paulo, where, according to navy Minister Amorim do Vale, the naval garrison was pro-Luz. Transport Minister Otávio Marcondes Ferraz, engineer from São Paulo, phoned Governor Jânio Quadros to advise of the government's plan to resist Lott, and he learned that all was quiet in the great industrial state.[16]

It was still only 7:00 A.M. that rainy morning when Carlos went aboard the *Tamandaré* with twenty-six other passengers who wanted to set up the federal government in São Paulo. Among the group were Luz, Marcondes Ferraz, Colonel Mamede, Justice Minister Prado Kelly, Agriculture Minister Munhoz da Rocha, Casa Militar head José Canavarro Pereira, and José Monteiro de Castro, who, as head of the Casa Civil, administered the presidential civilian staff. They gathered in the *praça d'armas,* the ship's most ornate room, under a portrait of Admiral Tamandaré. Pena Boto, navy Captain Sílvio Heck, and the other officers were above, at battle stations with sailors, when the *Tamandaré* got under way shortly after 9:00 A.M. Navy Minister Amorim do Vale remained behind to lead the whole fleet out of Guanabara Bay that evening.

The *Tamandaré* moved at only eight knots because two of its four boilers were not working. After it passed the *barra,* thus leaving the bay, warning shots were fired at it from Fort Leme on the orders of Lott, who opposed the departure of any of the squadron's ships. In the face of more shots from Leme, the *Tamandaré* kept under the protection of an Italian cargo ship that was leaving Rio. But soon the cruiser fell within the unobstructed range of Fort Copacabana, about nine thousand meters to the west. Fort Copacabana sent twelve shots in as many minutes, some going short and others long. The great splashes shook the ship, and the shells came close enough to fill the men aboard with apprehension and indignation.[17] Lott had ordered the forts to shoot directly on any departing Navy vessel that persisted in ignoring warning shots and signals,[18] but lieutenants at Fort Copacabana managed to miss the *Tamandaré* by small margins, while superior officers fumed. The crowd that had braved the rain to gather in the

Copacabana area was hardly impressed by the fort's accuracy, and Pena Boto, aboard the cruiser, remarked, "How poorly our army companions shoot."

Luz, like Pena Boto, opposed a retaliatory shelling by the cruiser lest it wreak destruction on crowded civilian areas in Rio. But he declared that "the mission must be fulfilled" and displayed a resoluteness that aroused the admiration of Lacerda, who had long considered the interim president a mediocre man.[19]

By 3:30 P.M. the *Tamandaré* was moving at sixteen knots (half its normal maximum speed) and Luz was in a good mood. About two hours later, however, he became depressed because the radio brought the news that Congress had deposed him. Legislation to declare him *impedido* (unable to govern) had been introduced at Lott's request and approved in both houses, after acrimonious debate, by the PSD-PTB-PSP-PRP-PTN-PR majorities. The nation's presidency was therefore in the hands of the next-in-line, Nereu Ramos, the pro-Kubitschek presiding officer of the Senate. Pena Boto, eager nevertheless to continue the sea voyage, assured Luz that they would be joined later by the whole fleet from Guanabara Bay. But Luz, fearful of a battle between the army and navy, sent a radio message to Amorim do Vale ordering the navy to remain in the bay.[20]

The *Tamandaré*'s passengers became more accustomed than they liked to meals of dried codfish. Some slept on sofas in the *praça d'armas* and others on cots in the warrant officers' mess.[21] Captain Sílvio Heck offered his cabin to Lacerda, who slept there after failing to persuade engineer Marcondes Ferraz to use it.

During the night, Pena Boto informed Luz that pro-Lott forces were in control of Santos. Luz, inclined to adhere to the original plan despite the news, put the question to a vote of the members of his government who were with him, and they all agreed not to turn back. But then Colonel Mamede pointed out that a landing in Santos, with the possible shedding of blood, could lead to prolonged civil war and prevent the military unity that was necessary for an eventual victory over the forces of corruption. Prado Kelly, impressed by the colonel's words, reversed his position. Except for Pena Boto, the others followed Prado Kelly's example. Carlos Lacerda, asked for his opinion, agreed with Mamede.[22]

Marcondes Ferraz told Carlos of his adventurous scheme for getting ashore incognito near Santos, dirtying his clothes, and hitchhiking a ride to the state capital, where he thought he might persuade Quadros to make the *Tamandaré*'s landing possible. Carlos told the distinguished engineer that, even if he succeeded in reaching São Paulo city, he would find Quadros unable to modify the resolve of the military forces in Santos to prevent a landing.[23]

Pena Boto was eager to take the *Tamandaré* to Bahia, where, he assured Luz, they would be well received at a large and friendly navy base. But Luz ordered a return to Rio and sent a message to Eduardo Gomes recommending that he abstain from further resistance in order to "avoid shedding the generous blood of Brazilians" and a clash within the military.[24]

8. Asylum in the Cuban Embassy (November 1955)

When the *Tamandaré* reached Rio on Sunday morning, November 13, the sun was shining again and the beaches were crowded. Bathers watched as the cruiser, demonstrating the anger of its officers, came as close as it could to Copacabana Fort while its loudspeaker, trained on the fort, blared the old navy song "Cisne Branco" (White Swan), played by the *Tamandaré* band.[1]

Shortly before noon the *Tamandaré* anchored in the bay and launches brought politicians aboard. Congressman Ovídio de Abreu (PSD, Minas), representing the Nereu Ramos government, negotiated with Luz, who was permitted to land after agreeing to resign the Chamber of Deputies presidency and take no legal action against the congressional *impedimento* vote.[2] Colonels Mamede and José Canavarro Pereira were arrested.

Among the UDN congressmen who came aboard were Afonso Arinos, Adauto Lúcio Cardoso, Juracy Magalhães, and Rafael Corrêa de Oliveira. Some of them conferred below with Prado Kelly while Carlos Lacerda, apparently exhausted and with circles under his eyes, spoke to Afonso Arinos on the deck. He invited the oppositionist leader to take over the directorship of the *Tribuna da Imprensa* and sought advice about what he should do after returning from the *Tamandaré* trip. Afonso Arinos, unwilling to be associated with the *Tribuna*, explained that running the newspaper would interfere with his parliamentary work. As for the future of Carlos, this had already been discussed in UDN circles, with the congressional bloc agreeing unanimously with party President Milton Campos' suggestion that Carlos should follow the example of Lantern Club President Amaral Netto, who found asylum in an embassy. Carlos has written that Afonso Arinos and Juracy Magalhães had the mission of persuading him to accept the UDN's decision "because the government said officially through General Flores da Cunha, one of the political harbingers of the coup, that it would not assume the responsiblity for my life."[3]

After a launch took them ashore, Afonso Arinos drove Carlos to the Peruvian embassy, while Adauto, Juracy Magalhães, and Rafael Corrêa de Oliveira followed in Adauto's station wagon. The Peruvian chargé d'affaires, unhappy at the idea of receiving Carlos, spoke of his need to consult his government. Afonso Arinos, using the embassy phone, called his friend Gabriel Landa, the Cuban ambassador. Landa, whose long tenure made him the dean of the ambassadors, was pleased to accede to Afonso Arinos' request, and so the UDN congressman took Carlos to the Cuban embassy, which occupied a floor in an apartment building in Copacabana.[4]

Already on November 12, Congressmen Adauto Lúcio Cardoso and Gabriel Passos (UDN, Minas) had presented the Supreme Court with a habeas corpus petition on Lacerda's behalf because, according to the press, a group of congressmen had been asking for his imprisonment. The PCB, not surprisingly, had included Lacerda's name on its list of those who, it said, should be punished by the new government. *Imprensa Popular* wrote that "the workers in the streets demand the immediate punishment of the *golpistas*"—the "vile traitors" who had prepared a "Saint Bartholomew Night massacre," that is, the men connected with the Lantern Club, "the Anti-Communist Crusade of Pena Boto," and the João Adil de Oliveira air force group.[5]

The situation seemed so explosive that on Sunday night, November 13, Cardinal Jaime de Barros Câmara visited Luz and appealed to him to abandon his plan to address Congress on the fourteenth. "Your presence could provoke hostile manifestations. The Communists could attack you. The government guarantees your life and rights but it cannot do so in the Chamber."[6] Luz refused to accept the cardinal's advice.

Afonso Arinos has written that Luz, in giving his speech in Congress on the fourteenth—courageously and firmly, but not defiantly—reached, "without doubt, the supreme moment of his long public life." Except for an unfriendly interruption by rash Congressman Leonel Brizola (PTB), mayor-elect of Porto Alegre, Luz's long account of his recent activities was delivered in an atmosphere of respect. Soon after, however, the Chamber was bedlam. Afonso Arinos could hardly be heard when he exclaimed that "the war ministry has transformed itself into a fortress of treason" and when he protested against the censorship of anti-Lott publications. During one bitter exchange on November 15, Flores da Cunha rushed from the presiding officer's table to the door of the Chamber accompanied by his son, who pulled out a revolver and flourished it in the air.[7]

Ambassador Landa was friendly to Carlos. Chatting with him one night about Cuban revolutions, he remarked that "you people tried to make a revolution without armed vehicles; you must have armed vehicles!" On the other hand, Landa's wife was anything but friendly. "She had been," Carlos said later, "a great friend of Getúlio and was associated with the *esquerda festiva* [festive Left] and joined people like Jorge Amado. . . . She had a horror of me, feeling I was a leading fascist." She was nonplussed with the arrival one day of a commission of women bearing a silver tray engraved with an appreciation to her for giving asylum to Congressman Carlos Lacerda. Messages of thanks, one signed by eighty men and women, were also received by the Landas.

Carlos' visitors were supposed to be restricted to members of his immediate family, but Ambassador Landa was broad-minded. When Raul Fernandes came to see Carlos, Landa resolved that he could hardly stop a former foreign minister from coming to his home. "I hope you two don't conspire," he said. Another visitor was former Foreign Minister João Neves da Fontoura.[8]

Still more visitors were admitted when Carlos, planning to go abroad, conferred with lawyer Fernando Cícero da Franca Velloso and others about the directorship of the *Tribuna.* The daily was allowed to resume publication on November 14, following an inspection of its files carried out under the direction of pro-Lott Colonel Jefferson Cardim de Alencar Osório.[9] Carlos, having failed to persuade Afonso Arinos to run it, turned to Dario de Almeida Magalhães, but the lawyer said he was too busy. Then Velloso phoned Congressman Aluísio Alves, who was in Belo Horizonte receiving treatment for tuberculosis. Aluísio Alves came at once to Rio and met at the

Flores da Cunha. (Drawing by Augusto Rodrigues in *Última Hora,* reproduced in Vol. 4 of Herman Lima, *História da Caricatura no Brasil*)

Cuban embassy with Carlos, Velloso, and Bishop José Távora. Despite the need of more medical treatment and time to direct the *Tribuna do Norte* of Natal, Aluísio Alves agreed to run the *Tribuna da Imprensa* as director; he was to be assisted by Elpídio Reis, who had become manager after the resignation of Carlos' older brother, Mauricinho.[10]

Ambassador Landa, at Carlos' request, petitioned for Brazilian foreign office papers that would allow his guest to leave Brazil. In the meantime, in Congress, Afonso Arinos, Adauto Lúcio Cardoso, and Mário Martins defended Carlos against the attacks of Brizola, who called him subversive, and Aarão Steinbruch, who accused "the enemy of the people" of having gone to foreign soil—the Cuban embassy—without furnishing the Chamber with the prior notice required of congressmen. Steinbruch, furthermore, proposed that the Brazilian government declare Landa *persona non grata* for having received Carlos.[11]

Lott, in a statement to the United Press, described Eduardo Gomes, Amorim do Vale, and Carlos Lacerda as "conspirators against the institutions." The PCB issued a manifesto giving full support to Lott for his actions against the "sinister fascist band" and declaring that the hospitalized Café Filho, "traitor" and "*golpista* leader," should not be allowed to return to the presidency.[12]

Preparing to go abroad, Carlos made arrangements for Letícia and the children to stay at the home of Fernando Cícero da Franca Velloso until the school schedule of the boys and the situation of Carlos would allow his family to join him. In a goodbye note to his mother, Carlos thanked her for all he owed her: "Life, your example, your inspiration, your love—I have lacked nothing and am a fortunate person. . . . Your whole life has been one of acquiescence to the brutality of facts. Today, once more, they impose themselves on our will. The so-called government of the people, by the people, and for the people has become a government of traitors, by traitors, and for traitors. I shall carry on with the struggle. I count on your judiciousness, your trust, your belief in your son who leaves you with this kiss of love and gratitude."[13]

After Landa secured the necessary permit for Carlos to go abroad, Carlos notified Congress of his intention. The notification, making no mention of a destination, brought a crowd on the afternoon of November 17 to the building in which the Cuban embassy was located. Landa, fearful of trouble, persuaded Police Chief Augusto Magessi to send a Special Police group to the area. The group kept reporters away from Carlos when he entered an embassy car that evening, together with Landa and Major Hermes da Fonseca Filho, Special Police commander. At the Galeão Airport, close to the Galeão Air Base, the police shielded Carlos from a crowd. Boarding a Pan American plane, he was heard to remark: "I have nothing to say except that I shall return. Viva Brazil!"[14]

Carlos left a written message, dated Galeão Airport, November 17, addressed to Aluísio Alves, Elpídio Reis, and their companions at the *Tribuna*. Published in the *Tribuna* on November 18, it said he was leaving "in order to continue the struggle in accordance with the new conditions created by the infamy of November 11." He emphasized the importance of the newspaper's survival and therefore instructed its employees to restrain their ire and bravura and remember that "small provocations are more dangerous than large-scale, vigorous, and necessary pronouncements, to be handled exclusively by the directorship." Carlos called for a firm resistance of the type that would not "increase the enemy's opportunity" at a time when traitors, cowards, opportunists, and corrupt people prevailed and Brazil was governed by "the regency of Gauleiter Nereu Ramos." He cited the "non-provocative courage" demonstrated in giving support to the "sublime" performance of the navy and to the "noble conduct" of Luz and his ministers aboard the *Tamandaré*, "under the command of one of the greatest heroes ever known to Brazil, the glorious Admiral Pena Boto."[15]

Speaking to reporters in Miami, Carlos said he was on his way to Cuba "to thank its authorities for the courtesies shown me by its embassy in Brazil." He said he would go on to New York where he would serve as a *Tribuna* correspondent and hoped to work for other Rio dailies. On November 19, while Carlos was in Havana, *O Globo* told its readers that Carlos would send articles to it and weekly recordings to Rádio Globo about international affairs and life in North America.[16]

Carlos, during his day in Havana, avoided expressing gratitude to Cuban dictator Fulgencio Batista. Instead, he visited the Havana newspapers and persuaded them to publish his appreciation to the Cuban people for having provided asylum. He stated that Nereu Ramos had been imposed by Lott and predicted that Lott's tanks would prevent the return of Café Filho from the hospital to Catete Palace.[17]

Lacking a visa for entering the United States, Lacerda phoned Landa, who, in turn, phoned the Cuban foreign ministry and persuaded it to make the necessary arrangements with the United States consulate. Carlos reached New York on November 19 and took a room in the Gorham, a small hotel close to Broadway. "Only then," he has written, "did I discover how exhausted I was."[18]

Why had Carlos gone into exile? The question has been raised by many, including Richard Bourne, who writes in his book about Latin American leaders that the need was debatable, "given that many in the *Tamandaré* affair were left unpunished." The British embassy, in messages to the foreign office in November 1955, concluded that Lacerda's departure "certainly damaged further his already greatly reduced prestige and influence." It pointed out, however, that he had recently been hanged in effigy and that the hatred of "many people on the left," who made him their main target, might have given him a "sticky" time in Brazil.[19]

In explaining his "exile," Lacerda admitted that "for the first time I was afraid of being killed." He cited the advice of *udenistas* who had told him, after the *Tamandaré* trip, that they had learned from a police *delegado* that his life and safety could not be guaranteed. His death may not have been "decreed," as Lacerda put it when replying to those who called him a coward;[20] but his position was hardly comparable with that of the other *Tamandaré* passengers, for the confusing events of November 1955 gave influence again to the very men (such as Euvaldo Lodi and Mendes de Morais) who, according to Gregório Fortunato, had urged the assassination of Lacerda in 1954.

For other reasons, too, he was ready to go abroad. Frequently he mentioned the exhaustion he felt upon approaching the end of what he called "the most terrible year of my life"—a year in which "I was called a falsifier and a traitor to Brazil." Writing from exile to Dom Hélder Câmara, he said that for several years he had put demands on his "body and mind" to a greater extent than anyone could normally endure.[21]

Lacerda's absence did not damage his prestige or influence and allowed him to make a long-awaited return to engage in another big battle that would have been premature had it come soon after the November 1955 coup and the inauguration of Kubitschek. Besides, as he saw it, the interval prevented the erosion of his prestige. He had, he wrote to Dom Hélder Câmara, his sister Vera, and friends, been for too long the sacrificial lamb, the recipient of all the hatred meant for others as well as himself. He explained to the archbishop that he had been the easiest one to attack and that it was therefore "natural and convenient to be away." Writing to Vera in February 1956 about his resolve not to return at that time, he said that to do so would mean getting uselessly burned while other oppositionists spared themselves. "The best service I can render now is not to let myself be used by those who have so far expended little." "I must," he wrote to Vera's daughter Lygia, "let time pass between the recent fusillade and a new phase of more efficient action . . . I am not going there to serve as a shock troop for third parties."[22]

The opportunity for a dramatic return to initiate a "new phase" was made possible during the last months of his exile when Lacerda obtained, from Argentina, fresh evidence to support his campaign against Goulart. Still abroad late in August 1956, he wrote in the *Tribuna:* "I have not wanted to live in Brazil as long as I could not prove the truth of my affirmations about the treason committed against Brazil by the band that has dominated it for a quarter of a century. That is why I expatriated myself."[23]

9. First Days in New York (November–December 1955)

Carlos had many friends in the United States, a result of visits to cover presidential elections and attend meetings of the Inter American Press Association, and his political and journalistic activities in 1953 and 1954 had made him well known in circles interested in South America. Writing to his mother from New York on November 27, 1955, he said he had more invitations than he could accept. One of the first he accepted was for a weekend in Connecticut with *Life* magazine's Andrew Heiskell and his wife, actress Madeleine Carroll. Carlos told his mother that the Heiskells had found a spacious house in Norwalk for him to rent, starting on December 23, and that it was only a one-hour train ride from New York.[1]

Carlos estimated that the monthly expenses for his family and himself, including the house rent of $300, would be $1,200, and he pointed out, in a letter to Fernando Velloso, that his income from the *Tribuna* and the Chamber of Deputies (half the regular pay, due to his absence) was by no means enough. He expected something for *O Globo* and *O Estado de S. Paulo* articles and told Velloso that he wished to supply unsigned articles to still another Brazilian newspaper and rent his house in Samambaia. A Brazilian in New York made arrangements for him to earn extra money by supplying Portuguese subtitles for wild westerns and other movies, at $200 per film, but months passed before this work began.[2]

Unexpectedly, a check for $730 reached Carlos from his father, Maurício de Lacerda, the inflaming orator and congressman of the pre-Vargas era who was working now as a lawyer for the Federal District government. A note, written by Maurício on December 13 and brought to New York by Senator Artur Bernardes Filho, explained to Carlos that the check was "for your Christmas with your wife and children—my grandchildren." The note, signed "your father and friend," closed with the hope that God would bring Carlos and his family a happy new year and a return to Brazil, "which I so much desire."[3]

Carlos had kept apart from his father since 1944, when Maurício's separation from Olga had become legal; and, in 1954, when Maurício had proposed a reconciliatory meeting, Carlos had refused, not wanting to hurt Olga.[4] Wrestling with the problem of whether to accept the check, Carlos spent many hours one night in New York conversing with journalist João Batista Barreto Leite Filho, who was on the Brazilian delegation to the United Nations. Barreto Leite, who felt that Carlos was trying to appease his conscience, kept insisting that Carlos should accept the money. Carlos wrote about the matter to his sister Vera in Rio and added: "Please show this letter to D. Hélder, with whom I spoke at length, last year, regarding the proposed visit of father to our home. I would like to have his advice."[5]

In a letter to 13-year-old Sebastião, Carlos told his son to remember, when he reached the United States, that the most important things to avoid were slipping on snowy streets and failing to say please ("the magic word that opens all doors"). "'Please, thank you, I am sorry' are indispensable, like salt for a meal or sugar in coffee."[6]

Diplomat José Osvaldo de Meira Penna, one of the members of the Brazilian delegation to the United Nations, arranged, at Carlos' request, for Carlos to speak at Professor Frank Tannenbaum's seminar at Columbia University. The seminar included several distinguished Latin American exiles, among them Alberto Lleras Camargo of Colombia and Carlos' friend Alberto Gainza Paz, who was about to return to post-Perón Argentina. Carlos' first talk about pre-1930 Brazil was received with more admiration than the emotional second one with its proposal that Brazil achieve democracy by a military intervention. Carlos, Meira Penna recalls, explained to horrified listeners that the military in Brazil "is different."[7]

Early in his exile, Carlos got in touch with Panair pilot Wilson L. Machado to serve as letter carrier because he feared his correspondence would fall into the hands of the Brazilian government. The pilot, who had offered his services after being captivated by Lacerda's speeches in 1954, agreed to receive letters from Lacerda's friends in Rio and mail them from Lisbon to the United States. Carlos would send his mail to Lisbon to be taken by Machado to Rio.[8]

The news from Brazil was not comforting for Carlos. Samuel and José Wainer were freed by a Supreme Court decision. Café Filho, having recovered his health, declared he would return to the presidency but was prevented from doing so by Lott's troops and was deposed by a vote of *impedimento* passed by the two houses of Congress during stormy sessions. While troops kept Café Filho confined to his apartment, Congress voted a state of siege for Brazil, and censorship was imposed on Rio newspapers. Afonso Arinos argued that nothing in Brazilian constitutional law authorized Congress to depose Café Filho, and the deposed president appealed to the Supreme Court. But the court could do nothing. As Justice Nelson Hungria wrote in his decision, "Against an armed insurrection, crowned with success, the only remedy is a counterrevolution by armed force. And this, positively, cannot be carried out by the Supreme Court."[9]

In the meantime General Maurell Filho, who had helped overthrow President Luz, sent Congress a new report about the Brandi letter that put some of the blame on Carlos. It said that the forgers, in carrying out their crime, had been stimulated by the "avidity" of political groups and some newspapers, such as the *Tribuna da Imprensa* and *O Globo,* whose "sensationalist political campaign" led to publishing reports without checking authenticity of sources.[10]

Journalists in the United States frequently asked Carlos to comment on Brazilian developments and accusations made against him in Brazil. Carlos did so late in November 1955, thus rejecting a suggestion, published earlier by *O Globo,* that he "follow the examples of Washington Luís and Otávio Mangabeira, who did not criticize the politics of their country during their exile." In his statement published in *O Globo* on December 1, Carlos pointed out that "the debate about the Brazilian situation in newspapers outside Brazil" was begun by War Minister Lott who "spoke to the foreign press in his interview with the United Press, making accusations against President Café Filho and his cabinet colleagues." "How," Carlos asked, "could I remain silent? I defended the behavior of my countrymen in order to establish the truth."[11]

In Rio on December 5, Lott gave an interview to *O Globo* in which he described Lacerda as having openly preached a coup against the will of the people in articles that would not have been tolerated in any country except Brazil. Maintaining that Lacerda sought to take some of the military "on the path of insanity," Lott nevertheless suggested that "the young man" should be viewed with compassion, being a mental case, the result of stresses experienced since infancy. "He had a dramatic youth," Lott explained, "in the Communist underground before he became converted to Christianity, but his behavior now demonstrates that he practices Catholicism according to the Marxist dialogue." The war minister pointed out that Lacerda's role in the events that included the murder of Major Vaz might have helped drive him insane. Expressing pity for Lacerda, Lott said that what was incomprehensible was that anyone should be influenced by his ideas. In reply to a question, the general asserted that he had never sought to arrest Lacerda and that his departure from Brazil was the result of "fear of his own shadow."[12]

Lacerda, in a letter written on December 14 to Lott, "Dictator of Brazil," expressed dismay at the *O Globo* interview and a subsequent explanatory note issued by the war minister. He wrote that Lott's treason to Luz and Café Filho, "the man who appointed you and had confidence in you," had been carried out to inaugurate "corruption and disorder," had no parallel in Brazil's history, and made the country the laughingstock of the world. "My indignation," Lacerda wrote, "appears to you to be a Communist characteristic and therefore Your Excellency would have arrested Jesus Christ when, in anger, he expelled the money changers from the temple."

Lacerda objected to a reference made by Lott to his father, Maurício de Lacerda, "in order to hurt me more" and wrote that "you must know that I have pride in the example of a public figure who, after more than twenty years of political activity, does not have in his record any treason, unworthiness, or corrupt act." Lacerda wrote that while Maurício, Juarez Távora, Eduardo Gomes, and Amorim do Vale had been "in anguish in prison," Lott, "general of the virgin sword," had made a career that was mediocre, passive, and accommodative.

Lacerda condemned Lott for "mixing Jesus Christ with Sigmund Freud in idiotic allusions to a guilt complex on my part for the death of Major Vaz." He argued that it was Lott, instrument of the assassins of Vaz, who should have a bad conscience. "The complex, Sr. Lott, is yours and flows from all your pores like fatty oil." Analyzing Lott's character, Lacerda found that pride, "the greatest of sins," made it unlikely that he would demonstrate remorse, "the only solution for the good of Brazil and rehabilitation of Your Excellency."[13]

10. In the Land of Uncle Sam (January–May 1956)

Letícia and the children arrived in New York by plane on December 15. In the Norwalk house on Christmas, when the Lacerdas were joined by the Heiskells and José Nabucos, the heating system broke down and they all suffered from the New England cold. The "consolation," Carlos said later, was that "hundreds of Christmas cards came from Brazil."[1]

In January, 17-year-old Sérgio and 13-year-old Sebastião started attending public school in Norwalk, and Carlos was soon writing his mother and sister about the accomplishments of the boys in school and in making friends despite the language problem. Four-year-old Maria Cristina, who did not go to school, was described by Carlos as "a charmer" who sometimes corrected his pronunciation of English.[2] To Cristina's delight, the "exile" afforded her good opportunities to have her father to herself. She joined him while he cooked, making dishes she considered terrific. It was a pastime he enjoyed and he whistled in the kitchen just as he had done while working in his flower garden at his Samambaia property.

The household included Dario de Almeida Magalhães' 25-year-old son Rafael, who had been assisting Carlos in his work since 1954 and was to act as a sort of secretary of Carlos.[3] Rafael joined Carlos and Sérgio on a train trip made in mid-February to Chicago, where Carlos, guest of the Chicago Council on Foreign Relations, gave two talks and a televised interview.

Carlos' work (and dental appointments) took him frequently to New York, where he made use of office space vacated by Argentine newspaper publisher Gainza Paz.[4] To avoid commuting by train, Carlos bought a car early in February, after the sale of his car in Rio. Back from Chicago, he used the car to drive with his family and Rafael to visit Canada. In Montreal they saw air force Major Gustavo Borges, who worked with the International Civil Aviation organization. In Ottawa they joined Brazilian Ambassador Afrânio de Melo Franco Filho, brother of Afonso Arinos and of José Nabuco's wife, Maria do Carmo. Straining the capacity of the new Plymouth, they returned to Norwalk with two of the Nabucos' five children, José (known as "Zezé") and Maria do Carmo (known as "Nininha").[5]

The winter weather in Connecticut, described as "unbearable" by Letícia, made it usually unattractive to go outdoors. But walks of one mile in the cold were necessary to buy food, when Carlos was away with the car, because the house was on the outskirts of the town.[6]

The heavy household chores made it necessary to take on a live-in maid, a girl from Guatemala. Letícia, who devoted much time to Maria Cristina, was not in the best of health. She suffered for a while from amoebic dysentery and was troubled by more serious hearing problems. Carlos was grieved to find an ear specialist pessimistic about curing the noise in the ears and the loss of hearing in one of them.[7]

Perhaps early letters to Brazil, trying to assure relatives and friends that all was well, contributed to a misunderstanding, and perhaps also, as Letícia suggested, "false friends" helped spread reports that the Lacerdas were enjoying a life of luxury in a great home. In letters written in March to Vera's 23-year-old daughter Lygia, Carlos and Letícia corrected this impression. Carlos wrote Lygia that "life here is not pleasant" but that he and his family were putting on "a good face to bad fortune." His letters made it clear that he did not relish returning to Brazilian political battles in which other oppositionists failed to be aggressive but that otherwise he longed to be back in his own country. "Sometimes," he wrote Vera's husband Odilon Lacerda Paiva, "it is difficult to remain here. There are days, like today, when I have a delirious desire to take the plane and return, even knowing what awaits me there. . . . But if that is my impulse, reason tells me to stay."[8]

Letícia wrote Lygia that they were in an "old" and "isolated" house, full of broken furniture and with very few blankets, old and torn. And she said that the "terrible climate," which left Maria Cristina "pale and without appetite," had allowed mother and daughter to take walks only five times in eleven weeks. "I have," she wrote, "been only twice to the movies and you know how much I love the cinema!" Her "only diversion" was the television set, around which the family gathered in the evenings.[9] One set came with the house. Publisher Alfredo C. Machado brought the Lacerdas another set, a gift from Roberto Marinho, director of *O Globo*. Carlos, admirer of Marinho, nominated him late in January for Columbia University's Maria Moors Cabot award.[10]

Respite from the cold was provided by a week at the Florida beach house of Marshall Field, Jr., reached after a scenic drive in which the young Nabucos participated. It was at the beach house that Sérgio got his start as a tennis player.[11]

Living expenses were a constant headache, with Letícia writing from Norwalk that the cost of kindergarten for Maria Cristina was beyond their means and with Carlos mentioning his "terrifying" dental bills and "another rent payment" that he was finding it difficult to make.[12] The rate of exchange became more and more unfavorable to the cruzeiro, and Carlos decided, late in March, to give up the Norwalk house when his contract ended late in May. Carlos, Letícia, and Maria Cristina would take an ocean liner to Lisbon, where the cost of living was lower than in the United States. The boys would return to Rio, resuming their education at the Andrews School, run by Alice Flexa Ribeiro. Sérgio would stay at the home of Dario de Almeida Magalhães,[13] and Sebastião would live with Vera and Odilon.

11. "Clarifying Public Opinion" about the Kubitschek Regime (January–June 1956)

In the United States, Carlos kept working away at articles to provide badly needed income. An article in the *New Leader* enlightened American readers about the Brazilian "crisis," while articles for Brazilians, such as those appearing under Lacerda's name in *O Estado de S. Paulo*, discussed the Kubitschek government's involvement with "coffee speculators" and the offers of Russia to assist Latin America. "If Russia really wants to help Brazil," Carlos wrote, it should "call off the activities of its fifth column."[1]

Carlos' columns in *O Globo*, "Um Brasileiro na Terra do Tio Sam" (A Brazilian in the Land of Uncle Sam), were signed Júlio Tavares, the pseudonym he had used when hiding in the 1930s. Appearing several times a week, they contained excerpts, some of them amusing, from American publications and occasional observations about life in the United States (such as the New Year office parties in New York) and politics there.[2]

Carlos used his *O Globo* column to attack Kubitschek and criticize the United States journalists for inadequate and inaccurate coverage of events in Brazil. He reprimanded *Time* and the *New York Times* for suggesting that Café Filho's illness may have been a sham. Writing later to Lygia, he said, "Newspapers like the *New York Times* are profoundly interested in the success of corruption in Brazil." He told her that if it were not for a few good friends and the need not to show weakness or lose face, he would stop trying to clarify public opinion.[3]

Early in January 1956, when President-elect Kubitschek arrived in the United States, Lacerda sought to clarify public opinion by writing a long, anti-Kubitschek letter to the *New York Times.* The letter, published on January 6, was written on behalf of "those who have been fighting consistently for democracy in Brazil, now damned by the soliloquies of Kubitschek's impresario, Gen. Henrique Lott, virtual dictator on the installment plan." Lacerda attributed Kubitschek's success to a putsch and said his visit to the United States coincided with the worsening of Brazil's state of siege and censorship. Kubitschek, Lacerda wrote, had been elected by an "illegal coalition" that opened the road to expanded activity of the Communist Party to take control of the masses "thanks to Russia's new tactics of a broad united front."[4]

Congresswoman Ivete Vargas (PTB, São Paulo), in the United States with the Kubitschek party, wrote a reply that the *Times* published on January 10. Pointing out that "the deputies who follow the example of Mr. Lacerda continue saying in the Chamber whatever they please," she wrote that Carlos Lacerda was "the only one who ran away. He is not a political exile; the Government pays no attention to him. He pretends to be victim of a political situation. However, he is only the victim of his own delirium. He speaks of democracy but used to preach dictatorship. His actions and attitudes, trying to discredit personalities and institutions, and above all provoking confusion in the country, serve Communist ideology perfectly."[5]

Kubitschek, after taking over the presidency on January 31, immediately signed decrees to end the state of siege on February 15 and do away with censorship. The Lantern Club was allowed to reopen on February 15.[6] But Lacerda, during his television interview in Chicago in mid-February, suggested that a revolution would be needed to overthrow Kubitschek, who, he declared, planned to perpetuate himself in the government by making use of electoral tricks. The accusation, which found its way to the Brazilian press, prompted *O Globo* to scold its "combative colleague." Marinho's daily reiterated its strong objection to having accusations against the Brazilian government made by Brazilians abroad. It was, *O Globo* wrote, "absolutely harmful" to have millions of Americans hearing such accusations on television before Kubitschek had committed any undemocratic act.[7]

The Lacerdas, when they reached Montreal on February 18, learned from Gustavo Borges, their host, about the uprising against the Kubitschek government, carried out in the Brazilian interior by a few air force officers. The uprising, known as the Jacareacanga revolt, was led by Major Haroldo Veloso with the help of Captain José Chaves Lameirão and was joined by Major Paulo Victor da Silva. In Norwalk, Carlos followed, with "increasing anguish" (he wrote to Lygia), the successful steps taken by Lott to subdue the uprising and capture Veloso,[8] who, like Paulo Victor da Silva, had been a member of the group of officers that had tried to protect Lacerda in August 1954. On March 6, a week after the capture, Congress adopted the Kubitschek administration's proposal to grant amnesty to all who had conspired against the government between November 10, 1955, and March 1, 1956.[9]

Government lawyers, however, continued with their legal case, underway since December, to convict the Lantern Club, Carlos Lacerda, and Amaral Netto of subversive activities. Carlos, discussing the case with journalists in Norwalk, said that the ones to be locked up were Lott and his group and that the Brazilian Supreme Court, in denying Café Filho his rights, had recognized that "the present regime is based on force." In his remarks to the American press, Carlos disparaged the Brazilian judiciary; but on March 19 the case against him, the Lantern Club, and Amaral Netto was dismissed because the judge found the government's accusations vague. Carlos, writing to Fernando Velloso, asked for an official, authenticated translation of the judge's decision for use at the April 5–10 meeting of the Inter American Press Association directors in Bermuda. He pointed out that several American newspapers had printed the accusations against him but that none had printed the judge's decision.[10]

While Carlos was in the United States, Dom Hélder Câmara published an interview giving his support to the Kubitschek administration. Carlos, who had never received a reply from Dom Hélder to the inquiry made by Vera regarding the check from Maurício, wrote to his "dear friend and pastor" to say what he thought about Kubitschek and Dom Hélder's position. He sent the letter to the *Tribuna*'s João Duarte, filho, with a note asking Duarte to deliver it to the archbishop and to publish it only if Dom Hélder agreed. But Carlos' letter was published, without Dom Hélder's permission, in the *Tribuna* on March 26. Dom Hélder's response was to give the press an open letter to Carlos that was published on April 2. It called Kubitschek "the legitimate president of Brazil" and said that Carlos had revealed himself to be an individual full of hate and ought to be quiet about Brazil while he was abroad.[11] So upset was Olga with the archbishop's public letter that she broke her rule of not involving herself in her son's disputes. "You have," she wrote to Dom Hélder, "taken advantage of my son's exile to accuse him of being a man full of hate. . . . Therefore I would like you to reply to this question: I, who was separated from the Church and became a believer again when his life was assaulted, want to know how you, who brought daily communion to his home, reconcile the communion which you provided with the accusation that he is a man full of hate?" After young Sebastião saw a copy of Olga's letter, he wrote to his grandmother to say how much he liked it; but, he added, "mind you don't take a liking to writing such letters and turn into a Sobral Pinto!" Dom Hélder did not reply to Olga. Lygia's younger brother Cláudio Lacerda Paiva, in his biography of Carlos, has written that "the greatest disappointment" during Carlos' exile was brought about by "one who was more than a friend, who was his pastor, and father-confessor, Dom Hélder Câmara." Cláudio also points out that the lawyers of Gregório Fortunato made use in court of Dom Hélder's letter calling Lacerda a man filled with hate.[12]

Before sailing to Portugal, Carlos wrote Dom Hélder a fifty-five-page letter in which he said, "You know I do not hate anyone. But you do not speak of the hatreds organized against me." Explaining that he had become the sacrificial lamb, Carlos wrote that people who did not dare attack Brigadeiro Eduardo Gomes, lest the armed forces react, attacked Carlos in order to put the reformist forces in disarray.

In this letter, which was published in the *Tribuna* on June 5, Carlos admitted that, in evaluating the roles of people in public life, he displayed sometimes "a certain intolerance and even a certain violence." These faults, he said, he hoped to overcome to the same extent that Brazil itself overcame the same faults. But, he added, what made it most difficult for him was the realization that men in high posts failed to assume their responsibilities. "My own error has been just the opposite; I take too much responsibility on my shoulders, more than they can bear, and I accept them sometimes in the place of other people. Therefore, for example, I let them consider me responsible for the suicide of Vargas, although I never betrayed him and always dealt frankly and loyally with him." Writing that he was also considered responsible for the regime that began on August 24, 1954, Carlos told the archbishop that he had had no influence in it, which was the reason it had "ended rather ingloriously at the hands of an audacious traitor."

In reply to Dom Hélder's admonition that he not speak on foreign soil about Brazil's blemishes, Carlos maintained that former President Washington Luís had kept quiet because of his temperament and the realization that his role was finished. It was necessary, Carlos insisted, to answer American newspaper stories depicting Lott as having prevented a coup by General Távora in connivance with the clergy. With Brazil sending Ernâni do Amaral Peixoto (Alzira Vargas' husband) as ambassador to Washington, Lacerda asked: "Do you not agree that I should explain here that Brazil is better than such a representative?"

Carlos wrote that if Kubitschek showed an interest in Dom Hélder's concern about the *favelados* (slum dwellers), the interest was false because the oligarchy wanted to keep the *favelados* in misery in order to make promises to them and win votes. Kubitschek administration advisers Augusto Frederico Schmidt and Armando Falcão were denounced by Carlos for being associated with Orquima, a company planning to export monazite sands containing strategically important thorium.

Carlos, who had been trying to write a small book about the need to reform Brazil,[13] told Dom Hélder (and the *Tribuna* readers) that Brazil lacked political parties. He explained that the PSD, stifling local democracy, used the national treasury to assure itself of a clientele and the PTB used the pension institutes to control wage earners and distribute jobs. Goulart's inheritance of Vargas' political assets was described as the result of a fraudulent testament letter "attributed to Vargas"—an infamous torch for civil war, which Carlos saw as more and more imminent. Lott's coup of November 1955 was described as Communism's greatest victory in South America.[14]

12. Criticizing the UDN and the *Tribuna* (February–July 1956)

Carlos reacted coldly to an appeal for his return, issued in February 1956 by some UDN leaders. The "owners of the UDN," he wrote to Fernando Velloso, wanted to lead him but he would not be led by them. "I shall not return to Brazil to be night watchman while the leaders sleep, sometimes lulled by their own speeches." "By no means," he added, "shall I go to Brazil to deal with Café Filho as a hero, or Prado Kelly as a great political leader, or Brigadeiro Eduardo Gomes (where is the Brigadeiro?) as chief. I prefer to die of hunger outside Brazil than participate in that stupid pantomime."

He wrote to Velloso that Prado Kelly, Milton Campos, and Adauto Lúcio Cardoso had "immense responsibility" for the return of the Getulistas, and he asked how Prado Kelly could head the UDN in Congress without explaining what he had done in the Café Filho justice ministry, "unaware of a conspiracy prepared since July and for a long time denounced by us."

Carlos informed Velloso that if he were to return to Brazil, his biggest battle would be "against allies rather than against the enemy." Adauto Lúcio Cardoso, he wrote, was "moved by casual civic bravura, but not by ideas, or a program, or political clearheadedness, for he has none of these things. He has no ideas and makes no effort to understand those of others." "Where," Carlos asked Velloso, "is General Juarez Távora? In what prison, in what exile is this great leader of the democratic and free armed forces? Is he at his home? In that case I'll remain in Norwalk, trying at least to prevent money from going to Kubitschek for corrupting and deceiving the people."

Afonso Arinos, Carlos lamented, had written in the *Atlantic Monthly* that Vargas had died, among other things, to defend the constitution. "For that type of Opposition, let them turn to my dear Afonso."

The coup of November 1955, Carlos also wrote to Velloso, could not possibly be considered "a consummated fact" and "must be denounced daily and with the greatest vehemence. Imagine a nation that receives a dagger in the back and then, with the handle of the dagger visible, gets up in the tribune and starts discussing appointments, projects, and paragraphs amending projects." He would, he vowed, do everything possible to overthrow the Kubitschek government but would return to Brazil only when he could join with others who were willing to face up to all their responsibilities.[1]

For a moment, late in February, Carlos was tempted to return to Brazil to rescue the *Tribuna da Imprensa,* "the only thing we have left."[2] But his sense of "duty" to remain abroad won the upper hand. He limited himself to sending "precise instructions" to the *Tribuna* and flooding Fernando Velloso with complaints about how it was managed during his absence.

The complaints usually followed disclosures of *Tribuna* deficits, such as the "stupefying" report, received from Elpídio Reis early in February, that the daily had lost half a million cruzeiros in a month. Carlos objected chiefly to the absences of Aluísio Alves, who, he felt, worked intensely at the *Tribuna* for only brief periods and then made trips, leaving the newspaper without continuous management and without proper control over expenditures.[3] Observing that the *Tribuna* was "disintegrating," Carlos pointed out that it lacked news, dealt with secondary matters on the first page, and was turning into an example of cheap, yellow journalism. He found the printing bad and the quality of paper the worst of any newspaper he received from Brazil. When he learned again in July of "alarming" losses, he attributed them in part to the devotion of too much paper to uninteresting reports ("propaganda of the British News Service") and long-winded articles about the theater and cinema. Carlos was struck by the small amount of advertising and resented receiving only a few reports from Elpídio about sales and subscriptions. He also complained that a letter from Luiz Ernesto Kawall, whom he considered a "splendid young man," made it clear that the São Paulo office was receiving no guidance. And when Carlos saw the way his "Reply to Dom Hélder" was printed by the *Tribuna,* he wrote to his mother that it was a "horror," with "punctuation marks that changed the meanings of sentences."[4]

In his "precise instructions" for the *Tribuna*'s orientation Carlos wrote that the *Tribuna* could not oppose foreign capital for Brazilian development, provided that Brazil had a government that was legitimate, honorable, and competent. Arguing that the Kubitschek administration had none of these virtues and was avid for get-rich-quick schemes instead of sound investments, Carlos concluded that the *Tribuna* would have to oppose any change to the Petrobrás Law that would allow foreign investments in petroleum extraction.

According to the "precise instructions," the United States government was guilty of financing corruption in underdeveloped countries, *Time* was guilty of lying to the American people on behalf of shady operators in control of Kubitschek, and former United States Ambassador James Kemper had obtained Goulart's approval for setting up one of his insurance companies in Brazil.

Carlos instructed the *Tribuna* to publish a warning of the consequences for those who might finance the "illegal" Kubitschek government: (*a*) nonrecognition of debts incurred by that government, (*b*) possible denunciation of agreements and confiscation of businesses resulting from negotiations with that government, and (*c*) the ill-will of Brazilian democrats.[5]

At the April 1956 meeting of stockholders of the Sociedade Anônima Editôra Tribuna da Imprensa, the "precise instructions" were approved unanimously. Carlos was reelected president, and Aluísio Alves and Fernando Velloso were chosen to serve with him in the directorship. The stockholders took note of an unusual development: the campaign to raise funds for another rotary press, undertaken by a group of women, or *mal-amadas*. The campaign, led by Hermínia Fernandes Lima, was a success and the much-needed new press was imported from Italy.[6]

Tribuna Editor-in-chief João Duarte, filho, could not be faulted for a lack of aggressiveness. His articles prompted Lott to see to it that he was the defendant in one government lawsuit after another. In mid-March the government arrested military officers, such as Admirals Amorim do Vale and Pena Boto, for giving the *Tribuna* interviews that it considered insolent.[7]

13. Police Action against the *Tribuna* and *Maquis* (August–September 1956)

After reaching Portugal by ship on June 13, Lacerda used the *Tribuna* to publish a long letter to Lott in which he proposed the resignations of Lott, Kubitschek ("nominal head of the government of Your Excellency"), and all who were governing the country. A regime of emergency, "the dream of the majority of Brazilians," was to be set up. It would include a Council of State, made up of "representatives of the principal parties and currents" and responsible for decreeing reforms—"better said, the true Revolution." Speculators, dishonest administrators, and shady dealers were to be tried and imprisoned. Venal and unqualified judges were to be dismissed, and Communist influence was to be eradicated from public administration.

Lacerda's letter, written when he was still hoping to complete the book he had started writing in Norwalk, gave some ideas of what he had in mind for Brazil. Electoral reform would establish the municipality as the "primary source of democratic power," with the voting there reserved to heads of families and with elections at higher levels handled in an indirect manner. Lacerda wrote that "universal suffrage, as carried out in Brazil, means, in practice, a dictatorship of ignorance and irresponsibility." Agrarian reform, seeking "recuperation of the land and its better distribution," would build up an agricultural middle class and be coupled with increased immigration of those "identified with Brazilian characteristics," especially the Portuguese. Lacerda also called for the expropriation, with indemnification, of lands around large cities for the formation of "green belts" of small-scale agricultural workers. Furthermore, he proposed a foreign policy revision designed to strengthen ties with "the western world to which we belong" and with the United States and to bring an end to the policy of begging for assistance "that does not assist anything and serves international dealers engaged in sharp practices."[1]

On August 24, second anniversary of the suicide of Vargas, Lacerda used the *Tribuna* again, this time to publicize his "Manifesto to the Brazilian People." The manifesto, which called Kubitschek "a frenzied exhibitionist" and Goulart "a traitor," alluded to "Communist control" over the dissemination of information. With the Communist version of Lott's coup prevailing in the world, Lacerda wrote, "the *New York Times* and *Pravda* have reached agreement for the first time."

The manifesto, chiefly a defense of Lacerda's conduct, said that the time was approaching for him to end an expatriation to which he had submitted himself in order to preserve, with his life, "the honor that was wounded by the infamy of those who dominate and degrade Brazil." For a man like himself, accustomed to risk his life every day, Lacerda said that to follow the path of preserving his life had not been easy. But, he pointed out, if he had been killed he would have been unable to prove his accusations against those who wanted to eliminate him and who portrayed him as a "frivolous destroyer and even a forger."

In a reference to the forgery charge, Lacerda said it had arisen because he had recognized the authenticity of the facts mentioned in the Brandi letter. He had, he explained, given Lott every opportunity to investigate the relations between the Vargas-Goulart group and the Perón group, but Lott, because he was conspiring or stupid, had thrown himself, headfirst, into the "river of mud." For himself, Lacerda wrote, the days that had followed had been "nightmarish" ones during which infamous enemies had shipwrecked "an entire life" that he had sought to have guided by loyal struggle and disinterested service.

In closing his manifesto, Lacerda promised to show that "you, Brazilian people, have been betrayed." And he promised to help heal the wounded nation—acting "with the care of a nurse and the humility of the Samaritan."[2]

In Rio on August 24, while authorities and others evoked the memory of Vargas, the police seized the edition of the *Tribuna* containing Lacerda's manifesto. With the help of squad cars, they prevented anyone from entering or leaving the *Tribuna* building. In the evening the police declared that the *Tribuna* could reappear if it did not carry articles by Lacerda attacking top government officials.[3] Circulation was resumed on the twenty-seventh.

O Estado de S. Paulo, which carried Lacerda's manifesto, was not molested.[4] But Rio Police Chief Augusto Magessi made trouble for the fortnightly *Maquis* on September 7, after it published a photograph of the *Tribuna*'s August 24 front page, leading the *Diário de Notícias* to proclaim that "forty thousand copies of *Maquis* were seized because of a photograph of an illegible manifesto." *Maquis,* whose circulation was close to 25,000, had been founded during Lacerda's exile by Amaral Netto, of the *Tribuna* and Lantern Club, and many of its writers were *Tribuna* employees. As the *Diário de Notícias* indicated, the size reduction rendered the Lacerda manifesto practically illegible. But Number 7 of *Maquis*, which published the objectionable photograph of the manifesto, also published articles repugnant to Kubitschek and Eastern Military Zone Commander Denys. Police Chief Magessi, besides ordering the seizure of all copies of *Maquis*, ordered the arrest of everyone found at the magazine's premises.[5]

While the political opposition and the press protested the police action, lawyers Dario de Almeida Magalhães, Sobral Pinto, and Adauto Lúcio Cardoso set to work defending *Maquis* and its personnel. Most of those arrested were released quickly. When Dario, a few days later, won a court order allowing the *Tribuna* to publish Lacerda's manifesto, Lacerda cabled his congratulations and expressed the hope that "the decision also applies to *Maquis*."[6]

Maquis received a court order allowing its eighth number to circulate. But its lawyers remained busy because circulation of the new number resulted in a lawsuit by General Mendes de Morais, who resented the magazine's statement that "Mendes de Morais and Meneses Cortes are strong candidates for the district's mayorship. The general is a thief. The colonel is not." Also Dario appealed for the release of the 26,600 copies of Number 7, seized on September 7, and sought 300,000 cruzeiros in damages.

On September 21, Police Chief Magessi learned of a court ruling favorable to Dario's appeal. Unwilling to abide by the ruling, he was dismissed by Kubitschek.[7] His replacement, Felisberto Batista Teixeira, had been a prominent police official during the Vargas dictatorship and, in November 1955, had participated in the coup of Lott and Denys.

14. Correspondence with Argentina about Goulart (July–September 1956)

Casa dos Cedros, the house the Lacerdas rented in mid-June in São João do Estoril, was a half-hour train ride from the center of Lisbon. It was near a beach, where the 5-year-old Maria Cristina spent much time, sometimes with a nursemaid because Letícia, as Carlos wrote to Fernando Velloso and Olga, continued to be in poor health. Maria Cristina, in a happy note to Sebastião (written by Letícia and illustrated by the young girl), advised that she and her father had learned to play golf.[1]

Affectionate letters to the boys from their parents were filled with admonitions and inquiries about school grades. Sebastião, whose continuing interest in music pleased his parents, was urged to spend his vacation with his grandmother Olga and cousin Gabriel (son of Mauricinho and Gilda) at Olga's home in Vassouras.[2]

Fernando Velloso, Sebastião's godfather, received a letter from Carlos asking him to make arrangements with Dario de Almeida Magalhães and Odilon and Vera, whereby "from now on they do not allow the boys to be on the streets after 8:00 P.M. or go around unaccompanied." The conduct of the boys, evidently not unlike that of their father in his younger days, prompted an irritated Carlos to tell Velloso that he understood that Sérgio was going out nights and frequenting bars and that Sebastião was planning pleasure trips "as though he had no exams to take." Carlos was so worried about the boys, the *Tribuna*, Letícia's health, and money matters and felt so deprived of company "of my own people," that he gave some thought in July to returning to Brazil. He was, he wrote, tired of waiting for "political decisions that don't come." "Personal factors," he pointed out, "have to be taken into consideration."[3]

But it was a political factor that almost brought Carlos by plane to Rio in mid-July. Learning that his leave from Congress might be considered to expire on July 18, he vowed to "save his mandate." He spent over two thousand escudos on urgent cables and spoke by phone, in an agitated state, to Odilon and Vera. Vera turned to UDN congressional leader Afonso Arinos, who arranged an extension. But money matters continued a problem. Carlos complained that Brazil's *Shopping News* and *O Estado de S. Paulo* owed him for articles and that Elpídio Reis always had to be reminded to send monthly remittances.[4]

Carlos, ever sensitive to steps taken against him behind his back, wrote to the widow of Major Vaz to warn her against "false friends," full of hatred for him, who might seek to seperate her from him and thus invalidate the sacrifice of Vaz. "The only thing left to complete the cycle of my suffering," he told Lygia Vaz, would be that "they poison you against me and say, for example, that I am away from it all, enjoying life, while Vaz is no longer with you and the children."

Carlos wrote to Lygia Vaz that he was to have been killed on November 11, 1955, as had been made clear when he had heard someone tell a general, "This time it won't be like August 5," 1954. But he insisted that his exile had little to do with his personal interest in living. It was inspired, he wrote, by the knowledge that his death would mean the disappearance of "the only thing that gave meaning to the sacrifice of Vaz: better days for all our children." He explained the continuation of his absence by writing that his return would unite, instead of divide, "the bloodthirsty enemy" and, in other circles, stimulate jealousy and incomprehension, leading to a repetition of the "isolation" he had experienced between August 24, 1954, and his exile. The time for verbal squabbles, he wrote, "is over." "Now it is a matter of articulating and unleashing a revolution that will clean up Brazil, elevate it, and prepare it for true democracy."

Carlos told Lygia Vaz that if, in the face of intrigues that sought to kill Vaz a second time, she felt his presence was necessary, he would return at once, preferring to face anything than lose her confidence. But he pleaded that she allow him to continue preparing, away from Brazil, for "what has to come" to fulfill the ideal of Vaz. "I never forget, Lygia, that, if I survived, it was for a purpose and it is to this purpose that I dedicate my life." Asking her to write, he told her that his correspondence was censored and that she should therefore give her reply to his sister, Vera, or Ruth Alverga.[5]

The mail for Carlos, given in Rio to the wife of Panair pilot Wilson Machado, included newspapers and magazines and reached such a size that War Minister Lott heard about it; suspicious of Machado, he sought information from Panair about his flight schedules. After that, Carlos took to asking Machado to memorize sensitive messages. Giving Machado one of these messages, a long one for a general about the Chinese Communist Party, Carlos said, "Wilson, you can't memorize it; you must live and feel what I am telling you."[6]

The expatriates were, of course, delighted to receive visitors from Brazil, such as Mauricinho, diplomat Newton Freitas, and Fernando and Carol Velloso. They dined out with them and showed them the sights. Carlos accompanied the Vellosos on a trip to Spain, and this, Letícia felt, was a good idea because, she wrote home, "he needs a little distraction."[7]

Early in his stay in Portugal, Carlos read a brief United Press item in the *Diário de Notícias* that referred to an investigation, carried out by the post-Perón government of Argentina, about the sale of Brazilian pinewood to the Perón government. The pine deal, according to the news from Argentina, involved a "foreign legislator," and therefore on July 5 Carlos wrote to Alberto Gainza Paz in Buenos Aires, asking him to advise whether the "foreign legislator" was a Brazilian and, if so, to find out his name.

Replying to Carlos on July 20, Gainza Paz wrote that while the official text, released to journalists about the investigation, simply mentioned "a foreign legislator," "everyone" knew his name was João Goulart. "Today," Gainza Paz added, "I can confirm that assertion, as you will verify, with the photocopies included in this envelope." The photocopies were of pages from a report of the Argentine Comisión Nacional de Investigaciones that mentioned a confidential memorandum of 1950 calling for the payment of one million Argentine pesos and sixty thousand dollars as a commission to João Goulart and Carlos Maura Ronchetti for arranging the sale of Brazilian pine to Argentina. The report of the Comisión Nacional de Investigaciones referred to testimony affirming that the payments, made in appreciation of Goulart's visits to Argentina, were to serve as contributions of the Argentine government "to the election campaign of Vargas."[8]

Carlos wrote to Gainza Paz again on August 27 to advise that, as a result of the photocopies, a parliamentary commission of inquiry (CPI) had been set up in the Brazilian Congress to look into the relations of Goulart and others with Peronism. Carlos told Gainza Paz that the majority of the CPI members, being men of Kubitschek and Goulart, wished to absolve Goulart and that Goulart, after denying everything, admitted only to having taken a step to help Brazilian pine producers. Carlos pointed out that the Argentine vice-president and foreign office denied, in strong terms, the authenticity of the document that Gainza Paz had copied with its references to Goulart.

"This places me," Carlos wrote, "in an uncomfortable position. I do not want to do anything that might hurt the position of the Argentine government. . . . I understand that it does not want complications with the present Brazilian government. But there are limits that it would be imprudent to exceed. Because, with those denials, the Argentine government is contributing to the victory of Peronism in Brazil."

Carlos pointed out that the CPI would want to know (*a*) from whom Carlos had received the photocopies and (*b*) why he believed them authentic. If, he asked, Gainza Paz was unwilling to have him violate professional secrecy by answering the first question, would he send information for satisfying the CPI on the second one? "Not only," Carlos wrote, "are my honor and my life itself at stake, but so also is the fate of Brazil as a democratic nation." Pleading for a prompt reply, he said he would return to Brazil with it and make "a decisive contribution to the liberation of my country and, in this way, to the tranquility of our continent."[9]

Gainza Paz, unwilling to have his name revealed, responded on September 5 by sending a draft of a suggested reply for Carlos to make to the CPI: "I can affirm, with my word of honor, that the photocopies correspond faithfully to a document signed by one of the investigating commissions. . . . The document is now among those being used in a legal case . . . in Buenos Aires. . . . I received the photocopies in my role of journalist and, for reasons of professional ethics, cannot reveal their origin. If one compares the photocopies with the text of newspaper publications in all the Buenos Aires dailies, one will see that the latter lacks only one word, the name of the legislator mentioned by witnesses before the investigating commission. *La Vanguardia* of Buenos Aires revealed that the eliminated name was that of Sr. Goulart. . . . I believe that if the government of Brazil or its legislative branch would say . . . that mention of the name . . . would not in any way affect the Brazilian people and authorities, the Argentine government could not deny a request for the complete text of the document in question."[10]

In Brazil the CPI was prevented from doing effective work because of the attitude of its proadministration majority. On September 20 the majority resolved that a trip by CPI members to Argentina would be "useless and unnecessary." *Udenistas,* however, sent Rio Municipal Councilman Raul Brunini on a secret mission to Buenos Aires with a letter to Gainza Paz and instructions to interview Argentine Vice President Isaac Rojas. "You have arrived too late," Rojas told Brunini, "because I discussed these matters a little with people from Chile and was therefore much criticized." Rojas said that he could speak officially only if the Brazilian CPI would present an official request. After Brunini pointed out that the make-up of the CPI made that impossible, Rojas spoke off-the-record, telling Brunini that everything the *udenistas* were claiming was "rigorously correct."[11]

In Brazil on September 21 the CPI majority seemed on the verge of approving the proposal of Benjamim Farah (PTB, Federal District) that the inquiry be terminated because the evidence showed that no Brazilian legislator had received the alleged commissions. UDN members Mário Martins and João Agripino objected strenuously and effectively, with Agripino pointing out that only four witnesses had been heard. After José Eduardo de Macedo Soares, brother of the foreign minister, wrote in the *Diário Carioca* that the accusation against Goulart should be dropped because it had been made by "*golpistas* and *lanterneiros,*" Agripino replied that his role on the CPI, assigned by the Chamber, had nothing to do with the origin of the accusation and that, in voting against closing the inquiry, he had been guided not by the testimony of João Duarte, filho, an accuser of Goulart, but by other evidence, such as that given by Goulart's former associate Carlos Maura Ronchetti. Ronchetti had admitted Goulart's role in the pine deal but had called it patriotic assistance to the timber industry.[12]

With Carlos preparing to return to Brazil, the Kubitschek administration proceeded to bar him from speaking on television or radio. The transport and public works ministry issued a *portaria* (directive), adding a new clause, Clause R, to the standard contract with those who had concessions to broadcast. The clause said merely that licencees would not be allowed to use their concessions for obscene programs or insults to the public authorities. The penalty for violating Clause R was a thirty-day suspension of the broadcasting concession.[13]

15. The Sword of Gold (November 1956)

Shortly before Carlos, Letícia, and Maria Cristina landed at the Galeão Airport at 2:00 A.M. on October 11, UDN leaders Otávio Mangabeira and Milton Campos hailed the approaching return of the "valiant fighter for the democratic cause." The Lantern Club furnished buses so that a crowd would be at the airport despite the inconvenient hour. Readers of the *Tribuna* were told that the recent exile would speak on Rádio Globo during the next few days, giving his impressions of Portugal and suggestions for a new Brazilian labor code.[1]

One of the readers of this news was Cleantho de Paiva Leite, *chefe de gabinete* (administrative chief) of the transport ministry. The minister, Lúcio Meira, agreed with him when he suggested that steps be taken to make sure that Lacerda did not broadcast. As Kubitschek was not in Rio, Meira consulted Lott, who expressed the same opinion. Cleantho then telephoned Roberto Marinho to point out that the thirty-day suspension penalty of the new Clause R would be applied if Carlos spoke on Rádio Globo. He added that the DOPS (Divisão de Ordem Política e Social of the police department) would be recording all Rádio Globo programs. Marinho said that Rádio Globo would abide by the ruling.[2]

When Congress met on October 11, Mário Martins opened a debate about Clause R by announcing that a radio station had been warned not to let Lacerda use its microphone. The debate was under way when Lacerda entered to resume his mandate. Commenting on one of the speeches, Lacerda politely cited freedom of expression in England. His remark induced Humberto Molinaro (PTB, Paraná) to point a finger at him and declare aggressively that "in England Your Excellency would already be in jail." Lacerda remained calm during the ensuing outbreak of exchanges. Refraining from attacking Molinaro, he spoke about British freedom to use radio and television.[3]

Later in the day, in the office of opposition leader Prado Kelly, Lacerda gave a press interview in which he was more aggressive. Always good for headlines when he spoke to the press, he said he could not recognize the Kubitschek administration as legitimate, and he called Kubitschek a "clown" who had begged for money in Washington. Explaining his exile, he said his death would have prevented him from revealing facts "much more significant than I could have imagined." "I have no doubt," he said, "that if I had remained in Brazil they would have closed the *Tribuna da Imprensa* and deprived me of my mandate." He promised to struggle against a press law recently proposed by the Kubitschek administration.[4]

Radio stations on the eleventh announced Lacerda's return but made no mention of his remarks. Admirers, at their radios to hear his comments on Portugal, heard, instead, a program of Portuguese music.[5] Only under very unusual circumstances when radios carried congressional debates would his voice be on the airwaves.

On Monday, the fifteenth, Lacerda's admirers packed the galleries of Congress to hear his first speech in Brazil for almost a year. He opened calmly enough, with praise for Aluísio Alves, João Duarte, filho, the political opposition, his *Tamandaré* comrades, and members of the Lantern Club. His statement that "if anyone in this country is without hatred, it is I" was greeted by guffaws from proadministration congressmen, whereupon he retorted that the response to his remark was a form of hatred. When he spoke of the "treason of the November movement," Congressman Humberto Molinaro, dressed in his major's uniform, yelled, "The traitor is you!" During the uproar that followed, someone snatched the major's briefcase, which was found to contain a revolver and a pistol, and this led to a scuffle in which journalists and the police participated. The major was so loudly booed from the galleries that the presiding officer threatened to have the visitors thrown out. Carlos, replying to the charge that he had been a coward in leaving Brazil, said that the spectacle being presented in the Chamber of Deputies helped explain his departure, and he reminded his listeners that the DOPS in November had said it could not guarantee protection of his life.

Lacerda discussed the evidence against Goulart, which "the Argentine government hides." Becoming animated, he spoke disparagingly of the Communist-supported pro-Lott Frente de Novembro (November Front) and Communist officers commanding troops. Colonel Henrique Oest, in command of troops in Alagoas, was accused by Lacerda of having delivered Communist Party orders for the 1935 uprising. "Do those who kill their brothers in uniform merit the confidence of the nation?" he asked.

Majority leader Tarcilo Vieira de Melo defended the government in a reply that drew loud objections from the galleries and applause from proadministration congressmen. Lacerda, Vieira de Melo said, had spoken in the name of the Lantern Club, not the UDN, and had returned to Brazil "preaching treason, disorder, and crime." When Lacerda left Tiradentes Palace, he was greeted by so large a crowd of supporters that traffic was tied up.

The UDN, contradicting Vieira de Melo, stood behind everything in Lacerda's speech. It was pleased that Lacerda had said he would no longer insist on an emergency regime, preferring to concentrate on denouncing Goulart and the administration's proposed press law.[6]

Catholic admirers of Lacerda attended a religious service held to express thanks for his return, and journalists spoke of the week starting October 15 as "Lacerda Week." The UDN of the Federal District honored him with a rally, whose speakers, introduced by Adauto Lúcio Cardoso, included Municipal Councilwoman Sandra Cavalcanti and Professor Raimundo Moniz de Aragão. Lacerda, in his response to the welcome, pleased Cariocas by arguing that Brazil had too many urgent problems to permit it to undertake a costly move of the capital from Rio.[7]

Enthusiastic crowds received him during the last week of October when he carried out an antigovernment speaking tour that took him to São Paulo city and towns in the state's interior and to Minas Gerais. Delivering a speech to the student UDN directorship in Belo Horizonte, he called Minas PSD leader Tancredo Neves a "rotten Mineiro" who had helped Vice President Goulart obtain quickly a ten million cruzeiro loan from the Bank of Brazil. A 23-year-old bureaucrat, displeased with the speech, tried to kill the orator with a knife but was thwarted by the police.[8]

None of the speeches was carried on the air. Lacerda therefore sent a telegram to Kubitschek, which appeared in the press, to protest the regulation that prevented him, journalist, congressman, and citizen, from broadcasting. But Kubitschek, as he told writer Josué Montello and others, felt that if Lacerda used the microphone he might bring about the fall of the government.[9] When the Chamber of Deputies voted on Lacerda's proposal that Transport Minister Lúcio Meira appear before it for questioning about Clause R, the proposal was defeated by a 120–54 vote.[10]

Lacerda, in speeches and articles, described the transport ministry's Cleantho de Paiva Leite as a "whelp of the Itatiaia Group," and he said that General Olímpio Mourão Filho, head of the government's Radio and Television Technical Commission, was "the author of the Cohen Plan that served as a pretext" for the coup that had ushered in Vargas' Estado Novo dictatorship in 1937. Mourão called Lacerda to his office to explain convincingly that he had not been responsible for the Cohen Plan. Describing himself as an old friend of Kubitschek, Mourão said that as long as he had an order from the president preventing Lacerda from broadcasting he would fulfill it.[11]

On October 29 the Frente de Novembro, which Lacerda had attacked in Congress on October 15, issued a controversial manifesto to "the people of the Federal district and the workers." It invited them to celebrate the first anniversary of the "military and popular" movement of November 11 by attending a rally at which Goulart would present a sword of gold to General Lott. Lacerda replied with the publication, before the rally, of a "Letter to the Brazilian generals." He explained to the generals that he ought to express his thoughts directly to the war minister but that Lott, full of resentments and incomprehension, responded to "loyal" attempts to enlighten him simply by initiating lawsuits, such as those brought in large number against João Duarte, filho, Rafael Corrêa de Oliveira, Amaral Netto, and Lacerda.

According to Lacerda's letter, Lott's recent declaration that only a few troop commanders were Communist Party members was beside the point because Moscow preferred non-Communist collaborators to party members and, as had been emphasized to Lacerda in 1954 at the War College (Escola Superior de Guerra), masked its true objectives with disguises featuring nationalism, populism, and even legalism. Communism, he warned, sought to wear the garb of respectability, use the "neurotics of Itatiaia," and form "popular militias" and "popular fronts."

"Today," Lacerda wrote, "the patio of the war ministry is inundated with bulletins of the Frente de Novembro. . . . It is the fifth column itself that commands the maneuver. The president of the republic extols this 'front.'" Lacerda described the army as becoming the "booty" of the political ambition of "factions that devastate it." "Better than I," he concluded, "Your Excellencies are in a position to know how disunion of the army occurred, due to personalism, incomprehension, and the activities of group against group."[12]

General Humberto Castello Branco, respected director of instruction at the War College, advised the organizers of the proposed pro-Lott rally that the association of the army with the Frente de Novembro was subversive and a breach of discipline, and he described the Frente as using methods typical of Communists and Nazis. Castello's views, published in *O Globo,* were supported by other generals and cited in the Senate by Daniel Krieger (UDN, Rio Grande do Sul). But of all the attacks on the sword of gold rally, Lott would remember Lacerda's as the most disconcerting.[13]

Lacerda attended a Mass in Calendária Church on November 10 to express thanks for the "exemplary and patriotic conduct" of the officers and crew of the *Tamandaré* in November 1955. On the eleventh he and 70-year-old Otávio Mangabeira joined a crowd that gathered in front of the residence of Admiral Amorim do Vale. Following speeches acclaiming the former navy minister, the crowd went to the nearby home of Castello Branco and sang the national anthem.[14]

Meanwhile, in front of the war ministry building, thousands of workers were on hand to hear Lott eulogized in verse and prose and see him receive the sword of gold from Goulart. One of the speakers, São Paulo's Mayor Vladimir de Toledo Piza, declared that Lott was clearly the man to take the place left vacant by Vargas' suicide. "The majority of the workers," *O Estado de S. Paulo* wrote depreciatingly, "were brought from São Paulo, Minas, and the state of Rio."[15]

Oppositionists in Congress and elsewhere reacted loudly to the sword of gold rally, and the military ministers spent the next days handing out punishments to officers for speaking on political matters. On November 19 the administration announced that the ruling against political pronouncements by military figures applied to those who had retired as well as those in active service. Távora, violating this order on the twenty-first, sent a lengthy "declaration" to the press revealing documents in which he had denounced the president and war minister. Then on the twenty-second he gave a radio-televison interview in which he discussed political matters and referred to his "declaration," already a press sensation.[16]

On November 23 the military ministers sentenced Távora to forty-eight hours of house arrest and arrested Colonel Nemo Canabarro Lucas, Frente de Novembro secretary, for giving a political interview to *Manchete.* At the same time the National Security Council (made up chiefly of the Kubitschek cabinet) closed down the Frente and the Lantern Club for six months.[17]

Veteran politician Otávio Mangabeira asserted on the twenty-third that the military crisis was the most serious to have occurred in the life of Brazil. Kubitschek, in a declaration made a few years later, said that the most critical moment of his administration took place on November 23, 1956. Revealing his apprehension about the situation that had existed in the armed forces, he said: "On that day I took office a second time. I had the impression that an August 24 was being prepared. But in a few hours everyone realized I was unwilling to commit suicide."[18]

Four hundred politicians, military officers, and writers, furious with the sword of gold affair and its aftermath, attended a lunch on November 24 to express their gratitude for the return of Lacerda to Brazil. UDN President Milton Campos, presiding at the lunch, called Lacerda a valorous collaborator in the democratic struggle and introduced the orators: São Paulo's Carlota Pereira de Queiroz (who praised the mother of Carlos), Pedro Aleixo of Minas, and Raimundo Padilha of Rio state. When Lacerda declared that "the struggle will continue," his listeners applauded deliriously and waved white handkerchiefs. He called the imprisonment of Távora "an appalling demonstration of bad faith and malice" and paid tribute to Pena Boto, Eduardo Gomes, and Manuel Bandeira, author of a poem mocking the sword of gold. The congressional majority, Lacerda said, had failed to enact educational reform and for over a year had blocked consideration of his proposed code that would free labor organizations from the labor ministry.[19]

As part of the continuing struggle, Lacerda kept hammering away at past understandings he believed to have existed between Goulart and the Perón administration. But Argentine President Pedro Aramburu made it clear that he was unwilling to release any documents that might mean "interference in the internal affairs of a friendly nation."[20]

Early in December, Lacerda received an assist from Gainza Paz, who told a *Tribuna* reporter: "I know that the Argentine investigating commission received testimony from people who confirmed accusations made about João Goulart receiving funds that he promised to use for the Vargas presidential campaign. These documents are official and so far have not been made public by the Argentine government." Despite these remarks, the majority members of the Brazilian CPI continued to block suggestions that it investigate in Argentina. On December 10 they brought the CPI to an end with the observation that nothing had been learned about the case. "A melancholy end," said minority members Mário Martins and João Agripino (UDN national secretary).[21]

VIII.

UDN Leader in Congress (1957–1959)

1. Lacerda Becomes UDN Congressional Leader (March 1957)

Early in 1957 Lacerda renewed his custom, initiated in 1954, of participating in *comícios em casa* (rallies at homes). They were meetings, generally held in apartment buildings and attended often by forty or fifty people, with the object of interesting entire families in the issues. Raul Brunini feels that Lacerda, successful in this respect, modified political practice.[1]

Brunini and Lacerda were accompanied by Haroldo Veloso, "hero" of the anti-Kubitschek uprising of 1956, when they held a *comício em casa* in Rio's Tijuca district in January 1957. Carlos asked his audience to follow the example of Veloso and said that plans to construct a new Brazilian capital would defraud the Cariocas. At a *comício em casa* in Petrópolis, held in the garden of a private house, he told an audience of several hundred that much investment, national and foreign, was needed, and that government-owned companies should be run by private enterprise and partly owned by it. He advocated new electoral practices with indirect elections, fewer political parties, and congressmen chosen from electoral zones instead of entire states.[2]

During the special session of Congress, which met between February 1 and March 15, 1957, lawmakers discussed the Kubitschek administration's decision to sign an agreement allowing the United States to set up a radar station on Fernando de Noronha Island for tracking guided missiles. The administration, choosing not to turn to Congress for approval, cited a clause in the Brazil–United States Military Accord of 1953 delegating authority to the president to execute the accord.[3]

Members of the Parliamentary Nationalist Front, founded in 1956 with considerable help from the PTB, objected to the tracking station agreement. Some of them, such as Bruzzi de Mendonça, Abguar Bastos, and Frota Moreira, met to consider legal action against the administration's plan. UDN congressional leader Afonso Arinos, after conferring with Prado Kelly, Olavo Bilac Pinto, Aliomar Baleeiro, and Rafael Corrêa de Oliveira, declared that the matter should be handled by Congress. Lacerda took the same position but made it clear in a speech in Congress that he favored the agreement with the United States, which, he said, would be a deterrent to Russian aggression.[4]

During the special session, political parties organized themselves for the forthcoming regular session that would last from mid-March 1957 through 1958. The PSD chose to continue with Ernâni do Amaral Peixoto as party president and Vieira de Melo as its leader in Congress. The UDN congressmen discussed candidates to replace Milton Campos as party president, Prado Kelly as leader of the congressional opposition bloc (the UDN and the small PL), and Afonso Arinos as UDN congressional leader. All who hoped to be chosen disclaimed any idea of collaborating with the government. They disagreed with Quadros spokesman Carlos Castilho Cabral, who favored a warm response to Kubitschek's appeal for fuller cooperation.[5]

Some, like UDN vice-leader Ernâni Sátiro (of Paraíba), felt that the next UDN president should come from the north and therefore favored João Agripino (of Paraíba), while others, arguing that a UDN president had never come from São Paulo, backed Herbert Levy or Antônio Pereira Lima. The strongest movement in January was the one launched by supporters of Senator Juracy Magalhães of Bahia. In February, however, it ran into trouble because Congressman Nestor Duarte (PL, Bahia) denounced Juracy for collaborating with the last Vargas government and accused him of having won his Senate seat by means of a deal with Goulart. Nestor Duarte, vice-leader of the PL, said that if Juracy became UDN president, the PL would end the alliance that had created the position of "leader of the opposition bloc."[6]

The continued existence of such a position was expected to open the way for a new UDN congressional leader because Afonso Arinos was scheduled to become leader of the two-party opposition bloc. In seeking to name his successor as UDN leader, the party found itself split between two hard-hitting anti-Getulistas, João Agripino and Aliomar Baleeiro. Baleeiro, a jurist from Bahia, broke the impasse by suggesting a list of three other possibilities: Lacerda and Adauto Lúcio Cardoso, both of the Federal District, and Bilac Pinto, a lawyer from Minas. Of the three, Lacerda seemed clearly the choice of a majority of the UDN congressmen but UDN Secretary Agripino reported that Bilac Pinto and Lacerda were in a tie. When the UDN congressmen met on March 19, Bilac and Lacerda offered to withdraw to prevent a struggle, but the pro-Lacerda sentiment was so evident that only Bilac withdrew.[7]

According to Lacerda's interpretation, Agripino had reported the Lacerda-Bilac tie in hope of becoming the leader himself. Lacerda also felt that the overwhelming pro-Lacerda sentiment resulted in part from support given by the *chapa branca* (white slate), made up of *udenistas* who planned to turn the violent opposition tactics of Lacerda into opportunities to give their own votes to the administration, or else refrain from voting, in return for Bank of Brazil loans and similar business advantages. The backing that Lacerda received from those who could be expected to refrain from participating in his most violent attacks on the administration led *Última Hora* to conclude that Lacerda had made a deal with the UDN moderates, or "realists," headed by José Cândido Ferraz, who wanted to make Juracy Magalhães party president.[8]

When the UDN *bancada* (congressional group) met on March 20 for a final vote on the leadership posts, Aliomar Baleeiro objected to the choice of Afonso Arinos to lead the UDN-PL opposition bloc. Afonso Arinos, he said, had not handled crises well and had been too gentle in personal contacts with members of the majority. But Baleeiro's proposal that a system of rotation be applied in selecting the opposition bloc leader was rejected by Milton Campos and Rafael Corrêa de Oliveira. In the end Afonso Arinos was chosen by acclamation.[9]

The only voice raised against making Lacerda the UDN leader was that of Gabriel Passos, of Minas, whose candidacy for UDN president was opposed by Lacerda and the *Tribuna* on the ground that he had collaborated with the Vargas dictatorship. Passos, a member of the Parliamentary Nationalist Front, which disliked Lacerda, spoke with vehemence, saying that Lacerda, as party leader, could not be expected to respect the line of the nationalists and might, with his newspaper, apply improper pressure on UDN congressmen. Lacerda replied that, although he would continue writing columns for the *Tribuna,* he would turn its directorship over to Aluísio Alves. Passos left the room and the choice of Lacerda as UDN leader was recorded as unanimous.[10]

Over two hundred UDN state representatives (forty from Minas) gathered in Rio early in April for the party's eleventh national convention. Juracy Magalhães saw the PL veto of his name as no reason to withdraw and, with Lacerda's help, easily won the UDN presidency, defeating Federal District Congressman Odilon Braga. The party adopted a program that, in the words of political scientist Maria Victoria de Mesquita Benevides, "emphasized liberal and private sector views" and welcomed foreign capital. As she points out, it called for autonomy for the Bank of Brazil, exchange reform, congressional control over the issuance of paper money, and the nationalization of radioactive materials.[11]

In backing Juracy Magalhães at the convention, Lacerda described the party as assuming a "realistic" stance. Catholic leader Gustavo Corção, analyzing Lacerda's role, wrote that Lacerda had many dangerous enemies but that his most dangerous enemy was himself. "Look, for example, at what is taking place in the UDN. While the bold UDN congressman confronts, with obviously superior skill, the maneuvers of Vieira de Melo in the Chamber of Deputies, he adopts, in the UDN directorship meetings and convention sessions, a line of conduct called realistic, parallel to the route followed by Vieira de Melo, and defends with ardor a candidate for the party presidency who maintains relations with Goulart."[12]

Lacerda, like others in the long-frustrated UDN, hoped that Juracy and the new pragmatic program would give the party an attractive image, useful when it turned, more assiduously than before, to find support in the streets and countryside. Speaking in Belo Horizonte, Lacerda said, "If we have one paramount task it is to remove the party from the mystique of glorious defeats."[13]

In pronouncements supposed to mollify the unhappy PL, the UDN said that its new president and program did not mean an abandonment of an intransigently oppositionist attitude. Juracy announced that he had received no appeals from the party's "realistic wing" to soften attacks on the government. The PL, however, decided to terminate its alliance with the UDN. Lacerda, in response, said that he and others had believed his election to the UDN leadership would preserve the alliance and that he was now resigning his leadership position. He planned, he added, to hand it over to Afonso Arinos, whose "leader of the opposition" post would disappear with the death of the UDN-PL alliance. Afonso Arinos, reportedly disillusioned with political activity, declined Lacerda's offer.[14]

The PL, reconsidering its position, took into consideration Lacerda's threat to leave his leadership post and the plan of Afonso Arinos to spend four months in Europe, thus placing the opposition leadership in the hands of the PL's Nestor Duarte. But what contributed most to the PL's decision to postpone breaking up the alliance was a determined effort of the administration to deprive Lacerda of his mandate. Under the rules governing procedures in the Chamber, the existence of an opposition bloc would be helpful to maneuvers for defending the mandate of the lively and controversial congressman from the Federal District.[15]

PL congressional leader Raul Pilla, miffed by the choice of Juracy to head the UDN, planned to advise the officers of the Chamber of the end of the UDN-PL alliance. Although he was usually unbending, he was persuaded by other PL members to hold off acting at least until after the battle on behalf of Lacerda's mandate.[16]

Lacerda therefore did not relinquish his leadership post. This may have been a disappointment to members of the UDN *chapa branca* who were beginning to resent his failure to socialize with them despite their contribution to his selection. Lacerda, having noted that the *chapa branca* "realists" met frequently at the Copacabana Palace Hotel bar, decided to address the problem there. After phoning Letícia to say he might not be home for forty-eight hours, he went to the bar, where he found Congressmen José Cândido Ferraz, Edilberto Ribeiro de Castro, and Virgílio Távora, Senator Dinarte Mariz, and most of the other adherents to the *chapa branca.* With them he drank, had a meal that lasted until 2:00 A.M., resumed drinking until 7:00 A.M., and then had beefsteaks at the home of Ribeiro de Castro. The congressmen shaved, attended a UDN meeting, and lunched until 5:00 P.M., when they resumed drinking at the Copacabana Palace bar. By 7:00 A.M. the next morning Lacerda had worn them out with his "Rasputinish" drinking ability and need for little sleep. He had also surprised them and overcome their resentment of his aloofness. But he pointed out, when he left, that they should understand that he could not carry on in such a way and be a good UDN congressional leader.[17]

2. Itamaraty's Secret Telegram 295 (April 1957)

The case of "the mandate of Carlos Lacerda" began formally on April 1 when Military Justice Prosecutor Ivo d'Aquino submitted a request to the Chamber of Deputies for the appearance of Lacerda before the military justice system to be tried for violating the National Security Law of 1953. The request cited Foreign Minister José Carlos de Macedo Soares, who declared that Lacerda, in quoting the ministry's secret Telegram 295, had made it possible to decipher Code S-7 used by Itamaraty (the foreign ministry). Itamaraty asserted that "the law does not permit congressional immunities to be applied in the case of crimes against the country's security."[1]

The contents of decoded secret Telegram 295 from the Brazilian embassy in Buenos Aires had been received by Lacerda from a reporter with ties to Itamaraty.[2] Lacerda first read the contents aloud on February 15 at a secret session of the Chamber of Deputies attended by José Carlos de Macedo Soares. Then, through Chamber First Secretary Wilson Fadul, Lacerda asked Itamaraty for copies of Telegrams 293 and 295, both about the Brazilian pine deal of 1950. Foreign Minister Macedo Soares, replying to Fadul on March 19, stressed Itamaraty's need to keep such communications secret.[3] Nevertheless, on March 27 Lacerda disclosed Telegram 295 during a congressional debate in which Goulart defender José Gomes Talarico (PTB, Federal District) had made a reference to the secret session of February 15. Because of this new disclosure, during a public session, the *Diário do Congresso Nacional* of March 28 published the telegram.[4] Sent from Buenos Aires in August 1956 by Ambassador João Carlos Muniz, it said:

> The naval attaché of this embassy has just been called by the vice-president of Argentina, who advised him that he has been informed by the Argentine naval attaché in Rio de Janeiro that some newspapers in Brazil are going to publish sensationally, the news that the Argentine vice-president will reveal the participation of the Brazilian vice-president in the much discussed sale of Brazilian pine, referred to in my Telegram 293. To the Brazilian naval attaché the Argentine vice-president expressed the desire that, in case such news is made public, the Brazilian government deny it in the most categoric manner. He advised that the Argentine embassy in Brazil has been instructed to issue a denial in case the above mentioned news is given out.[5]

Even before Vieira de Melo delivered his long speech of April 5, formally launching the battle in Congress, the press turned the affair into a heated national debate.

The proadministration *A Noite* assured its readers that Lacerda would be punished. Samuel Wainer's *Última Hora* wrote that Lacerda, in betraying his country, had reached his "supreme degradation" after a career of betraying the Communist Party, "with which he associated in order to inform against his companions," and after betraying *Tribuna* stockholders, associating with arms smugglers, and serving as accomplice of forgers in the Brandi letter "blackmail." As in the past, *Última Hora* called Lacerda "the crow," but now it also called him Judas Carlos Lacerda. He was nicknamed "the hyena of Lavradio Street" by the sensationalist *Código Secreto* (Secret Code), a magazine that sprang into existence at this time.[6]

Vice President João Goulart. (Hilde Weber drawing in Hilde Weber, *O Brasil em Charges, 1950–1985*)

Newspapers of the Chateaubriand chain, by far the most extensive in Brazil, were quick to call for severe punishment of Lacerda, who had recently written that Senator Francisco de Assis Chateaubriand used his Diários Associados chain to publish "intentionally false news" for the extraction of favors and money from those who feared its attacks. Calling Chateaubriand the "degrader" of journalism and the Senate, Lacerda had accused him of persecuting competitors, destroying reputations, and gaining appointments for immoral cronies. According to Lacerda, Chateaubriand had defamed the United States ambassador for failing to give him money and had been named ambassador to Great Britain by Kubitschek "as a price for not carrying out his threats to break with the government." Chateaubriand's *O Jornal,* of Rio, replied on April 4 with its article "Expulsion for the traitor," which said that prison sentences stipulated in the laws were too mild for Lacerda and that, in the past, men had been hanged and shot for crimes less serious than his latest assault on the national security and betrayal of his country.[7]

Lacerda, in a message to the friendly *O Estado de S. Paulo,* wrote that he did not know whether one should laugh or cry about the "delirious raving" of Military Prosecutor Ivo d'Aquino, who, he said, failed to understand that Itamaraty had several codes and frequently changed them. Ivo d'Aquino, Lacerda told *O Estado,* had found General Mendes de Morais innocent of persuading Gregório Fortunato to have Lacerda shot in 1954, and he added that the general, when mayor of Rio, had offered a "sinecure" to d'Aquino's son.[8]

Lacerda also attacked Vitor Nunes Leal, head of the presidential Casa Civil. In the *Tribuna* he described him as *desleal* (disloyal) to Kubitschek for devising a process, never previously used, to allow Congress to trample on the inviolability of congressional mandates. Lacerda called the step "simply a new chapter" in a series that had begun in August 1954 with the attempt to eliminate him physically; that attempt, he said, had been followed by charges that he opposed the republican institutions, by an "ostensive preparation" to assassinate him in November 1955, and by the "unconstitutional regulation" to keep his voice off the radio.[9]

Orating in Congress on April 2, Lacerda pointed out correctly that Telegram 295 merely authorized the Brazilian government to deny that the Argentine vice-president would reveal certain facts. But, he added, the response of Itamaraty had been to disavow the facts themselves in a declaration made "with spectacular display to the entire nation." "It seems," Lacerda told the Chamber of Deputies, "that I am being threatened with being shot as a traitor for stating that the nation is being betrayed."[10]

On April 5 majority leader Vieira de Melo had the attention of the nation when he presented the administration's case. Lacerda, he said, had endangered Brazil's entire system of communications with friendly nations, and he called his crime especially serious because he had been warned by the foreign minister not to commit it. The security law, Vieira de Melo pointed out, imposed two to six years' imprisonment for those who disclosed state secrets, with an additional 50 percent of the stipulated prison time in cases where warnings were given. He refuted statements already made by Herbert Levy (UDN, São Paulo) and Lacerda about the frequency of code changes, and he emphasized the time required and cost for setting up the code (1.5 million cruzeiros in 1942). Turning to "the inviolability of the mandate," the majority leader said it was intended to permit congressmen to express their ideas freely but not to allow state secrets to be disclosed. If a congressman disclosed state secrets in wartime, Vieira de Melo asked, "would he not have committed a monstrous crime?"[11]

Opposition leader Afonso Arinos had warned Lacerda not to disclose the telegram and had come to feel that Lacerda attacked alone and sought protection in a group.[12] But he undertook to defend him and interrupted the speech of the majority leader. Lacerda, Afonso Arinos told Vieira de Melo, had not published Telegram 295 in the *Tribuna* and therefore the whole question could be settled by a reprimand by the officers of Congress. Castilho Cabral, in another interruption, insisted that constitutional Article 44 left no doubt that the freedom of congressmen to express themselves in the Chamber was unrestricted. Vieira de Melo replied that no one had imagined that anyone would behave as Lacerda had done, committing "a crime of treason against the nation."[13]

Lacerda followed Vieira de Melo to the tribune. Analyzing the national security law, he said the national defense secrets mentioned in it did not depend on the opinion of the executive branch but were defined by Decree Law 27,583 of December 14, 1949, which listed fifteen items, none of which had been violated by him. Vieira de Melo, in one of the interruptions to Lacerda's speech, referred to Telegrams 293 and 295 in an effort to show that Goulart was not involved in the pine deal. Lacerda therefore asked the majority leader to read Telegram 293. Vieira de Melo refused on the ground that to do so would contribute to the disclosure of Itamaraty's Code S-7. This allowed Lacerda to argue that Vieira de Melo was contradicting his earlier statement about how the code had been completely broken. In conclusion, Lacerda said that on October 3, 1955, Lott had released the text of the coded telegram from Argentina about the Brandi letter (including a reference to the hour of the telegram's transmission) and should be considered as having committed a grave crime.[14]

The PTB was quick to subscribe to the administration's formula for having Congress, by a majority vote, strip Lacerda of his immunities from prosecution. The formula required 164 votes, which seemed well within reach considering that the PSD, with 114 congressmen, and the PTB, with 56, could count on other parties allied with the administration, as demonstrated in the votes expelling Carlos Luz and Café Filho from the Brazilian presidency. The opposition was made up of 74 UDN congressmen and 8 members of the PL.

Lacerda sought to arouse the fears of congressmen. Speaking with some of them, he said, "If you agree that congressional immunities can be violated because of a speech, you are going to set a very dangerous precedent." "Behind the cancellation of my mandate," he told the *Diário de Notícias,* "lies a plan to stab Congress."[15]

3. The Battle for Public Opinion (April–May 1957)

The forty-five-day struggle over Lacerda's mandate, the most sensational of his congressional career, was the principal topic throughout Brazil. Afonso Arinos has written that "through the press and radio, the debates reached every corner of the country. In practically every home in cities, towns, villages, and hamlets, on isolated *fazendas* of the backlands with their battery radios, the people turned their attention from other things, anxious, listening to speeches in Tiradentes Palace."[1]

In large cities, rallies were held in the streets. Thousands of Paulistas cheered Goulart when he proclaimed that the PTB was fulfilling its duty in condemning Lacerda for treason. In Rio during Holy Week, Goulart's supporters hung up hundreds of effigies of Judas, wearing shell-rimmed glasses and resembling Lacerda. At PTB-sponsored rallies in Rio, proadministration congressmen and labor leaders condemned Lacerda while shouting crowds demanded "imprisonment for the traitor."[2]

Lacerda spoke at meetings and rallies in Rio and elsewhere. At the Brazilian Press Association (ABI) on April 26, he told over a thousand supporters that the government machine was preparing to "grind up my flesh." Amaral Netto called the meeting a protest against an attempt to destroy democracy, and Raul Brunini, launching the slogan "Liberty with Lacerda," announced an outdoor rally to be held at the Esplanada do Castelo a week later. The *Tribuna,* in its list of artists and writers who were "mobilizing against the persecution of Lacerda," mentioned Adonias Filho, Afrânio Coutinho, Manuel Bandeira, Mário Pedrosa, Cândido Portinari, João Condé, and humorist Millôr Fernandes ("Vão Gogo").[3]

Students were divided. The president of the Centro Acadêmico Cândido de Oliveira, representing the law students in Rio, said Lacerda should be put on trial. Students who opposed this view answered a call of Rio's União Metropolitana dos Estudantes to join workers at a rally to defend congressional mandates. The rally, held at the headquarters of the National Union of Students (UNE), was almost disrupted by anti-Lacerda students associated with the Communist Party. But Lacerda restored order by asking the crowd to let the progovernment students be heard. When Lacerda spoke, he said he was not there to create an emotional climate. He discussed the secret telegrams and argued that, if the code had been broken, the government ought to reveal the text of Telegram 293.[4]

Although the Communist Party considered Lacerda a "detestable traitor," it liked neither the Kubitschek administration nor its manner of dealing with Lacerda, which, it said, denied the sanctity of legislative mandates and might make Lacerda a martyr, thus helping the "antinationalistic" forces for which he worked. It accused the administration of "violating labor union activities" and promising to turn Brazilian petroleum over to the American trusts. Foreign Minister Macedo Soares, it wrote, was as closely connected as Lacerda to Standard Oil and the Yankee embassy.[5]

Carlos' friend Marcelo Garcia, who was providing medical treatment for a daughter of Kubitschek, felt the president was making a mistake. In his own name (not that of Carlos), he appealed to Kubitschek to call off the fight in Congress and suggested that if Kubitschek would do so he would seek to persuade Carlos to modify his attacks to exclude personal ones against the president. But Kubitschek, using a bad name to describe Lacerda, expressed his determination to deprive him of his mandate.[6]

On April 6, Kubitschek asked Congress to authorize the expenditure of fifteen million cruzeiros for a new code. According to proadministration sources, diplomats reported that it would take six months to install it. Describing a woeful situation in which the Brazilian delegation to a joint commission in Washington was isolated from Itamaraty, these sources said: "The delegation has been unable to communicate with the ministry for about a month." Vieira de Melo, becoming more and more aggressive, told a radio audience that Lacerda's political career had been "an endless chain of crimes against the nation."[7]

Vieira de Melo's speeches did nothing to reverse a campaign already under way in *Correio da Manhã* to have him deposed as majority leader. Paulo Bittencourt's daily, despite its aversion to Lacerda, supported the inviolability of his mandate. *O Globo,* also opposing Vieira de Melo, wrote that his speech of April 5 lacked substance and was a bomb that failed to explode. Although it maintained that "the fiery leader of the UDN" had made a mistake in disclosing Telegram 295 publicly, *O Globo* claimed that he was fully protected by the constitution and that the whole "parliamentary institution" was being placed in jeopardy by the administration's performance.[8]

The *Diário Carioca,* directed by the foreign minister's brother and by Lacerda's old friend Horácio de Carvalho Júnior, continued to back the administration, along with *A Noite, Última Hora,* and the Chateaubriand chain. It published a series of anti-Lacerda articles by veteran journalist Danton Jobim, recipient of a Maria Moors Cabot journalism award. Jobim criticized Vieira de Melo for not organizing the government forces efficiently for the fight against Lacerda. And he found it inexplicable that "the great patriot," Eduardo Gomes, should have issued a declaration supporting the man who "revealed the secret code to foreigners." "Danton Jobim," Gustavo Corção wrote in *O Estado de S. Paulo,* "speaks of the crime of Lacerda. . . . But what was the crime? From what I understand, Lacerda denounced a crime and then proved that an official lie was used to cover it up."[9]

The governor of São Paulo, Jânio Quadros, issued a statement opposing "the annulment of the mandate of the leader of the UDN." Ademar de Barros, whose recent successful campaign for the São Paulo mayorship had been opposed by Quadros, gave his support to Vieira de Melo and praised Goulart.[10]

Ademar was regarded as the dominating figure in the PSP, the fourth largest party after the PSD, UDN, and PTB. But many of its thirty-two congressmen rebelled against his instructions to support Vieira de Melo. As for the PR (the fifth largest party, with nineteen congressmen), Senator Artur Bernardes Filho said its *deputados* could take any position they wished, whereas its congressional vice-leader, Raimundo de Sousa Brito, argued that Lacerda should be punished.[11] The PTN (whose six congressmen put it in seventh place, after the PL) was led in Congress by Castilho Cabral, who stated that the party opposed depriving Lacerda of his parliamentary immunity. Plínio Salgado's PRP (with three congressmen) condemned Lacerda's "unpatriotic" action and said he needed "civic reeducation," but it went on record as opposing the administration's plan. The three *deputados* of the PSB (Socialist Party) felt that Kubitschek was making a mistake.[12]

CONFRATERNIZAÇÃO

Ademar de Barros (*right*) gives his support to Goulart. (Drawing in *O Estado de S. Paulo*, May 3, 1957)

Late in April the administration strengthened its case by divulging a personal letter of October 28, 1955, from Raul Fernandes to Lacerda, in which Fernandes, foreign minister of Café Filho, refused to release copies of confidential papers about the activities of Peronists. Referring to a telegram that interested Lacerda, Fernandes had written: "You are familiar with the role that telegraphic codes play in diplomatic relations. With the coded texts circulating on telegraphic lines, shall people be allowed to discover the keys to our communications?"[13]

In *Última Hora* Otávio Malta quoted the *Diário Carioca* and Chateaubriand's *O Jornal* as saying that the Raul Fernandes letter demolished Lacerda. Predicting an inglorious end for the *corvo* (crow), *Última Hora* wrote that his last testament should read: "I, Carlos Lacerda, a vile traitor of the nation, the *Corvo* of Lavradio and the most perfect Judas on this planet, on going to the place where I should already have gone, cannot forget those who collaborated most efficiently with me in my arduous work of traitor." *Última Hora* also stated that the death of anti-Communist United States Senator Joseph McCarthy left Lacerda an orphan, and it ridiculed *Diário de Notícias* publisher João Ribeiro Dantas for opposing the suspension of Lacerda's mandate. "The position of Joãozinho," Otávio Malta wrote, "reminds us of places in the world where, for religious reasons, the killing of fleas, mosquitos, and other insects is prohibited."[14]

Última Hora defended Finance Minister José Maria Alkmin against attacks made by the *Tribuna* and wrote maliciously that Lacerda was offering to call off the attacks if the finance ministry would release from customs the 1956 Plymouth that he had purchased in New York early in 1956. Alkmin, accused by Lacerda of involvement in questionable financial operations, maintained that the importation of the car went beyond what was allowed to returning Brazilians. The politically astute finance minister amused congressmen when he listed some of the things Lacerda had been permitted to import: "a TV set, a freezer, a washing machine, a dryer, etc., etc." When Lacerda produced a foreign ministry document allowing importation of the Plymouth, Alkmin replied that the document was for statistical purposes only and that the finance ministry was in charge of the matter.[15]

Lacerda, discussing the controversy later, recalled a rude exchange in Congress during which he reacted to Alkmin's charge that he was a "smuggler of automobiles" by exhibiting all his car papers and retorting, "I am not a liar and you are." The Plymouth remained in customs for ten months on Alkmin's instructions and was in such bad condition when it was released that Lacerda sold it.[16]

4. The Justice Commission Votes against Lacerda (May 3, 1957)

Late in April the attention of Brazil turned to the twenty-five-man congressional justice commission, which had the task of giving the full Congress its opinion as to whether Lacerda's parliamentary immunity should be waived. The commission, headed by Antônio Oliveira Brito (PSD, Bahia), was dominated by the PSD-PTB coalition because of the distribution of its membership: PSD 9, UDN 6, PTB 5, PSP 2, PR 2, and PL 1.

The commission's *relator,* José Martins Rodrigues (PSD, Ceará), was preparing his report and opinion about the case of Telegram 295 when the government decided belatedly to add the case of the Brandi letter. Therefore Aarão Steinbruch (PTB, Rio state) became the commission's *relator* to study the request of the prosecuting attorney of the Federal District that Congress make Lacerda available to be tried for involvement in the criminal falsification of the letter.[1]

Lacerda, appearing before the justice commission, argued that he was not alone in having believed in the authenticity of the Brandi letter. To demonstrate that Generals Lott and Maurell had also considered it probably authentic, he played a phonograph record of Lott's October 3, 1955, announcement about Maurell's telegram from Buenos Aires. The majority's lack of interest in the recording was captured in an *O Estado de S. Paulo* drawing showing Aarão Steinbruch inattentive, Martins Rodrigues cutting his fingernails, and another progovernment congressman playing with a little paper boat. The UDN's scholarly Bilac Pinto set to work to present arguments as to why Lacerda should not be deprived of his congressional immunity in order to be tried for his role in the case of the forged letter.[2]

After the commission decided to vote first on the case of Telegram 295, *relator* Martins Rodrigues presented a twenty-page opinion favorable to the request of Ivo d'Aquino. He cited legal opinions and foreign legislation. Lacerda, he wrote, had not only violated his oath of office but had "profoundly endangered important negotiations about the defense of Brazil." The *relator*

In the congressional justice commission Lacerda plays a recording of Lott's words of October 3, 1955, about the Brandi letter. Aarão Steinbruch (*dark hair*) is next to Leoberto Leal, who tinkers with a paper boat while Martins Rodrigues (*far right, bottom*) cuts his fingernails. (Hilde Weber drawing in *O Estado de S. Paulo,* May 12, 1957)

argued that the nation, divided, shaken, and in suspense, would be distressed and incredulous if parliamentary prerogatives were carried to such an extreme as not to allow a judicial investigation.[3]

Lacerda prepared his own defense. He could have been a great lawyer but had shown no interest in finishing his law course in the 1930s. As a law student and a little later, he had occasionally defended destitute clients in the courts and always been successful. Now he threw himself into his own case with the intensity he had shown in 1934, when he had received an appeal to defend a prostitute accused of killing her newborn baby.

At the congressional library he learned what books Martins Rodrigues had borrowed; after the *relator* returned them, he took them to the library at the law office of Dario de Almeida Magalhães. There Lacerda and Dario's son Rafael looked up citations given by Martins Rodrigues and discovered that more extensive readings appeared to nullify some of the *relator*'s interpretations. They spent three days and nights preparing the defense, with Rafael's legal work accounting for about one-third of the 158-page document and Carlos' arguments occupying the remainder. Carlos pounded away on a law-office typewriter with such zest that he broke it.[4]

In the 158 pages, Lacerda covered a wide range of subjects, including Peronism and totalitarian doctrine. He quoted authorities who maintained that "venerable" Code S-7, fifteen years old, had been broken since at least 1953, and he maintained that the reading of the telegram at the secret session available to 326 congressmen, an act uncensured by the authorities, hardly left the telegram secret. Claiming that the government's position was inspired by political considerations, he said the people could no more believe in the "absurd" fifteen million cruzeiro cost of a new code than they could believe that the national security depended on Telegram 293 remaining a mystery. Senator Rui Barbosa, Lacerda pointed out, had also been threatened with a trial for treason for revealing confidential Itamaraty documents in 1919 and had, in his response, defended the right of the people to be informed about matters that the government was seeking to keep secret.[5]

The 158-page document pointed to flaws in references given by Martins Rodrigues. A fuller study of the democratic constitution of West Germany, it said, proved the opposite of what Martins Rodrigues tried to show. Past cases of the Brazilian government against José Carlos de Macedo Soares in 1923 and João Mangabeira in 1936 had occurred during a state of siege and a state of war and for this and other reasons were not comparable with the case of Telegram 295. As explained in Lacerda's defense document, Martins Rodrigues' statement about the position of Afrânio de Melo Franco in 1915 had failed to include an important paragraph, prompting Afrânio's son, Afonso Arinos, to publish a rectification in the *Tribuna*. And the *relator*'s inclusion of a quotation by Francisco Campos had led that jurist to give a reply that Lacerda furnished in his long defense statement, together with the news that Francisco Campos had agreed to defend him before the Supreme Court if the case went that far.[6]

Lacerda wound up his defense statement sensationally. "Telegram 295," he said, "is not in secret code. And the government knows that. It lied to the

Chamber, the nation, the army, the judiciary, the people, and this commission." He also declared that the telegram had been in the file of "reserved"—not "secret"—communications, available to many Itamaraty employees, "and I can say the same about Telegram 293." In his final sentence, he asserted that Telegram 293 gave the name of Goulart as the "Brazilian legislator" who had received money to be used in the Brazilian presidential election of 1950.[7]

On May 2, while Lacerda finished writing this long defense, scheduled for delivery that night, Juracy Magalhães spoke in the Senate, telling of messages of support for the UDN coming from all over Brazil. In the lower chamber, Afonso Arinos criticized Martins Rodrigues for having used "gymnastics and acrobatics" in his *relator*'s report. Addressing congressmen who belonged to the armed forces, the opposition leader asked why the military was forcing Congress to assume an attitude that he described as insane, unjust, and absurd. He maintained that if Congress followed the administration's wishes, the Supreme Court would eventually submit Congress to the greatest humiliation of its history by upholding the inviolability of parliamentary immunities.[8]

During ten hours, interrupted by time out for dinner, Lacerda read his 158-page defense. Returning home from the justice commission, he was unable to sleep and found relaxation in typing a play.[9]

The members of the justice commission presented their opinions on May 3 at a secret session. Like Prado Kelly, Milton Campos limited himself to a careful consideration of legal technicalities. He pointed out that parliamentary immunities were not held at the pleasure of congressional majorities but, rather, as a protection against them and that, if requests for violating the immunities were ever to be considered, the requests had to be submitted by judges and not by prosecuting attorneys such as Ivo d'Aquino. A study of the crime of treason, he said, showed that Lacerda had committed no such crime because his interest lay in correcting misinformation and not in willfully placing the national defense in danger.

When Ari Pitombo (PTB, Alagoas) delivered his vote in favor of the administration, his personal attacks on Lacerda were so violent that Adauto Lúcio Cardoso described the commission as disgracing itself and told its president, Oliveira Brito, that he would leave if "such insults" continued to be expressed.[10]

The votes favored the administration, fifteen to ten. Besides receiving all the PSD and PTB votes, the administration received one PR vote, that of lawyer Raimundo de Sousa Brito, of Bahia. In a comment on Lacerda's 158-page paper, he observed that even murderers were not granted unlimited time for presenting their defenses. The other PR member joined the UDN-PL coalition and so did the two PSP members (Osvaldo Lima Filho and Antônio Chagas Freitas).[11] The Kubitschek administration, disappointed in the smaller party votes, scheduled an early final vote by the full Chamber of Deputies.

The unsurprising verdict of the justice commission was followed in the evening by the Esplanada do Castelo rally, announced a week earlier by Raul

Statue of Rui Barbosa in the congressional justice commission; Rui is worried about the "illegal" steps taken by the commission's majority. (Hilde Weber drawing in *O Estado de S. Paulo*, May 3, 1957)

Brunini. Among those who spoke were Lacerda and five other UDN congressmen, Senator Juracy Magalhães, and several members of the Municipal Council. Another was PSD Congressman Euripides Cardoso de Menezes, who used scathing language to denounce fellow *pessedistas* who put party instruction above their personal wishes to vote to uphold congressional immunities.

Adauto Lúcio Cardoso compared the justice commission's verdict with the decision of Congress, prior to the establishment of the Estado Novo, that had sent four congressmen and one senator to prison. Municipal Councilwoman Sandra Cavalcanti argued that the government sought to crush the opposition by steps such as the one preventing broadcasts by "one of the most legitimate representatives of the people." Lacerda, who received a thunderous ovation, spoke of UDN legislative proposals about labor matters that the congressional majority was ignoring. Explaining the unusual brevity of his talk, he said he had to leave on a speechmaking trip that would take him to Santos, Belo Horizonte, and Niterói.[12]

The administration resolved to show that Lacerda, in his long defense, had lied in asserting that Telegram 293 contained the name of Goulart. On May 6, Vieira de Melo announced, Foreign Minister Macedo Soares would receive twelve congressional leaders at Itamaraty and confidentially show them "the exact text" of the telegram. After Afonso Arinos accepted the invitation, Lacerda went to his office to object violently to his "involving himself in a maneuver of the majority leader." Afonso Arinos, called a "dupe" by Lacerda and other oppositionist columnists, felt that a refusal to go to Itamaraty would look like a confession favorable to the majority.[13]

The visitors to Itamaraty were shown a copy of decoded Telegram 293 whereupon two of them asked about a blank space where apparently another name should have followed that of pine negotiator Carlos Maura Ronchetti. During a half-hour debate, Macedo Soares called in a technician who blamed the gap on decoding errors. After a further delay Itamaraty's chief of communications brought in what he said was the original precoded typescript, signed by Ambassador João Carlos Muniz. The visitors were also shown a coded version, which a cryptographer decoded for them. The documents mentioned a Brazilian who had been "a legislator," but Goulart's name was missing, as PSB leader José Antônio Rogê Ferreira announced after the visit.[14]

In Congress, Vieira de Melo said Lacerda's statement about Goulart being named in Telegram 293 was "an unadulterated lie, an unadulterated fabrication, an unadulterated slander, an unadulterated hoax, and an unadulterated act of meanness." *Última Hora* wrote that Lacerda, nothing more than a falsifier, had falsified secret Telegram 293. In the *Diário Carioca,* Danton Jobim wrote: "Today the UDN should cover its head with ashes,weeping in shame."

In the same newspaper, journalist Carlos Castello Branco described Lacerda as recalling copies of his forthcoming book containing the defense he had submitted to the justice commission. But the only effect of the Itamaraty visit on the book, *O Caminho da Liberdade,* was the addition of a footnote that said that Itamaraty "showed some congressmen three copies of Telegram 293, in translated text—but refused to show the coded text and the corresponding code."[15]

5. Closing Rallies (May 6–14, 1957)

At his home on the night of May 6, Afonso Arinos discussed plans to deflate the euphoria of the majority that had followed Vieira de Melo's latest speech about Telegram 293. He was joined by other *udenistas,* including Lacerda, "whose fatal ambition for fame and power," he writes, "always called for new crises in which his personal destiny became confused with the destiny of the institutions." When a reporter called at Afonso Arinos' residence, he found the men more optimistic than recent events appeared to justify. Lacerda told the reporter that the copies of Telegram 293, shown to congressmen at Itamaraty, seemed at variance with a copy he had.[1]

Afonso Arinos, speaking in Congress on May 7, admitted that Goulart's name was not in Telegram 293, but he maintained that other evidence left no doubt that Goulart was the "foreign legislator." He revealed that Ambassador João Carlos Muniz, in the telegram, had advised that the Argentine authorities would, if asked by Brazil, supply definitive clarifications about the whole matter. In appealing to the majority to accept the Argentine offer, Afonso Arinos said that Goulart might have had no dishonest intentions and had the obligation to defend his honor. The appeal, Afonso Arinos

The Lacerda Case. (Drawing in *O Estado de S. Paulo,* May 8, 1957)

writes, left the majority disoriented because it would be refused, thus weakening the case for punishing Goulart's accuser. He adds that his speech was praised enthusiastically by members of the opposition, with the exception of Lacerda, who felt insecure.[2]

Around the bust of Vargas in Cinelândia on the night of May 9, Lacerda's enemies held a fiery rally. Among the speakers at this "popular jury" trial were Congressmen Lutero Vargas, Ari Pitombo, and José Gomes Talarico, Porto Alegre Mayor Leonel Brizola, and former Aviation Minister Epaminondas Santos. They were constantly interrupted by cries of "Jail for the Assassin of Vargas" and "A Cage for the Crow."

Lutero Vargas, wildly acclaimed, said that it was not surprising that "the attacks on my father and me became more numerous and vehement when I presented Congress the project to nationalize banking assets. Nor can it be denied that the inspirer of the attacks was Lacerda, the agent of the international financial groups. His object was to destroy those who, like my father, became the symbols of the economic liberation of our country, of the Brazilian people." Lutero, as he reminded his audience, had set aside his congressional immunities when he testified in 1954 at the Galeão Air Base investigation about the assassination of Major Vaz. "In those days," Lutero stated, "Lacerda and his henchmen exceeded the limits of the constitution in doing all they wanted. Why does not Lacerda put aside his immunities just as, in those days, his yellow newspaper insisted be done by me and Congressman Euvaldo Lodi? Why?"

The crowd answered by shouting: "Because the Crow is a Traitor."

"A traitor," Lutero said, was what Lacerda had been called by Municipal Councilman Aristides Saldanha, "Lacerda's former Communist Party companion." Lacerda, according to Lutero, "betrayed his parents. He betrayed his companions. For a beefsteak he squealed on people who gave him hiding places from the police." Declaring that Lacerda had systematically attacked Petrobrás, Volta Redonda, and then Eletrobrás, Lutero asserted that "a subhuman of this type obviously cannot forgive my father, who gave his life for the political and economic emancipation of the Brazilian people." In conclusion, Lutero referred to Lacerda's "megalomania" and contended that it had reached a new high because he had compared himself with Rui Barbosa.

Leonel Brizola called Lacerda a simple thief, robber of the *Tribuna* shareholders. "When I was a congressman," he said, "I never tired of asking about the origin of his wealth. About his two country houses, his apartments, and the continued existence of his newspaper, famous for its deficits, deficits of readers and morals. But I never received a reply, not even when I discovered that Lacerda spent, on his propaganda and life of a nabob, the enormous sum of 1,500,000 cruzeiros. . . . In all the time I was in the Chamber of Deputies, I could never address him as Your Excellency. A criminal should be treated as such."

Brigadeiro Epaminondas Santos, in a reference to the murder of Major Vaz, said "*o corvo*," a coward, had left to his unfortunate fate the man who had protected him.[3]

In sharp contrast to the PTB-oriented Cinelândia crowd, audiences in São Paulo welcomed Lacerda when he appeared there at the side of Juracy Magalhães and Amaral Netto. Luís Martins wrote in *O Estado de S. Paulo* that the acclaim for Lacerda was "an eloquent demonstration of the repulsion felt for the project to cancel the mandate of Brazil's most voted-for congressman." Speaking at São Paulo's Engineering Institute on May 11, Lacerda blamed the "terrible wave" against him on the revenge of the Gregórios who had been restored to power and the "predominance of a group in the government that favors these corrupt ways in order to guarantee the impunity of its own corruption." To show that it was his foes and not himself who wished to end the Petrobrás monopoly, he referred to *Hanson's Latin American Letter*, published in the United States, which said that Washington "believes that if Lacerda can be smothered decisively, a great deal of steam will go out of the opposition and the Kubitschek administration will be able to get on with its decision to allow the foreign petroleum companies to begin effective exploitation and exploration in Brazil."[4]

After attending a rally in Salvador, Bahia, at the side of Aliomar Baleeiro, Lacerda returned to Rio to find both the administration and opposition nervous about the vote on his mandate. UDN President Juracy Magalhães, speaking to reporters on May 14, said: "I am pessimistic. . . . But I am absolutely certain that the habeas corpus petition we shall present to the Supreme Court will be granted unanimously." Prado Kelly told reporters that the congressional majority could make use of political commitments in seeking votes. But, he added, the Supreme Court considered only the juridical aspects "and in this area the opposition has an uncontestable superiority as demonstrated in the debates in Congress and especially in the justice commission." The habeas corpus petition had already been drawn up by Dario de Almeida Magalhães and Francisco Campos, author of the Estado Novo's Constitution of 1937.[5]

Pilot Wilson Machado—known as "Foguinho" by Lacerda's friends—was in Buenos Aires, having flown there on May 10 with an urgent message from Lacerda to Gainza Paz. Lacerda hoped for a revelation by Argentine President Pedro Aramburu. But Aramburu did not receive the Buenos Aires newspaper publisher and Brazilian pilot until May 18; and then all he would say was that he would make no declaration that might complicate matters for friends belonging to a friendly nation.[6]

6. The Vote of Congress (May 16, 1957)

Rafael de Almeida Magalhães, who helped organize rallies to support Lacerda, feels that Congress was brilliant during the era of Lacerda's leadership of the UDN.[1] It had many eminent men and distinguished speakers. The opposition played a dramatic card by having the oldest of them, 71-year-old Otávio Mangabeira, speak in Congress on May 14. The crowd in the packed galleries heartily applauded the renowned orator and anti-Getulista.

"If," Mangabeira said, "the government's request is denied, as law and good sense suggest, the matter will be ended. But if it is granted, the agitation will continue in the courts. . . . The Supreme Court will either guarantee the congressman his immunities, as I am convinced it will, and this will put the Chamber in an uncomfortable situation, or it will not guarantee inviolability of the mandate, putting the Supreme Court in an uncomfortable situation." Mangabeira predicted that Lacerda, if condemned, would speak to the nation from his cell through his newspaper. "Only a poor psychologist," he said, "can fail to perceive what will inevitably occur: a line of visitors at the prison door. The very paving stones in the streets will shout for amnesty and for the final acclaim, in the ballot boxes, of the name of the leader of the UDN."[2]

To follow Mangabeira to the tribune, the majority turned to 29-year-old Ivete Vargas (PTB, São Paulo), cousin of Lutero. She received an ovation when she said that Getúlio Vargas, "the leader of nationalism," preferred to offer his life as a holocaust rather than submit to "the heel of imperialism." She maintained that the egotistical groups that had created "total disorder" in 1954 were doing the same thing again in the hope of reaching power by subversive means. The congressional majority, she said, was asking no more than that the case of Lacerda go to the justice system where he would have the opportunity to prove his innocence.[3]

National interest in the congressional vote was such that the state legislature of Espírito Santo declared itself in favor of a public rally to support Lacerda.[4] The interest of the federal Chamber was demonstrated by the presence of 297 *deputados* on the afternoon of May 15, when Lacerda gave a speech that he said might be his last in the Chamber. As described by Afonso Arinos, Lacerda spoke in a careful, moderate, almost conciliatory manner "as always happens when he feels insecure." He revealed himself "as a victim, sacrificing himself to his executioners, with beautiful, calm words."[5]

Lacerda said that calculations made it seem probable that the vote would be unfavorable to him and therefore he was turning over to the UDN congressmen, the PL congressmen, and all the congressmen, the task of following up on the law projects he had introduced. Listing twenty-one in all, he placed special emphasis on the labor code he had proposed in June 1955, the work of "a team of the most competent specialists in social and labor law in Brazil." "I leave it, let us say, as a sort of open testament for the consideration . . . of the honorable Chamber of Deputies."

As for the telegram that had caused all the trouble, he said he could now affirm, "with absolute tranquility," that the text he had disclosed was not the literal translation of the original, but a mere paraphrase. "Last night I thought of presenting the proof for examination by the noble leaders of the majority. But, since all of us have slept little these last nights, . . . I decided that at this stage it would be perfectly useless and even prejudicial to introduce new evidence, even though definitive and conclusive. Already the noble majority leader has issued his command: the decision is political. Of what importance, then, are decisive proofs?"

Referring to the charge that he was a *golpista,* he said he had only carried out his duty to warn of what might happen to Brazil's "free institutions" with the return to power of those who had dominated the country for over a quarter of a century. He would, he said, be pleased if he could be shown to have been wrong. "But what have we seen? We have seen the return of those against whom I warned. . . . Machiavellianism dominates national life." He promised that if he were put in prison he would not fail to exercise his mandate there, perhaps with much more vigor, realism, and authenticity.

Turning to the teachings of Christ, Lacerda discussed sacrifices. Seeds, he pointed out, first have to "die in the dark earth," in order that plants might blossom. "If it is the wish of the majority, let it turn the present leader of the UDN into the example of a seed for a new and true democracy in Brazil, the one I promised to defend and shall defend at the cost of any sacrifice." The speech was followed by prolonged applause.[6]

Afonso Arinos and Vieira de Melo agreed that during the night session, which was to begin at 9:00 P.M., the only speeches would be by the two of them, with the opposition leader giving the first. Two hundred ninety-nine congressmen made their appearance, a record for a night session, because the long-awaited balloting was to follow the two speeches. Large crowds, unable to get into the already-filled galleries, occupied streets and squares in the neighborhood of Tiradentes Palace; like people all over Brazil, they listened to radios to follow what went on. Lacerda spent most of this time in the office of the opposition leader, listening to a broadcast of the proceedings, but he was on the floor of the Chamber when the majority leader spoke.[7]

Afonso Arinos opened his ninety-minute oration by remarking that the drama being enacted recalled the great days of the Chamber in the past, and he described Otávio Mangabeira, "the old tribune," as having reached "one of the pinnacles of his career of oratory . . . in issuing his unhappy warning." After calling the administration's solution juridically impossible, politically inopportune, and personally intolerable, Afonso Arinos objected emotionally to the "climate of oppression."[8]

Ari Pitombo, interrupting, spoke of the hatreds sown by Lacerda and the sacrifice made by Vargas; he would, he said, vote against Lacerda in order to honor the memory of Vargas. Áureo de Melo (PTB, Amazonas), in another interruption, expressed the need to "respond to hatred with hatred." Afonso Arinos observed that hatred was neither constructive nor a useful ingredient for a juridical debate, and he recalled that Vargas, in his farewell message, had said: "To hatred I reply with forgiveness." In his final exhortation, Afonso Arinos exclaimed: "I trust in Your Excellencies, I trust in Brazil, and, above all, I trust in God, who must turn his merciful eyes to this directionless country, to these forgotten men, to this abandoned place, to this land scorched by hatred."[9]

Following the applause for the opposition leader's speech, Vieira de Melo arose to the accompaniment of cheers from the congressional majority and boos from the galleries. While he repeated arguments already made, Lacerda interrupted to ask whether the word *secret* should be used for a message whose copies, one of which had reached him, circulated freely at Itamaraty.

Vieira de Melo quoted UDN jurist Pedro Aleixo, who, as majority leader in 1936, had defended stripping mandates from four congressmen, accused of conspiring against the regime. Prado Kelly pointed out that the crimes attributed to the four had been carried out when they were not acting as congressmen, and Afonso Arinos referred once more to the "state of war" in Brazil in 1936. Vieira de Melo, alluding to Lacerda's speech earlier in the day, stated that the telegram disclosed by the UDN leader had not been a paraphrase but the authoritative text, as recently demonstrated to congressmen who visited Itamaraty.[10]

The secret balloting was followed by the counting of the votes, one by one, in absolute silence. It was well past midnight when the number of votes opposing the administration reached the figure that guaranteed that the government would fail to muster 164.

Pandemonium took the place of anxious silence. While congressmen shouted and sang the national anthem, Lacerda entered triumphantly and embraced Afonso Arinos. Chamber of Deputies President Ulysses Guimarães (PSD, São Paulo) had so much trouble bringing about order that it was not until 2:15 A.M. that the voting was concluded and the final result announced: 152 favored the administration, 132 opposed it, and 13 voted in blank.[11]

Afonso Arinos, returning to the tribune, faced a throng that waved handkerchiefs. "Never in my long and active life," he said, "have I spoken to supporters and adversaries with greater justified jubilation than at this moment, nor with greater pride in belonging to this house of the national Congress." The victors, he said, were the constitution and the republic.[12]

Lacerda, accompanied by noisy supporters, went to the UDN headquarters. In his talk at the improvised celebration, he said: "If one can speak of a victory of the Brazilian people, it is the present one that guarantees them freedom of speech through their representatives." He expressed his conviction that the UDN had been strengthened and his hope that the UDN-PL alliance had been "consecrated by the sufferings of the battle."[13]

The Communist *Imprensa Popular* wrote that the outcome, surprising even Lacerda, could be attributed to the unconstitutionality of the government's case and the anti–Vieira de Melo position of "reactionary" PSD congressmen. Among them it included, without accurate knowledge of the recent secret balloting, Armando Falcão, Gustavo Capanema, and Horácio Lafer. *Última Hora* scolded "thirteen cowardly" PSD congressmen, members of the party's *ala velha* (old wing), who, it wrote, had made all the difference by voting in blank in order to defeat Vieira de Melo and the *ala moça* (youthful wing). According to *Última Hora,* a traitor and agent of the monopolies was "loose in the streets" because Congress had decided to let Lacerda "betray at will!"

While *Última Hora* berated "Horácio Lafer and his low-down, trashy followers," the *Diário Carioca* contended that the PTB also had its "traitors," such as José Alves de Azevedo. *Última Hora* agreed and wrote that PTB congressional leader João Batista Ramos was "simply irresponsible and lacking in intelligence."

"From this entire episode," the *Correio da Manhã* wrote, "the UDN must extract a valuable lesson—that it is impossible to continue being led by Carlos Lacerda; just as the PSD cannot continue being led by Vieira de Melo."[14]

7. From "National Pacification" to "Obstruction" (May–September 1957)

In Congress on May 16, Lacerda explained magnanimously that the UDN was refraining from boasting and was suppressing resentments so that everyone could work together on measures to benefit the nation. He said it was up to President Kubitschek to learn enough from the previous night's vote to allow the government to join the opposition in handling national problems. PTB leader Batista Ramos interrupted to express doubt that Lacerda, advocate of "the regime of exception" and representative of the UDN's "cruelest" wing, was sincere in suggesting pacification.[1]

Listing problems to be considered, Lacerda gave the UDN a proworker image. He asked why the government had prevented discussion of projects for an adjustable wage law, a family wage law, and a new labor code. He complained that Kubitschek, influenced by United States railroad experts, was depriving railroad workers of their rights, and he said that multiple exchange rates confiscated the earnings of farmers in order to finance what he called undesirable "monumental" projects being constructed simply to glorify Kubitschek. Asked about the vast electrification projects, he said he did not believe "the grandeur of Brazil is synonymous with the grandeur of the Furnas hydroelectric works," being started in Minas Gerais.

Turning to the petroleum question, Lacerda stressed the nationalist position of himself and his party. As the "firm, unshakable, and tenacious" defender of Petrobrás, Lacerda called attention to reports that international groups were infiltrating, "imposing themselves even within government circles." In addition, he spoke of Brazil's oil and gas concession in Bolivia, calling the Kubitschek government's approach to private investment for extraction there a "despicable case of the abandonment of the legitimate rights of Petrobrás . . . in order to benefit private groups, behind which international interests dance."[2]

While Lacerda offered UDN cooperation for a constructive "democratic dialogue," the PSD governor of Minas, José Francisco Bias Fortes, appealed for pacification. The PTB, however, continued eager to strip Lacerda of his parliamentary immunities so that he could be tried for his role in the Brandi letter affair. When Kubitschek asked government legislative leaders to drop the Brandi letter case, the PTB's Batista Ramos remained obstinate. Therefore the congressional justice commission discussed for a while longer the report of Relator Aarão Steinbruch. But the PSD members lost interest.[3]

Jânio Quadros, governor of São Paulo, liked Bias Fortes' pacification appeal. So did the president of the Minas UDN, Congressman José de Magalhães Pinto, whose wish to have meaningful discussions with the PSD of his state was supported by Afonso Arinos. Kubitschek let it be known that he, too, favored "understandings initiated by Governor Bias Fortes," but he said pacification was up to the parties.[4]

This led Lacerda to complain, at a UDN national directorship meeting, of the failure of the executive branch to take specific pacification steps. Possible steps were mentioned in a speech that he told the directorship he planned to give, accusing the executive branch of acts that barred him from radio broadcasts, that established a financial policy "disastrous" to coffee growers, and that stimulated military disunity by "persecuting capable and patriotic" officers. (João Adil de Oliveira, for example, was repeatedly denied promotion.)[5]

A majority of the Minas congressional contingent disliked Lacerda's proposed speech but in general his aggressiveness was hailed by the UDN *deputados,* most of whom had misgivings about pacification and hoped it would not mean collaborating in a cabinet reform contemplated by Kubitschek. Magalhães Pinto lost the first of many battles with Lacerda. He was even unable to persuade the UDN directorship that Lacerda should tone down expressions in his speech.[6]

In the speech, delivered on June 6, Lacerda said that during "almost twenty days of long and patriotic patience" he and his party had heard only vague expressions from Kubitschek together with constant references to the amnesty for the Jacareacanga rebels. The chief beneficiaries of the amnesty, Lacerda insisted, were "the conspirators, the insurrectionists who placed Kubitschek in the presidency by two coups in which the arms of the republic were used against the legitimate authority of the nation."

The administration, Lacerda said, felt that the UDN was endangering business dealers and pro-Communists associated with those in power. He called the "peace" of President Kubitschek "the peace of a person who does not know how to fight loyally, who does not know why he is fighting, . . . who does not know what new cabinet ministers to appoint because he does not know what the old ministers were doing." He added that "we never had the idea" of assisting Kubitschek in revising his "worn out, tired, and incompetent cabinet."[7]

Although former UDN President Milton Campos was from Minas, he joined the UDN majority in praising Lacerda's speech. Bilac Pinto, also from Minas, maintained that the administration was at fault for not "replying concretely to our proposal." The PTB's Batista Ramos, no advocate of pacification, was delighted with Lacerda's speech, and Cid Carvalho, PSD vice-leader, saw it as "unifying the majority and dividing the UDN." Congressman Horácio Lafer and other members of the so-called PSD old wing were disappointed and hoped, like Jânio Quadros, that the pacification idea of Bias Fortes would somehow go forward. But when the UDN national directorship met on June 12 it decided to consider pacification "definitely finished."[8]

If pacification needed a *coup de grâce,* it could be found in Lacerda's signed editorial of June 15 about Kubitschek, "The Foremost in Vulgarity" (O Cafajeste Máximo): "In the presidency is an unscrupulous, vulgar person. In the war ministry, which protects him, is a traitor full of remorse, who will have to betray several times to see if he can at least save face, now that everything else is lost." After Lott told Justice Minister Nereu Ramos that Lacerda had violated legislation regulating the press, the attorney general of the Federal District asked the Chamber of Deputies to deprive Lacerda of his immunities on account of O Cafajeste Máximo. But Vieira de Melo spoke convincingly to Kubitschek about the "inconvenience" of repeating the effort of May.[9]

Then Lacerda, asking Congress to let him dispense with his immunities, spoke of facing Lott in court. Congress, he said, had nine petitions filed against him by the war minister, leaving Rafael Corrêa de Oliveira, with only seven, "in manifest disfavor." "I hope," Rafael Corrêa said, "to catch up with Your Excellency." "I wish you luck," Carlos replied.[10]

In attacking the president in the *Tribuna* on June 15, Lacerda used the expression "sacrilegious Mass" when he mentioned the first Mass held in Brasília, where the administration planned to build, more quickly than Lacerda felt advisable, a new capital for the country. This jarring reference to the Mass, celebrated by São Paulo Cardinal Carlos Carmelo de Vasconcelos Mota together with five bishops and the papal nuncio, provoked scoldings from Vasconcelos Mota, Archbishop Hélder Câmara, and others. "This is not the first time," the cardinal said, "that we have been insulted by the gratuitous and anti-Christian insanity of the journalist." The Santa Catarina state legislature, in a telegram of support for the cardinal, expressed repulsion for the "crafty attack made by Carlos Lacerda on the clergy and Your Eminence." UDN President Juracy Magalhães declared that "when leader Carlos Lacerda, probably improperly, called the Brasília Mass sacrilegious, he sought to describe the sacrilege committed by the president of the republic who was present, looking over paragraphs of a speech he planned to give." Juracy added that if the cardinal had "a bad impression of the intentions of our companion, we *udenistas* must in humility ask forgiveness of His Eminence for the annoyance we involuntarily caused him."[11]

Lacerda flew to São Paulo on July 2 to discuss the matter with Cardinal Vasconcelos Mota. Accompanied by Roberto de Abreu Sodré, UDN leader in the São Paulo state assembly, he was received by the cardinal and Dom Paulo Rolim Loureiro at the Metropolitan Cathedral. He admitted having made a mistake in his reference to the Mass and the cardinal agreed to consider the matter closed. But Lacerda sought to defend, as Christian, his attacks on the Kubitschek government, which he maintained was illegal and harmful. The cardinal disagreed with Lacerda's conduct and was even reported in the press as having said "You are not a Christian." After the meeting, the cardinal told the press that he had explained that Catholics should consider the government legitimate and pray for those in authority and that in Brazil an atmosphere of love should replace the atmosphere of hate.[12]

The atmosphere in Congress became so acrimonious in August that the opposition resorted to what it called "obstruction": failing to be present when bills were to be voted. With normal absences, this made it so difficult to achieve a quorum that the *Tribuna* was able to boast on September 5 that legislative action had been paralyzed for seventeen days.[13]

The "obstruction," or "strike," by UDN and PL congressmen was a protest against a proposed electoral-law reform to relax the literacy requirement by allowing the vote to those who could do no more than sign their names on the registration forms. The opposition called the administration's proposal the "Fraud Project" and argued that the "scrawling" of what might be considered a signature did not constitute compliance with the constitutional provision about being able to read and write. Then Armando Falcão, on behalf of the administration, proposed a constitutional amendment to allow illiterates to vote. Lacerda replied that the government's attitude should be considered a confession of its inability to educate Brazilians.[14]

In mid-September leaders of the parties met and signed an agreement that ended the five-week-old "obstruction" and left the literacy requirement for the 1958 elections as the opposition had wished. Acting opposition leader Herbert Levy expressed his pleasure and said that during the battle "Carlos Lacerda never for a minute deserted his post." The *Tribuna*'s João Duarte, filho, gave credit to Lacerda for having suggested the agreement about the 1958 elections.[15]

8. The Caravana da Liberdade (May–December 1957)

Under the presidency of Juracy Magalhães, the UDN started a campaign in May 1957 to bring the party closer to the people. Excursions of speakers, almost always including Juracy and Lacerda, were undertaken on weekends, when the participants were not at work in the legislature. They allowed Lacerda to overcome, in small part, the handicap imposed by the regulation that prevented him from broadcasting.[1]

The campaign soon became known as the Caravana da Liberdade and hardly a weekend passed between June and December without trips to hold rallies, together with local UDN officers, in towns from the far north to Rio Grande do Sul. Lacerda, with his firm voice, dominated the campaigning. To new groups he revealed that he loved direct contact with the people and had the personality and oratorical skill to gain applause even from audiences that, at the outset, were determined to be hostile to him.[2]

The campaign was carried out in accordance with the UDN slogan, *Crescer Para Vencer* (Grow in Order to Win). To grow meant to eradicate the image of the party as an elite group uninterested in the common man and perhaps interested in conspiracy.[3] Tired of "glorious defeats," the UDN hoped that the Caravana would lay the groundwork for victories in the congressional and gubernatorial elections of October 1958 and contribute also to success in the presidential election of 1960.[4]

In the interior of São Paulo state, where Lacerda and Juracy were often accompanied by Herbert Levy and Roberto de Abreu Sodré, at least fifty rallies were held. Luiz Ernesto Kawall, of the *Tribuna*'s São Paulo office, recalls that Juracy went to bed regularly at 11:00 P.M., to be ready to start early the next morning, whereas Carlos, in need of little sleep, fraternized with students, reporters, and others far into the night. If Carlos was frequently vexed with what he called Juracy's "obsession" for being punctual for all appointments, Juracy also had complaints. "On the two or three occasions when I failed to show up," Carlos has said, "he was highly indignant because, modesty apart, I was a sort of star."[5]

According to Lacerda, the themes of the campaign were "the corruption of the government of Juscelino" and the inflation. Audiences understood him when he contended that wages were going up on a staircase and prices in an elevator. During a "Saturday and Sunday Caravana marathon" in much of the interior of Bahia, Aliomar Baleeiro discussed "fraud" in the foreign exchange market and Amaral Netto denounced "administrative scandals." In front of a banner proclaiming "The People Trust the Word of Carlos Lacerda," Lacerda told one of his Bahia audiences that "the people who called me a traitor on account of Telegram 295 say today I am an enemy of God." Among those who joined the Caravana in Rio state was the colorful, combative, and popular Tenório Cavalcanti, who wore his black cape and stirred the masses with tirades that Lacerda considered interminable.[6]

The campaigners emphasized their devotion to measures of interest to their audiences. Taxi drivers heard Herbert Levy report on Lacerda's law project to reduce the import duty on taxis by 50 percent. Railroad workers, pleased with a condemnation of Kubitschek's railroad labor proposals, decorated the speakers with the blue silk neckerchiefs of their union. Tenant farmers applauded calls for a "democratic agrarian reform."[7] Lacerda, who contended that Paraná Governor Moisés Lupion was a thief whose gangsters killed tenant farmers,[8] was one of the *udenistas* who visited fourteen Paraná municipalities during a weekend. Juracy, reporting in the Senate about the trip, pointed out that the campaign, inspired by "opposition and legality," was stimulating voter registration. The rally in Curitiba, he said, had been the largest held there in ten years.[9]

Leonel Brizola, mayor of Porto Alegre and brother-in-law of Goulart, sought to prevent the Caravana from coming to Rio Grande do Sul, where it had scheduled a rally in Santa Maria, a railroad center. In the words of Lacerda, Brizola "made threats, used the radio to instigate violence, and called for the death of UDN leaders."[10] After the Santa Maria PTB issued a proclamation asking the authorities to support the Caravana's opponents, hostile crowds demonstrated against Caravana members between the airport and the city and in front of the house where Juracy and Lacerda were guests. But Governor Ildo Meneghetti and General Osvino Ferreira Alves took steps to prevent clashes and the UDN rally was held. As he liked to do in Rio Grande do Sul, Lacerda spoke in Santa Maria of his Gaúcho great-grandfather, Sílvio dos Santos Paiva. And he put the responsibility for Vargas' suicide on the late president's close advisers. *O Estado do Rio Grande*, organ of the PL, praised Lacerda's conduct in the state's "strongest PTB center" and in the face of "cannibals" who had "promised to assassinate him." The *Diário da Manhã*, of Passo Fundo, Rio Grande do Sul, called Lacerda "the leader of the great sanitizing campaign against *gregorismo nacional*."[11]

During conversations on commercial planes, the 53-year-old Juracy sometimes suggested that he was nearing the end of his career and that the Caravana work should result in Lacerda becoming the UDN presidential candidate. Lacerda replied that he was not yet prepared for such a step and did not have enough national prestige to face a candidate to be named by Kubitschek. The UDN, he also said, was not yet strong enough to defeat a PSD-PTB alliance supported by Communists.[12]

The only radio station bold enough to broadcast Lacerda's Caravana speeches was Rádio Liberdade of Guaratinguetá, São Paulo. Its concession was quickly suspended by authorities who claimed it had been using an improper wave band. Therefore the UDN, citing the "punishment" of the station, intensified its propaganda on behalf of a radio and television law proposed by Prado Kelly. Lacerda, strong supporter of Prado Kelly's project, told the Inter American Press Association in Washington of his hope that Brazilian public pressure would result in its enactment. In Rio he wrote a preface to the *Tribuna*'s publication of Prado Kelly's study in which he complained that a government ruling had required Congressman Rubens Berardo (PTB, Federal District) to withdraw his offer to have a Berardo-Lacerda debate on the congressman's station, Rádio Continental.[13]

Herbert Levy, during a Caravana rally in São Paulo, criticized the

Juscelino Kubitschek, creator of Brasília. (Hilde Weber drawing in Hilde Weber, *O Brasil em Charges, 1950–1985*)

Kubitschek administration for paying Americans "fantastic prices" for steel frames for Brasília. But he made it clear that he approved of the rapid construction of the new capital. Levy's favorable view of Brasília was shared by many UDN congressmen who did not represent the Federal District, and Lacerda, during Caravana appearances, was restrained in expressing his misgivings about Brasília. In the *Tribuna,* however, he wrote that the time for Brasília had not come, especially as the federal budget for health services needed to be greatly increased, and he listed the "insanities of Brasília," such as the use of planes to carry bricks for construction before roads to the site had been built. He became piqued when Levy, in a congressional speech justifying Brasília, called Rio an ungovernable, dissolute city of nightclubs. Explaining to Levy that he rarely went to nightclubs, he said the inability of Paulista congressmen to resist temptation was no reason to construct a new capital. "Brasília," Lacerda said, "is the most expensive monument to folly and incompetence erected to this day."[14]

Exhaustion from Caravana and congressional work kept Carlos from participating in politics during the first two months of 1958. Hoping to avoid a complete collapse, he turned to sleep therapy with prescribed drugs, a cure he had learned was being utilized in Switzerland. His neighbors, Drs. Marcelo Garcia and Otávio Dreux, were cooperative. Carlos has written: "I went to bed, took the medicines, and began to sleep. I awoke without appetite, tasted a little food, carried out some routine hygiene, and went to sleep again." Letícia and a night nurse took turns watching over him.

One day he awoke with a stabbing pain in the side. For ten days, his son Sérgio recalls, Carlos was in a wretched condition, crying in agony and forced by the pain of breathing to sleep sitting up. It was not cancer, as

Carlos feared, or tuberculosis, as some thought possible, but pleurisy. After the pleurisy had been treated, Carlos returned to the sleep therapy.

Sometimes when he woke up he would leaf through a picture book and find that its colors seemed to multiply and the letters appear "three-fold, 350-fold." One morning he awoke to find himself in "absolute happiness" in a world he has described as "entirely new." "I never thought the white of the walls could be so alive. . . . A complete sense of well-being, a force both very light and very strong, seemed to hold me up above all uncertainties. . . . I did not have to think to reach conclusions, and the conclusions formed themselves as a chain with total indifference to logic. . . . I felt thoroughly lucid, able to understand everything, but at the same time separated from everything. . . . Just to be alive was good." Carlos went to the home of José and Maria do Carmo Nabuco to convalesce.[15]

Weak and thinner than usual, he returned to the Chamber of Deputies early in March 1958 to help elect Ranieri Mazzilli (PSD, São Paulo) to succeed Ulysses Guimarães, who was retiring from the Chamber presidency to run for the São Paulo governorship. The slate headed by Mazzilli included a *udenista* and was contesting the slate headed by Oliveira Brito, the justice-commission head who had worked to deprive Lacerda of his immunities in 1957. The Mazzilli slate won by a 150–120 vote.[16]

Lacerda defended the UDN's "realistic" line from the attacks of those who disliked the pragmatic alliances the party was making for the 1958 elections. One of the alliances he defended was with Ademar de Barros to obtain PSP support for Afonso Arinos, candidate for a Senate seat from the Federal District. The Mesquitas' *O Estado de S. Paulo,* no friend of Ademar de Barros, wrote that the UDN was compromising itself morally by its "matrimony" with the PSP. But Afonso Arinos, back from Europe and chosen a member of the Brazilian Academy of Letters, argued that the fragmentation of the political parties justified the UDN's interest in regional alliances.[17]

Adauto Lúcio Cardoso and former Senator Hamilton Nogueira joined the PL in condemning the UDN's "realism." "The new line," Adauto said, "contains the germ of destruction of the standard of political ethics that the UDN has been disseminating." Lacerda told Adauto he would not publish a reply because he was about to go to Switzerland to complete his medical treatment and participate in sessions of the Interparliamentary Union. He simply urged Adauto to discontinue his campaign against *realismo udenista.* Adauto, at a UDN national directorship meeting on March 12, announced he would yield to Lacerda's appeal, at least until new developments required him to speak out against excessive *realismo.* On the next day Carlos and 19-year-old Sérgio flew to Europe.[18]

9. The UDN's "Most Serious Crisis" (May–July 1958)

Writing to Fernando Velloso from Rome in April 1958, Carlos expressed satisfaction at the departure from the *Tribuna* of Aluísio Alves, candidate for reelection to Congress from Rio Grande do Norte. He said it marked the newspaper's return to its earliest position "without commitments to groups." No work performed for the *Tribuna,* he wrote, gave a person the right to use it for ends other than serving it and its readers.

In his letter, Carlos denounced Editor-in-chief João Duarte, filho. Duarte, he wrote, was "professionally a disaster for the newspaper," had reduced it to "an irresponsible lampoon," and had fostered intrigues and internal discontent. "What is worse, he has given the newspaper—whose strength lies in its unshakable and unquestionable integrity—a dubious reputation, to say the least."

In the past when Carlos had wanted to dismiss Duarte he had been restrained by his friendship for Velloso, who had argued against the step. Now, however, Carlos was determined to act, and an excuse for Duarte's removal from his post was found in the decision of Duarte to run for Congress in the Federal District. The *Tribuna,* Carlos wrote to Velloso, "cannot be the warrantor of the candidacy of a man who you and I and many people know has not been loyal, even to the newspaper." As for the *Tribuna,* Carlos explained to Velloso that "the hour is coming to prepare Sérgio to take my place, little by little, in the daily work. However, I must not leave him a ruined newspaper, but, rather, the newspaper which, although devoid of wealth, was virtuous."[1]

Returning to Brazil late in May, Lacerda found that *realismo udenista* had taken the form of UDN alliances with Goulart's Labor Party, the PTB, especially in the north. He was pained to find such an alliance being forged in Rio state, where the PSD-PTB coalition had fallen apart. As early as March, Rio state UDN leaders had felt that the PSD-PTB break might justify running a *udenista* for governor and they had asked Lacerda to be the candidate. He had cited his poor health and commitments to campaign for Afonso Arinos and others, and the Fluminense UDN had been quicker than Lacerda had wished to consider his reply a definite refusal.[2] During his absence, UDN municipal leaders in the state enthusiastically made local election arrangements with the PTB. Then the state leaders, arguing that the party's chief local enemy was the PSD, decided to support PTB gubernatorial candidate Roberto da Silveira, recently national secretary of the PTB. Silveira promised PTB backing for UDN municipal candidates and offered the UDN three cabinet posts in the state government he hoped to head.[3]

When Prado Kelly returned to Brazil late in May from the Interparliamentary Union meetings, he worked to have his party nominate its own man, Lacerda. Lacerda, in reply to reporters' questions, described himself as a fighter at the service of the UDN whenever it felt the need to struggle. He criticized the Fluminense UDN for lacking a fighting spirit. And he condemned the state government of Miguel Couto Filho, a former Vargas cabinet minister who had recently resigned the governorship to become the PTB senatorial candidate in a race in which he found himself supported by local UDN leaders. Lacerda made it clear that he would not be giving speeches at the side of Goulart and PTB candidates, such as Roberto da Silveira.[4]

On June 10 the UDN state convention ratified the alliance with the PTB.

Its delegates chose Miguel Couto Filho to be the UDN senatorial candidate and, by a 271–12 vote, named Silveira the party's candidate for governor. The outcome pleased Fluminense UDN President Paulo de Araújo, who had been offered the vice-gubernatorial nomination by the PTB, and it pleased UDN Congressmen Mário Guimarães and Alberto Torres. But Lacerda, Prado Kelly, and former Foreign Minister Raul Fernandes, noting that gubernatorial candidate Silveira was close to Goulart, were bitter. In the *Tribuna* Lacerda accused the PTB of having purchased representatives of the state UDN. He added that the directorship of the Fluminense UDN had committed a "felony without precedent in the political history of the country, manipulating a convention in which the *udenistas* were defeated by João Goulart and the corruption machine."[5]

At a UDN national directorship meeting on June 11, Lacerda exploded. He demanded that Congressmen Alberto Torres and Mário Guimarães be expelled from the party and announced his own intention to resign the congressional leadership and give up his mandate. Prado Kelly resolved to leave public life by refusing to run for Congress again. In response, Alberto Torres and Mário Guimarães pointed out that the fifty-two municipal directorships in Rio state, consulted before the convention, had welcomed the alliance because the PSD of Ernâni do Amaral Peixoto was disliked by the UDN rank and file.[6]

After UDN leaders in Rio state cited the UDN's "realistic" policy, Lacerda told the press that UDN-PTB alliances might be all right on the municipal level, where Communists found it difficult to infiltrate, but he drew the line at having any arrangement above that level, with the PTB or PSP. The PSP's Ademar de Barros had just made a deal with Goulart for PTB support in his quest for the São Paulo governorship, and Lacerda no longer defended an alliance with him. The PSP, he now said, "is another party not to be recommended to honest men and groups that combat corruption, graft, and the depravity of Brazilian public life."

Less "realistic" than he had been before going abroad, Lacerda insisted that the UDN adopt a "rigid definition" to limit interparty accords. Herbert Levy, also upset with the Fluminense UDN, argued that regional conventions should not approve accords before consulting the national directorship.[7]

Lacerda, furious at being called an agitator by UDN defenders of the Rio state alliance with the PTB, told journalists that his resignation from his leadership post would become effective within a few hours and that he would leave Congress after obtaining release from his commitment to work on the congressional commission investigating government fraud. However, in reply to Abreu Sodré's telegram of protest, he said: "My resignation from the leadership and departure from public life will take place only upon the exhaustion of all possibilities to reach a solution satisfactory to my conscience, which is to say satisfactory to the best interests of the party."[8]

One possibility, suggested by Afonso Arinos, was to run Eduardo Gomes for governor of Rio state. The idea delighted Lacerda, Prado Kelly, and Raul Fernandes and was even acceptable to Mário Guimarães. But the hesitant *brigadeiro* underwent minor surgery and could not be approached about political matters, on his doctors' orders.[9]

The UDN national directorship met almost daily to seek other solutions for what Afonso Arinos was calling "the most serious of all the crises ever faced by the UDN since its foundation." Juracy Magalhães said he would resign the UDN presidency if Lacerda left the congressional leadership. But João Agripino, condemning all resignation talk, argued that leadership posts were not the equivalent of paid jobs that could be abandoned. Juracy and Lacerda, he said, had the responsibility to complete work assigned them for strengthening the UDN and should not threaten to behave like José Américo and Otávio Mangabeira, who had weakened the party.[10]

Agripino's words served as a tonic. Lacerda and Juracy agreed not to resign. Juracy named Afonso Arinos arbitrator to report on Lacerda's twenty-page accusation against the Fluminense UDN and to negotiate with Ernâni do Amaral Peixoto to find a UDN-PSD gubernatorial candidate to replace Getúlio de Moura, the PSD candidate. But the report of Afonso Arinos, written after Getúlio de Moura refused to withdraw, left the situation unchanged.[11]

When the national directorship met on July 9 to consider the report of Afonso Arinos, Herbert Levy found himself seated next to Lacerda, who had called state UDN President Paulo de Araújo a traitor and used terms at least as abusive in the *Tribuna* to describe other Fluminense UDN leaders, many of them longtime admirers of Lacerda. "You are fortunate," Levy said to Lacerda, "because God endowed you with the talents of a genius. But you have acted like an idiot, a damn fool. You have bloodied the situation by hurting your greatest admirers and friends. Only you can save the situation."[12]

Lacerda, speaking at the meeting, expressed his sorrow at having "involuntarily" hurt his friends. The person who knew most certainly that he was at fault, he said, was himself. Speaking passionately, he begged forgiveness of companions with whom he had disagreed and lamented having insulted them in his newspaper. *Udenistas* embraced each other, and the meeting became so fraternal that Fluminense Congressmen Mário Guimarães and Tenório Cavalcanti delivered speeches praising the new spirit. The good faith of Alberto Torres, Mário Guimarães, and Rio state UDN President Paulo de Araújo was officially recognized. The decisions reached at the UDN state convention of June 10 were described as legitimate, but the regional directorship was urged to "reexamine them in search of a conciliatory formula."[13]

Paulo de Araújo, seeking a "conciliatory formula," consulted the municipal directorships and reported that the first replies indicated an overwhelming consensus in favor of the state organization's accord with the PTB. *Udenistas* who could not accept this position met at the home of Raul Fernandes to organize the UDN Defense Movement, a dissident group headed by Prado Kelly and Fernandes. Lacerda in mid-July participated in UDN Defense Movement speechmaking in opposition to Roberto da Silveira. The UDN state directorship therefore accused him of violating a national directorship recommendation that restraint be shown while the municipal directorships were being consulted.[14]

The UDN Defense Movement proposed that the UDN's Raimundo Padilha become PSD senatorial candidate to oppose former Governor Miguel Couto Filho, candidate of the UDN and PTB. But the PSD rejected Padilha, a former Green Shirt. It pointed out that his candidacy was unacceptable to its allies in the state: the PRP of Plínio Salgado and the PSP of Ademar de Barros. After that, the UDN dissidents sought to have Raul Fernandes run for the Senate with PSD backing; but the negotiation failed. Ernâni do Amaral Peixoto became the PSD candidate for the Senate.[15]

10. The Caminhão do Povo (August–October 1958)

Kubitschek, revamping his cabinet, replaced Foreign Minister José Carlos de Macedo Soares with Francisco Negrão de Lima in July 1958. Negrão, as mayor of the Federal District, had been so scathingly attacked in the *Tribuna* that he had written a venomous letter to Lacerda that was published in June in *Última Hora*. It described Lacerda as a vile coward whose behavior resembled that of the most sordid type of prostitute. Lacerda's "cynical and shameless lies," Negrão wrote, made him the most debauched scoundrel of Brazilian journalism. Negrão called his letter a descent into the mire in which Lacerda lived and said it was his final response

> to the miserable wretch who did not hesitate to besmirch his own father and was therefore despicable; the thief . . . who, according to an unrebutted accusation, stole the money of a magazine he edited as a young man; the traitor who squealed on his Bolshevik-adhering friends and described himself as a rogue full of unbearable remorse; the rascal who, according to another unanswered accusation, tried to cut his wrists to avoid military service; the blackmailer who established a business of defamation in search of political and social advantages; the infamous forger of the Brandi letter; the braggart and buffoon who boasted that by using blow after blow he would prevent the inauguration of men elected in 1955; and, lastly, the runaway of August 24 and November 11 who, lacking all moral fiber, was incapable of defending . . . what is dearest to all good people: the honor of his own home.[1]

As foreign minister, Negrão dedicated himself to promoting Operação Pan-Americana, launched by Kubitschek in June 1958 after hostile demonstrations against Vice President Richard Nixon in Peru and Venezuela had shown Latin American resentment of what was felt to be insufficient interest by the United States in dealing with underdevelopment in the continent. Lacerda, speaking of Operation Pan-America said: "Never have I seen a more stupid method of asking for money."[2]

Lacerda opposed loans from the United States to the Kubitschek government. Prior to the Brazilian visit of Secretary of State John Foster Dulles early in August, he wrote in the *Tribuna* that "the worst service Foster

Dulles could render Brazil, at this point, would be to loan it more money." If the Brazilian people could speak to Dulles, Lacerda wrote, they would tell him that "what is called private initiative here is frequently the right the state gives certain groups to enrich themselves." They would say "the Kubitschek government is the most corrupt of all those that have looted the country." Lacerda maintained that the men in the government, from the vice-president on down, were solidly anti–United States. Many of them, he stated, believed that Americans were idiots who could be induced by the threat of Communism to make it possible for Brazilians to live without working. According to Lacerda, the Brazilians were not basically anti-American but were being poisoned by Communists and their allies and by Brazilian business interests that feared foreign competition. He went on to warn that the popularity of the United States in Brazil would not be helped if Dulles associated himself with the Kubitschek government.

Lacerda was delighted with a photograph taken during the Dulles visit that showed Kubitschek, in front of Dulles, apparently pleading subserviently for money. After *Jornal do Brasil* ran the photograph in a seven-column front-page spread, Lacerda ran the picture in two issues of the *Tribuna* with comments each time. "It is," the *Tribuna* reported, "a complete verbal synthesis of all this stupidity of Operation Pan-America; it is the picture of the behavior of a government, of a group of men who have no composure." "Kubitschek's countenance is that of a subordinate, a beggar who transfers to another nation the responsibilities of Brazilians to defeat Communism in Brazil and put our house in order."[3]

Lacerda, on reassuming the UDN leadership in Congress in August, said he would lead a battle "for the liberation of the radio" from Clause R that prevented him from broadcasting. But little could be done in Congress to end the "Gag Regulation" because of the government's majority and because congressmen preferred to campaign than attend sessions. When a government broadcast said that General Olímpio Mourão Filho, in charge of implementing the Gag Regulation, was being accused by Lacerda of fabricating the Cohen Plan of 1937, Lacerda spoke in a rather empty Congress to demand a rectification. Lacerda's view, expressed more than once in Congress since 1956, was that the general had for years been falsely accused of responsibility for the plan—the unfounded Communist "plot"—that had helped Vargas usher in the Estado Novo.[4]

The Gag Regulation led Lacerda to announce that his campaign for reelection to Congress would be assisted by a "Voice of Silence" program. Rumored to consist of silent films of Lacerda to be shown on television, it was described by the *Tribuna* as something that would bring the "word" of Lacerda "to all Carioca homes." While the government and public wondered just what form the "Voice of Silence" program would take, a brisk business of selling phonograph records of Lacerda's speeches furnished funds for his reelection campaign.[5]

Adauto Lúcio Cardoso, seeking a ruling from the Superior Electoral Tribunal about the Gag Regulation, received an opinion from the attorney general of the republic, Carlos Medeiros Silva, stating that the government should not resort to prior censorship or pressure on radio or television stations. On September 1, the tribunal agreed with this view, in a unanimous decision that Municipal Councilwoman Sandra Cavalcanti called "one of the most brilliant in Brazilian justice."[6] Until election day, Clause R would not be used to restrict the broadcast of political speeches, and therefore the need for the "Voice of Silence" program was eliminated.

Lacerda, campaigning in an old truck in the Ipanema district on September 2, was cheered from the streets and windows of buildings when he announced that he would be broadcasting again, starting that evening on Rádio Eldorado. In his radio address, given somewhat emotionally in a hoarse voice, he said that the opposition's new opportunity would not be used to broadcast replies to the "insults and infamies of two years of total dictatorship" but, rather, to discuss the UDN program, including law projects pigeonholed by the congressional majority, such as his proposal of February 1955 requiring statements of personal wealth by administrators of government-controlled companies.[7]

Lacerda made plans to continue bringing the people the "Voice of Truth" on Rádio Eldorado, associated with *O Estado de S. Paulo,* and to broadcast daily on Rádio Globo. He even found Rio's two television stations, TV Tupi and TV Rio, unwilling to bar him although the first was controlled by the unfriendly Chateaubriand and the second could at any moment be deprived of its temporary permit to use the broadcasting channel of Rádio Mauá, radio outlet of the labor ministry.[8]

Lacerda's campaign in an old truck with a powerful loudspeaker, most frequently in the company of Senate candidate Afonso Arinos and Municipal Council reelection candidate Raul Brunini, was conceived in August. He presented the plan to Afonso Arinos when the two were sitting in a practically deserted Congress. They would, Lacerda suggested, campaign in the truck all over the Federal District, day after day. The senatorial candidate, in a difficult race against Lutero Vargas, agreed. "I and Afonso Arinos," Lacerda told Congress a few days later, "are going to the streets. We are going to make a campaign that will blow up this city."[9]

"Never," Afonso Arinos says, "have I experienced anything as stimulating, as fantastic." The Caminhão do Povo (Truck of the People) attracted enormous attention. Every afternoon the old truck, about to leave the square in front of the Chamber of Deputies, was surrounded by people, and, as it made its way from one stop to another, it was followed by a procession of cars driven by companions. Every day the *Tribuna* furnished the itinerary. After numerous stops and short speeches, the truck would reach a park, often in a suburb, for a principal rally. The candidates exchanged comments with the people about issues.[10] Among the candidates for the Municipal Council who often joined the Caminhão do Povo was Murilo Miranda, whose *Revista Acadêmica* had lasted from 1933 until 1946 and who had directed Rádio Roquete Pinto and the Municipal Theater. Carlos, praising his long-time friend, cited the nourishment and music Murilo Miranda had provided to workers as head of the government-subsidized restaurants of SAPS (Serviço de Alimentação da Previdência Social).[11]

After Afonso Arinos was brought to a Caminhão do Povo rally in the official car used by the opposition leader, *Última Hora* published a cartoon showing a paunchy Afonso Arinos emerging from an enormous Cadillac whose chauffeur was saying, "Congressman, now you can get on the truck." For the rest of the campaign, the opposition leader reached the truck by mingling with the common people on buses. According to *Última Hora,* which called the Caminhão do Povo the "Crow's Roost," *udenistas* fired gunshots at the jeep of a candidate who formed a group to follow the Roost and reply to "lies" expressed by Lacerda during his "gesticulations and monkeyshines."[12]

Occasionally, hostile audiences threw fruit or stones. Afonso Arinos, hit by a banana, picked it up, began to eat it, and expressed his thanks, provoking laughter. Hit by a stone, he called it a "PTB argument." But for the most part the audiences were so enthusiastic that Afonso Arinos became convinced that he would defeat Lutero Vargas, candidate of the PTB, Ademar de Barros, the illegal PCB, and Plínio Salgado's PRP. His optimism was in stark contrast to the view he had held when he had accepted the candidacy at the suggestion of Mário Martins.[13]

11. Carioca Voters Turn to Afonso Arinos, Lacerda, and Brunini (October 1958)

Lutero Vargas campaigned in Rio and São Paulo at the side of Ademar de Barros. But what caused a furor were Lutero's appearances at the side of Communist leader Luís Carlos Prestes, who had emerged from hiding after being acquitted of charges filed against him ten years earlier. Prestes' activities on behalf of PCB favorites, among them Lutero Vargas, Ademar de Barros, and Rio Grande do Sul gubernatorial aspirant Brizola, led Cardinal Jaime Câmara to issue a strong warning against alliances with Communists. Lutero, making more appearances with Prestes after the cardinal's declaration, was criticized by well-known Rio dailies such as *Correio da Manhã, Jornal do Brasil,* and *O Globo* (never by *Última Hora*). His Communist support, Lutero then explained, had been arranged by Vice President Goulart.

The vice-president, apparently none too pleased with Lutero's disclosure of his deal with the Communists, held a publicized conversation with the cardinal, in which he denied responsiblity for the appearances of Prestes at Lutero's side and said he would bring them to an end. But Prestes joined Lutero again on a speakers' platform. "I am," Lutero told the crowd, "very honored and happy to ally myself with the Communists. We are united, and here is the proof: Luís Carlos Prestes at my side." He went on to say that the PTB was allied with the Communists throughout the country in a nationalist movement to "oppose turning Brazil over to foreign imperialism."[1]

The cardinal's warning, heeded by the Kubitschek administration, was seconded by War Minister Lott. Majority leader Armando Falcão, after speaking with Kubitschek, issued a statement in the name of the PSD and the government condemning alliances with the Communists. This upset Lutero, who had been blaming the UDN for the fuss about the matter, and he had a bitter exchange with Falcão, who issued a written statement calling Lutero "a poor wretch deranged by alcoholism" and in need of a doctor. Lutero retorted that Falcão, "a thief," was in need of a jail cell and a striped prisoner's uniform.[2]

In not a few states, UDN candidates also accepted Communist support. Lacerda, however, declared in the Chamber of Deputies that it was the PTB that "really, with the usual few exceptions," had an accord "of national scope" with the Communists. The Communist Party, he told the almost vacant chamber, had resolved at its Fourth National Congress in 1954 to take over the PTB.[3]

Lacerda may have faced a larger audience when he met with the press in his apartment. Pacing back and forth and speaking quietly and deliberately, he called Brazil a nation afflicted by a "submarxist ideology" and therefore so scornful of moral values that "the greatest crimes are committed in the name of development." "For example," he said, "they say that coffee is holding us back and should be abandoned." "Perhaps," he suggested sarcastically, "the government would like to sell automobiles to the United States!" "Submarxist ideology," he also maintained, prevented a rational discussion of agrarian reform, which ought to give more attention to methods of land use than to the question of land ownership. Stating that "reform" and "revolution" were synonymous in Brazil, he argued that atomic energy development should be promoted in order to give the country an industrial revolution, such as petroleum and electricity had given the United States. When Lacerda spoke on TV Tupi, to an audience estimated at 300,000, he warned that the Communist menace was turning Brazil into "a new China."[4]

Lacerda did not limit himself to addressing large audiences. He turned once again, and for the last time, to *comícios em casa.* "Convince sixty people and they will convince an equal number," he said to fellow candidates, who followed his example and went from building to building.

The closing "victory parade" of the UDN lasted fourteen hours. Coming from rural areas and suburbs at sunset, the parade of candidates reached the densely populated section of tall buildings when lights were being turned on. From the windows and on the streets, the acclaim was stupendous. "Never," it has been reported, "had there been such a crowd on Avenida Nossa Senhora de Copacabana."[5]

The election returns gave Afonso Arinos 397,466 votes, Lacerda 143,012, and Brunini 24,261, making all three the most-voted-for candidates in their categories. The victory of Afonso Arinos, Brunini says, was considered "the most overwhelming of the epoch." In defeating Lutero Vargas in the Senate race, the congressman from Minas received more votes than had ever been given anyone in the electoral history of the Federal District.[6]

Última Hora regretted the election to the Senate of "the candidate of the reaction and *entreguismo.*"[7] But it found comfort in the gubernatorial victories of Leonel Brizola in Rio Grande do Sul and Roberto da Silveira in Rio state. Furthermore, in the new Chamber of Deputies, the UDN would have 70 members instead of 74, whereas the PTB representation would rise from

56 to 66 and that of the PSD from 114 to 115. The smaller parties, formerly represented by 82 congressmen, were reduced to 75.[8]

The UDN had many reasons to be cheerful. In Minas, where there was no gubernatorial race, Milton Campos defeated Artur Bernardes Filho in the Senate race. In Bahia, Juracy Magalhães was elected governor and Otávio Mangabeira senator. In São Paulo, Finance Secretary Carlos Carvalho Pinto, running on the UDN and other tickets and backed by Jânio Quadros, defeated Ademar de Barros for the governorship, and Father Benedito Calasans (known as "Carlos Lacerda in a cassock") was elected to the Senate.

Lacerda, in a post-election declaration, said he planned to bring the UDN forces together so that the party not "lose the victory." He would, he said, leave off being congressional leader in order to initiate a gigantic campaign throughout Brazil on behalf of *udenismo.* In Minas he hoped to persuade UDN Congressman Magalhães Pinto to abandon ideas of a UDN-PSD alliance ("parties of the center"). The UDN, Lacerda said, was a "growing child" whereas the PSD was "moribund."[9]

Jânio Quadros, running on the PTB ticket for congressman from Paraná, won an easy victory, which, together with Carvalho Pinto's triumph over Ademar de Barros, made Quadros a strong contender for the presidency in 1960. Lacerda said that Quadros' term in the governorship and choice for the state succession deserved respect, but he criticized his maverick tendencies. The time had passed, he said, when anyone could govern the country without a solid base or when candidates could be imposed on parties. A week later, in a *Tribuna* editorial, he attacked what he called the intrigues of "nationalists" who claimed that Quadros had refused to see him in São Paulo. It was, he wrote, too early for him to look up the popular former governor of São Paulo who had won a PTB congressional seat in Paraná. The purpose of his São Paulo trip, he explained, had been to argue that UDN support be given only to a presidential candidate faithful to the party program of democratic reform.

Well aware of the strength of Quadros, Lacerda pointed out that presidential hopeful Lott feared a Quadros candidacy and that Goulart, while recognizing Quadros as a hope for the PTB, was concerned lest Janismo spell the end of Janguismo. As for those who spoke of the "craziness" of Quadros, Lacerda wrote that neither he nor Quadros was "crazy, or at least as crazy as our adversaries claim."[10]

Murilo Miranda, the law school colleague of Carlos, won a Rio Municipal Council seat, but he showed little interest in politics. Another law school colleague, newspaper publisher Antônio Chagas Freitas (PSP), came in second to Lacerda in winning votes for reelection to the Chamber of Deputies. Carioca congressional candidates who also did well were Meneses Cortes (UDN), Elói Dutra (PTB), Mendes de Morais (PSP), Rubens Berardo (PTB), Adauto Lúcio Cardoso (UDN), and Sérgio Magalhães (PTB). João Duarte, filho, who lost his race, continued writing his "Tribuna Parlamentar" column in the *Tribuna;* but he was no longer a member of the management team, made up of Lacerda, Luís Brunini (brother of Raul), Odilon Paiva, Walter Cunto, and Mário Franqueira.[11]

12. The Roboré Agreement of 1958 (January 1959)

Lacerda was chosen by the UDN and PL to replace Senator Afonso Arinos as opposition leader in the lower house. João Agripino, of Paraíba, became UDN congressional leader.[1]

Late in 1958, before these changes occurred, Lacerda was approached by Congressman Sérgio Magalhães (PTB), one of the members of the Parliamentary Nationalist Front who were organizing a CPI (Parliamentary Commission of Inquiry) to study the dispute between Petrobrás President Janari Gentil Nunes and National Petroleum Council President José Alexínio Bittencourt. Sérgio Magalhães told Lacerda of his lack of confidence in the commission members and concern lest the commission fail in its work. "You have," he said, "much ability in this sort of thing." Lacerda, UDN leader, named himself to the commission, as Sérgio Magalhães wished.[2] Gabriel Passos (UDN), a founder of the Parliamentary Nationalist Front and leading advocate of the CPI, became *relator* of the commission.

The clash between army Colonels Janari Nunes and Alexínio Bittencourt stemmed from the March 1958 Roboré Agreement with Bolivia that revised the 1938 treaty giving Brazil rights to extract petroleum and gas from a concession in Bolivia. As Brazil had not carried out its obligations under the 1938 treaty, the area of the concession was reduced by the 1958 agreement. The new agreement, moreover, adhered to the latest Bolivian mining code by stipulating that the work on the concession was to be done by private Brazilian companies and not by Petrobrás.[3]

Petrobrás President Janari Nunes objected strenuously to the banishment of Petrobrás from Bolivia. On the other hand, Petroleum Council President Alexínio Bittencourt defended the Roboré Agreement as useful because of the failure of Petrobrás to produce much petroleum in Brazil, and he criticized Nunes' administration of the Brazilian government petroleum monopoly. As a result of the fight, both men lost their administrative posts in December 1958. Alexínio Bittencourt, who had been involved in the Roboré negotiations, turned over documents, consisting of almost a thousand sheets, to Lacerda.[4]

Defenders of Petrobrás, siding with Janari Nunes, considered the Roboré Agreement inimical to the government monopoly. The agreement, they felt, could put Petrobrás in a bad light and might require the diversion of funds that would otherwise be available to Petrobrás. They charged that Alexínio sought to help a Brazilian company being set up by the Capuava Refinery group, thus placing Brazil "at the mercy" of the Gulf Oil Company, which had relations with the refinery and was already operating in Bolivia. The Roboré Agreement was described as part of a maneuver devised by the big oil trusts with the help of some Brazilians "who place their immediate interests above the interests of the nation." The CPI itself was accused by Petrobrás lovers of "playing the game of Colonel Alexínio."[5]

Implementation of the Roboré Agreement fell to Roberto Campos, who had assumed the presidency of the BNDE (National Economic Development Bank) in June 1958, after its former president, Lucas Lopes, had become finance minister. Roberto Campos supported the idea of having Brazilian private companies, in need of financial and technical assistance in Bolivia, enter into risk contracts with foreign petroleum companies—which would have no equity but would participate in eventual profits in case exploration proved satisfactory.[6]

By the time Roberto Campos gave his erudite testimony to the CPI on January 17, he found himself opposed by Alexínio Bittencourt as well as Petrobrás. The colonel objected to the ideas Campos had about foreign financing. But, Campos explained in his testimony, risk contracts conformed to the financial and technical "principles" already drawn up by Alexínio Bittencourt and others for the guidance of those who were evaluating the half-dozen Brazilian companies on the BNDE's list. The risk contracts, Campos pointed out, would allow the risks to be shared while avoiding that Brazil, starved for foreign exchange, burden itself with added interest and amortization payments required by an increase in its foreign debt. Campos made it clear that conventional loans in hard currencies not only lacked these advantages but were unusual for such risky projects; if they could be obtained at all, it would probably be only because a Brazilian government bank guaranteed the financial performance of the borrowers. Campos shared Colonel Alexínio's belief that Brazil should have an inland supply of crude oil in wartime. But, he told the CPI, the colonel's failure to be realistic about the foreign exchange situation and the risks of exploration was creating exactly the conditions that would defeat execution of the Roboré Agreement.[7]

Lacerda, lavishing praise on Alexínio for his "great service" and courage in the face of slanders, received a letter from Raul Fernandes. The former foreign minister (and distant cousin of Carlos) had no great admiration for Alexínio, who, he wrote, was having disagreements with both Janari Nunes and the BNDE but was not, to the best of his knowledge, the object of slander. Fernandes, like Alexínio, cited the military importance of a source of petroleum not dependent on maritime delivery, and he pointed out that Argentina wanted to receive Bolivia's petroleum products. He also argued that if Petrobrás became involved in Bolivia, it would be financially less able to search for oil in Brazil. Furthermore, Fernandes defended the position of Roberto Campos. He wrote to Lacerda that the idea of preventing Brazilian private companies from associating with foreign capitalists, who would provide dollars, was a "high point of nationalist insanity." He added that "this business of exclusively Brazilian private capital for carrying out the Roboré Agreement is incomprehensible. No matter how much Colonel Alexínio wants to include this exclusivity in the agreement, I defy anyone to find such a stipulation in the document."[8]

But Lacerda assailed Roberto Campos. Speaking at a student meeting sponsored by the UNE, he described him as dominated by an "*entreguista* fanaticism" and said the BNDE's plan would transfer most of the profits to foreigners. The students, after hearing Lacerda, demonstrated so violently against Roberto Campos in front of the BNDE building that the authorities resorted to the use of tear gas.[9]

Campos has said that Lacerda "mobilized the students." In the *Tribuna,* however, Lacerda condemned the "grotesque manifestations" by young people, signs of totalitarian intolerance and of a "stupid, unpatriotic 'nationalism.'" Placing some of the blame on the Communists, he wrote that Luís Carlos Prestes opposed the agreement with Bolivia because Russia did not want Brazil strengthened by having a source of petroleum free from submarine warfare threats.[10]

Lacerda complained that the Communists, in stimulating disorders, wanted to turn the petroleum question into "a case for the police." Roberto Campos, too, appealed for less reliance on passion and ideology in handling discussions about "extremely delicate international problems." But, as researchers Plínio de Abreu Ramos and Dora Flaksman have written, the Roboré Agreement "inflamed political and military circles and led to particularly violent demonstrations in university circles." Arthur José Poerner, sympathetic to the views of the UNE-led, anti-Campos students, writes of the "serious" crisis, the newspaper headlines, and the traffic tie-ups brought about by defenders of Petrobrás.[11]

Lacerda upbraided Roberto Campos for giving an "exclusively economic" solution and for advancing a plan that he said was both "bad business" and "harmful to the national interest." Attacking the Kubitschek government, he said its errors were partly responsible for the clause preventing Petrobrás from entering Bolivia. Petrobrás, Lacerda told the readers of a UNE publication, would provide more petroleum if it had fewer "big bass drum nationalists." The students were informed by Lacerda that Petrobrás was "no worse" a solution to the petroleum problem than "the participation of private capital" and might be the better solution if it were administered honestly and competently. It would do a better job, he maintained, if it were less interested in disseminating pro-Petrobrás propaganda. "The only enemy of Petrobrás that can defeat it is the inefficiency provided in large measure by the demagogues who worship it."[12]

Janari Nunes denied having used Petrobrás funds to subsidize the press. Lacerda, after organizing a group to investigate carefully all publicity expenditures by Petrobrás, called Janari a liar and gave the CPI what he claimed was proof that Janari had subsidized "a bulletin of Russian propaganda." The sins of the Petrobrás administration, he wrote, would not have been revealed except for the CPI, the "patriotic" Colonel Alexínio, *Maquis* magazine, and the *Tribuna*.[13]

Late in January, the CPI approved the findings of a subcommission to which Lacerda belonged and which was headed by Oliveira Brito. The subcommission's conclusions, described by Lacerda as "necessarily bland to reflect the average opinion," expressed support for the monopoly of Petrobrás and urged it to give greater emphasis to the search for petroleum. As for the Roboré Agreement, the subcommission said that, in view of the impossibility of the participation of Petrobrás, the work should be done by private Brazilian companies, using financial assistance supplied by the government, together with conventional foreign loans guaranteed by Brazilian government banks. The subcommission wrote that the view of the BNDE, to allow foreign financing in return for a participation in the results, "is contrary to the interest of the country and prejudicial to the national economy, besides being harmful to the spirit of the Roboré Agreement."[14]

These findings echoed the views of Colonel Alexínio Bittencourt and were bitterly attacked by air force Colonel Anderson Mascarenhas, a passionate devotee of Petrobrás known for his poor opinion of Alexínio, Lacerda and the Roboré Agreement. Mascarenhas wrote that Lacerda, a liar and coward, was largely responsible for the "erroneous conclusions" adopted by the CPI.[15]

While Roberto Campos searched unsuccessfully for Brazilian companies able to execute the Roboré Agreement in accordance with the CPI guidelines, Lacerda continued his attack on the BNDE. Speaking at the Navy Club in March, he said that Brazil would have had "a bad agreement and a worse execution" had it not been for the vigilance exerted by Colonel Alexínio Bittencourt and those who foresaw the consequences of the criteria set up by Roberto Campos.[16] Nationalists, continuing to demonstrate against Campos, found it amusing to call him Bob Fields, the English-language equivalent of his name. They succeeded in driving him from office in July 1959.

It would be difficult to dispute the conclusion of the CPI that the Roboré Agreement was so different from the 1938 treaty that it constituted a new international understanding whose validity depended on legislative approval. But the achievement of that approval had become impossible even before the leading presidential hopefuls, in the latter part of 1959, attacked the Roboré Agreement.[17] Gas, discovered on the concession by the Gulf Oil Company in the early 1960s, was shipped to Argentina although Brazil would have been a more natural market.[18]

13. Directives and Bases for Education (1947–1961)

In Congress in 1957 Lacerda had introduced approximately twenty law projects, many of them seeking modest financial assistance for organizations he considered deserving, such as the Brazilian Academy of Letters, a cobblers' association aspiring to have a hospital, and a textile workers' union in need of a building. His proposal to have the government finance the acquisition of a thousand vehicles imported by taxi drivers was followed by a broader project to help others secure the tools of their trade. Several of his proposals, such as those to modify accident indemnification practices and to establish a pension institute for women doing domestic work, were also labor oriented. Among the few projects he presented in 1958 and 1959 was one to create a social security ministry for reorganizing and supervising the worker pension institutes. Most of Lacerda's proposals did not find their way out of the congressional commissions assigned to study them.[1]

Lacerda has written that his "principal work in Congress" was on behalf of a law providing the "directives and bases for education." It is therefore not surprising that in January 1959, when he received written questions from the UNE, he expressed disappointment to find the students asking about "exclusively political matters" and nothing about the proposed legislation.[2] At that time it appeared that Congress, after a delay of more than ten years, might act.

The 1946 Constitution called on Congress to "legislate about directives and bases for national education." It listed some rules, one of which required that primary education be obligatory, with public primary education given free of charge, and it stipulated that no less than certain percentages of federal and local tax receipts be spent on education. In declaring that "the states and the Federal District shall organize their systems of instruction," the constitution sought to avoid what many felt had been excessive centralization by the Estado Novo.[3]

As Dutra's education minister, Clemente Mariani formed a study commission in 1947. With its help he was able to send Congress a proposed Directives and Bases Law in 1948. His project, granting considerable power to the education ministry, disappointed defenders of decentralization. But it also disappointed the defenders of extreme centralization and its failure of passage was attributed to views expressed by Congressman Gustavo Capanema (PSD, Minas), who had headed the education ministry during the Estado Novo.[4]

When Lacerda assumed his congressional mandate in 1955 he sought to resurrect the Mariani project. He was told by Chamber of Deputies President Carlos Luz that the original copy, with the necessary signatures, had disappeared and that if he wished to save it he should present it as a new project under his own name. Thus Law Project 419, bearing Lacerda's name, was published in the *Diário do Congresso Nacional* of June 29, 1955. Not a few politicians maintained that his purpose was to advance a project associated with a former UDN minister, Mariani.[5]

From 1955 through 1957, Lacerda has written, nothing could be accomplished because of "the vested interests, political and financial pressures, the war between atheists and religious believers, and the struggle between different churches." Lacerda also blamed education ministry Chefe de Gabinete Celso Brant, who, he wrote, elected himself congressman in October 1958 "by using funds supposed to be allocated to scholarships." Congressmen showed little interest in May 1957 when discussion was begun about Law Project 2,222, produced by the congressional education commission.[6]

Outside Congress, however, the subject was much debated, especially in 1958. In the first part of the year, Catholic leaders Gustavo Corção, Alceu Amoroso Lima, and Archbishop Vicente Scherer advocated "freedom of instruction" in opposition to what churchmen were calling a "government monopoly" and the "socialist" ideas of Anísio Teixeira, director of Federal District education in the early 1930s. After the congressional education commission introduced a substitute proposal, Project 2,222-A, in June 1958, three cardinals and eighty-three bishops issued their Declaration of Goiânia defending private and religious education. Later in the year the UNE inaugurated a campaign on behalf of public education and the participation of students in the supervision of education.[7]

Lacerda, speaking in Congress in November 1958, pleased the defenders of private education and decentralization. Project 2,222-A, he said, favored a "totalitarianism" that would "divide Brazilians between manual and intellectual workers" by obliging children, at an early age, to decide whether to follow a path of culture or a technical profession. He attacked the centralization of the Mariani project and criticized the idea of legislating free federal university education in a country that "does not yet have enough free primary schooling to meet the needs of the people." Promising to present a substitute proposal, he called for a "dehydrated" law, "reduced to basic and fundamental expressions, to give the nation a definition of the concept of education." With that definition, he said, "we shall achieve decentralization . . . and freedom of instruction."[8]

The Lacerda *substitutivo,* also signed by Antônio Perilo Teixeira (UDN, Ceará), went to the congressional education commission on November 26, 1958. This project, Lacerda said, was the work of "a large group of educators." It adhered to the conclusions of a Congress of Private Schools, held in January 1948, and sought, wherever possible, to protect the private sector. It described education as "the inalienable and inviolable right of the family" and said the school "is, fundamentally, an extension and delegation" of that right. Opposing a government monopoly of instruction, it called for "equal conditions for public and private schools." Primary education, starting at the age of seven, would last for eight years in order to prevent the premature division of pupils into vocations. At the intermediate level, secondary or professional education would last a minimum of three years. Proof of completion of the secondary course would not be necessary for taking exams for admission to the top level of education.[9]

In December 1958, when the Chamber of Deputies was preparing to discuss Project 2,222-A, two new *substitutivos* appeared, both incorporating important ideas of the Lacerda proposal of November 26. One of them, known as the *substitutivo da comissão,* was a partial victory for the defenders of private education but did not go far enough to satisfy Lacerda and those who had campaigned since 1956 on behalf of the rights of private education.

During the congressional debate on December 11, Nestor Jost (PSD, Rio Grande do Sul) called Lacerda "exceedingly demagogic" and said the Lacerda *substitutivo* was full of absurdities, such as the provision that students could enter the top level of education without completing the secondary course. Lacerda argued that the *substitutivo da comissão* failed to place educational funds at the disposal of educators but retained them "in the hands of the education ministry." It was, he said, "a sort of declaration of war by the momentary majority of the congressional education commission"—a hodgepodge inspired by personal vanity or sensitivity about authorship.

Jost asked for an immediate vote on the various *substitutivos,* but Lacerda, seeking to gain time, proposed a forty-eight-hour postponement, and this was approved by a 124–40 decision. Despite assurances of Chamber of Deputies President Mazzilli of a new vote in forty-eight hours, the matter remained in abeyance until May 1959, by which time the Congress elected in October 1958 had been seated. In the meantime, on January 15, 1959, Lacerda presented his own second *substitutivo,* better organized than the first and with a few less reasons for objection by the defenders of public education. Lacerda's second *substitutivo,* unlike his first, would give some decision-making powers to the federal and regional educational councils.[10]

Preparing to defend his new *substitutivo* on a television program of the weekly "Gala Night" show, Lacerda learned that its producers could not obtain government approval for his appearance. To no avail Municipal Councilman Raul Brunini argued with General Olímpio Mourão Filho, head of the government's Radio and Television Technical Commission. "I consider it a crime," Brunini told the general, "not to allow Brazil to know about the Directives and Bases project of Congressman Lacerda, who finds himself forced to travel all over the country to explain it, like a traveling salesman, while the government has the use of every propaganda method to combat the principles established in it." The *Tribuna* wrote that Kubitschek himself, consulted by Mourão Filho, had issued the prohibition. Lacerda said his inability to use the radio and television "requires a new effort that I shall make as long as I have the energy." He had already given talks about his project in Belo Horizonte, Curitiba, and São Paulo. He received some help in São Paulo, when a former secretary of education of the state declared it absurd to describe Lacerda's *substitutivo* as "doing away with public schools." But sociologist Fernando de Azevedo, a founder of the University of São Paulo, organized a strong movement against what was called the "private school orientation" of Lacerda.[11]

Lacerda was defended by spokesmen of private school organizations and religious groups, such as the Confederation of Religious Believers. Father José Fonseca e Silva, a PSD congressman from Goiás, delivered a speech in which he said that although he strongly backed Kubitschek's political and economic policies, he was enthusiastic about what Lacerda was doing for decentralizing education and was therefore supporting him for the first time.[12]

In his work, Lacerda was assisted by Sandra Cavalcanti and Andrews School director and proprietor Carlos Flexa Ribeiro, the author of unsigned articles about the subject in *Correio da Manhã.* Lacerda also made use of ideas expressed in the past by Anísio Teixeira and others who now felt that decentralization would restrict government intervention on behalf of large-scale, free education for the masses. Writing in the *Tribuna* about the "pontiffs of official education," Lacerda mentioned those who did not want "religious schools, especially Catholic ones, to participate without discrimination" and Communists "who prefer . . . the type of school where students and instructors carry out strikes for the proletarization of teachers and the involvement of students in everything—except study."[13]

Opponents of Lacerda's ideas, worried lest his second *substitutivo* downgrade the role of public schools, drew up a new project early in 1959. Largely the work of Anísio Teixeira and known as the *substitutivo dos educadores,* it was presented by Congressman Celso Brant (PR, Minas) in May. It omitted reference to the "Christian concept of life," given in previous projects, and incorporated ideas that its authors found acceptable in the Mariani project of 1948 and the congressional education commission projects of 1958. It stipulated that curriculums of all top-level educational establishments would have to meet the approval of the education minister after he received the views of the National Education Council, made up entirely of members named by the president of the republic. According to University of São Paulo scholar João Eduardo Rodrigues Villalobos, the power given by this document to the minister could "frustrate all hopes of decentralized instruction, especially at the top level."[14]

The Chamber of Deputies discussion, which lasted for three weeks beginning on May 29, 1959, was about the *substitutivo dos educadores* and the second *substitutivos* of Lacerda and the congressional education commission. Jost argued that Lacerda sought to subvert the principle, upheld in all projects except his, that public schooling should be dominant. Lacerda tried to show that his proposal was not harmful to the expansion of public education. Comments by Professor Francisco San Tiago Dantas, recently elected to Congress and a friend of Carlos Flexa Ribeiro, led Lacerda to congratulate the new PTB congressman from Minas for believing that public and private education could be carried out, side by side, on an equal footing. The *Tribuna* proclaimed "San Tiago accepts the opinion of Lacerda."[15]

Lacerda could see the possibility of a compromise between his own proposals and those of the congressional education commission. But he had no use for the *substitutivo dos educadores* that he said renounced the past ideas of Anísio Teixeira and sociologist Fernando de Azevedo and would make the National Education Council a mere consultative "sponge" of bureaucratic "stuffed shirts." Speaking in Congress, he compared the anti-Catholicism of Anísio Teixeira with anti-Semitism and called it "detestable and anti-constitutional." "Anísio Teixeira," he said, "is an anti-Semite deflected from his course. . . . Since he is a liberal and it is bad to be anti-Semitic, he is against the Catholic Church." "His Lordship seeks to take vengeance on the Vatican by means of a system of teaching that assures every privilege for the central government," Lacerda said. As for Celso Brant, sponsor of the *substitutivo dos educadores,* Lacerda asked why he had not, as education ministry *chefe de gabinete,* provided "a little of the scholarship money that the whole world knows disappeared in the education ministry?"[16]

Seeking to clear up what he called misunderstandings, Lacerda said his own revised *substitutivo* would not superimpose private schooling on public schooling and was not, as claimed by Anísio Teixeira, excessively pro-Church. He said he could understand why "super-liberals" joined with Communists to oppose a project based on Christian philosophy but could not understand why student leaders worthy of that name "scheme against our project in meetings of students, who, to a large extent, remain unfamiliar with it." He directed attention to what he called the high cost of "official instruction" in comparison with private instruction.[17]

During the three weeks of congressional discussion, which ended in mid-June 1959, pronouncements and manifestos were made outside Congress and fifty-seven proposed amendments were considered in the congressional plenary sessions. The discussion was closed by a speech by Lacerda, described by Professor João Eduardo Rodrigues Villalobos as "the most beautiful from a formal point of view." Lacerda spoke of the background that had led to "the philosophy of totalitarian education, of education without God, of information accepted without questioning, of man uninterested in his origin and purposes." "We want," he said, "that this law, which the Chamber will vote, be the freedom certificate of Brazilian youth."[18]

While the congressional education commission sought to put together still another *substitutivo,* Fernando de Azevedo drew up a Manifesto of Educators to defend public schooling. Among its signers were Anísio Teixeira, Florestan Fernandes, Caio Prado Júnior, Nelson Werneck Sodré, Antônio Cândido de Melo e Souza, Darci Ribeiro, and Cecília Meireles. Its publication on July 1, 1959, led to the launching of the Campaign to Defend Public Schools, sponsor of conferences and rallies to oppose Lacerda's views. In *O Estado de S. Paulo,* which supported the campaign, University of São Paulo Professor Florestan Fernandes and others combatted the "freedom of instruction" ideas of Lacerda and the Catholic Church.[19]

The new law project, presented by the education commission on September 29, 1959, and revised in its final form on December 10, 1959, was approved, with practically no changes, by the Chamber of Deputies on January 22, 1960. It went further than the previous education commission projects in satisfying the interests of private education and the desires of the Catholic Church; and it contained many of the ideas expressed by Lacerda, such as the one about the school being "fundamentally an extension and delegation" of the rights of the family and the one prohibiting a "monopoly of instruction." The Federal Education Council, as the council was now to be called, was to consist of thirty members. Nine would be named by the president of the republic, and, in the case of the others, adequate representation was assured for private schools. Although Anísio Teixeira claimed that the Campaign to Defend Public Schools won a partial victory by preventing enactment of the "extreme form" of the Lacerda *substitutivo,* the victory belonged to the supporters of decentralization and private teaching.[20]

In 1960, while the measure awaited action in the Senate, the "defenders of public schools" continued to battle Catholics who advocated "freedom of instruction." They took their campaign to labor unions and, in February 1961, held a Labor Convention to Defend Public Schools at the headquarters of the huge São Paulo Metalworkers' Union. Although the Chamber of Deputies measure would give "preference" to public education in the allocation of public funds, these defenders complained that it allowed too much for the private sector. They proposed that public funds go exclusively to public schooling.[21]

The Communist *Novos Rumos* called Lacerda the "principal architect" of the Chamber of Deputies measure and wrote that his aim was to keep thirty million Brazilians illiterate and therefore out of political life, thus leaving his own "privileges" untouched. It argued that his original idea of allocating funds on the basis of the size of school enrollments would perpetuate the public sector's weakness in secondary education.[22]

Professor Darci Ribeiro, who was making plans for the new University of Brasília, published a letter to Lacerda in which he said the real purpose of the so-called defenders of the freedom of private instruction was to allow private schools to participate excessively in the distribution of public funds and escape "public control" in order to serve interest groups. He maintained that the private sector was already receiving "enormous" subsidies, which, if channeled to the public sector, would result in a desirable nationwide network of public secondary and technical schools. While presidential hopeful Jânio Quadros remained on the fence, General Lott, also seeking the presidency, echoed declarations of Darci Ribeiro and attacked the ideas of Lacerda and the measure passed by the Chamber of Deputies. Those who defended "family rights," Lott said, were using a "false position" as a justification for the private sector's use of funds that ought to go to the public school network.[23]

Lacerda accused Darci Ribeiro of misrepresenting his views in "television monologues"; but he asserted that election campaigning did not leave him enough time to appear with the professor in a public debate. Lacerda's suggestion that the defense of the directives and bases measure be undertaken instead by Sandra Cavalcanti was not well received by foes of Lacerda. It revealed, Darci Ribeiro wrote, that the "only domain" of Lacerda, a mere boaster, was "the monologue." According to *Novos Rumos,* Lacerda's refusal to debate left him unmasked as a coward and "agent of the industrialists of teaching."[24]

The Senate, thanks in part to the work of Relator Mem de Sá and Father Calasans, rejected a proposal that Calasans described as influenced by socialist or Communist ideas. In August 1961 the bill that had been passed in January 1960 by the lower house was accepted by the Senate with only minor modifications. Professor Luiz Antonio Cunha, sympathetic to the Campaign to Defend Public Schools, writes that the Law of Directives and Bases for Education, "of private education orientation," was finally sanctioned in December 1961.[25]

Lacerda has written that in order to get the project converted into law "I had to negotiate about the authorship of the *substitutivo* so that it ceased to be mine and became nobody's."[26] Lucia Hippolito, in her study of the career of Lacerda, writes that his role in putting together the education law was a unique one for him because, for the first time, he made use of politics to bring together the views of conflicting factions. She points out that he developed close contacts with members of other parties, accepted the collaboration of congressmen such as Aderbal Jurema of the PSD and San Tiago Dantas of the PTB, adopted suggestions, and gave attention to criticisms. "Handling adversaires not as enemies to be destroyed, Lacerda played the game of politics as it ought to be played in a democratic regime. Probably his attitude was responsible for the climate that prevailed during the discussion of the Law of Directives and Bases for Education, without doubt one of the most splendid moments of the Brazilian Congress since 1946."[27]

IX.

Backer of Quadros (1959–1960)

1. Lacerda's Decision to Support Quadros (February 1959)

Following the elections of October 1958, Lacerda announced that if it were up to him the UDN candidate for the presidential election of October 1960 would be UDN President Juracy Magalhães. But soon he was having second thoughts because it appeared that Jânio Quadros, 42 years old, had the mass support to win and that Juracy, as an opponent of Jânio, might provide the UDN with one more "glorious defeat."[1]

While Lacerda was uncertain whether the UDN and Quadros, a PTB congressman, could join forces, he was visited at his Tonelero Street apartment by two *udenistas* who wanted him to declare his support for Quadros: Roberto de Abreu Sodré, UDN leader in the São Paulo state legislature, and Father Antônio de Oliveira Godinho, a São Paulo drinking companion of Lacerda who had baptized Quadros' daughter and been elected in 1958 to the state legislature. They argued that Quadros would give Brazil a moral and austere administration and would, under any circumstances, win the presidential election. They found Lacerda sympathetic to their ideas.[2]

On behalf of Juracy Magalhães, eager to be the UDN presidential nominee, Lacerda was approached indirectly by Kubitschek. Kubitschek arranged for the presidential plane to bring Marcelo Garcia to Brasília. There, in the company of diplomat Hugo Gouthier, the president told the doctor that he was his only contact with Lacerda and revealed his idea of having Juracy serve as "national unity" candidate with the president's blessing. Garcia, reporting to Lacerda, said he believed such an arrangement would obligate Juracy to support the return of Kubitschek to the presidency in 1965. Lacerda replied that he would back Quadros because he wanted to succeed Quadros in the presidency.[3]

When Juracy told Lacerda that he had the support of Kubitschek and Goulart and would win the 1960 election for the UDN if Lacerda would help him obtain that party's nomination, he added that Lacerda could have any post he wished in a Juracy Magalhães administration. Juracy also referred to signs of instability in the character of Quadros. But Lacerda maintained that a UDN-PSD united front for Juracy, if successful, would mean a perpetuation of the "oligarchy." He also pointed out that it might well be unsuccessful at the polls, in which case Quadros would reach the presidency without any important "political instrument" and therefore without "the normal framework of the democratic process."[4]

In 1955 Lacerda had written that the "sinister" Quadros, a "delirious paranoid" and "virtuoso of felony," was worse than a dozen Ademars and was the Brazilian "political animal" who most reminded him of Hitler. Therefore when the UNE's *O Metropolitano* submitted its questions to Lacerda in January 1959, it asked whether the incompatibility between Lacerda and Quadros would make it difficult for the latter to be the UDN presidential candidate. Lacerda replied that the question was "well suited to a publication that is paid to attack the UDN and Jânio Quadros" and said it was too charged with false conjectures to be answered. He denied having any "personal incompatibility with Jânio Quadros."[5]

In his *Tribuna* editorials in mid-February, Lacerda called on Quadros to explain his position. He wrote that only Quadros could separate the UDN from the Quadros candidacy and added pointedly that "Sr. Kubitschek can never do it." Condemning the notion that the UDN seek the presidency "with the help of the PSD," Lacerda argued that such an arrangement would destroy all that the UDN had constructed and that it was impossible to have any confidence in the word of Kubitschek.

Lacerda warned his readers of the danger of Quadros embarking on a "personalistic adventure that would favor paternalism and *caudilhismo,* setting back the slow, contradictory, and bumpy march to democracy." Told that friends of Quadros wanted the candidate to steer clear of the UDN, Lacerda asked whether the idea came from Quadros and not just his friends. He sought to demolish the idea by arguing that neither small parties nor a wing of the PTB would provide Quadros with the "instruments of political action necessary to complement his immense popularity." Lacerda also wrote that if Quadros, on returning from his planned trip to Japan, found his candidacy encountering more difficulties "than at present" he could not say he had not been warned.[6]

Abreu Sodré brought Lacerda the suggestion of São Paulo Governor Carvalho Pinto that he meet with Quadros. "Roberto," Lacerda said, "You know me well enough to know I believe that if people quarrel on account of the public interest, they can make peace in the public interest." The meeting, he was told, would take place at Abreu Sodré's apartment in Santos on the morning of February 18.[7]

"Oh, my friend, what a happy reunion," Quadros exclaimed when he received Lacerda at the apartment. Quadros called himself "a *udenista* without a party card," and said "I don't want to assume party obligations, I want to be a popular candidate." Lacerda replied that Quadros' desire to be a popular candidate excited his interest. "I hope," he added, "that, as a popular candidate, you will take to the government the ideas we defend. If you give Brazil the government they say you gave São Paulo, I'll be satisfied."

Both men wanted an understanding. Quadros said he would receive, "willingly and with respect," the support of the UDN. He asked about the political situation in Rio and other places and spoke well of the political future of "that boy scout–like" Fernando Ferrari (PTB, Rio Grande do Sul), whose recent reelection to Congress made him Brazil's most voted-for congressman. The lively and cordial meeting delighted Abreu Sodré.[8]

Lacerda, surrounded by reporters after the meeting, was questioned again about his attacks on Quadros in 1955. "During the Távora campaign," he replied, "it is true that certain positions of Jânio Quadros displeased us. They gave the impression that he wished to remove the UDN from the campaign. At that time I criticized him severely, but it was nothing more than that." In reply to another question, Lacerda said he did not believe the official PTB would make Quadros its presidential candidate and that if a wing of the PTB did so it would not prevent the UDN from nominating him. Although he admitted that the UDN could not elect a president alone, he called it "the strongest force on which a president can count in carrying out an honest government."

That afternoon's *Tribuna* carried Lacerda's front page article, "Immediate alliance with Jânio Quadros." The article denied "Catete Palace propaganda" that he was backing Quadros in return for support for his own candidacy for the governorship of the state of Guanabara (to be created with the extinction of the old Federal District). "My candidate to govern the city of Rio," Lacerda wrote, "is Congressman Geraldo de Meneses Cortes, and I plan to present his name to the UDN." Lacerda also called it "nonsense" to insinuate that he was insisting on Quadros in order to become his vice-president. "If it depends on Jânio Quadros," he wrote, "the vice-presidential candidate of an alliance with him will be, I believe, Milton Campos."[9]

Lacerda failed in his wish to have the UDN support Quadros immediately. At the São Paulo city home of Abreu Sodré, where he was a guest, he pleaded his case to UDN leaders such as Juracy Magalhães, Antônio Carlos Magalhães (the Bahia congressman who headed Juracy's presidential campaign), Aliomar Baleeiro (another pro-Juracy Bahia politician), Adauto Lúcio Cardoso, and Fathers Godinho and Calasans. During the heated ten-hour discussion, Abreu Sodré tried, without success, to convince the Juracy people that the choice of the UDN was either defeat in 1960 or victory with Quadros.[10]

2. The UDN Convention of March 1959

With the UDN scheduled to hold its twelfth national convention in São Paulo starting on March 20, the Quadros candidacy was the subject of pronouncements. The most important was issued by the UDN of Minas, where Olavo Bilac Pinto, Milton Campos, and José Bonifácio de Andrada had spoken early in favor of the former governor of São Paulo. At the Minas UDN convention, held in the first week of March, state party leaders acclaimed a pro-Quadros resolution written by Afonso Arinos and Carlos Lacerda but said to have been written by José de Magalhães Pinto, outgoing president of the Minas UDN. Magalhães Pinto, congressman and banker, was nominated for the Minas governorship and became a strong candidate in the contest for the UDN presidency, to be decided in São Paulo later in the month.[1]

Quadros, visiting Rio before departing on a long trip abroad, met with Juracy Magalhães at Lacerda's apartment and declared he would withdraw his candidacy on returning from Japan if he found the Juracy candidacy "consolidated with the support of Catete Palace." In a statement for the *Tribuna* he called for "calm and reflection." Rio Grande do Sul Governor Brizola, also visiting Rio, said "the Lacerdistas have Jânio and we have Lott and Goulart." Communist spokesman Luís Carlos Prestes observed that "Jânio Quadros is merely the candidate of Carlos Lacerda and the international trusts."[2]

Lacerda worked for conciliation within the UDN. At a weekly party directorship meeting, held two days before the São Paulo national convention, he defended the two-year term of outgoing party President Juracy Magalhães in the face of attacks by Adauto Lúcio Cardoso. He worked to prevent the split developing between the supporters of the two candidates for the party presidency, Magalhães Pinto of Minas and Herbert Levy of São Paulo. Lacerda argued that no reason for a fight existed since both men favored Quadros. As for the desire of the Paulistas to have Levy in the party presidency, Lacerda pointed out that the Paulistas were going to have the prestige of placing their former governor in the presidency of the republic. Without success he urged Levy to withdraw.[3]

But Lacerda precipitated a fight at the party convention after outgoing party President Juracy Magalhães delivered his report. Declaring in a speech that the report "contained not one word critical of the government," Lacerda suggested that this lack was "the first result of the promises of the PSD" to support Juracy's presidential candidacy. Such a candidacy by the UDN, he said, was inadmissible because its only chance at the polls depended on the support of the government, the PSD, and the PTB, "in short, the forces of corruption." The only alternative, Lacerda said, was for the UDN to support Quadros immediately.

Juracy, in an emotional response, said Carlos was making a mistake in seeking to have the UDN act precipitously, thus eliminating the possibility of bringing forces together behind a candidate belonging to the party. He spoke of Lacerda's record of acting in a contradictory manner, initially opposing men and later praising them. Juracy also referred to his own past record as a 1930 revolutionary and his recent victory in winning the Bahia governorship. He exclaimed that he would not accept the charge of Lacerda that he was a traitor or government adherent. The crowd, including about three hundred delegates, rose to its feet to give a long ovation.

Lacerda denied having suggested that Juracy planned to betray the party. The Baiano, he told the *udenistas,* was no less endowed with honor and administrative talent than Jânio Quadros. But, he pointed out, the question of a presidential candidate had to be considered from a political, not sentimental, point of view. "It is necessary," Lacerda declared, "to march at once with Jânio Quadros, bearing in mind that any delay will result in the UDN having to back a victorious candidate at the tail end of events, leaving the upper hand to other parties." As a final argument, Lacerda said that a serious social convulsion threatened Brazil and that a great hope for social peace lay in the union of the UDN, party of the middle class, with Quadros, who could bring the working masses to the party. "The election of Jânio Quadros," Lacerda said, "will be an intermediate step leading to the conquest of Catete Palace afterwards by a UDN member. And this is the only stopgap mandate we shall permit."[4]

The supporters of Jânio seemed to have a majority. But the delegates, with UDN congressional leader João Agripino presiding, resolved to let the contest between the supporters of the two candidacies be settled at an "extraordinary convention to be held at a suitable time." A resolution, adopted unanimously, had Jânio in mind when it said the candidates must subscribe to the UDN program and Juracy in mind when it said they were required to oppose "the forces that have dominated the government for so many years." Lacerda told reporters that this meant no more talking to the president of the republic in the name of the party, thus restricting the negotiations that Juracy had been carrying out for his candidacy, "principally in the area of Catete Palace."[5]

The party program, to be sent by letter to the voyaging Jânio Quadros, spoke of the "Brazilian agrarian infrastructure which no longer supports the demographic pressure"; it required the UDN presidential candidate to promise, if elected, to give the country "detailed and realistic agrarian legislation, capable of bringing about a harmonious development, without the presently existing, dangerous social imbalances." The candidate was also to defend Petrobrás and work for reforms of education and foreign-exchange policy.[6]

Magalhães Pinto won the party presidency over Herbert Levy by a 204–79 vote. *O Estado de S. Paulo* reflected that a swift outcome in favor of Jânio might have been expected had Levy won but that the choice of Magalhães Pinto altered the picture because the Mineiro preferred to work out formulas of conciliation. To serve with Magalhães Pinto, Aluísio Alves was chosen secretary-general. Among the three new vice-presidents was Mário Martins, the anti-Quadros congressman who headed the Carioca UDN. Leandro Maciel, outgoing governor of Sergipe, became head of the UDN national council.[7]

A week later Lacerda reorganized the *Tribuna* management with the explanation that "the pressing demand to popularize my party, in the company of Juracy Magalhães, and illness, caused by fatigue, have kept me from my newspaper desk longer than I ever wanted." The reorganization brought in former Pernambuco Governor Carlos de Lima Cavalcanti, who would join Luís Brunini and Odilon Lacerda Paiva on the administrative side. It also brought in novelist Odilo Costa, filho, who had recently been instrumental in building up *Jornal do Brasil* and was expected to take much of the *Tribuna* editorial load from Lacerda's shoulders. The changes, Lacerda announced, would allow the continuation of work done earlier by Aluíso Alves, Mauricinho Lacerda, Elpídio Reis, and Ignácio Piquet Carneiro, men who had "dedicated themselves so much to assure the survival of this ship in days of storm and nights of treason" that had featured "the boldness of João Duarte, filho, . . . the dedication of Fernando Velloso, and the unforgettable assistance of Luís Camilo de Oliveira Neto."

Lacerda denied unfounded reports that the addition of Lima Cavalcanti and Odilo Costa, filho, had occurred because banker Magalhães Pinto had bought the *Tribuna.* He explained that the *Tribuna* had not been sold and added that his son Sérgio, 21 years old, would join it.[8]

3. Reflections about Salazar and Fidel Castro (April–May 1959)

Relations between Brazil and Portugal became strained after January 12, 1959, when General Humberto Delgado, recent opposition candidate for the Portuguese presidency, entered the Brazilian embassy in Lisbon and asked for asylum. Brazilian Ambassador Álvaro Lins, author of anti-Lacerda editorials in *Correio da Manhã* in 1955, learned that Delgado, recently deprived of his military rank, feared being arrested like other oppositionists who had joined him in calling on British leftist Aneurin Bevan to speak in Portugal.[1]

Lins was unable to persuade Portuguese Foreign Minister Marcelo Matias that Delgado should be considered as having found political *asilo* (asylum) and, as an *asilado,* should be granted a safe-conduct for reaching the airport, from which he wished to go to Brazil. Matias insisted that Delgado was simply a guest at the embassy, was not under arrest orders, and, if he wished to travel to Brazil, should first go home and request the necessary departure papers. Delgado, Matias said, should not be accompanied to the airport by the representative of any foreign power.

While the Portuguese police kept watch on the Brazilian embassy, a part of the press in Brazil used the incident to denounce the dictatorship of Antônio Salazar. Lins, whose position was attacked by the censored press of Portugal, maintained that the impasse was created by Salazar, whose ministers, such as Marcelo Matias, Marcelo Caetano, and Teotônio Pereira, served merely as puppets. But Lins was told that Salazar would discuss the Delgado matter with no Brazilian official, not even Kubitschek.[2]

Delgado was still in the Brazilian embassy on January 30 when Lacerda spoke in Congress, appealing to the Portuguese government for a safe-conduct for Delgado. Lacerda pointed out that he himself had found exile in Portugal, when his life had been in danger, and that the "voice of Brazil" had been the first to be raised on behalf of Portugal's claim to Goa. He explained to his listeners that various Portuguese military figures, suspected of subversive activities, had been dismissed from their posts and arrested, and he mentioned the case of Captain Henrique Galvão, who had been arrested and recently escaped. Joel Silveira, writing in the *Diário de Notícias,* expressed the fear that Delgado, if he remained in Portugal after leaving the Brazilian embassy, would be arrested within two weeks.[3]

The argument between Portugal and the Brazilian embassy about the status of Delgado was still unresolved in February when Assis Chateaubriand, Brazilian ambassador to Great Britain, arrived in Lisbon and conferred with Portuguese cabinet ministers. Chateaubriand felt that Lins should advise Delgado to go home, as the Portuguese authorities wished. Lins, who refused to agree, learned that Brazilian Foreign Minister Negrão de Lima was willing to accept the Portuguese proposal that would allow Delgado, a "guest" of the embassy, to leave for Brazil. Ambassador Lins argued that the imposition of conditions on Delgado's departure, whereby his host could not accompany him to the airport, made him an *asilado.* In his diary Lins wrote: "Kubitschek is not Brazil; and much less can Negrão de Lima be considered Itamaraty."

In the meantime, Captain Henrique Galvão, who had escaped from arrest, found asylum in the Argentine embassy. The Portuguese authorities, agreeing with Argentina that the captain was an *asilado,* said that the situation of Galvão, condemned to prison, was "completely different" from that of Delgado, "a citizen free to circulate."

Finally, in the middle of April, Negrão de Lima sent Antônio Mendes Viana, secretary-general of Itamaraty, to Lisbon to resolve the dispute. Mendes Viana was accompanied by João Ribeiro Dantas, director of the *Diário de Notícias.*[4]

Lacerda decided to go to Lisbon as a *Tribuna* reporter. Explaining his trip in a *Tribuna* article, he said: "We want to be in Portugal also as a voice of the opposition. . . . And, if it is not too presumptuous, to use what feeble possibilities we possess . . . to help reestablish normal relations between Brazil and Portugal." He described himself as having friends on both sides of the dispute. Praising Mendes Viana as a professional diplomat and disparaging Lins, he pointed out that the case was not for amateurs because it had to be resolved without humiliating either Delgado or Portugal.[5]

After reaching Lisbon on April 16, Lacerda accused the *Correio da Manhã* of stupidity and perfidy because it had written that he had been sent to Portugal by Negrão de Lima. But, he added, "Paulo Bittencourt knows, better than anyone, that the scorn I have for Negrão de Lima does not prevent me from serving Brazil, wherever and whenever I feel it necessary." When Lacerda called on Lins, the unhappy ambassador said he would not speak to him as the *Tribuna*'s reporter but that, as he was opposition leader in Congress, he would be given access to information and documents.[6]

With Itamaraty agreeing that Delgado was not a political *asilado,* Mendes Viana arranged for his departure by plane for Brazil on April 21. The former general, upon reaching Rio in the company of João Ribeiro Dantas, complained of having been persecuted in Portugal. *O Globo* wrote that in Brazil he ought not to combat the Portuguese government or cause it difficulties. But Lacerda pointed out that Portugal had never considered Delgado a political exile and therefore he was not subject to regulations applicable to that status, such as abstention from political activities.[7]

Appearing before the congressional diplomacy commission, headed by Raimundo Padilha, Lacerda reminded it that he had criticized the Senate for having given only superficial consideration to the nomination of Álvaro Lins as ambassador. He accused Lins of having committed a series of errors that "complicated the Delgado case." But he added that Delgado had shown no interest in a solution and that Chateaubriand had made matters worse by writing articles "attacking Álvaro Lins, Itamaraty, and Delgado." "As a journalist, he can write what he wants, but not as an ambassador."

Lacerda also told the congressional commission: "We must do everything possible to facilitate the dialogue between the Portuguese government and its opposition, not in order to install a new regime but to transform it so it will fulfill the ideal of the Luso-Brazilian community." He called the opposition to Salazar "an agglomeration of forces infiltrated by Masons and Communists, leaving Portugal today with the alternative of the permanence of the present regime or a new government whose composition will be so heterogeneous that no one can say what will prevail." He also called the commission's attention to "infiltration of a fascist character in Portuguese official circles."[8]

In the *Tribuna* Lacerda described the 70-year-old Salazar as "the most intelligent, the most lucid, the most implacably lucid of anachronisms." "My friends of the opposition," he wrote, "will perhaps be indignant if I say what I think in this regard, but I must say it: the work of Sr. Salazar will last much longer than his regime, and when no traces remain of the latter, much will remain from his effort to put order into political ideas. . . . A democracy, which will be born from the debris of the present conflict between capitalism and communism, will have much to learn from the ideas of Sr. Salazar." Lacerda called on Salazar to understand the point of view of his adversaries and to admit that the time had come for him to retire to save the best of his work; and he called on those adversaries to understand that "it is not by bravado, irrelevances, and contradictions but by an effort at political lucidity that democracy can be achieved without destroying the nation."[9]

Lacerda had hardly finished delivering his opinions about Salazar when Fidel Castro reached Brazil. Meeting him at the home of José Nabuco, Lacerda was captivated by—and decidedly outtalked by—the 32-year-old Cuban[10] and felt, whenever he questioned him, that he was "striking a match next to highly inflammable material." The torrent of Castro's arguments, Lacerda found, was convincing and, above all, fascinating. Lacerda was especially moved by Castro's sincerity. "I had the sensation," Lacerda disclosed, "of speaking with a man belonging to a species that appeared to have become extinct: the species of idealistic liberators."[11]

Lacerda sought to allay the reservations of those who faulted Castro for Communist connections and for the firing squads of Cuban revolutionaries that had shot hundreds of so-called enemies of the Cuban people. He quoted Castro as saying that he had no Communists in his government and enjoyed the almost unanimous support of the people, without class distinction. As for the shootings, Lacerda accepted Castro's argument that it was necessary to exterminate those who had robbed the country and served a wretched dictatorship. In the *Tribuna* Lacerda wrote: "I want to tranquilize frightened readers of press accounts and the naive souls who take offense at a reported shooting and do not see, or prefer not to see, the iniquities that destroy more than life, and the outrages that wound the very sources of life, acts that are not reported in such a sensational way."

Concluding his observations about Fidel Castro, Lacerda wrote that the Cuban revolutionary had given a new dimension to the history of the struggle for liberty in the Americas. "For men like Haroldo Veloso, there has been a victorious Jacareacanga," he added. Addressing Castro, Lacerda wrote: "May God recompense you. On behalf of the peoples of America you have achieved revenge for all the failures to act."[12]

If Lacerda was captivated by Fidel Castro, the Cuban was no less captivated by the younger daughter of the Nabucos. But the girl's mother, Maria do Carmo Melo Franco Nabuco, hardly considered the Cuban revolutionary the ideal suitor for Nininha. "Xandoca, open the door!" Fidel Castro screamed at the maid when he returned to the Nabuco home to see the girl. The door remained closed.[13]

4. Magalhães Pinto Irritates Lacerda (April–July 1959)

For the inauguration of Juracy Magalhães as governor of Bahia on April 8, UDN leaders went to Salvador. There, at Juracy's home, the incoming governor said to Levy, "Herbert, tell the group what you told me about the crazy behavior of Jânio." Lacerda has written that Levy, after hesitation and urging, "began to say things about Jânio that were profoundly indiscreet, obscene, and very unpleasant." Nevertheless, Levy and Abreu Sodré insisted that Jânio was an excellent administrator.[1]

From Bahia, Lacerda reported to the *Tribuna* that it would be an error to accept the view of those who described Juracy's presidential campaign as a struggle against the south by the northeast, afflicted by the "errors and plundering" of the Kubitschek government. The UDN, he insisted once again, should delay no longer in backing Quadros. To take a position after other parties had done so, he wrote, would mean "repeating the tremendous errors committed in the case of the Juarez Távora candidacy."[2]

But the UDN procrastinated. And while it did, Quadros wrote to Magalhães Pinto from New Delhi, India, on May 27, asking how things were going. On June 19, still waiting to hear from Magalhães Pinto, Quadros wrote to Lacerda from Istanbul, Turkey. "It seems licit," he wrote, "to believe that the UDN," with the support of Juracy and other leaders, "will back my candidacy. I consider this fact the greatest reward of a troubled public life—the maximum recompense to which I could aspire. If I can serve . . . , I shall serve with exemplary firmness, integrity, and dedication." He informed Lacerda that he planned to go to Israel at the invitation of its government following a visit he had made to Egypt, where he had been the guest of Nasser. He added that when he reached Rome he would decide, "in the light of developments and my remaining money," whether to visit Yugoslavia.[3]

Quadros was still in Istanbul when he received from Magalhães Pinto a list of twelve "pragmatic points" of the UDN, whose acceptance, in the words of Magalhães Pinto, was "indispensable" if the party was to support "a candidate outside its ranks." The list called for an agrarian reform and a foreign policy that would prevent Brazil from being a "yes man" of the United States or a satellite of Russia. And it included the UDN's nationalistic line about the petroleum monopoly and the preservation for Brazil of radioactive and atomic materials.[4]

In his reply from Rome, written on June 26, Quadros praised all the points. He said he had defended Petrobrás throughout his career and added that "my position on exchange reform, reform of social welfare, and education reform, all of which I consider indispensable and urgent, is sufficiently well known." Turning to other items on the UDN list of twelve, he promised to give special attention to the control of currency issuances, autonomy for unions, the cost of living problem, and economic development. Brazil's foreign policy, he wrote, should not depend on the foreign policy of other nations or be characterized by preferences or prejudices not corresponding to the real interests of the Brazilian people. As in other letters, Quadros expressed his esteem for Juracy Magalhães.[5]

While the UDN directors studied Quadros' reply, Nei Braga, Paraná congressman of the PDC (Christian Democratic Party), visited with Quadros in Rome. Back in Brazil early in July, Nei Braga reported that Quadros had accepted the program of the PDC. The press stated that Quadros' nomination in August or September by the PDC was assured and that his PDC running mate might be Fernando Ferrari, whom Quadros continued to praise when speaking with reporters abroad.[6]

Lacerda, who had been elected president of the Carioca UDN on June 19, became more and more irritated at Magalhães Pinto and the UDN directorship for not making up their minds. In the meantime Quadros, still in Rome, told reporters he had no interest in the views of Brazilian Communist leader Luís Carlos Prestes, whom he considered "defunct." Then, with his wife, mother, and 15-year-old daughter, he visited Yugoslavia, where he was the guest of Marshal Tito. Late in July he and *Diário de Notícias* Director João Ribeiro Dantas left Paris by air to spend a week in the Soviet Union. Before boarding the plane, Quadros declared that he personally favored a renewal of diplomatic relations between Brazil and the Soviet Union but that the decision was one for the Brazilian government and its security organizations to study and resolve. Quadros and Dantas, after visiting a nuclear plant in Leningrad, were received in Moscow by Nikita Khrushchev, with whom Quadros spoke about the need to establish direct Brazilian-Soviet commercial relations. "I have the impression," Quadros said in Moscow, "that Khrushchev was enthusiastic about the idea."[7]

In Brazil things went poorly for Lacerda. Magalhães Pinto pointed out that Quadros had not agreed that, if he were to be the UDN candidate, he should have but one running mate, to be named by the UDN. Magalhães Pinto also wanted Quadros to endorse the UDN gubernatorial candidates, one of whom was himself. Expressing pessimism about the status of negotiations with Quadros, Magalhães Pinto complained that representatives of Quadros were trying to prevent Quadros from becoming fully integrated into the

José de Magalhães Pinto. (Drawing by LAN on the cover of Sebastião Nery, *Folclore Político, 2*)

UDN party structure. The UDN president added that these matters had to be resolved before the party could set a nominating convention date, and he refused to yield to the plea of Lacerda that the convention be held in September, when Quadros was scheduled to return to Brazil.[8]

To make matters worse, Lacerda was in a fight with UDN congressmen belonging to the party's *chapa branca,* or "realistic wing." As opposition leader, he was struggling to defeat an administration-backed proposal for amending the constitution to create a new government organ of top advisers (*conselheiros*) that would include former presidents of Brazil. Lacerda remarked that some UDN congressmen, playing the government's game, "assiduously make trips to Catete Palace in search of official favors."[9]

In particular, Lacerda was troubled by Congressman José Cândido Ferraz (UDN, Piauí), who, on July 6, lunched at Laranjeiras Palace with Kubitschek, Juracy Magalhães, Juracy Magalhães Júnior, and Bahia cabinet member Rui Santos. On July 25, José Cândido Ferraz denied planning to expel Lacerda from the party and explained that expulsion had to be initiated by a regional directorship. But he added that "many *udenistas* are discontented with the methods that Carlos Lacerda has been forcing on the leadership of the opposition bloc." Lacerda, who wanted the party directorship to condemn publicly and officially any UDN *realista* who "violated the position" taken at the São Paulo national convention, said he intended to handle the problem at the first opportunity by establishing conditions under which he would remain in the party and in his opposition leadership post.[10]

During a conversation with Lacerda on the night of July 29, Magalhães Pinto accused the Carioca leader of creating crises. The discussion was so stormy that Lacerda followed it up with a letter in which he told the UDN president that he would leave the UDN. He would, he wrote, make this decision public after the battle to defeat the *conselheiros* amendment, "which we are carrying out in the Chamber of Deputies, clearly contrary to your wish." The resignation, Lacerda added, "leaves you free to make clandestine visits, as head of the principal opposition party and without its knowledge, to the head of the government—and what a head! and what a government!—in order to give him, as you say, advice. The adviser is he, not yet you, Magalhães. Your day will come very soon, but I do not want to be at your side that day. . . . All I have to say to you, and curtly, is that the creators of 'crises,' from Virgílio to me, make it possible for born statesmen like yourself to triumph."[11]

5. Conversations with Jânio in Europe (August 1959)

Early in August the UDN directorship resolved to send Lacerda and party Secretary Aluísio Alves to Europe to confer with Quadros about matters needing further clarification, such as its requirement that Quadros have but one running mate, chosen by the UDN. Quadros admirer Carlos Castilho Cabral concluded that the two emissaries represented the two factions in the UDN. Aluísio Alves, he has written, was close to Magalhães Pinto, was more favorable than Lacerda to the Juracy Magalhães candidacy, and had broken with Lacerda on the question of *Tribuna da Imprensa* policy.[1]

The Communist *Novos Rumos,* commenting on the forthcoming mission to Europe, wrote that Quadros, by negotiating in London with Lacerda and Aluísio Alves, would wipe out the propaganda advantages gained from visiting the Soviet Union. In London, *Novos Rumos* said, Quadros and Lacerda would make arrangements for an "antidemocratic conspiracy." It described Lacerdismo and the line of the Lantern Club as the "most reactionary" in Brazilian political life.[2]

In Rio, Lacerda expressed the hope that Juracy Magalhães would accept the vice-presidential nomination, and in Europe, Quadros voiced the same wish to Brazilian politicians, such as Adauto Lúcio Cardoso. But the governor of Bahia told Congressman Gabriel Passos, a UDN leader in Minas, that he planned to seek the presidential nomination for himself at the party convention. Besides, the PDC leadership was reported to be intransigent in demanding that Quadros' running mate be Fernando Ferrari.[3]

Aluísio Alves spoke with UDN governors in the northeast about ideas to explore with Quadros. In the meantime Lacerda conferred in São Paulo with Governor Carvalho Pinto and the presidents of the pro-Quadros PDC and PTN: Antônio Queiroz Filho and Emílio Carlos Kyrillos. While there he spoke also with Quadros confidant Francisco Quintanilha Ribeiro, who shared the command of the candidate's political work with São Paulo lawyer

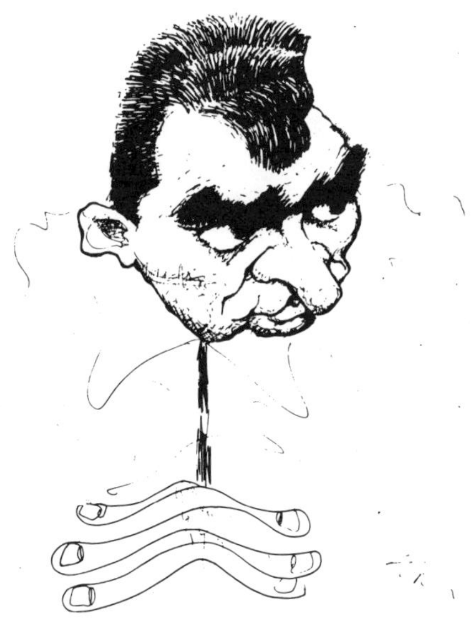

Aluísio Alves. (Drawing by LAN in Sebastião Nery, *Folclore Político, 2*)

Oscar Pedroso Horta. It was a two-man command that irritated Magalhães Pinto and was resented by Castilho Cabral, organizer and president of the independent Movimento Popular Jânio Quadros and unsuccessful advocate of having the PSD nominate Quadros.[4]

Lacerda and Aluísio Alves were met at the London airport shortly after midnight on August 15 by Quadros and his daughter and went to Quadros' hotel rooms for a discussion that lasted until 5:00 A.M. Quadros agreed that his running mate should be a UDN man, preferably Juracy. Aluísio Alves argued, with eloquence and apparent success, that much attention should be given during the campaign to the problems of the northeast. Lacerda, as communicative to the press as Quadros was uncommunicative, told reporters that the UDN had brought no demands but only suggestions.[5]

A few hours after the talk, the two emissaries of the UDN saw Quadros and his family off on a ship going to Vigo, on the northwest coast of Spain. Quadros, who had reportedly suffered a heart disturbance in London several days earlier, wanted rest and an opportunity to read the numerous documents brought from Brazil.[6]

With Aluísio Alves, Lacerda flew to Paris, and there he angrily denied press reports stating that no agreement had been reached in London. For him a high point of the brief Paris visit was a meeting with novelist André Malraux. Malraux, whom Lacerda found "extraordinarily intelligent and fascinating," was about to leave for Brazil and asked Lacerda for the expression that best described the spiritual attitude of the Brazilian people looking to the future. Lacerda suggested *L'Espoir* (Hope), the title of one of the author's novels. Malraux, inscribing each of two volumes of his collected works that he was giving Lacerda, wrote in one of them about "the hope that this meeting represents for the future of Brazil." In the other, the French novelist wrote that "perhaps one of the noblest functions of art is to make people aware of grandeur, of grandeur in themselves that they do not recognize."[7]

Meanwhile, in Vigo, Quadros let it be known that doctors had ordered a complete rest. He went to nearby La Toja, also on the Spanish coast, but found it an "inferno" because, he said, "every day I receive phone calls from reporters who do not realize I am convalescing from a heart condition." With his family he crossed into Portugal on August 23 and found the privacy he wanted at Gondarém, the property of Brazilian businessman João Carlos de Almeida Braga, near the border and a short distance from the town of Vila Nova Cerveira. Awaiting the arrival of the two UDN representatives, he studied more reports, these brought by a special emissary from Brazil. He conversed much with Antônio Carlos de Almeida Braga, brother of João Carlos, and showed no interest in leaving the place.[8]

Aluísio Alves, who had gone from Paris to Madrid, joined Lacerda in Lisbon on August 24. From there they want to Gondarém, where they spent three days. Lacerda, believing that the former governor's wife, mother, and daughter would like a change of scenery, offered to take them for a drive to the coast, but Jânio said, "My women do not go out without me."[9]

During the talks, Jânio said, "I want a *udenista* candidate as the single running mate of the ticket, and the choice is a problem of the party." He agreed to give immediate support to the UDN gubernatorial candidates who had possibilities of winning. And he promised to discuss with the party the cases of UDN candidates launched merely as gestures of protest and non-UDN candidates backed by the UDN.

Asked about "the command" of his campaign, Jânio pointed out that the campaign would be unusual in its length, lasting a year. He explained that in each state he planned to appear in the company of UDN candidates but wanted to give the command of the campaign to a committee made up of the presidents of all the parties supporting him. He pleased Lacerda when he said that as president he would seek to restore the federation, and he pleased Aluísio Alves by promising to emphasize, while campaigning, problems of the north and northeast, whose abandonment he attributed to excessive centralization. During a discussion about the nominating convention, Jânio told the UDN representatives that he expected to reach Santos by ship on September 21 or 22 and go on the twenty-fifth to his birthplace in Mato Grosso to await the "pronouncement of the party."[10]

Lacerda and Aluísio Alves went with the Quadros family by automobile to Oporto on a ride that made Jânio nervous because he thought Lacerda was driving too fast. During lunch in Oporto, Jânio said he planned to visit the shrine at Fatima. When Antônio Carlos de Almeida Braga remarked that Jânio had shown no interest in seeing the chapel at Gondarém, Jânio said a visit to Fatima would become known to everyone.[11] What surprised Lacerda was that Jânio spent as much time as he did complaining to members of the Portuguese press about what he called the mistreatment of a dog at Gondarém by João Carlos, thus embarrassing his recent host.[12]

In Oporto and Lisbon, Quadros and Aluísio Alves told reporters that a complete agreement had been reached between the UDN emissaries and the candidate. Quadros condemned the "nationalization" of industries but gave his full support to Petrobrás, calling petroleum a special case, and he reaffirmed his interest in seeing Brazilian-Soviet commercial and diplomatic relations established immediately.[13]

At the Rio airport, where Lacerda and Aluísio Alves arrived on August 29, Lacerda displayed his new pet, a young black crow (*corvo*). The bristly bird, Lacerda informed his greeters, was a present from a Portuguese friend. Explaining that his name was Vicente, Lacerda pointed out that "almost all crows have that name. When Saint Vincent was a prisoner, crows flew to heaven to find him food."[14]

The use of the term *corvo* as an epithet to describe Lacerda declined. The change, Lacerda has written, followed his adoption of Vicente.[15]

6. Lacerda Resigns as Opposition Leader (September 1959)

Reports by Lacerda and Aluísio Alves about Quadros' views were studied by national and local UDN leaders, and then, early in September, the party's national directorship met to decide what to do. The head of the Rio Grande do Sul section favored an immediate convention to nominate Quadros. But party President Magalhães Pinto pointed out that the party statutes required that he first consult all the state sections. He also expressed his regret at personal attacks by Lacerda in his newspaper against Juracy and those made by the Bahia section against Lacerda. The Bahia section and *udenistas* in the Bahia legislature were so infuriated by Lacerda's campaign against Juracy that they sent a telegram to the Bahia UDN congressmen suggesting they no longer accept Lacerda's leadership in the Chamber of Deputies.[1]

Magalhães Pinto, trying to act with "absolute neutrality," did not want to antagonize UDN northeastern Governors Dinarte Mariz, Luís Garcia, and Cid Sampaio, who appeared to favor Juracy Magalhães, opponent of an immediate convention. Lacerda, however, reached the conclusion that Magalhães Pinto, after achieving the party presidency, maneuvered against the Quadros candidacy.[2]

Lacerda resigned as opposition leader, giving some of his reasons in his letter of September 10 to Rondon Pacheco, of Minas, the interim UDN leader in Congress who had contributed to the battle that prevented passage of the *conselheiros* amendment. He wrote Rondon Pacheco about "slanders" against himself, made "coldly and deliberately" by UDN congressmen who hoped, he said, to aid the government in "systematically insulting the opposition leader." He mentioned also his dissatisfaction with the UDN, "paralyzed on account of personal ambitions." "This transformation of the UDN into a PTB, complete with collar and necktie," he told Rondon Pacheco, "appears to be such a serious error that I do not know which is greater: the moral failure . . . or the stupidity." Lacerda added that he hoped his "gradual retirement from public life" would be "a signal that the others, older and more tired, have also reached the hour for leaving the people in peace."[3]

In announcing his resignation publicly, Lacerda said he considered "the postponement of the UDN convention, or the failure to hold it at all, incompatible with commitments assumed by us, in the name of the party directorship, with Jânio Quadros." He was, he said bitterly, bringing an end to his effort to help the UDN become a democratic party and would return to journalism, "which is my profession, whereas politics is no profession for anyone." In other statements, he said he could be of more help to Quadros as a journalist than as a politician and would remain in the UDN as a voter and congressman.[4]

When a special UDN-PL commission (Magalhães Pinto, Rondon Pacheco, and Raul Pilla) sought Lacerda's return to the opposition leadership, he refused and repeated that the only solution for the "UDN crisis" was an immediate party convention. A little later he resigned from the presidency of the Federal District UDN with the explanation that he was morally obligated to give up the post until the representatives of the UDN "decide where they want to take the party: to an alliance with the forces of corruption or to a candidacy popular with its natural allies."[5]

Lacerda made this point when he met at a Botafogo apartment with officers attending the Army Staff School. General Rubens Resstel, then a major taking the staff school course, recalls that the officers, influenced by Colonels Newton de Oliveira Reis and Golberi do Couto e Silva, were inclined to support Juracy. They told Lacerda that Brazil needed reforms but not leftist reforms and they expressed concern about the activities of Communists during the Kubitschek administration. Lacerda convinced them that the solution lay in the election of Quadros. One army officer was so taken with Lacerda's discussion about Brazil's future that he said it was a shame Lacerda was not a presidential candidate.[6]

Quadros, who had booked passage to Brazil on the Italian vessel *Federico C*, leaving Lisbon on September 12, replied on September 10 to a letter Lacerda had written to him before resigning as opposition leader. Worried about Lacerda's combativity, he advised him to "be careful." "They seek," he wrote, "to take us to a crisis and that is *not* what we want. With the Lott candidacy becoming weak, I have the impression that another will appear, with a strange composition of forces and harmful to *udenista* unity. Therefore it is necessary to *temporize.* Do you understand? . . . The hour is one for prudence." Quadros told Lacerda to see Quintanilha Ribeiro "*at once* and work out with him the strategy for the future, which will be binding on me *also.*"[7]

While Quadros crossed the ocean with his family, his admirers in Rio prepared to greet him before the *Federico C* took him on to Santos. "As a symbol of the magnificence of his effort to clean up Brazil," they would present him with a hundred-kilogram broom, "the largest in the world." In the meantime in Congress, Quadros supporters denounced those who, they said, were hoping to avoid the direct presidential election by insincerely supporting Raul Pilla's proposed constitutional amendment to give Brazil a parliamentary form of government.[8]

During the stop of the *Federico C* at the Rio docks, Lacerda went aboard and spoke with the former São Paulo governor on a radio-television program that was not censored. In the course of the broadcast, journalist Hélio Fernandes asked Quadros if he was aware that three people, Lacerda, Hélio, and Hélio's brother Millôr Fernandes, were prohibited from speaking on television. The presidential hopeful denounced this "outrage" against democracy and the constitution and asked Lacerda if he could tell him the "justification" of the censorship. Lacerda said no justification existed and added that the fact that his reply to Quadros was being broadcast gave him an additional reason to be pleased with the welcoming ceremony. Quadros, on reaching São Paulo, announced that his campaign would start on October 17 in the seldom-visited territory of Acre, a location Lacerda had suggested.[9]

Gabriel Passos, one of the few Minas UDN leaders who favored Juracy, advised Magalhães Pinto again that Juracy would seek the presidential nomination at the convention. The UDN president, concluding his canvassing of the state sections, announced early in October that the convention would be held November 7 and 8. He attributed the new delay to a party statute requiring that no less than a month elapse between the announcement and the convention.[10]

Quadros, after calling on Kubitschek and promising to conduct a high-level campaign, joined Magalhães Pinto for a trip to Aracaju, Sergipe, to follow up on negotiations that former Sergipe Governor Leandro Maciel had been conducting with the Quadros people on behalf of the UDN governors of the northeast. At Aracaju on October 9, according to Lacerda, Pernambuco Governor Cid Sampaio made excessive demands in favor of the northeast and dealt with Quadros "as General Grant handled General Lee at the end of the war between the north and the south: the economic predominance of São Paulo was to end, etc. Jânio agreed to everything that Cid asked, evidently to have the support of the Pernambuco UDN, and then Cid returned to Pernambuco and read, on the radio or television, all that had been promised. . . . It made Jânio appear as a puppet, a stooge, of Cid Sampaio, and naturally Jânio was furious."[11] *Última Hora* wrote that Quadros, on returning from Aracaju, exclaimed that "the UDN and those migrants from the northeast will pay me dearly for their insolence." In São Paulo, Quintanilha Ribeiro called the story "totally false."[12]

That a northeasterner, probably Leandro Maciel, would become Quadros' running mate seemed likely after the Aracaju conference. But the situation was made awkward by the PDC on October 18, when it nominated Quadros for president and chose Fernando Ferrari to be his running mate.[13]

7. A Lively UDN Nominating Convention (November 7–8, 1959)

Before the UDN held its convention in Rio's Tiradentes Palace, the city was plastered with posters proclaiming that Juracy Magalhães was so clean that no broom was needed by the UDN. Among the rumors that filled the capital was one brought to Lacerda by Afonso Arinos and a northeastern governor about a plan to have the vice-presidential nomination go to Magalhães Pinto, whose good relations with Lott and Kubitschek were to be used to "tranquilize" the government in case Quadros won the presidential nomination. Lacerda, disgusted with the idea, told Magalhães Pinto he would seek the vice-presidential nomination himself just to oppose him. Magalhães Pinto denied the report and gave his support to Leandro Maciel although Lacerda would have preferred João Agripino, another northeasterner.[1]

The convention was about to begin on the afternoon of November 7, when Lacerda received a request from Quadros to join him at his Hotel Glória rooms. Quadros had been listening to Afonso Arinos relay Agripino's suggestion that the candidate make no campaign statements about the armed forces without first clearing them with the principal campaign advisers.[2] With the arrival of Lacerda, Quadros took him aside and said, "I can't put up any longer with the things I learned from Afonso Arinos, the things these people tell me, the conditions they want to impose. . . . Democracy under such conditions is impossible."

Lacerda tried to assure Quadros that all was well and that he would win the nomination, but the candidate remained indignant. Afonso Arinos, joining the pair, said it was time for the work to begin at the convention. But Quadros shocked the senator by saying, "I am no longer a candidate. Please be my representative because I don't wish to continue bothering Carlos, who, poor fellow, has been bothered too much by my candidacy. I want you, as UDN senator, to tell the gathering that I am no longer a candidate." Jânio spoke of returning to São Paulo and said many men in Brazil were in a better position to be president.

"Jânio," Lacerda said, "it seems to me you don't want to be tied to a single running mate, a UDN vice-presidential candidate, isn't that right?" "Perhaps," Quadros replied, "but that is not all. . . . I need freedom of movement." "I am not," Lacerda answered, "in a position to free you from commitments, but I think that if I'm going to accept your candidacy with the UDN, PDC, PL, PTN—not to mention I don't know how many other groups—your election will have such a popular character that you really won't depend on anyone. And I really do think you have a duty to work for the UDN candidacy." In the end Quadros agreed to make the "sacrifice."[3]

Magalhães Pinto went to the convention with the feeling that the agreement he had helped to work out with northeasterners for giving the vice-presidential nomination to Leandro Maciel would go a long way to unite the party. But when he reached Tiradentes Palace to preside over the initial proceedings he learned that five or six state sections felt that the party should not insist that Quadros fulfill a commitment in favor of the politically "inexpressive" Maciel.[4]

Magalhães Pinto, delivering his opening report about his recent conduct as party president, was interrupted by the entry of Lacerda, who was greeted by both an ovation and a shower of pro-Juracy leaflets thrown from the galleries. Juracy, addressing the delegates soon after Magalhães Pinto, claimed the party had succeeded in "growing in order to win" and should choose a presidential candidate from its own ranks rather than someone "who cannot feel the passion for our colors."

When Lacerda rose to reply, the chamber resounded with cheers and jeers. One congressman shouted, "A monster is at the tribune!" whereupon another added, "He is like Paulo Afonso Falls pouring out a torrent of words." After order had been restored, Lacerda praised the "Grow in Order to Win" slogan but said the growth should be with the people and not with Goulart and Kubitschek. He claimed that Quadros was providing the people, for the first time since they had "relearned democracy," an opposition candidate with the asset of an accomplished achievement in administration. "What convinced me was that accomplishment and not commitments that we did not and should not demand of him."[5]

Lacerda was interrupted by Governor Juracy Magalhães' finance secretary, Aliomar Baleeiro, whose face at that moment, Lacerda has said, was the face of one who wants to "chew someone up, the face of a cannibal in a rage."[6] Jânio Quadros, according to Baleeiro, was "nothing more than a political ballerina, to whom the head of John the Baptist should not be delivered." "Where," he asked Lacerda, "was Jânio Quadros when Juracy Magalhães was at your side" building up party support "from Rio Grande do Sul to the territory of Rio Branco?" Baleeiro also asked whether Quadros was not a congressman of the party headed by Goulart, and he added that Lacerda, in praising the probity of Quadros, was acting as though there were no men of probity in the UDN and was overlooking the role of Juracy as "an effective, vigorous, and upright administrator."[7]

Exclaiming "I am a *udenista,*" Baleeiro spoke of his past combats, often at the side of Lacerda. In those days, he said, he had "sought to mitigate the

Aliomar Baleeiro. (Drawing by Appe in *O Cruzeiro,* reproduced in Vol. 4 of Herman Lima, *História da Caricatura no Brasil*)

errors of Your Excellency." He was, he declared emotionally, warning him now that he was making a terrible mistake, one he would later repent.

José Bonifácio Coutinho Nogueira, young agriculture secretary of São Paulo, answered Baleeiro's "Where was Jânio Quadros?" question by stating that Quadros "was in the São Paulo government, carrying out the UDN program." Lacerda, agreeing with José Bonifácio, said that on November 11, 1955, Quadros was "defending the autonomy of São Paulo against the coup; he was not at a tribune, seeking your imprisonment like your state cabinet colleague, Vieira de Melo." Another speaker pointed out that Vieira de Melo, transport secretary of Governor Juracy Magalhães, had sought to cancel Lacerda's mandate.

Juracy, in one of his interruptions of Lacerda's speech, objected to Hilde Weber's political cartoon in that day's *Tribuna*, which seemed to show the UDN broom sweeping Juracy away. Lacerda replied that the figure being swept away was marked Ademar de Barros, but Juracy held the cartoon aloft to prove this was not so. Then Lacerda said the figure represented "spurious alliances to which I have alluded."

During Lacerda's exchange with Baleeiro the noise from the galleries had for a while made it impossible for speakers to be heard. Later, when it seemed that Lacerda might provoke serious disorder by turning his speech into a denouncement of Juracy, Governor Cid Sampaio made a plea in which he emphasized the importance of party unity. Lacerda concluded his speech without aggression.

Magalhães Pinto had yet to handle a document, in the possession of Lacerda and drawn up in part by Abreu Sodré, suggesting the withdrawal of the Leandro Maciel candidacy. The party president, learning that the document was to be presented to him, asked Minas UDN President Oswaldo Pieruccetti to give an oration extolling Maciel. The oration was well received as was another delivered in defense of Maciel by João Agripino, who had been chosen to take over as presiding officer.[8]

Pro-Quadros delegates, arriving the next afternoon to cast their votes, were applauded by mobs in the streets and crowds in the galleries. In Tiradentes Palace the three-minute ovation for Lacerda was in sharp contrast to the boos for pro-Juracy delegates Mário Martins, Gabriel Passos, and Seixas Doria (of Sergipe). In the balloting, Quadros defeated Juracy by 205 to 83 votes, and Maciel, unopposed, received 255 votes (but not the vote of Lacerda).[9]

At the night session, rose petals were thrown and hundreds of white handkerchiefs were waved when Quadros entered together with Leandro Maciel and Eduardo Gomes. Lacerda, in a speech to greet the delegates in the name of the Carioca *udenistas*, called Quadros the brother of Brazilians in every corner of the republic he would visit, starting with Acre. Lacerda spoke of the hopeful sentiments that could be detected on the sweaty faces of common men, looking forward to the "era of a truly new republic, with the dismissal of guile, deceit, trickery and everything that degraded and corrupted its predecessors, a republic of which this city may or may not be the capi-

Quadros adds the UDN to his party support. Lott nearby. (Hilde Weber drawing in *O Estado de S. Paulo,* November 10, 1959)

tal—a matter of the least importance—but a republic worthy of the Carioca people."

Quadros was deliriously acclaimed when he held aloft the flags of Brazil and the UDN and vowed that in his hands "the flag of the UDN will not fail." The acclaim continued throughout his delivery of a speech devoted principally to listing his dislikes (dictatorships, demagoguery, deceit, administrative disorder, and antisocial large landholdings) and his likes (sound money, Petrobrás, foreign policy without tutelage, free enterprise circumscribed for the common good, and the rule of the constitution). "Let us build," he concluded, "the republic of the dreams of its creators: Christian, indivisible, serene, prosperous, and democratic."[10] *Udenistas,* convinced that at long last they would win a national election, waved hundreds of brooms.

While the UDN held its convention, Carlos' father Maurício de Lacerda, a founder of the Carioca UDN, felt anxious about the health of Aglaiss Caminha, with whom he had been living for about three decades after leaving Olga. The 71-year-old orator had retired from his legal post in the Federal District government in 1958 and was working on his memoirs. Told that Aglaiss' heart condition would kill her, he was struck by a heart attack himself and died on November 23. Their son, Maurício Caminha de Lacerda, could not give the news to Aglaiss because of the seriousness of her condition. A letter, left by Maurício to Maurício Caminha de Lacerda urged him to harbor no grudges against Mauricinho, Vera, and Carlos, the children of Maurício and Olga.

The crowd that passed before the body of Maurício at the Municipal

Chamber building included Eduardo Gomes, Raul Pilla, Carlos Luz, and hundreds of admirers who recalled the stirring speeches made by the former congressman during the Old Republic. Among those who spoke at the burial, in the family plot at the São João Batista Cemetery, were Congressman Meneses Cortes and former journalist Hélio Silva, who had been writing about the Estado Novo in the *Tribuna.* The press carried tributes expressed by Otávio Mangabeira, Afonso Arinos, and others. An unsigned *Tribuna* editorial, "Champion of Public Liberties," reviewed the political activities of Maurício and concluded that the memory of them brought to mind an era of Brazilian public life, "made of sacrifices, flights of fancy, indefatigable vigilance, successive deceptions, unmatched eloquence, and unexcelled bravery."

Carlos, loyal to Olga, had seen little of his father, despite efforts at reconciliation by Maurício. However, according to the recollection of Maurício Caminha de Lacerda, the first four chapters of Maurício's memoirs were dictated at the home of Aglaiss to Carlos, who typed them. They appeared in the *Tribuna* on November 24, 25, 26, and 27, under the title of "Pages of the childhood of Maurício de Lacerda."[11]

8. The Candidate Resigns (November 25, 1959)

At Magalhães Pinto's Rio apartment on the night of November 9, Jânio Quadros assured Leandro Maciel and other *udenistas* that he would carry out his entire campaign at Maciel's side. He would, he said, work out some formula with Fernando Ferrari.[1]

A formula would be difficult to arrange. If politicians could dismiss Maciel as hardly a formidable opponent of Goulart, it was otherwise with Ferrari, whose prestige was at a peak. While the UDN held its convention, Ferrari handed the official wing of the PTB a spectacular defeat by securing, or helping secure, the election of his candidate as mayor of Porto Alegre. Arriving in Rio on November 9, he spoke with confidence about his recently formed Movimento Trabalhista Renovador (MTR). He called it a "true" labor movement capable of vastly increasing the ranks of the PDC. "At least half the present PTB voting strength," he said, "should join the PDC."[2]

Quadros, after campaigning with Maciel in Santa Catarina, met in São Paulo with Ferrari and PDC leaders to work out arrangements with them. In doing so, he announced his adherence to Ferrari's MTR and agreed that Ferrari might campaign at his side in the group scheduled to leave for Acre and other northern points on November 28. The presence of Ferrari, Jânio said, should not harm the UDN or affect his commitment to it.[3]

UDN leaders in Rio reacted violently and even threatened to leave any platform from which Ferrari might speak. They maintained that neither Ferrari, election opponent of Maciel, nor his labor wing had any organization in the north and wanted simply to make use of the UDN organization and Quadros' popularity. Then Quadros, resting in Santos, told reporters he was not adhering to the MTR and Ferrari would not accompany him to

Acre. On the next day Ferrari added to the confusion by saying he would make the trip to Acre. Magalhães Pinto pointed out that Jânio had agreed to have a single running mate, chosen by the UDN.[4]

In São Paulo on November 23, the Partido Trabalhista Nacional (PTN) nominated Quadros for president. Two days later Magalhães Pinto and Leandro Maciel came to São Paulo to discuss, at Quintanilha Ribeiro's home, the trip north. The presidential candidate, explaining his concessions to the PDC, said he found the PDC's André Franco Montoro insatiably ambitious and Ferrari, following the Porto Alegre election, intransigent. The *udenistas* resigned themselves to the presence of Ferrari in Acre and Maciel agreed to appear at Ferrari's side there. It was, Maciel felt, a harmonious meeting, due in part to his own concession. Others, such as Magalhães Pinto, agreed that it was a meeting "without incidents."[5]

Lacerda, although not present, described the scene to reporters as tragicomic and "worthy of an English humorist": "In the midst of attention to the present drama of Brazil—with the people in hunger and on the verge of desperation—the discussion was whether Sr. Leandro Maciel should speak at the UDN headquarters in Acre and Sr. Fernando Ferrari should speak on the platform or whether Sr. Fernando Ferrari should not speak on the platform but in the hotel; or whether Sr. Fernando Ferrari should go in the plane with Sr. Jânio Quadros, without later speaking on the platform, or whether, on the other hand, he should not travel with Sr. Jânio Quadros but should speak in the hotel, or at the UDN headquarters, or in some other place, or in no place. That is to say, an extremely polished, elegant, well-mannered duel about electoral touchiness occurred while the people were hoping these citizens would save Brazil."[6]

Quadros left the meeting after asking whether he should issue a written declaration calling Maciel his running mate. Then he wrote Maciel a warm letter, full of praise. He referred to him as "my candidate for the vice-presidency" and said he would not start campaigning unless they could do so together "from the first moment."[7]

But that evening Quadros wrote another letter, this one to Magalhães Pinto to announce his withdrawal as a candidate. He telephoned Quintanilha Ribeiro at 9:00 P.M., asking him to make the letter known to the press. In the letter, which Magalhães Pinto picked up later at the home of Abreu Sodré, Jânio said, "If it is difficult at this stage to achieve the indispensable harmony among the political currents and parties seeking new directions for Brazil," it "will be impossible" in the government to satisfy "the demands of the people and the needs of Brazilians." A letter from Jânio to Governor Carvalho Pinto, which appeared in the press a little later, called the resignation "unappealable" and said "It is better to be a free citizen than a prisoner in the presidency."[8]

Hundreds of thousands of Brazilians, in a campaign headed by the Movimento Popular Jânio Quadros, signed appeals to Quadros to return. The step he had taken, picturing himself unhappy with politicians, did nothing to dim his popularity, and the clamor for his return was intense.

Lacerda wrote in the *Tribuna* that Quadros was not alone in "reaching the limit of disgust. I, too. And many others." In his articles and declarations to the press, Lacerda assailed politicians and parties. Only several months later, in a letter to Júlio de Mesquita Filho, did he put the blame fully on the shoulders of Magalhães Pinto, whom he described as an evasive schemer and liar, favorable to a "national union" presidential candidacy "with Kubitschek & Co." "The episode of the resignation of Jânio Quadros," Lacerda contended in his letter to Mesquita, "was carefully put together by Magalhães Pinto." In explaining the charge, Lacerda wrote, somewhat weakly, that Magalhães Pinto "*knew* that Jânio Quadros had decided to resign if, in that indescribable conversation in São Paulo about the speakers' platform, no agreement was reached" and that the party president had failed to reveal, at a crucial moment, Jânio's wish to speak alone with Maciel.[9]

As Maciel maintained, Jânio's decision to resign may have been premeditated, and the presidential candidate may have resolved to do so even though the meeting at Quintanilha's home gave him less reason than he might have expected.[10] Lacerda, explaining the resignation to reporters on November 27, said it did not result from that "polite" scene but from many months in which Quadros was submitted to "a real process of maceration, flung from one side to another, solicited on all sides, forced to commit himself even with promises of appointments. . . . And during that time, Jânio Quadros was also submitted to the conceit, ambition, and crack-brained careerism of Fernando Ferrari." In the *Tribuna,* Lacerda said the Ferrari problem could have been avoided if the UDN had held its convention in August, and he called the Maciel candidacy an error. Writing about Maciel, whom he considered "a backland colonel without knowledge," he said he would not "reprimand the eminent Sergipe political chief. He will do so himself if his modesty allows. I simply understand that neither he nor anyone . . . can convince the electorate, even the exclusively *udenista* electorate, to vote for someone it does not know, merely in order to be agreeable to a social gathering of honorary political commanders."[11]

Lacerda told reporters that if Quadros did not withdraw his resignation "there will be no elections in Brazil." Discussing possible consequences, he spoke of military dictatorship and civil war. He issued an appeal to Quadros, whose whereabouts was unknown, calling him the last hope of the people. "All Brazilian politicians," he said, "should forget selfish ideas and give Jânio his post of commander and leader."[12]

Leandro Maciel, informed of Quadros' resignation, decided to submit his own and return to Aracaju. But when he learned what Lacerda was writing about him in the *Tribuna,* he changed his mind and called on the UDN to refute the Carioca congressman. In Rio, he released the contents of Jânio's letter of praise and said he would only withdraw if the party accepted Jânio's resignation.[13]

Juracy Magalhães, asked by reporters to comment on the situation, said: "Like all Brazilians, I learned, without surprise, the news of Jânio Quadros resigning his candidacy. Many more episodes will take place."[14]

9. The Candidate Reconsiders (December 5, 1959)

Magalhães Pinto, expressing "surprise and stupefaction," returned to Rio to confer with the UDN directorship. But before leaving for the national capital with Leandro Maciel, he phoned Lacerda, asking him to come to São Paulo. This Lacerda did on November 26, in the company of Napoleão de Alencastro Guimarães, a vice-president of the Movimento Popular Jânio Quadros.[1]

At the residence of lawyer Oscar Pedroso Horta, where Quadros supporters gathered, Lacerda found Quintanilha Ribeiro doubtful that Quadros would reconsider. A handwritten note from Quadros to Lacerda seemed to confirm Quintanilha's pessimism: "In all of this, believe me, it was an honor to know you better. I shall not forget our association. With my conscience at peace and with a position that is irrevocable, I know that you, later on, will be able to understand me."[2]

That understanding was to become an unsympathetic one, as is evident from Lacerda's account, given years later, about his moments at Pedroso Horta's residence on November 26, 1959. According to Lacerda's account, Pedroso Horta called Quadros "an unpredictable, crazy person"; and Lacerda added that Quintanilha Ribeiro, "one of Jânio's few sincere friends," could not be moved to reveal Jânio's hiding place even though Lacerda threatened to use television to "denounce that clown, that charlatan, that liar." The only result of the threat, Lacerda recalled, was such a large flow of tears from Quintanilha that the floor became wet. "I have never seen anyone cry so."[3]

Suddenly, Lacerda also recalled, a phone call for him from Jânio's daughter Dirce Maria ("Tutu") informed him that Jânio was at the home of industrialist Selmi Dei. Together with Quintanilha Ribeiro, Alencastro Guimarães, and the *Diário de Notícias'* João Ribeiro Dantas, Lacerda called on Quadros. When Quadros said, "I cannot submit to those people," Lacerda replied, "I have the same loathing for them, but either you dirty your hands or you don't enter political life. If we win a large vote, you can govern without commitments to anyone. Stop making promises to politicians and make them to the people." Quadros, stating that he had a more serious reason for resigning, took his guests to a bedroom where his wife, Eloá, was suffering from what Lacerda has said was an inflamed throat. "I have good reason to suppose the inflammation is cancer," Quadros said.[4]

Lacerda, who adds that Quadros' fear was fortunately unfounded, describes the lunch that followed, with Quadros "disclosing all his plans for the presidency," such as agreements with foreign creditors and labor union reform. Alencastro Guimarães said Quadros would receive votes of the Getulistas; and João Ribeiro Dantas, who hoped to become foreign minister, discussed African and Asian matters with Quadros at length.[5]

In Rio, Juracy supporter Mário Martins started a movement to hold a new UDN nominating convention. Therefore on November 27 Lacerda phoned Magalhães Pinto to ask for forty-eight hours to work out a solution, during which time UDN national directors were to make no pronouncements.[6]

Magalhães Pinto agreed. But Lacerda made no progress in his work. On the twenty-eighth Quadros released a "Proclamation to the Brazilian People" in which he said his resignation was irrevocable. He absolved the parties and their leaders from blame and spoke of his own temperamental weaknesses. He also declared that "in the web of hurt feelings, of frustrations, of suspicions that has become interwoven around me, I have no way of carrying out the electoral campaign, and if, by some miracle, I should carry it out, I would be unable to lead the nation with the freedom and security that are indispensable."[7]

Lacerda blamed the situation on Ferrari. Using a São Paulo radio and television broadcast (untroubled by censorship) to announce the completion of "the first part" of his work "to revive the Quadros candidacy," he called Ferrari a "progovernment man" trying to campaign on an opposition ticket. Then on the twenty-ninth, before returning to Rio, he told the press that Quadros, speaking with him on the previous night, had blamed the situation on Ferrari's intransigence. Ferrari's response was to announce that he would campaign without appearing with Quadros, whom he would continue to support.[8]

Meeting in Rio with the UDN directorship, Lacerda reported that he had found in Quadros a sincere person who was certainly not immature. He quoted Quadros as wishing to govern Brazil "in a revolutionary way and with the parties when they understand that they exist to serve the nation and not vice versa." Quadros, Lacerda also said, had admitted to having wrongfully made promises to reach the São Paulo governorship and had added, "Now I don't need to do so because I have a majority of the electorate." Lacerda blamed the crisis on the PDC, a "party of seven congressmen," whose Franco Montoro "is Jânio's greatest enemy."[9]

Lacerda told the UDN directors of his own dedication to the party, but in the *Tribuna* he attacked it. On the other hand, he suddenly heaped praises on Fernando Ferrari and Leandro Maciel. Ferrari, Lacerda wrote, had been "the victim of UDN demands" and had been so meritorious in agreeing to campaign on his own that he would probably be elected vice-president. *Tribuna* readers, who read on November 30 that Maciel was "unpardonably naïve," learned on December 1 that he and Lacerda had "settled their differences." "If he remains a candidate," Lacerda wrote, "he will have my vote. More than my vote, he has my respect."[10]

Lacerda called the UDN the party "from which I shall be expelled any day now," the party "that publishes denials, such as the one saying the president of the untouchable, oppositionist UDN was not with Sr. Kubitschek, a denial that is a lie because during the very week of the convention he was with him in the tabernacle of the opposition, which is now Catete Palace." With Magalhães Pinto in mind, he denounced those who used press agents and economic power, those who, being unable to speak, murmured and, being unable to unite, caused disunity. He reported that the UDN was at work on a formula, "an internal regulation for a brawl of politicians," that was unlikely to achieve its goal of persuading Quadros to renew his candidacy. "I have just about concluded," Lacerda wrote, "that Jânio Quadros ought not to return."[11]

The progovernment *Diário Carioca* wrote that Magalhães Pinto's success was not the result of economic power but of "pertinacity, good sense, and equilibrium, attributes that cause Carlos Lacerda so much horror." It added that Lacerda was attracted to *Janismo* (the Quadros movement) because it was unbalanced and exasperating and because he failed to understand that Quadros was simply using him. "When Jânio surprises him with a well-applied kick, Lacerda will not hesitate to use again, against his idol of today, the language that with so much inspiration he used in those days when he said Quadros was loathsome on the outside and loathsome on the inside."

"One cannot suppose," the *Diário Carioca* also wrote, that Lacerda "suffers remorse from time to time, for that would be to assume an ethical basis for his attitudes, whereas they have only a hysterical basis. His incoherence and folly have been exhaustively examined by the men who . . . were always perplexed to see the eulogies of yesterday transformed into the aggressions of today. . . . Leandro Maciel, who, in an interval of two or three days, has seen himself treated with indifference, with love, with hatred, and again with love, has completed a rapid and concentrated course about Carlos Lacerda."[12]

The Movimento Popular Jânio Quadros continued collecting signatures on its petitions to Quadros, while São Paulo Governor Carvalho Pinto continued to work with politicians on formulas for bringing the apparently temperamental candidate back to the electoral contest. Finally a formula, acceptable to Quadros, was revealed to party leaders in Rio on December 3. It required the four parties supporting Quadros (UDN, PDC, PTN, and PL) to sign a letter recognizing that Quadros supported only the vice-presidential candidate nominated by the UDN and that the PDC could have

Ademar de Barros, presidential candidate of the PSP. (Hilde Weber drawing in *O Estado de S. Paulo,* November 15, 1959)

its own vice-presidential candidate. It called for an interparty commission to plan the campaign and was accompanied by a protocol declaring that the PDC vice-presidential candidate would not participate in the rallies arranged by the commission. The formula left the UDN and Leandro Maciel well pleased.[13]

Quadros, on receiving the documents from Carvalho Pinto, wrote the São Paulo governor that his decision to resign, planned as an example of unselfishness, had been "exploited shamefully by ruthless adversaries, incapable of altruism." Noting that "the situation of the collectivity" was worsening day by day, Quadros wrote that he would run for president, "with a firmness and loyalty appropriate for the hopes of our people."[14]

Lacerda, who had returned to São Paulo, this time to autograph copies of his recently published *Xanam e Outras Histórias,* praised the "worthy decision" reached by "parties striving to save the country." Magalhães Pinto and the UDN, he said, had revealed their patriotism in signing the letter suggested by Carvalho Pinto.[15]

10. The Aragarças Revolt (December 3–4, 1959)

The political confusion brought about by the withdrawal of Quadros from the presidential race persuaded air force Lieutenant Colonel João Paulo Moreira Burnier and a few other conspirators that the time had come to carry out their long-postponed rebellion for the reformation of Brazil by a military "Revolutionary Command."[1] The plotters included air force Lieutenant Colonel Haroldo Veloso, the member of the 1954 Lacerda protection group who had led the Jacareacanga revolt of 1956, and army Colonel Luís Mendes da Silva, a World War II veteran.

On December 2, 1959, at Burnier's request, conspiring lawyer Luís Mendes de Morais Neto updated a draft of a manifesto he had prepared for Veloso earlier.[2] In its revised form it declared that force and corruption ruled the nation, which had reached an unparalleled state of disorder, and that "adepts of Communism, . . . in and out of public administration, seek to gain the maximum out of the misery and hunger of the people, in order to implant their regime of human slavery." Otávio Mangabeira was mentioned as having advised the young officers to revolt, and Quadros was said to have demonstrated that revolution was the only way to free Brazil from the group that dominated and ruined it. Dated December 3, the manifesto was signed the "Revolutionary Command."[3]

At about 4:00 A.M. on December 3, air force Colonel Gustavo Borges came to Lacerda's new apartment, at Praia do Flamengo 224, with a copy of the manifesto. He advised that Veloso and others were starting the rebellion by flying planes from Rio and Belo Horizonte to the interior and wanted to know if Lacerda would join them. Carlos told Letícia he was inclined to do so, but she convinced him that it would be useless and foolish. Then Carlos began to wonder whether the affair were not the result of provocative work by individuals who wanted the elections called off and had therefore infiltrated among his "brave companions" of the air force. He expressed this fear in making his decision known to his visitor and said that, after enough time had passed to allow the revolutionaries to get safely on their way, he would alert the country.[4]

After Borges left, Lacerda spoke with Eduardo Gomes, whose apartment was in the same building, and the *brigadeiro* phoned the Galeão Air Base and learned that three air force C-47s (DC-3s) had left Rio. Lacerda gave the planes a couple of hours and then phoned several congressmen and they came to his apartment. One was Chamber of Deputies First Secretary José Bonifácio de Andrada (UDN, Minas Gerais), who was asked by Lacerda to open the doors of Congress lest they be "closed for a long time." José Bonifácio phoned Chamber of Deputies President Ranieri Mazzilli, who in turn advised Justice Minister Armando Falcão.[5]

Soon UDN leader João Agripino arrived at the apartment with his brother, also a UDN congressman. Another who came at Lacerda's request was War Minister Lott's friend Bento Gonçalves Filho (PR, Minas Gerais), president of the Parliamentary Nationalist Front. Lacerda explained the situation to his political adversary and said steps should be taken so that a state of siege not be enacted as the result of an uprising that, while perhaps heroic, was irresponsible and politically dangerous. The nationalist congressman phoned the war minister from Lacerda's apartment and later called on him.[6]

By 8:30 A.M. the rebel planes, several from Rio and Belo Horizonte, had landed at Aragarças, a town of ten thousand on the Goiás–Mato Grosso border, three hundred miles west of the tumultuous construction activity of Brasília. They were joined by a Panair Constellation, whose commercial flight from Rio to Belém, Pará, had been interrupted because air force Major Éber Teixeira Pinto had used a revolver to force the pilot to fly with his thirty-five passengers to Aragarças. The conspirators wanted a craft with a long flight range. They also wanted Veloso, who had flown to Aragarças from Rio, to take control of areas in the north that he had dominated during his Jacareacanga revolt. But the rebel of 1956 could do nothing; he found government forces in control of the Jacareacanga airport and unfriendly rebels momentarily running things at Santarém, Pará.[7]

While the rebels at Aragarças were joined by the Panair Constellation, oppositionist congressmen conferred in Lacerda's congressional office.[8] Lacerda showed them the revolutionaries' manifesto, and he showed it also to Congressman Aderbal Jurema (PSD, Pernambuco), a friend from student days who had traveled with him in the northeast during the war. Aderbal's brother Abelardo Jurema (PSD, Paraíba) was the congressional majority leader.

In São Paulo, Jânio Quadros declared that "even the greatest courage, even the purest ideals" could not justify insurrection, and he called on his countrymen to adhere to constitutional ways and use the ballot boxes to achieve better days. Otávio Mangabeira, the only political figure to support the revolt openly, remarked in the Senate that Brazil needed men of character, like Veloso.[9]

On December 4, federal paratroopers moved on Aragarças and the rebels took flight in their planes, most of them going to Paraguay and Bolivia. Éber

Teixeira Pinto got aboard the Panair Constellation with its Belém-bound passengers and forced the pilot to take it to Buenos Aires.[10]

Kubitschek, in a radio address, said the Aragarças rebels, unlike those of Jacareacanga, would be rigorously punished. Lacerda, autographing copies of his book in São Paulo, remarked that he would believe in punishment for the rebels only when punishment was decreed for Vice President Goulart. "Sincerely and honestly," Afonso Arinos said, "we cannot declare that the young military men are criminals who should be cursed and punished by those responsible for the nation's political life."[11]

Although Kubitschek said no evidence existed to show that the political opposition had supported the uprising, congressmen belonging to the government majority tried to implicate Lacerda. Majority leader Abelardo Jurema, "speaking in the name of the government," blamed Lacerda directly.[12]

According to accounts in some of the press, Lacerda had known about the revolt three days before it took place. The Communists' *Novos Rumos* described Lacerda as "fully involved" in the uprising, designed to stage a coup if Jânio did not return to the presidential race and to create so much danger for the institutions that Jânio might decide to return. With Jânio's decision to return, *Novos Rumos* wrote, Lacerda and "other terrorists of the Lantern Club" abandoned the rebels to their fate and even denounced their plans in an effort to avoid being suspected of involvement. Thus, the Communist weekly wrote, Lacerda revealed once more his habit of squealing on associates.[13]

In Congress on December 7 Lacerda related what he had done on the morning of the uprising and said he could not remain silent while some accused him of involvement in the revolt and others called him a betrayer. Wishing to avoid naming the military officer who had visited him before dawn on the third, he made no mention of the visit and said that, after being awakened by a noise, he had found the revolutionary manifesto under the door of his apartment. Miguel Bahury (PSD, Maranhão) interrupted to say that Lacerda lived in a luxurious building that must have had a doorman or porter able to identify whoever left the manifesto at 4:00 A.M.[14]

"Perhaps," Bahury said, "my question is innocent, but it is very useful for revealing the position of Your Excellency." Lacerda provoked laughter by observing that "nothing Your Excellency does is innocent, you know that." Bahury kept pressing for information about Lacerda's "friend." "And if a friend were there," Lacerda replied, "does Your Excellency have the insolence to believe I would give you his name here?"

Bahury, denying insolence, expressed his belief that "Your Excellency, instead of being innocent, was involved in the bloody affair." He added that Lacerda had declared earlier that if Quadros did not withdraw his resignation within forty-eight hours, blood would flow. "Is this not an encouragement for attempted coups?" Bahury asked. Lacerda changed the subject by accusing Bahury of having used his mandate to obtain money from NOVACAP, the government company building Brasília. Bahury retaliated by accusing Lacerda of "living off a money-losing newspaper financed by the sale of stock to the unwary." He also called Lacerda a betrayer who had "squealed in the past when you were a Communist." During the exchange of insults, Bahury asked Lacerda to "answer my question and prove you're not a *golpista.*"

After José Bonifácio de Andrada, the presiding officer, brought the exchange to a close, Lacerda concluded his speech by stating that "within the government, more than outside it, forces can be found that are interested in provoking acts of desperation" with the single objective of guaranteeing that a clique, which held power thirty years, would "continue holding that power with impunity."[15]

Justice Minister Armando Falcão, addressing Congress for over two hours on December 10, made sensational charges based on subversive documents.[16] With the UDN worrying lest the administration call for a state of siege, Lacerda correctly pointed out that not all Falcão's documents were related to the Aragarças revolt, and he recalled the false Cohen Plan, used to usher in a state of siege.[17]

From La Paz, Bolivia, came the voice of Burnier: "Our movement achieved its objective with the decision of Jânio Quadros, who has popular support, not to withdraw." Burnier, Lacerda recalled later, "considered me a traitor at the time of Aragarças," and lawyer Luís Mendes de Morais Neto, who was jailed in Brazil in December 1959, continued, as before, to be unfriendly. But Veloso never criticized Lacerda.[18]

In December and January the government arrested air force officers felt to have favored the Aragarças uprising and it exerted pressure on Paraguay to expel the exiles, forcing Veloso and Luís Mendes da Silva to go to Argentina. In April 1960 the congressional majority blocked the opposition's proposal that the Aragarças rebels be granted amnesty. The rebels, planning to remain in exile until Quadros was victorious, signed a manifesto asking that no one support amnesty on their behalf. The ideals that had inspired them in 1959, they stated, continued strong.[19]

11. Absence from Brazil (December 1959–March 1960)

With the *Tribuna* about to observe its tenth anniversary in December 1959, Lacerda hoped Jânio Quadros would attend the commemorative lunch at the Engineers Club of Rio. Luiz Ernesto Kawall, of the *Tribuna*'s São Paulo office, arrived in Rio without the candidate but with a handwritten note from him. Read to the gathering by Roberto de Abreu Sodré, it described "the great Carlos Lacerda" and his fellow-workers at the *Tribuna* as "those few idealists and patriots to whom we already owe so much."[1]

The *Tribuna*'s Odilo Costa, filho, supporter of Juracy's bid for the presidential nomination, had left the *Tribuna* during the Aragarças uprising. This had opened the way for 21-year-old Sérgio Lacerda to become superintendent, serving on the directorship with *Tribuna* President Carlos Lacerda, Manager Luís Brunini, and Treasurer Odilon Lacerda Paiva.[2]

Odilon, a Lacerda cousin and the husband of Carlos' sister Vera, was a devotee of the Brazilian Socialist Party (PSB). More orderly in his work than

Carlos, the *Tribuna* treasurer had had his squabbles with his brother-in-law.[3] But despite his reserve, or more likely because of it, relations remained fairly satisfactory. They were mentioned by Carlos in a letter written to Odilon from Paris a few months after Sérgio became the *Tribuna diretor-superintendente.* Lacerda explained that he would have written earlier except for "that same shyness that affects our relations when we are together." He wrote that he detected in Odilon's reserve not only a character trait but also a feeling that Carlos was unappreciative of Odilon's cooperation, and he hastened to assure the *Tribuna*'s longtime officer that his cooperation "in my life and in our work, which is our newspaper," had been "decisive." He praised Odilon's dedication and said his presence provided perhaps the only tranquility in his turbulent life. Reflecting on that life, "with its high points and low points, its rewarding and bitter experiences, equally extreme," Carlos wrote that he was considering changing his ways, becoming less hyperactive.

"Now, with the entry of Sérgio," Carlos added, "I have been considering, and more than once, whether a *Tribuna* position might not also be of interest to Cláudio." Cláudio, the 19-year-old son of Odilon and Vera, had spoken as a boy about becoming a medical doctor, and Carlos mentioned this as a reason for not having brought the matter up earlier.[4] In 1960, Cláudio joined the *Tribuna.*

Lacerda's trip to Europe, made by plane on December 27, was ostensibly to attend a congress of the Moral Rearmament movement in Caux, Switzerland. The real reason for the trip, Lacerda confided to Júlio de Mesquita Filho, was to allow the UDN and particularly its president, Magalhães Pinto, to mend their ways while he remained silent.[5]

Lacerda was not silent before leaving. The press gave so much attention to his contention that the UDN was infected by the spirit of "national union" that Magalhães Pinto wrote Lacerda on December 21 to deny that the UDN had failed to play an oppositionist role. He could not, he also wrote, find "any basis for the divergences that, with so much emphasis, you proclaim are separating us." "Imagine, Carlos, if I were to accuse you of conspiring with the president of the republic against the candidate of the party you headed. You have said this about me."[6]

In a talk with Magalhães Pinto, Lacerda told him "everything I knew, everything I suspected, and everything I thought," undeterred by the arrival, during the conversation, of Afonso Arinos, who, without Lacerda's knowledge, had been invited by Magalhães Pinto. Lacerda told Magalhães Pinto that he could no longer have any trust in him and was going abroad to avoid creating a crisis in the UDN that might hurt the Quadros campaign.[7]

O Jornal, reporting on the talk, wrote that Lacerda had used violent language to attack Magalhães Pinto, Afonso Arinos, and Virgílio Távora. Virgílio Távora, the UDN representative on the Inter-party Commission for the Quadros campaign, responded with a statement in support of Magalhães Pinto.[8]

Lacerda left Brazil in the company of Letícia, Sebastião, and Edgar Flexa Ribeiro, son of the Andrews School proprietor. Before boarding the plane he told reporters that he would "return to join again the campaign of our candidate" after the UDN had reformed itself so that Quadros could have the liberty he needed to become really popular.[9]

On the next day, Magalhães Pinto, in a television speech, stated that "Carlos Lacerda, apparently recognizing his error, wanted to see me before he went to Switzerland, but I preferred to await his return." The UDN president was satisfied that the "friction provoked by Lacerda" had thus been brought to a close. The *Tribuna* at once denied that Lacerda had acknowledged making an error. And it accused Magalhães Pinto of using half-truths, as "has been done so frequently of late in certain areas of the party."[10]

At the Moral Rearmament Congress in Switzerland, Lacerda heard endless testimonies of young people who discussed their triumphs over bad habits. The testimonies and the fanaticism, stridently anti-Communist, bored him, and he left the congress after two days.[11] He was, however, anything but bored by the murder trial in Geneva of Pierre Jaccoud.

Jaccoud, former head of the Swiss Bar Association, was accused of the murder of the father of a young man who had been seeing a woman, with whom, it turned out, the distinguished and married barrister had been having a lengthy affair. As surprising pieces of evidence were presented, resulting at length in a conviction, the defendant was found to have acted in a manner completely at variance with his staid reputation. The trial was the sensation of Europe. Only the Swiss press and people, Lacerda found, rejected emotionalism.[12]

After leaving Switzerland for Austria, France, and Italy, Lacerda continued to follow the trial. His twenty-five *Tribuna* articles, "Drama of Passion in Switzerland," are the work of a first-rate reporter handling a fascinating crime.[13] *Paixão e Crime,* the publication of the articles in book form, may be the most difficult of Lacerda's books to lay aside.

In other articles Lacerda discussed the French possession of Algeria, where, he said, Francophiles had decided to follow the example of Algerian guerrillas who resorted to terrorism. He praised de Gaulle, "faced with the toughest days of his life," for insisting that peace precede any vote to settle Algeria's future status. "If de Gaulle fails," Lacerda wrote, "not only will France be destroyed and Algeria broken up, but the series of African nations that he is liberating will be turned over to Russia—and this, my dear friends, only six hours by plane from Recife."[14]

Lacerda's *Tribuna* articles from abroad touched on Brazilian affairs only when he discussed "the scandal of paper currency." He berated Finance Minister Sebastião Paes de Almeida for favoring two foreign currency printers, Thomas de La Rue of London and the American Banknote Company. After the Brazilian government pointed out that its Casa da Moeda was not yet able to issue urgently needed currency, Lacerda blamed "influential superbureaucrats" for obstinately failing to train Casa da Moeda personnel, and he obtained a letter from the National Bank of Austria offering to train Brazilian technicians free of charge.[15]

The four-month trip abroad, Sebastião recalls, became "one of those vacations in Europe" that Carlos so much enjoyed.[16] Needing little sleep and always on the go, Carlos was an avid tourist, eager to learn as much as he could wherever he traveled. He was fond of making purchases for his family, his friends, and himself and enjoyed dining with groups in well-known restaurants or restaurants he discovered. A congenial host or guest, he made friends easily while abroad and enjoyed partying all night with them.[17]

Letícia, less enthusiastic than Carlos about Paris,[18] was left with friends there early in March while Carlos attended a conference in Puerto Rico following the return of Sebastião and Edgar Flexa Ribeiro to Rio. For her the high point of the vacation was the visit to Italy, where her father had been born. Rome fascinated her.[19]

Despite royalties from *Xanam e Outras Histórias* and payments for articles and translations, the vacation added to the debt owed by Carlos to banks in Rio.[20]

12. Jânio and Others Write from Rio (February–March 1960)

While Lacerda refrained from commenting publicly from abroad on the UDN leadership, he received a flood of letters from Brazil describing disunity in the party. Congressman José Sarney (UDN, Maranhão), writing on February 6 at the suggestion of Sérgio Lacerda, informed Carlos about the "failure" of Quadros' far-flung campaign in the north. Sarney mentioned the "disappearance of opposition in the Chamber of Deputies with the avalanche of propaganda of Juscelino" about the vast highway program to connect Brasília with the north, and he told Lacerda that the UDN, identified by the government as opposed to development, ought to concentrate its attacks not on the development goals but on the amoral methods used, which were enriching a caste. To "reinvigorate" the opposition, Sarney disclosed, a group of *udenistas* was preparing a new movement and was writing Magalhães Pinto to ask that the party become more aggressive, lest it perish.[1]

This Bossa-Nova movement, headed by Sarney and Congressman Clóvis Ferro Costa, also from the far north, hoped to persuade the party to make itself attractive by advocating reforms inspired by a sense of social justice. According to a report sent to Lacerda by a political observer, the new movement was a reaction to the inability of the party to communicate with the people in the face of a "gigantic wave of government propaganda." Quadros himself, the report said, considered his northern excursion a failure, and Magalhães Pinto, seeking an improvement, had arranged to make Virgílio Távora, of Ceará, general coordinator of the Quadros campaign in the place of Quintanilha Ribeiro.[2]

When the UDN national directorship decided the party should continue having a representative on NOVACAP, the government company building Brasília, an angry Adauto Lúcio Cardoso resigned from the UDN directorship, on which he had served for twelve years, and the *Tribuna* accused the party of trying to give coverage to "the business deals and scandals of NOVACAP." Leaders of the Carioca UDN, unveiling a picture of Adauto in their headquarters, spoke of breaking with the party's national organization.[3]

Kubitschek shown as collapsing into scandals, such as those of NOVACAP, "constructor of holes and cesspools." Goulart whistling nearby. (Hilde Weber drawing in *O Estado de S. Paulo*, November 6, 1959)

Dinarte Mariz, UDN governor of Rio Grande do Norte, feared that Magalhães Pinto supported the bid of UDN Secretary-General Aluísio Alves to become the next governor and therefore he joined Lacerdistas who called on Magalhães Pinto to step aside. Writing to Lacerda, he said that Aluísio Alves, who had turned for support to the PSD because of the local situation, had just about moved the UDN headquarters to Armando Falcão's justice ministry. "In truth," he wrote, "Lott's campaign in Rio Grande do Norte is being carried out with the participation of the secretary-general of our party." Dinarte Mariz also felt that the UDN was giving no real support to Quadros and that Magalhães Pinto's party administration was unfavorably affected by his candidacy for the Minas governorship. He told the Rio press that after the murder of Virgílio de Melo Franco, the party had had only two outstanding figures, Juracy Magalhães and Carlos Lacerda, neither of whom was in the campaign.[4]

Minas Gerais, a leading beneficiary of the Kubitschek development programs, was of great importance to the Quadros campaign, and Magalhães Pinto's strength there could not be overlooked by *udenistas*.[5] As Lacerda learned from his anti–Magalhães Pinto correspondents, those who wished to overturn the party president had in mind another Mineiro, Pedro Aleixo, as a replacement. They also wanted Lacerda to return to the opposition leadership in Congress. "We of the opposition," an unhappy *udenista* campaigner wrote to Lacerda, "are in an ungoverned ship, in the midst of a tempest—and without a COMMANDER."[6] Lacerda, however, showed no sign of wanting to return to the struggle. Responding to Meneses Cortes' offer to step aside in his favor in the first election for a governor of Guanabara, Lacerda called himself "a man expelled from politics." He advised Meneses Cortes that he was not inclined to run for anything, with politics as they were.[7]

In March, Jânio Quadros made it clear he would not follow the example of Lott in declining Fidel Castro's invitation to spend a week in Cuba. "In the Antilles," he told reporters, "a fact of the greatest importance has occurred: power has been taken over by an honorable man, a courageous man, with whom we might disagree, but whose virtues we cannot deny."[8] Busy planning his trip, Quadros arranged to be accompanied by a group of over forty, including Afonso Arinos, Adauto Lúcio Cardoso, Castilho Cabral, the PDC's Paulo de Tarso Santos, and state legislators Francisco Julião (of the "peasant leagues") and Juracy Magalhães Júnior. Among the members of the press were João Ribeiro Dantas, Hélio Fernandes, Luís Carlos Mesquita, Carlos Castello Branco, and Murilo Melo Filho.

Quadros invited Sérgio Lacerda to join him on the Cuban trip, but Sérgio, much as he wanted to accept, declined because Carlos opposed Jânio's plan to visit Castro. Quadros told Sérgio he wanted also to invite writers Rubem Braga and Fernando Sabino, whom he did not know, and Sérgio brought them together with the candidate at the Lacerda apartment. Both accepted the invitation to accompany Quadros to Cuba.[9]

In the Lacerda apartment Jânio learned that Sérgio was going to Bahia to see his fiancée, a daughter of Clemente Mariani. And so, explaining that he had a bad wrist, he dictated to Sérgio a warm letter for delivery to Juracy Magalhães. In another letter dictated to Sérgio, this one for Carlos, Quadros said, "Your disapproval of my trip to Cuba arrived late or I would have considered it." This letter, dictated in the presence of Quintanilha Ribeiro, Rubem Braga, and Sebastião Lacerda, expressed Jânio's surprise at the length of time Carlos was remaining abroad. "You and a few others," he said, "threw me into this bonfire once again, after I had secured my freedom in a moment of rare courage. Only God knows the difficulties I have had in this struggle. Indifference, selfishness, ambitions, jealousy, and pure malice are causing me terrible damage, psychologically even more than electorally."

"Now," Quadros also dictated, "I read that you speak of desisting. I shall do nothing to impede your decision. What I affirm, however, is that you will not reach that decision without our both acting in that way together, such is the irritation and agony that afflicts me in this campaign. Note this well because it expresses how I feel." Quadros pointed out that Carlos had for years concerned himself with national politics, whereas he had limited himself to one state and therefore was not familiar with the injustices suffered by Carlos and could be excused for making errors in the larger area. But how, he asked, could he have consulted Carlos about such matters as the Cuban trip when he had not received a single line from him?[10]

While Carlos and Letícia traveled by ship to Brazil late in March, Quadros made his trip to Cuba, with the hearty approval of Magalhães Pinto, Leandro Maciel, and the newly formed Bossa-Nova renovating wing of the UDN.[11] For his Brazilian guests, Fidel Castro listed Cuba's principal export products (Raúl Castro adding "and revolution!").[12] Fidel had recently disappeared during a political squabble and then returned dramatically, "reclaimed by the people," apparently more popular than ever. Quadros, fascinated by the episode, kept asking Cubans for explanations.[13]

During the visit, the Cuban newspaper *Combate* quoted Quadros as saying that the Export-Import Bank of Washington was using a form of extortion against Brazil, whereupon Quadros denied making any statement about Brazilian affairs while outside the country. But João Ribeiro Dantas told journalists in Havana that the remark represented Quadros' "private opinion." When Quadros accepted an invitation to spend two days in Venezuela, reports blamed the curtailment of the Cuban trip on the Havana press, intent on publishing headlines making him appear hostile to the United States.[14]

Quadros said the reports were untrue. Back in Brazil he extolled Cuba, its "press freedom," and Castro, thus gaining support among student organizations and others leaning to the Left. To accuse the Cuban revolutionary government of being Communist, he said, was to reveal bad faith and ignorance because that government showed "absolute respect for property and juridical rules." He insisted that Che Guevara was not a Communist but, "very much to the contrary, first and foremost a democrat with socialist tendencies." Quadros declared that the enemies of Cuba's new regime, shot after judgments by "revolutionary tribunals," had been "really criminals."

It was, Quadros said, a serious error to judge Cuba at a distance and from newspaper stories. He added that, in order to speak about Cuban "reality," one had to visit Cuba, as he had done.[15]

13. While *Udenistas* Brawl, Maciel Resigns (April 1960)

Lacerda returned to Rio early in April in an aggressive mood. In his first appearance in Congress, he pleased his constituents by arguing that to move the capital to Brasília on the scheduled date of April 21 would be "a crime" because Brasília was in no condition to function. While seeking unsuccessfully to have a law enacted to keep Congress in Rio until after the October 3 elections, he pointed out that 150 million cruzeiros had been allocated to pay for dances and parties at the Brasília inauguration at a time when starving Ceará flood victims were still awaiting 80 million cruzeiros promised for their relief. Quadros, on the other hand, praised the transfer of the capital, and Magalhães Pinto announced that the UDN, cooperating with the "spirit of Brasília," would move its headquarters there.[1]

Renewing his attacks on Magalhães Pinto, Lacerda wrote that the Mineiro had failed to give promised support to Juracy Magalhães at the UDN convention and had then turned against Lacerda, thus defeating the two companions of the Caravana da Liberdade who had brought the UDN to the people. Full of praise for Leandro Maciel, he told the press that the first phase of the UDN plot to prevent Quadros' election would be Maciel's forced withdrawal. Magalhães Pinto, he wrote in the *Tribuna,* was using his bank, the Banco Nacional de Minas Gerais, to influence the press in favor of the Kubitschek administration. Journalists, "corrupted" by Magalhães Pinto, were described by Lacerda as hiding Magalhães Pinto's "scandalous" interest in the SIMCA motorcar company and spreading false rumors, such as a reported decision of Belo Horizonte *udenistas* to prohibit Lacerda from campaigning for Quadros in Minas.[2]

An irate Magalhães Pinto denied making use of "economic power" and pointed out that a debt of millions of cruzeiros, owed his bank by the *Tribuna*, did not prevent Lacerda's newspaper from attacking him daily and unfairly. He explained that his investment in SIMCA, which had helped bring the automobile company to Minas, had been made at the suggestion of the president of Brazil's National Steel Company.[3]

UDN congressional leader João Agripino was worried, as he wrote Lacerda, that the party was squabbling so ferociously that it might stupidly toss aside a victory it had a splendid chance to win. And he insisted that Lacerda was unjust in accusing his companions of being ineffective oppositionists.

Lacerda, in his response, called it unfair to blame him for the crisis. He described himself to Agripino as "merely one of the victims of the crisis" and wrote that he was being "smashed to pieces in the press" in an "unequal combat" carried on while his companions remained silent. With a continuation of the battle, he told Agripino, "I shall succumb, for I have not the resistance, not even financially, to carry on with this struggle."[4]

Agripino then spoke with Magalhães Pinto and persuaded him to set up a new UDN campaign commission, made up of Lacerda, Bilac Pinto, and Benedito Calasans. The new commission, Lacerda wrote to Júlio de Mesquita Filho, was to replace a former commission, headed by Magalhães Pinto and Aluísio Alves, that "never functioned in its four months." Presumably it was to work with the Inter-party Commission that, according to Lacerda, had also failed to function and was headed by Virgílio Távora, "a pillar of the Juracy candidacy who has joined the Magalhães Pinto scheme."[5]

The new commission, apparently a capitulation by Magalhães Pinto that put the command of the UDN campaign in Lacerda's hands, lasted less than a month. Lacerda attributed its short life to the displeasure expressed by Magalhães Pinto's "nationalist" supporters who had decided to portray the commission as composed of "men of the 'Right.'" The *Tribuna* faulted Gabriel Passos and "nationalists" of the Bossa-Nova.[6]

When Magalhães Pinto, meeting with Lacerda, offered to withdraw from the Quadros campaign and the Minas governorship race, Lacerda's reaction was to call the offer a threat to wreck Quadros' electoral base in Minas. But both Magalhães Pinto and Minas UDN President Oswaldo Pieruccetti told Quadros, in Rio for a rally on April 25, that they would definitely retire from the Quadros campaign unless Lacerda wrote Magalhães Pinto a letter retracting public statements injurious to the UDN president.[7]

The rally in Rio was held after Lacerda, to prevent a setback to the Quadros campaign, agreed to write the letter. It was the first rally at which the presidential candidate campaigned with Lacerda at his side. Lacerda, who had reassumed the presidency of the Carioca UDN, spoke to the thirty thousand applauding Cariocas about the need for a constitutional reform to guarantee for their new state, Guanabara, the receipt of municipal revenues and to avoid dividing it into municipalities, each with a legislature. Quadros called for an agrarian reform based on Christian principles and legal ways rather than the "revolutionary ways of Fidel Castro."[8]

Leandro Maciel was not among the speakers. With his campaign going poorly, he had decided to resign because, he complained bitterly, he had been "abandoned by the party." In his resignation statement, issued on the day of the Rio rally, he expressed his conviction that "flippancy, disloyalty, cunning, and subornation are, unfortunately, weapons that often lead to success in public life." He added that he had favored neither Magalhães Pinto nor Lacerda but had sought harmony.[9]

Lacerda's letter to Magalhães Pinto, written on the day of the rally, was not the retraction of injurious statements that the UDN president wanted. It said that before Magalhães Pinto reached a decision about withdrawing from the Minas gubernatorial race, he should understand that Lacerda was willing to make any sort of amends "that you or the Minas UDN consider necessary, for the sake of Jânio Quadros, whose position I have sought to spare." "I am," Lacerda wrote, "willing to withdraw or remain in politics, an activity I carry out with increasing discomfort and disgust; I am willing to speak or keep silent, leave the UDN or remain in it, write or not write." All he wanted, he pointed out, was Magalhães Pinto's guarantee that, despite appearances, his intentions were guided by the duties and ideals that had once brought them together. In conclusion Lacerda wrote that, although Magalhães Pinto had not given such a guarantee, he would dispense with it "as long as I do not receive the horrible proof that the worst of my assumptions is correct—that is, that your candidacy in Minas will be used as a threat to defeat our cause in a decisive moment."[10]

Lacerda was dismayed to find Magalhães Pinto giving the press "distorted passages" from the letter. When Quadros phoned Lacerda, before dawn on the twenty-sixth, to inform him of the press release, Lacerda told the presidential candidate it was a "glorification of Magalhães Pinto," deserving of ridicule.[11]

At the UDN national directorship meeting, called to handle the problem created by Maciel's resignation, Lacerda spoke of his "repulsion at the behavior of Magalhães Pinto" and demanded "an end to the wave of intrigues and outrages" that "sullied" the life of the UDN. Governors Juracy Magalhães and Cid Sampaio, assisted by Ceará's former Governor Paulo Sarasate, took Lacerda from the meeting room and pleaded that he avoid a clash "whose consequences cannot be foreseen." When they all rejoined the meeting, which Magalhães Pinto directed, Lacerda read the full text of his letter to the UDN president. He said he had gone to Europe to prevent the crisis, but it had broken out during his absence. Then he left the room with the explanation that he was not in agreement with decisions about to be reached. Following his departure, Minas UDN President Pieruccetti listed the troubles Lacerda had given the Minas UDN, starting with his opposition to the Maciel candidacy. Lacerda, he said, had suggested that Magalhães

Pinto withdraw from his election race and UDN post and had accused the UDN in Minas of threatening to deprive Quadros of his electoral base there.

Juracy reminded the gathering that the Minas UDN and Lacerda had been responsible for his defeat at the convention. After he urged that the two stop fighting, the directors adopted a resolution that he drew up with the help of the governors of Pernambuco and Santa Catarina. It recognized the "effort and dedication of Magalhães Pinto" and expressed confidence in "the performance of Carlos Lacerda, Bilac Pinto, and Benedito Calasans, members of the commission charged with directing the UDN campaign."[12]

Lacerda, in a telegram to Pedro Aleixo in Minas, said he might have to bow before the "threats" of Pieruccetti and Magalhães Pinto and refrain from campaigning for Quadros in Minas because he was unable to comply with the demands of the pair that he first give satisfaction to Magalhães Pinto and because his desistance from campaigning in Minas might be the price of preventing the Minas UDN from betraying Quadros and Brazil. He added that "Magalhães Pinto's DIP" (the initials of the censorship organization of the Vargas Estado Novo) had probably been at work in Minas, furnishing falsehoods with the help of the Kubitschek administration, and therefore he would appreciate it if Pedro Aleixo would arrange the publication, in newspapers "that still remain free," of the full text of his letter to Magalhães Pinto. Pedro Aleixo, replying on April 27, said he had attended a Minas UDN meeting at which everyone had agreed to avoid incidents that might hurt the Quadros campaign. He added that under the circumstances he had abstained from furnishing the full text of Lacerda's letter addressed to Magalhães Pinto—"a letter already known to almost all who attended the meeting."[13]

In Rio, Lacerda told the press that "the DIP of the president of the Banco Nacional de Minas Gerais" infamously twisted the truth when it asserted that Quadros was on Magalhães Pinto's side and that Lacerda, at the request of Quadros, had written a letter giving satisfaction to Magalhães Pinto. "The story," Lacerda told reporters, "has a grain of truth; the only thing is that things were completely different." In an editorial, Lacerda wrote that "the UDN crisis is largely due to the way the agents of Magalhães Pinto's economic group are completing, in the press and on the radio, Kubitschek's work of corruption." To get anything published in *Manchete* magazine, Lacerda wrote, one needed permission from Magalhães Pinto's bank or the presidential palace.[14]

After Magalhães Pinto was reported to have insisted that Gabriel Passos would make a good substitute for Leandro Maciel, the *Tribuna* suggested that his purpose was to prevent the vice-presidential candidacy from going to the party favorite, Senator Milton Campos. The Milton Campos candidacy, the *Tribuna* reported, "does not interest Magalhães Pinto politically because it could hurt his negotiations with the Minas PTB and PR about his gubernatorial candidacy."[15]

With most of the UDN leaders, including Lacerda, favoring Milton Campos, Cid Sampaio used Pedro Aleixo's telephone in Belo Horizonte to

A Communist view of Quadros. Courted by multinational girls (Esso, Hanna Mining, and the Light and Power Company), he is described as "the friend of the house (the White House)—and then? What do the girls demand?" (*Novos Rumos*, June 28–July 4, 1960)

speak to the Minas senator and former governor who was in Rome on a trip to attend an Interparliamentary Union conference. When Lacerda phoned Milton Campos a little later, the senator said he preferred not to run but would do so. "If all of you feel my acceptance can be useful to the country, I have no alternative."

Quadros announced that Campos would be his "only and legitimate" running mate. Before leaving to campaign in Minas, he sent warm telegrams to Lacerda and Magalhães Pinto, thanking each for support during his recent stay in the new state of Guanabara.[16]

X.

Candidate for Governor (1960)

1. Entering the Gubernatorial Race (May 1960)

Lacerda, with a recurrence of the throat problem that had troubled him in 1954, underwent X-rays and other tests starting on May 4, and they convinced physicians that an operation was necessary. The outcome of the operation seemed likely to determine whether he would acquiesce to the entreaties of admirers that he run for governor of Guanabara.

On May 10, the day before the operation, Lacerda wrote to the directorship of the Carioca UDN to say that in about ten days he would announce his decision. He pointed out that he lacked the financial resources of other aspirants and might still be affected by the government's ban on his use of radio and television. He suggested that the Carioca UDN consider someone other than himself. But he was by far the party's leading vote-getter in Rio, and, on May 11, all eight UDN municipal councilmen issued a manifesto calling on him to run for governor.[1]

Lacerda's throat trouble prevented him from joining the Quadros campaign in Rio state. Expressing his regret to one of the campaigners, he wrote that he would have welcomed the opportunity to attack Fernando Ferrari, "an impostor, much more so than João Goulart, who is at least authentic."[2] When Quadros visited Lacerda, at the time of the operation, Lacerda gave the presidential candidate a memorandum showing that if Guanabara were to receive three billion cruzeiros from the federal government, to pay for property expropriations, it could extend avenues and the Central do Brasil Railroad, bringing about a much-needed decongestion of traffic. On May 16 Quadros returned the memorandum with a handwritten note approving the plan and promising the money during his mandate "in installments compatible with the national resources."[3]

Lacerda was at home on the evening of the seventeenth, recovering from his operation, when the Carioca UDN directorship decided unanimously to present his name as its gubernatorial candidate at a convention to be held in a month. The directors, having disappointed the once-hopeful Meneses Cortes by their sudden decision, led a procession of about one hundred people to Lacerda's apartment. Lacerda told the gathering that although until then he had not been infected by the blue fly (the desire for high office) he now found himself bitten by it because the directorship had let the fly loose in his home.[4]

Concern about the condition of Lacerda's throat was pretty much dispelled because he launched into a thirty-minute speech to give the gathering an outline of his program for governing. He explained that the *favela* dwellers would be among those to benefit from his plan to improve transportation; and he revealed that Quadros had offered, if elected, to make three billion cruzeiros available for it.[5]

Quadros, visiting Lacerda at his apartment on May 19, publicly confirmed this sentiment. He declared: "Your government for the reconstruction and progress of the new state will have everything possible from my government." Well ahead in the polls, Quadros had by then become the choice of still another party, the Partido Republicano (PR), headed by Artur Bernardes Filho.[6]

Lacerda, announcing his candidacy in a manifesto on May 18, said he would begin his campaign by visiting *favelas*, thus replying to those who believed he was separated from the people "who most need our effort and understanding." Carrying out his promise on May 29, he surprised the *favelados* at the Vila do Vintém, where the PTB was strong. He listened to their grievances, spoke of his plans to improve transportation, and heard a *favelado* sing a samba written in his honor. Lacerda said he hoped at least to convert the Vila do Vintém (Village of the Penny) into the Vila do Cruzeiro.[7]

Following this visit, the first of many to the *favelas*, Lacerda learned that the government would no longer interpret Clause R of broadcasting concession contracts in a way to prevent him from using radio and television. At once he scheduled speeches on Rádio Eldorado and TV Rio for the night of May 30. Supporters, planning a popular outcry in case of a last-minute reimposition of censorship, used telephone books to make calls to thousands of homes to advise of Lacerda's return to broadcasting. In his speeches, which censors did not disturb, Lacerda described transportation, education, and the supply of food as Guanabara's chief problems.[8]

In giving attention to a few problems, instead of the list of twenty-two that he published in the *Tribuna*, Lacerda adopted the recommendation of his former schoolmate, Emil Farhat. Farhat, a veteran political campaigner who had become an executive of the McCann Erickson advertising firm, had come from São Paulo at Lacerda's request and reviewed Lacerda's extensive program for Guanabara. He had agreed that Guanabara had "a thousand problems" but suggested concentrating on a few, such as education, water supply, health, and transportation. After returning to São Paulo, Farhat learned that Lacerda had spoken violently against Kubitschek. He phoned Lacerda to say, "You are doing everything wrong. You are no longer candidate for the Municipal Council. Drop the big stick. Pick up a brick and say 'I am going to build.'" Lacerda did just that and, in his own words, created a "new image" of himself.[9]

Another Paulista who advised Lacerda was former Transport Minister

Otávio Marcondes Ferraz, the engineer responsible for the construction of the Paulo Afonso hydroelectric power station on the São Francisco River. Lacerda consulted him about building a Guanabara steel plant and about old plans to bring water to the city from the Guandu River through a forty-three-kilometer tunnel.[10]

While opponents of the Lacerda candidacy wrangled about who should run against him, Lacerda assembled a large and competent staff of advisers. His program for Guanabara, he explained at the UDN convention on June 17, was principally the work of Sandra Cavalcanti, Hamilton Nogueira, and Hélio Beltrão, with some collaboration by himself. Study groups were set up and their work was coordinated by Beltrão, president of the Brazilian Petroleum Institute, and Rafael de Almeida Magalhães, the 29-year-old lawyer (and able soccer player) who had helped defend Lacerda's mandate in 1957. While giving attention to campaign speeches and programs for the state, the coordinators kept in touch with about two hundred specialists who donated their time. Air force Colonel Gustavo Borges, a communications expert, had plenty of time because the Kubitschek administration refused to give him a military assignment. Other specialists included such eminent men as lawyers Temístocles Cavalcanti and Francisco Campos, economists Roberto Campos and Mário Henrique Simonsen, banker Otávio Gouveia de Bulhões, and engineer Glycon de Paiva. Lacerda, speaking with Glycon de Paiva in June at the home of lawyer Miguel Lins, asked him to serve in his state cabinet. For reasons of health, Glycon declined.[11]

A phone call from Rafael de Almeida Magalhães brought medical doctor Antonio Dias Rebello Filho into a group that studied problems of health with the help of Professor Raimundo Moniz de Aragão. In this field and others, studies made previously by Lacerda, during his term on the Municipal Council, were reviewed. Lacerda's longtime friend Marcelo Garcia, socialite and physician, concentrated on raising money for the campaign.[12]

Marcelo Garcia recalls that Congressman Antônio Chagas Freitas, whose crime-featuring *O Dia* outsold even *O Globo,* helped the Lacerda campaign by "preparing the ground for the *favela* type of people." If the *Tribuna*'s Walter Cunto, serving as the candidate's press adviser, had reason to be pleased with *O Dia,* he had equal reason to be exasperated with the widely read *Manchete* magazine. After he called Lacerda's attention to one of *Manchete*'s attacks, Lacerda, in a fury, phoned *Manchete* President Adolpho Bloch to express his indignation.[13]

Lacerda's statement to the UDN about his meager financial resources was confirmed when, as a candidate, he listed his assets and debts. His chief assets were the house he had built in 1952 in Samambaia and the recently purchased duplex apartment (used in part by Sérgio and Sebastião) at Praia do Flamengo. Despite the revenue received from the sale of the Tonelero Street apartment, he owed more than nine million cruzeiros for his residences. Communists, ignoring the debt and placing exaggerated values on Lacerda's assets, described the "*corvo* of Lavradio" as a man with a fortune, allied with "swindlers and assailants of the treasury of his political party."[14]

2. "The Devastated City and Its Reconstruction" (June–July 1960)

Shortly before Lacerda agreed to run for governor, he received a letter from Pedro Xavier d'Araújo, president of the local Partido Libertador (PL), to advise that the PL would join with the UDN in Guanabara if the UDN would cease acting as though it wanted "to struggle alone" and would consult the PL before taking positions. For example, Xavier d'Araújo wrote, "I do not see how to avoid having municipalities for the new state and do not see the dangers you speak of." Lacerda had no objection to consulting and certainly did not want the UDN to struggle alone. On June 3 the PL regional directorship resolved to present Lacerda's candidacy to its convention to be held on June 22, five days after the UDN convention.[1]

The Partido Trabalhista Nacional (PTN), of which São Paulo Congressman Emílio Carlos Kyrillos was national president, had no difficulty in settling on Lacerda's name, and it decided to hold its regional convention on June 11 and thus become the first party to nominate him. At meetings of the directorship of the local Partido Democrata Cristão (PDC), headed by Gladstone Chaves de Melo, the supporters of Lacerda overcame the objections of Fernando Ferrari supporters. A note, issued at the home of Juarez Távora, favored the nomination of Lacerda at the PDC convention, to be held on July 2.[2]

The last political party whose local directorship decided to support Lacerda was the Partido Republicano (PR). It settled the matter, by a 41-to-8 vote, on July 22, only eight days before its convention. Among the members of its directorship who brought the news to Lacerda was Hélio Walcacer, member of the Communist group with which Lacerda had associated in 1937. Walcacer had worked at the *Tribuna* for a while but, as Rio municipal councilman in 1955, had savagely assailed the Lantern Club.[3]

The Guanabara section of Ação Socialista, an organization in which Odilon Paiva was active but which had no party standing, proclaimed Lacerda its candidate on June 13. Another nonparty organization, the Movimento Popular Jânio Quadros (MPJQ) proved more difficult because its president, Carlos Castilho Cabral, felt that its support of Lacerda would cost Quadros 100,000 or 150,000 votes. Castilho Cabral also felt that Lacerda, "the uncontrollable *udenista* leader," resented his tendency to make decisions about the Quadros campaign in Guanabara. When the MPJQ, at the insistence of Quadros, finally came out in favor of Lacerda, it also expressed support for two other UDN gubernatorial candidates: Magalhães Pinto in Minas and Luís Cavalcanti in Alagoas.[4]

The nominating conventions were usually held in the Municipal Chamber, and at most of them Lacerda devoted his speech to one topic. On becoming the candidate of the PTN on June 11, he spoke about labor. He said his proposed labor code, introduced in Congress in 1955 and "sabotaged by those who consider themselves the owners of the worker," would give freedom to labor unions and extend labor legislation benefits to rural workers.

Mentioning other measures he had unsuccessfully sought to have enacted, he spoke of his plan to provide loans to "young professionals . . . , be they cobblers, doctors, dressmakers, taxi drivers, or painters," to enable them to buy the "tools of their trade," such as automobiles for taxi drivers. Another was the "basic reform" to create a social security ministry, "the only possible solution for the state of insolvency to which the pension institutes have been brought." Emphasizing his interest in labor, Lacerda said he had been brought up in the climate in which his father had helped enact laws about labor accidents, paid vacations, and pensions.[5]

Lacerda's UDN convention speech, "The Devastated City and Its Reconstruction," was given on June 17 and was a pledge to try to follow the example carried out in West Germany after its destruction by World War II. Speaking of his plan to demand that the federal government create "a free port in Rio de Janeiro," he called it the "minimum compensation for the harm resulting from the devastating series of evil deeds practiced on the city by the last federal administrations."[6]

In drawing a picture of the legacy received from those administrations, Lacerda furnished statistics about transportation, education, electric power, sewage, and the supply of food and water. He pointed out that over 100,000 children between the ages of 7 and 14 received no schooling, due to the lack of facilities, and that only 9 percent of those in primary schools completed the schooling. The sewage system, he reported, served only 1,300,000 of the city's 3,200,000 inhabitants, and the telephone system was so bad that 200,000 people were on the waiting list for instruments. For water supply, Lacerda declared it imperative to start work on the five-year Guandu project and other improvements, estimated to cost at least eight billion cruzeiros.[7]

Lacerda promised a sober, modest, and severe government—one that would "assign to private initiative what it must and can do," replacing "the delirium of assigning everything to the government, so that in the end the government is in charge of everything and does nothing." He wanted to create an industrial zone to prevent the exodus of industries and alleviate, in part, problems of the *favelados*. To finance the purchase of land in the zone and to guarantee other financings, he proposed transforming the Bank of the Municipality into an investment bank.

"We are," Lacerda told the *udenistas*, "the people of the Eighteen of the Fort, of Brigadeiro Eduardo Gomes. We are the people who elected Maurício de Lacerda in prison because he sacrificed himself for liberty, and we acclaimed Pedro Ernesto because he provided schools and hospitals. . . . Help me and I shall give you a city restored to happiness and to the charm of its former days."[8]

Discussing electric power at the PL convention on June 21, Lacerda blamed the Kubitschek government for the energy crisis he expected to occur in Guanabara in 1962 unless he could persuade the utility concessionaire, Rio–Light S.A., to install an oil-fueled thermoelectric plant. For the longer term he had two solutions. One was Guanabara's share of power to be produced at the Funil hydroelectric plant in Rio state. The other was nuclear power.

"Nuclear power," Lacerda said, "means for the twentieth century what coal meant to England in the eighteenth century and petroleum to the United States in the nineteenth century." Speaking of Quadros, who had sought a nuclear pilot plant for São Paulo and visited nuclear energy plants while abroad in 1959, Lacerda told the Libertadores, "I know of no one as interested in the idea of the great leap that Brazil must make with atomic power."[9]

"Today," Lacerda said to the PDC on July 2, "I shall discuss preventive and curative medicine, hygiene, hospitals, and health services." He suggested that three factors were principally responsible for poor public health in Rio: the use of untreated water, the precarious sewage system, and deficient garbage collection. A program to increase the equipment and personnel of existing hospitals, he said, was preferable to the more expensive path of building new ones. "Let us struggle," he said to the Christian Democrats, "as we have struggled in the opposition since 1947, but this time in the government, to develop in Rio the Right to Health as a basic right of the citizen along with the Right to Education."[10]

In his last convention speech, delivered to the PR on July 30, Lacerda discussed the transportation problems created by Guanabara's topography, disorganized development, and "abandonment" by the federal government. With people of the north zone spending two or three hours daily to get to and from work and sometimes using as many as three or four means of transport, he concluded that the Cariocas were "among the most patient people in the world." "But," he added, "their patience, instead of being a virtue, is an indication of failure. . . . They have become tired of complaining."

The orator promised to speed up the opening of tunnels for vehicles. Speaking of the cooperation he expected from the Quadros administration, he revealed that "the future president" had promised, in writing, to furnish funds to assist the start of the long-planned Metropolitano subway system. "In the opinion of specialists," Lacerda said, "the Metropolitano is the only effective and definitive solution to the problem of transporting masses over long distances, rapidly and cheaply, in cities with over two million inhabitants."[11]

At the headquarters of the Lacerda campaign, an old house on Almirante Tamandaré Street, publisher Alfredo C. Machado introduced Carlos to Marcos Tamoyo. Tamoyo, an engineer who had begun working for the city in 1950, had long advocated a roadway, 5,600 meters long and including 2,800 meters of tunnel under the Corcovado mountain, to make it unnecessary for traffic between the north and south zones to flow through Rio's congested downtown area. With the help of maps and blueprints he argued for his ambitious scheme. The candidate was noncommittal and never even asked a question. But when he spoke later on television, Carlos surprised Tamoyo; he defended the plan with explanations more convincing than those of its longtime advocate.[12]

3. Candidates on and against the Ticket (June–August 1960)

Before the Carioca UDN held its convention, its directors listed twenty-seven party members chosen to campaign for the thirty seats of the state constitutional assembly in the election of October 3. Thirteen more were to be chosen later by the UDN in consultation with other parties and groups, such as Ação Socialista.[1]

The original list included Aliomar Baleeiro, Afonso Arinos Filho (son of the senator), Frota Aguiar, Amaral Netto, Hélio Fernandes, Raul Brunini, jurist Temístocles Cavalcanti, and educators Raimundo Moniz de Aragão, Sandra Cavalcanti, and Carlos Flexa Ribeiro. Flexa Ribeiro and former Municipal Councilwoman Sandra Cavalcanti had been helping Lacerda with the proposed Law of Directives and Bases for Education and were among those Lacerda wished to see play a role in giving Guanabara a constitution.[2]

By September 3, the final date for listing assembly candidates, eleven parties had registered 381 contestants. The UDN had brought its list up to 40 by adding such names as Heber Horta Barbosa, president of Ação Socialista, Xavier d'Araújo, president of the Carioca PL, and 72-year-old Mozart Lago, journalist and former senator.[3]

During June the PTB, PSD, and PSB (Socialist Party) negotiated to find a single candidate to run against Lacerda. Hélio Fernandes, writing humorously in the *Diário de Notícias* on June 22, said the problem was "almost resolved" except for obstacles, such as Carioca PSD President Augusto Amaral Peixoto's veto of Ambassador Negrão de Lima (PSD), Negrão de Lima's veto of Sérgio Magalhães (PTB) and vice versa, vetos by the PTB and Ademar de Barros of Marshal Mendes de Morais (PSD), the veto by Mendes de Morais of Negrão de Lima, the veto by Goulart of Lutero Vargas (PTB), and the veto by the Catholics of Sérgio Magalhães.[4]

"The hesitant adversary," Lacerda said later, had a costly delay while it considered, among others, Aranha's son Osvaldo and engineer Hélio de Almeida, "who could have had a part of the PSD votes and certainly the votes of the PTB and the Communists, really very important at the time." Guilherme da Silveira ("Silveirinha"), owner of the Bangu textile plant and a friend of Lacerda, was asked to run against Lacerda by Lutero Vargas, Ademar de Barros, and Luís Carlos Prestes, whom he had known since 1928. He declined, telling them he was not a politician, and criticized their stand as being merely negative, that is, opposed to Lacerda.[5]

By early July the dispute was between former Mayor Mendes de Morais (PSD) and Chamber of Deputies Vice President Sérgio Magalhães, of the PTB's leftist *grupo compacto.* When the PSD nominated Mendes de Morais on July 4, the PTB and PSB were stunned. Quickly they nominated Sérgio Magalhães, whom Lacerda had come to regard as an honest congressman and unexciting speaker.[6]

Sérgio Magalhães discussed the problems of the new state with the PSB constitutional assembly candidates, one of whom was Lacerda's half-brother, *Correio da Manhã* columnist Maurício Caminha de Lacerda. Then, still in July, he announced his program. Neither this program nor his revised program of August differed much from the program of Lacerda. But they did not mention nuclear energy and they championed public education, saying that "education is not a business." Schooling and medical treatment, Sérgio Magalhães maintained, should be free of charge.[7]

The surprise entry in the gubernatorial race was the colorful Tenório Cavalcanti on the ticket of the small PRT (Partido Rural Trabalhista), a party associated with Hugo Borghi. Tenório, said to have been responsible for killings and to carry an automatic weapon next to a bulletproof vest under his black cape, lived in a fortress in Duque de Caxias, commanded a private militia, and owned the popular daily *Luta Democrática.* His principal political support was in the lowlands of Rio state, where his followers, including devotees of macumba, made him the most voted-for congressman from the state in 1958. But his articles and long speeches, in picturesque language and demanding all sorts of favors for the poor, gave him enormous popularity also in the *favelas* of Guanabara and strength in Rio's northern zone. As a candidate for governor in 1960, he promised, if elected, to open the prison gates so that all the convicts could go to agricultural areas and develop the "green belt" to provide food for the city.[8]

According to some accounts, the Tenório candidacy had been encouraged by UDN Congressman Mário Martins to draw votes away from Sérgio Magalhães. But Tenório entered the contest to win and was expected to garner support from much of the PSP. PSP leader Ademar de Barros, mayor of São Paulo, praised Tenório, who, in turn, gave support to Ademar's presidential bid.[9]

Arrangements for Jânio Quadros to lunch with Tenório in Caxias were

Tenório Cavalcanti. (Hilde Weber drawing in Hilde Weber, *O Brasil em Charges, 1950–1985*)

made late in July by MPJQ President Castilho Cabral, who was telling Quadros that Lacerdismo was prejudicial to his campaign and that he should not favor any one gubernatorial candidate. When Lacerda, eager to be Jânio's sole candidate for the Guanabara governorship, learned that Quadros had agreed to attend the lunch, he announced that he would resign his candidacy if Quadros thus assisted a UDN deserter who had a chance to win in Guanabara. Sérgio Lacerda, meeting Jânio at the Santos Dumont Airport, told him that fulfillment of the lunch date would mean they would not see each other again in Rio. The lunch was cancelled.[10]

Administration leaders, concerned lest a split of votes between Sérgio Magalhães and Mendes de Morais give the election to Lacerda, or possibly Tenório, studied formulas for the withdrawal of one of the so-called government candidates, or the withdrawal of both in favor of a "third" candidate. But nothing came of the talks. The PSD persisted with the Mendes de Morais candidacy although it was evident, as early as July, that it was attracting little interest.[11]

Lott and Goulart, arriving in Rio for a PSD-PTB rally at the Largo do Machado, had the problem of dealing with the scheduled presence of rivals Sérgio Magalhães and Mendes de Morais on the speakers' platform. The problem was settled by Sérgio Magalhães' PTB supporters, who physically attacked the members of a Mendes de Morais samba group at the rally, leading to stone throwing and turmoil, during which women and children were trampled. Mendes de Morais, receiving reports about the wounding of his followers, one of them a PSD municipal councilman, decided to remain at home rather than deliver his speech. The PSD, he said the next day, was disposed to "break definitely with the PTB," and he added that support for Ferrari, as an alternative to Goulart, was increasing in the PSD.[12]

On the national scene, however, the odds in favor of Jango Goulart were growing with the development of the Jan-Jan movement to elect Jânio and Jango. Goulart, after conversing with PR congressional leader Manoel Novais, expressed confidence that the Jan-Jan movement would win in the area of Bahia where Novais was influential. A little later, ten São Paulo state legislators gave impetus to the movement in their state, and their example was followed in labor circles in much of Brazil.[13]

Jânio Quadros, who extolled Vargas as a "great patriot" and a "great president," did nothing to stop the Jan-Jan movement.[14] After Lott-supporter Luís Carlos Prestes declared that Jânio, using João Ribeiro Dantas as intermediary, had turned to him for Communist support, Dantas was reported as confirming Prestes' statement. The independent *Correio da Manhã* accused Quadros of courting "Communists and leftists," adhering to the themes of "nationalists," and preaching "the revolution of Fidel Castro" in the Brazilian interior. "Has it now become impossible," it asked,"to win an election in Brazil without flattering the Left?"[15]

This was a problem that faced Lacerda especially in September when the contest became polarized, with the anti-Lacerda forces turning in increasing numbers to a single candidate, Sérgio Magalhães. The election for governorship, hard fought and close, developed into a battle in which the support-

A Communist view of Lacerda, from whose *Tribuna da Imprensa* lantern a powerful Uncle Sam emerges. (*Novos Rumos*, June 19–25, 1959)

ers of the PTB-PSB coalition, among them Luís Carlos Prestes and the Communists, described Lacerda as the favorite of the far Right. He was called a "McCarthyite," the would-be assassin of public education, and a neo-fascist who would use terrorist groups to pommel workers and make Guanabara the springboard for implanting dictatorship in Brazil. The electorate was repeatedly told that the *corvo* was the agent of the foreign-owned Rio–Light and Standard Oil and was receiving large contributions from them and from the United States government.[16]

Tenório Cavalcanti, in a poll conducted early in August, shared first place with Lacerda. But then a surge in favor of Sérgio Magalhães left Tenório in third place and the value of his candidacy to Lacerda became evident. Early in September, Lacerda told the anti-Lacerdistas that they could avoid voting for "the Communist candidate," Sérgio Magalhães, by turning to Tenório or Mendes de Morais. And he criticized the government for using threats to remove Tenório from the race. This was after Justice Minister Armando Falcão advised the popular Fluminense congressman that his election to the Guanabara governorship would limit his immunities to the geographical area of Guanabara, allowing him to be tried for crimes he was said to have committed in Rio state.[17]

4. Propaganda of the Left (August–September 1960)

On September 1, Lacerda inaugurated the first of the daily excursions of the Caminhão da Oposição (Truck of the Opposition), a replica of the Caminhão do Povo that had carried Afonso Arinos, Lacerda, and others to victory in 1958. Its schedule of trips to the suburbs was published each day in the *Tribuna.*[1]

Lacerda's speeches, on the Caminhão and elsewhere, were devoted to the improvements he planned to bring the new state and the need for them. On television he used a blackboard to present figures about the school shortage and describe his plans to finance the construction of fifty inexpensive public primary schools during his first year as governor. In the *Tribuna,* drawings by Hilde Weber depicted the challenges: a water faucet providing less than a trickle, piles of fly-infested garbage, a line of people waiting for a bus, and a candle used for illumination.[2]

Lacerda felt that such matters had become the chief concern of the voters, who, with the birth of their new state, found themselves with local interests to defend for the first time. He considered it an error of Sérgio Magalhães to speak at length "about imperialism and nationalism, that had nothing to do with the topics of nascent Guanabara."[3]

In the face of the strategy of some of the Communists, described by *Jornal do Brasil* as "seeking a violent reaction or, if possible, a dead body," Lacerda was careful.[4] An early example of his caution was his handling of the turmoil in August outside the Pedro II railroad station, where PTB-PCB enthusiasts were determined to disrupt a UDN rally. They set fire to the UDN propaganda stall and gained widespread applause by using a loudspeaker to attack Yankee capitalists, praise Luís Carlos Prestes, and advocate the extinction of the bourgeoisie and the massacre of Lacerda if he appeared. The opening speeches of the UDN rally, by Raul Brunini and Amaral Netto, were drowned out by hoots. Lacerda, arriving later, was insulted throughout his speech by remarks delivered on the loudspeaker of his adversaries. He seized a Brazilian flag and declared, "When they destroy our stall here, they burn a flag just like this one." He recommended that his supporters remain calm, leave the square after the rally, and give their answer in the ballot boxes. After he and the other UDN speakers left, the PTB-PCB zealots continued for several hours to stir up the crowd, but no combat occurred.[5]

Press attacks on Lacerda, led by *Última Hora* and *Novos Rumos,* took advantage of what could be culled from his controversial career, and few incidents were overlooked if they could be used against him or distorted for that purpose. Replying to the old charge that he was anti-Jewish, he explained in a Jewish weekly that his opposition in 1948 to the creation of the nation of Israel had been prompted by a concern for world peace and a fear that waves of anti-Semitism might result if Jews were considered to have their loyalties divided between Zionism and the countries in which they were born. He mentioned his anti-Nazi work and pointed out that three Jewish newspapers had been printed by the *Tribuna* press.[6]

The crow as depicted in the Communist press. (*Novos Rumos,* August 5–11, 1960)

In the Municipal Chamber, Jair Martins expressed surprise that Lacerda had recently visited synagogues "as though he were not the author of articles that sought to prevent Jews from coming to Brazil." Lacerda's so-called opposition to Jewish immigration was repeated during a debate in which a student dramatically quoted Lacerda as having written: "Well then, kill the Jews, finish with the Jews." Lacerda, greeting Jews on the occasion of their new year, denounced the "dishonest intentions of the young Communist" who, he pointed out, had taken his sentence from an argument made precisely because he had favored admitting Jewish refugees in Brazil.[7]

In one of his rebuttals to the attacks by *Última Hora,* Lacerda wrote that Samuel Wainer, a Jew, had been a traitor to his race because "he sold himself to the German embassy during the war in order to spread Nazi propaganda under the pretext that Stalin had made a pact with Hitler." Then *Última Hora* described Lacerda's life as a long series of betrayals. After calling him a traitor to the Aragarças rebels, it published its six-installment "Profile of a Candidate" about his so-called treacheries and cowardice, starting from his association with Communists in his youth. But for his "ravenous ambition" and Prestes' coldness toward him, *Última Hora* wrote, "Probably today we would have the Lantern Club leader within the PCB." The installment about "The False Catholic" found it fitting that he had been named in honor of Karl Marx and Friedrich Engels because "he was always a materialist." Horrified responses to his "sacrilegious Mass" remark, made in 1957, filled the installment.[8]

Novos Rumos, listing ten reasons to vote against Lacerda, called him the cowardly assassin of Vargas who had fled from Brazil "because the people, incensed, wanted to use their own hands to bring him to justice." Writing that "the author of the shameful Brandi letter" was a member of the "fascist Moral Rearmament," *Novos Rumos* added that Heinrich Himmler and Rudolf Hess had also been members and that founder Frank Buchman had said "Thank God for Hitler." According to *Última Hora,* Lacerda and his family had spent most of three months in a palatial hotel in Caux, Switzerland, with all expenses paid by Moral Rearmament.[9]

5. "The Thief of Chile Street" (September 1960)

In 1958 the Superintendency of Urbanization and Sanitization (SURSAN), commissioned to plan changes for downtown Rio following the demolition of the Santo Antônio Hill, studied a report of engineers and recommended that some of the buildings on Lavradio Street be torn down so that a wider thoroughfare could be made. Among the buildings were those belonging to the *Tribuna da Imprensa,* the Presbyterian Church, and the Masonic Order's Grande Oriente do Brasil. In exchange for these properties, the owners were to receive properties on Chile Avenue, which came into existence with the demolition of the hill. The property exchange plan was authorized by Law Number 3 passed by the Municipal Council on May 17, 1960.[1]

José Sette Câmara Filho, appointed governor of Guanabara in April 1960 by Kubitschek, was asked by Lacerda late in August to sanction Law Number 3. But the Left screamed against the property exchange plan, making it a campaign issue, and Sette Câmara's advisers reported that the law, if signed by the governor, would be too costly for the state. Lacerda, seeking to "defend the patrimony of 6,000 Brazilians, shareholders of the *Tribuna,*" tried to convince state authorities, whom he visited in the company of Rafael de Almeida Magalhães, that the property exchange plan was eminently fair. He pointed out that the plan, proposed by a pro-Kubitschek mayor in 1958 in the interest of the Federal District, had been found less costly than the alternative of paying the Presbyterian Church, the Masonic Order, and the *Tribuna* a total of 79 million cruzeiros, the official valuation put on the three properties. The state authorities, however, showed no inclination to proceed with the swap or pay cash to the *Tribuna,* whose property had been evaluated at 17.6 million cruzeiros by SURSAN in 1958.[2]

Sérgio Magalhães declared on September 2 that if he were elected governor he would not permit realization of "the shady *Tribuna da Imprensa* property deal in which Carlos Lacerda is involved." Jair Martins, a former *udenista,* raised a storm in the Municipal Chamber by calling Lacerda a swindler and impostor seeking to make a profit of 150 million cruzeiros for the *Tribuna.* In the halls of Congress, the PTB spoke of demanding the cancellation of Lacerda's mandate on the ground that the constitution prohibited congressmen from entering into contracts with government bodies such as SURSAN. The demand was made for publicity reasons, it being recognized that few congressmen would be available in Brasília.[3]

Lacerda challenged Sérgio Magalhães to debate the Chile Avenue matter on the "Gala Night" television program of Flávio Cavalcanti, produced by TV Rio. But the PTB gubernatorial candidate, explaining that he was not a television star and had another engagement, failed to show up at the appointed time on the night of September 5. Instead, a large group of law students and Communists, accompanied by *Última Hora* reporter Ib Teixeira, filled the auditorium. Shouting "Viva Sérgio" and calling Lacerda the "Thief of Chile Street," they made such an uproar that TV Rio called the police, and Flávio Cavalcanti had to alter his plan and interview Lacerda in a small studio.

The invaders, held back from the studio by the police and Lacerda supporters, carried on with their agitation outside the building while Lacerda replied to the questions of Flávio Cavalcanti. Remarking that Sérgio Magalhães "lacked the courage" to appear before the public to defend his accusations, Lacerda said that surely, under identical circumstances, "Marshal Mendes de Morais, of whom I am an enemy, or Tenório Cavalcanti, would have appeared." On leaving the building, he made his way through a mob holding up clenched fists and shouting "Thief of Chile Street!" *Jornal do Brasil* called the television show a degrading spectacle in which Carioca families, hoping to hear an informative debate, had witnessed, instead, personal attacks on Lacerda before he was forced to leave the auditorium.[4]

The repercussions were many. *Última Hora* reporter Ib Teixeira, claiming he had been prevented by Lacerda from debating with him on the "Gala Night" program, made an appearance later on TV Rio accompanied by Jair Martins. With hundreds of Lacerda foes in the auditorium to applaud, Ib Teixeira argued that Lacerda would "gain over 300 million cruzeiros with the incorporation of Chile Avenue and open the way for other property exchanges costing the state billions of cruzeiros." Sérgio Magalhães, in a widely published letter, mentioned his engagement at the law school on the night of the fifth and gave his reasons for opposing the *Tribuna* property exchange. He called it a deal in which "moral coverage" had been sought by including the Presbyterian Church and the Masonic Order together with the *Tribuna* and "the phantom Mário Pinotti Foundation" (assigned Chile Avenue Lot 18A).[5]

At Chile Avenue Lot 18, which SURSAN had assigned to the *Tribuna,* anti-Lacerda Young Workers (Mocidade Trabalhista) held a rally at which PTB state assembly candidate Roland Corbisier was the most aggressive of the eight speakers. He called Lacerda a coward and agent of foreign capitalism, whose supporters were "misguided fanatics suffering from Lacerditis." He defied Lacerda to debate the Chile Avenue case with him.[6]

Lacerda, accepting an invitation to address medical students, found an energetic opponent in the president of the student association, a pro-Communist who displayed maps and cited figures, furnished by *Última Hora,* about the proposed Chile Avenue transaction. The student was so persistent in interrupting Lacerda's attempts to speak that he was finally booed by colleagues. Lacerda condemned the demonstrators and insisted that the student association president be heard. The discussion ended with the association president joining in the applause given Lacerda for his presentation.[7]

The response of the law students to the September 5 "Gala Night" interview was a pronouncement in which their association, the Centro Acadêmico Cândido de Oliveira (CACO), disavowed the activities of law students at the interview. The CACO invited Lacerda to address the law school.[8]

When Sérgio Magalhães had spoken to the law students, law school Director Hermes Lima had been present and the audience had been respectful. But conditions were entirely different on the night of the sixteenth when Lacerda sought to discuss his program for the state. Not only was the director absent but also many of the twelve hundred students were agitators who shouted "Thief of Chile Street" and set off firecrackers. Lacerda supporters gained a pause in the melee by singing the national anthem. But when Lacerda resumed his effort to speak, asking for the sort of debate that was appropriate for the school, bedlam filled the room again. Students brought in a Sérgio Magalhães banner, prompting a brawl that sent four students to the hospital, among them the CACO president, struck by a club at the base of his skull. Before departing to give a television speech at TV Continental, Lacerda found an opportunity to answer a student who accused him of anti-Semitism.

Lacerda left an auditorium whose carpet had burns from firecrackers and many of whose chairs were broken. In his television address, described later by the *Jornal do Brasil* as the best of his campaign, he declared that the Communists, "whom I accuse of provoking the incidents, are irretrievable for democracy." He added that everyone should vehemently condemn the use the Communists were making of youth "through a sham nationalism."[9]

Afonso Arinos, who was at the law school meeting, affirmed that "this disgraceful agitation tells us how far the democratic spirit of education has degenerated among the students. I regret the omission of the school director, who withdrew, although he knew what was going to happen. As I am a colleague and friend of Professor Hermes Lima, it is with profound sadness that I witnessed his complete lack of concern about the educational and political behavior of the students." *O Globo* regretted that Lacerda had been unable to speak and denounced the "brutality . . . characteristic of the Iron Curtain regimes." The episode, *O Globo* wrote, was in contrast to the campaign that Lacerda, to the surprise of many, was conducting—a campaign in which he "is objectively discussing programs and viewpoints, and presenting a platform, elaborated with the advice of brilliant technicians in urban problems, that constitutes the greatest honor that the tribune and journalist could render to the political maturity and cultural advancement of those who seek to govern."[10]

6. The Human Side of the Candidate (August–September 1960)

When society columnist Ibrahim Sued interviewed Lacerda on television on September 7 to portray the human side of the candidate, the question that received the most publicity was that of the candidate's 9-year-old daughter, who was present. "When," Maria Cristina asked, "are we going to the movies together again?" The candidate smiled appealingly and said, "One of these days I'll skip a rally and we'll go." But the intensity of the campaign increased and Carlos, speaking each day at no fewer than two large rallies, failed to keep his promise to his daughter.[1]

On the Sunday morning following the Ibrahim Sued interview, Carlos took Letícia and Maria Cristina with him on a visit, well publicized in advance, to the Laranjeiras district where he had lived as a boy. There they attended Mass and walked through the streets with the vicar of the church. "This is more of a sentimental journey than an electoral meeting," Carlos remarked as the accompanying throng sang "Cidade Maravilhosa" and occupants of residences threw flowers and confetti. But the search for votes predominated. After Raul Brunini used a loudspeaker to announce "Here comes Lacerda! Viva Lacerda!" Carlos, standing on the top of a truck, spoke of his childhood in Laranjeiras and made a campaign speech in which he castigated Lott, "candidate of the Communists" and "inciter of the civil war of November 11."[2]

A few days later the human side of Carlos received rough treatment in an *O Cruzeiro* magazine article written by David Nasser, his former associate at *O Jornal.* Nasser made the point that Lacerda, "the slave of a morbid nature, really never had any friends" but that this trait would make him a good administrator of the city he had always faithfully defended. "If, dear reader, it were a matter of a fiancé for your daughter, Carlos Lacerda would be no good. But for the governorship he is excellent. He esteems no one. Not even himself."

Explaining that the heart of Lacerda had not always been so cold, Nasser mentioned his early passionate pro-Communist writings. But he maintained that Lacerda had never been "organically a man of the Left" and was instinctively a totalitarian "of the best style." "He would have been a fine Führer, swarthy, haughty, thundering, thrashing enemies, destroying obstacles. . . . The merit of this man is that he overcame his own nature and turned himself into one of the paladins of democracy. Being unable to destroy it, he took it as his mistress. He is a tragic figure."

As a friend, Nasser wrote, "Lacerda is horrible," and as a fellow political party member, "it must be unpleasant to deal with him." But, Nasser pointed out, the qualities to look for in an administrator were different ones: honesty, intelligence, and the ability to get things done. Praising Lacerda's honesty and intelligence, he wrote that the UDN candidate was likely to get things done because he was familiar with the needs of a city long scourged by venal politicians and would seek the best means to provide telephones, water, transportation, teaching, and hospital care.

If one were to vote with one's heart, Nasser wrote, probably no one would vote for Carlos Lacerda. "Therefore everyone should vote with his head. . . . Let us take advantage of his personal plan, which is to use Guanabara as a springboard for the bigger leap. Let us make use of his political ambition."

In the conclusion Nasser wrote: "I do not like Carlos Lacerda. Or, rather, I do not like his way of being, acting, and fighting. . . . But none of this is of the slightest importance. The nature of the struggle that he faced in a corrupt country . . . perhaps justifies his excesses. The truth is that he was able to remain unscathed—in his moral position and in his sometimes immoral method of battling. The story of his political contests has a bit of the missionary and the gangster in it. But, as in the case of Jânio Quadros—who one day will be the target of his unreasonable arrows—the life of Carlos Lacerda is a book of patriotism."[3]

A copy of Nasser's typescript was brought to Carlos by Dr. Antonio Dias Rebello Filho, who had been told tactfully by Nasser that it had been written to thrash Carlos and give him an opportunity to reply, thus helping his campaign. But Nasser's description of Lacerda as a man "incapable of keeping friendships" received wide publicity and was welcomed by his opponents.[4]

Lacerda, replying in a letter to Nasser that appeared in the next week's *O Cruzeiro,* said: "I think I am the person who has the most and best friends in this country." He mentioned anonymous friends among the multitude and friends from his youth and newspaper work. "The reason you consider me without friends is . . . that I am a man who decided to lose friends in order to preserve what justifies friendship."

Listing friends thus lost, Lacerda wrote of Communists "who deliberately hate me on orders of the Communist Party" and friends who failed to realize that friendship required condemning their political shortcomings when they harmed thousands of innocent people. Other friends, Lacerda told Nasser, had left him because they resented what they felt was his success in life. Furthermore, Lacerda admitted with regret to having often been inattentive to the immediate duties of friendship, such as sending presents. "And here," he added, "I make another confession that might make you laugh, David. I am a timid person." This timidity, he wrote, "often prevents me from forcing open the doors of other people. . . . And I do like a little solitude."

Lacerda denied having been passionate only in his youth and thanked God that he expected to die "with the capacity to be passionate, without which life becomes a desert of calculations and ambitions." As for his having "a totalitarian vocation," he blamed the allegation on Nasser's failure to distinguish between democracy and disorder or between democratic leaders and demagogues.

To Nasser's criticism of his inconsistencies, Lacerda replied that he had always been open to revising solutions for reaching his permanent goals, liberty and justice. "I sacrifice friends, time, repose, fortune, all that I have or might have, . . . in order to keep those goals in view."[5]

Lacerda, like most people, committed acts of carelessness and acts of surprising thoughtfulness in his relations with friends. An unusual example of the latter was his decision, during the heat of the campaign in September

1960, to spend some time at the side of Odilon Lacerda Paiva, who had fallen ill and needed comforting. This was all the more remarkable because Lacerda had such a strong aversion to calling on people who were sick that it was even said he never did so.[6]

During the governorship race, Carlos was deeply pained by the charge that he was anti-Jewish. In the *Tribuna* he wrote that he had never dreamed that the ferocity and unfairness of the electoral struggle would go so far as to lead people to consider him a racist. He could, he said, understand how the experience of the Jews did not allow them easy immunization against intrigue. But, he added, he hoped they would likewise understand how much he was "hurt by the injustice of the situation in which I am forced, during this entire campaign, to defend myself against a defaming suspicion that deviates from everything I have been in my life."[7]

Toward the end of the campaign, an exhausted Carlos dropped in at the São Bento Monastery to chat with Dom Lourenço de Almeida Prado, who had helped him find his way to Catholicism in 1948. "If things go as I expect," Carlos said, "I shall be elected governor. The thought scares me. I need your help." Dom Lourenço admitted that Carlos would face a difficult situation and that the Cariocas were rather ungovernable. "No," Carlos replied, "I'm not worried about that, I'm not worried about administration. I'm worried about myself, my temperament. This is why I need your help." Dom Lourenço spoke of the demands that his monastery duties, including running the São Bento School, made on his time but said he would help Carlos as much as he could. But Carlos never called on Dom Lourenço again.[8]

7. Missteps by the Leading Candidates (September 1960)

Sérgio Magalhães, "candidate of the PTB, the PSB, and all the nationalist fronts," stressed that he and his family had been brought up in the Catholic faith. "Unlike my UDN opponent," he said unfairly, "I am not an election-eve Catholic, a Catholic for reasons of expediency."

In accepting Communist votes, Sérgio Magalhães said he was following the example of *udenistas* such as Milton Campos, Cid Sampaio, Otávio Mangabeira, and Virgílio Távora. And he promised that, as governor, he would seek the collaboration of Archbishop Hélder Câmara in order to solve the problem of the *favelas*.[1]

On September 26, Sérgio Magalhães visited São Joaquim Palace to deliver a letter to the archbishop. The letter, which appeared in the Rio newspapers as material paid for by the campaign fund of its writer, called Dom Hélder the "Bishop of Development" and the "Bishop of the People" and praised him for recognizing the role played by labor in the creation of wealth. In closing, the PTB-PSD candidate declared that no one had the right to describe Vargas, Café Filho, or Kubitschek as Communists just because they had received Communist votes.[2]

On September 28, headlines in the Rio press revealed the reaction of Hélder Câmara, who said he had wanted to remain silent about the election but that Sérgio Magalhães himself, by giving publicity to a letter designed to deceive the electorate, had forced him to speak out lest the people be misled by it and by the candidate's "description of his visit to São Joaquim Palace." Dom Hélder stated succinctly that he agreed with Cardinal Jaime Câmara that "Sérgio Magalhães cannot receive the votes of Catholics on account of his position on divorce and Communism."[3]

In election campaigns, Lacerda said later, a step that you think will give good results sometimes does just the opposite. He was referring to the step he took on September 22 after Raul Brunini showed him a booklet said to have been printed at the Bankworkers' Pension Institute (IAPB). Lacerda, not yet fully recovered from a bad cold that had kept him out of the campaign for four days, was enraged by the booklet's insults, slandering Letícia and Sérgio Lacerda as well as members of the Quadros family. Deciding to be late for a rally, he set out impulsively for the IAPB printing shop, accompanied by companions such as Brunini and Edson Guimarães, candidates for the state constitutional assembly.[4]

At the printing shop the candidate and his friends found what they needed to prove that the printing had been done there with materials acquired thanks to the contributions of bank workers to their pension fund. In addition to two thousand kilograms of covers and pages, made from paper bought by the IAPB, they found the set type. And bags of trash revealed clippings from a magazine, *Brasil Nacionalista,* whose insulting verses about Quadros had been reproduced in the booklets.

At the request of Lacerda, an occupant of a nearby residence phoned the police and they sent an agent, who took charge of gathering evidence. The agent and Lacerda were setting out for the police station with some of their findings when administrators of the IAPB arrived, prompting Lacerda to tell the agent that it would be unwise to leave the IAPB administrators in a position to destroy further evidence. A struggle took place while Lacerda and his supporters reentered the shop against the will of the administrators, one of whom was General Felisberto Batista Teixeira, Rio police chief in 1956 and 1957 and a PTB candidate for the Guanabara constitutional assembly. The general drew his revolver, but Lacerda persuaded him to return it to its holster.

Street skirmishes between *petebistas* and *udenistas* came to an end when more police reached the scene. A judge had been sent for and when he arrived Lacerda explained the situation and Brunini requested an official investigation. The investigation was ordered quickly by President Kubitschek, who had not been spared by the booklets and who condemned the IAPB for using its press to print the slanders.[5]

Representatives of the PTB, PSB, and "nationalist committees" held a meeting at which they found Kubitschek guilty of "an act of treason." They blamed his reaction on misinformation given by PSD leaders and Justice Minister Armando Falcão and they urged Goulart to advise Kubitschek that the Rio police should be censured for giving support to Lacerda during his invasion of the IAPB.[6]

Lacerda and Brunini lost no time in going to court to present evidence against the pension institute, in the supposition that they might gain an electoral advantage by proving that supporters of Sérgio Magalhães had acted illegally. But, as Lacerda was forced to conclude, the whole episode was counterproductive and his impetuous dash to the IAPB helped his adversaries, who spread reports that he had "invaded a printing press of the workers" and, "with a group of hoodlums," had "thrashed workers." In response to the testimony of Brunini and Lacerda, an official of the IAPB told the court that the invasion was "a demonstration of real barbarism." "I was," he said, "cowardly assaulted by three of Lacerda's men."[7]

Lott, preparing to close his campaign in Rio, was scheduled to deliver a speech offering benefits to workers and condemning "the evil assault by Lacerda on a printing plant of the IAPB."[8] However, the speech was not given because, shortly before the Rio rally, a speakers' platform collapsed under the PTB-PSD presidential candidate, injuring his leg so badly that he had to abandon further appearances.

The rally, held at the Praça Rio Branco in the Esplanada do Castelo, featured speeches attacking the economic trusts that were said to favor the campaigns of Quadros and Lacerda. An actor, playing the part of a bearded Tiradentes, hero of an early Brazilian independence movement, entertained the crowd by responding to the antinationalist invective of a blond "Mr. Trust," played by another actor.[9]

This was the type of rally that did not appeal to Lacerda, who believed that political rallies (*comícios*) should be limited to political speeches. He did not favor turning them into "*showmícios*," a name sometimes given to political rallies that include entertainment by singers or actors.[10]

8. Farewell to the *Tribuna* (September 30, 1960)

As election day approached, Lacerda warned Quadros supporters not to wear miniature brooms on their lapels when they entered voting booths lest unfriendly officials annul their ballots on the ground that they were violating the law requiring that voting be secret. On the next day, September 29, brooms of all sizes were waved in the Praça da Bandeira when Quadros, accompanied by Milton Campos, Lacerda, and others, spoke in Rio at a rally described by the *Correio da Manhã* as the largest in the state's short history.[1]

Jânio, according to a *Correio da Manhã* survey, could expect 45 percent of the Guanabara vote compared with 27 percent for Lott; Milton Campos was shown to be well ahead of Goulart and Ferrari. As for the governorship race, the poll of the Instituto Brasileiro de Opinião Pública e Estatística (IBOPE) gave 40 percent of the state's vote to Lacerda, 27 percent to Sérgio Magalhães, 23 percent to Tenório Cavalcanti, and 5 percent to Mendes de Morais. *O Globo*'s canvassing showed Lacerda with 7,067 supporters, Sérgio Magalhães with 3,474, Tenório with 3,038, and Mendes de Morais with 814.[2] But preelection polls were known to be far from accurate, and it remained to be seen how far the surge for Sérgio Magalhães, still under way, would take him, bearing in mind that Lacerda-haters favoring Tenório were being persuaded to switch to Sérgio Magalhães.

The Sérgio Magalhães Caravana da Vitória, similar to the Lacerda Caminhão da Oposição, had been received with enthusiastic applause by onlookers in the last week. Before it departed on its final trip around Guanabara on September 30, the Sergistas held an enormous, spirited rally in Cinelândia, where one of the principal speakers was Carlos Marighella, appearing on behalf of "the Communists of Guanabara and Luís Carlos Prestes."

Lacerda, on the thirtieth, headed a parade of automobiles that circulated, like the Caravana da Vitória and the cars of the almost-forgotten Mendes de Morais, through a city that bade farewell to campaigning with all the commotion of a Carnaval Saturday. In crowded streets loudspeakers competed with each other and with small bands of music, while paper was thrown from windows and shouting campaign workers passed out handbills and pamphlets.[3]

In the evening, before facing television cameras for his final appeals, Lacerda visited the *Tribuna* to bid its employees farewell and turn its presidency over to his 21-year-old son Sérgio. In the crowd of two hundred in the reporters' room Carlos spotted veterans, who had joined the newspaper when it was launched in December 1949. Some, like Hilcar Leite, were no longer with the *Tribuna* but had come to wish him well. Carlos greeted them warmly. He said that Luiz Ernesto Kawall, the *Tribuna* secretary who had headed the São Paulo office, was like a son. Kawall, busy in Rio with press propaganda during the Lacerda campaign, gave Carlos a souvenir from the reporters: a copy of an "extra" edition, already dated October 4, announcing his victory in the governorship race.

Before Carlos addressed the gathering, he was greeted by Mário Franqueira, head of the *Tribuna* political section and the reporter with the longest service. On behalf of the *Tribuna* employees, Franqueira asked Carlos, "the superlative reporter," to supply "the greatest news story of his life: the redemption of Rio."

In this emotional setting, Carlos opened with a short prayer. Like some of the old-timers, Sérgio Lacerda was moved to tears during the ceremony in which his father did his leave-taking and promised to return after completing his term in the governor's chair in order to dedicate himself for the rest of his life to his profession. While serving as governor, he said, he would be a *Tribuna* reader, and he added, with a touch of humor, "You can interpret this as either a promise or a threat."

Carlos expressed full confidence in his son "principally because he has lived with me a long time—ever since he was born, I believe." "He possesses," Carlos declared, "management characteristics far superior to those I revealed here. I have faith in him principally because of the respect I know he has for all of you."

Upon entering the adjoining, smaller room in which he had worked, Carlos found the walls covered with placards, whose messages, some in verse, expressed hope for his return. He embraced fellow journalists and seated himself for the last time at the desk he had used since 1949. Then he left to resume his campaign by speaking without interruption on television until

6:00 A.M. on Saturday, October 1, when the election laws (and exhaustion) forced him to bring an end to broadcasting in the quest for votes.[4]

In a final press interview, published in *Jornal do Brasil* on Sunday, Lacerda demonstrated confidence in victory and satisfaction at having "resisted all provocations," thus showing the electorate that he had achieved "the maturity necessary for governing." As in his campaign speeches, he discussed his plans for reviving the state, which, he said, had been losing industry. Besides improving the state's infrastructure and creating an industrial zone, he proposed setting up a company, Companhia Progresso do Estado da Guanabara (COPEG), to help finance new industrial firms and carry out the state's economic development program.[5]

9. Victory by a Narrow Margin (October 1960)

On the eve of the elections, UDN President Magalhães Pinto praised Kubitschek for the atmosphere of liberty that prevailed for the voters. The elections were peaceful, but, on the day after they took place, Lacerda warned the nation that influential politicians, "linked directly to the Justice Ministry," were seeking to persuade electoral tribunal judges to alter the results. "This threat," he said "will be avoided only if the judges, most of them worthy of confidence, exert the utmost vigilance . . . , especially in Guanabara." *Última Hora* retorted that Lacerda was "unleashing electoral terror" by trying to frighten the judges, for his own benefit, while they were supervising the reporting of the results.[1]

Having denied that he would leave the state for Petrópolis after campaigning, Lacerda went with Letícia and some friends to the elegant Rio home of the rich aunt of an acquaintance, and there they followed broadcasts of the election news.[2] Letícia, contemplating the effect that a victory for Carlos might have on the family, was not eager to see her husband gain the governorship.[3]

From the beginning the reports contradicted the expectation of many that Lacerda, because of the division among his opponents, would win an easy victory. He has described the tenseness he felt for several days, during which the returns from the south of the city gave him a lead that sometimes seemed on the verge of being wiped out by the Sérgio Magalhães votes reported from the less-affluent districts. With each vote reported for Tenório Cavalcanti or Marshal Mendes de Morais, he rejoiced.[4]

Interest in the election had resulted in an unusually large turnout of registered voters in Guanabara (over 91 percent). It was apparent also, after the election, in the attention given, all over the city, to announcements made on portable radios, loudspeakers, and bulletin boards. *Última Hora* proclaimed that "The Duel between Sérgio and Lacerda Grips All of Brazil" and argued that the voters could be seen to have handed a "crushing political defeat" to Lacerda, "a dead weight in an electorate that voted en masse for Jânio Quadros and Milton Campos." Lacerda, it also wrote, had always been an "intransigent defender" of the thesis that a candidate should obtain an absolute majority before being declared victorious.[5]

With the results still incomplete, commentators suggested that Lacerda's invasion of the IAPB printing shop, a sign of immaturity, had cost him many votes. The *Tribuna da Imprensa* replied that the trouble had been caused by the failure of the press to report the incident fairly, a failure it blamed on Communist infiltration among reporters. "This is the truth," it wrote.[6]

The *Jornal do Brasil,* accused by the *Tribuna* of such infiltration, said it could understand the concern of Lacerdistas about the "surprising" election results but could not understand the *Tribuna*'s failure to appreciate that the *Jornal do Brasil* had provided "the best coverage" of the IAPB affair and had severely criticized the pension institute, the PTB, and Goulart. Perhaps, it wrote, the *Tribuna* considered the *Jornal do Brasil* reporting staff a "hotbed of Communists" because a preelection poll of *Jornal do Brasil* employees had given Sérgio Magalhães a slight edge. But, the *Jornal do Brasil* pointed out, the *Tribuna* should bear in mind that the same poll had revealed little support for Communist-backed Lott and Goulart.[7]

The final result of the October 3 governorship race, announced in the press on October 12, gave 356,722 votes to Lacerda, 331,592 to Sérgio Magalhães, 221,887 to Tenório Cavalcanti, and 51,503 to Mendes de Morais. Marcelo Garcia, who handled the finances of Lacerda's campaign, believes that if the campaign had lasted two or three more weeks, the victory would have gone to Sérgio Magalhães. Likewise, political scientist Gláucio Ary Dillon Soares, noting gains made by Sérgio Magalhães in the last three weeks of campaigning, feels that Sérgio Magalhães might well have won had the election occurred in November.[8]

According to the *Correio da Manhã,* Lacerda had good support from the middle class and was saved by the candidacy of Tenório Cavalcanti, "whose electorate is the same as that of the PTB candidate." *Última Hora,* pointing to returns that it said showed three out of four voters opposing Lacerda, expressed its fear of a "dictatorship against the people" by a "government of an inexpressive minority."[9]

Analyzing the 1960 returns, Gláucio Ary Dillon Soares finds that Lacerda had strong support among voters who favored foreign capital and who opposed state intervention in the economy. Breakdowns of voters by economic classes and importance of job positions led Soares to conclude that Lacerda was a class candidate, receiving even more votes from the upper classes than might have been expected to go to the parties nominating him but failing to show, in the lower classes, anything appreciably better than the conservative parties could have been expected to receive. "In the 1960s," Soares has also written, "it was only in the upper socio-economic groups that Lacerda found a response greater than expected; in the lower strata . . . the perspectives of Lacerda were worse than what could have been expected considering the support given to his party."

Soares also concludes that the votes given to Sérgio Magalhães indicate that the PTB-PSB candidate was not a class candidate, for they were distributed rather evenly between white-collar employees and manual laborers. Soares would guess, however, that Sérgio Magalhães' showing among voters in the lower classes might have been more positive had it not been for the bid by Tenório Cavalcanti, who, he finds, was definitely a class candidate, strong among laborers and the poor.[10]

On the national scene, the "fenômeno Jânio Quadros" swept Brazil more vigorously than it had swept São Paulo before. Quadros received close to six million votes, nearly equaling the combined total cast for Lott and Ademar de Barros. Goulart, by edging past Milton Campos, won the vice-presidency once again. In Minas Gerais the governorship went to Magalhães Pinto.

The makeup of the Guanabara thirty-man constitutional assembly was not as unfavorable to Lacerda as pictured by *Última Hora,* which called attention to the defeats of some of the candidates favored by Lacerda, such as educators Carlos Flexa Ribeiro and Raimundo Moniz de Aragão. The UDN, with nine seats, emerged as the largest party and was followed by the PTB with six seats and the PSD with four. Each of five smaller parties (PR, PRT, PSP, PSB, and PTN) would have two representatives, and the PDC one. PSB candidate Maurício Caminha de Lacerda was not elected.[11]

Lutero Vargas, recipient of 11,386 votes, was the most popular constitutional assembly candidate of the PTB, whose delegation (including Roland Corbisier and journalist José Saldanha Coelho) could be expected to attack Lacerda savagely. Heading the PSD list were former Education Secretary Gonzaga da Gama Filho, winner of 15,343 votes, and Lopo Coelho, winner of 8,215 votes. Lopo Coelho, a congressman in the 1950s, had served earlier in high posts under President Dutra and more recently been secretary of agriculture, industry, and commerce in what had been the Federal District.[12]

On an individual basis the election for the Guanabara constitutional assembly was a resounding triumph for Amaral Netto. The *udenista* who had worked on the *Tribuna* and founded the violently anti-Kubitschek *Maquis*

Carlos Lacerda. (Drawing by Appe in *O Cruzeiro,* reproduced in Vol. 4 of Herman Lima, *História da Caricatura no Brasil*)

magazine and Lantern Club was given 35,203 votes, more than twice the number received by his closest rival. To serve with him on the UDN *bancada,* the voters chose Aliomar Baleeiro, Temístocles Cavalcanti, Afonso Arinos Filho, Jorge Valadão, Sandra Cavalcanti, Lígia Lessa Bastos, Raul Brunini, and Frota Aguiar.[13]

Former Finance Minister Eugênio Gudin, in his *O Globo* column, praised the "first class men" chosen for the constitutional assembly, mentioning Temístocles Cavalcanti, Aliomar Baleeiro, Lopo Coelho, Amaral Netto, and Gladstone Chaves de Melo (PDC). "Only a small residue of the old vulgar herd," he said, "succeeded in gaining admittance to this assembly of regeneration."[14] It was to be an assembly in which the combined strength of the parties that had nominated Lacerda would be fourteen, less than a majority. Therefore, while jurist Temístocles Cavalcanti worked on a draft of a state constitution, Lacerda met at the Praia do Flamengo apartment with the future *udenista constituintes* in order to discuss an alliance. The group abandoned the idea of having Aliomar Baleeiro become assembly president and agreed on the PSD's Lopo Coelho, who could provide two assembly votes besides his own[15] and thus give the incoming administration a majority, even if it was not a closely knit one. Amaral Netto was the choice to head the UDN *bancada.*

10. Preparing to Tour the World (October 1960)

It was the season for victorious politicians, such as Jânio Quadros, José de Magalhães Pinto, and Carlos Lacerda, to make extended trips abroad.

For Lacerda, planning an ambitious trip that would take him to the United States, Japan, Taiwan, and Europe, the situation was complicated because the organization of the new state of Guanabara was far from complete. When Lacerda left Rio for New York on October 28 with his son Sérgio and press secretary Walter Cunto, he did not know the date of his inauguration. The PSD, in no hurry to have Lacerda take over from Kubitschek appointee Sette Câmara, had been arguing that the incoming administration of Guanabara should take office on January 31, 1961, when the new president of Brazil would be sworn in. Late in September, however, the Regional Electoral Tribunal (TRE) ruled that the new governor and the constitutional assembly should be inaugurated ten days after the TRE handed out, probably late in November, the certificates of election.[1]

The PTB, unsuccessful in getting the Guanabara gubernatorial election annulled for what it called fraud, urged its constitutional assemblymen to turn to the labor unions, factories, and *favelas* to gain popular backing for limiting the governor's term to two years. The UDN, defending a five-year term, cited the law written by PTB Congressman San Tiago Dantas and adopted by the federal government in April 1960 to create the new state.[2]

Lacerda has written that the San Tiago Dantas Law, despite the talent of its author, was an "insanity" that produced "a fetus, not even a new born child!"[3] Whatever the cause, much remained to be settled, such as whether

Guanabara, like other states, should be divided into municipalities, each with a mayor and municipal council.

The most serious pending problem was the status (if any) of the Rio Municipal Council, whose fifty members had been elected in October 1958 to serve until January 1963. This notorious "Gilded Cage" had passed a law, just before the October 1960 elections, that would increase by nine billion cruzeiros the wages of the state's ninety thousand employees. To save the state from bankruptcy, Sette Câmara vetoed most of the increases, but the Gilded Cage overrode the vetoes. It had, of course, no sympathy for the plan of the newly elected constitutional assembly to make itself the exclusive state legislature and close down the Municipal Council. The Municipal Council, determined to fight the plan in court with the help of lawyers Sobral Pinto and Hariberto de Miranda Jordão (Wainer's former lawyer), quoted the San Tiago Dantas Law, which gave the Municipal Council exclusive legislative and veto powers until the new constitution was promulgated and which stipulated that the fifty municipal councilmen should thereafter join the thirty constitutional assemblymen to form the new legislature.[4]

The status of the Military Police of the old Federal District was another organizational problem. In October, when Justice Minister Armando Falcão sought to "federalize" the Military Police force of Guanabara, placing it under the control of the government of the nation, Lacerda received a letter from officers of that six-thousand-man troop saying they would agree to nothing but "federalization." Lacerda called Falcão's proposal unconstitutional.[5]

Before going abroad, Lacerda met frequently at his apartment with his early choices for administrative posts (some yet to be created), such as Hélio Beltrão, chosen to direct planning, and Rafael de Almeida Magalhães, chosen to administer the governor's office. Lacerda, who enjoyed writing notes, dictated a stream of them to his secretary, Ruth Alverga, with instructions for his new team about inauguration plans and future government steps. In his note for Carlos Flexa Ribeiro, the incoming education secretary, Lacerda asked him to consult Aderbal Jurema, "the best education secretary Pernambuco ever had."[6]

Also before going abroad, Lacerda called on General Odílio Denys, who had carried out the November 11, 1955, "coup of Lott" and, in February 1960, replaced Lott as Kubitschek's war minister. Lacerda wanted to take to Quadros in Portugal the assurance of the war minister that the president-elect would be inaugurated. Denys told Lacerda that although "some of us are a little worried about his temperament, we have no hostility." The army, he said, would respect the will of the people and hoped to help Quadros "bring about the government he promised."

The conversation, at the marshal's apartment, was mostly about November 1955, with Lacerda remarking that he himself had not had the forces necessary to carry out the coup that Denys now accused him of having wanted. "The UDN leaders," Lacerda told Denys, "planned to adopt my point of view in case it worked out. As it did not work out, some of them took refuge in a comfortable legalism and left me all by myself."

Denys said, "You people, especially you, misled yourselves about military forces when you plotted a revolution. I never gave the matter much importance, but Lott did." Asked by Lacerda to explain his lack of concern, Denys replied that he had learned in military school not to worry about what the adversary wants to do but only about what the adversary is able to do. "That," Lacerda said, "is a good lesson for me and I shall remember it the rest of my life."[7]

EPILOGUE

Governor-Elect

Following Denys' assurances about the inauguration of Jânio, coups were not on Lacerda's mind. As the incoming governor of Guanabara, he had his heart set on giving the state the administration he had been describing almost daily during four months of campaigning. Political power, he often said, was attractive to him only because it gave him the opportunity to be constructive and serve the people. "It amazes me to see people do everything possible to achieve power and then . . . limit themselves to the enjoyment of the privileges and honors that it offers."[1]

Reviewing the career of his father, Maurício de Lacerda, Carlos wrote in 1967 that the opposition congressman and orator of the 1920s had considered public life a grant, or trusteeship, to be used constructively, not a claim for personal advantage. Unfortunately, Carlos added, Maurício had been denied the opportunity of becoming, as he had seemed destined, the creator of great projects; he had been left—unjustly, according to Carlos—with the reputation of being a politician and writer who knew only how to destroy, "the same reputation that people wanted to fasten on me." "But I had what was denied him, the opportunity to demonstrate that I was able to do what I demanded of others and refrain from doing what I condemned in others."[2]

During his years as a journalist and congressman Lacerda had achieved such fame for savage attacks that many questioned whether he had the qualifications necessary to provide a constructive administration. In trying to convince the electorate that Kubitschek and his team were forever at fault, he had sometimes taken positions that an impartial observer can only consider to be unfair. But it would be wrong to conclude that Lacerda lacked the ability to be objective just because he played the role of oppositionist to the hilt in a setting in which the political combatants of all stripes were more concerned with fighting than fairness. In considering what was in store for Guanabara, the characteristics revealed by the journalist-congressman that were important were boundless energy and enthusiasm.

Lacerda's dynamism augured well for the incoming administration. He had never been known to shy away from making decisions and, according to everything that was known about his temperament, would be likely to insist that they be carried through with speed and excellence. He was an impatient leader who combined passion for great projects with an eye for detail and a dislike of routine.

Lacerda possessed a vast amount of firsthand knowledge of conditions in the new state. A Carioca by birth, he had spent most of his life in Rio and had studied the problems as a journalist, municipal councilman, and congressman. Experts, called in during the recent campaign to propose solutions to the problems, found him a quick reader and intelligent listener, who captured the necessary details with amazing speed. He showed vision rather than intransigence during discussions with these advisers.

The large team of advisers reflected well his ability to attract talent. After he made his first selections for executive positions in the new government, *O Globo* wrote of "the care and impartiality with which Lacerda chose his immediate collaborators, honest and capable people."[3]

While directing his newspaper, Lacerda had built up an effective team, inspired and loyal. Subordinates, it is true, found him always demanding, sometimes difficult to work for, and occasionally explosive. He loathed mediocrity. His dedication, demonstrated during the extremely long hours he worked, was frequently infectious, and, when it was not, he could be expected to react, berating or dismissing employees who failed to measure up to his standards. As David Nasser had written during the recent election campaign, Lacerda would not let friendships stand in the way of giving the new state an administration that was dynamic and honest.

The denouncer of dishonest politicians was determined to keep a sharp eye out to make certain that his own administration was free of taint. Appalled by idleness, he promised a healthy upheaval for a government apparatus whose payroll included workers whose chief task was to receive paychecks. Eugênio Gudin, welcoming the new chief executive of Guanabara, called him "a citizen who personifies moral cleanliness and therefore war against the sordid political practices and swindling implanted on this poor city for over half a century."[4]

Lacerda was so eager to be scrupulous that he withdrew, before going abroad, his offer of the finance secretaryship to Congressman Raimundo Padilha. Having learned that *Última Hora* was prepared to publish a headline revealing that the finance post was going to a man who was in default on payments owed to the Bank of the Municipality, Lacerda spoke with Padilha, who explained that his lack of resources had not allowed him to liquidate a loan made necessary by the unsuccessful business venture of a son. Lacerda wrote to Padilha that he could not appoint him, bearing in mind "the example that must be given" not just to enemies but above all to friends and "considering public opinion in general." "I cannot begin the government with an act that I would condemn in any governor."[5]

Lacerda decided that it would be best for his family that he not reside in Guanabara Palace. Feeling that the children of Vargas had not benefited from palace life, he said to his niece Lygia, "Look at Vargas, who put his children in the palace." So careful was Carlos that he had family squabbles. One of the worst was with his mother, Olga, on the day he assumed the governorship. Olga, returning from a beauty parlor and putting on a new dress for the occasion, was ordered by Carlos to resign from her job in the municipal finance secretaryship. It was a job she had secured through her many friends in the municipal offices after years of work for the municipality but was one of those that required little more than collecting wages. She reacted to her son's demand with abundant tears and reminders of her long life of sacrifices, and Carlos had to deal with her more carefully before she would consent to his request, wipe away her tears, and attend the inaugural ceremony.[6]

"Lacerda," Rafael de Almeida Magalhães has written, "had a marvelous side, that of irreproachable honesty; I never saw him arranging to find employment for anybody, not even for his former teacher. But he also had the somber, personalistic side of *'l'état c'est moi.'*"[7]

The personalistic side of Lacerda, mentioned by Rafael, was in strong evidence during his two terms in Congress. Both before and after he achieved his leadership posts, he defined, and identified himself with, the positions he felt his party should assume. In doing so with passion, Lucia Hippolito writes, he contributed to the polarization of Brazil, becoming a point of reference for describing concepts, such as rightism and leftism, *golpismo* and legalism. "Positions with respect to Lacerda were used to classify people, characterize them, place them in categories."[8]

Failing, in his first year in Congress, to achieve his radical political objectives, Lacerda came to regard his fellow *udenistas* as timid politicians who would have sided with him had his views prevailed and were content to use him as the "sacrificial lamb," the main target to be attacked. Carlos had displayed a human capacity to see himself as a martyr ever since childhood, when he had found that spankings had given an iridescence to the halos he had pictured above his head.

After assuming leadership posts in the congressional opposition, Carlos had some success in gaining his party's acceptance of his views, thus provoking José Cândido Ferraz and other *udenista* friends of Kubitschek to complain of "the methods that Carlos Lacerda has been forcing on the leadership of the opposition bloc." An examination of Lacerda's methods reveals, however, that the weapon he most frequently used was his extraordinary power to persuade. The orator who could alter the opinions of large audiences, and whose arguments were found by Afonso Arinos to be "almost always brilliant" and more effective than his own, was a master convincer. Hugo Levy, who assisted Lacerda in his work in Congress, recalls that the UDN leader was so convincing in argument that some of his congressional opponents feared talking with him because they did not want to be seduced.[9]

When arguments failed, Lacerda occasionally turned to another weapon, the personalistic one of making his point dramatically by threatening to resign his leadership post and even his party membership. Resignation threats were effective moves for men such as Quadros and Lacerda, whose records as vote-getters and orators were impressive enough to give them leverage in a weak political party system. Nor were the threats to be taken lightly when they were made by political titans tempted by the vision of gaining the support that an apparent sacrifice might bring while retiring from a difficult affray (but not from the war).

If, as journalist Prudente de Moraes, neto believed at the time, Brazilians wanted to feel they were really being governed,[10] the choices of Quadros and Lacerda appeared to have been good ones. It remained to be seen, however, whether *"l'état c'est moi"* philosophy could be adapted to political conditions that demanded a certain amount of conciliation. Lacerda, as congressman, had seldom been willing to be conciliatory. He was loath to make deals or even hide his contempt for mediocrity. As incoming governor, he had no intention of adhering to the custom of handing out jobs for the sake of pleasing state legislators or other people of influence. Governor Lacerda, former Public Works Secretary Enaldo Cravo Peixoto says, "was a very bad politician" because he did not handle the legislators tactfully and "refused, absolutely, to take care of any political request." The governor also surrendered the executive's traditional prerogative of naming state attorneys and notary publics with an eye on gaining political advantages; he saw to it that these appointments were determined by *concursos* (competitive examinations).[11]

To the traits of Lacerda that suggested trouble on the local level can be added his tendency to be hypercritical of superiors. He had made life difficult for presidents of the UDN as well as presidents of the republic and their ministers. Because the relationships of states to the central government were important for financial and other reasons, Guanabara seemed likely to be affected if its new governor persisted in being a thorn in the side of those who governed Brazil.

After Lacerda was elected governor, Roberto de Abreu Sodré liked to tell him that he would do well to concentrate on administering the state, for an exemplary term in Guanabara Palace would go a long way toward bringing him the UDN presidential nomination in 1965. It would be ludicrous to believe that Lacerda did not have his eye on the presidency, much as he might deny it and speak of wanting to return to journalism. But he also regarded the opportunity to be constructive in Guanabara as an end in itself—a new challenge in his life of adventures and one to be handled with his usual vigor.

It might have been assumed that Lacerda's role of assailant of the top authorities would be altered as a result of the inauguration in January 1961 of Jânio Quadros, for whom he professed a warm friendship. But how would the touchy Quadros react to Lacerda's view that friendship was no reason to discard frank criticism and that he was performing a useful service in condemning what he felt were faults? After all, the condemnation was so often done in public and in such strong language that the service was seldom appreciated.

Lacerda, who had spent a lifetime becoming a national figure by combating federal administrations, would soon again take the lead in stirring up Brazil whenever he felt the country ought to share his indignation. No longer handicapped by the radio and television censorship imposed on him during the Kubitschek administration, he was to gain the reputation, while governor, of being the "overthrower of presidents."

He deserves, however, to be better known as the man who gave Guanabara a spectacularly constructive administration. Despite handicaps caused by his refusal to ingratiate himself with men of political influence on the local or national level, he made good on his campaign promises to the Cariocas. With imagination and energy, he handled the innumerable problems whose solutions could hardly be deferred, such as those related to education, health, water supply, sewage, housing, and transportation. In addition he built up a vigorous state bank and advanced Rio as a cultural center. From his administration the Cariocas received attractive parks and playgrounds and a city that was much cleaner and more beautiful than it had been.

"Lacerda," Ayrton Baffa writes, "was the ablest governor that this crazy city of Rio de Janeiro has known in its contemporary history." In the words of Congressman Laerte Vieira, he was an "unusual administrator" whose "complete dedication, indomitable dynamism, capacity for work, sure command, vision, and foresight shook up archaic processes and found a substitute for the corrupt bureaucratic machine, thus achieving, with perfect rigor and smoothness, a great work that penetrated all sectors of public administration." In the opinion of Sobral Pinto, Lacerda's accomplishments as governor surprised even his friends.[12]

Notes

NOTE: References to CPDOC are to the Centro de Pesquisa e Documentação de História Contemporânea do Brasil in the Instituto de Direito Público e Ciência Política, Fundação Getúlio Vargas, Rio de Janeiro. References to CCL and LFC are to the Carlos Lacerda collection in the library of the University of Brasília and to the papers in the hands of the Lacerda family in Rio de Janeiro. References to DFR are to Daphne F. Rodger.

Prologue

1. José Honório Rodrigues, introduction to Carlos Lacerda, *Discursos Parlamentares,* p. 26. Dario de Almeida Magalhães, in Lourenço Dantas Mota, compiler, *A História Vivida,* vol. 2, p. 221.

2. Paulo Pinheiro Chagas, *Esse Velho Vento da Aventura: Memórias,* p. 330.

3. Afonso Arinos de Melo Franco, *Diário de Bolso seguido de Retrato de Noiva,* p. 16.

4. José Honório Rodrigues, introduction to Carlos Lacerda, *Discursos Parlamentares,* p. 28.

5. *Última Hora,* May 16, 1957.

6. Aspásia Camargo, Maria Tereza Lopes Teixeira, and Maria Clara Mariani, *O Intelectual e o Político: Encontros com Afonso Arinos,* p. 155.

7. David Nasser, "Elogio ao Adversário," *O Cruzeiro,* September 7, 1960.

I. Son of Maurício (1914–1931)

1. Family Background (1860–1900)

1. John Dos Passos, *Brazil on the Move,* p. 143.

2. Carlos Lacerda, "Rosas e Pedras do Meu Caminho," Chapter 1 (*Manchete* 782, April 15, 1967), pp. 25–26. Carlos Lacerda, *A Casa do Meu Avô,* pp. 77, 78, 150.

3. Carlos Lacerda, "Rosas e Pedras do Meu Caminho," Chapter 1, pp. 25–26. Flávio Galvão, "Sebastião de Lacerda, Juiz do Supremo Tribunal Fe-

deral," *Revista do Tribunal de Contas do Município de São Paulo,* vol. 8, no. 25 (April 1979), p. 30.

4. Galvão, "Sebastião de Lacerda," p. 28.
5. Carlos Lacerda, *A Casa do Meu Avô,* pp. 33, 76, 77.
6. Vera Lacerda Paiva, letter to JWFD, Rio de Janeiro, May 8, 1984.
7. Carlos Lacerda, *A Casa do Meu Avô,* pp. 76, 105.
8. Maurício de Lacerda, "Memórias," handwritten, in the Carlos Lacerda collection at the University of Brasília (henceforth called CCL).
9. Ibid. Carlos Lacerda, *A Casa do Meu Avô,* p. 76.

2. A Multitude of Relatives (1900–1914)

1. Carlos Lacerda, "Rosas e Pedras de Meu Caminho," Chapter 2 (*Manchete* 783, April 2, 1967), p. 26. Carlos Lacerda, *A Casa do Meu Avô,* p. 95. Cláudio Lacerda, "Lacerda: Uma Vida de Lutas," *Fatos & Fotos,* Chapter 2, p. 5.
2. Maurício de Lacerda, *Entre Duas Revoluções,* pp. 36–38.
3. Maurício de Lacerda and Olga Caminhoá Werneck, correspondence, 1907–1909, in CCL.
4. Carlos Lacerda, notes about his family, in CCL.
5. Galvão, "Sebastião de Lacerda," p. 39.
6. Carlos Lacerda, *A Casa do Meu Avô,* pp. 104–105. Odilon Lacerda Paiva, interview, Rio de Janeiro, August 5, 1984.
7. Sebastião Lacerda, interview at Chácara Lacerda (in Sebastião de Lacerda, Rio de Janeiro), July 3, 1983.
8. Carlos Lacerda, *A Casa do Meu Avô,* p. 120.

3. Maurício Enters Politics (1910–1918)

1. Maurício de Lacerda, *Entre Duas Revoluções,* p. 40.
2. Ibid., p. 51.
3. Carlos Lacerda, "Rosas e Pedras do Meu Caminho," Chapter 1, p. 23. "Perfil de um candidato," Part 3, *Última Hora,* September 21, 1960. Lucia Hippolito, "Carlos Lacerda, Ascensão e Queda da 'Metralhadora Giratória': Esboço de biografia política" (Rio de Janeiro: typewritten, June 1978), p. 3.
4. Fernando de Lacerda, letter to Sebastião de Lacerda, n.d., in CCL.
5. Carlos Lacerda, interview, Washington, D.C., September 17, 1968. Carlos Lacerda, "Rosas e Pedras do Meu Caminho," Chapter 2, p. 25. Fernando de Lacerda, letter to Sebastião de Lacerda, Rio de Janeiro, July 8, 1912, in CCL.
6. Carlos Lacerda, notes about his family, in CCL. Carlos Lacerda, interview, Rio de Janeiro, July 3, 1971. Paulo de Lacerda, letters to Sebastião de Lacerda, 1917, and letter to Sebastião de Lacerda, Mogi Mirim, January 15, 1919, in CCL.
7. Fernando de Lacerda, letters to Sebastião de Lacerda, Rio de Janeiro, October 2, 1912, and October 11, 1915, in CCL.
8. Cláudio Lacerda, "Lacerda: Uma Vida de Lutas," Chapter 1, p. 8. Mau-

rício de Lacerda, *Entre Duas Revoluções*, pp. 40–44. Maurício de Lacerda, *Segunda República*, p. 246.

9. *Na Barricada*, 1, no. 6 (September 23, 1915). *Correio da Manhã*, May 20, 1917. Nelson Werneck Sodré, *A História da Imprensa no Brasil*, p. 363.

10. Olga Caminhoá Werneck Lacerda, letter to Sebastião de Lacerda, March 14, 1914, in CCL.

11. Carlos Lacerda, "Rosas e Pedras do Meu Caminho," Chapter 2, p. 26.

12. Maurício de Lacerda, *Entre Duas Revoluções*, p. 67.

13. *O Estado de S. Paulo*, November 15, 1918. Carioca: Native or resident of the city of Rio de Janeiro.

14. Maurício de Lacerda, letter to Olga Lacerda, Paris, December 13, 1918.

15. Vera Lacerda Paiva, letter to JWFD, May 8, 1984. Carlos Lacerda, "Rosas e Pedras do Meu Caminho," Chapter 2, p. 26. Diary of Clara Freitas quoted in Cláudio Lacerda, "Lacerda: Uma Vida de Lutas," Chapter 2, p. 5.

4. Tribune of the Proletariat (1919–1924)

1. Maurício de Lacerda, *Entre Duas Revoluções*, pp. 54–55.

2. Ibid., p. 67.

3. Ibid., pp. 58, 92, 67. Maurício de Lacerda, *Segunda República*, p. 247.

4. Maurício de Lacerda, "O Congresso Operário," *Voz do Povo*, 1, no. 9 (February 14, 1920).

5. Maurício de Lacerda, "No Eito da Leopoldina," *Voz do Povo*, 1, no. 16 (February 22, 1920).

6. Maurício de Lacerda, *Entre Duas Revoluções*, pp. 58–59. Fluminense: Native or resident of the state of Rio de Janeiro (sometimes referred to as Rio state).

7. Maurício de Lacerda, *Entre Duas Revoluções*, pp. 138–139.

8. Ibid., pp. 136–137, 135. Maurício de Lacerda, *História de uma Covardia*, pp. 47–48.

9. Maurício de Lacerda, *Entre Duas Revoluções*, pp. 117, 111. Cláudio Lacerda, "Lacerda: Uma Vida de Lutas," Chapter 3. Maurício de Lacerda entry in *Dicionário Histórico-Biográfico Brasileiro, 1930–1983.*

10. Maurício de Lacerda, autobiographical notes in the files of *O Estado de S. Paulo.*

11. Maurício de Lacerda, *Entre Duas Revoluções*, pp. 151–153, 158.

12. Otávio Brandão, interview, Rio de Janeiro, November 14, 1970.

13. Maurício de Lacerda, *Entre Duas Revoluções*, pp. 161–164.

5. Carlos and His Relatives (1919–1924)

1. Maurício Caminha de Lacerda, interview with Daphne F. Rodger (henceforth shown as DFR), Rio de Janeiro, April 7, 1983.

2. Carlos Lacerda, *A Casa do Meu Avô*, p. 135.

3. Ibid. Cláudio Lacerda, "Lacerda: Uma Vida de Lutas," Chapter 2, p. 4. Vera's expression was found by her in a book about child psychology.

4. Vera Lacerda Paiva, letter to JWFD, May 8, 1984, pp. 3, 6. Vera Lacerda Paiva, interview with DFR, Rio de Janeiro, February 7, 1983.

5. Carlos Lacerda, *A Casa do Meu Avô,* p. 86.

6. Vera Lacerda Paiva, interview with DFR, Rio de Janeiro, February 13, 1983.

7. Vera Lacerda Paiva, interview with DFR, February 7, 1983. See Carlos Lacerda, *A Casa do Meu Avô,* p. 86.

8. Carlos Lacerda, Notebook 4 (handwritten while in hiding, early 1936), pp. 823–827. See pp. 4–5 of Vera Lacerda Paiva's typewritten transcription.

9. Carlos Lacerda, "José Conta o Seu Roubo," in *Xanam e Outras Histórias,* pp. 29–42. Carlos Lacerda, "Rosas e Pedras do Meu Caminho," Chapter 4 (*Manchete,* May 6, 1967), p. 31.

10. Austregésilo de Athayde, interview with DFR, Rio de Janeiro, March 21, 1983.

11. Vera Lacerda Paiva, letter to JWFD, May 8, 1984, and interview, August 5, 1984. Carlos Lacerda, interviews, September 17, 1968, and July 3, 1971.

12. Comments of Léa Paiva Borges Carneiro, given to DFR during interview with Vera Lacerda Paiva, February 13, 1983.

13. Carlos Lacerda, *A Casa do Meu Avô,* p. 81.

14. Marcos [Carlos Lacerda], *O Quilombo de Manoel Congo* (see "Dedicatória"). Marcos [Carlos Lacerda], "Tia Colodina," *Revista Acadêmica,* 2, 13 (August 1935). See also Carlos Lacerda, *A Casa do Meu Avô,* pp. 99–107. The real name of Colodina was Claudina.

15. Carlos Lacerda, *A Casa do Meu Avô,* pp. 120–121.

16. Ibid., pp. 47, 163.

17. Ibid., pp. 77, 35–36, 37. Carlos Lacerda, "Rosas e Pedras do Meu Caminho," Chapter 1, p. 29; Chapter 12 (*Manchete,* July 1, 1967), p. 110.

18. Carlos Lacerda, *A Casa do Meu Avô,* p. 149. Fernando de Lacerda, letter to Sebastião de Lacerda, 1923, in Carlos Lacerda, "Rosas e Pedras do Meu Caminho," Chapter 3 (*Manchete,* April 29, 1967), p. 30. Vera Lacerda Paiva, letter to JWFD, May 8, 1984.

19. Carlos Lacerda, letter to Olga Lacerda, in Carlos Lacerda, "Rosas e Pedras do Meu Caminho," Chapter 1, p. 24.

6. The Death of Sebastião (July 5, 1925)

1. Carlos Lacerda, "Rosas e Pedras do Meu Caminho," Chapter 3 (*Manchete,* April 29, 1967) and Chapter 4 (*Manchete,* May 6, 1967), p. 28.

2. Maurício de Lacerda, *História de uma Covardia,* pp. 401–402, 103.

3. Maurício Caminha de Lacerda, interview, Rio de Janeiro, August 29, 1984.

4. Galvão, "Sebastião de Lacerda," pp. 39–40, 43. Maurício de Lacerda, *História de uma Covardia,* p. 104.

5. Galvão, "Sebastião de Lacerda," p. 41.

6. Ibid. Carlos Lacerda, *A Casa do Meu Avô,* p. 24.

7. Maurício de Lacerda, *História de uma Covardia,* pp. 111, 436–437.
8. Ibid., pp. 436–439. Galvão, pp. 42–43. Carlos Lacerda, *A Casa do Meu Avô,* p. 152.
9. *Correio da Manhã,* July 7, 1925.
10. Carlos Lacerda, *A Casa do Meu Avô,* p. 42.

7. Hard Times for the Family (1925–1927)

1. Carlos Lacerda, *A Casa do Meu Avô,* p. 42.
2. Carlos Lacerda, "Rosas e Pedras do Meu Caminho," Chapter 3, p. 31.
3. Vera Lacerda Paiva, letter to JWFD, May 8, 1984, p. 3.
4. Charles Pullen Hargreaves, "Carlos Lacerda," typewritten recollections, Rio de Janeiro, January 28, 1983.
5. Ibid. Carlos Lacerda, "Rosas e Pedras do Meu Caminho," Chapter 4, p. 29; Chapter 3, p. 31.
6. Otávio Brandão, interview, Rio de Janeiro, November 14, 1970.
7. Carlos Lacerda, *Depoimento,* p. 29. Carlos Lacerda, interviews, Washington and Rio de Janeiro, September 17, 1968, and July 3, 1971.
8. Maurício de Lacerda, *História de uma Covardia,* pp. 153, 127, 157. *O Estado de S. Paulo,* September 19, 24, 1925. Cláudio Lacerda, "Lacerda: Uma Vida de Lutas," Chapter 3, p. 3.
9. Carlos Lacerda, "Rosas e Pedras do Meu Caminho," Chapter 3, p. 31.
10. Cláudio Lacerda, "Lacerda: Uma Vida de Lutas," Chapter 3, pp. 4, 3.
11. "Carta de Maurício de Lacerda aos Diretores do Centro Eleitoral do 2º Distrito," *5 de Julho,* no. 23 (May 18, 1925).
12. Maurício de Lacerda, letter to Agripino Nazaré, March 10, 1926, in Maurício de Lacerda, *Entre Duas Revoluções,* appendix ("Da Masmorra"), pp. 40–44. Cláudio Lacerda, "Lacerda: Uma Vida de Lutas," Chapter 3, p. 6.
13. Maurício de Lacerda, letters to Everardo Dias and Otávio Brandão, in Maurício de Lacerda, *Entre Duas Revoluções,* appendix ("Da Masmorra"), pp. 140–152, 152–154. Report of speech by Maurício de Lacerda, *Correio da Manhã,* February 9, 1927. Maurício de Lacerda, *Entre Duas Revoluções,* pp. 191–192.
14. *A Nação,* January 3, February 12, 1927. Maurício de Lacerda, *História de uma Covardia,* p. 376. Otávio Brandão, interview, Rio de Janeiro, August 30, 1970. Cláudio Lacerda, "Lacerda: Uma Vida de Lutas," Chapter 4, p. 6.

8. Pio Americano and Forquilha (late 1920s)

1. Carlos Lacerda, "Rosas e Pedras do Meu Caminho," Chapter 3, p. 31.
2. Carlos Lacerda, *A Casa do Meu Avô,* p. 105.
3. Vera Lacerda Paiva, letter to JWFD, Rio de Janeiro, July 14, 1984.
4. Carlos Lacerda, *A Casa do Meu Avô,* p. 20. Carlos Lacerda, "Rosas e Pedras do Meu Caminho," Chapter 4, pp. 29–31.
5. Ibid.
6. Emil Farhat, interview, São Paulo, August 2, 1983.

7. Carlos Lacerda, letters to Delmira Cruz, Rio de Janeiro, December 12, 1927, and Comércio, December 30, 1927, in CCL.

8. Carlos Lacerda, "Rosas e Pedras do Meu Caminho," Chapter 2, p. 24.

9. Emil Farhat, interview, August 2, 1983, and interview with DFR, São Paulo, March 11, 1983.

10. *Correio da Manhã,* December 22, 1928. Carlos Lacerda, *Depoimento,* p. 27.

11. Carlos Lacerda, interview, September 17, 1968.

12. Carlos Lacerda, autobiographical notes in small black binder in CCL. Olga Caminhoá Werneck Lacerda, letter to her children, The Hague, September 15, 1928, in CCL.

13. Carlos Lacerda, "Rosas e Pedras do Meu Caminho," Chapter 1, p. 27.

14. Carlos Lacerda, autobiographical notes in small black binder in CCL. Carlos Lacerda, "Rosas e Pedras do Meu Caminho," Chapter 3, p. 30. Carlos Lacerda, letter to Olga Lacerda, Rio de Janeiro, August 6, 1928, in CCL.

15. Léa Paiva Borges Carneiro, handwritten notes, Rio de Janeiro, February 13, 1983. Carlos Lacerda, *A Case do Meu Avô,* p. 105.

16. Carlos Lacerda, "Rosas e Pedras do Meu Caminho," Chapter 3, p. 30. Léa Paiva Borges Carneiro, handwritten notes.

17. Vera Lacerda Paiva, letter to JWFD, May 8, 1984, p. 8. Carlos Lacerda, Notebook 4 (handwritten while in hiding, December 1935–January 1936), p. 535. See p. 12 of Vera Lacerda Paiva's typewritten transcription.

9. Maurício, Carlos, and the 1930 Revolution (1928–1930)

1. João Batista Barreto Leite Filho, interviews with Luís Carlos Prestes and Maurício de Lacerda, *O Jornal,* April 6, 8, 1928.

2. Maurício de Lacerda, *Segunda República,* pp. 58–59.

3. Otávio Brandão, interviews, Rio de Janeiro, November 14, 1970, June 27, 1971, and letter to JWFD, Rio de Janeiro, May 25, 1971.

4. Leôncio Basbaum, *Uma Vida em Seis Tempos: Memórias,* pp. 53, 64, 67–68. Eliezer Pacheco, *O Partido Comunista Brasileiro (1922–1964),* p. 231.

5. *O Jornal,* June 1, 1930. *Correio da Manhã,* June 6, 1930.

6. Affonso Henriques, *Vargas o Maquiavélico,* pp. 79–82. Gaúcho: Native or resident of Rio Grande do Sul. Mineiro: Native or resident of Minas Gerais.

7. Charles Pullen Hargreaves, "Carlos Lacerda," p. 2. Maurício de Lacerda, *Segunda República,* p. 212.

8. Cláudio Lacerda, "Lacerda: Uma Vida de Lutas," Chapter 4, pp. 2, 3. Maurício de Lacerda, *Segunda República,* pp. 206, 213.

9. Carlos Lacerda, "Rosas e Pedras do Meu Caminho," Chapter 5 (*Manchete,* May 13, 1967), pp. 27–28.

10. Ibid. Maurício de Lacerda, *Segunda República,* pp. 219–221.

11. Carlos Lacerda, "Rosas e Pedras do Meu Caminho," Chapter 5, p. 29.

10. The Uruguay Trip and Its Aftermath (1930–1931)

1. Cláudio Lacerda, "Carlos Lacerda: Uma Vida de Lutas," Chapter 3, p. 3.
2. Carlos Lacerda, "Rosas e Pedras do Meu Caminho," Chapter 5, p. 29.
3. Ibid.
4. Ibid.
5. Maurício Paiva de Lacerda, *A Evolução Legislativa do Direito Social Brasileiro,* p. xxxii (see also preface by Maurício Caminha de Lacerda, p. xix).
6. Maurício de Lacerda, *Segunda República,* pp. 249–255.
7. Ibid., pp. 256–261.
8. Ibid., pp. 254–255.
9. Maurício Caminha de Lacerda, interview, August 29, 1984, and interview with DFR, April 7, 1983. Vera Lacerda Paiva, letter to JWFD, May 8, 1984, and interview with DFR, Rio de Janeiro, September 1, 1985.
10. Maurício de Lacerda, *Segunda República,* pp. 322–327. "Factos Policiaes," *O Jornal,* January 20, 1931.
11. Maurício de Lacerda, *Segunda República,* pp. 333, 336, 308–309. Maurício Caminha de Lacerda, preface to Maurício Paiva de Lacerda, *A Evolução Legislativa,* pp. xii–xiii.
12. *Diário de Notícias,* May 15, 16, 17, June 10, 1931. Maurício de Lacerda, *Segunda República,* pp. 349–385.
13. Prefeitura Municipal, *A Questão do Morro de Santo Antonio, Contrato da Companhia Industrial Santa Fé: Relatório Preliminar do 2º Procurador dos Feitos da Fazenda Municipal* (Rio de Janeiro: Jornal do Brasil, 1932). Maurício Caminha de Lacerda, preface to Maurício Paiva de Lacerda, *A Evolução Legislativa,* p. xi.
14. *Diário de Notícias,* June 2, 1931.

II. Crusader for Communism (1931–1939)

1. The First Publications of Carlos (1931–1934)

1. Carlos Lacerda, *Depoimento,* p. 29. Antonio Carlos Villaça, *O Livro de Antonio,* p. 44.
2. Carlos Lacerda, "Rosas e Pedras do Meu Caminho," Chapter 4, pp. 29–31. Carlos Lacerda, autobiographical notes in small black binder, in CCL.
3. *Diário de Notícias,* July 30, 31, August 12, 1931.
4. Ibid., August 29, 1931, January 7, 12, 15, 22, 23, 1932.
5. *Para Todos,* January 2, 1932. Luís Martins, *Um Bom Sujeito,* p. 23.
6. *Para Todos,* January 16, 1932. *Diário de Notícias,* January 9, 1932. Luís Martins, *Um Bom Sujeito,* p. 23.
7. Marcos Carneiro de Mendonça, interview with DFR, Rio de Janeiro, February 4, 1983.
8. Carlos Lacerda, "Anna Amélia Queiroz Carneiro de Mendonça," in *Em Vez: Crônicas,* pp. 43–47. Marcos Carneiro de Mendonça, interview with DFR.

9. Carlos Lacerda, "coitadinha da realidade brasileira," *rumo,* 1, no. 1 (May 1933), pp. 20–21; *rumo,* 1, nos. 5, 6 (September–October 1933), no. 4 (August 1933). Carlos Lacerda, "itinerário de um problema," *rumo,* 1, no. 3 (July 1933), p. 12.

10. Vera Lacerda Paiva, interview with DFR, January 30, 1983.

11. *sensacionalismo* (Rio de Janeiro: Casa do Estudante do Brasil; distrib. Freitas Bastos & Cia., 1933), pp. 103–105, 141–145.

12. *Diário de Notícias,* January 16, 1932 (*página de educação*). Article about Cecília Meireles, *Leia Livros,* March 1984. Carlos Lacerda, "Rosas e Pedras do Meu Caminho," Chapter 5, pp. 22, 24.

13. Carlos Lacerda, "Anna Amélia Queiroz Carneiro de Mendonça," in *Em Vez: Crônicas,* p. 44.

14. Evandro Lins e Silva, letter to Sérgio Lacerda, Rio de Janeiro, May 5, 1980, p. 3.

15. Carlos Lacerda, "rasgando a camisa verde-oliva," *rumo,* 2, no. 8 (June 1934). Carlos Lacerda, "'Voz do Oeste'—Plínio Salgado," *rumo,* 2, nos. 9, 10 (July–August 1934).

16. L. M. [Luís Martins], "Murilo Miranda," *O Estado de S. Paulo,* May 2, 1971. Yedda Braga Miranda, "Lembranças," foreword to Mário de Andrade, *Cartas a Murilo Miranda,* p. 5.

17. Carlos Lacerda, "S. Bernardo e o Cabo da Faca," *Revista Acadêmica,* no. 9.

2. Carlos, Law Student (1932–1934)

1. Evandro Lins e Silva, interview, Brasília, October 17, 1965.

2. Edmundo Moniz, interview with DFR, Rio de Janeiro, February 6, 1983.

3. Ivan Pedro de Martins, interview with DFR, London, June 13, 1985. Arthur José Poerner, *O Poder Jovem,* p. 134.

4. Carlos Lacerda, "Na Tribuna da Imprensa," *Correio da Manhã,* September 30, 1947.

5. Evandro Lins e Silva, letter to Sérgio Lacerda.

6. Ibid. Carlos Lacerda, *Depoimento,* p. 28.

7. Vera Lacerda Paiva, interview, Rio de Janeiro, July 22, 1984, and interviews with DFR, Rio de Janeiro, July 26, August 25, 1985, February 12, 1989. Marcos Madeira, interview with DFR, August 23, 1985.

8. Evandro Lins e Silva, letter to Sérgio Lacerda.

9. Ibid. Carlos Lacerda, "As confissões de Lacerda," *Jornal da Tarde,* May 27, 1977. Carlos Lacerda, "Tristão com o Nariz na Porta," *Revista Acadêmica,* July 12, 1935. José Maria Bello, *Memórias,* pp. 214–216. Hermes Lima, *Travessia: Memórias,* pp. 75–85. Carlos Lacerda, in *Depoimento,* pp. 28–29, says Hermes Lima's winning thesis was a plagiarism, as Alceu Amoroso Lima later demonstrated to Carlos Lacerda.

10. Carlos Lacerda, "Rosas e Pedras do Meu Caminho," Chapter 3, pp. 24, 26. Evandro Lins e Silva, letter to Sérgio Lacerda. Vera and Odilon Lacerda Paiva, interview with DFR, February 7, 1983.

11. Vera Lacerda Paiva, letter to JWFD, Rio de Janeiro, May 8, 1984.

12. Vera Lacerda Paiva, letter to JWFD, Rio de Janeiro, March 20, 1984.
13. Marcos [Carlos Lacerda], *O Quilombo de Manoel Congo*, pp. 5, 7, 8, 50.
14. Cláudio Lacerda, "Lacerda: Uma Vida de Lutas," Chapter 5, p. 5.
15. Carlos Lacerda, letters to Maurício de Lacerda and João, Forquilha, January 14, 1934, in CCL.
16. Carlos Lacerda, *Depoimento*, p. 35.
17. Edmundo Moniz, interview with DFR.
18. Appointment of Maurício Lacerda Filho by the *interventor federal* of the Federal District, September 4, 1934, in CCL.
19. Carlos Lacerda, "Rosas e Pedras do Meu Caminho," Chapter 3, p. 28. Carlos Lacerda, *A Casa do Meu Avô*, pp. 11–12. Vera Lacerda Paiva, interview with DFR, Rio de Janeiro, February 18, 1989.

3. Communism Beckons (1932–1934)

1. Everardo Dias, letter to Eponina Dias, January 13, 1933.
2. Edmundo Moniz, interview with DFR. See references to Olga Lacerda's letters to Antônio Bello in Maurício Lacerda Filho, letter to Carlos Lacerda, Rio de Janeiro, January 2, 1943, in CCL.
3. Carlos Lacerda, "A Reforma Universitária," in *Palavras e Ação*, p. 89.
4. Ivan Pedro de Martins, interview with DFR, June 13, 1985. José Honório Rodrigues, *Chagas Freitas e o Rio de Janeiro*, p. 46. Carlos Lacerda, *Depoimento*, p. 29.
5. Carlos Lacerda, *Depoimento*, p. 43. Carlos Lacerda, "Rosas e Pedras do Meu Caminho," Chapter 6 (*Manchete*, May 20, 1967), p. 23. Carlos Lacerda, "Na Tribuna da Imprensa," *Correio da Manhã*, September 30, 1947.
6. Otávio Malta, interview. Rio de Janeiro, October 9, 1968. Carlos Lacerda, interview, Washington, D.C., September 17, 1968. Cláudio Lacerda, "Lacerda: Uma Vida de Lutas," Chapter 4, p. 6.
7. Ivan Pedro de Martins, interview with DFR.
8. Vera Lacerda Paiva, interview, Rio de Janeiro, August 5, 1984. Cláudio Lacerda, "Lacerda: Uma Vida de Lutas," Chapter 4, p. 6.
9. Poerner, *O Poder Jovem*, p. 133. Jorge Amado, letter to Luís Henrique Dias Tavares, Bahia, November 2, 1985. Ivan Pedro de Martins, "A Flecha e o Alvo" (unpublished manuscript of book), pp. 127–129. Ivan Pedro de Martins, interview with DFR.
10. Ivan Pedro de Martins, interview with DFR. Ivan Pedro de Martins, "A Flecha e o Alvo," pp. 73–74.
11. Carlos Lacerda, preface to Ilha Ehrenburg, *Fevereiro Sangrente: A Revolução de 1934 na Austria*, translated by Carlos Lacerda, pp. 5–18 (see pp. 7, 16–18).

4. The Aliança Nacional Libertadora (1935)

1. Eliezer Schneider, interview with DFR, Rio de Janeiro, July 15, 1985.
2. Cláudio Lacerda, "Lacerda: Uma Vida de Lutas," Chapter 4, p. 6.
3. Ivan Pedro de Martins, interview with DFR.

4. "A reunião de hontem, no João Caetano," *Correio da Manhã,* March 31, 1935.

5. Carlos Lacerda, interview, Rio de Janeiro, July 3, 1971. Carlos Lacerda, *Depoimento,* p. 42.

6. Ivan Pedro de Martins, "A Flecha e o Alvo," pp. 148–149.

7. Ibid., pp. 152–153.

8. *A Manhã,* July 30, 1935.

9. Maurício de Lacerda entry in *Dicionário Histórico-Biográfico Brasileiro. A Manhã,* October 6, May 26, 1935. Otávio Malta, interview, Rio de Janeiro, October 9, 1968, and interview with DFR, Rio de Janeiro, March 17, 1983.

10. Carlos Lacerda, "Quaes os Livros Necessários à Formação de uma Cultura Socialista?" *Revista Acadêmica,* 2, no. 11 (May 1935). Carlos Lacerda, "In Memoriam de Murillo Mendes," *Revista Acadêmica,* 2, no. 11.

11. Maurício de Lacerda entry in *Dicionário Histórico-Biográfico Brasileiro.* Otávio Malta, interview with DFR, March 17, 1983.

12. *A Manhã,* May 26, 1935. Carlos Lacerda, *Depoimento,* p. 44. Carlos Lacerda, "Rosas e Pedras do Meu Caminho," Chapter 6 (*Manchete,* May 20, 1967), p. 25.

13. *A Manhã,* July 6, 1935.

14. Carlos Lacerda, "Rosas e Pedras do Meu Caminho," Chapter 9 (*Manchete,* June 10, 1967), p. 105. Robert M. Levine, *The Vargas Regime: The Critical Years, 1934–1938,* p. 102. *International Press Correspondence* (periodical of the Executive Committee of the Communist International, Vienna, Berlin, London), August 28, 1935.

15. *A Manhã,* July 30, August 1, July 24, 1935. Carlos Lacerda, "Exame de Escriptores," *A Manhã,* November 10, 1935.

16. João Condé, interview, Rio de Janeiro, August 11, 1983, and interview with DFR, March 23, 1983.

17. Febus Gikovate, interview, São Paulo, November 21, 1968. Carlos Lacerda, "Rosas e Pedras do Meu Caminho," Chapter 9, p. 105.

18. Carlos Lacerda, "Rosas e Pedras do Meu Caminho," Chapter 9, pp. 105–106. Carlos Lacerda, *Depoimento,* p. 41. *International Press Correspondence,* December 2, 1935.

19. *Marcha,* Rio de Janeiro, 1, nos. 1–5 (October 16–November 22, 1935) (see no. 5, p. 16). Marcos [Carlos Lacerda], "Frente Única em Todos os Sectores," *Marcha,* no. 5.

20. *A Manhã,* November 12, 1935. Maurício de Lacerda, letter to Luís Carlos Prestes, November 15, 1935, in Eurico Bellens Porto, *A Insurreição de 27 de Novembro: Relatório,* p. 139.

5. In Hiding (1935–1936)

1. Paulo and Aparecida Mendes de Almeida, interview, São Paulo, July 26, 1983.

2. Carlos Lacerda, "Rosas e Pedras do Meu Caminho," Chapter 9, p. 106.

3. Ibid. Carlos Lacerda, small black binder, in CCL.

4. Carlos Lacerda, "Rosas e Pedras do Meu Caminho," Chapter 9, p. 106.
5. Ibid.
6. Ibid.
7. Carlos Lacerda, *Depoimento*, p. 36.
8. Ibid. Carlos Lacerda, "Rosas e Pedras do Meu Caminho," Chapter 9, p. 107. Júlio Tavares (Carlos Lacerda), "Novidades de um velho caderno," unpublished typewritten article in Walter Cunto Collection, Rio de Janeiro.
9. Vera Lacerda Paiva, letter to JWFD, May 8, 1984. Carlos Lacerda, small black binder, in CCL. Carlos Lacerda, "Rosas e Pedras do Meu Caminho," Chapter 3, p. 28. Cláudio Lacerda, "Lacerda: Uma Vida de Lutas," Chapter 5, pp. 2–3.
10. Vera Lacerda Paiva, letter to JWFD, July 14, 1984.
11. Cláudio Lacerda, "Lacerda: Uma Vida de Lutas," Chapter 5, p. 3.
12. Ibid. Carlos Lacerda, "Rosas e Pedras do Meu Caminho," Chapter 6, p. 27. Carlos Lacerda, Notebook 3, pp. 533, 624, 805 (see pp. 11, 28, 67 of Vera Lacerda Paiva's transcription), and Notebook 4, pp. 992–995 (transcription pp. 55–56).
13. Carlos Lacerda, Notebook 3, p. 806 (transcription p. 67), and Notebook 4, pp. 992–994 (transcription p. 55).
14. Carlos Lacerda, Notebook 4, pp. 1024, 896–908 (transcription pp. 64, 26–30).
15. Carlos Lacerda, Notebook 3, pp. 628, 683–693 (transcription pp. 28–29, 32–39).
16. Carlos Lacerda, *Depoimento*, p. 41. See Samuel Wainer, *Minha Razão de Viver: Memórias de um Repórter*, pp. 76–77.
17. Caio Júlio César Tavares [Carlos Lacerda], "Spengler e a Paz" and "Usina—um Livro para Sempre," *Revista Acadêmica*, 3, no. 19 (June 1936) and 3, no. 20 (July 1936). *Revista Acadêmica*, 3, no. 23 (November 1936).
18. Carlos Lacerda, "Cultura y Revolución," *Unidad*, Buenos Aires, 1, no. 3 (April 1936).
19. Carlos Lacerda, small black binder, in CCL. Carlos Lacerda, "Rosas e Pedras do Meu Caminho," Chapter 6, p. 27. Cláudio Lacerda, "Lacerda: Uma Vida de Lutas," Chapter 5, p. 3.
20. Carlos Lacerda, "Rosas e Pedras do Meu Caminho," Chapter 6, pp. 27–28.

6. *O Rio* (1937)

1. Carlos Lacerda, preface to *O Rio*, p. 19. Editor's note about Moacir Werneck de Castro at end of Moacir Werneck de Castro, "Mário de Andrade no Rio," *Revista do Brasil*, 1, no. 2 (1984), shows that Moacir's article, "A Revolução Praieira," was published in *Problemas* (of São Paulo), nos. 2 and 4 of 1937. Carlos Lacerda, interview, September 17, 1968. Maurício Caminho de Lacerda, interview with DFR, Rio de Janeiro, March 28, 1983.
2. Vera Lacerda Paiva, interview, August 5, 1984. Cláudio Lacerda, "Lacerda: Uma Vida de Lutas," Chapter 4, p. 4.
3. Carlos Lacerda, *A Casa do Meu Avô*, pp. 80–81. Carlos Lacerda, interview, September 17, 1968.

4. Carlos Lacerda, declaration, *A Gazeta,* São Paulo, July 28, 1937. Mário Domingues, "'O Rio' no Regina," *Correio da Noite,* September 15, 1937.

5. Carlos Lacerda, *O Rio* (illustrated by Livio Abramo), p. 94.

6. Ibid., p. 141.

7. Ibid., p. 8.

8. Carlos Lacerda, letter to Vera Lacerda Paiva, April 30, 1937, in CCL.

9. *O Estado de S. Paulo,* June 12, 15, July 1, 1937. Filinto Müller, report to Vargas, Rio de Janeiro, June 18, 1937, in Hélio Silva, *1937: Todos os Golpes se Parecem,* pp. 577–582.

10. Carlos Lacerda, letter to Letícia Abruzzini, date unclear, in the Lacerda family collection (henceforth called LFC). Carlos Lacerda, Notebook 3, pp. 808–810 (transcription p. 68) and Notebook 4, p. 921, dated February 13, 1936 (transcription p. 34). Maurício Caminha de Lacerda, preface to Maurício Paiva de Lacerda, *A Evolução Legislativa,* p. xi.

11. Program of Companhia de Arte Dramática Álvaro Moreyra, "O Rio, Quatro Quadros de Júlio Tavares." M.W., "'O Rio' de Júlio Tavares," *Revista Acadêmica,* no. 29 (August 1937). Vera Lacerda Paiva, telegram to Olga Lacerda, July 29, 1937, in CCL.

12. M.W., "'O Rio' de Júlio Tavares." For more about Álvaro Moreyra and the newspapers, see "Cia. de arte dramática Álvaro Moreyra," *Revista Acadêmica,* no. 30 (September 1937). Paulista: Pertaining to, or native of, São Paulo.

13. Mário Domingues, "'O Rio' no Regina." *Correio da Manhã,* September 15, 1937.

14. Ibid. Mário Nunes, "'O Rio'—4 atos de Júlio Tavares," *Jornal do Brasil,* September 15, 1937. *A Pátria, O Globo, A Vanguarda, O Paiz, O Imparcial, Diário de Notícias,* all of September 16, 1937. Graciliano Ramos, "O Rio" (newspaper clipping dated Rio de Janeiro, September 17, 1937, source not shown, in CCL).

7. The Merry Smile of Ziloca (1937)

1. Carlos Lacerda, "Rosas e Pedras do Meu Caminho," Chapter 8 (*Manchete,* June 3, 1967), pp. 25–26. Carlos Lacerda, preface to *O Rio,* p. 20.

2. Gilberto Trompowisky, "O Nome da Semana: Dona Letícia de Lacerda" (newspaper clipping, no source shown), in CCL. Carlos Lacerda, "Rosas e Pedras do Meu Caminho," Chapter 8, p. 25.

3. Carlos Lacerda, letters to Letícia Abruzzini, in LFC (see Carlos Lacerda letters of July 2, 18, August 4, 5, 8, 1937, and letter of December 25, 1937, quoting from Letícia's letter of July 23, 1937).

4. Cláudio Lacerda, "Lacerda: Uma Vida de Lutas," Chapter 6, p. 1. Carlos Lacerda, *Desafio e Promessa: O Rio São Francisco,* p. ix.

5. Carlos Lacerda, *Depoimento,* p. 37.

6. Carlos Lacerda, letters to Letícia Abruzzini, Belo Horizonte, August 15, 1937, Pirapora, August 21, 1937, and Juazeiro, September 11, 1937, in LFC.

8. Bahia (1937)

1. Carlos Lacerda, *Depoimento,* p. 37. "No caderno de anotações, a autocrítica," *Jornal do Brasil,* May 22, 1977.
2. Carlos Lacerda, "O S. Francisco e o Integralismo: II, A Ação," *Diretrizes,* no. 5 (August 1938), pp. 27–28.
3. [Carlos Lacerda], "O Rio S. Francisco," *O Observador Econômico e Financeiro,* February 1939, pp. 80–116 (see p. 92). "No caderno de anotações, a autocrítica."
4. Carlos Lacerda, letters to Letícia Abruzzini, aboard ship and in Juazeiro, September 11, 1937, in LFC.
5. "No caderno de anotações, a autocrítica."
6. Carlos Lacerda, *Desafio e Promessa,* p. ix. Carlos Lacerda, "O S. Francisco e o Integralismo: I, O Ambiente," *Diretrizes,* no. 4 (July 1938), pp. 38–39.
7. Carlos Lacerda, "Rosas e Pedras do Meu Caminho," Chapter 8, p. 25. Carlos Lacerda, preface to *O Rio,* pp. 17–18. Carlos Lacerda, *Depoimento,* pp. 38–39.
8. Carlos Lacerda, "Rosas e Pedras do Meu Caminho," Chapter 8, p. 25.
9. Communism file of Carlos Lacerda, in CCL. Fernando Bueno, L. M. de Souza, and Guimarães Padilha, *Êsse Incrível Lacerda,* p. 14.
10. Carlos Lacerda, *Depoimento,* pp. 39–40.
11. Carlos Lacerda, letters to Letícia Abruzzini, Casa de Correção, Rio de Janeiro, November 23, 1937, and Comércio (Sebastião de Lacerda), December 25, 1937, in LFC.

9. Marriage (March 1938)

1. Carlos Lacerda, *A Casa do Meu Avô,* p. 95.
2. Carlos Lacerda, letter to Letícia Abruzzini, Comércio (Sebastião de Lacerda), December 25, 1937, in LFC.
3. Ibid., January 12, 1938, in LFC.
4. Carlos Lacerda, *A Casa do Meu Avô,* p. 95. Maurício Paiva de Lacerda, letter to Carlos Lacerda, Chácaras Lacerda, March 16, 1939, in CCL.
5. Carlos Lacerda, letters to Letícia Abruzzini, January 17, 19, 1938, in LFC. Carlos Lacerda, *A Casa do Meu Avô,* p. 81.
6. Carlos Lacerda, letter to Olga Lacerda, January 19, 1938, in CCL.
7. Carlos Lacerda, letter to Letícia Abruzzini, January 20, 1938, in LFC.
8. Evandro Lins e Silva, letter to Sérgio Lacerda, pp. 2, 17. Wainer, *Minha Razão de Viver,* p. 53. Maurício Caminha de Lacerda, interview with DFR, March 28, 1983.
9. Letícia Abruzzini, letter to Carlos Lacerda, Valença, January 19, 1938, in LFC. Carlos Lacerda, letter to Letícia Abruzzini, January 20, 1938, in LFC.
10. Carlos Lacerda, letter to Letícia Abruzzini, January 19, 1938, in LFC.
11. Carlos Lacerda, *A Casa do Meu Avô,* p. 61. Maria Cristina Lacerda Simões Lopes, interview with DFR, Rio de Janeiro, March 24, 1983.

12. Carlos Lacerda, *A Casa do Meu Avô,* pp. 61–62. Vera Lacerda Paiva, interview with DFR, February 18, 1989. Carlos Lacerda, letter to Olga Lacerda, January 19, 1938, in CCL. Carlos Lacerda, "Rosas e Pedras do Meu Caminho," Chapter 8, p. 26. Maurício Caminha de Lacerda, interview, Rio de Janeiro, August 29, 1984. Carlos Lacerda, letter to Olga Lacerda, April 14, 1938, in CCL.

13. Carlos Lacerda, *A Casa do Meu Avô,* pp. 61–62.

14. Carlos Lacerda, letter to Olga Lacerda, April 14, 1938.

15. Carlos Lacerda, "Na Tribuna da Imprensa," *Correio da Manhã,* September 30, 1947.

10. Writers and Beer Drinkers (1938–1939)

1. Fernando Cícero da Franca Velloso, letter to JWFD, Rio de Janeiro, October 1, 1984. Carlos Lacerda, *Depoimento,* p. 47. Samuel Wainer, interview, Rio de Janeiro, September 28, 1968. Moacir Werneck de Castro, typewritten note to JWFD, Rio de Janeiro, August 1989.

2. Carlos Lacerda, "Rosas e Pedras do Meu Caminho," Chapter 6, p. 26.

3. Carlos Lacerda, "O São Francisco: esse desconhecido," *Diretrizes,* no. 3 (June 1938). Carlos Lacerda, "O S. Francisco e o Integralismo," *Diretrizes,* nos. 4, 5 (July, August, 1938).

4. Carlos Lacerda, *Depoimento,* p. 47. Carlos Lacerda, "Rosas e Pedras do Meu Caminho," Chapter 6, pp. 23–24.

5. "Ligeira palestra com o dr. Carlos de Lacerda, da Imprensa Carioca," *Diário da Tarde,* Florianópolis, Santa Catarina, October 6, 1938.

6. Carlos Lacerda (name not shown), "A Colonização Allemã no Brasil," *O Observador Econômico e Financeiro,* October 1938, pp. 107–139 (see p. 138). Carlos Lacerda, "Resumo Histórico de um Problema Brasileiro," *Diretrizes,* 1, no. 9 (November 1938), pp. 21–25. Armando Daudt d'Oliveira, interview, Rio de Janeiro, August 10, 1983. Epaminondas Moreira do Valle, interview with DFR, July 26, 1985.

7. [Carlos Lacerda], *Desafio e Promessa,* p. ix. [Carlos Lacerda], "O Rio S. Francisco," *O Observador Econômico e Financeiro,* February 1939, pp. 80–116.

8. Carlos Lacerda, *Depoimento,* p. 48. Samuel Wainer, interview, September 28, 1968. Wainer, *Minha Razão de Viver,* pp. 48–53.

9. Orígenes Lessa, *O Índio Cor de Rosa: Evocação de Noel Nutels,* p. 60.

10. Ibid. Samuel Wainer, interviews, Rio de Janeiro, September 28, 1968, and São Paulo, July 14, 1979. Emil Farhat, interview with DFR, São Paulo, March 11, 1983.

11. Wainer, *Minha Razão de Viver,* p. 52. Otávio Malta, interview with DFR, Rio de Janeiro, March 17, 1983.

12. Guilherme Figueiredo, interview, Rio de Janeiro, July 24, 1984. Moacir Werneck de Castro, "Mário de Andrade no Rio," *Revista do Brasil,* 1, no. 2 (1984). Yedda Braga Miranda, interview, Rio de Janeiro, July 28, 1984.

13. Charles Richard Carlisle, ed., *Tesserae: A Mosaic of Twentieth Century Brazilian Poetry,* p. ix.

14. Guilherme Figueiredo, "Prefácio importantíssimo," in "Cobras e lagartos," typed manuscript, 28 pp., Rio de Janeiro, 1984 (see p. 22).
15. Moacir Werneck de Castro, "Mário de Andrade no Rio," p. 65.
16. Guilherme Figueiredo, interview. Figueiredo, "Prefácio Importantíssimo," p. 25. Mário de Andrade, *Cartas a Murilo Miranda,* p. 117, note 89.
17. Luís Martins, *Um Bom Sujeito,* pp. 23, 34.

11. Expulsion from the Communist Party (February 1939)

1. Carlos Lacerda, "Na Tribuna da Imprensa," *Correio da Manhã,* September 30, 1947.
2. Carlos Lacerda, *Depoimento,* p. 47.
3. Ibid., p. 48. João Batista Barreto Leite Filho, typewritten notes for JWFD, Rio de Janeiro, August 1981, says that Lacerda, in telling the story, spoke of Odete de Carvalho e Souza (who, in 1961, was succeeded as ambassador to Israel by Barreto Leite Filho).
4. Carlos Lacerda, "Rosas e Pedras do Meu Caminho," Chapter 6, p. 24. Carlos Lacerda, *Depoimento,* p. 48. Carlos Lacerda, "Na Tribuna da Imprensa," *Correio da Manhã,* September 30, 1947.
5. Carlos Lacerda (name not shown), "A Exposição Anti-Communista," *O Observador Econômico e Financeiro,* 3, 36 (January 1939), pp. 124, 139.
6. Ibid., pp. 141–142, 152.
7. Otávio Malta, interview with DFR, March 17, 1983.
8. Carlos Lacerda, "Na Tribuna da Imprensa," *Correio da Manhã,* September 30, 1947. Carlos Lacerda, "Rosas e Pedras do Meu Caminho," Chapter 3, p. 26.
9. Carlos Lacerda, "Rosas e Pedras do Meu Caminho," Chapter 3, p. 26.
10. Carlos Lacerda, "A Exposição Anti-Communista," pp. 139, 142. "Desmascarando um provocador," *Revista Proletária,* nos. 13, 14 (February–March 1939), pp. 16–17 (see p. 16).
11. Carlos Lacerda, *Depoimento,* p. 49. Carlos Lacerda, "Rosas e Pedras do Meu Caminho," Chapter 6, p. 26. Carlos Lacerda, "Na Tribuna da Imprensa," *Correio da Manhã,* September 30, 1947. Carlos Lacerda, interview, September 17, 1968.
12. João Batista Barreto Leite Filho, typewritten notes, August 1981, and interview, Rio de Janeiro, August 12, 1981. Emil Farhat, interview, São Paulo, August 2, 1983. Edgar Flexa Ribeiro, interview, Rio de Janeiro, July 8, 1983.
13. Samuel Wainer, interview, September 28, 1968. Wainer, *Minha Razão de Viver,* pp. 71–72.
14. Ibid.
15. Carlos Lacerda, early poems, in the Arquivo Mário de Andrade at the Instituto de Estudos Brasileiros of the University of São Paulo.
16. "Desmascarando um provocador," *Revista Proletária.*
17. Carlos Lacerda, "Rosas e Pedras do Meu Caminho," Chapter 6, p. 26.
18. Vera Lacerda Paiva, letter to JWFD, Rio de Janeiro, July 14, 1984, and interview, August 5, 1984.

19. Wainer, *Minha Razão de Viver,* pp. 72–73, and interview, September 28, 1968. Carlos Lacerda said (interview, September 17, 1968) that eventually Moacir Werneck de Castro ceased speaking with him.

20. Carlos Lacerda, interview, September 17, 1968. Carlos Lacerda, *Depoimento,* p. 44. Vera Lacerda Paiva, letter to JWFD, May 8, 1984.

21. Carlos Lacerda, "Na Tribuna da Imprensa," *Correio da Manhã,* September 30, 1947.

III. Crusader for Democracy (1939–1945)

1. With Inter-Americana (1940–1941)

1. Maurício Paiva de Lacerda, letters to Carlos Lacerda, March 16, 24, 1939, in CCL.

2. Carlos Lacerda, letter to Olímpio Guilherme, November 16, 1939, in CCL. Fernando Cicero da Franca Velloso, letter to JWFD.

3. Fernando Goldgaber, letters to JWFD, September 30, December 1, 1984. Oswaldo Alves, letter to Goldgaber, n.d. Israel Pedrosa, letter to Goldgaber, October 20, 1984.

4. Carlos Lacerda, letter to Letícia Lacerda, June 1940, in CCL.

5. Carlos Lacerda, letter to Mário de Andrade, São Paulo, October 11, 1941, in CCL. Moacir de Werneck Castro, *Mário de Andrade: Exílio no Rio,* pp. 136, 178–182.

6. Carlos Lacerda, "A penetração japoneza no Brasil," *O Radical,* December 17, 18, 20, 21, 23, 24, 27, 28, 30, 31, 1941, and January 1, 1942.

7. Carlos Lacerda, letter to Olímpio Guilherme, November 16, 1939.

8. Rubem Braga, letters to Carlos Lacerda, São Paulo, October 7, 1940, and November 7, 1941, in CCL.

9. Cláudio Lacerda, "Lacerda: Uma Vida de Lutas," Chapter 6, p. 7.

2. Friendships in São Paulo (1939–1942)

1. Paulo and Aparecida Mendes de Almeida, interview. Hermínio Sacchetta, interviews, São Paulo, November 5, 1968, and August 19, 1979.

2. Paulo and Aparecida Mendes de Almeida, interview. Carlos Lacerda, "Programa: Teatro dos Mil e Um Contos," expressing plans and purpose, in CCL. Carlos Lacerda, handwritten notes, in CCL. "Paulo Mandes: 40 anos de crítica," *Folha de S. Paulo,* January 7, 1979.

3. Paulo Mendes de Almeida, letter to Carlos Lacerda, July 2, 1939, in CCL. Paulo and Aparecida Mendes de Almeida, interview.

4. Paulo Mendes de Almeida, letter to Carlos Lacerda, São Paulo, April 5, 1939, in CCL.

5. Luís Martins, *Um Bom Sujeito,* pp. 87, 71–73, 83. "Carta coletiva a Carlos Lacerda," Santa Tereza do Alto, September 30, 1940, signed by Luís Martins, Emiliano Di Cavalcanti, Noemia, and Tarsila do Amaral, in CCL. Luís Martins, letter to Carlos Lacerda, São Paulo, October 29, 1941, in CCL.

6. Babá [Clara Freitas], letter to Zila [Letícia] and Carlos Lacerda, Rio de Janeiro, October 6, 1941, in CCL.

7. Arnaldo Pedroso d'Horta, observations in Vera d'Horta Beccari, *Lasar Segall e o Modernismo Paulista,* p. 156. Yedda Braga Miranda, interview. Paulo Mendes de Almeida, letters to Carlos Lacerda, São Paulo, July 2, 1939, February 15, 1940, January 27, 1941, and letters to Zila [Letícia], January 27, 1941, February 11, 23, September 21, 1942, in CCL.

8. Carlos Lacerda, "Morreu Monteiro Lobato," "Na Tribuna da Imprensa," *Correio da Manhã,* July 6, 1948. Carlos Lacerda, "Rosas e Pedras do Meu Caminho," Chapter 8, p. 26. "A Exposição, Modas para Senhoras e Crianças" (newspaper advertisement clipping), in CCL. "No Sítio do Pica-Pau Amarelo: 1º programa: Narizinho no Reino das Águas Claras," typescript, in CCL.

9. Carlos Lacerda, "Rosas e Pedras do Meu Caminho," Chapter 8, pp. 23, 26. Cláudio Lacerda, "Lacerda: Uma Vida de Lutas," Chapter 6, p. 7.

10. Paulo and Aparecida Mendes de Almeida, interview. Carlos Lacerda, "Rosas e Pedras do Meu Caminho," Chapter 8, p. 26.

11. Luís Martins, *Um Bom Sujeito,* p. 84. "Paulo Mendes: 40 anos de crítica."

12. Alfredo Mesquita, interview, São Paulo, July 24, 1983.

13. Ibid. *O Rio,* preface, pp. 14–15.

14. Vera Lacerda Paiva, interview with DFR, February 13, 1983, and letter to JWFD, May 8, 1984.

15. Carlos Lacerda, *Depoimento,* pp. 82–83. Hélio Fernandes, interview, Rio de Janeiro, August 1, 1984.

3. Union with Vargas for the War Effort (1942–1943)

1. Carlos Lacerda, "Sinceridade e Poesia," *Revista Acadêmica,* May 1942. Carlos Lacerda, "Bernanos, um Espírito que se Perdeu a Si Mesmo," *Revista Acadêmica,* no. 61 (August 1942).

2. "Declaracão de Princípios," *Diretrizes,* June 11, 1942. Eurico Gaspar Dutra, letter to Getúlio Vargas, Rio de Janeiro, June 15, 1942, in Vargas papers at the Centro de Pesquisa e Documentação de História Contemporânea do Brasil at the Fundação Getúlio Vargas, Rio de Janeiro (henceforth shown as CPDOC).

3. Carlos Lacerda, "Rosas e Pedras do Meu Caminho," Chapter 8, p. 23. Carlos Lacerda, letter to Joaquim Rolla, Rio de Janeiro, August 5, 1942, in CCL. Meridional salary mentioned in Carlos Lacerda, small black binder, in CCL. Vera Lacerda Paiva, letter to JWFD, May 8, 1984.

4. Carlos Lacerda, "Rosas e Pedras do Meu Caminho," Chapter 9 (*Manchete,* June 10, 1967), p. 107.

5. Ibid. Companhia Editôra Nacional, letters to Haydée Fonseca and Carlos Lacerda, São Paulo, September 19, 25, in CCL.

6. Carlos Lacerda, letter to Alcides Etchegoyen, Rio de Janeiro, November 4, 1942, in CCL.

7. "PCB: Fernando de Lacerda e sua Concepção de União Nacional," *Diretrizes,* May 27, 1943, in Edgard Carone, *A Terceira República (1937–1945),* pp. 500–507.

8. Moacir Werneck de Castro, interview, Rio de Janeiro, July 2, 1979. Carlos Lacerda, "Os Intelectuais e a União Nacional," *Revista Acadêmica,* no. 62 (November 1942).

9. Samuel Wainer, interviews, Rio de Janeiro and São Paulo, September 28, 1968, July 14, 1979. Moacir Werneck de Castro, interviews, Rio de Janeiro, December 2, 1967, July 2, 1979. Wainer, *Minha Razão de Viver,* pp. 73–74.

10. Carlos Lacerda, letter to Alcides Etchegoyen, November 4, 1942.

11. Carlos Lacerda, small black binder, in CCL.

12. Samuel Wainer, interviews, September 28, 1968, July 14, 1979. Wainer, *Minha Razão de Viver,* p. 66. "PCB: Fernando de Lacerda e sua Concepção de União Nacional."

13. "Carlos Lacerda concede a *Cultura* palpitante entrevista," *Cultura,* Belo Horizonte, September 1943, Carlos Lacerda, *Depoimento,* pp. 158–159.

14. Carlos Lacerda, "Carta do Energúmeno à Estrela de 'A Manhã,'" *Diário Carioca,* December 5, 1943. Carlos Lacerda, "Rosas e Pedras do Meu Caminho," Chapter 8, p. 27. "Ponto de Vista," Suplemento Literário of *Diretrizes,* December 16, 1943, p. 16. Carlos Lacerda, letter to Maurício Lacerda Filho, Rio de Janeiro, December 16, 1943, in CCL.

4. Working for Chateaubriand (1943–1944)

1. Joel Silveira, interview, Rio de Janeiro, August 26, 1983. Joel Silveira, "Carlos Lacerda, amigo bissexto," *O Liberal,* Belém, August 18, 1977. Mara Caballero, "Joel Silveira revive em livro a luta dos pracinhas na Itália," *Jornal do Brasil,* December 19, 1983.

2. Joel Silveira, interview. Mara Caballero, "Joel Silveira." Carlos Lacerda, "Rosas e Pedras do Meu Caminho," Chapter 9, p. 108.

3. Carlos Lacerda, "Rosas e Pedras do Meu Caminho," Chapter 9, p. 108.

4. William Wieland, letter to Carlos Lacerda, American Embassy, Rio de Janeiro, January 19, 1944, in CCL. Carlos Lacerda, "Rosas e Pedras do Meu Caminho," Chapter 9, pp. 109–110.

5. Carlos Lacerda, "Rosas e Pedras do Meu Caminho," Chapter 9, p. 111.

6. Ibid., pp. 111–112. Carlos Lacerda, small black binder, in CCL.

7. Carlos Lacerda, "Rosas e Pedras do Meu Caminho," Chapter 9, p. 111. Décio de Almeida Prado, letter to Carlos Lacerda, São Paulo, March 21, 1944, in CCL. Carlos Lacerda, letter to Décio de Almeida Prado, Rio de Janeiro, March 23, 1944, in CCL.

8. Samuel Wainer, interview, September 28, 1968. Wainer, *Minha Razão de Viver,* pp. 60–61, 67–68.

9. Geraldo Ferraz, *Depois de Tudo* (São Paulo: Paz e Terra, 1983), pp. 123–124.

10. "Dia D—A nossa artilharia esmaga os nazistas," *O Jornal,* May 21, 1944. Carlos Lacerda, "Rosas e Pedras do Meu Caminho," Chapter 9, p. 108.

11. Austregésilo de Ataíde, interview with DFR.

12. Carlos Lacerda, "Alguns Problemas de Jornal," *Publicidade,* June 1944. Carlos Lacerda, "Matéria Paga," *Publicidade,* December 1944.

13. Carlos Lacerda, "Alguns Problemas de Jornal." Carlos Lacerda, letter to Leão Gondim de Oliveira, Rio de Janeiro, July 21, 1944. One milreis had been renamed the cruzeiro in 1942.

14. David Nasser and Jean Manzon, "O café vai desaparecer do mundo, proclama o interventor de São Paulo," *O Jornal,* November 30, 1944. David Nasser, "As Grandes Amizades (9): Meu Amigo, Carlos Lacerda," *Manchete,* no. 802 (September 2, 1967).

15. Carlos Lacerda, letter to Assis Chateaubriand, Rio de Janeiro, November 30, 1944, in CCL. Note, signed "Ed." to "Sr. Leão," November 1944, in CCL. Assis Chateaubriand, letter to Carlos Lacerda, December 12, 1944, in CCL.

5. At the First Writers' Congress (January 1945)

1. Boletim Secreto de Informações 14, War Ministry, 2nd Military Region, Estado Maior Regional, 2nd Section, December 22, 1944, and Bulletin 97, Delegacia de Segurança Política, September 28, 1944, both in Vargas papers, in CPDOC. Carolina Nabuco, *A Vida de Virgílio de Melo Franco,* pp. 159–163.

2. Carlos Lacerda, *Depoimento,* p. 366.

3. Nabuco, *A Vida de Virgílio de Melo Franco,* p. 165.

4. Antônio Cândido de Melo e Souza, interview, São Paulo, August 7, 1981.

5. Figueiredo, "Prefácio importantíssimo," p. 26. See the testimonies of Joel Silveira, Jorge Amado, Guilherme Figueiredo, Manoel Gomes Maranhão, Moacir Werneck de Castro, Pompeu de Souza, and Nelson Werneck Sodré in Joel Silveira and Geneton Moraes Neto, *Hitler-Stálin: O Pacto Maldito e Suas Repercussões no Brasil.*

6. Carlos Lacerda, "Rosas e Pedras de Meu Caminho," Chapter 8, p. 27. Luís Martins, *Um Bom Sujeito,* pp. 14, 37.

7. Luís Martins, *Um Bom Sujeito,* p. 110.

8. Luiz Ernesto Kawall, interview with DFR, São Paulo, March 11, 1983.

9. *Primeiro Congresso Brasileiro de Escritores, promovido pela Associação Brasileira de Escritores (ABDE), São Paulo, Janeiro 22 a 27, 1945* (proceedings, Biblioteca da Escola de Comunicações e Artes, Universidade de São Paulo, Ref. No. 6090), pp. 49–50.

10. Ibid., p. 62.

11. Ibid., pp. 78–80.

12. Ibid., pp. 131–135, 118–122, 72–73. See also Carlos Guilherme Mota, *Ideologia da Cultura Brasileira (1933–1976),* pp. 148–151.

13. *Primeiro Congresso Brasileiro de Escritores,* pp. 144–146.

14. Nabuco, *A Vida de Virgílio de Melo Franco,* p. 165.
15. *Primeiro Congresso Brasileiro de Escritores,* p. 155.

6. The Interview with José Américo (February 1945)

1. Luiz Felippe de Oliveira Penna, interviews, Rio de Janeiro, August 11, 16, 1983.
2. Ibid.
3. *Correio da Manhã,* February 8, 1945.
4. "A situação: Declarações do Sr. José Américo," *Correio da Manhã,* February 22, 1945.
5. Carlos Lacerda, commenting on José Américo, in "A mão extendida e a liquidação moral," *Correio da Manhã,* May 27, 1945. Hélio Silva, *1945: Porque Depuseram Vargas,* p. 84 (testimony of Juracy Magalhães).
6. Luiz Felippe de Oliveira Penna, interviews. Carlos Lacerda, "Rosas e Pedras do Meu Caminho," Chapter 9, p. 113.
7. Hélio Silva, *1945: Porque Despuseram Vargas,* pp. 84–85.
8. Maurício Caminha de Lacerda, interview, Rio de Janeiro, August 29, 1984. "Declaração do Sr. Maurício de Lacerda," *Correio da Manhã,* February 21, 1945.
9. Luiz Felippe de Oliveira Penna, interviews. Carlos Lacerda, "Rosas e Pedras do Meu Caminho," Chapter 9, p. 113.
10. *O Globo,* February 22, 1945.
11. Lucia Hippolito, "Carlos Lacerda, Ascensão e Queda da 'Metralhadora Giratório,'" p. 13. Nabuco, *A Vida de Virgílio de Melo Franco,* p. 167. *O Globo,* February 22, 1945.
12. *Correio da Manhã,* March 8, 1945.
13. Carlos Lacerda, *Depoimento,* p. 66.
14. José Alberto Gueiros, interview with DFR, Rio de Janeiro, March 23, 1983.

7. The Break with Prestes (April–July 1945)

1. Moacir Werneck de Castro, interview, Rio de Janeiro, July 2, 1979.
2. Samuel Wainer, interview, São Paulo, July 14, 1979. Wainer, *Minha Razão de Viver,* p. 83.
3. *Correio da Manhã,* May 16, 1945. Carlos Lacerda, *Depoimento,* pp. 129–130.
4. Alfredo Mesquita, letter to Carlos Lacerda, Livraria Jaraguá, São Paulo, June 7, 1945, in CCL.
5. Carlos Lacerda, "A mão extendida e a liquidação moral."
6. Carlos Lacerda (name not shown), "Salvo Melhor Juizo," *7 Dias em Revista,* 1, no. 1 (June 14, 1945) (also in other numbers). Epaminondas Moreira do Valle, interview with DFR, Rio de Janeiro, July 26, 1985. Fernando Cícero da Franca Velloso, letter to JWFD.
7. Carlos Lacerda, "Sobre uma união democrática," *Correio da Manhã,* June 17, 1945.

8. Carlos Lacerda, letter to Osório Borba, Rio de Janeiro, July 27, 1945, in CCL.

8. Unsuccessful Playwright (October–November 1945)

1. Alfredo Mesquita, interview.
2. Carlos Lacerda, "A Bailarina Solta no Mundo," typewritten, in CCL.
3. Alfredo Mesquita, interview.
4. Alfredo Mesquita, letter to Carlos Lacerda, October 5, 1945. *Diário Carioca,* October 3, 10, 1945.
5. Carlos Lacerda, "Amapá ou O Lobo Solitário," typewritten, in CCL. See also brief description in Programa, Grupo Universitário de Teatro, October 10, 1945.
6. *O Estado de S. Paulo,* May 22, 1977 (quoting Décio de Almeida Prado). Athos Abramo, "Duas representações do Grupo Universitário de Teatro" (newspaper clipping), in CCL.
7. Carlos Lacerda, quoted in *Jornal de São Paulo,* October 28, 1945. Carlos Lacerda, letter to Olga Lacerda, Louveira, November 1, 1945. Programa, Grupo de Teatro Experimental, November 13, 1945.
8. Alfredo Mesquita, interview. "Lacerda—O teatrólogo" (quoting Alfredo Mesquita). "Palcos e Circos" (newspaper clipping), in CCL. *Diário da Noite,* November 19, 1945 (signed BET).

9. "Fiuza, the Rat" (November–December 1945)

1. Carlos Lacerda, *O Rato Fiuza,* pp. 12–13. *Diário Carioca,* November 17, 1945, p. 3, lists the five possibilities considered by the PCB as Luís Frederico Carpenter, Francisco Prestes Maia, Abraão Ribeiro, Caio Prado Júnior, and Yeddo Fiuza.
2. Osvaldo Peralva, interview, Rio de Janeiro, September 14, 1963. Hélio Silva, *1945: Porque Depuseram Vargas,* p. 278.
3. *Diário Carioca,* November 21, 1945.
4. Maurício Caminha de Lacerda, letter to JWFD, January 27, 1985.
5. Hugo Borghi entry in *Dicionário Histórico-Biográfico Brasileiro.*
6. Carlos Lacerda, *O Rato Fiuza,* pp. 13–14.
7. Vera Lacerda Paiva, letter to JWFD, May 8, 1984.
8. Carlos Lacerda, *O Rato Fiuza,* pp. 17–18.
9. Cláudio Lacerda, "Lacerda: Uma Vida de Lutas," Chapter 7, p. 3.
10. Ibid. Carlos Lacerda, "Fiuza a serviço do integralismo," *Diário Carioca,* November 22, 1945. Carlos Lacerda, *O Rato Fiuza,* p. 13.
11. Carlos Lacerda in *Diário Carioca,* November 22, 29, 27, 30, 23, 1945.
12. Joel Silveira, interview.
13. Carlos Lacerda in *Diário Carioca,* November 25, 28, 30, December 1, 1945.
14. Ibid.; also November 22, 1945.
15. Carlos Lacerda in *Diário Carioca,* December 1, 1945.
16. *Tribuna Popular,* November 19, 1945.

17. Ibid., November 23, 30, December 1, 1945.

18. Carlos Lacerda, "Entre Eduardo Gomes e o integralismo há um rato," *Diário Carioca,* December 2, 1945. Carlos Lacerda, *O Rato Fiuza,* pp. 15, 115 (footnote). *Diário Carioca,* November 29, 1945.

10. The Defeat of the UDN (December 1945)

1. Carlos Lacerda, "Os brasileiros silenciosos," *Correio da Manhá,* November 30, 1945, reprinted in Carlos Lacerda, *O Rato Fiuza,* pp. 117–127.

2. Nabuco, *A Vida de Virgílio de Melo Franco,* pp. 198–202.

3. Maurício Caminha de Lacerda, letter to JWFD.

4. "Lições do Pleito," editorial, *Diário Carioca,* December 7, 1945. José Bonifácio Nogueira, "Redenção política do Brasil," *O Globo,* October 9, 1960.

5. Carlos Lacerda, *Depoimento,* pp. 34, 46.

6. Carlos Lacerda in *Diário Carioca,* December 29, 14, 21, 1945.

7. Nabuco, *A Vida de Virgílio de Melo Franco,* pp. 198–202.

8. *Diário Carioca,* December 21, 28, January 3, 1945.

9. John Dos Passos, *Brazil on the Move,* p. 140.

10. *Diário Carioca,* January 3, 1945.

IV. Indefatigable Columnist (1946–1949)

1. Launching "Na Tribuna da Imprensa" (1946)

1. Cláudio Lacerda, "Lacerda: Uma Vida de Lutas," Chapter 7, p. 4.

2. Carlos Lacerda, "Carta ao homem lívido," in "Na Tribuna da Imprensa," *Correio da Manhã,* February 24, 1946. (As this column always appeared in the *Correio da Manhã,* the newspaper reference for it is omitted in the following notes.)

3. Hugo Borghi quoted in Carlos Lacerda, "A Nação contra Ugo Borghi," in "Na Tribuna da Imprensa," March 29, 1946.

4. *O Estado de S. Paulo,* March 10, June 5, 1946. Carlos Lacerda, "Na Tribuna da Imprensa," July 5, 1946.

5. Carlos Lacerda, *Depoimento,* p. 64. Carlos Lacerda, "A Nação contra Ugo Borghi."

6. Hélio Rodrigues, letter to Carlos Lacerda, Santos, January 23, 1946. Carlos Lacerda, "Censura da censura," *Diário Carioca,* January 4, 1946.

7. Carlos Lacerda, "Na Tribuna da Imprensa," May 21, February 15, 1946.

8. Carlos Lacerda, "Carta ao Presidente sobre a situação nacional," in "Na Tribuna da Imprensa," May 12, 1946.

9. Carlos Lacerda, "Na Tribuna da Imprensa," July 4, 5, 1946. About "Rebeco": Vera Lacerda Paiva, interview, August 5, 1984; Cláudio Lacerda, "Lacerda: Uma Vida de Lutas," Chapter 7, p. 4. The movie was based on the novel *Rebecca* by Daphne du Maurier.

10. Carlos Lacerda, "Na Tribuna da Imprensa," July 6, 1946.

11. "A Tentativa de Sequestro de Carlos Lacerda," *Correio da Manhã,* July 6, 1946. Carlos Lacerda, "Na Tribuna da Imprensa," July 6, 1946.

2. Studying European Cooperatives (July–August 1946)

1. Carlos Lacerda, "Na Tribuna da Imprensa," September 30, 1947. Carlos Lacerda, *Como Foi Perdida a Paz,* p. 9.
2. Correspondence in CCL.
3. Carlos Lacerda, letters to Fernando Cícero da Franca Velloso, London, July 13, 27, 1946, in the Velloso collection.
4. Carlos Lacerda, letters to Velloso, London, July 29, 1946, in the Velloso collection. Carlos Lacerda, "Primeiras impressões de Londres," *Correio da Manhã,* July 28, 1946.
5. Carlos Lacerda, letter to Olga Lacerda, Stockholm, August 19, 1946, in CCL. Virgílio de Melo Franco, letter to Carlos Lacerda, Rio de Janeiro, July 28, 1946, in CCL. Carlos Lacerda, letter to Velloso, London, July 13, 1946.
6. Carlos Lacerda, letter to Velloso, Stockholm, August 5, 1946, in the Velloso collection.
7. The Co-operative Party, letters to Carlos Lacerda (signed Jack Bailey and A. E. Oram), London, July 19, 1946, in CCL. Carlos Lacerda, letters to Velloso, London, July 13, 21, 29, 1946, in the Velloso collection.
8. Carlos Lacerda, postcard to Odilon, Vera, Lygia, Cláudio, and Olga, Luleå, Sweden, August 12, 1946, in LFC. Thomas Harris (Reuters Pressbyra Aktiebolag), letter to Carlos Lacerda, Stockholm, August 12, 1946, in CCL. Richard Sterner, letter to Carlos Lacerda, Stockholm, August 16, 1946, in CCL. Carlos Lacerda, letter to Velloso, Stockholm, August 19, 1946, in the Velloso collection.
9. Carlos Lacerda, letter to Velloso, Stockholm, August 19, 1946. Carlos Lacerda, "Na Tribuna da Imprensa," September 30, 1947. Carlos Lacerda, *Como Foi Perdida a Paz,* p. 9. Carlos wrote an introduction to the second edition (1948) of Valdiki Moura, *Notícia do Cooperativismo Brasileiro.*

3. Trieste and the Paris Peace Conference (August–October 1946)

1. Carlos Lacerda, letters to Fernando Cícero da Franca Velloso, Paris, August 21, 22, 1946, in the Velloso collection.
2. João Batista Barreto Leite Filho, interview, Rio de Janeiro, July 1, 1983.
3. Carlos Lacerda, "Na Tribuna da Imprensa," August 28, 1947.
4. Samuel Wainer, interview, São Paulo, July 14, 1979.
5. Carlos Lacerda, *Como Foi Perdida a Paz,* pp. 105, 104.
6. Ibid.
7. Carlos Lacerda, in *Correio da Manhã,* September 30, 1947, October 8, 12, 1946. See also Carlos Lacerda, *Como Foi Perdida a Paz,* pp. 107, 113–115.
8. Carlos Lacerda, *Como Foi Perdida a Paz,* p. 120.
9. Ibid., pp. 133–140.

10. Ibid., pp. 120–121, 136, 124.

11. Ibid., p. 127. Wainer, *Minha Razão de Viver,* p. 99.

12. Carlos Lacerda, "O Fracasso da Conferência," *Correio da Manhã,* October 11, 1946. See also Carlos Lacerda, *Como Foi Perdida a Paz,* pp. 185–189.

13. Ibid. Carlos Lacerda, "Balanço da Delegação Brasileira," in *Como Foi Perdida a Paz,* pp. 181–185 (see also pp. 155–156).

14. Carlos Lacerda, in *Correio da Manhã,* September 30, 1947.

15. Carlos Lacerda, *Como Foi Perdida a Paz,* pp. 172, 170, 150–155.

16. Lygia Paiva Derizans and Cláudio Lacerda Paiva, interview, Rio de Janeiro, August, 8, 1983. Cláudio Lacerda, "Lacerda: Uma Vida de Lutas," Chapter 7, p. 4.

17. Carlos Lacerda, "Na Tribuna da Imprensa," September 30, 1947.

4. Election to the Municipal Council (January 1947)

1. Nabuco, *A Vida de Virgílio de Melo Franco,* p. 207.

2. Carlos Lacerda, "Na Tribuna da Imprensa," December 3, 1946.

3. Carlos Lacerda, "O Movimento Renovador e a reforma social," in "Na Tribuna da Imprensa," November 15, 1947. Sílvio Frank Alem, "A Contribuição à História dos Socialismos no Brasil: A Construção do Partido Socialista Brasileiro (1945–1947)" (João Pessoa: Núcleo de Documentação e Informação Histórica Regional, Universidade Federal da Paraíba, May 1984), pp. 65, 71, 88, quoting *Vanguarda Socialista,* November 22, 27, 1946.

4. Hilcar Leite, interview, Rio de Janeiro, July 5, 1983. Carlos Lacerda, "O Movimento Renovador e a reforma social." Gustavo Corção, "Em quem não devemos votar," in "Na Tribuna da Imprensa," January 12, 1947.

5. *Correio da Manhã,* January 9, 10, 12, 1947. Carlos Lacerda, "Na Tribuna da Imprensa," January 5, 11, 1947.

6. Carlos Lacerda, "Na Tribuna da Imprensa," January 5, 11, 1947.

7. *Correio da Manhã,* January 9, 10, 14, 1947.

8. *Tribuna Popular,* January 16, 11, 1947.

9. Carlos Lacerda, *Depoimento,* p. 76.

10. *Correio da Manhã,* March 13, 1947.

11. *Tribuna Popular,* January 15, February 6, 1947.

12. Carlos Lacerda, "Na Tribuna da Imprensa," February 8, 1947.

13. *Correio da Manhã,* February 11, 1947.

14. Carlos Lacerda, "Rosas e Pedras do Meu Caminho," Chapter 9, p. 105.

15. *Correio da Manhã,* February 7, 27, 1947.

16. Ibid., March 14, 1947. Carlos Lacerda, "A reconquista da cidade," in "Na Tribuna da Imprensa," January 14, 1947.

5. The PCB's Loss of Legality and Representation (1947–1948)

1. Hélio Silva, *1945: Porque Depuseram Vargas,* pp. 336, 383–402.

2. Carlos Lacerda, "Na Tribuna da Imprensa," April 11, 15, 16, 17, 1947.

3. Carlos Lacerda, "Na Tribuna da Imprensa," May 8, 1947. "A sessão da Câmara Municipal," *Correio da Manhã,* May 10, 1947.

4. Carlos Lacerda, "O Movimento Renovador e a reforma social." Heráclito Fontoura Sobral Pinto, letter to Carlos Lacerda, Rio de Janeiro, May 10, 1947, in CCL.

5. Carlos Lacerda, letter to Sobral Pinto, Rio de Janeiro, May 28, 1947, in CCL.

6. Carlos Lacerda, "Na Tribuna da Imprensa," June 11, 12, 1947.

7. Carlos Lacerda, "Na Tribuna da Imprensa," September 30, August 28, September 7, 1947. Luís Carlos Prestes, in hiding early in 1936, encouraged the PCB leadership to kill Elza Fernandes, believed to be giving the police information about Communists.

8. Luís Martins, *Um Bom Sujeito,* pp. 124–125.

9. Luís Martins, "Um grave incidente," *O Estado de S. Paulo,* October 21, 1947.

10. Luís Martins, *Um Bom Sujeito,* pp. 125–126. Carlos Lacerda, "Rosas e Pedras do Meu Caminho," Chapter 2, p. 22.

11. *Correio da Manhã,* October 22, 1947. Carlos Lacerda, "Sobre o rompimento," in "Na Tribuna da Imprensa," October 21, 1947.

12. *Correio da Manhã,* October 21, 23, 1947. Carlos Lacerda, "Na Tribuna da Imprensa," October 24, 1947.

13. Carlos Lacerda, "Na Tribuna da Imprensa," May 11, December 28, 1947.

14. *Correio da Manhã,* January 8, 1948.

6. Combative Municipal Councilman (1947)

1. *Câmara do Distrito Federal,* Law Projects 18, 23, 16A of March 18, 17, 1947 (in folder "Carlos Lacerda, vereador," in the Walter Cunto collection).

2. Carlos Lacerda, "O destino da cidade ocupada," in "Na Tribuna da Imprensa," June 8, 1947. Walter Cunto, interview, Rio de Janeiro, August 14, 1984. *Correio da Manhã,* June 26, 1947.

3. *Correio da Manhã,* July 31, 1947. Carlos Lacerda, "Na Tribuna da Imprensa," September 14, 1947.

4. Carlos Lacerda, *Depoimento,* p. 229. Carlos Lacerda, "Na Tribuna da Imprensa," September 23, August 15, September 14, 25, 26, 1947. *Câmara do Distrito Federal,* Law Project 146 of June 17, 1947 (in folder "Carlos Lacerda, vereador," in the Walter Cunto collection).

5. Carlos Lacerda, "Na Tribuna da Imprensa," September 11, 27, November 11, 1947.

6. Carlos Lacerda, "Na Tribuna da Imprensa," June 26, 27, 1947.

7. *Correio da Manhã,* July 1, 18, 1947. Rui Barbosa, article of November 2, 1898, reprinted in "Na Tribuna da Imprensa," July 2, 1947.

8. Carlos Lacerda, "Na Tribuna da Imprensa," November 11, 1947. "Os Vereadores," editorial, *Correio da Manhã,* November 29, 1947.

9. Carlos Lacerda, "Na Tribuna da Imprensa," November 25, 26, 1947.

Adauto Lúcio Cardoso, letter to Secretaria Geral da Comissão Executiva da U.D.N., Seção Distrito Federal, *Correio da Manhã,* November 30, 1947. "A crise na UDN carioca," *Correio da Manhã,* December 4, 1947.

10. Carlos Lacerda, letter to A Comissão Executiva da UDN, Seção Distrito Federal, in "Na Tribuna da Imprensa," December 5, 1947.

11. Lygia Paiva Derizans and Vera Lacerda Paiva, interview with DFR, Rio de Janeiro, August 25, 1985.

12. *Correio da Manhã,* December 16, 19, 1947.

13. Ibid., December 9, 1947. Carlos Lacerda, letter to the president of the Câmara do Distrito Federal, in "Na Tribuna da Imprensa," December 23, 1947.

14. *Câmara do Distrito Federal,* no. 4–5, of April 2, 1948, reporting on December 1947 (in folder "Carlos Lacerda, vereador," in the Walter Cunto collection).

15. Carlos Lacerda, "Na Tribuna da Imprensa," November 15, 20, 1947. The manifesto drafting commission of the Movimento Renovador consisted of Adauto Lúcio Cardoso, Alceu Amoroso Lima, Alfredo Lage, Carlos Lacerda, Eduardo Borgerth, Gustavo Corção, Heráclito Sobral Pinto, José Fernando Carneiro, Marino Bomilcar Besouchet, and Mário Pedrosa. Eduardo Borgerth, diary, entries for 1946 and 1947.

7. Visit to the Arab World (February–March 1948)

1. Carlos Lacerda, *Uma Luz Pequenina.* The seven stories and others were published in *Xanam e Outras Histórias.* Carlos Drummond de Andrade comments about *Uma Luz Pequenina* in *Revista Acadêmica,* no. 69 (December 1947).

2. Carlos Lacerda, "Na Tribuna da Imprensa," January 16, 1948.

3. Ibid., February 21, 1948. Carlos Lacerda, *O Brasil e o Mundo Árabe,* pp. 81, 95.

4. Carlos Lacerda, *O Brasil e o Mundo Árabe,* pp. 110–121.

5. Ibid., pp. 17–18, 103.

6. Carlos Lacerda, "Na Tribuna da Imprensa," May 16, 1948.

7. Carlos Lacerda, *O Brasil e o Mundo Árabe,* pp. 72, 138, 143–144.

8. Carlos Lacerda, letter to Olga Lacerda, Beirut, February 24, 1948, in CCL.

9. Carlos Lacerda, *O Brasil e o Mundo Árabe,* pp. 193, 187–188.

10. Carlos Lacerda, small black binder, in CCL. Carlos Lacerda, *O Brasil e o Mundo Árabe,* p. 11.

11. Carlos Lacerda, *O Brasil e o Mundo Árabe,* pp. 15–17. Carlos Lacerda, "Na Tribuna da Imprensa," May 16, 1948.

12. Wainer, *Minha Razão de Viver,* pp. 107–111.

13. Carlos Lacerda, *Depoimento,* pp. 403–404.

8. Municipal Thugs Pummel Carlos (April 1948)

1. Carlos Lacerda, "O petróleo brasileiro e o sr. Hermes Lima," in "Na Tribuna da Imprensa," April 6, 1948.

2. Carlos Lacerda, "Na Tribuna da Imprensa," April 6, 7, 11, 13, 1948.
3. Cláudio Lacerda, "Lacerda: Uma Vida de Lutas," Chapter 7, p. 7.
4. Carlos Lacerda, "Rosas e Pedras do Meu Caminho," Chapter 2, p. 22. Carlos Lacerda, "Carta ao Presidente da República," in "Na Tribuna da Imprensa," April 16, 1948.
5. *Correio da Manhã,* April 18, 1948. Carlos Lacerda, "Na Tribuna da Imprensa," April 20, 21, 1948. Carlos Lacerda, "Solidariedade ao difamador," *Tribuna da Imprensa,* May 3, 1950.
6. "Na Tribuna da Imprensa" (apparently not written by Lacerda), April 23, 1948. Carlos Lacerda, "Na Tribuna da Imprensa" (Rádio Mayrink Veiga speech of April 17), April 20, 24, 1948.
7. Carlos Lacerda, "Rosas e Pedras do Meu Caminho," Chapter 2, p. 22.
8. Ibid.
9. *Correio da Manhã,* April 18, 1948. Afonso Arinos de Melo Franco, interview, Rio de Janeiro, July 29, 1984.
10. Carlos Lacerda, "Rosas e Pedras do Meu Caminho," Chapter 2, p. 22.
11. *Correio da Manhã,* April 20, 1948.
12. Ibid., April 23, 1948. Carlos Lacerda, "Rosas e Pedras do Meu Caminho," Chapter 2, p. 23.
13. *Correio da Manhã,* April 27, 20, 23, 1948.
14. Ibid., April 25, 1948.
15. Carlos Lacerda, "Na Tribuna da Imprensa," May 14, 1948, January 29, 1949. Carlos Lacerda, "Rosas e Pedras do Meu Caminho," Chapter 2, p. 22.
16. *Correio da Manhã,* May 26, 1950. *Tribuna da Imprensa,* May 17, 18, 19, 23, 25, 1950.
17. *Tribuna da Imprensa,* May 17, 1950. Carlos Lacerda, *Depoimento,* p. 84.
18. Afonso Arinos de Melo Franco, interview, July 29, 1984. Walter Cunto, interview, Rio de Janeiro, August 7, 1983.

9. Conversion to Catholicism (1948)

1. Marcos Madeira, interview with DFR.
2. Carlos Lacerda, "Na Tribuna da Imprensa," June 11, 16, 17, 18, 19, 1948.
3. Antonio Carlos Villaça, transcript of interview taped by the Sociedade dos Amigos de Carlos Lacerda (received by JWFD March 1986), p. 12. Villaça, interview with DFR, Rio de Janeiro, August 17, 1985.
4. Carlos Lacerda, *Depoimento,* p. 50.
5. Heráclito Fontoura Sobral Pinto, interview, Rio de Janeiro, July 8, 1983.
6. Epaminondas Moreira do Valle, interview with DFR.
7. Carlos Lacerda, "Na Tribuna da Imprensa," January 12, 1947. Gustavo Corção entry in *Dicionário Histórico-Biográfico Brasileiro.*
8. Carlos Lacerda, "Rosas e Pedras do Meu Caminho," Chapter 7 (*Manchete,* May 27, 1967), p. 38.
9. Ibid. Graça Carvalho Pierotti, interview with DFR, Rio de Janeiro, September 1, 1986.
10. "Benedito que converteu Lacerda rezou missa de 7º dia," *Jornal do*

Brasil, May 28, 1977. Lourenço de Almeida Prado, interview, Rio de Janeiro, August 15, 1983. Carlos Lacerda, *Depoimento,* p. 47. Heráclito Fontoura Sobral Pinto, interview, July 8, 1983.

11. Lourenço de Almeida Prado, interview, August 15, 1983. Carlos Lacerda, "Rosas e Pedras do Meu Caminho," Chapter 2, p. 27.

12. Lourenço de Almeida Prado, interview, August 15, 1983, statement in *Jornal do Brasil,* May 28, 1977, and letter to Carlos Lacerda, September 26, 1948, in Carlos Lacerda, "Rosas e Pedras do Meu Caminho," Chapter 7, p. 38. Antonio Carlos Villaça, transcript of interview taped by the Sociedade dos Amigos de Carlos Lacerda, p. 16.

13. Maria Cristina Lacerda Simões Lopes, interview, August 8, 1983.

14. Antonio Dias Rebello Filho, *Carlos Lacerda, Meu Amigo,* pp. 82–83.

15. Carlos Lacerda, "A Via Sacra," in ibid., pp. 83–89 (see pp. 86, 88, 89).

16. Carlos Lacerda and Corrêa Pinto, *Duas Cartas em Tôrno de uma Idéia,* pp. 23, 10, 13.

17. Carlos Lacerda, "Rosas e Pedras do Meu Caminho," Chapter 7, pp. 38–39.

10. Predicting the Election of Dewey (October–November 1948)

1. Carlos Lacerda, in *Correio da Manhã,* December 1, 2, 3, 4, 5, 8, 9, 10, 11, 1948.

2. Carlos Lacerda, in *Correio da Manhã,* December 8, 1948.

3. Carlos Lacerda, in *Correio da Manhã,* December 8, 11, 1948.

4. Carlos Lacerda, letters to Sérgio Lacerda, New York, November 8, 1948, in CCL, and to Fernando Cícero da Franca Velloso, New York, October 5, 1948, in Velloso collection.

5. Carlos Lacerda, letter to Olga Lacerda, New York, October 15, 1948, in CCL.

6. Carlos Lacerda, in *Correio da Manhã,* October 12, September 30, 1948.

7. Carlos Lacerda, letter to Fernando Velloso, October 5, 1948.

8. Carlos Lacerda, in *Correio da Manhã,* September 30, 1948, quoting an American friend about Truman. Carlos Lacerda, "O Brasil na Conferência de Chicago," *Correio da Manhã,* September 22, 1948.

9. Carlos Lacerda, letter to Fernando Velloso, October 5, 1948. Carlos Lacerda, in *Correio da Manhã,* October 29, September 29, 30, 1948.

10. Carlos Lacerda, letter to Olga Lacerda, October 15, 1948.

11. Carlos Lacerda, in *Correio da Manhã,* November 4, 5, 1948.

12. *Correio da Manhã,* October 30, 1948. Nabuco, *A Vida de Virgílio de Melo Franco,* pp. 233–241. Carlos Lacerda, letters to Olga Lacerda, New York, November 8, 29–30, 1948, in LFC. Carlos Lacerda, letters to Sérgio Lacerda, New York, one without date, in LFC, and the other an addition to his letter of November 8, 1948, to Olga Lacerda.

11. Communists Disrupt the ABDE (March–April 1949)

1. Carlos Lacerda, "Na Tribuna da Imprensa," January 12, 1949.

2. Ibid., December 28, 1948, February 17, March 10, January 7, 1949.

3. Carlos Lacerda, letter to UNE President Genival Barbosa, in "Na Tribuna da Imprensa," February 17, 1949.
4. Carlos Lacerda, "Na Tribuna da Imprensa," December 29, 1948.
5. Afonso Arinos de Melo Franco, *A Escalada: Memórias,* pp. 165–169.
6. Ibid. Carlos Lacerda, "Na Tribuna da Imprensa," March 27, 31, 1949.
7. Article about Carlos Drummond de Andrade, *Jornal do Brasil,* Caderno B, September 29, 1984. Carlos Drummond de Andrade, declaration, *Diário de Notícias,* April 29, 1949. Carlos Lacerda, "Na Tribuna da Imprensa," March 26, 1949. Afonso Arinos de Melo Franco, interview, Rio de Janeiro, August 25, 1984. Melo Franco, *A Escalada,* pp. 165, 167.
8. Melo Franco, *A Escalada,* pp. 167–168. Carlos Lacerda, "Na Tribuna da Imprensa," March 26, 1949.
9. Melo Franco, *A Escalada,* pp. 168–169. Carlos Lacerda, "Na Tribuna da Imprensa," March 29, 30, 1949.
10. Melo Franco, *A Escalada,* p. 169.
11. Ibid., p. 170. Carlos Lacerda, "Na Tribuna da Imprensa," April 8, 1949. Melo Franco, interview, August 25, 1984.
12. Melo Franco, *A Escalada,* p. 170. *Correio da Manhã,* April 8, 1949. *Diário de Notícias,* April 29, 1949.
13. Melo Franco, *A Escalada,* p. 170. *Diário de Notícias,* April 29, 1949.
14. Carlos Lacerda, in *Tribuna da Imprensa,* April 15, 1950.

12. Carlos Leaves the *Correio da Manhã* (April 1949)

1. Quotation from the law project, in Carlos Lacerda, "Na Tribuna da Imprensa," February 4, 1949. Carlos Lacerda, "Na Tribuna da Imprensa," February 20, 1949.
2. Carlos Lacerda, "Na Tribuna da Imprensa," February 19, 1949.
3. Carlos Lacerda, "Na Tribuna da Imprensa," February 16, 1949.
4. Carlos Lacerda, "Na Tribuna da Imprensa," February 16, April 24, 26, 23, 1949. Carlos Lacerda, "Rosas e Pedras do Meu Caminho," Chapter 5 (*Manchete,* May 13, 1967), p. 26.
5. Carlos Lacerda, "Na Tribuna da Imprensa," April 24, 26, 27, 1949.
6. *Correio da Manhã,* April 27, 1949.
7. P. B., "Na Tribuna da Imprensa," May 1, 1949. Carlos Lacerda, "Rosas e Pedras do Meu Caminho," Chapter 5, p. 26. Carlos Lacerda, *Depoimento,* pp. 74–75.
8. P. B., "Na Tribuna da Imprensa," May 1, 1949.

V. Director of a New Newspaper (1949–1953)

1. Prescription for Better Journalism (1949)

1. Aluísio Alves, interview, Rio de Janeiro, August 17, 1983. Luiz Felippe de Oliveira Penna, interview, August 11, 1983. Carlos Lacerda, letter to Letícia Lacerda, Rio de Janeiro, February 12, 1949, in LFC.
2. "História do Pato Feio," *Tribuna da Imprensa,* December 24, 1959.
3. Odilon and Vera Lacerda Paiva and Lygia Paiva Derizans, interview,

Rio de Janeiro, July 22, 1984. Carlos Lacerda, "Bem-vindos à *Tribuna da Imprensa*," *Tribuna da Imprensa*, April 2, 1959. Cláudio Lacerda, "Lacerda: Uma Vida de Lutas," Chapter 8, p. 2.

4. Carlos Lacerda, speech at the *assembléia geral extraordinária* of the Sociedade Anônima Editôra Tribuna da Imprensa, July 9, 1953, *Tribuna da Imprensa*, June 17, 1954 (see p. 5, column 3).

5. Luiz Felippe de Oliveira Penna, interview, August 11, 1983.

6. "Tribuna da Imprensa: ata da assembléia geral da constituição" of September 2, 1949, *Diário Oficial*, December 7, 1949 (see p. 16,767).

7. "História do Pato Feio." Carlos Lacerda, *Depoimento*, p. 100, quoting Alceu Amoroso Lima. José Luiz Moreira de Souza, interview, Rio de Janeiro, August 16, 1983. Aluísio Alves, interview.

8. *Tribuna da Imprensa*, October 30, 31, 1951. "Tribuna da Imprensa: ata da assembléia geral da constituição" (see p. 16,775). Cláudio Lacerda, "Lacerda: Uma Vida de Lutas," Chapter 8, p. 12.

9. Carlos Lacerda, *A Missão da Imprensa*, p. 66.

10. Ibid., pp. 9–13.

11. Ibid., pp. 29–30.

12. Ibid., pp. 32–33.

13. Ibid., pp. 65–66.

14. Ibid., pp. 60, 29.

15. Ibid., pp. 65, 20–26.

16. Ibid., p. 61.

17. Ibid., p. 62.

2. Launching the *Tribuna da Imprensa* (December 27, 1949)

1. Aluísio Alves, interview.

2. Thomas Leonardos, interview, Rio de Janeiro, August 6, 1984. Dario de Almeida Magalhães, interview, Rio de Janeiro, July 7, 1983. *Estatutos da Sociedade Anônima Editôra Tribuna da Imprensa* (n.d.). Carlos Lacerda, speech at the *assembléia geral extraordinária* (see p. 5, column 4). Samuel Wainer, interview, September 28, 1968.

3. "Tribuna da Imprensa: ata da assembléia geral da constituição" (see p. 16,767). *Estatutos da Sociedade Anônima Editôra Tribuna da Imprensa.*

4. Ibid.

5. Heráclito Fontoura Sobral Pinto, interview, Rio de Janeiro, July 8, 1983.

6. Carlos Lacerda, speech at the *assembléia geral extraordinária* (see p. 4, column 3). Stefan Baciu, *Lavradio, 98*, pp. 40–42. Walter Cunto, interview, Rio de Janeiro, August 7, 1983. Dario de Almeida Magalhães, interview. Cláudio Lacerda, "Lacerda: Uma Vida de Lutas," Chapter 8, p. 2.

7. José Maria Homem de Montes, interview, São Paulo, July 26, 1983.

8. Samuel Wainer, interview, September 28, 1968. "Garantia para anunciantes e leitores: Código de ética comercial da 'Tribuna da Imprensa,'" *Tribuna da Imprensa*, December 27, 1949, 2nd section, p. 1.

9. Hilcar Leite, interview. *Tribuna da Imprensa*, December 27, 1949, 1st section, p. 4. Walter Cunto, handwritten notes for JWFD, Rio de Janeiro, Au-

gust 7, 1983. Cláudio Lacerda, "Lacerda: Uma Vida de Lutas," Chapter 8, p. 2.

10. "História do Pato Feio." Cláudio Lacerda, "Lacerda: Uma Vida de Lutas," Chapter 8, p. 2.

11. *A Direção* (the Directorship), "Afinal começamos," and *O redator de plantão* (the editor of this number), note for readers, *Tribuna da Imprensa,* December 27, 1949. *Tribuna da Imprensa,* June 17, 1954, p. 5, column 4.

12. Walter Ramos Poyares, interview with DFR, Rio de Janeiro, July 30, 1985.

13. Carlos Lacerda, *Depoimento,* p. 196. Carlos Lacerda, speech at the *assembléia geral extraordinária* (see p. 4, columns 5, 6). "A Tribuna da Imprensa responde às perguntas dos democratas de Última Hora," *Tribuna da Imprensa,* October 31, 1951. Ruth Alverga, transcript of interview taped by the Sociedade dos Amigos de Carlos Lacerda, p. 4.

14. Ayrton Baffa, "A Metralhadora Giratória Disparada com Dois Dedos," *Revista de Comunicação,* vol. 5, no. 19 (September 1989).

15. Raul de Sá Barbosa, interview with DFR, Rio de Janeiro, January 18, 1983.

16. Ruth Alverga, transcript of interview, pp. 3–4.

17. Baffa, "A Metralhadora Giratória." Murilo Melo Filho, "Lacerdista, Durante Sete Anos," typewritten, p. 2.

18. Cláudio Lacerda, "Lacerda: Uma Vida de Lutas," Chapter 8, p. 3. Carlos Lacerda, speech at the *assembléia geral extraordinária* (see p. 4, columns 4, 5). Carlos Lacerda, "Rosas e Pedras do Meu Caminho," Chapter 10 (*Manchete,* June 17, 1967), pp. 113, 115.

19. Baciu, *Lavradio, 98,* p. 171. Hilde Weber, *O Brasil em Charges, 1950–1985* (São Paulo: Circo Editorial, 1986).

20. Odilon and Vera Lacerda Paiva, interview, Rio de Janeiro, August 5, 1984.

21. Marcelo Garcia, interview, Rio de Janeiro, August 18, 1983.

22. Ruth Alverga, transcript of interview, pp. 1, 2, 6. Ruth Alverga, interview, Rio de Janeiro, August 7, 1983, and interview with DFR, Rio de Janeiro, March 30, 1983. Baciu, *Lavradio, 98,* p. 50.

23. Baciu, *Lavradio, 98,* p. 50.

3. Assaulted by an Air Force Colonel (May 14, 1950)

1. *Tribuna da Imprensa,* May 23, 1950, quoting article published on May 11.

2. *Diário de Notícias* and *Correio da Manhã,* May 16, 1950.

3. Ibid. *Tribuna da Imprensa,* May 15, 1950. *Correio da Manhã,* May 26, 1950.

4. *Correio da Manhã,* May 16, 1950.

5. *Tribuna da Imprensa,* May 16, 19, 1950.

6. Ibid., May 17, 18, 23, 24, 1950.

7. Ibid., May 25, 1950.

8. *Correio da Manhã,* May 26, 1950. *Diário de Notícias,* May 27, 1950.

9. *Tribuna da Imprensa,* May 18, 19, 20, 30, 1950. Carlos Lacerda, "Rosas e Pedras do Meu Caminho," Chapter 2, p. 23.

4. Presidential Election (October 1950)

1. Carlos Lacerda, "A candidatura do Brigadeiro e a TI," *Tribuna da Imprensa,* April 17, 1950.
2. *Tribuna da Imprensa,* March 13, 15, 21, April 13, 1950.
3. Carlos Lacerda, *Depoimento,* p. 98.
4. Carlos Lacerda, "Despedida à UDN," *Tribuna da Imprensa,* July 20, 1950. *Tribuna da Imprensa,* May 11, 12, 13, 1950.
5. Carlos Lacerda, *Depoimento,* p. 100. *Tribuna da Imprensa,* May 20, July 1, August 3, July 17, 14, 1950.
6. Carlos Lacerda, "Despedida à UDN." *Tribuna da Imprensa,* July 14, 20, 21, 1950.
7. Carlos Lacerda, "Despedida à UDN." *Tribuna da Imprensa,* June 14, 1950.
8. *Tribuna da Imprensa,* July 20, 21, 24, 28, 29–30, June 20, October 6, 1950. Carlos Lacerda, *Depoimento,* p. 100.
9. Ibid.
10. *Tribuna da Imprensa,* June 1, 1950. Carlos Lacerda, "Com o Brigadeiro apesar de tudo," *Tribuna da Imprensa,* August 3, 1950.
11. Carlos Lacerda, "Em busca da Cidade das Meninas," *Tribuna da Imprensa,* August 30, 1950.
12. *Tribuna da Imprensa,* September 4, 1950.
13. Carlos Lacerda, *Depoimento,* pp. 101–102.
14. Hippolito, "Carlos Lacerda, Ascensão e Queda," pp. 27–28. *Tribuna da Imprensa,* January 19, 1951, October 10, 1950, January 16, 1951.
15. Jeff Bingaman, "The Strategy of Political Opposition: An Analysis of the Political Life of Carlos Lacerda," typewritten, 50 pages, Stanford Law School, October 30, 1967 (copy in CCL), citing *New York Times,* October 14, 1950.
16. Carlos Lacerda, "Agora será diferente," *Tribuna da Imprensa,* October 16, 1950.

5. Vargas Returns to the Presidency (1951)

1. *Tribuna da Imprensa,* January 22, 24, 1951.
2. Ibid., January 18, March 26, April 11, January 31, 1951.
3. Ibid., January 25, 29, February 1, 1951. Carlos Lacerda, *Depoimento,* p. 121.
4. Ruth Alverga, interview with DFR, March 30, 1983. Carlos Lacerda, "Rosas e Pedras do Meu Caminho," Chapter 9, p. 111. Carlos Lacerda, "Oração pela criança nova," typewritten poem, May 15, 1951, in LFC. Lourenço de Almeida Prado, interview.
5. *Tribuna da Imprensa,* April 19, February 3–4, 1951.
6. Ibid., December 6, 1951.

7. Ibid., December 4, 5, 6, July 20, August 28, 1951.
8. Ibid., July 4, 14–15, 1951.
9. Ibid., July 22, August 10, 4–5, 1951.
10. Ibid.
11. Ibid., August 9, October 20–21, 1951.
12. Ibid., November 6, 14, October 31, August 1, 9, 1951.
13. Ibid., December 7, 1951.
14. Ibid., December 12, 1951.
15. Ibid., December 13, 19, 8–9, 7, 17, 1951.
16. Ibid., December 7, 12, 1951.

6. The Specter of *Última Hora* (1951–1952)

1. *Tribuna da Imprensa,* August 9, 1951.
2. Samuel Wainer, in Câmara dos Deputados, *Autos do Inquérito Instaurado pela Comissão Parlamentar de Inquérito Instituída pela Resolução nº 313 de 27 de Maio de 1953,* p. 6. Samuel Wainer, "O Dia em que Getúlio me Mandou Fazer um Jornal," *Playboy* (Brazil), nº 93 (April 1983), pp. 134, 136.
3. Wainer, *Minha Razão de Viver,* p. 128.
4. Ibid., pp. 129–131. Câmara dos Deputados, *Autos do Inquérito,* pp. 56, 6–15. Samuel Wainer, letter to Alzira Vargas do Amaral Peixoto, May 1953 (CPDOC Ref. GV 53.05.00/3) in Adelina Maria Alves Novaes e Cruz, Célia Maria Leite Costa, Maria Celina Soares d'Araújo, and Suely Braga da Silva, compilers, *Impasse na Democracia Brasileira, 1951–1955: Coletânea de Documentos,* pp. 234–236. *Diário Carioca,* quoted in *Tribuna da Imprensa,* June 25, 1953.
5. Câmara dos Deputados, *Autos do Inquérito,* pp. 6–15. Wainer, *Minha Razão de Viver,* p. 134.
6. Luthero Vargas, *Getúlio Vargas: A Revolução Inacabada,* pp. 244–246. Câmara dos Deputados, *Autos do Inquérito,* pp. 19–21, 187–191, 285 (testimonies of Francisco Matarazzo Júnior, August 14, 1953, and Carlos Lacerda, September 2, 1953). *Tribuna da Imprensa,* August 27, 1952.
7. Câmara dos Deputados, *Autos do Inquérito,* pp. 17–19. Carlos Lacerda, in *Tribuna da Imprensa,* March 10, 1952.
8. Paulo Silveira, interview, Rio de Janeiro, July 22, 1984. Wainer, *Minha Razão de Viver,* pp. 144, 134. *Última Hora* entry in *Dicionário Histórico–Biográfico Brasileiro.* Herman Lima, *História de Caricatura no Brasil,* vol. 4, p. 1620.
9. Samuel Wainer and Francisco Matarazzo Júnior, testimonies in Câmara dos Deputados, *Autos do Inquérito,* pp. 16, 189.
10. *Tribuna da Imprensa,* July 11, 24, October 27–28, 30, 1951. Carlos Lacerda, testimony, June 9, 1953, Câmara dos Deputados, *Autos do Inquérito,* p. 25. *Tribuna da Imprensa,* November 6, 5, 1951.
11. *Tribuna da Imprensa,* March 12, 13, 1952. Walter Cunto, comments in Ruth Alverga, transcript of interview, p. 10.
12. *Tribuna da Imprensa,* October 31, 1951.

13. Carlos Lacerda, "Relatório aos acionistas," *Tribuna da Imprensa,* March 14, 1952.

7. *Bamba* and Other Headaches (1951–1952)

1. Ruth Alverga, interview with DFR, March 30, 1983.
2. Graça Carvalho Pierotti, interview with DFR.
3. *Bamba,* vol. 1, no. 1 (June 10, 1951). Cláudio Lacerda, "Lacerda: Uma Vida de Lutas," Chapter 8, pp. 3–4.
4. *Tribuna da Imprensa,* June 22, 1951.
5. Carlos Lacerda, "Relatório aos acionistas." *Tribuna da Imprensa,* July 13, 1951. Graça Carvalho Pierotti, interview with DFR.
6. Ruth Alverga, interview with DFR, March 30, 1983.
7. Carlos Lacerda, letter to Hélder Câmara, Rio de Janeiro, December 19, 1952, in CCL.
8. Lourenço de Almeida Prado, letter to Carlos Lacerda, April 17, 1952, in CCL. Carlos Lacerda, letter to Lourenço de Almeida Prado, Rio de Janeiro, July 30, 1952, in CCL.
9. Walter Cunto, transcript of interview taped by the Sociedade dos Amigos de Carlos Lacerda, p. 4.
10. Carlos Lacerda, "Relatório aos acionistas."
11. Hernâni Donato, "Carlos Lacerda Planeja Fundar em São Paulo a Revista 'Veja,'" typewritten notes for JWFD, São Paulo, August 1984.
12. Maurício Lacerda Filho, letter to Carlos Lacerda, Rio de Janeiro, April 14, 1952, in CCL. Sérgio Lacerda, letter to his parents, n.d., in CCL.
13. João Condé, interview, Rio de Janeiro, August 11, 1983.
14. Carlos Lacerda, letter to Andrew Heiskell, Rio de Janeiro, July 29, 1952, in CCL. See also letters of Heiskell and Alberto Gainza Paz to Carlos Lacerda, August and September 1952, in CCL.
15. *Tribuna da Imprensa,* October 30, 1952.
16. John Dos Passos, *Brazil on the Move,* pp. 140–141.

8. Widely Heralded Prisoner (December 1952)

1. *Tribuna da Imprensa,* September 20–21, 22, 24, 25, 1952.
2. Ibid., September 26, 27–28, October 1, September 20–21, 1952.
3. Ibid., September 27–28, 30, October 1, 2, 4–5, 1952. Carlos Lacerda, letter to José Picorelli, Rio de Janeiro, November 6, 1952, in CCL.
4. Carlos Lacerda, telegram to Francisco Negrão de Lima, Rio de Janeiro, November 29, 1952, in CCL.
5. *Tribuna da Imprensa,* December 2, 1952. Bueno et al., *Êsse Incrível Lacerda,* pp. 11–12.
6. Wainer, *Minha Razão de Viver,* p. 140.
7. *Tribuna da Imprensa,* December 2, 1952. Bueno et al., *Êsse Incrível Lacerda,* pp. 11–12.
8. *Tribuna da Imprensa,* December 2, 1952.
9. Ibid., December 2, 3, 1952. *O Estado de S. Paulo,* December 3, 1952.

10. *O Estado de S. Paulo,* December 3, 1952.
11. *Tribuna da Imprensa,* December 3, 4, 1952.
12. Ibid., December 3, 1952.

9. "Help Your Brother" (February–March 1953)

1. *Tribuna da Imprensa,* August 17, 1951. Carlos Lacerda, *Visão da Sêca no Nordeste: Um Relato, um Testemunho, um Programa,* pp. 27–28.
2. Ibid. *Tribuna da Imprensa,* August 27, 1951.
3. Carlos Lacerda, "Como lutar contra a sêca," typewritten, 48 pages, (talk at the Brazilian Press Association [ABI], March 23, 1953) (see pp. 4–6).
4. Carlos Lacerda, *Visão da Sêca no Nordeste,* pp. 33–38, 47.
5. Victor Coelho Bouças, interview, Rio de Janeiro, August 2, 1984.
6. Carlos Lacerda, *Visão da Sêca no Nordeste,* pp. 55–62.
7. *Tribuna da Imprensa,* March 9, May 16–17, 1953. Carlos Lacerda, "Como lutar contra a sêca," p. 4.
8. *Tribuna da Imprensa,* February 12, 13, 20, 21–22, 23, 1951.
9. Carlos Lacerda, "Rosas e Pedras do Meu Caminho," Chapter 10 (*Manchete,* June 17, 1967), pp. 118–119.
10. Ibid. Carlos Lacerda, *Depoimento,* pp. 114–116.
11. Ibid.
12. *Tribuna da Imprensa,* February 24, 25, 28, March 2, 7–8, 10, 20, 1953.
13. Carlos Lacerda, *Depoimento,* p. 116. Raul Brunini, taped interview, Rio de Janeiro, March 9, 1989 (see pp. 1, 6 of transcript).

10. Precarious Relations with Jânio Quadros (1953)

1. Carlos Lacerda, in *Tribuna da Imprensa,* July 26–27, 1952.
2. Afonso Arinos de Melo Franco, "A UDN e o Acôrdo Militar Brasil–Estados Unidos," *Tribuna da Imprensa,* December 1, 1952. Carlos Lacerda, in *Tribuna da Imprensa,* January 23, 1953. *Tribuna da Imprensa,* February 5, 1953.
3. *Tribuna da Imprensa,* March 19, 1953.
4. Ibid., March 21–22, 1953. Viriato de Castro, *O Fenômeno Jânio Quadros,* p. 70.
5. Luiz Ernesto Kawall, interview, São Paulo, July 31, 1983.
6. *Tribuna da Imprensa,* February 10, 11, 1953. Ademarismo: support for, and practices of, São Paulo politician Ademar de Barros.
7. Ibid., March 26, 28, 31, 1953.
8. Carlos Lacerda, *Depoimento,* p. 198. Luiz Ernesto Kawall, interview, July 31, 1983.
9. Jânio Quadros, "Mensagem aos Cariocas," *Tribuna da Imprensa,* April 22, 1953. Carlos Lacerda, "Um dia com Jânio Quadros," *Tribuna da Imprensa,* April 22, 1953.
10. Carlos Lacerda, "Rosas e Pedras do Meu Caminho," Chapter 11 (*Manchete,* June 24, 1967), p. 109.
11. Cruz et al., *Impasse na Democracia Brasileira,* pp. 337–340. *Tribuna*

da Imprensa, November 17, September 16, December 9, 1953. Carlos Lacerda, "Rosas e Pedras do Meu Caminho," Chapter 11, p. 111.

12. *Tribuna da Imprensa,* December 9, 1953. Carlos Lacerda, *Depoimento,* pp. 207–208. Carlos Lacerda, "Rosas e Pedras do Meu Caminho," Chapter 11, p. 111.

13. Ibid. *Tribuna da Imprensa,* December 12–13, 14, 1953.

VI. Dethroner of Vargas (1953–1954)

1. Congress Investigates the Wainer Group (June–November 1953)

1. "Esbanjavam o dinheiro do Banco do Brasil," *Tribuna da Imprensa,* May 20, 1953.

2. *Tribuna da Imprensa,* May 25, 23–24, 22, 1953.

3. Cláudio Lacerda, "Lacerda: Uma Vida de Lutas," Chapter 8, p. 5. Armando Falcão, interview, Rio de Janeiro, August 26, 1983. Newspaper clippings in file about Wainer, at *O Estado de S. Paulo.*

4. Armando Falcão said (interview, August 26, 1983) he received many more than 110 signatures but some signers retracted. Carlos Lacerda, "Rosas e Pedras do Meu Caminho," Chapter 10, p. 114. Samuel Wainer, letters to Getúlio Vargas and Alzira Vargas do Amaral Peixoto, in Cruz et al., *Impasse na Democracia Brasileira,* pp. 240, 234–237.

5. Luthero Vargas, *Getúlio Vargas: A Revolucão Inacabada,* pp. 244–245. *Tribuna da Imprensa,* May 28, 31, 1953. Hélio Fernandes, interview.

6. Câmara dos Deputados, *Autos do Inquérito.* Marcos de Sousa Dantas, letter to *Correio da Manhã,* November 12, 1953.

7. Luthero Vargas. *Getúlio Vargas: A Revolucão Inacabada,* pp. 244–246. Wainer, *Minha Razão de Viver,* pp. 158–161.

8. Letters to Carlos Lacerda, 1953, in CCL. Baciu, *Lavradio, 98,* p. 89.

9. Wainer, *Minha Razão de Viver,* p. 166–167.

10. Marvin Alisky, *Latin American Media: Guidance and Censorship,* p. 97. Marcelo Garcia, interview. *Tribuna da Imprensa,* June 22, 1953.

11. *Tribuna da Imprensa,* July 20, 1953.

12. Carlos Lacerda, "Rosas e Pedras do Meu Caminho," Chapter 10, p. 115. Baciu, *Lavradio, 98,* p. 90. *Tribuna da Imprensa,* December 3, 1953.

13. Wainer, *Minha Razão de Viver,* p. 197. *Diário Carioca,* July 8, 1953. *O Jornal,* July 19, 1953. *Diário de Notícias,* July 28, 1953. PCB manifesto in *Problemas,* no. 46 (May–June 1953), pp. 1–4 (see p. 3). *Imprensa Popular,* September 15, 1953, May 27, 1954.

14. Carlos Lacerda, in Câmara dos Deputados, *Autos do Inquérito,* pp. 24–29. Samuel Wainer, in Câmara dos Deputados, *Autos do Inquérito,* pp. 82, 56. *Correio da Manhã,* June 26, 1953.

15. *O Estado de S. Paulo,* July 7, 1953. *Diário de Notícias,* July 14, 1953. *Correio da Manhã,* July 17, 1953. *Última Hora,* July 16, 1953. Câmara dos Deputados, *Autos do Inquérito,* p. 4. *Última Hora,* July 20, 1953.

16. Câmara dos Deputados, *Autos do Inquérito,* pp. 4, 132. *Tribuna da*

Imprensa, July 29, 1953. *Última Hora,* July 28, 1953. *Correio da Manhã* and *O Tempo,* August 6, 1953. *Folha de S. Paulo,* August 11, 1953.

17. Eddy Dias da Cruz [Marques Rebello], in Câmara dos Deputados, *Autos do Inquérito,* pp. 296–298. *Diário Carioca,* July 31, 1953. Wainer, *Minha Razão de Viver,* pp. 169–171.

18. *Tribuna da Imprensa,* September 1, 11, 14, 1953. Marcos de Sousa Dantas, letter to *Correio da Manhã.*

19. Marcos de Sousa Dantas, letter to *Correio da Manhã. Tribuna da Imprensa,* September 9, 10, 1953.

20. *Tribuna da Imprensa,* October 28, November 13, 1953. Carlos Lacerda, telegram to Marcos de Sousa Dantas, November 25, 1953, in CCL.

21. Cruz et al., *Impasse na Democracia Brasileira,* pp. 242–246. Hariberto de Miranda Jordão, *O Caso da Última Hora: Resposta ao Relatório da Comissão Parlamentar de Inquérito. Tribuna da Imprensa,* December 7, 1953. Luthero Vargas, *Getúlio Vargas: A Revolução Inacabada,* pp. 218, 282, 284, 243. Hélio Silva, *1954: Um Tiro no Coração,* p. 207.

22. *Tribuna da Imprensa,* April 1, May 6, 17, June 23, 1954.

2. "Samuel Wainer, Born in Bessarabia" (1953–1954)

1. Carlos Lacerda, testimony at criminal court hearings, March 1954, in *Tribuna da Imprensa,* March 16, 1954.

2. Walter Cunto, interview, Rio de Janeiro, August 7, 1983.

3. *Diário de S. Paulo* and *Tribuna da Imprensa,* July 15, 1953. Samuel Wainer, *Minha Razão de Viver,* p. 196.

4. Carlos Lacerda, testimony at criminal court hearings, March 1954. Ruth Alverga, interviews, Rio de Janeiro, August 7, 1983, August 16, 1984. *Diário da Noite,* July 18, 1953. *Tribuna da Imprensa,* July 18–19, 1953. *O Jornal,* July 19, 1953. See also Armando Falcão, *Tudo a Declarar,* pp. 59–79 ("O Caso da *Última Hora*").

5. *Correio da Manhã,* August 20, 1953.

6. Carlos Lacerda, testimony at criminal court hearings, March 1954. Wainer, *Minha Razão de Viver,* pp. 188–189.

7. *Tribuna da Imprensa,* July 20, 1953.

8. Carlos Lacerda, "Rosas e Pedras do Meu Caminho," Chapter 10, p. 114. David Nasser, "Meu Amigo, Carlos Lacerda." *Tribuna da Imprensa,* March 16, 1954, July 21, 22, 1953.

9. *Tribuna da Imprensa,* August 29, 1953.

10. *O Jornal,* July 23, 1953. *Tribuna da Imprensa,* July 29, 1953.

11. Carlos Lacerda, "Rosas e Pedras do Meu Caminho," Chapter 10, p. 114. Carlos Lacerda, letter to Fernando Bastos Ribeiro, Delegado do 2º Distrito, Rio de Janeiro, August 4, 1953, in CCL.

12. *Última Hora,* August 2, 1953.

13. *Tribuna da Imprensa,* August 10, September 10, 1953. *O Estado de S. Paulo,* November 29, 1956.

14. *Tribuna da Imprensa,* September 9, 1953, August 21–22, 16, Sep-

tember 11–12, 16, 1954. Clube da Lanterna entry in *Dicionário Histórico-Biográfico Brasileiro.*

15. *Tribuna da Imprensa,* August 29, September 29, 1953.

16. Ibid., September 29, October 2, 1953. Richard Bourne, *Political Leaders of Latin America,* p. 221. Carlos Lacerda, letter to Letícia Lacerda, Mexico City, October 7, 1953, in LFC. Letícia Lacerda, letter to Carlos Lacerda, Rio de Janeiro, September 30, 1953, in LFC.

17. William W. White, letter to Carlos Lacerda, Washington, D.C., July 29, 1953, and Andrew Heiskell, letter to Carlos Lacerda, New York, July 30, 1953, both in CCL. *Tribuna da Imprensa,* October 16, 1953.

18. Carlos Lacerda, speech at the *assembléia geral extraordinária* (see p. 4, column 5).

19. *Tribuna da Imprensa,* September 16, 1953. Carlos Lacerda, letter to John Klem (of the Editors Press Service, New York), Rio de Janeiro, February 15, 1954, in CCL.

20. *Tribuna da Imprensa,* March 19, 20, April 28, 27, 1954. Evandro Lins e Silva, interview, August 2, 1984.

21. *Tribuna da Imprensa,* February 13–14, 1954. Paulo Silveira, interview.

22. *Tribuna da Imprensa,* March 4, 5, 1954.

3. Trying to Impeach Vargas (April–June 1954)

1. Hélio Fernandes, interview.

2. *Tribuna da Imprensa,* December 2, 1953.

3. Ibid., April 5, June 25, 1954.

4. Ibid., June 2, 5–6, July 5, 6, 9, 1954. *Correio da Manhã,* March 25, 1954. *O Estado de S. Paulo,* March 25, 1954, May 22, 1977. Carlos Lacerda, *Depoimento,* pp. 121–123. Carlos Lacerda, "Rosas e Pedras do Meu Caminho," Chapter 5, p. 25.

5. *Tribuna da Imprensa,* December 4, 1953.

6. Epitácio Caó, *Carreirista da Traição,* pp. 80, 101.

7. *Tribuna da Imprensa,* February 25, March 4, June 1, 1954. Melo Franco, *A Escalada,* pp. 269–283. Villaça, interview with DFR, August 17, 1985.

8. *Tribuna da Imprensa,* June 24, 1954. *Última Hora,* June 28, July 2, 5, 1954.

9. *Tribuna da Imprensa,* March 8, 9, 1954. Carlos Lacerda, *O Caminho da Liberdade: Discurso na Comissão de Justiça da Câmara dos Deputados,* pp. 189–190. Juan Perón, *Discurso Pronunciado por el Excelentísimo Señor Presidente de la Nación General Juan Perón en la Escuela Nacional de Guerra,* pp. 15–18. (Restricted Copy No. 0426, well marked, is in the Walter Cunto collection.)

10. *Tribuna da Imprensa,* March 15, April 3–4, 1954.

11. Ibid., April 9, 8, 5, May 6, 1954.

12. Melo Franco, *A Escalada,* pp. 288–289. *Tribuna da Imprensa,* June 1, 1954. *Última Hora,* June 5, 7, 1954.

13. *Última Hora,* June 11, 1954. *Tribuna da Imprensa,* June 15, 1954.
14. *Tribuna da Imprensa,* June 16, 17, 30, July 1, 1954. Melo Franco, *A Escalada,* p. 289.

4. "The Crow" (May–July 1954)

1. *Tribuna da Imprensa,* May 22–23, May 15–16, 1954. *Última Hora,* May 13, 14, 1954. *Imprensa Popular,* May 26, 16, 18, 1954.
2. *Tribuna da Imprensa,* May 22–23, 24, 1954.
3. Ibid., May 26, 27, 1954.
4. Ibid. *Imprensa Popular,* May 27, 1954.
5. Wainer, *Minha Razão de Viver,* p. 181. Paulo Silveira, interview.
6. *Última Hora,* May 25, 26, 27, 1954.
7. Luthero Vargas, *Getúlio Vargas: A Revolução Inacabada,* pp. 278–280. *Última Hora,* May 29, 31, June 1, 10, 1954.
8. *Última Hora,* May 31, 1954. *Tribuna da Imprensa,* July 6, 1954.
9. *Última Hora,* July 9, 12, 1954. *Tribuna da Imprensa,* July 12, 13, 14, 1954.
10. *Tribuna da Imprensa,* June 12, 13, 14, July 27, 1954.

5. Candidate Lacerda and the Air Force Majors (January–August 1954)

1. *Tribuna da Imprensa,* January 29, February 13–14, 1954.
2. Carlos Lacerda, letter to Maurício Joppert, in *Tribuna da Imprensa,* March 12, 1954.
3. Carlos Lacerda, drafts of manifesto of the Aliança Popular Contra o Roubo e o Golpe, in CCL (see also the program for legislative action of the Aliança Popular, *Tribuna da Imprensa,* July 9, 1954).
4. *Tribuna da Imprensa,* February 24, 1954. Carlos Lacerda, letter to Maurício Joppert, in *Tribuna da Imprensa,* March 12, 1954.
5. *Tribuna da Imprensa,* August 3, September 3, 14, June 3, 4–5, 11, October 1, 1954. *Última Hora,* June 1, 2, 10, 1954.
6. *Tribuna da Imprensa,* June 3, July 16, June 9, 1954.
7. Ibid., August 2, September 11–12, 1954.
8. Ibid., September 13, 1954. Viriato de Castro, *O Fenômeno Jânio Quadros,* p. 105. Prestes Maia entry in *Dicionário Histórico-Biográfico Brasileiro.*
9. *Tribuna da Imprensa,* July 6, 15, August 1, 2, 1954. *Última Hora,* July 17, 27, 28, 1954.
10. Gustavo Borges, interview, Rio de Janeiro, August 14, 1983.
11. Carlos Lacerda, *Depoimento,* pp. 127–128. Gustavo Borges, interview.
12. *Tribuna da Imprensa,* August 10, 1954.
13. Gustavo Borges, interview.
14. Cláudio Lacerda, "Lacerda: Uma Vida de Lutas," Chapter 9, p. 2.
15. Carlos Lacerda, *Depoimento,* pp. 132–133.

6. "My Friend Vaz Is Dead" (August 5, 1954)

1. "Cinco homens, cinco destinos," *Jornal do Brasil,* August 5, 1984. F. Zenha Machado, *Os Últimos Dias do Govêrno de Vargas,* p. 12. Testimony at Galeão Air Base of João Valente de Sousa about the receipt of 100,000 cruzeiros from SESI for the guard, *Tribuna da Imprensa,* September 4–5, 1954. Hugo Baldessarini, *Crônica de uma Época (De 1850 ao Atentado contra Carlos Lacerda): Getúlio Vargas e o Crime de Toneleros,* p. 179.

2. Lutero Vargas, testimony as reported in *O Estado de S. Paulo,* September 9, 1954. Baldessarini, *Crônica,* pp. 176, 179–180. F. Zenha Machado, *Os Últimos Dias,* pp. 69, 60.

3. Gregório Fortunato, testimony as reported in *O Estado de S. Paulo,* September 28, 1954, and in Baldessarini, *Crônica,* pp. 279, 327.

4. *O Estado de S. Paulo,* September 17, 18, 28, 1954. Baldessarini, *Crônica,* pp. 224, 228, 324–337.

5. Climério Euribes de Almeida, testimony as reported in *O Estado de S. Paulo,* September 17, 1954. "Cinco homens, cinco destinos." *O Estado de S. Paulo,* August 18, 20, September 17, 22, 1954. Baldessarini, *Crônica,* pp. 174, 185. John V. D. Saunders, "A Revolution of Agreement among Friends: The End of the Vargas Era," *Hispanic American Historical Review,* 44, no. 2 (May 1964), p. 200.

6. Baldessarini, *Crônica,* pp. 184–185, 200. Climério Euribes de Almeida, testimony as reported in *O Estado de S. Paulo,* September 17, 23, 1954. The amount "promised" Alcino is given as 500,000 cruzeiros in "Relatório dos Oficiais da Aeronáutica . . . , Lido durante a Reunião Realizada no Clube da Aeronáutica do Dia 21 de Agosto," F. Zenha Machado, *Os Últimos Dias,* pp. 149–155. Alcino João do Nascimento (testimony as reported in *O Estado de S. Paulo,* August 20, 1954) spoke of 500,000 cruzeiros. F. Zenha Machado, *Os Últimos Dias,* p. 19. Alcino João do Nascimento, testimony as reported in *O Estado de S. Paulo,* September 23, 1954.

7. Alcino João do Nascimento and Climério Euribes de Almeida, testimonies as reported in *O Estado de S. Paulo,* August 20, September 17, 1954. *Tribuna da Imprensa,* July 12, August 2, 1954. Cláudio Lacerda, "Lacerda: Uma Vida de Lutas," Chapter 9, p. 2. Baldessarini, *Crônica,* p. 188.

8. José Cândido Moreira de Souza, interview with DFR, Rio de Janeiro, August 27, 1986. Carlos Lacerda, *Depoimento,* p. 132. Climério Euribes de Almeida and Nelson Raimundo de Sousa, testimonies reported in *O Estado de S. Paulo,* September 17, 23, 1954. F. Zenha Machado, *Os Últimos Dias,* p. 16.

9. Carlos Lacerda, "Rosas e Pedras do Meu Caminho," Chapter 10, p. 115. Gustavo Borges, interview. Carlos Lacerda, testimony given in Miguel Couto Hospital, *O Globo,* August 5, 1954, reproduced in Hélio Silva, *1954: Um Tiro no Coração,* pp. 216–217.

10. Gustavo Borges, interview. George Sumner Filho, interview with DFR, Rio de Janeiro, March 16, 1989. Carlos Lacerda, *Depoimento,* pp. 133–134.

11. Borges, interview. Hélio Silva, *1954: Um Tiro no Coração,* p. 217.

12. Baldessarini, *Crônica*, p. 194. Testimonies of Climério Euribes de Almeida and Alcino João de Nascimento, as reported in *O Estado de S. Paulo*, September 17, August 20, 1954. Carlos Lacerda, *Depoimento*, p. 134. Report of Armando Nogueira, reproduced in Carlos Lacerda, "Rosas e Pedras do Meu Caminho," Chapter 10, p. 116.

13. Borges, interview. Sumner Filho, interview with DFR.

14. Armando Falcão, interviews, Rio de Janeiro, November 30, 1966, August 26, 1983. Falcão, *Tudo a Declarar*, pp. 83–97 ("O Crime da Rua Tonelero").

15. Ibid. Cláudio Lacerda, "Lacerda: Uma Vida de Lutas," Chapter 9, p. 3. Carlos Lacerda, *Depoimento*, p. 135.

16. F. Zenha Machado, *Os Últimas Dias*, p. 8.

17. Maurício Caminha de Lacerda, interview with DFR, April 7, 1983.

7. Investigation of the Crime (August–October 1954)

1. *O Estado de S. Paulo*, August 6, 1954. *Tribuna da Imprensa*, August 5, 1954.

2. Bourne, *Political Leaders of Latin America*, p. 221. F. Zenha Machado, *Os Últimos Dias*, p. 12.

3. *O Estado de S. Paulo*, August 7, 1954.

4. Ibid., August 10, 1954. Melo Franco, *A Escalada*, pp. 317–322.

5. Borges, interview. F. Zenha Machado, *Os Últimas Dias*, p. 43.

6. F. Zenha Machado, *Os Últimos Dias*, pp. 15–16, 20. Alcino João do Nascimento, testimony as reported in *O Estado de S. Paulo*, August 20, 1954.

7. F. Zenha Machado, *Os Últimos Dias*, pp. 23–28.

8. *O Estado de S. Paulo*, August 11, 1954. Baldessarini, *Crônica*, p. 209. Cláudio Lacerda, "Lacerda: Uma Vida de Lutas," Chapter 9, p. 3. Hélio Silva, *1954: Um Tiro no Coração*, pp. 226–227, quoting Carlos Lacerda.

9. *Tribuna da Imprensa*, August 14–15, 1954. Hélio Silva, *1954: Um Tiro no Coração*, p. 235.

10. *O Estado de S. Paulo*, August 14, 15, 1954. F. Zenha Machado, *Os Últimos Dias*, pp. 46–49. *Tribuna da Imprensa*, August 14–15, 1954.

11. *Tribuna da Imprensa*, August 17, 18, 1954. *O Estado de S. Paulo*, August 18, 1954. Saunders, "A Revolution of Agreement among Friends," p. 199.

12. F. Zenha Machado, *Os Últimos Dias*, p. 58. Baldessarini, *Crônica*, pp. 215–216, 324–326. *Tribuna da Imprensa*, August 23, 1954.

13. Baldessarini, *Crônica*, pp. 215–216, 326–329. *Tribuna da Imprensa*, October 1, 1954. *O Estado de S. Paulo*, October 1, 15, 1954.

14. Carlos Lacerda, *Depoimento*, p. 138, quoting Mendes de Morais. *O Estado de S. Paulo*, September 18, October 15, 1954.

15. Cláudio Lacerda, "Lacerda: Uma Vida de Lutas," Chapter 9, p. 5. Baldessarini, *Crônica*, p. 324.

16. Carlos Lacerda, *Depoimento*, p. 138.

17. *O Estado de S. Paulo,* October 2, 7, 1954. Evandro Lins e Silva, interview, Rio de Janeiro, August 25, 1983. Ângelo Mendes de Morais entry in *Dicionário Histórico-Biográfico Brasileiro.*

18. "Cinco homens, cinco destinos." Carlos Lacerda, *Depoimento,* p. 141 (editor's note).

8. Demanding the Resignation of Vargas (August 1954)

1. Baciu, p. 104. *Tribuna da Imprensa,* August 23, 1954.

2. *Tribuna da Imprensa,* August 9, 1954. Camargo et al. *O Intelectual e o Político,* p. 248. Hélio Silva, *1954: Um Tiro no Coração,* pp. 240–241. *Imprensa Popular,* August 10, 1954. F. Zenha Machado, *Os Últimos Dias,* pp. 33–34.

3. *Tribuna da Imprensa,* August 10, 1954.

4. Ibid., August 16, 10, 1954.

5. F. Zenha Machado, *Os Últimos Dias,* pp. 38, 36–37.

6. Ibid. Carlos Lacerda, "Rosas e Pedras do Meu Caminho," Chapter 10, p. 118. João Café Filho, *Do Sindicato ao Catete: Memórias Políticas e Confissões Humanas,* vol. 1, pp. 304–305. Carlos Lacerda, *Depoimento,* pp. 145–146.

7. *Imprensa Popular,* August 12, 1954. Carlos Lacerda, *Depoimento,* p. 146.

8. *Tribuna da Imprensa,* August 13, 1954. F. Zenha Machado, *Os Últimos Dias,* p. 41.

9. Camargo et al., *O Intelectual e o Político,* pp. 150, 256. Melo Franco, *A Escalada,* pp. 327–333.

10. Josué Montello, in *Diário da Manhã,* August 14, 1954, reproduced in Josué Montello, "A palavra de Carlos Lacerda," *Jornal do Brasil,* May 8, 1984. Josué Montello, speech at the Academia Brasileira de Letras, July 16, 1959, reproduced in Josué Montello, *A Oratória Atual do Brasil.* Marcelo Garcia, interview. Fernando Pedreira, quoted in "Um Terremoto," *Jornal do Brasil* (page about "Lacerda/70 anos"), April 30, 1984. José Américo de Almeida, "Mérito da entrevista foi de Lacerda," *O Globo,* May 22, 1977. Antônio Carlos Villaça, "A veemência e a ironia," *Jornal de Letras,* August 1982.

11. *O Estado de S. Paulo,* August 15, 1954. F. Zenha Machado, *Os Últimos Dias,* p. 50.

12. *Imprensa Popular,* August 19, 7, 6, 8, 11, 21, 1954. *Diário de S. Paulo,* August 24, 1954 (quoting Prestes). *Tribuna da Imprensa,* August 16, 1954. See also PCB manifesto of July 1954 in *Problemas,* no. 61 (September 1954), pp. 1–7.

13. Luiz Carlos Prestes, "A Situação de Fernando Lacerda perante o Partido," *Problemas,* no. 61, pp. 12, 19, 11, and "Resolução do Comitê Central do P.C.B.," *Problemas,* no. 61. *Tribuna da Imprensa,* August 28–29, 1954. *Imprensa Popular,* August 8, 1954.

14. F. Zenha Machado, *Os Últimos Dias,* p. 62, 64. José Queiroz Júnior, *Memórias sôbre Getúlio,* p. 163–165. *Tribuna da Imprensa,* August 13, 20, 1954. *O Estado de S. Paulo,* August 21, 1954.

15. *Tribuna da Imprensa,* August 20, 21–22, 1954. *O Estado de S. Paulo,* August 22, 1954.

16. F. Zenha Machado, *Os Últimos Dias,* p. 71. *O Estado de S. Paulo,* August 24, 1954. Bento Munhoz da Rocha Netto, *Radiografia de Novembro,* pp. 118–119.

17. F. Zenha Machado, *Os Últimos Dias,* pp. 81–82.

18. *O Estado de S. Paulo,* August 24, 1954. Café Filho, *Do Sindicato ao Catete,* pp. 346–347.

19. Baciu, *Lavradio, 98,* p. 105. Café Filho, *Do Sindicato ao Catete,* p. 345. Melo Franco, *A Escalada,* p. 345. Carlos Lacerda, *Depoimento,* p. 146.

9. "Death to Lacerda" (Late August 1954)

1. F. Zenha Machado, *Os Últimos Dias,* pp. 53, 129. Queiroz Júnior, *Memórias sôbre Getúlio,* p. 161.

2. Carlos Lacerda, *Depoimento,* pp. 147–149. Carlos Lacerda, "Rosas e Pedras do Meu Caminho," Chapter 10, pp. 117, 119.

3. Ibid.

4. Osvaldo G. Aranha, interview, Rio de Janeiro, July 2, 1963.

5. "Documento Interno do PCB, Editado pelo Comité Central sob o Título 'O Golpe e a Posição do Partido,' com Ordem para Ser Discutido nos Orgãos de Base," typewritten, 5 pp., August 1954, in *O Estado de S. Paulo* files about Communism in Brazil. *O Estado de S. Paulo,* August 25, 27, 1954.

6. Report of the Freedom of the Press Commission of the Inter American Press Association, read at the Tenth Inter American Press Association Conference, Rio de Janeiro, October 7, 1954, in *O Estado de S. Paulo,* October 8, 1954. *O Estado de S. Paulo,* August 25, 1954. Paulo Brandi, *Vargas: Da Vida para a História,* p. 298.

7. *Tribuna da Imprensa,* August 26, 1954. Brandi, *Vargas,* p. 298. *O Estado de S. Paulo,* August 25, 27, 1954. *Imprensa Popular,* August 25, 1954.

8. *Tribuna da Imprensa,* August 26, 31, 1954. Carlos Lacerda, "Rosas e Pedras do Meu Caminho," Chapter 10, p. 117. Carlos Lacerda, *Depoimento,* p. 147. Report of the Freedom of the Press Commission of the Inter American Press Association, read at the Tenth Inter American Press Association Conference. Baciu, *Lavradio, 98,* p. 106. Ruth Alverga, transcript of interview taped by the Sociedade dos Amigos de Carlos Lacerda, p. 7.

9. *Tribuna da Imprensa,* August 26, 1954.

10. Ibid. *O Estado de S. Paulo,* August 27, 1954. Baciu, *Lavradio, 98,* p. 105. Wainer, *Minha Razão de Viver,* p. 205. Brandi, *Vargas,* p. 298.

11. *Tribuna da Imprensa,* August 26, 1954.

12. Café Filho, *Do Sindicato ao Catete,* vol. 2, p. 389. Carlos Lacerda, *Depoimento,* p. 148. *Tribuna da Imprensa,* September 6, 1954. Carlos Lacerda, in *Tribuna da Imprensa,* August 27, 1954.

13. Carlos Lacerda, in *Tribuna da Imprensa,* August 27, September 6, 1954.

14. José Soares Maciel Filho, interview, Rio de Janeiro, March 14, 1965. Lutero Vargas, in *Manchete,* April 6, 1983. Alzira Vargas do Amaral Peixoto, "A Vida de Getúlio" (narrated to Raul Giudicelli), *Fatos & Fotos,* Chapter 13, October 5, 1963. Hélio Silva, *1954: Um Tiro no Coração,* pp. 224, 268, 283, 286. Francisco Dória, "Secretário redigiu ícone populista," *Jornal do Brasil,* August 27, 1989.

15. *The Observer* (London), August 29, 1954. Sumner Filho, interview with DFR.

16. Luiz Carlos Prestes, "Informe de Balanço de Comité Central," prepared for the PCB's Fourth National Congress, held in November 1954, reproduced in Inquérito Policial Militar 709, *O Comunismo no Brasil,* vol. 1, p. 214. *Última Hora,* September 10, 1954. *Imprensa Popular,* August 27, 28, 1954, including quotation from *O Radical.*

17. Carlos Lacerda, in *Tribuna da Imprensa,* August 28–29, 1954. *Tribuna da Imprensa,* August 30, 1954.

18. *Tribuna da Imprensa,* August 31, 1954. Carlos Lacerda, letter to Olga Lacerda, September 1, 1954, in CCL.

10. Most Voted-for Congressman (October 1954)

1. *Tribuna da Imprensa,* August 30, September 6, 3, 1954. Carlos Lacerda, *A Linha de Yenan e as Fôrças Armadas,* p. 19.

2. Carlos Lacerda, in *Tribuna da Imprensa,* September 4–5, 3, 1954.

3. *Tribuna da Imprensa,* September 14, 13, 11–12, August 30, 1954. *O Estado de S. Paulo,* October 2, 1954.

4. Carlos Lacerda, *Depoimento,* pp. 148–149. *Tribuna da Imprensa,* October 1, 1954.

5. *O Estado de S. Paulo,* October 8, 1954. Café Filho, *Do Sindicato ao Catete,* p. 472.

6. Viriato de Castro, *O Fenômeno Jânio Quadros,* p. 106. *O Estado de S. Paulo,* October 7, 1954.

7. *O Estado de S. Paulo,* October 8, 12, 9, 10, 1954. *New York Times,* October 10, 1954.

8. *O Estado de S. Paulo,* October 21, 1954. Carlos Lacerda, "Rosas e Pedras do Meu Caminho," Chapter 11 (*Manchete,* June 24, 1967), p. 107.

9. *Tribuna da Imprensa,* October 12, 19, 1954.

Intermission. Journalist and Orator

1. Carlos Lacerda, *Depoimento,* pp. 148–149.

2. Ibid., p. 149.

3. Nasser, "Meu Amigo, Carlos Lacerda."

4. Fernando Pedreira quoted in "Um Terremoto," *Jornal do Brasil,* Caderno B ("Lacerda/70 anos"), April 30, 1984.

5. David Nasser, "Falta Lacerda," *Manchete,* no. 1431 (September 22, 1979).

6. Josué Montello, speech at the Academia Brasileira de Letras, July 16, 1959, reproduced in Montello, *A Oratória Atual do Brasil.*

7. Villaça, "A veemência e a ironia."

8. See Juracy Magalhães, quoted in Abelardo Jurema, *Juscelino & Jango, PSD & PTB,* p. 24, and Melo Franco, *A Escalada,* pp. 366–367.

9. Samuel Wainer, interviews, September 28, 1968, and July 14, 1979.

10. Maurício Lacerda Filho, letter to Diretoria da Sociedade Anônima Editôra Tribuna da Imprensa, Rio de Janeiro, May 5, 1955, in CCL. Carlos Lacerda and Maurício Lacerda Filho, handwritten notes, January 1955, in CCL.

VII. Advocate of an Emergency Regime (1955–1956)

1. The Etelvino Lins Candidacy (April–June 1955)

1. Carlos Lacerda, *Depoimento* p. 149.

2. Ibid., p. 154.

3. Ibid., p. 174. Carlos Lacerda, "Rosas e Pedras do Meu Caminho," Chapter 11, p. 105.

4. Carlos Lacerda, letter to Etelvino Lins, Lisbon, November 29, 1954, in Cruz et al., *Impasse na Democracia Brasileira,* pp. 361–362 (see also p. 356).

5. *O Estado de S. Paulo,* December 28, 1954.

6. *Tribuna da Imprensa,* March 17, 1955. Carlos Lacerda, *Depoimento,* pp. 250, 150. "Entrevista de Carlos Lacerda ao jornal dos estudantes," *Tribuna da Imprensa,* January 19, 1959 (reply to Question 1). Carlos Lacerda, *A Linha de Yenan e as Fôrças Armadas,* p. 14. "Carta de Carlos Lacerda ao General Teixeira Lott," *Tribuna da Imprensa,* July 13, 1956 (p. 7 of the separately printed version).

7. *Tribuna da Imprensa,* February 7, March 11, 17, 1955.

8. Ibid., February 3, 4, 1955. Cruz et al., *Impasse na Democracia Brasileira,* p. 335. Etelvino Lins entry in *Dicionário Histórico-Biográfico Brasileiro.* Etelvino Lins, manifesto, *Tribuna da Imprensa,* June 25–26, 1955.

9. *Tribuna da Imprensa,* April 11, 1955. Viriato de Castro, *O Fenômeno Jânio Quadros,* pp. 129–132. Café Filho, *Do Sindicato ao Catete,* vol. 2, pp. 519–520. Juarez Távora, *Uma Vida e Muitas Lutas: Memórias,* vol. 3, *Voltando à Planície,* pp. 47–51.

10. Etelvino Lins, manifesto. Etelvino Lins, *Um Depoimento Político: Episódios e Observações,* pp. 75, 69. José Eduardo Prado Kelly, interview, Rio de Janeiro, October 8, 1965.

11. *Tribuna da Imprensa,* April 30, May 5, 1, 1955.

12. Juarez Távora, interview, Rio de Janeiro, November 27, 1967. Távora, *Uma Vida e Muitas Lutas,* vol. 3, pp. 59–67.

13. *Tribuna da Imprensa,* May 13, 9, April 6, June 2, 24, 1955.

14. Ibid., June 6, 9, 1955.

15. Etelvino Lins, manifesto. Aluísio Alves, "A atitude do Etelvino Lins," *Tribuna da Imprensa,* June 23, 1955.

16. *Tribuna da Imprensa,* June 24, 1955.
17. Ibid., June 28, 1955.

2. The Panair Strike (January–March 1955)

1. *O Estado de S. Paulo,* February 19, 15, 1955, Paulo Sampaio, "A Greve Parcial na Panair do Brasil," *O Estado de S. Paulo,* March 1, 1955.
2. *O Estado de S. Paulo,* February 17, 1955. Law Project 22 of the Câmara dos Deputados, 1955. Carlos Lacerda, *Depoimento,* p. 194.
3. *O Estado de S. Paulo,* February 15, 19, 1955.
4. Paulo Sampaio, "A Greve Parcial na Panair do Brasil."
5. Carlos Lacerda, *Depoimento,* pp. 194–195. *Tribuna da Imprensa,* February 8, 1955.
6. *O Estado de S. Paulo,* March 6, 1955.
7. Gustavo Borges, letters to Carlos Lacerda, including letter, Montreal, April 28, 1955, and Panair do Brasil CPI documents, in CCL. Carlos Lacerda, *Depoimento,* p. 195.
8. Carlos Lacerda, *Depoimento,* p. 195. Paulo Sampaio, letter to CPI President Armando Falcão, Rio de Janeiro, May 5, 1955, in CCL.
9. Carlos Lacerda, *Depoimento,* p. 223. Rebello Filho, *Carlos Lacerda, Meu Amigo,* p. 191 (footnote) (see also *O Estado de S. Paulo,* June 19, 1957, quoting João Batista Ramos).
10. *Tribuna da Imprensa,* September 26, 1955.
11. Maria Fernanda, conversation with DFR, Rio de Janeiro, August 15, 1985.
12. Conversations with Maria Abreu Sodré (São Paulo, July 21, 1983) and others.

3. Contentious Congressman (July–September 1955)

1. Chagas, *Esse Velho Vento da Aventura,* p. 330.
2. Sérgio Lacerda, interview, Rio de Janeiro, August 22, 1988. Carlos Lacerda, *Discursos Parlamentares,* p. 15 of Nota do Editor.
3. Carlos Lacerda, *Discursos Parlamentares,* pp. 115–136 (see pp. 135, 128–129, 130, 134).
4. Melo Franco, *A Escalada,* pp. 366–367.
5. *Correio da Manhã,* August 6, 1955. Cruz et al., *Impasse na Democracia Brasileira,* pp. 395–400.
6. *O Estado de S. Paulo,* August 9, 11, 12, 1955.
7. *Câmara dos Deputados* Law Projects, 7, 9, 17, 22, 26, 48, 86, 170, 201, 229, 342, 360, 419, 429, and 495 of 1955 (see also Carlos Lacerda, *Discursos Parlamentares,* pp. 200–202).
8. *Câmara dos Deputados* Law Projects 17, 26 (February 1955). José Eduardo Prado Kelly, interview. Afonso Arinos de Melo Franco, interview, Brasília, October 16, 1965. José Maria Alkmin, interview, Brasília, October 15, 1965. (See also Carlos Lacerda, *Discursos Parlamentares,* pp. 77–111.)

9. Adauto Lúcio Cardoso, interview, Rio de Janeiro, December 15, 1965. *O Estado de S. Paulo,* September 20, 1955.

10. Interviews, José Maria Alkmin, Afonso Arinos de Melo Franco, and José Eduardo Prado Kelly, October 15, 16, 8, 1965. Afonso Arinos de Melo Franco, *A Escalada,* p. 374.

11. *O Estado de S. Paulo,* August 11, September 1, 1955. *Imprensa Popular,* September 2, 1955.

12. *O Estado de S. Paulo,* September 6, 1955.

13. *Imprensa Popular,* September 15, 1955. *Tribuna da Imprensa,* September 14, 1955. *O Estado de S. Paulo,* September 22, 1955.

14. Heráclito Fontoura Sobral Pinto, *Lições de Liberdade,* p. 28.

15. *Tribuna da Imprensa,* September 2, 10–11, 1955.

4. The Brandi Letter (September–October 1955)

1. Emílio Maurell Filho, in *Tribuna da Imprensa,* November 1, 1955. "O depoimento de Carlos Lacerda," *O Estado de S. Paulo,* October 30, 1955. Cláudio Lacerda, "Lacerda: Uma Vida de Lutas," Chapter 10, p. 3.

2. Maurell Filho, in *Tribuna da Imprensa,* November 1, 1955.

3. *Tribuna da Imprensa,* September 17–18, 1955.

4. Maurell Filho, in *Tribuna da Imprensa,* November 1, 1955. Luiz Felippe de Oliveira Penna, interview, August 16, 1983.

5. *O Estado de S. Paulo,* September 21, 1955. Maurell Filho, in *Tribuna da Imprensa,* November 1, 1955.

6. *Tribuna da Imprensa,* September 17–18, 1955.

7. Ibid., September 19, 1955. *O Estado de S. Paulo,* September 20, 22, 1955. Cláudio Lacerda, "Lacerda: Uma Vida de Lutas," Chapter 10, p. 3. Maria Alayde Albite Ulrich, "Carlos Lacerda e a UDN" (master's thesis, Pontifícia Universidade Católica do Rio Grande do Sul, 1984), p. 91.

8. *Imprensa Popular,* September 21, 27, 1955.

9. *O Estado de S. Paulo,* September 23, 20, 22, 30, 1955.

10. *Tribuna da Imprensa,* September 23, 1955. *Imprensa Popular,* September 27, 1955.

11. *Tribuna da Imprensa,* September 28, 26, 1955.

12. Ibid., September 29, 26, 1955. *O Estado de S. Paulo,* September 28, 1955.

13. *Tribuna da Imprensa,* October 3, 1955. *O Estado de S. Paulo,* October 4, 1955.

14. *O Estado de S. Paulo,* October 2, 5, 1955. *Tribuna da Imprensa,* November 1, 1955.

15. *O Estado de S. Paulo,* October 18, 1955. Emílio Maurell Filho, interview, Rio de Janeiro, October 11, 1965.

16. Emílio Maurell Filho, in *Tribuna da Imprensa,* November 1, 1955.

17. *Última Hora,* November 1, 1955. *Imprensa Popular,* November 1, 6, 1955.

18. *Tribuna da Imprensa,* October 19, 21, 1955.

19. Ibid., November 3, 1955.
20. "Carta de Carlos Lacerda ao General Teixeira Lott," *Tribuna da Imprensa,* July 17, 1956 (see p. 2 of separately printed copy of the letter).
21. José de Segadas Viana, letter to Carlos Lacerda, Rio de Janeiro, October 10, 1955, in Walter Cunto collection (see Brandi Letter folder).
22. *O Estado de S. Paulo,* October 29, 30, 1955. Cláudio Lacerda, "Lacerda: Uma Vida de Lutas," Chapter 10, p. 3.
23. *O Globo,* November 1, 2, 1955.

5. The October 1955 Elections

1. *Imprensa Popular,* September 11, 1955. Carlos Lacerda, "A atitude do povo," *Tribuna da Imprensa,* September 12, 1955.
2. *Tribuna da Imprensa,* September 29, 1955. Osvaldo Maia Penido, interviews, Rio de Janeiro, September 6, 1963, October 10, 1967. Mário Schenberg (interview, São Paulo, November 14, 1966) said that he arranged for Kubitschek to meet with Pedro Pomar, who did the talking on behalf of the PCB.
3. Carlos Lacerda, "A situação do povo," *Tribuna da Imprensa,* September 12, 1955.
4. *O Estado de S. Paulo* and *Tribuna da Imprensa,* September 20, 1955.
5. Távora, *Uma Vida e Muitas Lutas,* vol. 3, p. 85. *Tribuna da Imprensa,* September 20, 23, 1955.
6. Távora, *Uma Vida e Muitas Lutas,* vol. 3, p. 85.
7. Viriato de Castro, *O Fenômeno Jânio Quadros,* pp. 133, 137. *Jornal do Commercio,* Rio de Janeiro, October 2, 1955.
8. *O Estado de S. Paulo,* October 4, 5, 1955.
9. Ibid., October 6, 7, 1955. *Imprensa Popular,* October 6, 1955.
10. *Tribuna da Imprensa,* October 5, 1955.

6. "Kubitschek Will Not Be President" (October 1955)

1. *Tribuna da Imprensa,* October 10, 1955.
2. Melo Franco, *A Escalada,* pp. 375–376 (including memorandum from Raul Fernandes). *O Estado de S. Paulo,* October 11, 12, 14, 1955. Carlos Pena Boto and Cruzada Brasileira Anticomunista, message, *O Globo,* October 14, 1955, reproduced in Joffre Gomes da Costa, *Marechal Henrique Lott,* p. 264.
3. *Correio da Manhã,* October 13, 14, 1955. Carlos Lacerda, "Os males do alcoolismo," *Tribuna da Imprensa,* October 15, 1955.
4. *O Estado de S. Paulo,* October 15, 13, 1955. *Tribuna da Imprensa,* October 17, 1955. José Loureiro Júnior, *O Golpe de Novembro e Outros Discursos,* p. 29.
5. Plínio Salgado, interview, Brasília, October 14, 1965. Carlos Lacerda, *Depoimento,* p. 160. Carlos Lacerda, "Rosas e Pedras do Meu Caminho," Chapter 11, p. 106.
6. Henrique Baptista Duffles Teixeira Lott, "Depoimento Prestado ao Juiz

da 11ª Vara Criminal a Respeito do 11 de Novembro de 1955," in Gomes da Costa, *Marechal Henrique Lott,* pp. 501–508 (see p. 508). Edmundo Jordão Amorim do Vale, interview, Rio de Janeiro, September 7, 1963. *Tribuna da Imprensa,* October 21, 1955. *O Estado de S. Paulo,* November 6, 1955.

7. Café Filho, *Do Sindicato ao Catete,* vol. 2, p. 537. *Jornal do Commercio,* Rio de Janeiro, October 17–18, 1955. "Depoimento de Lott," *Manchete,* November 19, 1955 (see first page of the article). *Tribuna da Imprensa,* October 19, 1955.

8. *Tribuna da Imprensa,* October 21, 22–23, 1955.

9. Clube da Lanterna, manifesto of October 12, 1955, given on pp. 7–10 of Fidélis Amaral Netto, *O Clube da Lanterna e a Legalidade Vigente: Parte Escrita do Depoimento Prestado pelo Jornalista Amaral Netto, Presidente do Clube da Lanterna, na Delegacia de Ordem Política e Social, em 9 de Dezembro de 1955, perante o Delegado Olavo Rangel.*

10. *Tribuna da Imprensa,* October 21, 1955.

11. Ibid., October 22–23, 1955. *O Estado de S. Paulo,* October 25, 27, November 5, 1955. Melo Franco, *A Escalada,* p. 379.

12. *Tribuna da Imprensa,* October 25, 1955. *O Estado de S. Paulo,* October 25, 1955. Evandro Lins e Silva, interview, Rio de Janeiro, August 2, 1984. *Diário Carioca,* June 6, 1956. *Tribuna da Imprensa,* November 8, 4, 1955 (quoting Evandro Lins e Silva and *Time*).

13. Carlos Lacerda, letter to Marshall Field, Jr., Rio de Janeiro, October 31, 1955, in CCL. *O Estado de S. Paulo,* October 8, 1955.

7. Lott's Coup (November 11, 1955)

1. Carlos Lacerda, in *Tribuna da Imprensa,* November 1, 1955, and on Rádio Globo, November 7, 1955, as reported in *Tribuna da Imprensa,* November 8, 1955. Carlos Lacerda, "A lição de Canrobert—antes que seja tarde," *Tribuna da Imprensa,* November 3, 1955.

2. *Tribuna da Imprensa,* November 3, 1955.

3. Henrique Lott, interview, Rio de Janeiro, August 27, 1963.

4. Carlos Lacerda, "A hora das forças armadas," *Tribuna da Imprensa,* November 4, 1955.

5. Távora, *Uma Vida e Muitas Lutas,* vol. 3, pp. 90–91.

6. *O Estado de S. Paulo,* November 8, 11, 1955. Otávio Marcondes Ferraz, interview, São Paulo, August 9, 1963.

7. Carlos Lacerda, "A hora das forças armadas."

8. Heráclito Fontoura Sobral Pinto, interview, Rio de Janeiro, July 8, 1983. Carlos Lacerda, letter to Sobral Pinto, Rio de Janeiro, November 8, 1955 (in the collection of Fernando Cícero da Franca Velloso).

9. Melo Franco, *A Escalada,* p. 378.

10. Carlos Lacerda, "Não podem tomar posse," *Tribuna da Imprensa,* November 9, 1955. Carlos Lacerda, quoted Gomes da Costa, *Marechal Henrique Lott,* p. 287.

11. Henrique Lott, interview, August 27, 1963. Gomes da Costa, *Marechal Henrique Lott,* p. 303.

12. *Tribuna da Imprensa,* November 6, 1955. *O Estado de S. Paulo,* November 12, 1955. Carlos Lacerda, letter to Hélder Câmara, reproduced in *Tribuna da Imprensa,* June 5, 1956 (see p. 31 of typewritten copy, n.d., in CCL).

13. Carlos Lacerda, letter to Hélder Câmara (see p. 31 of typewritten copy). Carlos Lacerda, "Rosas e Pedras do Meu Caminho," Chapter 2, p. 26. Carlos Lacerda, *Depoimento,* p. 160. Melo Franco, *A Escalada,* p. 382.

14. Carlos Lacerda, letter to Hélder Câmara, typewritten copy, p. 32. Melo Franco, *A Escalada,* p. 383.

15. *O Globo,* November 11, 1955.

16. Carlos Lacerda, letter to Hélder Câmara, typewritten version, p. 32. Carlos Lacerda, *Depoimento,* p. 161. Carlos Pena Boto, interview, Rio de Janeiro, October 27, 1965. Otávio Marcondes Ferraz, interview, São Paulo, August 9, 1963.

17. Pena Boto, interview, October 27, 1965. Otávio Marcondes Ferraz, interview, August 9, 1963.

18. Henrique Lott, interview, August 27, 1963.

19. Carlos Lacerda, *Depoimento,* p. 164. Pena Boto, interview, October 27, 1965. Carlos Lacerda, interview, Rio de Janeiro, September 23, 1975.

20. Pena Boto, interview, October 27, 1965. Gomes da Costa, *Marechal Henrique Lott,* p. 316. According to *O Globo* (November 12, 1955), the legislative decisions to depose Carlos Luz received a 185–72 vote in the lower house and a 44–9 vote in the Senate. PTN: Partido Trabalhista Nacional. PR: Partido Republicano.

21. Gualter Maria Menezes de Magalhães and Telmo Becker Reifschneider, interview, aboard the *Tamandaré,* Rio de Janeiro, December 6, 1965.

22. Carlos Lacerda, *Depoimento,* pp. 165–167.

23. Ibid., pp. 167–168.

24. Pena Boto, interview, October 27, 1965. *O Globo,* November 12, 1955.

8. Asylum in the Cuban Embassy (November 1955)

1. Pena Boto, interview, October 27, 1965.

2. Carlos Luz, speech in the Chamber of Deputies, November 14, 1955, in Munhoz da Rocha, *Radiografia de Novembro,* Appendix 21, pp. 133–153. *Impedimento* vote: vote declaring the president *impedido* (unable to govern).

3. *O Estado de S. Paulo,* November 15, 1955. Melo Franco, *A Escalada,* p. 389. *Tribuna da Imprensa,* November 14, 16, 1955. Carlos Lacerda, "Rosas e Pedras do Meu Caminho," Chapter 11, p. 108.

4. Melo Franco, *A Escalada,* pp. 389–390.

5. *O Globo, O Estado de S. Paulo,* and *Imprensa Popular,* November 15, 1955.

6. Carlos Luz, speech of November 14, 1955 (see Munoz da Rocha, *Radiografia de Novembro,* pp. 152–153).

7. Melo Franco, *A Escalada,* pp. 390, 392 (note 93), 393.

8. Carlos Lacerda, *Depoimento,* pp. 171, 170. Letters to Ambassador and Sra. Gabriel Landa, November 1955, in CCL.

9. *Tribuna da Imprensa,* November 17, 1955.

10. Aluísio Alves, interview. Fernando Cícero da Franca Velloso, interview, Rio de Janeiro, August 16, 1983. *O Estado de S. Paulo,* November 19, 1955. *Tribuna da Imprensa,* November 18, 1955.

11. *O Estado de S. Paulo,* November 17, 1955.

12. *O Globo,* November 16, 1955. *O Estado de S. Paulo,* November 18, 1955.

13. Fernando Cícero da Franca Velloso, interview, August 16, 1983. Carlos Lacerda, letter to Olga Lacerda, Rio de Janeiro, November 16, 1955, in CCL.

14. Carlos Lacerda, *Depoimento,* p. 171. *O Estado de S. Paulo,* November 18, 19, 1955. *O Globo* and *Tribuna da Imprensa,* November 18, 1955.

15. "Mensagem de Carlos Lacerda," *Tribuna da Imprensa,* November 18, 1955. *Gauleiter:* a German term for a district leader of the Nazi party.

16. *O Estado de S. Paulo,* November 19, 20, 1955. *O Globo,* November 19, 1955.

17. Carlos Lacerda, *Depoimento,* p. 172. *O Estado de S. Paulo,* November 20, 1955.

18. Carlos Lacerda, *Depoimento,* p. 172. John S. Knight, letter to Carlos Lacerda, Chicago, November 21, 1955, in CCL. Carlos Lacerda, "Rosas e Pedras do Meu Caminho," Chapter 11, p. 108.

19. Bourne, *Political Leaders of Latin America,* p. 225. British embassy in Brazil, letters to the British foreign office, Rio de Janeiro, November 24, 28, 1955, in the Public Record Office, London.

20. *O Estado de S. Paulo,* October 12, 16, 1956.

21. Ibid. Carlos Lacerda, "Rosas e Pedras do Meu Caminho," Chapter 11, p. 106. Carlos Lacerda, letter to Hélder Câmara (see pp. 39–40 of typewritten copy).

22. Carlos Lacerda, letter to Hélder Câmara, typewritten copy, pp. 39–40. Carlos Lacerda, letter to Carlos Alberto Aulicino, Norwalk, Connecticut, January 20, 1956 (in collection of Carlos Alberto Aulicino, São Paulo). Carlos Lacerda, letters to Vera Lacerda Paiva, Norwalk, February 7, 17, 1956, in CCL. Carlos Lacerda, letter to Lygia Paiva, Norwalk, March 4, 1956, in CCL.

23. Carlos Lacerda, in *Tribuna da Imprensa,* August 24, 1956.

9. First Days in New York (November–December 1955)

1. Carlos Lacerda, letter to Olga Lacerda, New York, November 27, 1955, in CCL. Carlos Lacerda, *Depoimento,* p. 172.

2. Carlos Lacerda, letters to Fernando Cícero da Franca Velloso, New York, December 2, 20, 1955, in collection of Velloso. Carlos Lacerda, *Depoimento,* p. 174. Carlos Lacerda, letter to Vera Lacerda Paiva, Norwalk, February 7, 1956, in CCL.

3. Carlos Lacerda, "Explicação ao leitor que não é daquele tempo," in Maurício de Lacerda, *História de uma Covardia,* pp. 7–10.

4. Cláudio Lacerda, "Lacerda: Uma Vida de Lutas," Chapter 10, p. 5.

5. Ibid. João Batista Barreto Leite Filho, interview, Rio de Janeiro, July 24, 1984.

6. Carlos Lacerda, letter to Sebastião Lacerda, New York, December 8, 1955.

7. José Osvaldo de Meira Penna, interview, Brasília, July 15, 1983. José Osvaldo de Meira Penna, *O Dinossauro,* pp. 120–121.

8. Wilson L. Machado, "Algumas lembranças de um amigo," typewritten, Curitiba, October 1988, p. 1.

9. *O Estado de S. Paulo,* November 24, 1955. *O Globo,* November 25, December 7, 13, 17, 1955.

10. *O Globo,* November 29, 1955.

11. Ibid., December 1, 1955.

12. Henrique Lott, in *O Globo,* December 5, 1955.

13. Carlos Lacerda, letter to "H. D. Teixeira Lott, Ditador do Brasil," New York, December 14, 1955, copy in files of Alfredo C. Machado, Rio de Janeiro.

10. In the Land of Uncle Sam (January–May 1956)

1. *O Globo,* December 16, 1955. Carlos Lacerda, *Depoimento,* p. 172.

2. Carlos Lacerda, letter to Vera Lacerda Paiva, Norwalk, February 7, 1956, in CCL. Carlos Lacerda, letter to Olga Lacerda, Norwalk, January 30, 1956, in CCL.

3. Rafael de Almeida Magalhães, interview, Rio de Janeiro, August 17, 1983. Dario de Almeida Magalhães, interview.

4. Júlio Tavares [Carlos Lacerda], "Um Brasileiro na Terra do Tio Sam," *O Globo,* January 9, 1956, in LFC.

5. Carlos Lacerda, letters to Vera Lacerda Paiva, February 7, 17, 1956, in CCL. Carlos Lacerda, letter to Fernando Velloso, New York, December 2, 1955, in the Velloso collection. Gustavo Borges, interview, Rio de Janeiro, August 14, 1983. Sérgio Lacerda, interviews, Rio de Janeiro, August 17, 22, 1988.

6. Letícia Lacerda, letter to Lygia Paiva, Norwalk, March 8, 1956, in LFC.

7. Carlos Lacerda, letters to Olga Lacerda, Norwalk, January 30, February 6, 1956, and to Vera Lacerda Paiva, Norwalk, February 7, 1956, in CCL.

8. Carlos Lacerda, letter to Lygia Paiva, Norwalk, March 4, 1956, and to Odilon Lacerda Paiva, Norwalk, March 22, 1956, in CCL.

9. Letícia Lacerda, letter to Lygia Paiva, March 8, 1956. Carlos Lacerda, letter to Olga Lacerda, January 30, 1956.

10. Carlos Lacerda, *Depoimento,* p. 174. Carl W. Ackerman, Dean of the Graduate School of Journalism of Columbia University, letter to Carlos Lacerda, New York, February 2, 1956, in CCL.

11. Sérgio Lacerda, interview, August 17, 1988.

12. Léticia Lacerda, letter to Lygia Paiva, March 8, 1956. Carlos Lacerda, letter to Lygia Paiva, March 4, 1956.

13. Carlos Lacerda, letter to Fernando Velloso, Norwalk, March 27, 1956, in the Velloso collection. Carlos Lacerda, letter to Olga Lacerda, May 13,

1956, in CCL. Rafael de Almeida Magalhães, interview, August 17, 1983. Edgar Flexa Ribeiro, interview, Rio de Janeiro, August 15, 1983.

11. "Clarifying Public Opinion" about the Kubitschek Regime (January–June 1956)

1. Carlos Lacerda, letter to Judith Keig of the Chicago Council on Foreign Relations, Norwalk, February 2, 1956, in CCL. Carlos Lacerda, in *O Estado de S. Paulo,* March 28, February 9, 1956.

2. Júlio Tavares [Carlos Lacerda], "Um Brasileiro na Terra do Tio Sam," *O Globo,* January 6, 7, 9, 14, 16, 17, 25, 26, February 1, 1956.

3. Ibid., January 7, 14, 1956. Carlos Lacerda, letter to Lygia Paiva, March 4, 1956.

4. Carlos Lacerda, letter to the editor of the *New York Times,* Norwalk, January 3, 1956, published January 6, 1956.

5. Ivette Vargas, letter to the editor of the *New York Times,* New York, January 7, 1956, published January 10, 1956.

6. Edgard Carone, *A República Liberal, II: Evolução Política (1945–1964),* p. 115. *O Globo,* February 17, 1956.

7. *O Globo,* February 20, 1956.

8. Rafael de Almeida Magalhães, interview, August 17, 1983. Carlos Lacerda, letter to Lygia Paiva, March 4, 1956.

9. Haroldo Veloso and Juscelino Kubitschek entries in *Dicionário Histórico-Biográfico Brasileiro. O Estado de S. Paulo,* March 3, 1956.

10. Fidélis Amaral Netto, *O Clube da Lanterna,* pp. 11–12. Carlos Lacerda, letter to Olga Lacerda, January 30, 1956. "Declarações de Carlos Lacerda," *O Estado de S. Paulo,* February 28, 1956. *O Estado de S. Paulo,* March 20, 1956. Carlos Lacerda, letter to Fernando Velloso, New York, March 23, 1956, in the Velloso collection.

11. Carlos Lacerda, *Depoimento,* p. 173. *Tribuna da Imprensa,* March 26, April 2, 1956.

12. Carlos Lacerda, *Depoimento,* p. 173. Sebastião Lacerda, letter to Olga Lacerda ("Dinda"), Norwalk, May 23, 1956. Cláudio Lacerda, "Lacerda: Uma Vida de Lutas," Chapter 10, p. 5.

13. For references to the proposed book, see Carlos Lacerda, letter to Vera Lacerda Paiva, February 17, 1956, and to Lygia Paiva, March 4, 1956, and Letícia Lacerda, letter to Olga Lacerda, Estoril, June 16, 1956, in CCL. Lacerda planned to call his book "A Reforma do Brasil."

14. Carlos Lacerda, letter to Hélder Câmara (see pp. 25, 8, 29, 11–12, 15–17, 27, 35, 37, 38–46 of the typewritten copy). For Armando Falcão's reply to the accusation about the Orquima business connection (made by the *Tribuna da Imprensa*) see *O Estado de S. Paulo,* April 4, 1956.

12. Criticizing the UDN and the *Tribuna* (February–July 1956)

1. Carlos Lacerda, letters to Fernando Velloso, Norwalk, February 17, 27, 1956, in the Velloso collection.

2. Carlos Lacerda, letter to Fernando Velloso, February 9, 1956, in the Velloso collection.

3. Ibid. Carlos Lacerda, letter to Fernando Velloso, Lisbon, July 21, 1956, in the Velloso collection.

4. Ibid. Carlos Lacerda, letter to Olga Lacerda, Estoril, June 16, 1956, in CCL.

5. Carlos Lacerda, "Instruções precisas," typewritten, February 1956, in the Velloso collection.

6. Newspaper clipping, no source shown, April 20, 1956, in the Velloso collection. Cláudio Lacerda, "Lacerda: Uma Vida de Lutas," Chapter 8, p. 2. Walter Cunto, interview, Rio de Janeiro, August 7, 1983.

7. Carlos Lacerda, *A Linha de Yenan e as Forças Armadas,* p. 19. *O Estado de S. Paulo,* March 14, 1956.

13. Police Action against the *Tribuna* and *Maquis* (August–September 1956)

1. Carlos Lacerda, letter to General Teixeira Lott, version published in *Tribuna da Imprensa,* July 13, 1956 (see pp. 3, 4, 5, 7).

2. Carlos Lacerda, "Manifesto de Carlos Lacerda ao Povo Brasileiro," *Tribuna da Imprensa,* August 24, 1956.

3. Tad Szulc, "Brazilian Police Seize Newspaper," *New York Times,* August 25, 1956.

4. Ibid. See also Tad Szulc, "Ban on Rio Paper Abashes Regime," *New York Times,* August 26, 1956.

5. *Maquis,* September 5, 1956. "*Maquis* Penhorado Agradece," *Maquis,* probably early October 1956. Baciu, *Lavradio, 98,* pp. 110–111. *O Estado de S. Paulo,* dateline Rio de Janeiro, September 7, 1956. Amaral Netto and Batista Teixeira entries in *Dicionário Histórico-Biográfico Brasileiro.*

6. Carlos Lacerda, cable, Paris, September 12, 1956, in "*Maquis* Penhorado Agradece."

7. "*Maquis* Penhorado Agradece." Dario de Almeida Magalhães, in *O Estado de S. Paulo,* July 30, 1978. *O Estado de S. Paulo,* September 21, 1956.

14. Correspondence with Argentina about Goulart (July–September 1956)

1. Letícia Lacerda, letters to Sebastião Lacerda, Estoril, June 14, 16, 1956, and letters to Olga Lacerda, Estoril, June 16, 1956, in CCL. Carlos Lacerda, letters to Olga Lacerda, Lisbon, June 16, August 10, 1956, and to Sebastião Lacerda, Lisbon, June 21, 1956, in CCL. Carlos Lacerda, letter to Fernando Velloso, Lisbon, July 15, 1956, in the Velloso collection. Maria Cristina Lacerda, letter to Sebastião Lacerda, Estoril, July 9, 1956, in CCL.

2. Carlos Lacerda, letters to Sebastião Lacerda, July 15, August 5, 1956, in CCL. Letícia Lacerda, letters to Sebastião Lacerda, June 25, July 25, August 3, 16, 1956, in CCL.

3. Carlos Lacerda, letters to Fernando Velloso, Lisbon, July 5, 15, 1956, in the Velloso collection.

4. Carlos Lacerda, letters to Fernando Velloso, Lisbon, July 19, 21, 1956, in the Velloso collection. Vera Lacerda Paiva, interview with DFR, Rio de Janeiro, January 30, 1983.

5. Carlos Lacerda, letter to Lygia Vaz, Lisbon, July 21, 1956, in the collection of Lygia Vaz Brito e Cunha.

6. Wilson L. Machado, "Algumas lembranças de um amigo," p. 2.

7. Letícia Lacerda, letters to Sebastião Lacerda, August 3 and n.d. (early August), 1956, in CCL. Carlos Lacerda, letter to Olga Lacerda, August 10, 1956. Lisbon newspaper clipping, no source shown, dateline Braga, August 22, 1956, in the Velloso collection, Letícia Lacerda, letter to Sebastião Lacerda, Estoril, September 7, 1956, in CCL.

8. Carlos Lacerda, *O Caminho da Liberdade,* p. 44 and appendix. Alberto Gainza Paz, letter to Carlos Lacerda, Buenos Aires, July 20, 1956, in CCL.

9. Carlos Lacerda, letter to Alberto Gainza Paz, Lisbon, August 27, 1956, in CCL.

10. Alberto Gainza Paz, letter to Carlos Lacerda, Buenos Aires, September 5, 1956, in CCL. Carlos Lacerda, *O Caminho da Liberdade,* p. 45.

11. Raul Brunini, taped interview, Rio de Janeiro, March 9, 1989 (see pp. 24–26 of transcript). Raul Brunini, interview, Rio de Janeiro, August 1, 1989.

12. *O Estado de S. Paulo,* September 21, 22, October 10, 1956. Carlos Lacerda, *O Caminho da Liberdade,* p. 46.

13. Cleantho de Paiva Leite, interview, Rio de Janeiro, August 14, 1984.

15. The Sword of Gold (November 1956)

1. *O Estado de S. Paulo,* October 11, 1956. Cleantho de Paiva Leite, interview. Carlos Lacerda, telegram to Juscelino Kubitschek, *O Estado de S. Paulo,* October 24, 1956.

2. Cleantho de Paiva Leite, interview.

3. *O Estado de S. Paulo,* October 12, 1956.

4. Ibid. *New York Times,* October 12, 1956.

5. *New York Times,* October 12, 1956. Cleantho de Paiva Leite, interview.

6. *O Estado de S. Paulo,* October 16, 1956.

7. Ibid., October 17, 18, 20, 24, 1956.

8. *O Estado de S. Paulo,* October 26, 30, 1956. *Jornal do Commercio,* October 31, 1956.

9. Carlos Lacerda, telegram to Juscelino Kubitschek, *O Estado de S. Paulo,* October 24, 1956. Josué Montello, "A palavra de Carlos Lacerda."

10. *O Estado de S. Paulo,* November 6, 1956.

11. Carlos Lacerda, *A Linha de Yenan e as Forças Armadas,* p. 51. Carlos Lacerda, "Carta de Carlos Lacerda aos generais brasileiros," *O Estado de S. Paulo,* November 11, 1956. Carlos Lacerda, *Depoimento,* p. 276.

12. Carlos Lacerda, "Carta aos generais brasileiros," in *A Linha de Yenan e as Forças Armadas,* pp. 17–26.

13. Humberto de Alencar Castello Branco, letter to Senhores Membros do Comitê Auxiliar do Distrito Federal da Frente de Novembro, Rio de Janeiro,

November 8, 1956, in Castello Branco collection (File L1) at the CPDOC. Daniel Krieger, interview, Brasília, October 21, 1975. Henrique Lott, interview, Rio de Janeiro, October 13, 1975.

14. *O Estado de S. Paulo,* November 11, 13, 1956.

15. Gomes da Costa, *Marechal Henrique Lott,* p. 366. *O Estado de S. Paulo,* November 13, 1956.

16. *O Estado de S. Paulo,* November 22, 24, 1956. Távora, *Uma Vida e Muitas Lutas,* vol. 3, pp. 119–120. Gomes da Costa, *Marechal Henrique Lott,* pp. 373–374.

17. *O Estado de S. Paulo,* November 21, 22, 24, 1956. "Declarações do Deputado Tenório Cavalcanti," *O Estado de S. Paulo,* November 25, 1956. Nemo Canabarro Lucas entry in *Dicionário Histórico-Biográfico Brasileiro.*

18. *O Estado de S. Paulo,* November 24, 1956. Juscelino Kubitschek in *O Cruzeiro,* April 2, 1960, p. 91 (quoted in Gomes da Costa, *Marechal Henrique Lott,* p. 376).

19. *O Estado de S. Paulo,* November 25, 1956.

20. Ibid., October 20, 1956.

21. Ibid., December 8, 11, 1956.

VIII. UDN Leader in Congress (1957–1959)

1. Lacerda Becomes UDN Congressional Leader (March 1957)

1. Raul Brunini, taped interview (see pp. 4–6 of transcript).

2. Newspaper clippings (probably from the *Tribuna da Imprensa*), January 23, February 18, 1957, in the Walter Cunto collection.

3. *O Estado de S. Paulo,* January 8, 1957.

4. Ibid., January 8, 20, 1957. Partido Trabalhista Brasileiro and Frente Parlamentar Nacionalista entries in *Dicionário Histórico-Biográfico Brasileiro.* Carlos Lacerda, *Discursos Parlamentares,* pp. 165–180.

5. *O Estado de S. Paulo,* February 7, 8, 1957, December 29, 1956.

6. Ibid., January 9, 15, February 26, March 27, 1957.

7. Ibid., March 14, 20, 1957.

8. Carlos Lacerda, *Depoimento,* p. 177. *Última Hora,* April 8, 1957.

9. *O Estado de S. Paulo,* December 22, 1956, February 12, March 20, 21, 1957.

10. Ibid., March 21, 1957. *Tribuna da Imprensa,* March 21, 1957.

11. *O Estado de S. Paulo,* April 5, 9, 1957. Maria Victoria de Mesquita Benevides, *A UDN e o Udenismo: Ambigüidades do Liberalismo Brasileiro (1945–1965),* p. 203.

12. Gustavo Corção, "Antíteses," *O Estado de S. Paulo,* April 13, 1957.

13. Benevides, *A UDN e o Udenismo,* pp. 104–105. *Tribuna da Imprensa,* March 18, 1957.

14. *O Estado de S. Paulo,* April 11, 25, 1957.

15. Ibid., April 12, 23, 1957.

16. Ibid., April 9, 25, 1957. Afonso Arinos de Melo Franco, interview, Rio de Janeiro, July 29, 1984.

17. Carlos Lacerda, *Depoimento,* p. 178.

2. Itamaraty's Secret Telegram 295 (April 1957)

1. *O Estado de S. Paulo,* April 3, 1957. *Última Hora,* April 2, 1957.

2. Cláudio Lacerda, "Lacerda: Uma Vida de Lutas," Chapter 10, p. 6.

3. Copies of documents in files about Carlos Lacerda at *O Estado de S. Paulo,* including request for information sent by the Chamber of Deputies and reply from José Carlos de Macedo Soares, March 19, 1957 (sent to Wilson Fadul).

4. Cláudio Lacerda, "Lacerda: Uma Vida de Lutas," Chapter 10, p. 6. Carlos Lacerda, *O Caminho da Liberdade,* p. 48. Carlos Lacerda, "Parecer do Relator Martins Rodrigues," in *O Caminho da Liberdade,* pp. 195–210 (see p. 195).

5. Cláudio Lacerda, "Lacerda: Uma Vida de Lutas," Chapter 10, p. 6. Carlos Lacerda, *O Caminho da Liberdade,* p. 60 (footnote).

6. *A Noite* clipping in *O Estado de S. Paulo* files about Carlos Lacerda. *Última Hora,* April 3, 22, 1957. *Código Secreto* (Rio de Janeiro magazine), no. 1 (1957), p. 22.

7. Carlos Lacerda, "Chateaubriand, digno representante de Kubitschek," *Tribuna da Imprensa,* March 18, 1957 (see also March 13). "Expulsão para o traidor," *O Jornal,* April 4, 1957.

8. *O Estado de S. Paulo,* April 3, 1957.

9. Carlos Lacerda, "Na batalha de meu mandato joga-se a sorte do regime," *Tribuna da Imprensa,* April 5, 1957.

10. *Tribuna da Imprensa,* April 3, 1957.

11. "Libelo do líder da maioria contra o Sr. Carlos Lacerda," *Jornal do Commercio,* April 6, 1957.

12. Melo Franco, *A Escalada,* p. 419.

13. "Libelo do líder da maioria contra o Sr. Carlos Lacerda."

14. Ibid. *O Estado de S. Paulo,* April 6, 1957.

15. Carlos Lacerda, *Depoimento,* p. 184. *Jornal do Commercio,* April 13, 1957. *Diário de Notícias* clipping in *O Estado de S. Paulo* files about Carlos Lacerda.

3. The Battle for Public Opinion (April–May 1957)

1. Melo Franco, *A Escalada,* p. 421.

2. *Última Hora,* May 6, April 22, May 10, 1957.

3. *Tribuna da Imprensa,* April 27–28, 8, 1957.

4. *Última Hora,* April 22, 1957. *Tribuna da Imprensa,* April 25, 26, 1957.

5. *Imprensa Popular,* May 4, 5, 11, 14, 16, 1957.

6. Marcelo Garcia, interview.

7. *Última Hora,* April 10, 11, 1957. *O Estado de S. Paulo,* April 28, 1957.
8. *Última Hora,* April 24, 1957. *O Globo,* April 8, 1957.
9. Danton Jobim, in *Diário Carioca,* April 16, 17, 1957. *Última Hora,* April 24, 1957. Gustavo Corção, in *O Estado de S. Paulo* (clipping, n.d., in files about Carlos Lacerda).
10. *O Estado de S. Paulo,* April 24, May 5, 1957. *Última Hora,* May 6, 1957.
11. *O Estado de S. Paulo,* May 4, 5, 1957. *Última Hora,* April 20, 1957.
12. *O Estado de S. Paulo,* May 5, 1957. Cory Porto Fernandes, interview, São Paulo, August 21, 1984.
13. Carlos Lacerda, *Depoimento,* p. 180. Copies of documents in *O Estado de S. Paulo* files about Carlos Lacerda.
14. *Última Hora,* May 1, 3, April 22, May 4, 16, 1957.
15. Ibid. April 9, 1957. Carlos Lacerda, letter to Henrique Lott, July 13, 1956, and "Instruções precisas" to *Tribuna da Imprensa,* February 1956 (for criticism of Alkmin). *O Estado de S. Paulo,* March 16, 1957. Carlos Lacerda, quotation (April 10, 1957) in Ulrich, "Carlos Lacerda e a UDN," p. 142. *Tribuna da Imprensa,* March 8, 9–10, 14, 1957.
16. Carlos Lacerda, *Depoimento,* p. 176. Sérgio Lacerda, interview, August 17, 1988.

4. The Justice Commission Votes against Lacerda (May 3, 1957)

1. *Tribuna da Imprensa,* April 27–28, 1957. *O Estado de S. Paulo,* May 3, 1957.
2. *Tribuna da Imprensa,* April 27–28, 1957. *O Estado de S. Paulo,* May 3, 1, 1957.
3. *Tribuna da Imprensa,* April 27–28, 1957. "Parecer do Relator Martins Rodrigues," in Carlos Lacerda, *O Caminho da Liberdade,* pp. 195–210.
4. Carlos Lacerda, *Depoimento,* p. 180. Rafael de Almeida Magalhães, interviews, August 17, 1983, August 9, 1989.
5. Carlos Lacerda, *O Caminho da Liberdade,* pp. 41, 81–82, 127, 74–76.
6. Ibid., pp. 137, 147, 138–141.
7. Ibid., p. 170.
8. *O Estado de S. Paulo,* May 3, 1957.
9. Ibid., May 4, 1957. Marcelo Garcia, interview.
10. "Voto do Deputado Milton Campos em Nome da Oposição," in Carlos Lacerda, *O Caminho da Liberdade,* pp. 213–214. *O Estado de S. Paulo,* May 4, 1957. *O Globo,* May 4, 1957.
11. *O Estado de S. Paulo* and *Última Hora,* May 4, 1957.
12. *O Estado de S. Paulo,* May 4, 1957. *Pessedista:* associated with the PSD.
13. *O Estado de S. Paulo,* May 7, 1957. Melo Franco, *A Escalada,* p. 422.
14. *O Estado de S. Paulo,* May 7, 1957. Melo Franco, *A Escalada,* p. 422.
15. *O Estado de S. Paulo,* May 7, 1957. *Última Hora,* May 7, 8, 1957 (including quotations from *Diário Carioca*). Carlos Lacerda, *O Caminho da Liberdade,* p. 106 (footnote).

5. Closing Rallies (May 6–14, 1957)

1. Melo Franco, *A Escalada,* p. 422. *O Estado de S. Paulo,* May 7, 1957.

2. *O Estado de S. Paulo,* May 8, 1957. Melo Franco, *A Escalada,* pp. 424–425.

3. *Última Hora,* May 10, 1957.

4. Luís Martins, in *O Estado de S. Paulo,* May 14, 1957. *O Estado de S. Paulo,* May 12, 1957. *Hanson's Latin American Letter,* quoted in Carlos Lacerda, *O Caminho da Liberdade,* pp. 249–254 (see p. 249).

5. *O Estado de S. Paulo,* May 12, 15, 1957. Dario de Almeida Magalhães, interview.

6. Wilson L. Machado, "Algumas lembranças de um amigo," p. 3.

6. The Vote of Congress (May 16, 1957)

1. Rafael de Almeida Magalhaẽs, interview, August 17, 1983.

2. *O Estado de S. Paulo,* May 15, 1957.

3. Ibid. *Última Hora,* May 15, 1957.

4. *O Estado de S. Paulo,* May 16, 1957.

5. Melo Franco, *A Escalada,* p. 425.

6. *O Estado de S. Paulo* and *Jornal do Commercio,* May 16, 1957. Carlos Lacerda, *Discursos Parlamentares,* pp. 199–208.

7. Melo Franco, interview, Rio de Janeiro, July 29, 1984. *Correio da Manhã,* May 16, 1957. Melo Franco, *A Escalada,* p. 427.

8. Melo Franco, *A Escalada,* pp. 425–428.

9. Ibid. *Correio da Manhã,* May 16, 1957.

10. Melo Franco, *A Escalada,* p. 428. *Correio da Manhã, Última Hora,* and *O Estado de S. Paulo,* May 16, 1957.

11. Melo Franco, *A Escalada,* p. 428. *Correio da Manhã,* May 16, 1957.

12. Melo Franco, *A Escalada,* pp. 428–429. *Correio da Manhã,* May 16, 1957.

13. Ibid. *O Estado de S. Paulo,* May 17, 1957.

14. *Imprensa Popular,* May 17, 1957. *Última Hora,* May 16, 17, 1957 (including quotations from other newspapers). Armando Falcão stated (interview, Rio de Janeiro, August 3, 1989) that he followed the leadership of Vieira de Melo and voted accordingly.

7. From "National Pacification" to "Obstruction" (May–September 1957)

1. *O Estado de S. Paulo,* May 17, 1957. Carlos Lacerda, *Discursos Parlamentares,* pp. 211–235. In a tribute to Congressman Yukishigue Tamura, Lacerda, in his speech, denounced "those skeptics, disbelievers, or false sociologists who have so frequently spoken of difficulty in the assimilation of Japanese immigrants." Thus he parted company with ideas expressed in his series of articles, "The Japanese Penetration of Brazil," published just after the Japanese attack on Pearl Harbor.

2. Ibid. *Tribuna da Imprensa,* December 10, 23, 1957.

3. *O Estado de S. Paulo,* May 17, 22, 23, 1957.
4. Ibid., June 8, 7, 6, 1957.
5. Ibid., June 6, July 7, 29, 1957. Carlos Lacerda, *Discursos Parlamentares,* pp. 262–263.
6. *O Estado de S. Paulo,* June 7, 1957.
7. Ibid. Carlos Lacerda, *Discursos Parlamentares,* pp. 259–280.
8. *O Estado de S. Paulo,* June 7, 8, 13, 1957.
9. "Age Lott contra Carlos Lacerda," *Jornal do Commercio* clipping, n.d., in Carlos Lacerda file at *O Estado de S. Paulo. O Estado de S. Paulo,* July 3, 5, 1957.
10. *Tribuna da Imprensa,* July 6–7, 1957.
11. *Folha da Noite,* June 21, 1957. "Brasília," *Tribuna da Imprensa,* editorial, July 2, 1957. Rafael Corrêa de Oliveira, "A Missa," *O Estado de S. Paulo,* June 27, 1957. *O Estado de S. Paulo,* June 30, 1957. *Última Hora,* September 21, 1960.
12. Rafael Corrêa de Oliveira, "A Missa." *Diário Popular,* July 3, 1957. *Folha da Noite,* July 4, 5, 1957. *O Estado de S. Paulo,* July 5, 1957.
13. *Tribuna da Imprensa,* September 5, 1957.
14. Ibid., September 4, 5, 3, 1957.
15. Ibid., September 19, 20, 1957. João Duarte, filho, in ibid., September 12, 1957.

8. The Caravana da Liberdade (May–December 1957)

1. Otávio Soares Dulci, *A UDN e o Anti-Populismo no Brasil,* pp. 150–151. *O Estado de S. Paulo,* June 6, 1957. Carlos Lacerda, *Depoimento,* p. 197.
2. Luiz Ernesto Kawall, interview, São Paulo, July 25, 1983. Nelson Pereira, interview, São Paulo, August 4, 1983. Armando Daudt d'Oliveira, interview.
3. Rafael de Almeida Magalhães, interview, Rio de Janeiro, August 17, 1983.
4. Carlos Lacerda, *Depoimento,* p. 200. *O Estado de S. Paulo,* June 6, 1957.
5. Luiz Ernesto Kawall, interview, July 25, 1983. Juracy Magalhães, "Juracy esclarece depoimento de Lacerda," *O Estado de S. Paulo,* July 20, 1977. Carlos Lacerda, *Depoimento,* pp. 197–198.
6. Carlos Lacerda, *Depoimento,* pp. 198–200. *Tribuna da Imprensa,* July 2, 18, 20–21, 23, 1957.
7. *Tribuna da Imprensa,* July 8, 9, October 8, 1957.
8. Carlos Lacerda, *A Linha de Yenan e as Fôrças Armadas,* p. 49.
9. *Tribuna da Imprensa,* July 8, 1957.
10. Carlos Lacerda, *A Linha de Yenan e as Fôrças Armadas,* p. 49.
11. *Tribuna da Imprensa,* September 21–22, 1957. Newspaper clipping probably from *Tribuna da Imprensa,* October 26, 1957, in the Walter Cunto collection.
12. Carlos Lacerda, *Depoimento,* p. 200.
13. Cleantho de Paiva Leite, interview, Rio de Janeiro. *Tribuna da Imprensa,* December 3, October 11, 18–19, 1957.

14. *Tribuna da Imprensa,* July 9, 2, 1957. Carlos Lacerda, *Depoimento,* pp. 195–196. Bourne, *Political Leaders of Latin America,* p. 226.
15. Carlos Lacerda, "Rosas e Pedras de Meu Caminho," Chapter 8 (*Manchete,* June 3, 1967), pp. 22–23. Sérgio Lacerda, interview, Rio de Janeiro, August 22, 1988.
16. *O Estado de S. Paulo,* March 2, 4, 5, 7, 11, 12, 1958.
17. Ibid., March 4, 9, 5, 1958.
18. Ibid., March 5, 6, 11, 12, 13, 14, 15, 1958.

9. The UDN's "Most Serious Crisis" (May–July 1958)

1. Carlos Lacerda, letter to Fernando Velloso, Rome, April 14, 1958.
2. Mário Guimarães, declaration, *O Estado de S. Paulo,* June 13, 1958. Herbert Levy, interview, São Paulo, August 1, 1983.
3. *O Estado de S. Paulo,* May 15, 1958. Mário Guimarães, declaration.
4. *O Estado de S. Paulo,* May 27, June 3, 1958. José Eduardo Prado Kelly entry in *Dicionário Histórico-Biográfico Brasileiro.*
5. Roberto da Silveira, statement, *O Estado de S. Paulo,* June 19, 1958. *O Estado de S. Paulo,* May 15, 1958. "Nota da Tribuna da Imprensa," *O Estado de S. Paulo,* June 12, 1958.
6. *O Estado de S. Paulo,* June 12, 1958. José Eduardo Prado Kelly entry in *Dicionário Histórico-Biográfico Brasileiro.*
7. *O Estado de S. Paulo,* June 12, 18, 13, 1958.
8. Ibid., June 12, 15, 1958. *Tribuna da Imprensa,* June 17, 1958.
9. *Tribuna da Imprensa,* June 16, 1958. *O Estado de S. Paulo,* June 15, 17, 18, 19, 1958.
10. *O Estado de S. Paulo,* July 10, June 20, 1958.
11. Ibid., June 20, 27, July 1, 6, 8, 10, 1958.
12. Ibid., July 8, 1958. Herbert Levy, interview. Herbert Levy, speech in the Chamber of Deputies, June 29, 1977, printed in *Diário do Congresso Nacional,* vol. 32, no. 71 (June 30, 1977), pp. 5,680–5,681 (see p. 5,681).
13. Herbert Levy, interview. *O Estado de S. Paulo,* July 12, 17, 1958.
14. *O Estado de S. Paulo,* July 17, 18, 19, 1958.
15. Ibid., August 22, 23, 26, 29, September 3, 4, 1958. *Jornal do Brasil,* September 25, 1958.

10. The Caminhão do Povo (August–October 1958)

1. Francisco Negrão de Lima, letter to Carlos Lacerda, *Última Hora,* June 6, 1958.
2. Carlos Lacerda, "Entrevista de Carlos Lacerda ao jornal dos estudantes," *Tribuna da Imprensa,* January 19, 1959.
3. Carlos Lacerda, "O que o povo diria ao Sr. Dulles," *Tribuna da Imprensa,* August 4, 1958. *Time,* August 18, 1958. *Tribuna da Imprensa,* August 9–10, 7, 1958.
4. *Última Hora,* September 22, 1958. *O Estado de S. Paulo,* August 2, 10, 15, 1958. *Tribuna da Imprensa,* August 25, September 11, 1958.

5. *Tribuna da Imprensa,* September 1, 2, 1958. *O Estado de S. Paulo,* September 2, 9, 1958. Cláudio Lacerda, "Lacerda: Uma Vida de Lutas," Chapter 10, p. 7.

6. *O Estado de S. Paulo,* August 27, September 3, 1958. *Tribuna da Imprensa,* August 29, September 2, 3, 1958. *Jornal do Brasil,* September 2, 3, 1958.

7. *Tribuna da Imprensa,* September 3, 1958.

8. Ibid., September 4, 17, 1958. *Jornal do Brasil,* September 5, 4, 1958.

9. Camargo et al., *O Intelectual e o Político,* p. 155. Melo Franco, *A Escalada,* p. 446.

10. Camargo et al., *O Intelectual e o Político,* p. 155. Melo Franco, *A Escalada,* pp. 446–447. Raul Brunini, interview, Rio de Janeiro, August 12, 1983, and taped interview (see pp. 3–4 of transcript).

11. *Tribuna da Imprensa,* September 23, 1958.

12. Raul Brunini, interview, August 12, 1983. Camargo et al., *O Intelectual e o Político,* p. 156. *Última Hora,* September 29, 1958.

13. Melo Franco, *A Escalada,* p. 447, and interview, Rio de Janeiro, July 29, 1984. *Tribuna da Imprensa,* October 8, 1958. *Última Hora,* September 22, 1958.

11. Carioca Voters Turn to Afonso Arinos, Lacerda, and Brunini (October 1958)

1. *Jornal do Brasil,* September 16, 17, 18, 1958. *Correio da Manhã,* September 27, October 2, 1958. *O Globo,* September 27, 1958.

2. *Correio da Manhã,* September 24, 1958. *Jornal do Brasil,* September 20, 1958.

3. *Correio da Manhã,* October 2, 1958. *Jornal do Brasil,* September 11, 1958.

4. *Jornal do Brasil,* September 2, 1958. *Tribuna da Imprensa,* September 16, 1958.

5. Raul Brunini, taped interview (see pp. 5–6 of transcript). *Tribuna da Imprensa,* October 1, 1958. Melo Franco, *A Escalada,* p. 449. Raul Brunini, interview, August 12, 1983.

6. Cláudio Lacerda, "Lacerda: Uma Vida de Lutas," Chapter 10, p. 7. Raul Brunini, interview, August 12, 1983. Melo Franco, *A Escalada,* p. 451.

7. *Última Hora,* October 6, 1958. *Entreguismo:* the turning over of Brazilian assets to foreigners.

8. Manuel Vega-Palacin, "Elections, Parties, and Congress: Brazil, 1945–1964," Ph.D. dissertation, the University of Texas at Austin, 1981, p. 17.

9. *O Estado de S. Paulo,* October 8, 1958. About Calasans, see Carlos Castilho Cabral, *Tempos de Jânio e Outros Tempos,* p. 114.

10. Carlos Lacerda, interview with *O Estado de S. Paulo,* in *Tribuna da Imprensa,* October 10, 1958. *Tribuna da Imprensa,* October 16, 1958.

11. Yedda Braga Miranda, interview. *Tribuna da Imprensa,* October 8, November 21, 1958.

12. The Roboré Agreement of 1958 (January 1959)

1. *O Estado de S. Paulo,* February 17, 1959.

2. Cláudio Lacerda, "Lacerda: Uma Vida de Lutas," Chapter 11, p. 2.

3. Carlos Lacerda, in *Tribuna da Imprensa,* January 22, 1959. Gabriel Passos, *Estudos sôbre o Acordo de Roboré,* pp. 83–133.

4. Janari Nunes, Alexínio Bittencourt, and Acordo de Roboré entries in *Dicionário Histórico-Biográfico Brasileiro.* Carlos Lacerda, *Discursos Parlamentares,* p. 725. Carlos Lacerda, *Depoimento,* pp. 193–194.

5. Anderson Oscar Mascarenhas, *Roboré, um Torpedo contra a Petrobrás,* pp. 120, 185, 38.

6. Roberto Campos, interview, Rio de Janeiro, December 23, 1974.

7. Roberto Campos, "A Questão do Petróleo Boliviano," in *Economia, Planejamento, e Nacionalismo,* pp. 217–253.

8. Raul Fernandes, letter to Carlos Lacerda, Vassouras, January 17, 1959, in CCL.

9. *Tribuna da Imprensa,* January 24–25, 30, 1959.

10. Roberto Campos, interview. Carlos Lacerda, in *Tribuna da Imprensa,* January 30, 1959. *PCB: Vinte Anos de Política: Documentos, 1958–1979,* p. 59.

11. *Tribuna da Imprensa,* January 30, 1959. Roberto Campos, *Economia, Planejamento, e Nacionalismo,* p. 253. Acordo de Roboré entry in *Dicionário Histórico-Biográfico Brasileiro.* Poerner, *O Poder Jovem,* p. 196.

12. *Tribuna da Imprensa,* January 30, 22, 24–25, 1959. Carlos Lacerda, "Entrevista de Carlos Lacerda ao jornal dos estudantes."

13. *Tribuna da Imprensa,* December 19, 1958. Carlos Lacerda, "O que o povo precisa saber sôbre o caso do petróleo na Bolivia," *Tribuna da Imprensa,* January 23, 1959.

14. *Tribuna da Imprensa,* January 30, 1959.

15. Mascarenhas, *Roboré, um Torpedo contra a Petrobrás,* pp. 223–226.

16. Roberto Campos, interview. *Tribuna da Imprensa,* March 20, 1959.

17. Gabriel Passos, *Estudos sôbre o Acôrdo de Roboré,* pp. 7–55. Acordo de Roboré entry in *Dicionário Histórico-Biográfico Brasileiro.*

18. Roberto Campos, interview.

13. Directives and Bases for Education (1947–1961)

1. *Câmara dos Deputados* Law Projects 2266, 2272, 2275, 2282, 2418, 2855, 2894, 3150, 3183, 3203, 3212, 3309, 3310, 3426, 3460, 3504, 3616, 3634, and 3638 of 1957; Project 4688 of 1958; Project 3 of 1959.

2. Carlos Lacerda, "Rosas e Pedras do Meu Caminho," Chapter 1, p. 23. Carlos Lacerda, "Entrevista de Carlos Lacerda ao jornal dos estudantes."

3. Brazilian Constitution of 1946, Article 5 (Clause XV, Subsection d) and Articles 166–175. Carlos Flexa Ribeiro, interviews, Rio de Janeiro, July 5, 1983, August 26, 1984.

4. João Eduardo Rodrigues Villalobos, *Diretrizes e Bases da Educação:*

Ensino e Liberdade, pp. 41–47. Carlos Flexa Ribeiro, interviews, July 5, 1983, August 26, 1984.

5. Carlos Lacerda, *Discursos Parlamentares* (speeches of May 15, 1957, November 3, 1958), pp. 202, 600. Carlos Lacerda, in *Tribuna da Imprensa,* April 4–5, 1959. *Diário do Congresso Nacional,* June 29, 1955. Villalobos, *Diretrizes e Bases,* pp. 68, 97.

6. Carlos Lacerda, in *Tribuna da Imprensa,* April 4–5, 1959. Villalobos, *Dietrizes e Bases,* p. 75. Carlos Lacerda, *Discursos Parlamentares,* p. 601.

7. Villalobos, *Diretrizes e Bases,* pp. 83–86, 91–93. *O Estado de S. Paulo,* November 7, 1958.

8. Carlos Lacerda, *Discursos Parlamentares,* pp. 599, 602–604, 610–611. Villalobos, *Diretrizes e Bases,* p. 94. Ulrich, "Carlos Lacerda e a UDN," pp. 268–269.

9. Villalobos, *Diretrizes e Bases,* pp. 101, 35, 106, 103, 104–106. Carlos Lacerda, *Discursos Parlamentares* (speech of December 11, 1958), p. 715. Ulrich, "Carlos Lacerda e a UDN," pp. 281–283.

10. Villalobos, *Diretrizes e Bases,* pp. 113, 118, 116, 111–113. Carlos Lacerda, *Discursos Parlamentares,* pp. 715, 718. *Tribuna da Imprensa,* December 12, 1958.

11. *Tribuna da Imprensa,* May 16–17, 18, 19, 21, April 4–5, 1959. Luiz Antonio Cunha, "Em Defesa do Ensino Público," *Ciência Hoje,* vol. 3, no. 13 (July–August 1984) (see p. 48).

12. *Tribuna da Imprensa,* December 19, 20–21, 1958, January 22, 27, 1959. Villalobos, *Diretrizes e Bases,* p. 99. José Fonseca e Silva, in Carlos Lacerda, *Discursos Parlamentares,* p. 759.

13. Carlos Lacerda, *Depoimento,* p. 218. Carlos Flexa Ribeiro, interviews, July 5, 1983, August 26, 1984. Carlos Lacerda, in *Tribuna da Imprensa,* April 4–5, 1959. Villalobos, *Diretrizes e Bases,* pp. 122–123.

14. "Lacerda: Anticatolicismo de Anísio parece com anti-semitismo," *Tribuna da Imprensa,* June 4, 1959. Villalobos, *Diretrizes e Bases,* pp. 120–123.

15. Villalobos, *Diretrizes e Bases,* pp. 122–125, 110. *Tribuna da Imprensa,* June 5, 1959.

16. Carlos Lacerda in *Tribuna da Imprensa,* June 3, 4, 1959.

17. Carlos Lacerda in *Tribuna da Imprensa,* June 3, April 4–5, 1959. Villalobos, *Diretrizes e Bases,* p. 149.

18. Villalobos, *Diretrizes e Bases,* pp. 135, 131, 130.

19. Luiz Antonio Cunha, "Em Defesa do Ensino Público." Lei de Diretrizes e Bases entry in *Dicionário Histórico-Biográfico Brasileiro.* Villalobos, *Diretrizes e Bases,* p. 147 (note 19).

20. Villalobos, *Diretrizes e Bases,* pp. 135–141, 146. Luiz Antonio Cunha, "Em Defesa do Ensino Público," p. 48

21. Luiz Antonio Cunha, "Em Defesa do Ensino Público." Villalobos, *Diretrizes e Bases,* pp. 141, 152.

22. "Lacerda Não Quer Escola Para Todos," *Novos Rumos,* August 5–7, 1960. *Novos Rumos,* June 10–16, 1960.

23. Darci Ribeiro, letter to Carlos Lacerda, Rio de Janeiro, June 6, 1960, in *Novos Rumos,* June 10–16, 1960.

24. Ibid. *Tribuna da Imprensa,* June 6, 1960. "Darci Ribeiro Responde a Carlos Lacerda: Fanfarrão e Pusilânime," *Novos Rumos,* June 10–16, 1960.
25. Villalobos, *Diretrizes e Bases,* pp. 157–160, 164–165. Luiz Antonio Cunha, "Em Defesa do Ensino Público."
26. Carlos Lacerda, "Rosas e Pedras do Meu Caminho," Chapter 1, p. 23.
27. Hippolito, "Carlos Lacerda, Ascensão e Queda," pp. 49, 50.

IX. Backer of Quadros (1959–1960)

1. Lacerda's Decision to Support Quadros (February 1959)

1. Mário Victor, *Cinco Anos que Abalaram o Brasil: De Jânio Quadros ao Marechal Castelo Branco,* p. 38.
2. Antônio de Oliveira Godinho, interview, São Paulo, July 24, 1983. Roberto de Abreu Sodré, interview, São Paulo, August 3, 1983. Herbert Levy, interview.
3. Marcelo Garcia, interview.
4. Carlos Lacerda, "Rosas e Pedras do Meu Caminho," Chapter 11 (*Manchete,* June 24, 1967), p. 112.
5. Caó, *Carreirista da Traição,* p. 196. Carlos Lacerda, "Entrevista de Carlos Lacerda ao jornal dos estudantes."
6. Carlos Lacerda, in *Tribuna da Imprensa,* February 13, 16, 17, 1959.
7. *Tribuna da Imprensa,* February 19, 20, 1959. Carlos Lacerda, *Depoimento,* p. 202. Carlos Lacerda, "Rosas e Pedras do Meu Caminho," Chapter 11, p. 112.
8. Ibid. Fernando Ferrari entry in *Dicionário Histórico-Biográfico Brasileiro.*
9. *Tribuna da Imprensa,* February 18, 1959.
10. Ibid., February 20, 1959. Roberto de Abreu Sodré, interview.

2. The UDN Convention of March 1959

1. *Tribuna da Imprensa,* February 19, 20, March 4, 7–8, 9, 1959. Carlos Lacerda, letter to Júlio de Mesquita Filho, Rio de Janeiro, April 26, 1960, in CCL.
2. *O Estado de S. Paulo,* March 10, 1959. *Tribuna da Imprensa,* February 25, March 10, 1959.
3. *O Estado de S. Paulo,* March 19, 1959. Carlos Lacerda, letter to Júlio de Mesquita Filho, April 26, 1960.
4. *O Estado de S. Paulo,* March 22, 1959.
5. *Tribuna da Imprensa,* March 23, 1959. *O Estado de S. Paulo,* March 22, 24, 1959.
6. *Tribuna da Imprensa,* March 23, 1959. *O Estado de S. Paulo,* June 28, 1959.
7. *Tribuna da Imprensa,* March 23, 1959. *O Estado de S. Paulo,* March 24, 1959. Mário Martins entry in *Dicionário Histórico-Biográfico Brasileiro.*

8. Carlos Lacerda, "Bem-vindos à *Tribuna da Imprensa*," newspaper clipping, April 2, 1959, in Velloso collection.

3. Reflections about Salazar and Fidel Castro (April–May 1959)

1. Álvaro Lins entry in *Dicionário Histórico-Biográfico Brasileiro. Tribuna da Imprensa,* April 29, 17, 1959. Álvaro Lins, *Missão em Portugal,* p. 133.
2. Álvaro Lins, *Missão em Portugal,* pp. 80–133 (see pp. 159–160, 251, 169–170).
3. Carlos Lacerda, *Discursos Parlamentares* (speech of January 30, 1959), pp. 751–756. Joel Silveira, quoted in Álvaro Lins, *Missão em Portugal,* p. 266.
4. *Tribuna da Imprensa,* April 17, 1959. Álvaro Lins, *Missão em Portugal,* pp. 205, 236–237, 320, 322, 321, 268, 309, 283.
5. *Tribuna da Imprensa,* April 15, 1959.
6. Ibid., April 16, 17, 20, 1959. Álvaro Lins, *Missão em Portugal,* p. 333.
7. *Tribuna da Imprensa,* April 29, 22, 25–26, 1959.
8. Ibid., April 29, 1959.
9. Ibid., April 28, 1959.
10. Antônio Carlos de Almeida Braga, interview, New York, September 2, 1988.
11. *Tribuna da Imprensa,* May 6, 1959.
12. Ibid., May 7, 6, 1959.
13. Gabriel Lacerda, conversation, Rio de Janeiro, August 22, 1988.

4. Magalhães Pinto Irritates Lacerda (April–July 1959)

1. Carlos Lacerda, "Rosas e Pedras do Meu Caminho," Chapter 11, p. 112. Carlos Lacerda, *Depoimento,* pp. 202–203.
2. *Tribuna da Imprensa,* April 8, 1959.
3. Ibid., June 3, 1959. Jânio Quadros, letter to Carlos Lacerda, Istanbul, Turkey, June 19, 1959, in CCL.
4. "Relatório político do Sr. Magalhaēs Pinto," delivered at the UDN nominating convention, Rio de Janeiro, November 7, 1959, published in *O Estado de S. Paulo,* November 8, 1959. Magalhães Pinto's letter to Jânio Quadros, transcribed in the "Relatório político," was dated June 11, 1959.
5. "Relatório político do Sr. Magalhães Pinto." *O Estado de S. Paulo,* June 28, 1959.
6. *O Estado de S. Paulo,* July 2, 8, 25, 1959.
7. Victor, *Cinco Anos que Abalaram o Brasil,* p. 42. *Tribuna da Imprensa,* June 20–21, 1959. *O Estado de S. Paulo,* July 11, 19, 24, 28, August 4, 1959.
8. *O Estado de S. Paulo,* July 30, 1959.
9. Ibid., July 29, 31, August 12, July 26, 1959.
10. Ibid., July 7, 26, 28, 1959.

11. Carlos Lacerda, letter to José de Magalhães Pinto, Rio de Janeiro, July 30, 1959, in CCL.

5. Conversations with Jânio in Europe (August 1959)

1. *O Estado de S. Paulo,* August 6, 1959. Castilho Cabral, *Tempos de Jânio e Outros Tempos,* p. 163.
2. *Novos Rumos,* August 14–20, 1959.
3. *O Estado de S. Paulo,* August 11, 13, 9, 1959.
4. Ibid., August 9, 7, 1959. Castilho Cabral, *Tempos de Jânio e Outros Tempos,* pp. 160, 149–152, 137, 146–147, 166.
5. *O Estado de S. Paulo,* August 15, 16, 1959.
6. Ibid., August 12, 16, 19, 1959.
7. Ibid., August 19, 30, 1959. Carlos Lacerda, letter to Raul Pilla, in *O Estado de S. Paulo,* September 12, 1959.
8. *O Estado de S. Paulo,* August 18, 20, 23, 25, 27, 31, 1959. Antônio Carlos de Almeida Braga, interview.
9. *O Estado de S. Paulo,* August 30, 1959. Carlos Lacerda, *Depoimento,* p. 246.
10. *O Estado de S. Paulo,* September 2, 1959.
11. Carlos Lacerda, *Depoimento,* p. 246. Antônio Carlos de Almeida Braga, interview.
12. Carlos Lacerda, *Depoimento,* p. 246.
13. *O Estado de S. Paulo,* August 28, 29, 1959.
14. Ibid., August 30, 1959.
15. Carlos Lacerda, "Rosas e Pedras do Meu Caminho," Chapter 2 (*Manchete,* April 22, 1967), p. 23.

6. Lacerda Resigns as Opposition Leader (September 1959)

1. *O Estado de S. Paulo,* September 2, 1959. "Relatório político do Sr. Magalhães Pinto." *Tribuna da Imprensa,* September 1, 10, 11, 1959.
2. *Tribuna da Imprensa,* September 10, 11, October 2, 1959. Carlos Lacerda, letter to Júlio de Mesquita Filho, Rio de Janeiro, April 26, 1960, in CCL.
3. Rondon Pacheco entry in *Dicionário Histórico-Biográfico Brasileiro.* Carlos Lacerda, letter to Rondon Pacheco, São Paulo, September 10, 1959, in CCL.
4. *Tribuna da Imprensa,* September 10, 11, 15, 1959.
5. Ibid., September 23, 24, 1959, October 17–18, 1959.
6. Rubens Resstel, interview, São Paulo, August 4, 1983.
7. Jânio Quadros, letter to Carlos Lacerda, Lisbon, September 10, 1959, in CCL.
8. *Tribuna da Imprensa,* September 17, 19–20, 18, 24, 1959.
9. Ibid., September 22, 23, 1959. Carlos Lacerda, *Depoimento,* p. 203.
10. *O Estado de S. Paulo,* November 3, 1959. *Tribuna da Imprensa,* September 29, 30, October 3–4, 1959.

11. *Tribuna da Imprensa,* October 9, 10, 1959. Carlos Lacerda, *Depoimento,* p. 203.
12. *Tribuna da Imprensa,* October 15, 1959.
13. Ibid., October 13. André Franco Montoro, statement, *O Estado de S. Paulo,* December 4, 1959.

7. A Lively UDN Nominating Convention (November 7–8, 1959)

1. Carlos Lacerda, letter to Júlio de Mesquita Filho, April 26, 1960.
2. Melo Franco, *A Escalada,* p. 460.
3. Carlos Lacerda, *Depoimento,* pp. 208–209. In this quotation of Lacerda, as given in *Depoimento,* Lacerda referred to accepting ". . . the candidacy of the UDN, PDC, PR, PTN, and I don't know what others." The PR, pro-Kubitschek, was considered pro-Lott at that time. Hilde Weber's cartoon in *O Estado de S. Paulo,* November 10, 1959, shows party preferences.
4. *O Estado de S. Paulo,* November 6, 8, 1959.
5. Ibid., November 8, 1959.
6. Carlos Lacerda, *Depoimento,* p. 209.
7. Aliomar Baleeiro entry in *Dicionário Histórico-Biográfico Brasileiro. O Estado de S. Paulo,* November 8, 1959.
8. Aliomar Baleeiro entry in *Dicionário Histórico-Biográfico Brasileiro. O Estado de S. Paulo,* November 8, 1959.
9. Ibid., November 10, 1959.
10. Ibid., Victor, *Cinco Anos que Abalaram o Brasil,* pp. 49–52.
11. Maurício Caminha de Lacerda, interviews with DFR, Rio de Janeiro, March 28, April 7, 1983. *Tribuna da Imprensa,* November 23, 24, 25, 26, 27, 1959, including "Páginas da infância de Maurício de Lacerda."

8. The Candidate Resigns (November 25, 1959)

1. *O Estado de S. Paulo,* November 10, 1959.
2. Ibid.
3. Ibid., November 17, 19, 20, 1959.
4. Ibid., November 21, 22, 1959.
5. Ibid., November 22, 28, 27, 1959. Victor, *Cinco Anos que Abalaram o Brasil,* p. 60.
6. *O Estado de S. Paulo,* November 28, 1959.
7. Castilho Cabral, *Tempos de Jânio e Outros Tempos,* p. 171. Jânio Quadros, letter to Leandro Maciel, November 25, 1959, in *O Estado de S. Paulo,* November 28, 1959.
8. Jânio Quadros, letters to José de Magalhães Pinto, November 25, 1959, and to Carlos Alberto de Carvalho Pinto, November 27, 1959. See Castilho Cabral, *Tempos de Jânio e Outros Tempos,* p. 171, and Victor, *Cinco Anos que Abalaram o Brasil,* pp. 56–58, 60.
9. *Tribuna da Imprensa,* November 27, 1959. Carlos Lacerda, letter to Júlio de Mesquita Filho, Rio de Janeiro, April 26, 1960, in CCL.

10. Leandro Maciel, quoted in Castilho Cabral, *Tempos de Jânio e Outros Tempos,* p. 173, and in *O Estado de S. Paulo,* November 27, 1959.

11. *O Estado de S. Paulo,* November 28, 1959. Carlos Lacerda, *Depoimento,* pp. 206, 203. *Tribuna da Imprensa,* November 27, 1959.

12. *O Estado de S. Paulo,* November 27, 1959.

13. Ibid., November 28, 1959.

14. Victor, *Cinco Anos que Abalaram o Brasil,* p. 61.

9. The Candidate Reconsiders (December 5, 1959)

1. Victor, *Cinco Anos que Abalaram o Brasil,* p. 60. Carlos Lacerda, letter to Júlio de Mesquita Filho, April 26, 1960, in CCL.

2. *O Estado de S. Paulo,* November 27, 1959. Jânio Quadros, note to Carlos Lacerda, November 26, 1959, in CCL.

3. Carlos Lacerda, *Depoimento,* p. 204.

4. Ibid., pp. 204–205. Carlos Lacerda, "Rosas e Pedras do Meu Caminho," Chapter 11, p. 114.

5. Ibid.

6. *O Estado de S. Paulo,* November 28, 1959.

7. Ibid., November 28, 29, 1959.

8. Ibid., November 29, 1959. *Tribuna da Imprensa,* November 28–29, 1959.

9. *O Estado de S. Paulo,* December 2, 1959.

10. *Tribuna da Imprensa,* November 30, December 1, 1959.

11. Ibid., December 1, 1959.

12. "Nossa Opinião: O janista Lacerda," *Diário Carioca,* December 2, 1959.

13. *O Estado de S. Paulo,* December 4, 5, 6, 1959.

14. Ibid., December 6, 1959.

15. *Correio Paulistano,* December 5, 1959. *Tribuna da Imprensa,* December 5–6, 1959.

10. The Aragarças Revolt (December 3–4, 1959)

1. Copies of proposed revolutionary decrees, in files of Luís Mendes de Morais Neto.

2. Luís Mendes de Morais Neto, interviews, October 19, November 25, 1966. Haroldo Veloso, interviews, Marietta, Georgia, January 6, 7, 1966. Lacerda, in his speech in Congress, December 7, 1959, reported in *Tribuna da Imprensa,* December 8, 1959, called Colonel Mendes da Silva an "authentic hero" of the FEB (the Brazilian Expeditionary Force that fought in Italy in World War II).

3. *Correio da Manhã* and *Tribuna da Imprensa,* December 4, 1959.

4. Letícia Lacerda, conversation with DFR, Rio de Janeiro, March 1989. Carlos Lacerda, *Depoimento,* p. 188. Carlos Lacerda, speech in Congress, December 7, 1959.

5. *O Jornal* and *O Estado de S. Paulo,* December 4, 1959. Carlos Lacerda, speech in Congress, December 7, 1959.

6. Ibid. Carlos Lacerda, *Depoimento,* p. 190.

7. "A Rebelião de Aragarças," *Mundo Ilustrado,* December 19, 1959. Glauco Carneiro, *História das Revoluções Brasileiras,* vol. 2, pp. 519–531. Haroldo Veloso, interviews, January 6, 7, 1966.

8. Carlos Lacerda, speech in Congress, December 7, 1959.

9. *Correio da Manhã* and *O Estado de S. Paulo,* December 4, 1959. Aragarças Revolt entry in *Dicionário Histórico-Biográfico Brasileiro.*

10. "A Rebelião de Aragarças."

11. *Correio Paulistano,* December 5, 1959. *Correio da Manhã,* December 4, 1959.

12. *Tribuna da Imprensa,* December 5–6, 1959. *Correio da Manhã* and *O Estado de S. Paulo,* December 4, 1959.

13. *O Jornal,* December 4, 1959. *Novos Rumos,* December 11–17, 1959.

14. Carlos Lacerda, *Depoimento,* p. 188. Carlos Lacerda, speech in Congress, December 7, 1959.

15. *Tribuna da Imprensa* and *O Estado de S. Paulo,* December 8, 1959.

16. *Tribuna da Imprensa* and *Diário do Congresso Nacional,* December 11, 1959.

17. *Tribuna da Imprensa,* December 15, 16, 1959. *Diário de Notícias,* December 13, 1959.

18. France Presse release, La Paz, December 17, 1959. *Tribuna da Imprensa,* December 17, 1959. Carlos Lacerda, *Depoimento,* p. 191.

19. *Tribuna da Imprensa,* December 19–20, 1959, January 9–10, 11, 13, 1960. Haroldo Veloso, interviews, January 6, 7, 1966. Regarding exiles in Bolivia, see *O Estado de S. Paulo,* April 26, 1960. The manifesto of exiles, issued in Buenos Aires, was dated April 12, 1960.

11. Absence from Brazil (December 1959–March 1960)

1. Luiz Ernesto Kawall, interview, São Paulo, July 31, 1983. Jânio Quadros note to the *Tribuna da Imprensa,* December 23, 1959, in CCL.

2. Walter Cunto, interview, Rio de Janeiro, August 14, 1984. *Tribuna da Imprensa,* December 3, 4, 1959.

3. Vera Lacerda Paiva, interview, Rio de Janeiro, August 25, 1988.

4. Carlos Lacerda, letter to Odilon Lacerda Paiva, Paris, March 17, 1960, in LFC. Vera Lacerda Paiva, Odilon Lacerda Paiva, and Lygia Paiva Derizans, interview, Rio de Janeiro, July 22, 1984.

5. *Tribuna da Imprensa,* December 21, 28, 1959. Carlos Lacerda, letter to Júlio de Mesquita Filho, Rio de Janeiro, April 26, 1960, in CCL.

6. José de Magalhães Pinto, letter to Carlos Lacerda, Belo Horizonte, December 21, 1959, in CCL.

7. Carlos Lacerda, letter to Júlio de Mesquita Filho, Rio de Janeiro, April 26, 1960.

8. *Tribuna da Imprensa,* December 24, 1959.

9. Ibid., December 28, 1959.

10. Ibid., December 29, 1959.
11. Sebastião Lacerda, interview, August 15, 1988.
12. Carlos Lacerda, "Começa o julgamento," *Tribuna da Imprensa,* February 2, 1960.
13. Carlos Lacerda, *Paixão e Crime: O Processo do Dr. Jaccoud.*
14. Carlos Lacerda, in *Tribuna da Imprensa,* February 5, 6–7, 4, 1960.
15. Carlos Lacerda, in *Tribuna da Imprensa,* February 10, 27–28, March 7, 8, 1960.
16. Sebastião Lacerda, interview, August 15, 1988.
17. João Condé, interview, Rio de Janeiro, August 11, 1983.
18. Letícia Lacerda, interview with DFR, Rio de Janeiro, January 5, 1988.
19. Letícia Lacerda, letter to Sebastião Lacerda, Paris, March 7, 1960, in CCL. Gilberto Trompowisky, "O Nome da Semana: Dona Letícia de Lacerda," newspaper clipping, in CCL.
20. *Tribuna da Imprensa,* August 7, 1960.

12. Jânio and Others Write from Rio (February–March 1960)

1. José Sarney, letter to Carlos Lacerda, Rio de Janeiro, February 6, 1960, in CCL.
2. "Bossa-Nova" da UDN entry in *Dicionário Histórico-Biográfico Brasileiro.* Benevides, *A UDN e o Udenismo,* p. 115. Letter on *Tribuna da Imprensa* stationery (signature illegible) to Carlos Lacerda, Rio de Janeiro, February 5, 1960, in CCL.
3. *Tribuna da Imprensa,* February 11, March 8, 9, 1960.
4. *Correio da Manhã,* March 23, 25, 1960. Dinarte Mariz, letter to Carlos Lacerda, Rio de Janeiro, March 23, 1960, in CCL.
5. *Novos Rumos,* April 22–28, 1960. *Correio da Manhã,* March 24, 1960.
6. Letter on *Tribuna da Imprensa* stationery (signature illegible) to Carlos Lacerda, Rio de Janeiro, February 23, 1960, in CCL.
7. *Correio da Manhã,* March 9, 1960.
8. Ibid., March 24, 25, 1960.
9. Sérgio Lacerda, interview, Rio de Janeiro, August 17, 1988.
10. Jânio Quadros, letter to Carlos Lacerda, Rio de Janeiro, March 24, 1960, in CCL.
11. *Tribuna da Imprensa,* March 8, February 18, 1960. *Correio da Manhã,* March 15, 1960.
12. Castilho Cabral, *Tempos de Jânio e Outros Tempos,* p. 189.
13. Prudente de Moraes, neto, interview, Rio de Janeiro, August 31, 1963.
14. *Correio da Manhã,* April 1, 2, 1960.
15. Ibid., April 7, 1960. *Tribuna da Imprensa,* April 7, 1960.

13. While *Udenistas* Brawl, Maciel Resigns (April 1960)

1. *Tribuna da Imprensa,* April 2, 5–6, 1960. *Correio da Manhã,* April 5, 22, 1960.

2. *Tribuna da Imprensa,* April 11, 2, 1960. *Correio da Manhã,* April 9, 1960.

3. *Correio da Manhã,* April 6, 1960. *Tribuna da Imprensa,* April 12, 1960.

4. João Agripino, letter to Carlos Lacerda, Rio de Janeiro, April 11, 1960, in CCL. Carlos Lacerda, letter to João Agripino, Rio de Janeiro, April 12, 1960, in CCL.

5. Carlos Lacerda, letter to Júlio de Mesquita Filho, Rio de Janeiro, April 26, 1960, in CCL. *Tribuna da Imprensa,* April 28, 1960.

6. *Correio da Manhã,* April 14, 1960. *O Estado de S. Paulo,* May 7, 1960. Carlos Lacerda, letter to Júlio de Mesquita Filho, April 26, 1960. *Novos Rumos,* April 22–28, 1960.

7. Carlos Lacerda, letter to Júlio de Mesquita Filho, April 26, 1960. Carlos Lacerda, letter to José de Magalhães Pinto, Rio de Janeiro, April 25, 1960, in CCL.

8. *Correio da Manhã,* April 26, 1960. *O Estado de S. Paulo,* April 20, 1960. *Tribuna da Imprensa,* April 25, 1960.

9. *Tribuna da Imprensa,* April 19, 1960. *Correio da Manhã,* April 26, 1960.

10. *Correio da Manhã,* April 27, 1960. Carlos Lacerda, letter to José de Magalhães Pinto, April 25, 1960.

11. *Tribuna da Imprensa,* April 26, 1960. *Correio da Manhã,* April 27, 1960.

12. *Correio da Manhã,* April 27, 1960.

13. *Tribuna da Imprensa,* April 26, 1960. Pedro Aleixo, letter to Carlos Lacerda, Belo Horizonte, April 27, 1960, in CCL.

14. *Tribuna da Imprensa,* April 26, 29, 1960.

15. Ibid., April 28, 1960.

16. Ibid., April 28, 29, 30, May 3, 6, April 27, 1960.

X. Candidate for Governor (1960)

1. Entering the Gubernatorial Race (May 1960)

1. Carlos Lacerda, letter to Newton Tornaghi, Rio de Janeiro, May 4, 1960, in CCL. Carlos Lacerda, letter to Diretório da UDN, Secção do Rio de Janeiro, May 10, 1960, in CCL. *O Estado de S. Paulo,* May 12, 1960.

2. Carlos Lacerda, letter to Newton Tornaghi, May 4, 1960.

3. Carlos Lacerda, memorandum to "President Jânio Quadros," Rio de Janeiro, May 11, 1960, and notations of Jânio Quadros on it, May 16, 1960, in CCL.

4. Castilho Cabral, *Tempos de Jânio e Outros Tempos,* pp. 197–198. *Tribuna da Imprensa,* May 18, 1960.

5. *Tribuna da Imprensa,* May 18, 1960.

6. *Tribuna da Imprensa,* May 20, 16, 1960.

7. Ibid., May 19, 30, 1960.

8. Ibid., May 31, 1960. *Jornal do Brasil,* October 2, 1960.

9. Carlos Lacerda, "Isto eu prometo," *Tribuna da Imprensa,* June 2, 1960. Emil Farhat, interview, São Paulo, August 2, 1983, and interview with DFR,

São Paulo, March 11, 1983. Carlos Lacerda, *Depoimento,* p. 216.

10. Otávio Marcondes Ferraz, interview, São Paulo, August 2, 1983. Carlos Lacerda, *Agua Afinal,* phonograph record (produced by Teleplan). Rebello Filho, *Carlos Lacerda, Meu Amigo,* p. 59 (quoting Ayrton Baffa). *O Globo,* September 8, 1960.

11. Carlos Lacerda, *O Poder das Idéias,* p. 109. Rafael de Almeida Magalhães, interview, Rio de Janeiro, August 17, 1983. "Chefe de Gabinete," *Jornal do Brasil,* October 23, 1960. Gustavo Borges, interview, Rio de Janeiro, August 14, 1983. Glycon de Paiva, letter to Carlos Lacerda, Rio de Janeiro, June 13, 1960, in CCL. Carlos Lacerda, letter to Glycon de Paiva, Rio de Janeiro, June 27, 1960, in CCL.

12. Rebello Filho, *Carlos Lacerda, Meu Amigo,* pp. 34–35. Carlos Lacerda, *Depoimento,* p. 215. Marcelo Garcia, interview. Carlos Lacerda, *Depoimento,* p. 214.

13. André de Séguin des Hons, "Os Diários do Rio de Janeiro: 1945–1982" (master's thesis, history department, Universidade Federal do Rio de Janeiro, January 1982), pp. 174–177, 234. Marcelo Garcia, interview. Walter Cunto, interview, Rio de Janeiro, August 7, 1983, and interview with DFR, Rio de Janeiro, March 25, 1983.

14. "Os bens de Lacerda," *Tribuna da Imprensa,* August 17, 1960. *Novos Rumos,* August 26–September 1, 1960.

2. "The Devastated City and Its Reconstruction" (June–July 1960)

1. Xavier d'Araújo, letter to Carlos Lacerda, May 5, 1960, in CCL. *Tribuna da Imprensa,* June 3, 1960.

2. *Tribuna da Imprensa,* June 7, 10, 11–12, 13, 29, 1960. *O Estado de S. Paulo,* June 15, 1960.

3. *Correio da Manhã,* July 23, 1960. Rebello Filho, *Carlos Lacerda, Meu Amigo,* p. 179. *Tribuna da Imprensa,* October 21, 22–23, 1955.

4. *Tribuna da Imprensa,* June 14, August 2, 1960. Castilho Cabral, *Tempos de Jânio e Outros Tempos,* pp. 193–205.

5. *Tribuna da Imprensa,* June 13, 1960. Eventually Lacerda's proposal to assist taxi drivers was enacted.

6. Carlos Lacerda, *O Poder das Idéias,* pp. 125, 112–116.

7. Ibid., pp. 117–118, 121–122, 116.

8. Ibid., pp. 127, 130–131.

9. Ibid., pp. 158, 160–162. *Tribuna da Imprensa,* June 22, 1960.

10. Carlos Lacerda, *O Poder das Idéias,* pp. 162, 166, 170, 175.

11. Ibid., pp. 134–136, 138, 133, 144, 145, 148.

12. Alfredo C. Machado, interview, Rio de Janeiro, August 8, 1989.

3. Candidates on and against the Ticket (June–August 1960)

1. *Tribuna da Imprensa,* June 17, 1960.

2. Ibid. *Jornal do Brasil,* October 23, 1960. Edgar Flexa Ribeiro, interview, Rio de Janeiro, July 8, 1983.

3. *Correio da Manhã,* September 4, 1960. *Tribuna da Imprensa,* September 2–3, 1960. *Jornal do Brasil,* September 18, 1960.

4. Hélio Fernandes, in *Diário de Notícias,* reprinted in *Tribuna da Imprensa,* June 22, 1960.

5. Lacerda, *Depoimento,* pp. 214, 292. Guilherme da Silveira, interview, Rio de Janeiro, August 30, 1984.

6. *Correio da Manhã,* July 3, 5, 7, 9, 1960. Sérgio Magalhães entry in *Dicionário Histórico-Biográfico Brasileiro.* Carlos Lacerda, *Depoimento,* pp. 193, 214–215.

7. *Correio da Manhã,* July 9, September 24, July 31, August 8, 1960.

8. Ibid., July 8, 22, September 10, 1960. *Diário de Notícias,* July 22, 1960. *Jornal do Brasil,* October 2, 1960, June 20, 1982. Israel Beloch, *Capa Preta e Lurdinha: Tenório Cavalcanti e o Povo da Baixada,* p. 55. Tenório Cavalcanti file at archive of *O Estado de S. Paulo. Visão,* October 25, 1982. Carlos Lacerda, *Depoimento,* pp. 198, 214.

9. *Jornal do Brasil,* June 20, 1982. Mário Martins entry in *Dicionário Histórico-Biográfico Brasileiro. Correio da Manhã,* July 13, 26, 1960.

10. *Diário de Notícias,* July 22, 1960. Sérgio Lacerda, interview, Rio de Janeiro, August 17, 1988. Castilho Cabral, *Tempos de Jânio e Outros Tempos,* pp. 200–205 (see letter, Castilho Cabral to Jânio Quadros, Rio de Janeiro, June 6, 1960, on p. 201).

11. *Correio da Manhã,* July 13, 20, 19, 1960.

12. Ibid., August 24, 30, 1960.

13. Ibid., August 13, 25, 30, 1960.

14. Ibid., August 13, 1960. Thomas E. Skidmore, *Politics in Brazil: An Experiment in Democracy,* p. 190.

15. *Jornal do Brasil,* September 23, 1960. *Correio da Manhã,* editorial, August 9, 1960.

16. *Jornal do Brasil,* September 22, 1960. *Última Hora,* September 5, 1960. *Novos Rumos,* September 30–October 6, August 12–18, August 26–September 1, 1960.

17. *Jornal do Brasil,* October 2, 1960. *Correio da Manhã,* September 4, 2, 1960.

4. Propaganda of the Left (August–September 1960)

1. *Correio da Manhã,* September 1, 1960. *Tribuna da Imprensa,* September 3–4, 1960.

2. *Tribuna da Imprensa,* August 8, 12, 13–14, 15, 16, 1960.

3. Carlos Lacerda, *Depoimento,* p. 215.

4. Luís Gutemberg, article about the Lacerda campaign, *Jornal do Brasil,* October 2, 1960.

5. Ibid. *Correio da Manhã,* August 19, 20, 1960.

6. Carlos Lacerda in *Aonde Vamos,* reprinted in *Tribuna da Imprensa,* October 1–2, 1960.

7. *Última Hora,* September 14, 1960. *O Globo,* September 17, 22, 1960.

8. Carlos Lacerda, "A Ofensiva Comunista," in *Tribuna da Imprensa,* September 3, 1960. *Correio da Manhã* and *Jornal do Brasil,* September 4, 1960. *O Globo,* September 5, 1960. *Última Hora,* September 16, 1960. "Perfil de um Candidato," *Última Hora,* September 19, 20, 21, 22, 23, 26, 1960 (see September 20, 21).

9. *Novos Rumos,* September 30–October 6, 1960. *Última Hora,* September 23, 1960.

5. "The Thief of Chile Street" (September 1960)

1. *Tribuna da Imprensa,* September 5, 1960. *Correio da Manhã,* September 27, 1960. *Jornal do Brasil,* September 6, 1960. *Última Hora,* September 1, 1960.

2. Ibid.

3. *Correio da Manhã,* September 3, 1960. *Última Hora,* September 3, 1960. *Jornal do Brasil,* September 16, 1960. *O Globo,* September 17, 1960.

4. *Última Hora* and *O Globo,* September 6, 1960. *Jornal do Brasil,* September 9, 1960.

5. *Última Hora* September 6, 13, 1960. *Correio da Manhã,* September 6, 1960.

6. *Jornal do Brasil,* September 14, 1960. *Última Hora,* September 15, 1960.

7. *Jornal do Brasil,* October 2, 1960 (article by Luís Gutemberg).

8. Ibid., September 11, 15, 1960.

9. *Correio da Manhã,* September 17, 1960. *O Globo,* September 17, 19, 1960. *Jornal do Brasil,* September 17, October 2, 1960 (article by Luís Gutemberg).

10. *O Globo,* September 17, 19, 1960.

6. The Human Side of the Candidate (August–September 1960)

1. *O Globo,* September 8, 1960. *Jornal do Brasil,* October 2 (article by Luís Gutemberg), September 11, 1960.

2. *Jornal do Brasil,* September 11, 1960. *Tribuna da Imprensa* and *O Globo,* September 12, 1960.

3. David Nasser, "Elogio ao Adversário."

4. Rebello Filho, *Carlos Lacerda, Meu Amigo,* p. 40.

5. Carlos Lacerda, "Vida Pública: Resposta a David Nasser," *O Cruzeiro,* September 24, 1960, reproduced in Carlos Lacerda, *Palavras e Ação,* pp. 97–107.

6. Cláudio Lacerda, "Quem realmente conheceu este homem?" *Jornal da Tarde,* May 23, 1977. Antonio Dias Rebello Filho and Lígia Gomide, interview with DFR, Rio de Janeiro, March 26, 1983.

7. *Tribuna da Imprensa,* October 1–2, 1960.

8. Lourenço de Almeida Prado, interview. Lourenço de Almeida Prado, letter to Carlos Lacerda, Rio de Janeiro, May 19, 1967, in CCL.

7. Missteps by the Leading Candidates (September 1960)

1. *Última Hora,* September 13, 16, 1960.
2. *Correio da Manhã,* September 27, 1960.
3. *Jornal do Brasil* and *Correio da Manhã,* September 28, 1960.
4. Carlos Lacerda, *Depoimento,* p. 216. *Jornal do Brasil,* September 18, 20, 21, October 2 (article by Luís Gutemberg), September 23, 1960. *Tribuna da Imprensa,* September 23, 1960.
5. *Tribuna da Imprensa,* September 23, 1960. *Jornal do Brasil,* September 23, 25, 1960. *Petebista:* associated with the PTB.
6. *Jornal do Brasil,* September 25, 1960.
7. Carlos Lacerda, *Depoimento,* p. 216. *O Globo,* September 23, 1960.
8. *Jornal do Brasil,* September 27, 1960.
9. Ibid., September 28, 1960.
10. Raul Brunini, taped interview (see p. 29a of transcript).

8. Farewell to the *Tribuna* (September 30, 1960)

1. *Tribuna da Imprensa,* September 28, 1960. *Correio da Manhã,* September 29, 30, 1960.
2. *Correio da Manhã,* September 20, 21, 1960. *Jornal do Brasil,* October 1, 1960. *O Globo,* September 27, 1960.
3. *Correio da Manhã,* September 22, 30, October 1, 1960, *Jornal do Brasil,* September 30, October 1, 1960.
4. *Tribuna da Imprensa,* October 1–2, 1960. Hilcar Leite, interview. Luiz Ernesto Kawall, interview, São Paulo, July 25, 1983. *Jornal do Brasil,* October 1, 2, 1960.
5. *Jornal do Brasil,* October 2, September 28, 1960.

9. Victory by a Narrow Margin (October 1960)

1. *Correio da Manhã,* October 1, 4, 1960. *Jornal do Brasil,* October 5, 1960. *Última Hora,* October 6, 1960.
2. *Correio da Manhã,* October 4, 1960. Carlos Lacerda, *Depoimento,* p. 217.
3. Léticia Lacerda, conversation with DFR, Rio de Janeiro, January 5, 1988, and March 1989.
4. Carlos Lacerda, *Depoimento,* p. 217.
5. *Correio da Manhã,* October 18, 5, 1960. *Última Hora,* October 7, 1960.
6. *Tribuna da Imprensa,* October 7, 1960.
7. *Jornal do Brasil,* October 8, 1960.
8. *Correio da Manhã,* October 13, 1960. According to the figures of the Regional Electoral Tribunal, announced in November, Lacerda received 357,126 votes and Sérgio Magalhães 333,690 (see *Tribuna da Imprensa,* November 10, 1960). Marcelo Garcia, interview. Gláucio Ary Dillon Soares, "As Bases Ideológicas do Lacerdismo," *Revista Civilização Brasileira,* vol. 1, no. 4 (September 1965), p. 59 (footnote 18).

9. *Correio da Manhã,* October 9, 1960. *Última Hora,* October 11, 1960.

10. Gláucio Ary Dillon Soares and Nelson do Valle e Silva, "O Charme Discreto do Socialismo Moreno," *Dados: Revista de Ciências Sociais,* vol. 28, no. 2 (1985), p. 256. Dillon Soares, "As Bases Ideológicas do Lacerdismo," pp. 58, 59. See also Guita Grin Debert, *Ideologia e Populismo,* p. 96.

11. *Última Hora,* October 11, 1960. *Tribuna da Imprensa,* November 10, 1960. *Correio da Manhã,* October 9, 1960. *O Globo,* December 6, 1960.

12. *Tribuna da Imprensa,* November 10, 1960.

13. Ibid.

14. Eugênio Gudin, "Govêrno Bossa Limpa," *O Globo,* December 9, 1960.

15. *Correio da Manhã,* October 25, 26, 1960. Rafael de Almeida Magalhães, interview, Rio de Janeiro, August 17, 1983.

10. Preparing to Tour the World (October 1960)

1. *Jornal do Brasil,* September 15, 1960. *Tribuna da Imprensa,* September 26, 27, 1960. *Correio da Manhã,* September 27, 1960. See Paulo Konder Bornhausen, letter to Carlos Lacerda, Joinville, October 27, 1960 (in CCL), about his plan to be in Rio for Lacerda's "inauguration on November 15."

2. *Correio da Manhã,* October 12, 21, 25, 1960. *Tribuna da Imprensa,* November 24, 1960.

3. Carlos Lacerda, *Depoimento,* p. 196.

4. *Tribuna da Imprensa,* November 22, 7, 5–6, 8, 11, 14, 26, 27, 17, 1960, March 22, 1961. *Correio da Manhã,* October 15, 21, 25, 18, December 31, 1960. Mario Lorenzo Fernandez, letter to Carlos Lacerda, Rio de Janeiro, November 6, 1960, in CCL. *O Globo,* December 6, 13, 16, 12, 1960.

5. Carlos Lacerda, *Depoimento,* p. 273. *Correio da Manhã,* October 19, 27, 1960.

6. Carlos Lacerda, letters to Hélio Beltrão, Rafael de Almeida Magalhães, Carlos Flexa Ribeiro, José Cândido Moreira de Souza, Victor Bouças, Rio de Janeiro, October 22, 24, 26, 27, 1960, in CCL.

7. Carlos Lacerda, "Rosas e Pedras do Meu Caminho," Chapter 11 (*Manchete,* June 24, 1967), p. 107. Carlos Lacerda, *Depoimento,* pp. 241–242.

Epilogue. Governor-Elect

1. Carlos Lacerda, *Depoimento,* p. 219.

2. Carlos Lacerda, "Rosas e Pedras de Meu Caminho," Chapter 2, p. 25.

3. *O Globo,* December 6, 1960.

4. Gudin, "Govêrno Bossa Limpa."

5. Carlos Lacerda, *Depoimento,* p. 217. Carlos Lacerda, letter to Raimundo Padilha, Rio de Janeiro, October 28, 1960, in CCL.

6. Lygia Paiva Derizans and Vera Lacerda Paiva, interview with DFR, Rio de Janeiro, August 25, 1985.

7. Rafael de Almeida Magalhães, quoted in Marília Pacheco Fiorillo, "O Esperto Charme da Burguesia," *Status*, no. 142 (May 1986), p. 32.

8. Hippolito, "Carlos Lacerda, Ascensão e Queda," pp. 83–84.

9. Hugo Levy, interview with DFR, Rio de Janeiro, March 7, 1989.

10. Prudente de Moraes, neto, interview.

11. Hugo Levy, Rafael de Almeida Magalhães, and Edgar Flexa Ribeiro, interviews, Rio de Janeiro, August 1, 9, 19, 1989. Alcino Salazar, interview taped by the Sociedade dos Amigos de Carlos Lacerda (see pp. 5–7 of transcript). Hugo Levy, interview with DFR. Enaldo Cravo Peixoto, interview taped by the Sociedade dos Amigos de Carlos Lacerda (see p. 2 of transcript).

12. Baffa, "A Metralhadora Giratória." Laerte Vieira, speech in the Chamber of Deputies, June 29, 1977, printed in *Diário do Congresso Nacional*, vol. 32, no. 71 (June 30, 1977), pp. 5,672–5,674 (see p. 5,673). Heráclito Fontoura Sobral Pinto, interview taped by the Sociedade dos Amigos de Carlos Lacerda (see p. 2 of transcript).

Sources of Material

Agripino, João. Letters to Carlos Lacerda. CCL.

Aleixo, Pedro. Letters to Carlos Lacerda. CCL.

Alem, Sílvio Frank. "A Contribuição à História dos Socialismos no Brasil: A Construção do Partido Socialista Brasileiro (1945–1947)." Typewritten, 90 pages. João Pessoa: Núcleo de Documentação e Informação Histórica Regional, Universidade Federal da Paraíba, May 1984.

Alisky, Marvin. *Latin American Media: Guidance and Censorship.* Ames, Iowa: Iowa State University Press, 1981.

Alkmin, José Maria. Interview, Brasília, October 15, 1965.

Almeida, Climério Euribes de. Testimony at the Galeão Air Base as reported in *O Estado de S. Paulo,* September 17, 23, 1954.

Almeida, José Américo de. "A Situação: Declarações do Sr. José Américo." *Correio da Manhã,* February 22, 1945.

———. "Mérito da entrevista foi de Lacerda." *O Globo,* May 22, 1977.

Almeida, Paulo Mendes de. Letters to Carlos and Letícia Lacerda. CCL.

——— and Aparecida Mendes de Almeida. Interview, São Paulo, July 26, 1983.

Alverga, Ruth. Transcript of interview taped by the Sociedade dos Amigos de Carlos Lacerda.

———. Interviews, Rio de Janeiro, August 7, 1983, and August 16, 1983, and interview with DFR, Rio de Janeiro, March 30, 1983.

Alves, Aluísio. "A atitude do Etelvino Lins." *Tribuna da Imprensa,* June 23, 1955.

———. Interview, Rio de Janeiro, August 17, 1983.

Alves, Oswaldo. Letter to Fernando Goldgaber, n.p., n.d.

Amado, Jorge. Letter to Luís Henrique Dias Tavares, Bahia, November 2, 1985.

Amaral Netto, Fidélis. *O Clube da Lanterna e a Legalidade Vigente: Parte Escrita do Depoimento Prestado pelo Jornalista Amaral Netto, Presidente do Clube da Lanterna, na Delegacia de Ordem Política e Social, em 9 de Dezembro de 1955, Perante o Delegado Olavo Rangel.* Rio de Janeiro, 1956.

Andrade, Carlos Drummond de. Comments about Carlos Lacerda, *Uma Luz Pequenina,* in *Revista Acadêmica,* no. 69 (December 1947).

———. Declaration. *Diário de Notícias,* April 29, 1949.

Andrade, Mário de. *Cartas a Murilo Miranda.* Rio de Janeiro: Editora Nova Fronteira, 1981.

Antas, Luiz Mendes. *Dicionário de Siglas e Abreviaturas: Descodificação.* São Paulo: Traço Editora, 1984.

[Aragarças Rebellion.] "A Rebelião de Aragarças." *Mundo Ilustrado,* December 19, 1959.

———. Revolutionary decrees of plotters, in possession of Luís Mendes de Morais Neto.

Aranha, Osvaldo G. Interview, Rio de Janeiro, July 2, 1963.

Araújo, Xavier d'. Letter to Carlos Lacerda, May 5, 1960, CCL.

Athayde, Austregésilo de. Interview with DFR, Rio de Janeiro, March 21, 1983.

Aulicino, Carlos Alberto. Collection of letters from Carlos Lacerda, São Paulo.

———. Interview, São Paulo, July 28, 1983.

Baciu, Stefan. *Lavradio, 98.* Rio de Janeiro: Editoria Nova Fronteira, 1982.

Baffa, Ayrton, "A Metralhadora Giratória Disparada com Dois Dedos." *Revista de Comunicação,* vol. 5, no. 19 (September 1989).

Baldessarini, Hugo. *Crônica de uma Época (De 1850 ao Atentado contra Carlos Lacerda): Getúlio Vargas e o Crime de Toneleros.* São Paulo: Companhia Editora Nacional, 1957.

Bamba. Children's weekly published in Rio de Janeiro by Editôra Tribuna da Imprensa, 1951–1952.

Barbosa, Raul de Sá. Interview with DFR, Rio de Janeiro, January 18, 1983.

Barbosa, Rui. Article of November 2, 1898, reprinted in "Na Tribuna da Imprensa," *Correio da Manhã,* July 2, 1947.

Basbaum, Leôncio. *Uma Vida em Seis Tempos: Memórias.* São Paulo: Editora Alfa-Omega, 1976.

Beccari, Vera d'Horta. *Lasar Segall e o Modernismo Paulista.* São Paulo: Brasiliense, 1984.

Bello, José Maria. *Memórias.* Rio de Janeiro: Livraria José Olympio Editôra, 1958.

Beloch, Israel. *Capa Preta e Lurdinha: Tenório Cavalcanti e o Povo da Baixada.* Rio de Janeiro: Editora Record, 1986.

Benevides, Maria Victoria de Mesquita. *A UDN e o Udenismo: Ambigüidades do Liberalismo Brasileiro (1945–1965).* São Paulo: Editora Paz e Terra, 1981.

Bingaman, Jeff. "The Strategy of Political Opposition: An Analysis of the Political Life of Carlos Lacerda." Typewritten, 50 pages. Stanford Law School, October 30, 1960. Copy in CCL.

Bittencourt, Paulo. "Na Tribuna da Imprensa," *Correio da Manhã,* May 1, 1949.

Borgerth, Eduardo. Diary. Handwritten. Entries for 1946 and 1947.

Borges, Gustavo. Letters to Carlos Lacerda. CCL.
———. Interview, Rio de Janeiro, August 14, 1983, and handwritten notes for JWFD.
Bornhausen, Paulo Konder. Letter to Carlos Lacerda, Joinville, October 27, 1960. CCL.
Boto, Carlos Pena. Message in *O Globo,* October 14, 1955. Reproduced in Joffre Gomes da Costa, *Marechal Henrique Lott,* p. 264.
———. Interview, Rio de Janeiro, October 27, 1965.
Bouças, Victor Coelho. Interview, Rio de Janeiro, August 2, 1984.
Bourne, Richard. *Political Leaders of Latin America,* New York: Alfred A. Knopf, 1970.
Braga, Antônio Carlos de Almeida. Interview, New York, September 2, 1988.
Braga, Rubem. Letters to Carlos Lacerda, São Paulo, October 7, 1940, November 7, 1941, CCL.
Branco, Humberto de Alencar Castello. Letter to Senhores Membros do Comitê Auxiliar do Distrito Federal da Frente de Novembro, Rio de Janeiro, November 8, 1956. Castello Branco collection (File L1). CPDOC.
Brandão, Otávio. Interviews, Rio de Janeiro, August 30, November 14, 1970, June 27, 1971, and letter to JWFD, Rio de Janeiro, May 25, 1971.
Brandi, Paulo. *Vargas: Da Vida para a História.* Rio de Janeiro: Zahar Editores, 1983.
British embassy in Brazil. Letters to the British foreign office, Rio de Janeiro, November 1955. Public Record Office, London.
Brunini, Raul. Taped interview with Letícia Lacerda, Vera Lacerda Paiva, Cláudio Lacerda Paiva, Lamy Cunto, and DFR, Rio de Janeiro, March 9, 1989. Transcript by DFR.
———. Interviews, August 12, 1983, August 1, 1989.
Bueno, Fernando, L. M. de Souza, and Guimarães Padilha. *Êsse Incrível Lacerda.* Rio de Janeiro: Editôra Iniciativa, n.d.
Caballero, Mara. "Joel Silveira revive em livro a luta dos pracinhas no Itália." *Jornal do Brasil,* December 19, 1983.
Cabral, Carlos Castilho. *Tempos de Jânio e Outros Tempos.* Rio de Janeiro: Editôra Civilização Brasileira, 1962.
Café Filho, João. *Do Sindicato ao Catete: Memórias Políticas e Confissões Humanas.* 2 vols. Rio de Janeiro: Livraria José Olympio Editôra, 1966.
Câmara do Distrito Federal. Official publication. Issues of 1947.
Câmara dos Deputados. *Autos do Inquérito Instaurado pela Comissão Parlamentar de Inquérito Instituída pela Resolução nº 313 de 27 de Maio de 1953.* Rio de Janeiro: Departamento de Imprensa Nacional, 1954.
———. *Deputados Brasileiros, 1826–1976: Obra Comemorativa do Sesquicentenário da Câmara dos Deputados.* Brasília: Centro de Documentação e Informação, Câmara dos Deputados, 1976.
———. See Fleischer, David V.
Câmara dos Deputados. Official publication printing law projects. Issues of 1955–1959.
Camargo, Aspásia, Maria Tereza Lopes Teixeira, and Maria Clara Mariani.

O Intelectual e o Político: Encontros com Afonso Arinos. Brasília: Dom Quixote Editora Senado Federal and CPDOC/Fundação Getúlio Vargas, 1983.

Campos, Milton. "Voto do Deputado Milton Campos em Nome da Oposição," in Carlos Lacerda, *O Caminho da Liberdade,* pp. 213–214.

Campos, Roberto. *Economia, Planejamento, e Nacionalismo.* Rio de Janeiro: APEC Editôra, 1963.

———. Interview, Rio de Janeiro, December 23, 1974.

Caó, Epitácio. *Carreirista da Traição.* 2nd ed. N.p.: Edições Gernasa, 1964.

Cardoso, Adauto Lúcio. Letter to Secretaria Geral da Comissão Executiva da U.D.N., Seção Distrito Federal, *Correio da Manhã,* November 30, 1947.

———. Interview, Rio de Janeiro, December 15, 1965.

Careta. Rio de Janeiro magazine, published 1908–1960.

Carlisle, Charles Richard, ed. *Tesserae: A Mosaic of Twentieth Century Brazilian Poetry.* Fort Worth: Latitudes Press, 1983.

Carneiro, Glauco. *História das Revoluções Brasileiras.* Vol. 2. Rio de Janeiro: Edições O Cruzeiro, 1965.

———. *Luzardo: O Último Caudilho.* Vol. 2. Rio de Janeiro: Editora Nova Fronteira, 1978.

Carneiro, Léa Paiva Borges. Comments and handwritten note for DFR at interview, Rio de Janeiro, February 13, 1983.

Carone, Edgard. *A República Liberal, II: Evolução Política (1945–1964).* São Paulo: Difel/Difusão Editorial, 1985.

———. *A Terceira República (1937–1945).* São Paulo: Difel/Difusão Editorial, 1976.

Casa do Estudante do Brasil, ed. *sensacionalismo.* Rio de Janeiro: Casa do Estudante do Brasil; distrib. Freitas Bastos & Cia, 1933.

Castro, Moacir Werneck de. *Mário de Andrade: Exílio no Rio.* Rio de Janeiro: Editora Rocco, 1989.

———. Articles in *Revista Acadêmica, Marcha, Problemas* (of São Paulo), and *Revista do Brasil.*

———. Interviews, Rio de Janeiro, December 2, 1967, July 2, 1979, August 5, 10, 1989, and typewritten note for JWFD, Rio de Janeiro, August 1989.

Castro, Viriato de. *O Fenômeno Jânio Quadros.* 3rd ed. São Paulo: Palácio do Livro, 1959.

Cavalcanti, Tenório. "Declarações do Deputado Tenório Cavalcanti." *O Estado de S. Paulo,* November 25, 1956.

Chagas, Paulo Pinheiro. *Esse Velho Vento da Aventura: Memórias.* Rio de Janeiro and Brasília: Livraria José Olympio Editora and Ministério da Educação e Cultura, 1977.

Chateaubriand Bandeira de Melo, Francisco de Assis. Letters to Carlos Lacerda, Rio de Janeiro, November 30, December 12, 1944. CCL.

(*Cinco de Julho*) *5 de Julho.* Clandestine weekly published in Rio de Janeiro in support of the military rebellion of 1924–1927.

Código Secreto. Rio de Janeiro magazine. No. 1, 1957.

Communist Party, Brazilian. *PCB: Vinte Anos de Política: Documentos, 1958–1979.* São Paulo: Livraria Editora Ciências Humanas, 1980.

Communist Party of Brazil. "Documento Interno do PCB, Editado pelo Comitê Central sob o Título 'O Golpe e a Posição do Partido' com Ordem para Ser Discutido nos Órgãos de Base." Typewritten, five pages, August 1954. Copy in Communism in Brazil files at *O Estado de S. Paulo.*

Companhia Editôra Nacional. Letters to Haydée Fonseca and Carlos Lacerda, São Paulo, September 19–25, 1942, in CCL.

Condé, João. Interview, Rio de Janeiro, August 11, 1983, and interview with DFR, March 23, 1983.

Conniff, Michael L. *Urban Politics in Brazil: The Rise of Populism, 1925–1945.* Pittsburgh: University of Pittsburgh Press, 1981.

Constituições do Brasil. São Paulo: Saraiva, 1963.

Co-operative Party, The. Letters to Carlos Lacerda, London, July 1946. CCL.

Corção, Gustavo. "Antíteses." *O Estado de S. Paulo,* April 13, 1957.

———. "Em que não devemos votar." "Na Tribuna da Imprensa," *Correio da Manhã,* January 2, 1947.

Correio da Manhã. Rio de Janeiro newspaper.

Correio da Noite. Rio de Janeiro newspaper.

Correio Paulistano. São Paulo newspaper.

Costa, Joffre Gomes da. *Marechal Henrique Lott.* Rio de Janeiro, 1960.

Cruz, Adelina Maria Alves Novaes e, Célia Maria Leite Costa, Maria Celina Soares d'Araújo, and Suely Braga da Silva, compilers. *Impasse na Democracia Brasileira, 1951–1955: Coletânea de Documentos.* Rio de Janeiro: Editora da Fundação Getúlio Vargas, 1983.

Cruzeiro, O. Rio de Janeiro weekly magazine.

Cultura. Belo Horizonte publication.

Cunha, Luiz Antonio, "Em Defesa do Ensino Público." *Ciência Hoje,* vol. 3, no. 13 (July–August 1984).

Cunha, Lygia Vaz Brito e. Interviews, Rio de Janeiro, August 9, 1983, August 13, 1989.

Cunto, Lamy. Interviews, Rio de Janeiro, August 6, 12, 1989.

Cunto, Walter. Comments in Ruth Alverga, transcript of interview taped by the Sociedade dos Amigos de Carlos Lacerda.

———. Transcript of interview taped by the Sociedade dos Amigos de Carlos Lacerda.

———. Files of Carlos Lacerda papers and tapes of Carlos Lacerda speeches.

———. Interviews, Rio de Janeiro, August 7, 1983 (and handwritten notes for JWFD), August 14, 1984, and interview with DFR, Rio de Janeiro, March 25, 1983.

Dados: Revista de Ciências Sociais. Publication of the Instituto Universitário de Pesquisas do Rio de Janeiro.

Dantas, Marcos de Sousa. Letter to *Correio da Manhã,* November 12, 1953 (published in *Correio da Manhã* at that time).

Debert, Guita Grin. *Ideologia e Populismo.* São Paulo: T. A. Queiroz Editora, 1979.

Derizans, Lygia Paiva. Interviews, Rio de Janeiro, August 8, 1983, July 22, 1984, and interviews with DFR, Rio de Janeiro, August 25, 1985, February 12, 1989.

Diário Carioca. Rio de Janeiro newspaper.
Diário da Noite. São Paulo newspaper.
Diário da Tarde. Florianópolis, Santa Catarina, newspaper.
Diário de Notícias. Rio de Janeiro newspaper.
Diário de S. Paulo. São Paulo newspaper.
Diário do Congresso Nacional. Brazilian government publication.
Diário Oficial. Brazilian government publication.
Diário Popular. São Paulo newspaper.
Dias, Everardo. Letter to Eponina Dias, Rio de Janeiro, January 13, 1933. In possession of Eponina Dias Alcoforado, São Paulo.
Dicionário Histórico-Biográfico Brasileiro, 1930–1983. Rio de Janeiro: Editora Forense-Universitária Ltda., 1984.
Diretrizes. Rio de Janeiro magazine run by Samuel Wainer in the late 1930s and early 1940s.
Donato, Hernâni. "Carlos Lacerda Planeja Fundar em São Paulo a Revista 'Veja.'" Typewritten notes for JWFD. São Paulo, August 1984.
Dória, Francisco. "Secretário redigiu ícone populista." *Jornal do Brasil,* August 27, 1989.
Dulci, Otávio Soares. *A UDN e o Anti-populismo no Brasil.* Belo Horizonte: Editora Universidade Federal de Minas Gerais, 1986.
Dutra, Eurico Gaspar. Letter to Getúlio Vargas, Rio de Janeiro, June 15, 1942. Vargas papers, CPDOC.
Ehrenburg, Ilya. *Fevereiro Sangrento: A Revolução de 1934 na Austria.* Preface and translation by Carlos Lacerda. 2nd ed. Rio de Janeiro: Alba, n.d.
Estado de S. Paulo, O. São Paulo newspaper.
———. Reports of Galeão Air Base testimonies (about the Tonelero Street crime) of Lutero Vargas, Gregório Fortunato, Climério Euribes de Almeida, Alcino João do Nascimento, and Nelson Raimundo de Sousa, August 20, September 9, 17, 23, 1954.
———. Files in the archives of the newspaper.
Falcão, Armando. *Tudo a Declarar.* Rio de Janeiro: Editora Nova Fronteira, 1989.
———. Interviews, Rio de Janeiro, November 30, 1966, August 26, 1983, August 3, 1989.
Farhat, Emil. Interview, São Paulo, August 2, 1983, and interview with DFR, São Paulo, March 11, 1983.
Fatos & Fotos. Rio de Janeiro magazine.
Fernanda, Maria. Conversation with DFR, Rio de Janeiro, August 15, 1985.
Fernandes, Cory Porto. Interview, São Paulo, August 21, 1984.
Fernandes, Hélio. Interview, Rio de Janeiro, August 1, 1984.
Fernandes, Raul. Letter to Carlos Lacerda, Vassouras, January 17, 1959. CCL.
———. Memorandum. In Afonso Arinos de Melo Franco, *A Escalada.* Pp. 375–376.
Fernandez, Mario Lorenzo. Letter to Carlos Lacerda, Rio de Janeiro, November 6, 1960. CCL.

———. Interviews, Rio de Janeiro, August 23, 1988, August 23, 1989, and interview with DFR, September 2, 1985.

Ferraz, Geraldo. *Depois de Tudo.* São Paulo: Paz e Terra, 1983.

Ferraz, Otávio Marcondes. Interviews, São Paulo, August 9, 1963, and August 2, 1983.

Figueiredo, Guilherme. "Prefácio Importantíssimo" to "Cobras e Lagartos." Typewritten, 28 pages. Rio de Janeiro, 1984.

———. Interview, Rio de Janeiro, July 24, 1984.

Finatto, Adelar. *Álvaro Moreyra.* Porto Alegre: Tchê! Comunicações Ltda., 1985.

Fleischer, David V. *Deputados Brasileiros: Repertório Biográfico dos Senhores Deputados, Abrangendo o Período de 1946–1967.* Brasília: Coordenação de Publicações, Centro de Documentação e Informação, Câmara dos Deputados, 1981.

Folha da Noite. São Paulo newspaper.

Folha de S. Paulo. São Paulo newspaper.

Fortunato, Gregório. Testimony at the Galeão Air Base. In *O Estado de S. Paulo,* September 28, 1954, and in Hugo Baldessarini, *Crônica de uma Época.*

Franco, Afonso Arinos de Melo. *A Escalada: Memórias.* Rio de Janeiro: Livraria José Olympio Editôra, 1965.

———. "A UDN e o Acôrdo Militar Brasil–Estados Unidos." *Tribuna da Imprensa,* December 1, 1952.

———. *Diário de Bolso seguido de Retrato de Noiva.* Rio de Janeiro: Editora Nova Fronteira, 1979.

———. See Camargo, Aspásia et al.

———. Interviews, Brasília, October 16, 1965, and Rio de Janeiro, July 29, August 25, 1984.

Franco, Virgílio de Melo. *A Campanha da UDN.* Rio de Janeiro: Valverde, 1946.

———. Letter to Carlos Lacerda, Rio de Janeiro, July 28, 1946. CCL.

Freitas, Clara [Babá]. Letter to Carlos and Letícia Lacerda, Rio de Janeiro, October 6, 1941. CCL.

Galvão, Flávio de Almeida Prado. "Sebastião de Lacerda, Juiz do Supremo Tribunal Federal." *Revista do Tribunal de Contas do Município de São Paulo,* vol. 8, no. 25 (April 1979).

———. Comments for JWFD. Typewritten, 10 pages. São Paulo, August 1988.

Garcia, Marcelo. Interview, Rio de Janeiro, August 18, 1983.

Gardner, Mary A. *The Inter American Press Association: Its Fight for Freedom of the Press, 1926–1960.* Austin and London: University of Texas Press, 1967.

Gazeta, A. São Paulo newspaper.

Gikovate, Febus. Interview, São Paulo, November 21, 1968.

Giudicelli, Raul. See Peixoto, Alzira Vargas do Amaral.

Globo, O. Rio de Janeiro newspaper.

Godinho, Antônio de Oliveira. Interview, São Paulo, July 24, 1983.
Goldgaber, Fernando. Letters to JWFD, Rio de Janeiro, September 30, December 1, 1984.
Gomide, Lígia. Interview with DFR, Rio de Janeiro, March 26, 1983.
Gudin, Eugênio. "Govêrno Bossa Limpa." *O Globo,* December 9, 1960.
Gueiros, José Alberto. Interview with DFR, Rio de Janeiro, March 23, 1983.
Guimarães, Mário. Declaration. *O Estado de S. Paulo,* June 13, 1958.
Gutemberg, Luís. Article about Carlos Lacerda's campaign for governor. *Jornal do Brasil,* October 2, 1960.
Hargreaves, Charles Pullen. "Carlos Lacerda." Typewritten recollections, 2 pages. Rio de Janeiro, January 28, 1983.
Harris, Thomas. Letter to Carlos Lacerda, Stockholm, August 12, 1946. CCL.
Heiskell, Andrew. Letters to Carlos Lacerda, CCL.
Henriques, Affonso. *Vargas o Maquiavélico.* São Paulo: Palácio do Livro, 1961.
Hippolito, Lucia. "Carlos Lacerda, Ascensão e Queda da 'Metralhadora Giratória': Esboço de biografia política." Typewritten, 94 pages. Rio de Janeiro, June 1978.
Hons, André de Séguin des. "Os Diários do Rio de Janeiro, 1945–1982." Master's thesis. Rio de Janeiro: Universidade Federal do Rio de Janeiro, November 1982.
Imparcial, O. Rio de Janeiro daily newspaper.
Imprensa Popular. Rio de Janeiro Communist newspaper.
Inquérito Policial Militar No. 709 (Military Police Investigation 709). *O Comunismo no Brasil.* Vol. 1. Rio de Janeiro: Biblioteca do Exército, 1966.
Inter American Press Association, Freedom of the Press Commission. Report read at the Tenth Conference of the association, Rio de Janeiro, October 7, 1954. Published in *O Estado de S. Paulo,* October 8, 1954.
International Press Correspondence. Periodical of the Executive Committee of the Communist International. Vienna, Berlin, London.
Jordão, Hariberto de Miranda. *Agravo de Instrumento No. 4.861 (Competência do Juízo em Matéria de Nacionalidade): Memorial do Agravante, Samuel Wainer.* Rio de Janeiro, 1954.
———. *O Caso da Última Hora: Resposta ao Relatório da Comissão Parlamentar de Inquérito.* Rio de Janeiro, 1953.
———. *O Executivo Movido pelo Banco à ERICA é um Caso Típico de Abuso de Direito: Contestação da ERICA.* Rio de Janeiro, 1954.
Jornal, O. Rio de Janeiro newspaper.
Jornal da Tarde. São Paulo newspaper.
Jornal de São Paulo. Newspaper established by Hermínio Sacchetta and others.
Jornal do Brasil. Rio de Janeiro newspaper.
———. "Cinco homens, cinco destinos," August 5, 1984 (about the Tonelero Street crime of 1954).
———. "Lacerda/70 anos," April 30, 1984.
Jornal do Commercio. Rio de Janeiro newspaper.

Jurema, Abelardo. *Juscelino & Jango, PSD & PTB.* Rio de Janeiro: Editora Artenova, 1979.
Kawall, Luiz Ernesto. Interviews, São Paulo, July 25, 31, August 3, 1983, and interview with DFR, São Paulo, March 11, 1983.
Kelly, José Eduardo Prado. Interview, Rio de Janeiro, October 8, 1965.
Knight, John S. (Editor and publisher, *Chicago Daily News*). Letter to Carlos Lacerda, Chicago, November 21, 1955.
Krieger, Daniel. Interview, Brasília, October 21, 1975.
Lacerda, Carlos. "A Bailarina Solta no Mundo." Typewritten theatrical piece, CCL.
———. *A Casa do Meu Avô.* Paperback edition. Rio de Janeiro: Editora Nova Fronteira, 1977.
———. *Agua Afinal.* Phonograph record, produced by Teleplan.
———. *A Linha de Yenan e as Fôrças Armadas.* Rio de Janeiro: Tribuna da Imprensa, 1957.
———. "Amapá ou O Lobo Solitário." Typewritten theatrical piece, CCL.
———. *A Missão da Imprensa.* Rio de Janeiro: Livraria AGIR Editora, 1950.
———. "A penetração japoneza no Brasil." Daily articles in *O Radical,* December 17, 1941–January 1, 1942.
———. "A Ponte sôbre o Atlântico." Typewritten theatrical piece, an early version of "Amapá ou O Lobo Solitário." CCL.
———. "As confissões de Lacerda." *Jornal da Tarde,* May 27–June 15, 1977.
———. *A Tranquila Certeza de Segall.* Booklet giving speech in the Câmara dos Deputados, August 7, 1957, N.p.: Edição do Museu Lasar Segall, 1964.
———. Autobiographical notes in small black binder. CCL.
———. *Como Foi Perdida a Paz.* São Paulo: Instituto Progresso Editorial, 1947.
———. "Como Lutar contra a Sêca." Typewritten, 48 pages. Talk at the Brazilian Press Association (ABI), March 23, 1953.
———. *Depoimento.* Rio de Janeiro: Editora Nova Fronteira, 1977.
———. *Desafio e Promessa: O Rio São Francisco.* Rio de Janeiro: Distribuidora Record, 1964.
———. *Discursos Parlamentares.* Rio de Janeiro: Editora Nova Fronteira, 1982.
———. Drafts of manifesto of the Aliança Popular Contra o Roubo e o Golpe. CCL.
———. Early poems. Arquivo Mário de Andrade, Instituto de Estudos Brasileiros, University of São Paulo.
———. *Em Vez: Crônicas.* Rio de Janeiro: Editora Nova Fronteira, 1975.
———. "Explicação ao Leitor que Não É Daquele Tempo." In the Editora Nova Fronteira edition (1980) of Maurício de Lacerda, *História de uma Covardia.* Pp. 7–10.
———. "Instruções precisas." Typewritten, February 1956. Velloso collection.
———. Introduction to 2nd edition of Valdiki Moura, *Notícia do Cooperativismo Brasileiro.* São Paulo: Instituto Progresso Editorial, 1948.
———. Law Projects submitted as city councilman (given in pages of the

Câmara do Distrito Federal of 1947 collected in folder "Carlos Lacerda, vereador," in the Walter Cunto collection, Rio de Janeiro) and as federal congressman (given in pages of the *Câmara dos Deputados* of 1955–1959 and the *Diário do Congresso Nacional* of 1955, collected in folder "Deputado Carlos Lacerda, Projetos," found at Carlos Lacerda's Rocio residence and presently in collection of JWFD in Austin).

———. Letters and other papers. CCL, LFC, and Walter Cunto collection, Rio de Janeiro.

———. "Na Tribuna da Imprensa." Daily column in *Correio da Manhã,* 1946–1949.

———. Notebooks 3 and 4. Handwritten, December 1935–March 1936. Vera Lacerda Paiva's typewritten transcriptions.

———. [Júlio Tavares, pseud.]. "Novidades de um Velho Caderno." Typewritten. Walter Cunto collection, Rio de Janeiro.

———. Notes about the Lacerda family. CCL.

———. *O Brasil e o Mundo Árabe.* Rio de Janeiro, 1948.

———. *O Caminho da Liberdade: Discurso na Comissão de Justiça da Câmara dos Deputados.* 2nd ed. Rio de Janeiro, 1957.

———. *O Poder das Idéias.* Rio de Janeiro: Distribuidora Record, 1962.

———. [Marcos, pseud.]. *O Quilombo de Manuel Congo.* Rio de Janeiro: Editôra Revista Acadêmica [1935].

———. *O Rato Fiuza.* Rio de Janeiro: Editora Moderna, 1946.

———. *O Rio.* São Paulo: [Editôra Gaveta/Livraria Jaraguá] 1943.

———. *Paixão e Crime: O Processo do Dr. Jaccoud.* Rio de Janeiro: Editôra Nova Fronteira, 1965.

———. *Palavras e Ação.* Rio de Janeiro: Distribuidora Record, 1965.

———. Preface to Ilya Ehrenburg, *Fevereiro Sangrento: A Revolução de 1934 na Austria,* translated by Carlos Lacerda. Rio de Janeiro: Alba, n.d.

———. *Retrato da Cidade Devastada e Sua Reconstrução.* Booklet giving speech at the Convenção da UDN Carioca, June 17, 1960. Rio de Janeiro: Editora Rio–São Paulo, 1960.

———. "Rosas e Pedras do Meu Caminho." Twelve autobiographical articles. *Manchete,* nos. 782–793 (April 15–July 1, 1967).

———. Testimony at criminal court hearings, March 1954. *Tribuna da Imprensa,* March 16, 1954.

———. Testimony in Câmara dos Deputados, *Autos do Inquérito Instaurado pela Comissão Parlamentar de Inquérito Instituída pela Resolução nº 313 de 27 de Maio de 1953.*

———. [Júlio Tavares, pseud.]. "Um Brasileiro na Terra do Tio Sam." Series of articles. *O Globo,* 1956.

———. *Uma Luz Pequenina.* Rio de Janeiro: Editôra Revista Acadêmica, 1948.

———. "Vida Pública: Resposta a David Nasser." *O Cruzeiro,* September 24, 1960. Reproduced in Carlos Lacerda, *Palavras e Ação.*

———. *Visão da Seca no Nordeste: Um Relato, um Testemunho, um Programa.* Rio de Janeiro: Tribuna da Imprensa, 1951.

———. *Xanam e Outras Histórias.* São Paulo: Livraria Francisco Alves, 1959.

———, and Corrêa Pinto. *Duas Cartas em Tôrno de uma Idéia.* Rio de Janeiro, 1951.

———. Interviews, Rio de Janeiro, October 11, 1967, July 3, 1971, September 23, 1975, Washington, D.C., September 17, 1968, Tucson, February 17, 18, 1976.

Lacerda, Cláudio. "Lacerda: Uma Vida de Lutas." Serialized biography. *Fatos & Fotos,* nos. 1142–1161 (1983).

———. "Quem realmente conheceu este homem?" *Jornal da Tarde,* May 23, 1977.

Lacerda, Fernando de. Declarations in *International Press Correspondence,* August 8, 1935.

———. Interview in *Diretrizes,* May 27, 1943.

———. Letters to Sebastião de Lacerda, Rio de Janeiro, July 8, October 2, 1912, October 11, 1915, and n.d. CCL.

Lacerda, Gabriel. Conversation, Rio de Janeiro, August 22, 1988.

Lacerda, Letícia Abruzzini. Conversations with DFR, Rio de Janeiro, January 5, 1988, and March 1989.

———. Letters. LFC and CCL.

Lacerda, Maria Cristina. Letter to Sebastião Lacerda, Estoril, July 9, 1956. CCL.

Lacerda, Maurício Caminha de. Preface to Maurício Paiva de Lacerda, *A Evolução Legislativa do Direito Social Brasileiro.*

———. Letter to JWFD, January 27, 1985.

———. Interview, Rio de Janeiro, August 29, 1984, and interviews with DFR, Rio de Janeiro, March 28, April 7, 1983.

Lacerda, Maurício Paiva de. *A Evolução Legislativa do Direito Social Brasileiro.* Rio de Janeiro: Editora Nova Fronteira, 1980.

———. Articles in *Voz do Povo,* 1920.

———. Autobiographical notes in files of *O Estado de S. Paulo.*

———. Correspondence with Olga Caminhoá Werneck, 1907–1909, and letter to Olga Lacerda, Paris, December 13, 1918. Correspondence with Carlos Lacerda. CCL.

———. *Entre Duas Revoluções.* Rio de Janeiro: Livraria Editora Leite Ribeiro; distrib. Freitas Bastos, Spicer & Cia., 1927.

———. *História de uma Covardia.* Rio de Janeiro: Editora Leite Ribeiro, 1927; Editora Nova Fronteira, 1980.

———. Letter to Diretores do Centro Eleitoral do 2º Distrito. *5 de Julho,* no. 23 (May 18, 1925).

———. "Memórias." Handwritten. CCL.

———. "Páginas da infância de Maurício de Lacerda." *Tribuna da Imprensa,* November 24, 25, 26, 27, 1959.

———. *Segunda República.* Rio de Janeiro: Livraria Editora Freitas Bastos, 1931.

———. See Prefeitura Municipal.

Lacerda, Olga Caminhoá Werneck. Correspondence with Maurício de Lacerda, 1907–1909. CCL.

———. Letter to Sebastião de Lacerda, March 14, 1914, and letter to her children, The Hague, September 15, 1928. CCL.

Lacerda, Paulo de. Letters to Sebastião de Lacerda, 1917, and letter to Sebastião de Lacerda, Mogi Mirim, January 15, 1919. CCL.

Lacerda, Sebastião. Interviews, Sebastião de Lacerda, Rio de Janeiro, July 3, 1983, and Rio de Janeiro, August 15, 1988.

Lacerda, Sérgio. Letters to his parents. CCL.

———. Interviews, Rio de Janeiro, August 17, 22, 1988, July 31, August 21, 1989.

Lacerda Filho, Maurício. Letters to Carlos Lacerda, Rio de Janeiro, January 2, 1943, April 14, 1952, and January 1955, and letter to the Diretoria da Sociedade Anônima Editôra Tribuna da Imprensa, Rio de Janeiro, May 5, 1955. CCL.

Leia Livros. São Paulo magazine.

Leite, Cleantho de Paiva. Interview, Rio de Janeiro, August 14, 1984.

Leite, Hilcar. Interview, Rio de Janeiro, July 5, 1983.

Leite Filho, João Batista Barreto. Interviews with Luís Carlos Prestes and Maurício de Lacerda. *O Jornal,* April 6, 8, 1928.

———. Typewritten notes for JWFD, Rio de Janeiro, August 1981.

———. Interviews, Rio de Janeiro, August 12, 1981, July 1, 1983, July 24, 1984.

Leonardos, Thomas. Interview, Rio de Janeiro, August 6, 1984.

Lessa, Orígenes. *O Índio Cor de Rosa: Evocação de Noel Nutels.* Rio de Janeiro: Editora Codecri, 1978.

Levine, Robert M. *The Vargas Regime: The Critical Years, 1934–1938.* New York and London: Columbia University Press, 1970.

Levy, Herbert. Speech in the Chamber of Deputies, June 29, 1977. *Diário do Congresso Nacional,* vol. 32, no. 71 (June 30, 1977), pp. 5,680–5,681.

———. Interview, São Paulo, August 1, 1983.

Levy, Hugo. Interview, Rio de Janeiro, August 1, 1989, and interview with DFR, Rio de Janeiro, March 7, 1989.

Liberal, O. Belém, Pará, newspaper.

Lima, Francisco Negrão de. Letter to Carlos Lacerda. *Última Hora,* June 6, 1958.

Lima, Herman. *História da Caricatura no Brasil.* 4 vols. Rio de Janeiro: Livraria José Olympio Editôra, 1963.

Lima, Hermes. *Travessia: Memórias.* Rio de Janeiro: Livraria José Olympio Editora, 1974.

Lins, Álvaro. *Missão em Portugal.* Rio de Janeiro: Editôra Civilização Brasileira, 1960.

Lins, Etelvino. Manifesto. *Tribuna da Imprensa,* June 25–26, 1955.

———. *Um Depoimento Político: Episódios e Observações.* Rio de Janeiro: Livraria José Olympio Editôra, 1977.

Lopes, Maria Cristina Lacerda Simões. Interview, Rio de Janeiro, August 8, 1983, and interview with DFR, Rio de Janeiro, March 24, 1983.

Lott, Henrique Baptista Duffles Teixeira. "Depoimento de Lott." *Manchete,* November 19, 1955.

———. "Depoimento Prestado ao Juiz da 11ª Vara Criminal a Respeito do 11 de Novembro de 1955." In Joffre Gomes da Costa, *Marechal Henrique Lott.* Pp. 501–508.

———. Interviews, Rio de Janeiro, August 27, 1963, October 13, 1975.

Loureiro Júnior, José. *O Golpe de Novembro e Outros Discursos.* Rio de Janeiro: Livraria Clássica Brasileira, 1957.

Luz, Carlos. Speech in the Chamber of Deputies, November 14, 1955. In Bento Munhoz da Rocha Netto, *Radiografia de Novembro,* Appendix 21, pp. 133–153.

Maça, A. Rio de Janeiro weekly magazine.

Machado, Alfredo C. Interviews, Rio de Janeiro, July 7, 1983, August 8, 1989 (and some papers).

Machado, F. Zenha. *Os Últimos Dias do Govêrno de Vargas.* Rio de Janeiro: Editora Lux, 1955.

Machado, Wilson L. "Algumas lembranças de um amigo." Typewritten, Curitiba, October 1988.

Maciel Filho, José Soares. Interview, Rio de Janeiro, March 14, 1965.

Madeira, Marcos. Interview wtih DFR, Rio de Janeiro, August 23, 1985.

Maffei, Eduardo. "Brasil Gerson e Seus Históricos Passos." *Voz da Unidade,* February 5, 1982.

Magalhães, Dario de Almeida. "O Povo Não Escolhe Pior do que as Elites." In Lourenço Dantas Mota, compiler, *A História Vivida,* vol. 2.

———. Interview, Rio de Janeiro, July 7, 1983.

Magalhães, Gualter Maria Menezes de, and Telmo Becker Reifschneider. Interview aboard the *Tamandaré,* Rio de Janeiro, December 6, 1965.

Magalhães, Juracy. "Juracy esclarece depoimento de Lacerda." *O Estado de S. Paulo,* July 20, 1977.

Magalhães, Rafael de Almeida. Quote. In Marília Pacheco Fiorillo, "O Esperto Charme da Burguesia." *Status,* no. 142 (May 1986). P. 32.

———. Interviews, Rio de Janeiro, August 17, 1983, August 9, 1989.

Magalhães, Sérgio. *Pela Abolição dos Privilégios às Empresas Estrangeiras: Coletânea de Projetos de Lei—4ª Legislatura.* Rio de Janeiro: João Paulo Moreyra, 1959.

Malta, Otávio. Interview, Rio de Janeiro, October 9, 1968, and interview with DFR, Rio de Janeiro, March 17, 1983.

Manchete. Rio de Janeiro weekly magazine.

Manhã, A. Rio de Janeiro newspaper, 1935 (pro–Aliança Nacional Libertadora).

Manzon, Jean, and David Nasser. "O Café Vai Desaparecer do Mundo, Proclama o Interventor de São Paulo." *O Jornal,* November 30, 1944.

Maquis. Rio de Janeiro fortnightly magazine, run by Fidélis Amaral Netto.

Marcha. Rio de Janeiro antifascist newspaper that published five numbers in October and November 1935.

Mariz, Dinarte. Letter to Carlos Lacerda, Rio de Janeiro, March 23, 1960. CCL.

Martins, Ivan Pedro de. "A Flecha e o Alvo." Manuscript of a book. Copy in collection of JWFD.
———. Interview with DFR, London, June 13, 1985.
Martins, Luís. Letters to Carlos Lacerda. CCL.
———. *Noturno da Lapa.* Rio de Janeiro: Editôra Civilização Brasileira, 1964.
———. *Um Bom Sujeito.* São Paulo: Paz e Terra, 1983.
———. "Um grave incidente." *O Estado de S. Paulo,* October 21, 1947.
———. [L. M.]. Articles in *O Estado de S. Paulo.*
Mascarenhas, Anderson Oscar. *Roboré, um Torpedo contra a Petrobrás.* São Paulo: Editôra Fulgor, 1959.
Matarazzo Júnior, Francisco. Testimony. In Câmara dos Deputados, *Autos do Inquérito Instaurado pela Comissão Parlamentar de Inquérito Instituída pela Resolução nº 313 de 27 de Maio de 1953.*
Maurell Filho, Emílio. Statements. *Tribuna da Imprensa,* November 1, 1955.
———. Interview, Rio de Janeiro, October 11, 1965.
Mellão Neto, João. *Jânio Quadros: 3 Estórias para 1 História.* São Paulo: Editora Renovação Ltda., 1982.
Melo Filho, Murilo. "Lacerdista, Durante Sete Anos." Typewritten, 5 pages.
Mendonça, Marcos Carneiro de. Interview with DFR, Rio de Janeiro, February 4, 1983.
Mesquita, Alfredo. Letters to Carlos Lacerda, Livraria Jaraguá, São Paulo, June 7, October 5, 1945. CCL.
———. Quoted in "Lacerda—O teatrólogo," *O Estado de S. Paulo,* May 22, 1977.
———. Interview, São Paulo, July 24, 1983.
Mesquita, Ruy. Interview, São Paulo, July 22, 1983.
Miranda, Yedda Braga. "Lembranças." Foreword to Mário de Andrade, *Cartas a Murilo Miranda.*
———. Interview, Rio de Janeiro, July 28, 1984.
Moniz, Edmundo. Interview with DFR, Rio de Janeiro, February 6, 1983.
Montello, Josué. *A Oratória Atual do Brasil.* Rio de Janeiro: DASP, 1959.
———. Article. *Diário da Manhã,* August 14, 1954. Reproduced in Josué Montello, "A palavra de Carlos Lacerda," *Jornal do Brasil,* May 8, 1984.
Montes, José Maria Homem de. Interview, São Paulo, July 26, 1983.
Montoro, André Franco. Statement. *O Estado de S. Paulo,* December 4, 1959.
Moraes, neto, Prudente de. Interview, Rio de Janeiro, August 31, 1963.
Moraes Neto, Geneton. See Silveira, Joel.
Morais Neto, Luís Mendes de. Collection, in his files, of proposed revolutionary decrees drawn up for anti-Kubitschek military officers.
———. Interviews, Rio de Janeiro, October 19, November 25, 1966.
Mota, Carlos Guilherme. *Ideologia da Cultura Brasileira (1933–1976).* 4th ed. São Paulo: Editora Ática, 1980.
Mota, Lourenço Dantas, compiler. *A História Vivida.* Vol. 2. São Paulo: O Estado de S. Paulo, 1981.

Moura, Valdiki. *Notícia do Cooperativismo Brasileiro.* 2nd ed. São Paulo: Instituto Progresso Editorial, 1948.
Mundo Ilustrado. Rio de Janeiro weekly magazine.
Na Barricada. Rio de Janeiro anarchist newspaper, 1915.
Nabuco, Carolina. *A Vida de Virgílio de Melo Franco.* Rio de Janeiro: Livraria José Olympio Editôra, 1962.
Nação, A. Rio de Janeiro newspaper of Leônidas de Rezende and Maurício de Lacerda, closed by the Bernardes government in 1924. It reappeared, January–August 1927, as the Communist organ.
Nascimento, Alcino João do. Testimony as reported in *O Estado de S. Paulo,* August 20, 1954, and testimony at the Galeão Air Base as reported in *O Estado de S. Paulo,* September 23, 1954.
Nasser, David. "As Grandes Amizades (9): Meu Amigo, Carlos Lacerda." *Manchete,* no. 802 (September 2, 1967).
———. "Elogio ao Adversário." *O Cruzeiro,* September 17, 1960.
———. "Falta Lacerda." *Manchete,* no. 1431 (September 22, 1979).
——— and Jean Manzon. "O Café Via Desaparecer do Mundo, Proclama o Interventor de São Paulo." *O Jornal,* November 30, 1944.
Nery, Sebastião. *Folclore Político, 2.* Rio de Janeiro: Editora Record, 1976.
New York Times, The. New York newspaper.
Nogueira, José Bonifácio. "Redenção Política do Brasil." *O Globo,* October 9, 1960.
Noite, A. Rio de Janeiro newspaper that closed down in December 1957.
Novos Rumos. Rio de Janeiro Communist weekly newspaper.
Observador Econômico e Financeiro, O. Rio de Janeiro magazine founded by Valentim Bouças in 1936.
Observer, The. London newspaper.
Oliveira, Armando Daudt d'. Interview, Rio de Janeiro, August 10, 1983.
Oliveira, Rafael Corrêa de. "A Missa." *O Estado de S. Paulo,* June 27, 1957.
Pacheco, Eliezer. *O Partido Comunista Brasileiro (1922–1964).* São Paulo: Editora Alfa-Omega, 1984.
Paiva, Cláudio Lacerda. Interview, Rio de Janeiro, August 8, 1983.
———. See Lacerda, Cláudio.
Paiva, Glycon de. Letter to Carlos Lacerda, Rio de Janeiro, June 13, 1960. CCL.
Paiva, Odilon Lacerda. Interviews, Rio de Janeiro, July 22, August 5, 1984.
Paiva, Vera Lacerda. Letters to JWFD, Rio de Janeiro, March 20, May 8, July 14, 1984.
———. Telegram to Olga Lacerda, July 29, 1937. CCL.
———. Interviews, Rio de Janeiro, July 22, August 5, 1984, August 25, 1988, and interviews with DFR, Rio de Janeiro, January 30, February 7, 13, 1983, July 26, August 25, September 1, 1985, February 12, 18, March 1989.
Para Todos. Rio de Janeiro weekly magazine.
Passos, Gabriel. *Estudos sôbre o Acôrdo de Roboré.* São Paulo: Editôra Fulgor, 1960.
Passos, John Dos. *Brazil on the Move.* Garden City: Doubleday & Company, 1963.

Pátria, A. Rio de Janeiro newspaper.
Paz, Alberto Gainza. Letters to Carlos Lacerda, Buenos Aires, July 20, September 5, 1956. CCL.
Pedreira, Fernando. Remarks in "Um Terremoto," *Jornal do Brasil,* Caderno B ("Lacerda/70 anos"), April 30, 1984.
Pedrosa, Israel. Letter to Fernando Goldgaber, October 20, 1984.
Peixoto, Alzira Vargas do Amaral. "A Vida de Getúlio," narrated to Raul Giudicelli, chapter 13. *Fatos & Fotos,* October 5, 1963.
Peixoto, Enaldo Cravo. Transcript of interview taped by the Sociedade dos Amigos de Carlos Lacerda.
Penido, Osvaldo Maia. Interviews, Rio de Janeiro, September 6, 1963, October 10, 1967.
Penna, José Osvaldo de Meira. *O Dinossauro.* São Paulo: T. A. Queiroz Editor, 1988.
———. Interview, Brasília, July 15, 1983.
Penna, Luiz Felippe de Oliveira. Interviews, Rio de Janeiro, August 11, 16, 1983.
Peralva, Osvaldo. Interview, Rio de Janeiro, September 14, 1963.
Pereira, Nelson. Interview, São Paulo, August 4, 1983.
Perón, Juan. *Discurso Pronunciado por el Excelentísimo Señor Presidente de la Nación General Juan Perón en la Escuela Nacional de Guerra.* Buenos Aires, 1953.
Pierotti, Graça Carvalho. Interview with DFR, Rio de Janeiro, September 1, 1986.
Pinto, Corrêa, and Carlos Lacerda. *Duas Cartas em Tôrno de uma Idéia.* Rio de Janeiro, 1951.
Pinto, Heráclito Fontoura Sobral. Letter to Carlos Lacerda, Rio de Janeiro, May 10, 1947. CCL.
———. *Lições de Liberdade.* Belo Horizonte: Editora Comunicação, Universidade Católica de Minas Gerais, 1977.
———. Transcript of interview taped by the Sociedade dos Amigos de Carlos Lacerda.
———. Interviews, Rio de Janeiro July 8, August 25, 1983.
Pinto, José de Magalhães. Letters to Carlos Lacerda. CCL.
———. "Relatório Político de Sr. Magalhães Pinto." Speech delivered at the UDN nominating convention, Rio de Janeiro, November 7, 1959. *O Estado de S. Paulo,* November 8, 1959.
Poerner, Arthur José. *O Poder Jovem.* Rio de Janeiro: Editôra Civilização Brasileira, 1968.
Polícia do Distrito Federal, Delegacia de Segurança Política. Boletim 97, September 28, 1944. Vargas papers, CPDOC.
Porto, Eurico Bellens. *A Insurreição de 27 de Novembro: Relatório.* Rio de Janeiro: Imprensa Nacional, 1936.
Poyares, Walter Ramos. Interview with DFR, Rio de Janeiro, July 30, 1985.
Prado, Décio de Almeida. Letter to Carlos Lacerda, São Paulo, March 21, 1944. CCL.

Prado, Lourenço de Almeida. Letters to Carlos Lacerda, Rio de Janeiro, April 17, 1952, May 19, 1967. CCL.
———. Statement. *Jornal do Brasil,* May 28, 1977.
———. Interview, Rio de Janeiro, August 15, 1983.
Prefeitura do Município de São Paulo, Secretaria Municipal de Cultura. *História das Eleições: Memória da Democracia.* São Paulo: Departamento do Patrimônio Histórico, 1985.
Prefeitura Municipal. *A Questão do Morro de Santo Antonio, Contrato da Companhia Industrial Santa Fé: Relatório Preliminar do 2º Procurador dos Feitos da Fazenda Municipal.* Rio de Janeiro: Jornal do Brasil, 1932.
Prestes, Luiz Carlos. "A Situação de Fernando Lacerda Perante o Partido." *Problemas,* no. 61 (September 1954).
———. "Informe de Balanço do Comitê Central." Prepared for the PCB's Fourth National Congress, held in November 1954. Reproduced in Inquérito Policial Militar No. 709, *O Comunismo no Brasil,* vol. 1, p. 214.
Primeiro Congresso Brasileiro de Escritores. See Writers' Congress, First.
Problemas. São Paulo antifascist monthly magazine, established in August 1937.
Problemas. Rio de Janeiro Communist Party monthly magazine, established in August 1947.
Programa, Companhia de Arte Dramática Álvaro Moreyra, 1937. "*O Rio,* quatro quadros de Júlio Tavares."
Programa, Grupo de Teatro Experimental (São Paulo), November 13, 1945. "*A Bailarina Solta no Mundo,* farse em dois atos de Carlos Lacerda. Ensaios e direção de Alfredo Mesquita."
Programa, Grupo Universitário de Teatro (São Paulo), October 10, 1945. "*Amapá* de Carlos Lacerda, peça em três quadros e um 'ballet.'"
Publicidade. Rio de Janeiro magazine.
Quadros, Jânio. "Mensagem aos Cariocas." *Tribuna da Imprensa,* April 22, 1953.
———. Letters to Carlos Lacerda. CCL.
Queiroz Júnior, José. *Memórias sôbre Getúlio.* Rio de Janeiro: Editorial COPAC, 1957.
Radical, O. Rio de Janeiro newspaper.
Rebello, Marques [pseud. of Eddy Dias da Cruz]. Testimony. Câmara dos Deputados, *Autos do Inquérito Instaurado pela Comissão Parlamentar de Inquérito Instituída pela Resolução nº 313 de 27 de Maio de 1953.*
Rebello Filho, Antonio Dias. *Carlos Lacerda, Meu Amigo.* 2nd ed. Rio de Janeiro: Editora Record, 1981.
———. Interview, Rio de Janeiro, August 7, 1983, and interview with DFR, Rio de Janeiro, March 26, 1983.
Reifschneider, Telmo Becker. See Magalhães, Gualter Maria Menezes de.
Resstel, Rubens. Interview, São Paulo, August 4, 1983.
Revista Acadêmica. Rio de Janeiro magazine.
Revista do Brasil. Publication of the Departamento de Cultura, of the Secretaria de Ciência e Cultura do Estado do Rio de Janeiro, Vol. 1, no. 2 (1984).

Revista de Comunicação. Quarterly magazine published by Agora Comunicação Integrada Ltda.

Revista Proletária. Rio de Janeiro monthly organ of the PCB's Central Committee.

Ribeiro, Carlos Flexa. Interviews, Rio de Janeiro, July 5, 1983, August 26, 1984.

Ribeiro, Darci. Letter to Carlos Lacerda, June 6, 1960. *Novos Rumos,* June 10–16, 1960.

Ribeiro, Edgar Flexa. Interviews, Rio de Janeiro, July 5, 8, August 15, 1983, August 19, 1989.

Rocha Netto, Bento Munhoz da. *Radiografia de Novembro.* 2nd ed. Rio de Janeiro: Editôra Civilização Brasileira, 1961.

———. Interview, Curitiba, November 28, 1965.

Rodrigues, Hélio. Letter to Carlos Lacerda, Santos, January 23, 1946. CCL.

Rodrigues, José Honório. *Chagas Freitas e o Rio de Janeiro.* Rio de Janeiro, 1982.

———. Introduction to Carlos Lacerda, *Discursos Parlamentares.*

Rodrigues, Martins. "Parecer do Relator." In Carlos Lacerda, *O Caminho da Liberdade.* Pp. 195–210.

rumo. Rio de Janeiro monthly magazine, 1933–1934, originally of the Casa do Estudante do Brasil.

Sacchetta, Hermínio, Interviews, São Paulo, November 5, 1968, August 19, 1979.

Salazar, Alcino. Transcript of interview taped by the Sociedade dos Amigos de Carlos Lacerda.

Salgado, Plínio. Interview, Brasília, October 14, 1965.

Sampaio, Paulo. "A Greve Parcial na Panair do Brasil," *O Estado de S. Paulo,* March 1, 1955.

———. Letter to Armando Falcão (president of the Parliamentary Commission of Inquiry investigating Panair do Brasil), Rio de Janeiro, May 5, 1955. CCL.

Sarney, José. Letter to Carlos Lacerda, Rio de Janeiro, February 6, 1960. CCL.

Saunders, John V. D. "A Revolution of Agreement among Friends: The End of the Vargas Era." *Hispanic American Historical Review,* 44, no. 2 (May 1964), pp. 197–213.

Schenberg, Mário. Interview, São Paulo, November 14, 1966.

Schneider, Eliezer. Interview with DFR, Rio de Janeiro, July 15, 1985.

(*Sete Dias em Revista*) *7 Dias em Revista.* Rio de Janeiro weekly magazine published in the mid-1940s.

Silva, Evandro Lins e. Letter to Sérgio Lacerda, 20 pages, Rio de Janeiro, May 5, 1980.

———. Interviews, Brasília, October 17, 1965, Rio de Janeiro, August 25, 1983, August 2, 1984.

Silva, Hélio. *1937: Todos os Golpes se Parecem.* Rio de Janeiro: Editôra Civilização Brasileira, 1970.

———. *1945: Porque Depuseram Vargas,* Rio de Janeiro: Editora Civilização Brasileira, 1976.

———. *1954: Um Tiro no Coração.* Rio de Janeiro: Editora Civilização Brasileira, 1978.
Silva, Nelson do Valle e. See Soares, Gláucio Ary Dillon.
Silveira, Guilherme da. Interview, Rio de Janeiro, August 30, 1984.
Silveira, Joel. "Carlos Lacerda, amigo bissexto." *O Liberal,* Belém, August 18, 1977.
———. Interview, Rio de Janeiro, August 26, 1983.
——— and Geneton Moraes Neto. *Hitler-Stálin: O Pacto Maldito e Suas Repercussões no Brasil.* Rio de Janeiro: Editora Record, 1990.
Silveira, Paulo. Interview, Rio de Janeiro, July 22, 1984.
Silveira, Roberto da. Statement. *O Estado de S. Paulo,* June 19, 1958.
Skidmore, Thomas E. *Politics in Brazil: An Experiment in Democracy.* New York: Oxford University Press, 1967.
Soares, Gláucio Ary Dillon. "As Bases Ideológicas do Lacerdismo." *Revista Civilização Brasileira,* vol. 1, no. 4 (September 1965).
——— and Nelson do Valle e Silva. "O Charme Discreto do Socialismo Moreno." *Dados: Revista de Ciências Sociais,* vol. 28, no. 2 (1985).
Sodré, Maria Abreu. Interview, São Paulo, July 21, 1983.
Sodré, Nelson Werneck. *A História da Imprensa no Brasil.* Rio de Janeiro: Editôra Civilização Brasileira, 1966.
Sodré, Roberto de Abreu. Interview, São Paulo, August 3, 1983.
Sousa, João Valente de. Testimony at the Galeão Air Base. In *Tribuna da Imprensa,* September 4–5, 1954.
Sousa, Nelson Raimundo de. Testimony at the Galeão Air Base. In *O Estado de S. Paulo,* September 17, 1954.
Souza, Antônio Cândido de Melo e. Interview, São Paulo, August 7, 1981.
Souza, José Cândido Moreira de. Interview with DFR, Rio de Janeiro, August 27, 1986.
Souza, José Luiz Moreira de. Interview, Rio de Janeiro, August 16, 1983.
Status. Brazilian magazine.
Stern, Irwin, editor-in-chief. *Dictionary of Brazilian Literature.* Westport, Connecticut: Greenwood Press, 1988.
Sterner, Richard. Letter to Carlos Lacerda, Stockholm, August 16, 1946. CCL.
Sumner Filho, George. Interview with DFR, Rio de Janeiro, March 16, 1989.
Távora, Juarez. *Uma Vida e Muitas Lutas: Memórias.* Vol. 3, *Voltando à Planície.* Rio de Janeiro: Biblioteca do Exército Editora, 1977.
———. Interview, Rio de Janeiro, November 27, 1967.
Time. Weekly magazine.
Tribuna da Imprensa. Rio de Janeiro newspaper.
Tribuna da Imprensa, Sociedade Anônima. *Estatutos da Sociedade Anônima Editora Tribuna da Imprensa.* N.d.
Tribuna Popular. Rio de Janeiro Communist newspaper, 1945–1947.
Trompowisky, Gilberto. "O Nome da Semana: Dona Letícia de Lacerda." Newspaper clipping. CCL.
Ulrich, Maria Alayde Albite. "Carlos Lacerda e a UDN." Master's thesis.

Porto Alegre: Pontifícia Universidade Católica do Rio Grande do Sul, 1984.

Última Hora. Rio de Janeiro newspaper.

Unidade. Magazine "por la Defensa de la Cultura: Órgano de la Agrupación de Intelectuales, Artistas, Periodistas y Escritores (AIAPE)." Buenos Aires. Vol. 1, no. 3 (April 1936).

Vale, Edmundo Jordão Amorim do. Interviews, Rio de Janeiro, September 7, 1963, November 10, 1965.

Valle, Epaminondas Moreira do. Interview with DFR, July 26, 1985.

Vanguarda A. Rio de Janeiro newspaper.

Vanguarda Socialista. Rio de Janeiro weekly, directed by Mário Pedrosa, that began publication late in 1945.

Vargas. Luthero. *Getúlio Vargas: A Revolução Inacabada.* Rio de Janeiro, 1988.

———. Testimony at the Galeão Air Base. In *O Estado de S. Paulo,* September 9, 1954.

Vaz Júnior, Rubens Florentino. Interviews, Rio de Janeiro, August 9, 1983, August 13, 1989.

Vega-Palacin, Manuel. "Elections, Parties, and Congress: Brazil, 1945–1964." Ph.D. dissertation, The University of Texas at Austin, 1981. Ann Arbor: University Microfilms International, 1981.

Velloso, Fernando Cícero da Franca. Collection of newspaper clippings and letters from Carlos Lacerda, Rio de Janeiro.

———. Letter to JWFD, Rio de Janeiro, October 1, 1984.

———. Interviews, Rio de Janeiro, August 16, 1983, August 15, 1984.

Veloso, Haroldo. Interviews, Marietta, Georgia, January 6, 7, 1966.

Viana, José de Segadas. Letter to Carlos Lacerda, Rio de Janeiro, October 10, 1955. Brandi Letter folder, Walter Cunto collection, Rio de Janeiro.

Victor, Mário. *Cinco Anos que Abalaram o Brasil: de Jânio Quadros ao Marechal Castelo Branco.* Rio de Janeiro: Editôra Civilização Brasileira, 1965.

Vieira, Laerte. Speech in the Chamber of Deputies, June 29, 1977. *Diário do Congresso Nacional,* vol. 32, no. 71 (June 30, 1977), pp. 5,672–5,674.

Villaça, Antônio Carlos. "A Veemência e a Ironia," *Jornal de Letras,* August 1982.

———. *O Livro de Antonio.* Rio de Janeiro: Livraria José Olympio Editora, 1974.

———. Transcript of interview taped by the Sociedade dos Amigos de Carlos Lacerda.

———. Interview with DFR, Rio de Janeiro, August 17, 1985.

Villalobos, João Eduardo Rodrigues. *Diretrizes e Bases da Educação: Ensino e Liberdade.* São Paulo: Livraria Pioneira Editôra and Editôra da Universidade de São Paulo, 1969.

Visão. Weekly magazine.

Voz da Unidade. São Paulo Communist weekly published in the 1980s.

Voz do Povo. Rio de Janeiro proletarian daily, 1920.

Wainer, Samuel. Letters to Alzira Vargas do Amaral Peixoto and Getúlio Vargas, in Adelina Maria Alves Novaes e Cruz et al., compilers, *Impasse na democracia brasileira, 1951–1955: Coletânea de documentos,* pp. 234–237, 240.

———. *Minha Razão de Viver: Memórias de um Repórter.* Rio de Janeiro: Editora Record, 1987.

———. "O Dia em que Getúlio me Mandou Fazer um Jornal." *Playboy* (Brazil), no. 93 (April 1983).

———. Testimony. In Câmara dos Deputados, *Autos do Inquérito Instaurado pela Comissão Parlamentar de Inquérito Instituída pela Resolução nº 313 de 27 de Maio de 1953.*

———. Interviews, Rio de Janeiro, September 28, 1968, São Paulo, July 14, 1979.

War Ministry, 2nd Military Region, Estado Maior Regional, 2nd Section. Boletim Secreto de Informações 14, December 22, 1944. Vargas papers, CPDOC.

Weber, Hilde. *O Brasil em Charges, 1950–1985,* São Paulo: Circo Editorial, 1986.

White, William W. Letter to Carlos Lacerda, Washington, D.C., July 29, 1953. CCL.

Wieland, William. Letter to Carlos Lacerda, American embassy, Rio de Janeiro, January 19, 1944. CCL.

Writers' Congress, First. *Primeiro Congresso Brasileiro de Escritores Promovido pela Associação Brasileira de Escritores (ABDE), São Paulo, Janeiro 22 a 27, 1945,* proceedings. Biblioteca da Escola de Comunicações e Artes, Universidade de São Paulo (Ref. No. 6090).

Index